Roman Civilization
Volume I

ROMAN CIVILIZATION

SELECTED READINGS

Edited by

Naphtali Lewis and Meyer Reinhold

VOLUME I

THE REPUBLIC AND THE AUGUSTAN AGE

THIRD EDITION

COLUMBIA UNIVERSITY PRESS • NEW YORK

COLUMBIA UNIVERSITY PRESS
New York   Oxford
Copyright © 1990 Columbia University Press
All rights reserved

Library of Congress Cataloging-in-Publication Data

Roman civilization : selected readings / edited by Naphtali Lewis and
Meyer Reinhold. — 3d ed.
p.   cm.
Includes bibliographical references.
Contents: v. 1. The Republic and the Augustan Age — v. 2. The Empire.
ISBN 0–231–07054–3 (set). — ISBN 0–231–07055–1 (pbk. : set)
1. Rome—Civilization—Sources.   I. Lewis, Naphtali.
II. Reinhold, Meyer
DG13.L4   1990

937—dc20   90–33405
                                                               CIP

Vol. 1
67995

Casebound editions of Columbia University Press books are Smyth-sewn
and printed on permanent and durable acid-free paper
∞
Printed in the United States of America
c 10 9 8 7 6 5 4 3 2 1

CONTENTS

PREFACE

Roman Civilization has now served an entire generation of students and teachers. The time is ripe for an updated revision that takes into account the new finds and prolific scholarship of the past thirty-odd years, as well as new areas of interest and emphases that have developed in the study of Roman antiquity. Accordingly, the two volumes of the present edition include many important documents, inscribed on stone or bronze, or written on papyrus or ostraca, that have been published since the appearance of our previous editions. As before, many of these are here available for the first time in English translation. We offer also a new chapter on women, two new chapters on coins, and an added final chapter that carries the coverage of the fourth century beyond Constantine the Great to the consolidation of Christian society and the capture and sack of Rome by the Goths under Alaric. As before, our sources, literary and nonliterary, carry the story from Rome's modest beginnings on the famous seven hills to its far-flung, multifaceted imperial grandeur, with selections from the activities of the highest levels of government to those of the lives of the humblest peasants and slaves.

As we observed in the preface of our first edition, "There is no need to review here in detail the editorial problems that attend the attempt to compress within these two volumes a body of fairly representative excerpts from the riches of the written records of Rome's thousand-year history. We recognize that every condensation involves a process of interpretation, and that it would be impossible to find agreement among scholars on what is indispensable in such a compilation of selections.

"The procedure which we adopted as being, in our opinion, the most fruitful, is to present the materials in topical chapters arranged chronologically, and in the selection of texts, to exclude snippets, however classic, to avoid duplication of materials from different periods, and to limit markedly technical or rhetorical pieces and purely narrative passages—such as descriptions of the endless wars and battles of Roman history—to a very few examples, in order to give more space and greater emphasis to texts illustrating the political, administrative, religious, economic, military, social, and cultural aspects of Roman civilization. Where possible, we have let the record speak for itself; where necessary, we have equipped the texts with introductions and a minimum of explanatory notes."

As for the English translations of Latin and Greek texts, those not otherwise attributed include a few from the public domain but are preponderantly our own. We are also indebted for borrowed materials to the following publishers and/or authors: Harvard University Press—divers volumes of the Loeb Classical Library; Oxford University Press—R. H. Barrow, *Symmachus, Relation II* (1973), R. Ireland, *De Libris Bellicis* (1979), M. Whittaker, *Tatian's Oratio ad Graecos* (1987); Johns Hopkins University Press—G. Luck, *Arcana Mundi* (1985), O. Temkin, *Soranus, Gynaecology* (1956); Noyes Press—J. R. Bram, *Firmicus Maternus, Mathesis* (1975): Fathers of the Church Press—B. M. Peebles, *Sulpicius Severus, Writings* (1949); Paulist Press—P. G. Walsh, *Paulinus of Nola, Poems* (1975); and R. T. Ridley for his splendid translation of Zosimus' *New History*. The above supplement the permissions acknowledged in the preface to our previous editions.

Our commentaries assume that the reader will have ready access to general works on Roman history and to an atlas of classical geography. Our Introduction does not attempt a formal survey of Greek, Roman, and Early Christian literary history but aims rather at sketching for readers a background and perspective for the sources they will actually encounter in the two volumes.

The complexities and similarities of the official imperial nomenclature frequently make it difficult for the reader to recognize which of several emperors is meant in a given text. In such cases we have adopted the typographical device of setting in small capitals the name by which the emperor in question is commonly known today—e.g., Tiberius Claudius Caesar Augustus Germanicus, or Emperor Caesar Marcus Aurelius Antoninus [Caracalla] Augustus.

The bibliographies, brought up to date, are less extensive but more pointed than those of the second edition. They are aimed at assisting the English-speaking student and general reader who may wish to probe further into one or another element of the subjects treated in the various chapters. The bibliographies are, accordingly, limited to books and articles in English.

It is appropriate that we record here our thanks to Roxanne Gentilcore and Dorothy S. Stewart for dedicated assistance in the preparation of the bibliographies and the indexes, respectively, to Christopher A. Tuttle for expeditious production of multiple copies of the huge typescript, and to the editorial staff of Columbia University Press.

April 1990   N. L.

M. R.

ABBREVIATIONS USED IN CITATION OF SOURCES

ADA	Regia Academia Italica, *Acta Divi Augusti,* Pars Prior (Rome, 1945)
AE	*L'Année Epigraphique* (Paris, 1888–)
CIL	*Corpus Inscriptionum Latinarum* (16 vols., Berlin, 1863–)
Dessau	H. Dessau, *Inscriptiones Latinae Selectae* (3 vols., Berlin, 1892–1916)
Dittenberger	W. Dittenberger, *Sylloge Inscriptionum Graecarum* (3d ed., 4 vols., Leipzig, 1915–1924)
FIRA	*Fontes Iuris Romani Antejustiniani* (2d ed., 3 vols., Florence, 1940–1943)
IG	*Inscriptiones Graecae* (14 vols., Berlin, 1873–)
IGRR	*Inscriptiones Graecae ad Res Romanas Pertinentes* (3 vols., Paris, 1906–1927)
LCL	Loeb Classical Library
OGIS	W. Dittenberger, *Orientis Graeci Inscriptiones Selectae* (2 vols., Leipzig, 1903–1905)
RDGE	R. K. Sherk, *Roman Documents from the Greek East* (Baltimore, 1969)
ROL	E. H. Warmington, *Remains of Old Latin* (4 vols., Cambridge, Mass., 1935–1940; Loeb Classical Library)
SEG	*Supplementum Epigraphicum Graecum* (Leiden, 1923–)

ROMAN CIVILIZATION

VOLUME I

The Republic and the Augustan Age

INTRODUCTION: THE SOURCES

ROMAN HISTORIOGRAPHY

Roman literature began in 240 B.C.; its historiography began a few decades later, in the aftermath of the Second Punic War against Carthage. Thus, the history of Rome did not begin to be systematically written until the end of the third century B.C., when Rome had already become the dominant power in the Mediterranean world. The pioneer historians were for the most part Roman senators who sought to reconstruct Roman history from its origins to their own times. They did so with a Roman and class bias and a principal focus on public affairs both at home and abroad. Before them, Greek historians had directed only scant attention to the institutions and growing might of the Italian city on the Tiber and seven hills. In the absence of formal history the early Roman historians called upon several principal resources that left a permanent impress on Roman historical writing: the official records of events kept by the priestly bodies and the methods and principles of contemporary Greek (Hellenistic) historiography.

Like the ancient Jewish people, the Romans became conscious of their historical importance late in their development. Faced with the task of reconstructing the first five hundred years of their history, Roman writers fell back upon a host of legends and oral traditions of both native and Greek origin; family records of noble houses; extant inscribed documents, such as treaties and laws; and the archives of the priestly colleges, above all the *annales* compiled by the *pontifex maximus* (chief pontiff) in connection with his duties as regulator of the calendar. This annual record of the names of magistrates and memorable events briefly noticed did not become part of the official state archives until 320 B.C. For the centuries preceding that date the *annales* were "reconstructed" in the interest of important Roman families, to form a continuous list of magistrates. The introduction of falsifications was facilitated by the general destruction of Rome during the Gallic invasion of 390 B.C., in which no doubt many, though certainly not all, records perished. Subsequently, with the development of historical writing, the keeping of these pontifical records was abandoned. About 120 B.C. the entire text, known as *Annales Maximi* (Pontifical Chronicles), was compiled and published in eighty books by Publius Mucius Scaevola, then chief pontiff.[1]

Servius,[2] *Commentary on Vergil,* Aeneid I. 373

There is this difference between annals and history; history belongs to those times which we saw or could see . . . but annals belong to those times which our age did not experience. Hence Livy is both annalist and historian. Nevertheless, these terms are easily confused.

Now the annals used to be prepared in the following way. The *pontifex maximus* had every year a whitened tablet, on which he used to place at the top the names of consuls and the other magistrates and to note memorable events that had occurred at home and abroad, on land and on sea, day by day. Through the diligence of the chief pontiff the ancients compiled the annual commentaries in eighty books, and called them *Annales Maximi* from the *pontifices maximi* by whom they were made.

Aulus Gellius, *Attic Nights* II. xxviii. 6

In the Fourth book of his *Origins* Cato says: "I do not intend to write the kind of thing that appears on the tablet of the *pontifex maximus*—when grain was dear, or when the darkness or something else obscured the light of the sun or moon."

---

1. In 18/17 B.C. the Emperor Augustus ordered the preparation and inscription on an arch in the Roman Forum of the records now known, from their location in modern times, as the *Fasti Capitolini* (published in *CIL,* vol. I, and more recently in *Inscriptiones Italiae,* vol. XIII, part 1 [Rome, 1947]). These contain (1) an annual list of high officials, together with brief notices of some memorable events, from the beginning of the Republic to Augustus' own time (this list was subsequently kept up to date until A.D. 13); and (2) a list of all triumphs celebrated from regal times to 19 B.C., after which date that honor was reserved as a prerogative of the emperor.

2. Maurus Servius Honoratus, a learned grammarian of the late fourth century A.D. His best-known work, the *Commentary on Vergil,* is extant in a shorter and in an expanded version; the latter is used here. Biographical data on the other authors cited here and below will be found on pp. 10–30.

Livy, *History of Rome* VI. i. 1–3

I have set forth in the five preceding books the history of the Romans, their foreign wars and domestic dissensions, from the founding of the city to its capture, first under the kings, then under consuls, dictators, decemvirs, and consular tribunes. These matters are enveloped in obscurity both by reason of their great antiquity, like far-off objects which can be descried only with difficulty, and also because written records, the only trustworthy memorials of events, were in those times few and scanty, and such records as did exist in the *Pontifical Chronicles* and in public and private archives nearly all perished in the burning of the city. From its second beginning, when the city was reborn from its roots, so to speak, in more luxuriant and fruitful growth, a clearer and more reliable account of political and military history can be set forth.

Rome's first formal historians quite naturally followed the annalistic pattern of the pontifical records. Indeed, the annalistic structure made its appearance even in early Roman epic poems, such as the *Annals* of Ennius and the *Punic War* of Naevius, and it remained a permanent feature of Roman historical writing. While all Roman historical works composed before the middle of the first century B.C. are now lost except for fragments, most of our extant sources for the regal and republican periods (e.g., Livy, Dionyius of Halicarnassus, Plutarch, Appian, Cassius Dio, Valerius Maximus) are based on the work of these early annalistic writers.

In the first place, these pioneers wrote down and fixed for all time the traditional account of Roman history for the period before the Second Punic War (218–201 B.C.), when contemporary data began to be accumulated. They reconstructed the past out of legends, the vainglorious archives of noble families, and the official and falsified pontifical annals. This material contains a basic core of historical fact, much embellishment, and much pure fiction; for the early annalists felt no restraint about inventing material to fill out gaps in their information. An especially common practice was to retroject into dimmer periods various social, economic, political, and military events of more recent or contemporary times. Moreover, the Roman annalists down to the middle of the first century B.C. were all men of affairs belonging to the senatorial order, the ruling class of the Roman Republic; in consequence, they cast the historical framework that they created in the social and political perspectives of their class. Roman historiography was colored also by the fact that, in its beginnings, it sought to demonstrate the resources and might of the Roman state and to justify in influential Greek circles the measures taken by Rome in handling world affairs.

Thus the first Roman historian, Quintus Fabius Pictor (c. 200 B.C.), wrote his *Annals* of Rome in the Greek language, and, with the notable exception of Cato, his immediate successors continued this practice. With Lucius Cassius Hemina (c. 150 B.C.), in whose times Roman overlordship over the Hellenistic world had become an established fact, Latin supplanted Greek as the language of Roman annalistic literature.[3] Next Gnaeus Gellius, who wrote c. 150–120 B.C., abandoned the earlier concise method for a treatment of Roman history on a vast scale, running to at least ninety-seven books. Thereafter this expansive style became an orthodox technique in Roman historiography, as the monumental works of Livy and Cassius Dio reveal. The worst aspects of the Roman annalists manifested themselves in the Sullan period, when such writers as Quintus Claudius Quadrigarius and Valerius Antias, who became notorious for their falsifications, presented a version of Rome's past that resembled a kind of historical romance. An evanescent phenomenon, also in the Sullan period, was the rewriting of the annals of Rome by Gaius Licinius Macer, who colored the national history with the social and political viewpoints of the antisenatorial faction.

In short, as a result of falsifications and distortions, of nationalistic and sociopolitical tendentiousness, Roman historical writing made little qualitative, though some stylistic, progress, down to the so-called Golden Age of Latin literature—the age of Cicero and Caesar. Educated Romans of that period were conscious of the unreliability of the established traditions concerning early Roman history and of the technical and stylistic deficiencies of the annals of the two preceding centuries.

Livy, *History of Rome* VIII. xl. 3–5

It is difficult to decide which account, or which authority, to prefer to which. The record, I am convinced, has been falsified by funeral eulogies and by untrue inscriptions on ancestral portraits, as each family with deceptive falsehood appropriated to itself a tradition of great deeds and official distinctions. That is why the records of private careers and of public events are so much confused. And there is no such thing as a contemporary writer of those days on whose authority one might rely.

3. On Cato, who had earlier written in Latin, see p. 10.

Cicero, *Brutus* XVI. 62; From *LCL*

Of these [funeral orations] some are, to be sure, extant, which the families of the deceased have preserved as trophies of honor and for use on the death of a member of the same family, whether to recall the memory of the past glories of their house or to support their own claims to noble origins. Yet by these laudatory speeches our history has become quite distorted; for much is set down in them which never occurred— false triumphs, too large a number of consulships, false relationships, and transfers of patricians to plebeian status, in that men of humbler birth professed that their blood blended with a noble family of the same name, though in fact quite alien to them; as if I [Marcus Tullius], for example, should say that I was descended from Manius Tullius the patrician, who was consul with Servius Sulpicius ten years after the expulsion of the kings.

Plutarch, *Life of Numa* i. 1–2

Though genealogies from the beginning to King Numa seem to be set down accurately, yet there is a vigorous dispute concerning the time in which he reigned. But a certain writer named Clodius, in a book entitled *Examination of Chronology,* maintains that the ancient records were lost when the city was sacked by the Gauls and that those which are now extant were forged to flatter the pride of some men by inserting their names among the first families and the most illustrious houses, though in reality they had no claim to it.

Cicero, *Laws* I. ii. 5; From *LCL*

Atticus. There has long been a desire, or rather a demand, that you[4] should write a history. For people think that, if you entered that field, we might rival Greece in this branch of literature also. And to give you my own opinion, it seems to me that you owe this duty not merely to the desire of those who take pleasure in literature, but also to your country, in order that the land which you have saved you may also glorify. For our national literature is deficient in history, as I realize myself, and as I frequently hear you say. But you can certainly fill this gap satisfactorily, since, as you at least have always believed, this branch of literature is closer than any other to oratory [cf. below].

Of even greater importance in molding the general pattern of Roman historiography as it matured was the influence of the principles and

4. Atticus addresses himself to Cicero.

methods of the Hellenistic Greek historians, whom, almost from the
start, Roman historians used as their models. Thus among the Romans,
as among the Greeks, history was regarded not as a social science but as
a branch of literature. The Greek historians and their Roman imitators
were primarily literary artists, not scholars; their efforts were dominated
not by scientific methodology, but by canons of artistic form. Specifically, history was conceived as a branch of, or something akin to,
rhetoric. Hence no need was felt even by great historians like Sallust,
Livy, and Tacitus, when they were not dealing with contemporary
events, to base their presentation on primary sources. Furthermore,
stylistic homogeneity was a more important aim than strict fidelity to
the facts, with the result that historical documents, for example, were
not reproduced in their original form but paraphrased, and speeches and
letters, attributed to historical personages but in reality the free creations
of the writers, were incorporated into the narrative for heightened effect.
"We concede to rhetoricians," says Cicero, "the privilege of distorting
history in order to produce a more effective narrative."[5]

Other characteristics, too, were inherited by the Romans from the
Hellenistic historians. From this source came the application to Roman
historiography of some of the techniques of the Greek drama and the
emphasis upon the role of individuals in the course of events, with the
resultant subordination or neglect of broad historical forces. Greek in
origin, also, was the utilitarian concept of history as a practical guide for
men of affairs, and the conscious moralizing purpose of providing through
history ethical lessons for the edification of the reader. Above all, the
patriotic motif was kept constantly in the foreground by the historians
of Rome. A final influence, which makes itself increasingly felt in the
last two centuries B.C., was the scholarly antiquarianism fostered by the
Greek Peripatetic school, and this concept of "history for its own sake"
eventually brought into being a new, escapist literary genre—encyclopedic, quasi-historical—that enjoyed a vigorous life beginning in the
troubled times of the dying Republic and continuing through the Empire.

Aulus Gellius, *Attic Nights* v. xviii. 6–9; From *LCL*

Thus history, it is said, is the setting forth or description—call it what
you will—of events, but annals set down the events of many years
successively, with observance of the chronological order. . . . I quote a

5. Cicero, *Brutus* xi.42.

passage of some length from the First Book of [the *Histories* of] Sempronius Asellio [lived c. 160–c. 90 B.C.], in order to show what his opinion is of the difference between history and annals.

"Between those," he says, "who have desired to leave us annals and those who have tried to write the history of the Roman people, there was this essential difference. The books of annals merely made known what happened and in what year it happened, which is like writing a diary. . . . For my part, I realize that it is not enough to make known what has been done, but that one should also show with what purpose and for what reason things were done." A little later in the same book Asellio writes: "For annals cannot in any way make men more eager to defend their country, or more reluctant to do wrong. Furthermore, to write over and over again in whose consulship a war was begun and ended, and who in consequence entered the city in triumph, and in that book not to state what happened in the course of the war, what decrees the senate made during that time, or what law or bill was passed, and with what motives these things were done—that is to tell stories to children, not to write history."

The classic expression of all the major characteristics of Roman historiography as it evolved in the last two centuries B.C. is found in Livy, whom the Romans considered their most distinguished historian. His most comprehensive statement of aims and attitudes is contained in the famous preface to his work.

Livy, History of Rome, Preface; From LCL

Whether I am likely to accomplish anything worthy of the labor, if I record the achievements of the Roman people from the foundation of the city, I do not really know, nor if I knew would I dare avouch it; perceiving as I do that the theme is not only old but hackneyed through the constant succession of new historians, who believe either that in their facts they can produce more authentic information or that in their style they will prove better than the rude attempts of the ancients. Yet, however this may be, it will be a satisfaction to have done myself as much as lies in me to commemorate the deeds of the foremost people of the world; and if in so vast a company of writers my own reputation should be obscure, my consolation would be the fame and greatness of those whose renown will throw mine into the shade. Moreover my subject involves infinite labor, seeing that it must be traced back above seven hundred years, and that proceeding from slender beginnings it has so increased as now to be burdened by its own magnitude; and at the same time I doubt not that to most readers the earliest origins and the period immediately succeeding them will give little pleasure, for they will be in haste to reach these modern times, in which the might of a people which has long been powerful is working its own undoing. I myself, on the contrary, shall see in this an additional reward for my toil, that I may avert my gaze from the troubles which our age has been witnessing for so many years, so long at least as I am absorbed in the recollection of the brave days of old, free from every care which, even if it could not divert the historian's mind from the truth, might nevertheless cause it anxiety.

Such traditions as belong to the time before the city was founded, or rather was presently to be founded, and are rather adorned with poetic legends than based upon trustworthy historical proofs, I purpose neither to affirm nor to refute. It is the privilege of antiquity to mingle divine things with human, and so to add dignity to the beginnings of cities; and if any people ought to be allowed to consecrate their origins and refer them to a divine source, so great is the military glory of the Roman people that when they profess that their father and the father of their founder was none other than Mars, the nations of the earth may well submit to this also with as good a grace as they submit to Rome's dominion. But to such legends as these, however they shall be regarded and judged, I shall for my own part attach no great importance. Here are the questions to which I would have every reader give his close attention—what life and morals were like; through what men and by what policies, in peace and in war, empire was established and enlarged; and then let him note how, with the gradual relaxation of discipline, morals first gave way, as it were, then sank lower and lower, and finally began the downward plunge which has brought us to the present time, when we can endure neither our vices nor their cure.

What chiefly makes the study of history wholesome and profitable is this, that you behold the lessons of every kind of experience set forth as on a conspicuous monument; from these you may choose for yourself and for your own state what to imitate, from these mark for avoidance what is shameful in the conception and shameful in the result. For the rest, either love of the task I have set myself deceives me, or no state was ever greater, none more righteous or richer in good examples, none ever was where avarice and luxury came into the social order so late, or where humble means and thrift were so highly esteemed and so long held in honor. For true it is that the less men's wealth was, the less was their greed. Of late, riches have brought in avarice, and excessive pleasures the longing to carry wantonness and license to the point of personal ruin and universal destruction.

With the decline of the Republic and the concentration of power in the hands of the emperor, literature became increasingly the province of professional littérateurs. As restraints upon freedom of expression grew, literature developed an increasing emphasis on matters of form and was more and more characterized by antiquarianism, "art for art's sake," dilettantism, and rhetorical display. The influence of the prevailing rhetorical education, with its emphasis on artificial declamation, became universal. The political oratory of the last two centuries of the Republic received its death blow with the establishment of the Principate; the accumulated technical skills of the art of rhetoric became a vehicle for imperial pronouncements, for showpieces by professional rhetoricians, for arguments in law cases, and for prolix and fulsome panegyrics of the emperors. Historiography continued along the lines laid down during the Republic, with these differences: its rhetorical, belletristic, ethical approach is heightened; Roman writers who concern themselves with the imperial period focus their attention on the city of Rome and the emperor's court, neglecting the broader aspects of the Empire as a whole, and cater to the public taste for gossip and scandal about the court; and contemporary history in general ceases to be written. The last-named tendency was fostered during the Augustan Age by the official policy of celebrating and reviving the pristine virtues and customs of the earlier Roman, a policy that inevitably operated to imbue history with antiquarianism. In addition, the scholarly encyclopedic movement of the declining Republic flourished. The learning of the period expressed itself also in a number of technical treatises on various subjects; among those extant are books on architecture, medicine, agriculture, and water supply. Finally, the growing cosmopolitanism of the Roman Empire resulted in the disappearance of significant differences between Greek and Roman writers, except that universal history continued to be almost exclusively the field of the Greeks.

Under the Empire official control of information began, and access to the truth was more difficult than under the Republic.

Cassius Dio, *Roman History* LIII. xix. 3–5

But from this time most things began to be done secretly and *in camera,* so that anything made public is distrusted, being in any case beyond verification. For it is suspected that everything that is said and done has been accommodated to the wishes of emperors or deputies. As a result much that never happened is rumored, much that actually happened is never known, and with nearly every event a version gains currency that is different from the way it in fact happened.

WRITERS OF THE REPUBLICAN PERIOD

The conspectus that follows is intended not to outline the literary history of the Roman Republic and Empire, but to provide the reader with concise information on the significance and thinking of the authors whose works figure importantly in the present collection of sources.

CATO

(234–149 B.C.)

Marcus Porcius Cato of Tusculum was the founder of Latin prose literature. A soldier-statesman of extensive military and administrative experience, he was in his public career and his thinking the exponent of the austere ancient Roman virtues and the spokesman of the ultraconservative, narrowly nationalistic reaction against the rising tide of Hellenism and the inevitable transformation of Roman life under the impact of wealth and power of empire. Himself a member of the possessing and ruling class, even if he was a "new man" [see introduction to § 155], he exhibited the traditional Roman practicality and dogmatism. In keeping with his aggressive nationalism, he alone among the historians of his generation wrote his work in Latin.

His sole surviving work, the oldest extant Latin prose work, is his *De Agricultura* (On Agriculture), a manual on farm management for absentee landowners written c. 160 B.C. Comprising 162 brief chapters, this treatise is a precious source for the economic, social, and religious institutions of the second century B.C. Cato wrote this guide to serve the needs of the increasingly numerous owners of latifundia who were as yet inexperienced in the operation of these large estates that were developing in the transformation of Italian agriculture from subsistence farming to one of the most important sources of income for the Roman ruling class. It is especially important for its evidence on the beginnings of "plantation" slavery in Italy.

POLYBIUS

(c. 200–c. 117 B.C.)

Polybius of Megalopolis in southern Greece, "the sun in the field of Roman history," as Mommsen called him, is our most trustworthy authority for the period from the beginning of the Second Punic War to the middle of the second century B.C. Of his *Histories,* a general history of the Mediterranean world in forty books, covering the years 220–146 B.C., with a two-book introduction on antecedent events, only the first five books (to 216 B.C.) survive entire, together with excerpts and fragments of the rest. The son of one of the leaders of the Achaean League, he took an active part in the political and military affairs of his native Achaea in the era when the Greeks were faced with the problem of adjusting themselves to the realities of Roman overlordship. Deported to Italy in 166 B.C. as one of 1,000 Achaean hostages, he remained in Rome for over a decade, observing the character and institutions of the conquerors of the Mediterranean and winning the friendship of the scions of the Roman nobility, in particular of Scipio the Younger. His expatriation served to inculcate on him an admiration for Roman imperialism as a blessing to the world and a desire to expound to his fellow Greeks the rapid rise of Rome to worldwide hegemony in the short span of fifty-three years (220–168 B.C.)—"a thing unexampled in history"—and the futility of continuing their resistance to such might.

Polybius is a unique figure in ancient historiography, for, contrary to traditional practices, he did not propose to produce a work of literary art, explicitly rejected rhetoric and the techniques of tragic drama, and introduced few speeches in his work. A historian's historian, he brought to his subject a combination of political realism, military experience, personal knowledge of topography, and a conviction of the organic unity of history. Thus he chose the year 220 B.C. as starting point because "since that time history has been a kind of organic whole, and the affairs of Italy and Africa have been interconnected with those of Asia and Greece, all moving toward one end," namely, Roman world empire.[6]

In his constant effort to probe the causes and interrelations of events, Polybius developed a series of theories of historical causation as he progressively modified his interpretation of the Roman rise to power. At first he saw *Tyche* (Chance, Fortune), an unpredictable, superhuman power, as the prime motive force in history. Later, as his admiration for the Romans grew, he attributed their world hegemony to human causality—the national character and institutions of the Romans. Finally, presumably as he lived to observe the growing corruption of the Roman aristocracy, he modified his earlier views and fell back upon a form of the mechanistic Stoic concept of Fate and the operation of recurrent historical cycles.[7]

6. Polybius I. iii. 4.
7. The continuator of Polybius' history was the Greek polymath Posidonius of Apamea (c. 135–

CICERO

(106–43 B.C.)

Marcus Tullius Cicero of Arpinum "is the supreme index to his age. He is in contact with all its interests. His works, therefore, form a history of his era—of its politics and society as well as its literature and knowledge."[8] A gifted speaker and brilliant lawyer, equipped with the finest education available at that time, he came into the public eye early and rose rapidly through the lower magistracies to the consulship (63 B.C.), although he was a "new man." As consul he suppressed the revolutionary conspiracy of Catiline. Subsequently his political enemies brought about his exile, but he was restored after a year and a half through the influence of Pompey the Great. But though he served a year as governor of Cilicia in 51–50 B.C., he remained in political eclipse, playing the part of elder statesman and devoting most of his time to the practice of law and to literary composition. He returned briefly to a position of political leadership and prominence after the assassination of Caesar, when his outspoken attacks on Antony in his fourteen *Philippics* led to his proscription by the Second Triumvirate and his brutal assassination by Antony's soldiers.

The fifty-seven extant speeches of Cicero constitute one of our richest contemporary sources for the period 81–43 B.C. They are concerned with civil and criminal cases and with political affairs. For all their prolixity and partisanship—in his orations as an advocate he employs all the devices of a skilled lawyer; in his public addresses he is the defender of the vested interests of the ruling and propertied classes—they provide accurate factual material in many areas, such as Roman law and the judicial system, political institutions and constitutional history, economic and social life, taxation, public finances, and provincial administration.

Equally important is the extensive body of letters collected and pub-

---

c. 50 B.C.), whose universal history of the period from 136 to 82 B.C. exerted a tremendous influence on later authors. His work, a retrogression from the standards set by Polybius, combined the Roman oligarchical and the Stoic points of view. He was primarily a moralist and was probably the first to enunciate the idea, which quickly became conventional, of the superior virtues of the older Romans and the degenerative effects of luxury and vice upon the Romans of the last century of the Republic (cf. §§ 80, 96, 170, 171).

8. J. W. Duff, *A Literary History of Rome from the Origins to the Close of the Golden Age,* 3d ed. (London, 1960), p. 256.

lished after his death. The 864 extant letters (774 from the pen of Cicero, 90 from his correspondents) are addressed to, or written by, various friends and members of his household (the sixteen books *Ad Familiares*), to his friend and publisher Atticus (the sixteen books *Ad Atticum*), to his brother Quintus (three books), and to Brutus (two books). Some are dated as early as 68 B.C., but the bulk belongs to the last decade of his life. In his letters Cicero reveals himself as does no other Roman whose works survive; all the political great pass before us in a variegated panorama; we penetrate into large affairs and small—into the private life of his times, the intellectual and business interests, the political maneuverings of the upper classes.

Besides being a practical man of affairs, Cicero was also a scholarly idealist, and in the years of his exile and political eclipse he devoted himself to the composition of treatises on political theory, rhetoric, and philosophy. His *De Republica,* in six books, of which about one third is extant, and his *De Legibus* (Laws), in at least five books, of which three are extant, take as their models Plato's dialogues of the same titles, but they reveal a political philosophy combining idealism and actual Roman practices. His works on oratory, the most important of which are the *Orator, Brutus,* and *De Oratore* (On Oratory), are valuable sources for Roman education, the history of oratory, and forensic techniques. His philosophic essays are marked by no great profundity or originality of thought; in them Cicero sought to transmit to the Romans his own interests in speculative thought and to popularize Greek philosophy by presenting it in the Latin language and adapting it to Roman needs. Leaning toward eclecticism, he poured his studies of Greek ethics, theology, and epistemology into his treatises on *Old Age, Friendship, The Nature of the Gods, Divination, The Ends of Good and Evil, Duties,* and the famous *Tusculan Disputations,* as well as into a number of minor essays.

CAESAR

(100–44 B.C.)

Gaius Julius Caesar, the most important political and military figure of the middle of the first century B.C., prepared two tracts in the heat of his military campaigns. His *Commentarii de Bello Gallico* (Commentaries on the Gallic War)—military memoirs in seven books on his policies toward and campaigns against the Gauls, Germans, and Britons in 59–

52 B.C.—were written not as history but as political pamphlets.[9] Caesar sought through the speedy publication of these memoirs to maintain *in absentia* his political prestige in Rome, to justify his unauthorized acts in leading his troops outside the province assigned to him, and to defend his policies toward the peoples beyond the Alps. Simple and unrhetorical, his *Gallic War* reveals the military genius of the author, provides invaluable information on Roman military institutions, and contains the earliest extant accounts of the ethnology and culture of the Gauls, Germans, and Britons. His second set of memoirs, the *Commentarii de Bello Civili* (Commentaries on the Civil War), in three books, is one of our prime sources for the events of 49–48 B.C. As in his earlier work, Caesar's basic purpose in writing the *Civil War* was a political one, to justify before the Roman public his war against Pompey and his adherents.[10]

VARRO

(116–27 B.C.)

Marcus Terentius Varro of Reate is the dean of Roman antiquarians. Though he had a public career during the civil war period, he was essentially a learned encyclopedist—"the most erudite of the Romans," Quintilian calls him. His gigantic output, comprising seventy-four works in about 620 books, accumulated and marshaled information in almost all fields of learning. Of his *Roman Antiquities* in forty-one books, only tiny fragments survive. Of his *De Linguia Latina* (The Latin Language) in twenty-five books, six books are extant. This work is an etymological study of the origins of Latin words, often faulty in method, but containing valuable *obiter dicta* on many aspects of Roman history and society. Only his *De Re Rustica* (On Landed Estates), in three books, has come down to us intact. Together with Cato's *De Agricultura* this treatise is our prime source for the management and operation of the large estates in Italy under the Republic.

---

9. One of his officers, Aulus Hirtius, completed the story, carrying it down to 50 B.C. in an eighth book.

10. The *Civil War,* too, is incomplete. The authorship of the three supplementary books on the wars in Egypt, Africa, and Spain in 48–45 B.C. is a vexed question.

SALLUST

(86–c. 35 B.C.)

Gaius Sallustius Crispus of Amiternum in the Sabine country, after an active public career as an adherent of Julius Caesar, retired from politics after Caesar's assassination and devoted himself to writing history. Of his *Histories,* in five books, covering the years 78–67 B.C., a few fragments and excerpts remain. But his two extant monographs on *The Jugurthine War* and *The Catilinarian War* establish his position as one of the great Roman historians. Despite his moralizing emphasis on the evils of greed and ambition, his carelessness in matters of chronology, his geographical inaccuracies, and a predilection for analysis and comparison of personalities, Sallust is unique among extant Roman historians in abandoning the annalistic method for the historical monograph and in his application of Thucydidean realism and Polybian standards to his subject matter. The poet Martial called him "the first in Roman history." It must be understood, however, that Sallust was primarily a political pamphleteer in his *Jugurtha* and *Catiline.* In these two historicopolitical tracts he sought to defend the policies and leaders of the antisenatorial opposition by revealing the corruption and incompetence of the *optimates* and by countering the propaganda directed against Caesar. Yet his pamphlets afford us a lucid picture of the international and internal consequences of the partisan strife of the last century of the Republic.

DIODORUS

(c. 80–c. 29 B.C.)

Diodorus of Sicily, a Greek writer about whom little is known, is the author of the *Historical Library,* a general world history in forty books covering the period from mythological times to 60 B.C. Books I–V, XI–XX, and fragments from the rest have survived. These provide some useful information about Roman history, especially for the years 480–302 B.C. But in the main Diodorus' work is a dull, inaccurate chronicle of information culled from secondary sources that attempts mechanically to present the history of the Mediterranean world area by area and year by year. Like most historians in antiquity, Diodorus reveals a pragmatic, ethical view of history and an emphasis upon the role of the "strong man."

WRITERS OF THE IMPERIAL PERIOD

VERGIL

(70–19 B.C.)

Publius Vergilius Maro, from the region of Mantua in Cisalpine Gaul, the leading poet of the Augustan Age, poignantly and sensitively reflects the contradictions between the official façade of ideals and the disillusioning realities of the Augustan Age. A scholar and man of letters, he became a member of the literary circle gathered by Augustus' intimate adviser Maecenas, and devoted his mature years to a profound effort to probe whether the "new order" of Augustus was the highest stage of social evolution. Combining Greek literary tradition with a Roman perspective, he produced the *Eclogues* (or *Bucolics*), ten pastoral poems; the *Georgics,* four books in praise of Italy and agriculture; and the great nationalist and philosophical epic the *Aeneid,* in twelve books. An artificial product, heavily indebted to Greek epic poetry, drama, and philosophical speculation, the *Aeneid,* though cast in the form of a legendary epic, is nonetheless superficially a vehicle for the Augustan themes of peace, national unity and duty to the state, moral rearmament through the revival of the "Roman virtues" and the ancestral piety and religion, and Rome's "enlightened" imperial destiny under the guidance of the imperial family. Despite this, Vergil's *Aeneid* is pervaded by an atmosphere of gloom and doubt, for, using the yardstick of Greek philosophic and political speculation and the concept of the "common humanity of man" to appraise the world order constructed by the Romans of the Republic and reorganized by Augustus, he could not reconcile the differences between what he desired and what he glorified, between unattainable ideals and the realities of his material world.

HORACE

(65–8 B.C.)

Quintus Horatius Flaccus of Venusia in southern Italy, the son of an exslave, was introduced by his friend Vergil into Maecenas' literary coterie. With the collapse of Brutus' lost cause, which he had espoused, he made his peace with the new regime of Augustus and abandoned politics. Content henceforth in the comfortable existence provided by Maecenas' subsidies, he devoted himself completely to the enjoyment of life and to the composition of poetry of great technical perfection, which gives us glimpses of the society, politics, religion, and literary and intellectual life of the Augustan Age. Horace's *Satires* and *Epodes* belong to his earlier period. The *Odes,* lyric poems on a variety of themes including national topics, are his masterpiece. Literary criticism and familiar philosophical reflections of no great profundity form the contents of his *Epistles,* the poems of his last years. He is also the author of the *Carmen Saeculare* (Secular Hymn), written on the occasion of Augustus's celebration of the Secular Games in 17 B.C.

DIONYSIUS OF HALICARNASSUS

(c. 60/55 B.C.–after 7 B.C.)

Dionysius, who came to Rome from Halicarnassus c. 30 B.C., was a Greek teacher of rhetoric and a distinguished literary critic. In addition to work in these fields he wrote the *Roman Antiquities,* in twenty books, an annalistic history of Rome from the legendary beginnings to 264 B.C. Books I–X and most of Book XI (to 446 B.C.) are extant, as well as fragments of the rest. This work, produced under the influence of the atavistic movement of the Augustan period and employing as sources the prosenatorial annalists of the Sullan period, is a markedly rhetorical, prolix, antiquarian reworking of the annals of early Rome. Much space is devoted to tiresome, unhistorical speeches. Nevertheless, Dionysius is not entirely without historical acumen, and he is at times our only or best source for early Roman institutions and traditional history.

LIVY

(59 B.C.–A.D. 17)

Titus Livius of Patavium (Padua) in northern Italy is the greatest of the annalists of Rome. His *History of Rome* to 9 B.C. (entitled *Ab Urbe Condita,* "From the Founding of the City"), in 142 books, supplanted all previous chronicles and gave to the history of the Roman Republic the perspectives and form that it retained until the beginnings of modern criticism in the nineteenth century. Of this "colossal masterpiece," as the German historian Niebuhr called it, there are extant Books I–X (beginnings to 293 B.C.), XXI–XLV (218–167 B.C.), and fragments from and summaries of the rest.[11]

Essentially a literary artist and court historian, without a fundamental grasp of geography, military science, or politics, Livy brought to bear upon the historical traditions of Rome[12] an unexcelled narrative skill, a superb prose style, and all the techniques of rhetoric and drama, to create what was virtually a prose epic of the glories of Rome's past. His basic aim was not critical inquiry, but moral reform through lessons to be drawn from an idealized past, through emphasis on ancient virtues, heroism, patriotic sacrifice, and religious piety. Insufficiently critical of his sources, and making no pretension to a systematic philosophy of history, Livy selected and emphasized what suited his purposes, infusing his history with his ethical aim and a prosenatorial bias. Eloquent but fictitious speeches and elaborate but generically similar descriptions of battles abound in Livy's history, and in the early books he recounts at great length many traditional Roman legends. Nevertheless, for many periods of the Republic Livy is our best or only authority.

PROPERTIUS

(c. 50–before 2 B.C.)

Sextus Propertius, one of the leading poets of the Augustan Age, scion of one of the leading Italian families of Assisi, became a member of the literary circle of Maecenas. He wrote mostly love poems to his beloved "Cynthia" that provide pictures of contemporary life and thought. In his later years he turned from erotic poetry to Augustan and national themes.

---

11. Because of the great size and cost of Livy's history, a number of abridgments and summaries of abridgments were made in later centuries. The most valuable of these is the *Periochae* (Résumés), based on an epitome of the first century A.D. and extant for all books except CXXXVI and CXXXVII. Based on Livy's work are also, among others, the compendia of Cassiodorus, Florus, Eutropius, Orosius, and Rufius Festus.

12. His principal sources were the early annalists, Polybius and other Greek writers, and some official documents.

OVID

(43 B.C.–A.D. 18)

Publius Ovidius Naso of Sulmo in central Italy was a fashionable literary dilettante in the Rome of the Augustan Age. In addition to a considerable body of erotic and mythological poetry, he composed a versified calendar, the *Fasti,* which describes (from an antiquarian point of view) anniversaries and religious festivals of the first half of the year. This work contains valuable material on legends, folklore, religion, and social customs. In the last decade of his life, after he was exiled by Augustus for moral reasons to Tomi, on the west coast of the Black Sea, he wrote the *Tristia* (Laments) and *Epistulae ex Ponto* (Letters from the Black Sea), poems in which, while expressing his misery because of his separation from the cosmopolitan atmosphere of Rome, he gives us a few glimpses of conditions in a peripheral region of the Roman Empire.

VITRUVIUS

(Period of Augustus)

Vitruvius Pollio, an architect and military engineer about whom almost nothing is known, is the author of the sole surviving Roman treatise on architecture, *De Architectura,* in ten books (written c. 25–23 B.C.). Vitruvius was an expert technician who was involved in the beautification of Rome under Augustus. His work deals in detail not only with architecture and town-planning, but also with water supply, devices for telling time, machines, and war engines.

STRABO

(c. 64 B.C.–c. A.D. 21)

Strabo, a Greek scholar from Amasia in the Roman province of Pontus, was a historian and geographer. His *General History,* continuing Polybius to the end of the Republic, is lost. His extant *Geography,* in seventeen books, written as an aid for men of affairs (either for Romans, for whom he had a high admiration, or for Asiatic Greeks), is a mine of information not only on the geography of the known world, but also on political and economic history.

SENECA THE ELDER

(c. 55 B.C.–c. A.D. 37–41)

Lucius Annaeus Seneca, the elder, of Córdoba in Spain, the father of the philosopher (see p. 21), is the author of a collection of *Controversiae* (Debates) and *Suasoriae* (Pleadings), which he wrote from memory to preserve the teaching methods and styles of the rhetoricians of the late Republic and early Empire. He gives us eighty-one subjects assigned to students for preparation and delivery — criminal, civil, and social themes, all based on hypothetical laws and situations.

VELLEIUS

(Before 20 B.C.–after A.D. 30)

Velleius Paterculus of Campania, a retired army officer, is the author of a *Compendium of Roman History* in two books. Book I, from the beginnings to 146 B.C., is preserved in small part; Book II, preserved intact, covers the period from 146 B.C. to A.D. 30. Velleius' amateur condensation of Roman history lacks historical depth, is highly rhetorical and subjective, biographical in method, frankly pro-aristocratic, and profuse in its adulation of the imperial family, in particular of the Emperor Tiberius, under whom Velleius had a long military service. Yet the *Compendium* is our best extant abridgement of Roman history; it is valuable for data on Roman colonies and provincial history and for providing the best existing connected account of events from 168 B.C. to A.D. 30, being especially full for the reign of Augustus and most of that of Tiberius.

PHILO

(c. 20 B.C.–c. A.D. 40)

Philo Judaeus, the distinguished Jewish theologian-philosopher of Alexandria, is the author of numerous Greek works in which he sought to reconcile Jewish theology with Hellenic philosophy. There are also extant two political tracts from his pen: *Against Flaccus,* which expounds the grievances of the Jewish community against the governor of Egypt, providing valuable information on the administration of Egypt and on the place of the Jews in the Roman Empire; and *Embassy to Gaius,* an account of a delegation (of which he was a member) sent by the Jewish community of Alexandria in A.D. 39–40 to voice its grievances to the Emperor Caligula. The latter work is especially important for its first-hand picture of the mad Caligula and for the Jewish resistance to emperor worship.

VALERIUS MAXIMUS

(Period of Tiberius)

Valerius Maximus, about whose life nothing is known, is the author of *Facta et Dicta Memorabilia* (Memorable Deeds and Sayings) in nine books. This work is a miscellany of facts and anecdotes, intended to serve as a repertory for rhetoricians and teachers. Though Valerius relies chiefly on the annalists and is shallow, uncritical, superstitious, and rhetorical, his work preserves for us much valuable information on Roman history and institutions.

SENECA THE YOUNGER

(c. 4 B.C.–A.D. 65)

Lucius Annaeus Seneca from Córdoba in Spain, son of Seneca the rhetorician (see p. 20), was a prominent figure in the reigns of Claudius and Nero, serving as tutor and adviser to the latter. He was subsequently implicated in the conspiracy of Piso against Nero and was ordered to commit suicide. Seneca is our best source for Roman Stoicism. Of his voluminous moral and philosophical works the following are extant: twelve so-called *Dialogues, On Clemency* (two books), *On Benefits* (seven books), and 124 *Moral Epistles*. His *Natural Questions,* regarded during the Middle Ages as a reference book on cosmology and physics, is of little value as a source for the Roman knowledge of natural science. The *Apocolocyntosis* (Pumpkinization) is a witty, cynical satire on the deification of the Emperor Claudius. Seneca is the author also of eight tragedies, artificial closet dramas based on fifth-century Greek plays and reworked by the application of Roman rhetoric and Stoic philosophy.

PETRONIUS

(Period of Nero [?])

Petronius Arbiter, about whom little is known, was probably connected with the court of Nero. His one surviving work, which is not preserved entire, is the *Satyricon,* a realistic picaresque novel revealing—from the point of view of a witty, cynical aristocrat—phases of contemporary Italian life. It is a very valuable document for the social and economic history of the early Empire.

COLUMELLA

(Period of Nero)

Lucius Junius Moderatus Columella, from Gades (modern Cadiz) in Spain, was a retired army officer who became a practical farmer in Italy. His *De Re Rustica* (On Landed Estates), in twelve books, and his *De Arboribus* (On Arboriculture), in one book, constitute our most comprehensive source for Roman agricultural techniques and the management of large estates. It is especially valuable, when compared with the earlier similar works of Cato and Varro, for an understanding of the changes in agricultural economy that occurred in the early Empire.

PLINY THE ELDER

(A.D. 23–79)

Gaius Plinius Secundus, of Como in northern Italy, had an active public career and was in the last years of his life a close associate of the Emperor Vespasian. He lost his life while serving as admiral of the fleet evacuating refugees from the eruption of Mt. Vesuvius in A.D. 79. Pliny was also an encyclopedic scholar, whose lost works, in 102 volumes, dealt with military science, history, education, and language. His one surviving work, the *Natural History* in thirty-seven books, is a huge compilation at secondhand of the prevailing scientific knowledge of the early Empire, containing 20,000 items derived from 2,000 volumes by 100 principal authors. While Pliny's work is marred by bookishness, credulity, and the pseudoscience of the times, the *Natural History* is a mine of information about many aspects of Roman social, religious, economic, and political institutions.

QUINTILIAN

(A.D. *c. 30–c. 96*)

Marcus Fabius Quintilianus, born in Spain, was the most successful and most distinguished professor of oratory in Rome. His career was climaxed by his appointment to a chair of rhetoric subsidized by the Emperor Vespasian and to the post of tutor of the children of the Flavian dynasty. His *Institutio Oratoria* (Institutes of Oratory), in twelve books, an epoch-making and influential work, was the product of his pedagogical experience and constitutes our most important authority on Roman education. While much of this treatise on the education of the orator from infancy to the polished graduate deals with highly technical aspects of rhetoric, it is extremely valuable for its information on the methods and content of Roman education, for details of Roman law, and for Quintilian's acute, and now classic, literary judgments. Attributed to him but spurious are two collections of *Declamationes,* 19 long and 145 shorter rhetorical exercises similar to those of Seneca the Elder, on imaginary points of law.

FRONTINUS

(A.D. *c. 40–103/104*)

Sextus Julius Frontinus had a distinguished career that included the governorship of Britain and the office of water commissioner of the city of Rome. His works are characterized by typical Roman practicality. The *Stratagems,* in three books (there is a fourth by an unknown author), intended to illustrate principles of military science for army officers, is a collection of anecdotes from Greek and Roman history on successful military artifices. Much more valuable is his *De Aquis Romae* (The Water Supply of Rome), in two books, a technical work on the aqueducts and pipes supplying the residents of Rome, written on the basis of his personal experience as administrator, an accurate knowledge of the legislation concerning the city's water supply, and much diligent research.

JOSEPHUS

(A.D. 37/38–c. 100)

Flavius Josephus, born Joseph ben Matthias, was a prominent Jewish Pharisee, a man of affairs and diplomat who, despite a pro-Roman bias acquired after a visit to Rome, was reluctantly drawn into the Jewish revolt of A.D. 66–70 as a general of his people's forces. Taken prisoner, he became the interpreter and adviser of Titus and was subsequently granted Roman citizenship and attached on terms of great intimacy to the Flavian house. In Rome he devoted the remainder of his career to the writing of history. His *magnum opus* is the *Jewish Antiquities,* from the Creation to A.D. 65, in twenty books. The *Jewish War,* in seven books, was written to point up the futility of further resistance to the might of Rome; *Against Apion,* in two books, is a defense of Judaism against the detractions of anti-Semites; and his *Autobiography* is a defense of his own conduct during the Jewish revolt. Josephus is more propagandist than historian. Yet, though his works are highly rhetorical, exaggerated, and biased, they provide valuable information on Roman imperial policy and administration and insight into the attitudes of subject peoples of the Empire toward Roman rule.

MARTIAL

(A.D. 38/41–c. 100)

Marcus Valerius Martialis, from Bilbilis in Spain, spent thirty-five of his mature years at Rome as a man of letters, moving in the highest levels of Roman society. His fifteen books of verse *Epigrams,* skillfully wrought miniatures of the cosmopolitan life of the capital, reveal a realistic knowledge of all strata of society in the Flavian Age. These thumbnail sketches of all manner of men, women, and customs provide us with valuable details on the social and private life of imperial Rome.

DIO CHRYSOSTOM

(A.D. c. 40–c. 120)

Dio Cocceianus Chrysostomus of Prusa in Bithynia belonged to a wealthy provincial family. His fame as a traveling lecturer brought him to Italy, where he associated with the imperial court. Exiled by Domitian from

Italy and Bithynia for fourteen years, he later enjoyed the favor of Nerva and Trajan. Much of his time was spent as a public figure in his native Prusa. Of his voluminous writings much is lost. His numerous extant orations consist of sophistic showpieces, moral discourses, and political addresses. The latter, though highly artificial (like all Dio's work), provide valuable information about contemporary society and local affairs in the Greek cities of Asia Minor.

PLUTARCH

(A.D. *c. 46–c. 126*)

A wealthy man of letters and occasional public lecturer, Plutarch spent most of his life in his native town of Chaeronea in central Greece but went on several embassies to Rome. The bulk of his writings is contained in the *Moralia* (Moral Essays), a collection of more than sixty treatises on a variety of topics, especially ethical questions. More important as a source for Roman civilization are his classic *Parallel Lives,* fifty biographies of eminent Greek and Roman soldiers and statesmen, most of them arranged in Greek–Roman pairs followed by summary comparisons. However, since these were written as moral lessons rather than as historical essays, one must not expect to find in them thorough compilations of factual data or evidences of critical research. Plutarch's sources were secondary (principally the annalists for Roman material), and his methods were those of the hero worshiper and sentimental moralist— anecdotal, antiquarian, dramatic, and digressive. Nevertheless, Plutarch's *Lives* have preserved much valuable material on phases of Roman society, institutions, and history from the legendary foundations of the city of Rome to the early Principate.

TACITUS

(A.D. *c. 55–120*)

Publius(?) Cornelius Tacitus, member of a distinguished Roman family, was a lawyer with a long legal and political career before he became a historian. As a literary artist and as a historical realist he is the leading figure in Roman historiography. His earliest work is the *Dialogus de Oratoribus* (Dialogue on Oratory), a monograph on the decline of oratory in the imperial period. Next came the *Agricola* and the *Germania*. The former, a biography of his father-in-law, who distinguished himself (among other things) as governor of Britain, is valuable for details of imperial administration and the consolidation of Roman rule in Britain; the latter is a scholarly monograph of outstanding value on the ethnography, the political and military institutions, the economic life, and the religion and customs of the Germanic tribes at the end of the first century A.D.

The two most significant works of Tacitus, written in the full maturity of his literary and historical powers, are his *Annales*[13] in eighteen books, covering the history of the years A.D. 14–68, and his *Historiae,* presumably in twelve books, dealing with the events of the years A.D. 69–96. Of the *Annals* there are extant Books I–IV, the beginning of Book V, Book VI, the second half of Book XI, and Books XII–XVI (A.D. 14–29, 31–37, and 47–66); of the *Histories* only Books I–IV and the first part of V (A.D. 69–70). These two works, both annalistic in structure, constitute our most trustworthy source for the history of the early Principate, largely because of the basic accuracy of the facts and the critical realism of the author. Yet Tacitus was fundamentally a literary artist with a superb narrative skill and a unique style deliberately cultivated for maximum effect. His approach to history was the ethical one characteristic of antiquity. Gloomy, cynical, satirical, he captures the mind and emotions of the reader by dosing his facts with a clever and effective, if unhistorical, admixture of gossip, rumor, innuendo, and speculation. His psychological insight into character is profound, but his excessive speculation on individual motivation frequently results in distortion. In addition, his emphasis on the individual in history and his concentration on Rome and the imperial court circumscribe his historical vision. He is openly biased in favor of a moderate aristocratic republic, and this political prejudice, too, distorts his historical analyses. The profound dislocation of Tacitus' superficially happy times is reflected in his confused philosophy of history. As moving forces in history he accepts indiscriminately predestination, chance, free will, and divine intervention. Moreover, the contradictions and inconsistencies in Tacitus are due not only to this lack of an organic theory of historical causation, but also to the conflict between his prejudices and the facts and to the conflicting evidence of his sources, which he neglected or failed to resolve.

---

13. The accepted title, for which, however, there is no ancient authority.

PLINY THE YOUNGER

(A.D. *61/62–c. 114*)

Gaius Plinius Caecilius Secundus, of Como in northern Italy, was the nephew and adopted son of Pliny the Elder (see p. 22). A wealthy, learned man of affairs, littérateur, and lawyer, he had a long public career at Rome, culminating in the governorship of Bithynia (A.D. 111–113). Of his writings there are extant the *Panegyricus,* a fulsome, rhetorical oration delivered in the senate in honor of Trajan on the occasion of Pliny's elevation to the consulship (A.D. 100), and 368 *Letters* arranged in ten books. The 121 letters of Book x are from his official correspondence, when governor of Bithynia, with the Emperor Trajan; they constitute a prime source of our knowledge of Roman provincial administration. The remainder, written between A.D. 97 and 109 with a view to eventual publication, are really miniature essays on a variety of topics, and they provide a panorama of the life and manners of his age as seen through the eyes of a cultured gentleman of the Roman ruling class.

JUVENAL

(A.D. *c. 60–c. 140*)

Decimus(?) Junius Juvenalis, about whose life very little is known that is certain, was trained in rhetoric and had a military career. His sixteen *Satires* present a grim, cynical, pessimistic picture of the immorality and degeneracy of the Roman upper classes in the late first and early second centuries. His moral indignation, stemming largely from disappointment in his personal career, produced an exaggerated documentation of the evils of his age. But he is a valuable source for many realistic, if overdrawn, details of contemporary society.

SUETONIUS

(A.D. *c. 69–c. 150*)

Gaius Suetonius Tranquillus came of a wealthy Roman family; little else is known of his life, except that he practiced law and was for a time a secretary of the Emperor Hadrian. In his writing he was essentially an antiquarian, "the Varro of the imperial period." Of his numerous works there are extant part of the *De Viris Illustribus* (Biographies of Famous

Men—grammarians, rhetoricians, and poets), and the *Vitae Duodecim Caesarum* (Lives of the Twelve Caesars), biographies of Julius Caesar and the first eleven emperors (Augustus to Domitian). Suetonius set a new vogue in historical writing, which retained thereafter for centuries his biographical approach and method. His *Lives* are monotonously constructed, anecdotal, with little psychological or political understanding. His method is that of cataloguing a multitude of brief, often disjointed facts, interspersed with bits of scandal and backstairs gossip. Like Tacitus, he concentrates his attention on the individual (the emperor) and on the imperial court, to the exclusion of broader historical movements.

APPIAN

(A.D. *c. 95–c. 165*)

Appian of Alexandria, a lawyer by profession, was a Romanized Greek who was active in the Roman civil service. A dilettante in the field of history, he undertook to rewrite the history of Rome on a new principle, namely, along geographical lines. The result was his *Roman History* in twenty-four books, of which the following are extant: Preface, fragments of Books I–V, Book VI (wars in Spain), Book VII (Hannibalic War), Book VIII (Punic Wars), Book IX (Illyrian Wars), Book XI (Syrian Wars), Book XII (Mithridatic Wars), and Books XIII–XVII (Civil Wars, 133–35 B.C.). Books XIII–XVII form a unit commonly cited by the title *Civil Wars,* Books I–V. Though based on secondary and tertiary sources, lacking historical breadth and critical independence, and devoted almost exclusively to military history, Appian's work is, in the present state of our sources, extremely valuable for the internal affairs of Rome in the century from the Gracchi to the end of the Republic, thus helping to bridge the gap between Polybius' *Histories* and the writings of Cicero.

FLORUS

(*Time of Hadrian*)

(Lucius Annaeus?) Florus, about whom little is known except that he was born in Africa, was a man of letters whose one extant work is an *Epitome of Roman History* in two books, from the beginnings to the Age of Augustus. Devoted mostly to military events and leaning heavily on

Livy, Florus' abridgement is essentially a panegyric of Rome—rhetorical, moralistic, excessively brief, inaccurate in detail, but serviceable where there are lacunae in our other sources.

FRONTO

(A.D. *c.* 100–166/167)

Marcus Cornelius Fronto of Numidia was the foremost master of the art of rhetoric of his time, who, after a public career in Rome, became the tutor of Marcus Aurelius and Lucius Verus. His *Letters*, a collection of instructional correspondence with his two imperial pupils, are pedantic and fulsome, but they provide us with a valuable picture of Marcus Aurelius, the imperial court, and the education of the time.

GELLIUS

(A.D. *c.* 123–*c.* 169)

Aulus Gellius, of Italian origin, was a lawyer with an antiquarian bent. While still a student in Athens, he began the preparation of a work entitled *Noctes Atticae* (Attic Nights), in twenty books. This is a miscellany on a great variety of topics and is of especial value because, in his love of accumulating information, Gellius excerpted passages and details from many earlier authors whose works are now lost.

APULEIUS

(A.D. *c.* 125–*c.* 171)

Lucius(?) Apuleius, from Madaura in Africa, was a member of the provincial aristocracy, a brilliant lawyer, and a traveling lecturer. He was an opponent of Christianity and his principal literary interests lay in the mystical religions of his age, in magic, and in philosophy. Extant from his pen are the *Apologia,* a speech defending himself against a charge of practicing magic; the *Florida* (Purple Patches), excerpts from his lectures and philosophical writings; and the *Metamorphoses,* or *Golden Ass,* a picaresque romance of exquisite beauty and continuing popularity. Apuleius' works are a valuable source for the social life and religious interests of the second century in the provinces.

PAUSANIAS

(Time of Marcus Aurelius)

Pausanias, a Greek traveler and geographer, of whose life nothing is known, published in A.D. 174 a *Description of Greece* in ten books, intended as a tourist guidebook to Greece and to Greek antiquities. The historical digressions in this work contain useful information on Greece under Roman domination.

CASSIUS DIO

(A.D. 164/165–after 229)

Cassius Dio Cocceianus, a native of Bithynia, is the "Greek Livy." A bicultural Roman senator, with experience in the highest levels of imperial administration under seven emperors from Commodus to Severus Alexander, he devoted twenty-two years of his life to writing his *Roman History,* his *magnum opus.* In eighty books it covered about 1,000 years of Roman history from its origins to his own day. Together with many fragments, about one third of this vast work has survived. Particularly full are the books for the years 69 B.C. to A.D. 46 and for 217–219.

Dio's *History* is of uneven merit. Characteristic are his annalistic method, rhetorical style, and many fictitious speeches. Despite many shortcomings, Cassius Dio's *Roman History* is indispensable for many periods of Rome's long history, especially for the Augustan Age and his own times. To Dio his *History* contained an essential usable past as guide for the perilous times in which he lived, when, as he lamented, the Principate took an ominous turn "from a monarchy of gold to one of iron and rust." Committed to the monarchy and to the interests of his own class, he extracted from Rome's history lessons for his own critical age. The gaps in Dio's *History* are partially filled by the epitomes of the Byzantine compilers Zonaras (early twelfth century) and Xiphilinus (late eleventh century), upon which we chiefly rely for the material of Books I–XXI and LXI–LXXX, respectively.

ATHENAEUS

(Early third century)

Athenaeus was born at Naucratis in Egypt, of Greek origin. He migrated to Rome, where he poured his antiquarian erudition into an encyclopedic work, the *Deipnosophistae* (Savants at Dinner). This learned miscellany is a storehouse of factual information, quotations from earlier authors, and anecdotes on the most varied social and literary topics, with particular emphasis on gastronomy.

HERODIAN

(A.D. c. 165–c. 255)

Herodian was a Syrian Greek in the Roman civil service. His *History* in eight books, an account of the successors of Marcus Aurelius to the accession of Gordian III (A.D. 180–238), is the work of a second-rate historian. He was sincere in his work and often possessed personal knowledge of events he recorded; but his history is biographical in character, rhetorical and moralistic. With all its deficiencies, however, Herodian's work embodies a good deal of material for which it is our sole extant source.

EUTROPIUS

(Reign of Valens [A.D. 364–378])

Eutropius, about whom little is known, is the author of a *Breviarium ab Urbe Condita* (Compendium of Roman History) to A.D. 364. Carefully compiled from secondary sources (in the main) and following the established tradition of Roman history, Eutropius' simple narrative, covering about twelve centuries, is of value in filling in existing gaps in our earlier sources.

THE "HISTORIA AUGUSTA"

The *Lives of the Caesars,* probably the product of the middle of the fourth century, is a collection of thirty imperial biographies from Hadrian to Carinus, the emperors from A.D. 117 to 284. (The lives for the period

244–253 are lost.) These biographies, which have been labeled "little better than literary monstrosities," are assigned by the tradition of the manuscripts to six different authors, but a widely held modern theory attributes the whole collection to a single writer. Modeled on Suetonius' biographical method, they are extremely untrustworthy (especially the later ones), emphasize trivial personal anecdotes, and are lacking in historical sense, critical ability, and respect for the truth. They contain over 150 alleged documents of all kinds, almost all of which are suspect as forgeries or outright fabrications.

AMMIANUS MARCELLINUS

(A.D. *c. 330–c. 395*)

Ammianus Marcellinus, the last great historian in antiquity, was born into an upper-class family in Antioch and made his career in the Roman army. Writing in Latin, he produced a *History* in continuation, and in the style, of Tacitus. Of his thirty-one books the first thirteen are lost; the surviving eighteen cover the years A.D. 353–378, for which period they are our principal source. Himself a pagan, Ammianus idolized the Emperor Julian, whose only fault he found to be his intolerance toward Christians. In Ammianus' view, "the decision of divine will . . . increased Rome from its cradle and promised that it would be eternal" (XIX. X. 4).

MACROBIUS

(A.D. *c. 400*)

The life of Ambrosius Theodosius Macrobius, the "Latin Athenaeus," is little known. The principal work of this antiquarian polymath and Vergil scholar, the *Saturnalia* in seven books, of a fictitious dialogue and symposium, is a vast miscellany of information on Roman antiquities, comparable to the *Attic Nights* of Aulus Gellius (see p. 29). It is especially valuable because of its excerpts from earlier works now lost and for the intellectual interests of the pagan aristocracy in the late Empire.

JULIAN

(A.D. *332–363*)

Julian "the Apostate," successor of Constantius II, was Roman emperor from 361 to 363. While officially proclaiming freedom of worship throughout the empire, he energetically strove to restore the ancestral polytheism and was even impelled to persecute Christians. A pupil of Libanius, he is the author of scores of *Letters,* many of them anti-Christian, all of them illustrative of his great learning and his interest in matters philosophical and antiquarian.

LIBANIUS

(A.D. *314–393*)

A Greek native of Antioch, where he spent most of his life, Libanius was a professor of rhetoric, orator, and man of letters. Though a zealous pagan, he was favored by the Emperors Constantius II and Theodosius; and though he eulogized the Emperor Julian, he was not unsympathetic to Christians. His extant works, reflecting the ideals of the urban upper classes of the eastern provinces, consist of 1,500 letters and sixty-four speeches, a veritable mine of information about late antiquity.

SYMMACHUS

(A.D. *c. 340–402*)

Quintus Aurelius Symmachus, the greatest orator of his time, held high posts in the imperial administration, including the consulship. Extant are many of Symmachus's letters, some state papers, and panegyrics of Valentinian I and of Gratian, which are major sources of information for the period. He was a traditionalist in pagan religion, and was a moderate anti-Christian.

CLAUDIAN

(A.D. *c. 370–404*)

Claudius Claudianus, a native of Egypt, was an influential court poet of late antiquity, the last Latin poet writing in the classical mode. He wrote in many classical genres, including epics.

ZOSIMUS

(Fifth Century)

Zosimus, a Greek historian of the late fifth–early sixth centuries, was a convinced pagan, who nevertheless held high imperial offices. His *New History* in six books, after quickly sketching past history from the Trojan War, concentrates on the period A.D. 305–410, for which it is one of our most important sources. Zosimus' underlying theme is the collapse of the Roman Empire, which he attributes in part to the weakness of the Roman rulers in admitting barbarians into Roman lands and military units, but primarily to the neglect of the pagan gods under the Christian emperors. Hence his special hostility to Constantine, whom he calls "the initiator of impiety."

XIPHILINUS AND ZONARAS

See Cassius Dio (p. 30).

CHRISTIAN WRITERS

JUSTIN MARTYR

(A.D. c. 100–c. 165)

Justinus Flavius, a native of Palestine and a convert to Christianity, is one of the earliest Christian writers. Of his works only the *Dialogue* and *Apology* have survived. The latter is especially valuable because of its description of early Christian worship and its analysis of the charges of crime and immorality leveled against the Christians.

TERTULLIAN

(A.D. c. 155/60–c. 222/30)

Quintus Septimius Florens Tertullianus, the founder of Western Christian theology and the first great personage of Latin Christianity, was born at Carthage and after his conversion became a priest. Of his voluminous apologetic, doctrinal, moral, and polemical writings, thirty-one works are extant. Particular interest attaches to his *Ad Nationes* (To the

Pagans), in two books, and to his *Apology,* which are concerned with the defense of Christian life against popular charges of criminality, immorality, and disloyalty to the imperial government.

CYPRIAN

(A.D. *c. 210–258*)

Thascius Caecilius Cyprianus, bishop of Carthage, was a prolific writer. For the student of Roman civilization the most instructive of his extant works are his *Letters,* mostly on church management and discipline; *De Lapsis* (On Those Who Have Lapsed from the Faith), dealing with conditions during the persecutions of the middle of the third century; *Ad Donatum* (To Donatus), on the vanity of worldly things, which presents a good picture of the pagan world of his time; and *De Ecclesiae Unitate* (On the Unity of the Catholic Church), his most important work.

MINUCIUS FELIX

(A.D. *c. 240*)

Marcus Minucius Felix, probably a Roman lawyer, is the author of the dialogue *Octavius.* This "finest of Latin apologies for Christianity" is a defense of the new religion against an attack upon it made by Fronto (see p. 29).

LACTANTIUS

(A.D. *c. 245/50–c. 325*)

Lucius Caecilius Firmianus Lactantius, the "Christian Cicero," was born at Carthage. He was converted to Christianity after a career as a professor of rhetoric and later was appointed tutor to Emperor Constantine's son Crispus. Of his many extant works the most famous is the *Institutiones Divinae* (Divine Institutes), in seven books, a defense of Christian doctrine against pagan religion. His *De Mortibus Persecutorum* (On the Deaths of the Persecutors) is valuable not only for the history of the persecutions from Nero to Galerius, but also for its precious contemporary description of Diocletian's economic and social reorganization of the Roman Empire.

EUSEBIUS

(A.D. *c. 260–339/40*)

Eusebius, bishop of Caesarea in Palestine, is the "Father of Church History." His *Ecclesiastical History* to A.D. 324, in ten books, is a mine of information about Christian antiquity, the persecutions, and the intellectual and institutional evolution of the Church. Extant also are his *Chronicon* in two books, a chronological table epitomizing universal history, and a *Life of Constantine* in four books, a glorification of the first Christian emperor.

AUGUSTINE

(A.D. *354–430*)

Aurelius Augustinus (St. Augustine), the "Christian Plato," was born in Numidia, had a career as professor of rhetoric in Carthage and Italy, where he was converted to Christianity, and later became bishop of Hippo in Africa. His vast literary product, totaling 118 works, consists of controversial books, doctrinal treatises, philosophical and rhetorical essays, biblical exegesis, sermons, and letters. Most famous are his spiritual autobiography, the *Confessions,* in thirteen books, and *De Civitate Dei* (The City of God), in twenty-two books. The latter work, a definitive reply to pagan attacks, is valuable not only for early Christian life and thought, but also for the numerous details of Roman history and religion that it contains.

OROSIUS

(*Early fifth century*)

Paulus Orosius, a native of the Iberian Peninsula, studied for a time with St. Augustine. He is the author of the first Christian universal history, the *Historiae adversus Paganos* (History Against the Pagans), in seven books. Based on secondary sources, rhetorical, distorted, diffuse, often erroneous and contradictory, Orosius' history of the world was essentially apologetic in purpose. He selected and emphasized the calamities and disasters of past history to support his thesis that the crisis of the

Roman Empire in his time was not due to the spread of Christianity and the abandonment of pagan religion, and that under a divine providence a better world was in the making.

JEROME

(A.D. *c. 345–420*)

Eusebius Hieronymus (St. Jerome), the famed Christian scholar, was the most learned man of his time, an ardent controversialist in his championing of Catholicism and the ascetic way of life. His most famous work is the translation of the New Testament into Latin (The Vulgate). Numerous letters of his survive.

LEGAL SOURCES

ROYAL ORDINANCES

The earliest Roman law of which we have any record is a collection of the enactments of the prerepublican kings, said to have been compiled by a *pontifex* named Papirius about the end of the regal period (510 B.C.). These laws are concerned largely with religion and related public matters; therefore, while they gave official sanction to a number of enduring customs, because of their basically sacral nature they had little importance in the development of Roman law in the Republic and Empire. See further § 8, where a selection from these royal ordinances is given.

THE TWELVE TABLES (450–449 B.C.)

Roman legal sources proper begin with the Twelve Tables. These laws, essentially a codification of existing custom, dealt with procedures in litigation, family relations, debt, land and other property matters, delicts, and a number of matters of public and sacred law. They are reproduced and discussed more fully in § 32.

LEGISLATION (LEGES, PLEBISCITA)

The most direct source of law is, of course, legislation. Under the Republic the only laws, in the strict sense of the word *(leges latae)*, were the enactments of the popular assemblies. The legislative assembly of the early Republic was the *comitia centuriata* (§ 27), in which the citizens voted in military units called centuries. Although this body continued to exercise certain traditional functions, from the third century B.C. on the most important legislative body of the Roman Republic was the *comitia tributa,* in which the vote was by tribes (i.e., by regional units). In addition to participating in these general assemblies, the plebeian citizens developed a separate conclave *(concilium plebis)* for the more effective assertion of their rights and demands. The resolutions of this plebeian assembly were known as *plebiscita*. In 287 B.C. the so-called struggle of the orders culminated in the Hortensian Law (§ 42), which decreed that *plebiscita* were to be as fully valid as *leges* proper. Therefore the plebeian and tribal assemblies became practically indistinguishable, and *plebiscita* were frequently loosely referred to as *leges.*

JUDICIAL EDICTS (EDICTA MAGISTRATUUM)

Among the prerogatives of the Roman magistrates who held the *imperium*—the consuls and praetors—was the right of issuing judicial edicts *(ius edicendi)*. In 367 B.C., when it had become apparent that the two consuls could no longer discharge all the executive functions of the expanding Roman state, the office of praetor was created to assume the supervision of the administration of justice (§ 38). Within a few years it became the custom for the praetor, on entering office, to issue an edict in which he set forth the principal rules of legal procedure that would prevail under his jurisdiction.[14] Since many of these rules were naturally retained and repeated each year by successive praetors, these became established with the passage of time as standard practice, and this continuing part of the praetor's edict came to be known as "the traditional edict" *(edictum tralaticium)*. Clearly, these edicts were not acts of legisla-

---

14. This initial proclamation did not, of course, preclude a praetor's right to issue additional regulations during his term of office if circumstances required. The praetor, it should be noted, was not a trial judge but more like a present-day minister of justice, or the Attorney General of the United States.

tion, but statements of procedures to be followed in the administration of the law. Yet, through this control of the operation and enforcement of the law, in the last century of the Republic the praetors—elected administrative officers who were often without legal training—became the most important agency of legal development.[15]

This power of the praetors came to an end *c.* A.D. 125, when the Emperor Hadrian assigned Salvius Julianus, the leading jurist of the time, to systematize the various praetorial edicts in permanent form, the so-called *Edictum Perpetuum.* Thereafter the praetors continued the formality of proclaiming their annual edicts, but they no longer had the power to introduce changes or innovations; this was henceforth the exclusive prerogative of the emperor.

ROMAN AND NON-ROMAN LAW
(IUS CIVILE, IUS GENTIUM)

The body of laws and customs peculiar to Rome and Roman citizens was known as *ius civile.* The expansion of Roman dominion and the resulting increased intercourse with foreigners led in 241 B.C. to the creation of a second praetor *(praetor peregrinus)* to supervise litigation in which aliens *(peregrini)* were involved. The first praetor (henceforth called *praetor urbanus)* continued to operate in the realm of *ius civile;* but since the latter was the exclusive privilege of Roman citizens, the *praetor peregrinus* issued a separate edict, based in large measure on "the law which natural reason has established among all men"[16]—*ius gentium.*

The source and nature of this body of law, which the Romans regarded as based on principles of common humanity and therefore universally applicable, have been variously explained by modern scholars. The prevailing view holds that in origin *ius gentium* consisted essentially of the simple legal rules observed by the peoples of central Italy. According to this view *ius civile* obviously included parts of *ius gentium,* plus certain elements of specifically Roman origin. What is certain at all events is that with the passage of time Roman law was increasingly influenced by the law of the subject peoples of the Empire, especially the

---

15. The latitude which this system left unscrupulous praetors desirous of serving private or special interests is fairly obvious. The best known case of its abuse is that of the notorious Verres (§§ 139, 143, 144).

16. Justinian, *Institutes* I. ii. I.

Greeks. "And so the Roman people too," wrote Justinian's compilers, "employs in part its own law, and in part the law common to all men."[17]

DECREES OF THE SENATE (SENATUS CONSULTA)

The senate was originally an advisory council to the Roman kings, and then to the Republican magistrates who succeeded the kings. In addition, it exercised a certain supervision over legislation, since enactments of the popular assemblies were usually submitted to it for preliminary approval. But, although it had no official legislative or executive power, the senate was able—both by virtue of the fact that it was the only permanent organ of the Roman government and by skillful political manipulation—to extend its supervisory and advisory control of magistrates and people to such a degree that from the end of the third century B.C. on it was in effect the real policy-making body of the Roman Republic. Its resolutions *(senatus consulta),* though strictly speaking only advices or instructions to magistrates on law enforcement, came to be phrased with all the finality of formal legislation and to have, for all intents and purposes, the force of law.

Under the Empire the popular assemblies were gradually abolished and *senatus consulta* became formal legislative enactments, but they were limited to such matters as the emperor chose to submit for the senate's rubber stamp of approval. Indeed, as the Principate evolved into overt monarchy it was the proposal made to the senate by the emperor *(oratio principis),* rather than the formality of its enactment by the Senate, that came to be referred to as the act of legislation. This frank recognition of reality appears *c.* A.D. 200; and the latest recorded *senatus consultum* dates from the reign of Probus (A.D. 276–282). With the accession of Diocletian soon afterward and the establishment of a frankly absolutistic monarchy, the emperor became the sole legislative authority of the Roman government.

IMPERIAL LEGISLATION (PRINCIPUM PLACITA)

Before Diocletian there was no constitutional basis for the emperor's legislative authority; but the imperial regime, although founded on the fiction of the "restored Republic," provided the emperor with such vast

17 Ibid

special powers that he was from the beginning of the Principate the supreme legislative authority in the state. Augustus, carefully avoiding the open manifestations of monarchy, preferred to effect and formalize his legislation through the traditional republican channels of the popular assemblies and the senate. However, immediately after his reign these republican pretenses began to disappear. In Tiberius' reign the powers of the assemblies were sharply curtailed and the Senate began to lose the modicum of authority that Augustus had left it. Hadrian, as noted earlier, flatly proclaimed his exclusive authority over the praetor's edict. A century later the noted jurist Ulpian penned the classic formulation of the situation: "What the emperor has determined has the force of law since . . . the people has transferred to him all its power and authority."[18] In this same third century the emperor, who had previously been declared subject to the laws, was proclaimed to be above the law. The culmination of this process was the complete elimination of the Senate as a legislative source and the emergence of the absolute monarchy under Diocletian.

The emperor's "legislative" acts, known as *constitutiones,* were of four types:

1. *Edicta.* These were statements, usually on novel matters and broad in scope, and had the force of statutes to all intents and purposes.

2. *Rescripta.* These were replies by the emperor to inquiries from officials and to petitions from individuals. Some rescripts applied only to the case at issue; others established precedents for the future. Whatever the intention of the issuing emperor, the tendency to regard and use all rescripts as precedents was naturally very strong, and this practice was finally validated by Justinian.

3. *Decreta.* These were judicial decisions of the emperor, either in cases of first instance or on appeal. Beginning with Diocletian, such decisions were usually rendered by rescript.

4. *Mandata.* These were administrative orders prepared in the imperial chancellery for governors setting out for their provinces, to brief them on the current status of important legal principles that they would need to apply in the exercise of the offices. *Mandata* were thus not new imperial enactments (and therefore not *constitutiones,* strictly speaking), but they incorporated already existing *constitutiones.* As such they frequently served jurists and nonjurists alike as convenient up-to-date sources of law.

18. Justinian, *Digest* I. iv. I *prooemium* (=*Institutes* I. ii. 6).

Unless specifically delimited, *constitutiones* apparently remained valid until expressly repealed or superseded.

INTERPRETATION BY JURISTS
(RESPONSA PRUDENTIUM)

The earliest interpreters of Roman law were the *pontifices,* the overseers of the rituals and taboos from which law in Rome, as in most primitive societies, arose. The college of pontiffs kept their rules and traditions secret until *c.* 300 B.C., when plebeians finally gained admittance to the pontificate and published its legal arcana, thereby destroying what had until then been a patrician monopoly manipulated against the commons. This secularization of the law gave rise to a new class of interpreters and elaborators of legal doctrine, the *iurisprudentes.* These men pursued their juristic activity neither by virtue of any official position nor in anticipation of consultation fees; their qualification, as characterized by one of their number, was "a conception of the good and the fair, separating right from wrong."[19] During the Republic the weight of their opinion depended entirely on their reputation. Under the Empire a kind of official recognition was accorded certain jurists in the form of an honorific privilege known as *ius respondendi,* "the right of giving [juristic] response"; and from the time of Hadrian at least, leading jurists were generally members of the emperor's advisory *consilium.* The era of the great jurists came to an end *c.* A.D. 250, when the Principate collapsed in anarchy, and with its passing ended the "classical age" of Roman law.

The jurists' activities may be classified under three major headings:

1. They advised magistrates and private individuals on points of law and procedure, on the conduct of litigation (they did not, however, plead), and on the drafting of legal instruments.

2. They gave instruction not by lecturing, but by allowing young men to be present at their consultations. This attendance at juristic consultations was regarded in the Republic and Empire as the most important part of the training for a legal and public career.

3. They produced an enormous legal literature. Their earliest works were commentaries on specific laws, case books, and collections of forms for legal and business use. The first systematic and scientific legal

19. Ulpian, in *Digest* I. i. I. I.

treatise, involving a theoretical approach and an analysis of general principles, was attributed to Quintus Mucius Scaevola, under whom Cicero studied; and it is probably no accident that Scaevola is the earliest writer quoted in Justinian's *Digest*. In the 300 years that followed, Roman jurists produced a great variety and quantity of legal works, from general handbooks of instruction *(institutiones)* to specialized monographs. Most of these works are preserved only in citations in the *Digest*. Of the few that have survived the most valuable is the *Institutes* of Gaius. This work, written *c* A.D. 160, was the chief source for the *Institutes* of Justinian. Other extant juristic works are the *Sententiae,* or "Opinions," of Paulus (*c.* A.D. 200); a book of *Regulae,* or "Rules," sometimes attributed to the famous jurist Ulpian but actually part of an epitome prepared A.D. 320–342 by an unknown writer; and a third-century treatise, commonly called *Comparison of Roman and Mosaic Law*.

CODIFICATIONS

The era of the jurists was succeeded by an age of codification, culminating in the sixth century in the comprehensive *Corpus Juris Civilis*. This development is not hard to understand. By A.D. 250 Roman law was a vast and constantly growing congeries of statutes, decisions, and other legal records. The great jurists had, by their teaching, consultations, and writings, helped their contemporaries to thread a course through this legal maze. With the disappearance of these commentators, practitioners turned to codifications for assistance in keeping abreast of the law.

The earliest of these codes were two private compilations, the *Codex Gregorianus* and the *Codex Hermogenianus*. While neither of these is extant, we know that they were published A.D. *c.* 291–295, that they gave a systematic presentation of the *constitutiones* from Hadrian to Diocletian, and that they are the source on which later compilations drew for earlier imperial enactments. The next important code was an official collection ordered by the Emperor Theodosius II and published in A.D. 438. This *Codex Theodosianus,* which is extant in considerable part, contained all the *constitutiones* from the time of Constantine. Finally, in the sixth century, Justinian assigned to a commission headed by Tribonian the task of preparing a definitive codification, superseding all previous compilations. This *Corpus Juris Civilis,* the direct ancestor of most modern European civil codes, is extant in its entirety and consists of four parts:

1. *Code* (first issued A.D. 529; only the revised edition of 534 is extant)

—a collection in twelve books of all important *constitutiones* from Hadrian to Justinian that were still in force, corrected, and modified to bring them up to date.

2. *Digest* or *Pandects* (A.D. 533)—the most important part of the whole work, a codification in fifty books of the writings of the jurists (2,000 treatises were perused), modified to take account of later legislation and to avoid redundancies, conflicts, and repetition of matter already in the *Code*.

3. *Institutes* (A.D. 533)—an introduction to Roman law for beginners (still used today for that purpose). The plan and much of the content of this book are derived from Gaius; most of its material is to be found also in the *Code* or *Digest*.

4. *Novels*—new *constitutiones* issued by Justinian himself in the twelve years after A.D. 534. This collection is not part of the great compilation directed by Tribonian. The most used form of this collection is the so-called *Authenticum,* in which Justinian's original Greek texts are accompanied by Latin translations.[20]

INSCRIPTIONS

A vast body of written and inscribed documents salvaged from the ruins of the ancient world helps us in some measure to overcome the incompleteness and to correct the subjectivity of the strictly literary sources on Roman civilization. An invaluable storehouse of primary materials is the accumulation of inscriptions on stone, metal, and other durable materials, which today numbers over 100,000 in Latin, and many thousands more in Greek but pertaining to Roman affairs (many of them translations of official documents and communications received in the Greek-speaking part of the Empire from the Roman government). Each year a considerable number of additional inscriptions continues to be unearthed. Preserved sometimes in fragmentary condition and sometimes intact, these inscriptions range in size from the most exiguous remnants to such extensive documents as the *Fasti Capitolini* [see note 1], the *Deeds of the*

---

20. In order to achieve a consistent and up-to-date *Corpus,* Justinian's compilers, as mentioned above, did not hesitate to alter earlier texts when they found it necessary. Similar intrusive or altered matter is found also in the extant works of the jurists, all of which have come down to us in manuscripts considerably later in date than the original publications. These adulterations of text are known technically as *interpolations.* Much progress has been made in the past hundred years in identifying these interpolations and in reconstructing the original texts of the juristic works and of the *constitutiones* compiled in the first three centuries of the Christian era.

Deified Augustus (§ 195) and Diocletian's *Edict on Maximum Prices* (vol. 2, § 123).

The science of epigraphy is of comparatively recent date. Collections of Latin inscriptions began to be made as early as the time of Charlemagne, but their study was not put on a scientific basis until the nineteenth century. Thus access to this rich epigraphical material is still largely reserved to specialists. Few translations have been made, and those that do exist have appeared in such scattered publications as to be virtually inaccessible to students and laymen interested in Roman antiquity. One of the aims of the present collection of sources is to remedy this deficiency, within the limits of these volumes, for the English-speaking public.

Official documents of the Roman Republic and Empire were regularly inscribed for permanent record; among the extant inscriptions are numerous examples of treaties, laws and plebiscites, decrees of the senate, edicts and communications of Roman magistrates and foreign powers, pronouncements and enactments of the Roman emperors and dedications to them, military documents (especially veterans' diplomas), and calendars and *fasti*—to mention a few of the more important types. In addition, there are huge quantities of honorary and commemorative inscriptions, of business and personal records, even scribblings on walls (so-called *graffiti*), relating to private individuals of low as well as high station.

Indeed, from the second century B.C. to the end of the Roman Empire, there is hardly any aspect of Roman civilization that is not illuminated by the inscriptions.[21] They provide in particular a corrective to the upper-class perspectives of the literary sources by affording insights into the private lives, occupations, and thinking of the common people. Moreover, it is largely through the inscriptions that the main lines of the social and economic history of the Roman Empire have been reconstructed. The entire field of Roman law has been enriched by inscriptional evidence. Inscriptions have shed great light in the areas of international affairs; the administration of Rome, Italy, and the provinces of the Empire; the exploitation of subject peoples; the careers of major and minor personages of Roman officialdom; taxation and other fiscal matters; the extension of Roman citizenship; and the progress of urbanization. The internal administration of Roman municipalities is illustrated

---

21. Inscriptions of the Republican period constitute only a small fraction of the total now extant; the overwhelming majority belong to the period of the Empire.

by a host of epigraphical documents. A great many yield detailed information on the powers of the Roman emperors, the imperial civil service, the growth and administration of the emperor's personal domains, and the emergence of quasi-feudal relationships such as the colonate. They have also provided valuable information on religious institutions, and a very numerous group documents the spread of Christianity in the Roman world.

PAPYRI AND SIMILAR DOCUMENTS

For ordinary official, business, and personal needs, the Roman world employed a writing paper made by pressing together two transverse layers of thin strips cut from the papyrus plant and laid side by side. Papyrus documents are associated primarily, though not exclusively, with Egypt. The Nile delta, where the plant grew in abundance, retained throughout antiquity a practical monopoly of papyrus manufacture, which was invented by the Egyptians *c.* 3000 B.C., and it is from the desert sands of Egypt, where they lay for centuries protected from the deteriorating effects of air and water, that nearly all of the ancient papyri now extant have been recovered.[22]

Papyrus was put up and sold in roll form *(volumen),*[23] which could be used whole or from which pieces could be cut as desired. For jottings, memoranda, and similar purposes, the Romans frequently used small wooden tablets with surfaces thinly waxed (or sometimes merely smoothed), either singly or strung together in a pad; this pad of superimposed tablets was the forerunner of the *codex,* or modern book form, which came into use for both papyrus and parchment in the course of the first century B.C. or A.D. and which had completely supplanted the roll for literary works by the fourth century.[24] Parchment, though employed mostly for literature, was used also for documents in some parts of the Empire, especially in areas such as Asia Minor, where large-scale sheep-raising afforded an abundance of the raw material. Finally,

22. A few papyrus finds have been made outside Egypt, notably at Herculaneum (see note 26), at Dura-Europus in the Syrian desert, in Israel at Nessana in the southern desert (the Negev) and in a cave of the Judaean desert, and (carbonized) in a tomb in Macedonia, all of which afforded moisture-free conditions similar to those of the Egyptian desert.

23. Hence ancient literary works were customarily separated into volumes, or books.

24. The lectionary use of the Gospels and other books of early Christianity was an important factor fostering this development, since the desired passage could be found more quickly in the *codex* than in the *volumen* form.

there are important records of antiquity preserved on ostraca, or pot-sherds, which were widely used in the Eastern Mediterranean in pre-Roman and Roman times for brief notations of all kinds.[25] In the Hellen-istic and Roman periods ostraca were used most often for tax receipts, presumably because the taxpayer had to furnish the material for the receipt, and any household could provide a supply of broken bits of pottery.

The study of ancient documents preserved on these materials, known as papyrology from the most usual of them, is the newest of the auxil-iary sciences of classical scholarship, having developed only in the last hundred years. To be sure, ancient papyri began to be recovered in the Mediterranean area as early as the eighteenth century, both in Her-culaneum[26] and in Egypt. But systematic excavation for and scientific study of papyri began only in the 1880s, after Egyptian peasants turned up hundreds of pieces one year while digging for fertilizer in the refuse dumps of buried ancient towns. Since then numerous archaeological expeditions and continued activity by native diggers have yielded an almost unbelievably rich harvest of papyri and other finds. Thousands of papyri and ostraca have already been published; many thousands more repose still unpublished in many museums, libraries, and private collections in the Near East, Europe, and the United States.

When Alexander the Great conquered the Persian Empire (of which Egypt was then a part), Greek became both the language of officialdom and the *lingua franca* of commerce in the ancient Near East, and it continued throughout the period of Roman rule to be the universal language of the eastern Mediterranean. In this area Latin was used almost exclusively by those agencies directly connected with and re-sponsible to Rome, notably the offices of the provincial governors and the army units stationed at strategic points. Accordingly, almost all the papyri, ostraca, etc., of the Roman period are written in Greek. The comparatively few Latin pieces deal mostly with the army and to a lesser extent with the imperial administration.

Unlike literary works and epigraphic records, papyrus documents

25. The well-known Athenian practice of ostracism employed ostraca (on which the intended victim's name was scratched or written) as ballots.

26. Beginning in 1752, some 800 papyrus rolls were found in the excavation of Herculaneum. Like other cellulose substances, they were carbonized by the volcanic matter that covered the town in the famous eruption of Vesuvius in A.D. 79. The rolls were obviously part of a library. Because of the difficulty of opening the almost petrified rolls, comparatively few of these texts have been read to date; the published fragments, however, show that this was a library of philosophical and other literary works (mostly Greek, some Latin), including many now lost.

were not composed with an eye to posterity. They are, for the most part, the papers of everyday activity: business contracts, tax receipts, personal letters—in short, everything from imperial constitutions and other official records to shopping lists and similar personal trivia. Thus these documents, as broad in their range as life itself, enable us to view the many-faceted life in a Roman province in its living, pulsating reality, and in particular to penetrate into the activities, thoughts, and emotions of the provincial masses, who appear in literature only as seen through the eyes of the educated upper classes. The papyri have been particularly informative in matters of law, administration, economics, society, and private life. A considerable number of the details revealed by these texts are, to be sure, peculiar to Egypt or even to a given locality in Egypt; but, even though Egypt occupied a unique status among the Roman provinces, being officially the personal domain of the Roman emperor, it was nonetheless a Roman province, and much can be learned from the papyri which is germane to the history of the Roman Empire as a whole.

COINS

Rome's need for coined money arose with the spread of her power and interests through the Italian peninsula and the concomitant transformation of her internal economy. The earliest Roman coinage was issued *c.* 300 B.C., at first only in bronze but very soon after in silver and gold as well. Subsequent expansion and conquests overseas provided the Romans with vastly increased supplies of precious metals. But it was not until the time of Augustus that Roman coinage was issued in regular and steady supply. During the Republic coins were minted only at intervals and to meet specific needs—those of public largess and the ordinary requirements of trade, and above all those of the endless wars.

For republican and imperial times alike these coins, by their legends and their pictorial representations, illuminate innumerable details of Roman history and historical tradition, mores, domestic politics, provincial administration, foreign policy, religion, buildings and monuments, wars and triumphs. Indeed the Roman coins may be said to provide us with an incomplete, to be sure, but representative pictorial history of Roman civilization.

The coins are instructive also by the geographic distribution of the finds. For example, the mute yet eloquent testimony of coin hoards buried for safekeeping in the soil of France in the fourth and fifth centuries A.D. frequently date and localize a barbarian invasion or similar alarm. Moreover, while the great majority of Romans coins have naturally been found within the territorial confines of the Roman Empire, specimens have been unearthed all the way from Scandinavia to India. The numbers and dates of the coins in these finds faithfully reflect the extension of the commerce of the Roman Empire in the first two centuries of the Principate and its contraction thereafter. A particularly striking case in point is the large number of coins of Augustus and his immediate successors found in India, recalling the Elder Pliny's complaint that in the middle of the first century A.D. foreign trade with the East drained the empire of 100,000,000 sesterces in specie annually.[27]

See further chapter 10.

27. *Natural History* XII. xli. 84. This huge figure may indeed be, as many modern scholars have thought, somewhat exaggerated, but the coins show that Pliny's statement resides upon a serious basis of fact.

FROM THE BEGINNINGS TO 509 B.C.

1. ITALY

THE PEOPLES OF ITALY AND ITS PHYSICAL GEOGRAPHY

Pliny, *Natural History* III. v. 38–40, 43–45; From *LCL*

After this comes Italy, its first people being the Ligurians, after whom come Etruria, Umbria, and Latium, where are the mouths of the Tiber and Rome, the capital of the world, sixteen miles from the sea. Afterwards comes the coast of the Volsci and of Campania, then of Picenum and Lucania and the Bruttii, the southernmost point to which Italy juts out into the sea from the almost crescent-shaped chain of the Alps. After the Bruttii comes the coast of Magna Graecia,[1] followed by the Sallentini, Paediculi, Apuli, Paeligni, Frentani, Marrucini, Vestini, Sabini, Picentes, Gauls, Umbrians, Tuscans, Venetians, Carni, Iapudes, Histri, and Liburni.[2] I am well aware that I may with justice be considered ungrateful and lazy if I describe in this casual and cursory manner a land which is at once the nursling and the mother of all other lands, chosen by the providence of the gods to make heaven itself more glorious, to unite scattered empires, to make manners gentle, to draw together in converse by community of language the jarring and uncouth tongues of so many nations, to give mankind civilization, and in a word to become throughout the world the single fatherland of all the races. But what am I to do? The great fame of all its places—who could touch upon them

---

1. The southern coastal region of Italy, dotted with Greek colonies established there c. 750–500 B.C.

2. Pliny proceeds counterclockwise around Italy. Distances are given in Roman miles (see Glossary).

all?—and the great renown of the various things and peoples in it give me pause. In that list even the city of Rome alone . . . what elaborate description it merits! . . .

In shape, then, Italy much resembles an oak leaf, being far longer than it is broad, bending towards the left at its top and ending in the shape of an Amazon's shield, the projection in the center being called Cocynthos [now Punta di Stilo] while it sends out two horns along bays of crescent shape, Leucopetra [now Capo delle Colonne] on the right and Lacinium [now Capo dell'Armi] on the left. Its length extends for 1,020 miles, beginning from Aosta at the foot of the Alps and passing through Rome and Capua in a winding course to the town of Reggio situated on its shoulder, where begins the curve, as it were, of the neck. . . . The breadth varies, being 410 miles between the rivers Var and Arsa where they flow into the Tuscan Sea and the Adriatic, but at about the middle, in the neighborhood of the city of Rome, from the mouth of the River Pescara, which flows into the Adriatic Sea, to the mouths of the Tiber, its breadth is 136 miles, and a little less from Castrum Novum on the Adriatic to Palo on the Tuscan Sea, in no place exceeding a width of 200 miles. The circuit of the entire coast from the Var round to the Arsa is 2,049 miles. Its distances from the countries that surround it are as follows: from Istria and Liburnia in certain places, 100 miles; from Epirus and Illyricum, 50 miles; from Africa, according to Marcus Varro, less than 200; from Sardinia, 120; from Sicily, 1½; from Corcyra, less than 80; from Issa,[3] 50.

THE RESOURCES OF ITALY

Pliny, *Natural History* XXXVII. xiii. 77

Having now treated all the works of nature, I think it would be appropriate to conclude with a judgment, as it were, on her bounties and on the countries which produce them. My conclusion is that on the whole earth, wherever the vault of heaven extends, the country which is the most beautiful and which deservedly holds first place in all the products of nature is Italy, the ruler and second parent of the world; recommended as she is by her men and women, her generals and soldiers, her slaves, her preeminence in the arts, and the renown of her brilliant men, by her situation, too, her healthful and temperate climate, the easy access which she offers to all peoples, her many-harbored coasts and favorable

3. Island in the Adriatic, now Vis, Yugoslavia; its Italian name is Lissa.

winds; advantages, all of them, due to her situation, lying as she does midway between the east and the west, and extended in the most favorable of all positions. Add to this the abundant supply of her waters, the healthfulness of her wooded groves, the repeated intersections of her mountain ranges, the mildness of her wild animals, the fertility of her soil, the richness of her pastures. She is surpassed by no land in any of those products which human life ought not to feel in want of: cereals, wine, olive oil, wool, flax, clothing, cattle. As for horses, none are preferred to the native breed for training for three-horse races; while for mines of gold, silver, copper, and iron, so long as it was legal to work them, Italy was second to no land. At the present day, teeming as she is with these treasures, she lavishes upon us, as the whole of her bounties, her various liquids and the flavors of her cereals and fruits [see further § 166 on agriculture in Italy].

2. THE ETRUSCANS

The origin of the Etruscans, the neighbors of the Romans in the region from the Tiber River to the Arno now known as Tuscany, remains the most knotty question of early Italian history. The theory that they came to Italy as migrants from Lydia in Asia Minor was current at least as early as the fifth century B.C., when Herodotus recorded it in his *History* (I. xciv). As the first of the following three selections shows, however, this theory did not win universal acceptance even in ancient times. There are about 10,000 Etruscan inscriptions, written in the Greek alphabet, but in an obscure language. On the basis of extensive archaeological remains, Etruscologists are generally inclined to the view that it was largely an indigenous Italic culture, with exotic elements. "Most of the obscurities of Etruscan history derive from the fact that it reaches us from an alien and largely hostile tradition, recorded when Etruria was already a spent force" (*Oxford Classical Dictionary*, 2d ed., p. 410). The cultural influence of the Etruscans on Rome, particularly on her religious, military, and political institutions, was impressive.

Dionysius of Halicarnassus, *Roman Antiquities* I. xxx. 1–3; From *LCL*

I am convinced that the Pelasgians are not the same as the Tyrrhenians. And I do not believe, either, that the Tyrrhenians were a colony of the Lydians; for they do not use the same language as the latter, nor can it be alleged that, though they no longer speak a similar tongue, they still retain some other indications of their mother country. For they neither worship the same gods as the Lydians nor make use of similar laws or institutions, but in these very respects they differ more from the Lydians than from the Pelasgians. Indeed, those probably come nearest to the truth who declare that the nation migrated from nowhere else, but was native to the country, since it is found to be a very ancient nation and to agree with no other either in its language or in its manner of living. And there is no reason why the Greeks should not have called them by this name, both from their living in towers[4] [*tyrrheis* in Greek] and from the name of one of their rulers. The Romans, however, give them other names: from the country they once inhabited, named Etruria, they call them Etruscans, and from their knowledge of the ceremonies relating to divine worship, in which they excel others, they now call them Tuscans.[5]

Livy, *History of Rome* v. xxxiii. 7–10; From *LCL*

The Tuscan sway, down to the rise of the Roman domination, stretched over a wide expanse of land and sea. How great their power was on the upper and lower seas, by which Italy is surrounded like an island, is apparent from the names, since the Italian peoples have called one of them Tuscan, the general designation of the nation, and the other Hadriatic, from Hatria, an Etruscan colony; and the Greeks call the same seas Tyrrhenian and Adriatic. In the lands which slope on either side towards one of these seas they had twice twelve cities; first the twelve on this side of the Apennines, towards the lower sea; to which afterwards they added the same number beyond the Apennines, sending over as many colonies as there were original cities, and taking possession of all the region beyond the Po River (except the angle belonging to the Veneti who dwell about the gulf) as far as the Alps.

Diodorus of Sicily, *Historical Library* v. xl. 1–2; From *LCL*

It remains for us now to speak of the Tyrrhenians. This people, excelling as they did in manly vigor, in ancient times possessed great territory and founded many notable cities. Likewise, because they also availed them-

---

4. This version of the origin of the name *Tyrrhenian* appears already in the fifth century B.C. (Herodotus I. xciv).

5. This ancient "etymology" regarded the name Tuscan as derived from the Greek verb *thyo*, "to sacrifice." The prevalent view today is that *Tusci* stems from *Tursci* (whence *Etursci*, which became *Etrusci*), where *turs* is the same element that appears in the Greek *Tyrsenoi*, the older form of *Tyrrhenoi*.

selves of powerful naval forces and were masters of the sea over a long period, they caused the sea along Italy to be named Tyrrhenian after them; and, also perfecting the organization of land forces, they were the inventors of the *salpinx,* as it is called, a discovery of the greatest usefulness in war and named after them the "Tyrrhenian trumpet." They were also the authors of the dignity that surrounds the heads of the state, providing their rulers with lictors and an ivory stool[6] and a toga with a purple band;[7] and in connection with their houses they invented the peristyle, a useful device for avoiding the confusion connected with the attending throngs; and these things were adopted for the most part by the Romans, who added to their embellishment and transferred them to their own political institutions. Letters and the teaching about nature and the gods they also brought to greater perfection, and they elaborated the art of divination by thunder and lightning more than all other men; and for this reason the Romans, who rule practically the entire inhabited world, show honor to these men even to this day and employ them as interpreters of the omens of Jupiter as they appear in thunder and lightning.[8]

3. ADVANTAGES OF THE SITE OF ROME

Cicero, *Republic* ii. v–vi; From *LCL*

How, then, could Romulus have acted with a wisdom more divine, both availing himself of all the advantages of the sea and avoiding its disadvantages, than by placing his city on the bank of a never-failing river whose broad stream flows with unvarying current into the sea? Such a river enables the city to use the sea both for importing what it lacks and for exporting what it produces in superfluity; and by means of it likewise the city can not only bring in by sea but also obtain from the land, carried on its waters, whatever is most essential for its life and civilization. Consequently it seems to me that Romulus must at the very beginning have had a divine intimation that the city would one day be the seat and hearthstone of a mighty empire; for scarcely could a city

---

6. This stool was called by the Romans *sella curulis,* "curule chair." For the lictors, see Glossary.

7. Called by the Romans *toga praetexta.* See Glossary.

8. On the importance of divination among the Romans, see § 177.

placed upon any other site in Italy have more easily maintained our present widespread dominion.

As to the natural defenses of the city itself, who is so unobserving as not to have a clear outline of them imprinted upon his mind? The line and course of its walls were wisely planned by Romulus and the kings who succeeded him, being so placed on the everywhere steep and precipitous hillsides that the single approach, which lies between the Esquiline and the Quirinal hills, was girt about by a huge rampart facing the foe and by a mighty trench; and our citadel [the Capitoline Hill] was so well fortified by the sheer precipices which encompass it and the rock which appears to be cut away on every side that it remained safe and impregnable even at the terrible time of the advent of the Gauls [for the Gallic invasion see § 14]. In addition, the site which he chose abounds in springs and is healthful, though in the midst of a pestilential region; for there are hills, which not only enjoy the breezes but at the same time give shade to the valleys below.

4. FOUNDATION LEGENDS

For pre-Republican Rome the archaeological evidence is our principal reliable source. The historical value of the numerous foundation legends is negligible. "The evidence they supply is less valuable for the beginnings of Roman history than for the entry of Rome into the intellectual heritage of Greece" (*Cambridge Ancient History,* 7:369). Largely created by Greek imagination in the fifth and fourth centuries B.C. and harmonized with the native Romulus legends, they were absorbed into the Roman annalistic tradition.

Livy, *History of Rome* I. i–vii (abridged); From *LCL*

First of all, then, it is generally agreed that when Troy was taken, vengeance was wreaked upon the other Trojans, but that two, Aeneas and Antenor, were spared all the penalties of war by the Achaeans, owing to long-standing claims of hospitality, and because they had always advocated peace and the giving back of Helen. They then experienced various vicissitudes. . . . Aeneas . . . guided by fate to undertakings of greater consequence [than Antenor], came . . . [to Latium in Italy]. Landing there, the Trojans, who, after their all but immeasurable wanderings, had nothing left but their swords and ships, were driving booty from the fields, when King Latinus and the aborigines, who then occupied the country, rushed down from their city and their fields to repel with arms the violence of the invaders. . . . Latinus was told that the people were Trojans and their leader son of Anchises and Venus; that their city had been burnt, and that, driven from home, they were looking for a dwelling place and a site where they might build a city. . . . Aeneas became a guest in the house of Latinus; there the latter, in the presence of his household gods, added a domestic pact to the public one, by giving his daughter in marriage to Aeneas. This event removed any doubt in the minds of the Trojans that they had brought their wanderings to an end at last in a permanent and settled habitation. They founded a town, which Aeneas named Lavinium, after his wife. In a short time, moreover, there was a male scion of the new marriage, to whom his parents gave the name of Ascanius.

[United by Aeneas, the Trojans and aborigines, renamed Latins, were forced into war by the Rutulians, led by King Turnus, previously betrothed to Lavinia. Turnus was supported by the Etruscans under King Mezentius. The Latins were victorious, but both Latinus and Aeneas lost their lives in the war. Aeneas' son, Ascanius, when he reached manhood left Lavinium and founded a new city, Alba Longa. There follows the traditional line of kings to Numitor.]

Amulius drove out his brother Numitor and ruled in his stead. Adding crime to crime, he destroyed Numitor's male issue; and Rhea Silvia, his brother's daughter, he appointed a Vestal under the pretense of honoring her, and by consigning her to perpetual virginity, deprived her of the hope of children. But the Fates were resolved, as I suppose, upon the founding of this great city, and the beginning of the mightiest of empires, next after that of Heaven. The Vestal was ravished, and having given birth to twin sons, named Mars as the father of her doubtful offspring, whether actually so believing, or because it seemed less wrong if a god were the author of her fault. But neither gods nor men protected the mother herself or her babes from the king's cruelty; the priestess he ordered to be manacled and cast into prison, the children to be committed to the river. It happened by singular good fortune that the Tiber, having spread beyond its banks into stagnant pools, afforded nowhere any access to the regular channel of the river, and the men who brought the twins were led to hope that being infants they might be drowned. . . . The story goes that when the floating basket in which the children had been exposed was left high and dry by the receding water, a she-wolf, coming down out of the surrounding hills to slake her thirst, turned her steps towards the cry of the infants, and with her teats gave them suck so gently that the keeper of the royal flock found her licking them with her tongue.[9] Tradition assigns to this man the name of Faustulus, and adds that he carried the twins to his hut and gave them to his wife Larentia to rear. Some think that Larentia, having been free with her favors, had got the name of "she-wolf" among the shepherds, and that this gave rise to this marvelous story.

> [The youth of Romulus and Remus is described, and how Remus was captured and turned over to Amulius, how the identity of the twins was revealed, how Amulius was killed and the kingdom restored to their grandfather Numitor.]

The Alban state being thus turned over to Numitor, Romulus and Remus were seized with the desire to found a city in the region where they had been exposed and brought up. And in fact the population of Albans and Latins was too large. . . . Since the brothers were twins, and respect for their age could not determine between them, it was agreed that the gods who had those places in their protection should choose by augury who should give the new city its name, and who should govern it when built. Romulus took the Palatine for his augural quarter, Remus the Aventine. Remus is said to have been the first to receive an augury, from the flight of six vultures. The omen had been already reported when twice that number appeared to Romulus. Thereupon each was saluted king by his own followers, the one party laying claim to the honor from priority, the other from the number of the birds. They then engaged in a battle of words and, angry taunts leading to bloodshed, Remus was struck down in the affray. The commoner story is that Remus leaped over the new walls in mockery of his brother, whereupon Romulus in great anger slew him, and in menacing wise added these words withal, "So perish whoever shall leap over my walls!"[10] Thus Romulus acquired sole power, and the city, thus founded, was called by its founder's name.

---

9. The famous Capitoline wolf, a product of Etruscan art of the fifth century B.C., has no connection with the Romulus-Remus legend. The twins that now form a part of the statue were added during the Italian Renaissance. The earliest known plastic representation of the legend is the bronze statue of the wolf suckling twin boys set up in the Forum at Rome in 296 B.C.

10. This part of the legend was devised to illustrate the sanctity of the *pomerium,* on which see § 6.

5. The Seven Kings of Rome

"In the beginning," says Tacitus in the opening words of his *Annals,* "kings ruled the city of Rome." Though most of the kings recorded by name were historical personages, no reliable record of their reigns can be reconstructed. Many of the religious, social, and political institutions of republican Rome obviously originated in the regal period, but the details of the traditional accounts were mostly fabricated by annalists and antiquarians.

Eutropius, *Compendium of Roman History* I. i–viii

The Roman Empire—human memory can hardly recall any empire smaller in its beginnings or larger in its growth throughout the whole world—has its origin from Romulus, who was born (together with his twin brother Remus) the son of Rhea Silvia, a Vestal Virgin, and, according to belief, of Mars. At the age of eighteen, while engaged in brigandage among shepherds, he founded a small town on the Palatine Hill, on the 21st of April, in the third year of the Sixth Olympiad, and the 394th after the destruction of Troy.[11]

After the foundation of the city, which he called Rome after his own name, he proceeded about as follows. He enrolled as citizens a great number of the neighboring people and chose a hundred of the elders whose advice he could employ in conducting all business and whom he named senators on account of their age. Then, since he himself and his people had no wives, he invited the peoples near the city of Rome to an exhibition of games, and seized their young women.[12] After war broke out because of the injustice involved in the seizure, he conquered the inhabitants of Caenina, Antemnae, Crustumerium, the Sabine country, Fidenae, and Veii. All these towns surround the city of Rome. And when he disappeared in a sudden storm, he was believed to have been carried off to the gods in the thirty-seventh year of his reign, and he was deified. Then Rome was ruled by senators for five-day periods, and a full year passed under their administration.[13]

Then Numa Pompilius was elected king. He, it is true, waged no wars, but was no less beneficial to the state than Romulus. For he

11. April 21, 753 B.C., the traditional date of the founding of Rome.
12. The famous "rape of the Sabine women"; the story may be read in detail in Livy I. ix–xiii.
13. The traditional origin of the *interregnum*, the stopgap period when there was no chief magistrate. Cf. Dionysius of Halicarnassus, *Roman Antiquities* II. lvii. 1–2.

established laws and customs for the Romans, who because of the frequency of their battles were already regarded as brigands and semi-civilized; and he marked off the year, which had previously been confused because of lack of regulation, into ten months;[14] and he established at Rome an endless number of religious rites and temples. He died a natural death in the forty-third year of his reign.

He was succeeded by Tullus Hostilius. This king resumed warfare, conquered the Albans who are situated twelve miles from Rome, and the people of Veii and Fidenae, six and eight miles respectively from Rome. He also enlarged the city by adding to it the Caelian Hill. After a reign of thirty-two years, he was struck by lightning and burned to death together with his house.

After him Ancus Marcius, grandson of Numa on his daughter's side, received the *imperium*. He waged war against the Latins, added the Aventine Hill and the Janiculan Hill to the city, and founded a city [Ostia] on the seacoast at the mouth of the Tiber sixteen miles from Rome. He died a natural death in the twenty-fourth year of his reign.

Next Tarquinius Priscus became king. He doubled the number of senators, built the *circus* at Rome, and established the Roman Games, which still continue in our times. He likewise conquered the Sabines and annexed to the territory of Rome a considerable amount of territory removed from them. He was the first to enter the city in triumph. He built walls and sewers, and began the construction of the Capitol. He was killed in the thirty-eighth year of his reign by the sons of Ancus, the king whom he had succeeded.

After him Servius Tullius, son of an aristocratic woman who was however a captive slave girl, received the *imperium*. He also subjugated the Sabines, added three hills, the Quirinal, Viminal, and Esquiline, to the city, and constructed ditches around the wall. He was the first to order a census, which up to that time had been unknown throughout the entire world. Under him, when all had been subjected to the census, Rome had 83,000 citizens, including those in the rural districts. He was criminally killed by his son-in-law Tarquin the Proud, son of the king whom he himself had succeeded, and by his own daughter, to whom Tarquin was married.

Lucius Tarquinius the Proud, the seventh and last of the kings, conquered the Volsci, a people not far from the city in the direction of Campania, subjected the towns of Gabii and Suessa Pometia, made

14. The calendar of the early period was a twelve-month lunar calendar. See § 9.

peace with the Etruscans, and built the temple of Jupiter on the Capitoline.[15] Afterwards, while assaulting Ardea, a town situated eighteen
miles from Rome, he lost his power. For after his son, who was also
called Tarquin, had violated a very well-known and very chaste woman,
Lucretia, the wife of Collatinus, she complained to her husband, father,
and friends of the violence done to her, and committed suicide in sight
of all. For this reason Brutus, likewise a relative of Tarquin, aroused the
populace and deprived Tarquin of his power. Soon the army too, which
was besieging the town of Ardea with him, deserted; and when, on
coming to the city, the king found the gates closed and himself shut out,
he went into exile with his wife and children, after he had reigned
twenty-four years. Thus Rome was a monarchy, under seven kings, for
243 years, while as yet the territory of Rome extended at most just about
fifteen miles.

6. THE POMERIUM: FOUNDING AND GROWTH OF THE CITY OF ROME

Italic towns were founded with religious ceremonies attributed by the
ancient authors to Etruscan origin. The boundary line, or *pomerium,* of the
proposed site was formally laid down and marked off by stones. The
urban territory thus delimited was ceremonially inaugurated as a *templum,*
or rectangular area of sacred character within whose bounds the auspices
could be taken. The *pomerium* thus had important juridical, religious, and
political implications, for it served as a sort of religious frontier, separated
the *urbs* (city) from the *ager publicus* (public land), and marked the limit of
the jurisdiction of the urban magistrates as well as of the extra-urban
power of those invested with military authority. The extension of the
pomerial line tended to keep pace with the growth of the city.

Livy, *History of Rome* I. xliv

To accommodate such a large population it was apparent that the city
too had to be enlarged. He [Servius Tullius] added two hills, the Quirinal and the Viminal; then next he enlarged the Esquiline, and he himself
lived there, in order to give respectability to the place. He surrounded

15. The Capitol, which housed the Etruscan trinity of Jupiter, Juno, and Minerva, was one of the
earliest temples built in Rome. Dedicated in 509 or 507 B.C. and presided over by Jupiter Optimus
Maximus (Jupiter Best and Greatest), it remained the central shrine of the Romans throughout their
history.

the city with an embankment and both ditches and a wall;[16] thus he extended the *pomerium.* Those who consider solely the etymology of the word *pomerium* interpret it to be *postmoerium* (the space behind the wall); it is, however, rather the space on both sides of the wall, the place which formerly the Etruscans, when they founded cities, used to consecrate with augural rites,[17] fixing definite boundaries on both sides with boundary stones, at the points where they intended to construct a wall, so that on the inside no buildings should be extended to the fortifications (which now commonly are actually attached to them), and so that on the outside there should extend some ground untouched by human labor. This space, which it was forbidden either to inhabit or to plow, was called by the Romans *pomerium* as much because it is behind the wall as because the wall is behind it, and as the city grew, those consecrated boundaries were always extended as far as the fortification walls were to be advanced.

Aulus Gellius, Attic Nights XIII. xiv. 1–3; From LCL

The augurs of the Roman people who wrote books *On the Auspices* have defined the meaning of *pomerium* in the following terms: "The *pomerium* is the space within the rural district designated by the augurs along the whole circuit of the city without the walls, marked off by fixed bounds and forming the limit of the city auspices." Now the most ancient *pomerium,* which was established by Romulus, was bounded by the foot of the Palatine Hill. But that *pomerium,* as the Republic grew, was extended several times and included many lofty hills. Moreover, whoever had increased the domain of the Roman people by land taken from an enemy had the right to enlarge the *pomerium.*

7. The End of the Monarchy at Rome

The rape of Lucretia is one of the best known of Roman legends. Through the romantic web of the story, which is merely fictional embroidery supplied by a later age, there emerges clearly enough the essential political

16. Remains of such a fortification wall (seventh/sixth century?) have been discovered.

17. Cf. Servius, *Commentary on Vergil,* Aeneid v. 755: "Cato says in his *Origins* that this was the custom. Founders of a city yoked a bull on the right, a cow on the inner side, and, girded Gabinian fashion, that is, with the toga partly covering the head and partly tucked up, they used to hold the curved plow handle so that all the earth fell on the inner side; and thus by constructing a ditch, they marked out the site of the walls, raising the plow at the locations of the gates."

fact, which there is no reason to question: about the end of the sixth century B.C. there occurred at Rome a local revolution, such as other Etruscan-dominated cities also witnessed in this era of declining Etruscan power, by which the aristocratic families overthrew the royal dynasty and assumed control of the state.

Dionysius of Halicarnassus, *Roman Antiquities* IV. lxxxiv. 2–5; From *LCL*

When Brutus[18] had done haranguing [the citizenry assembled in the Forum], they all cried out, as from a single mouth, to lead them to arms. Then Brutus, pleased at this, said, "On this condition, that you first hear the resolution of the senate and confirm it. For we have resolved that the Tarquinii and all their posterity shall be banished both from the city of Rome and from all the territory ruled by the Romans; that no one shall be permitted to say or do anything about their restoration; and that if anyone shall be found doing anything contrary to these decisions he shall be put to death. If it is your pleasure that this resolution be confirmed, divide yourselves into your *curiae* and give your votes; and let the exercise of this right be the beginning of your liberty." This was done; and all the *curiae* having given their votes for the banishment of the tyrants, Brutus again came forward and said, "Now that our first measures have been confirmed in the manner required, hear also what we have further resolved concerning the form of our government. It was our decision, upon considering what magistracy should be in control of affairs, not to establish the kingship again, but to appoint two annual magistrates to hold the royal power, these men to be whomever you yourselves shall choose in the *comitia,* voting by centuries. If, therefore, this also is your pleasure, give your votes to that effect." The people approved of this resolution likewise, not a single vote being given against it. After that Brutus, coming forward, appointed Spurius Lucretius as *interrex* to preside, according to ancestral custom, over the *comitia* for the election of magistrates. And he, dismissing the assembly, ordered all the people to go promptly in arms to the field[19] where it was their custom to elect their magistrates. When they were come thither, he chose two men to perform the functions which had belonged to kings —Brutus and Collatinus [Lucretia's husband]; and the people, being called by centuries, confirmed their appointment. Such were the measures taken in the city at that time.

18. Lucius Junius Brutus, the traditional founder of the Republic.
19. Campus Martius, "Field of Mars." See Glossary.

8. Customs and Ordinances of Prerepublican Rome

Roman tradition speaks of a body of *leges regiae,* or "royal laws," promulgated by Romulus and the succeeding kings and codified by one Papirius in the reign of Tarquinius Superbus. The authenticity of these "laws" and the legislative authority by which they were issued, the reality and date of the Papirian collection, and many other questions concerning the validity of this Roman tradition have been much discussed in recent years. The prevailing view among modern legal scholars is that these "laws," though in most cases ascribed to mythical kings, do in fact embody customs and institutions going back to prerepublican times. Since they either are clearly sacral in nature or belong to the borderland between law and religion, it is further thought that these ordinances stemmed from a sacerdotal rather than a political authority, possibly that of the king acting in his capacity as religious head of the state. These measures have little importance in the subsequent development of Roman law, but they are valuable for the glimpses they provide of Roman society in the regal period. A representative selection from these *leges regiae* follows.

Various sources, collected in *FIRA,* I, 3–18; Translation partly from *LCL*

After Romulus had distinguished those of superior rank from their inferiors, he next established laws by which the duties of each were prescribed. The patricians were to be priests, magistrates, and judges, and were to assist him in the management of public affairs, devoting themselves to the business of the city. The plebeians were excused from these duties, as being unacquainted with them and, because of their small means, wanting leisure to attend to them, but were to apply themselves to agriculture, the breeding of cattle, and the exercise of gainful trades. . . . He placed the plebeians as a trust in the hands of the patricians, by allowing every plebeian to choose for his patron any patrician whom he himself wished. . . .

The regulations which he then instituted concerning patronage and which long continued in use among the Romans were as follows. It was the duty of the patricians to explain to their clients the laws, of which they were ignorant; to take the same care of them when absent as present, doing everything for them that fathers do for their sons with regard to money and to the contracts that related to money; to bring suit on behalf of their clients when they were wronged in connection with contracts and to defend them against any who brought charges against them; and, to put the matter briefly, to secure for them both in private and in public affairs all that tranquility of which they particularly stood in need. It was the duty of the clients to assist their patrons in providing dowries for their daughters upon marriage if the fathers had not sufficient means; to pay their ransom to the enemy if any of them or of their children were taken prisoner; to discharge out of their own purses their patrons' losses in private suits and the pecuniary fines which they were condemned to pay to the state, making these contributions to them not as loans but as thank-offerings; and to share with their patrons the costs incurred in their magistracies and dignities and other public expenditures, in the same manner as if they were their relations.

Romulus by a single law . . . led women to behave themselves with modesty and great decorum. The law was to this effect, that a woman joined to her husband by holy matrimony should share in all his possessions and sacred rites. The ancient Romans designated holy and lawful marriages by the term "farreate,"[20] from the sharing of *far* . . . for this was the ancient and, for a long time, the ordinary food of all the Romans, and their country produces an abundance of excellent spelt. . . . The participation of the wives with their husbands in this holiest and first food and their union founded on the sharing of all their fortunes took its name from this sharing of the spelt and forged the bond of an indissoluble union, and there was nothing that could annul these marriages. This law obliged both the married women, as having no other refuge, to conform themselves entirely to the temper of their husbands, and the husbands to rule their wives as necessary and inseparable possessions. Accordingly, if a wife was virtuous and in all things obedient to her husband, she was mistress of the house to the same degree as her husband was master of it, and after the death of her husband she was heir to his property in the same manner as a daughter was to that of her father; that is, if he died without children and intestate, she was mistress of all that he left, and if he had children, she shared equally with them. But if she did any wrong, the injured party was her judge and determined the degree of her punishment. Some offenses, however, were

---

20. This solemn religious ceremony, officiated over by the *pontifex maximus* (high priest), was usually known as *confarreatio*.

judged by her relations together with her husband; among them was adultery, or if it was found she had drunk wine. . . . For Romulus permitted them to punish both these acts with death, as being the gravest offenses women could be guilty of, since he looked upon adultery as the source of reckless folly, and drunkenness the source of adultery. And both these offenses continued for a long time to be punished by the Romans with merciless severity [cf. § 191]. The wisdom of this law concerning wives is attested by the length of time it was in force; for it is agreed that during the space of five hundred and twenty years no marriage was dissolved at Rome.[21]

He also enacted certain laws, among them a severe one which forbids a wife to divorce her husband, but permits a husband to cast aside his wife for poisoning his children or counterfeiting his keys,[22] and for adultery; but if a man should for any other reason send his wife away, the law prescribes that half of his property shall belong to his wife, and the other half be consecrated to Ceres; and whoever puts away his wife must make a sacrifice to the gods of the lower world.

But the lawgiver of the Romans [Romulus] gave virtually full power to the father over his son during his whole life, whether he thought proper to imprison him, to scourge him, to put him in chains and keep him at work in the fields, or to put him to death, and this even though the son were already engaged in public affairs, though he were numbered among the highest magistrates, and though he were celebrated for his zeal for the commonwealth . . . [cf. Valerius Maximus in § 146]. And not even at this point did the Roman lawgiver stop in giving the father power over the son, but he even allowed him to sell his son, without concerning himself whether this permission might be regarded as cruel and harsher than was compatible with natural affection. . . . He even gave leave to the father to make a profit by selling his son as often as three times, thereby giving greater power to the father over his son than to the master over his slaves. For a slave who has once been sold and has later obtained his liberty is his own master ever after, but a son who had once been sold by his father, if he became free, came again

---

21. According to one tradition the first divorce of a confarreate marriage took place in 231 B.C. But that date is probably wrong. Livy states (*History of Rome* IX. xliii. 25) that Lucius Annius divorced his wife in 307/6 B.C.

22. The text here is corrupt. Perhaps this should read: "for using poisons, for substituting children."

under his father's power, and if he was a second time sold and a second time freed, he was still, as at first, his father's slave; but after the third sale he was freed from his father. . . . [This law was modified by] Numa Pompilius, the successor of Romulus, as follows: "If a father gives his son leave to marry a woman who by the laws is to be the sharer of his sacred rites and possessions, he shall no longer have the power of selling his son."

Numa also regulated the periods of mourning according to ages. For instance, for a child of less than three years there was to be no mourning at all; for one older than that the mourning was not to last more months than the child had lived years, up to ten; and no age was to be mourned longer than that, but ten months was the period set for the longest mourning. This is also the period during which women who have lost their husbands remain in widowhood, and she who took another husband before this term was out was obliged by the laws of Numa to sacrifice a pregnant cow.

A regal ordinance forbids the burial of a woman who has died during pregnancy until the offspring is first removed from her; anyone who acts otherwise is regarded as having destroyed the hope of a living being together with the pregnant woman.

The king[23] summoned an assembly of the people and declared, "In accordance with the law I appoint duovirs to pass judgment on Horatius for treason." The law in its dread formulation read: "Let the duovirs pass sentence for treason; if he appeals from the duovirs, let the appeal be heard; if they are upheld on appeal, his head shall be covered, he shall be suspended by a rope from a gallows, he shall be scourged whether inside or outside the *pomerium*."[24]

Servius Tullius permitted even manumitted slaves to enjoy equal rights of citizenship, unless they choose to return to their own countries.

23. Tullus Hostilius, the successor of Numa. Cicero (*In Defense of Rabirius* iv. 13) attributes this "formulation of torture" to the tyrannical Tarquinius Superbus, but this may be a striving for rhetorical effect.

24. According to one view, what is meant is not that the culprit was hanged, but that he was tied to a barren tree and scourged to death. This passage is from the story of Horatius, whose crime was the killing of his sister; perhaps in this early period all crimes deserving of capital punishment were subsumed under the heading of treason, i.e., an offense against the state.

For he ordered these freedmen to report the value of their property in the census along with all the other free men, he distributed them among the four city tribes . . . and he admitted them to participation in all public matters on an equal footing with the other plebeians.

But of all Numa's measures the one most admired is his distribution of the people according to their crafts. . . . Those so distributed were flute-players, goldsmiths, carpenters, dyers, leather-workers, leather-dressers, coppersmiths, and potters. The remaining crafts he lumped together, and made one group out of them all. To each group he assigned appropriate social gatherings, assemblies, and religious rites.

9. THE ROMAN CALENDAR

The Roman calendar, commonly called the Calendar of Numa, is the oldest extant record of Roman civilization. It can be reconstructed in general from the extant Roman urban calendars (of which there are at least twenty-five), and is based on a twelve-month lunar year of 355 days, with provision for an intercalary month of twenty-two or twenty-three days every two years. The year was divided into eight-day periods, lettered A through H, each ninth day being a market day *(nundinae)*. The months were divided by the phases of the moon, as follows: new moon—Kalends; first quarter—Nones (always the ninth day before the Ides); full moon—Ides. Each day has a mark of religious significance attached to it. The recurrent symbols are: F = *fastus,* a day on which it was proper to transact business in court; C = *comitialis,* a day on which *comitia* (public assemblies) might meet, or "assembly day" (also proper to transact business in court); N = *nefastus,* a day on which it was improper to transact legal business or to hold assemblies; NP, meaning uncertain, perhaps = NFP, *nefastus, feriae publicae,* no legal or assembly business, public holiday; EN = *endotercisus,* i.e., *fastus* in the middle of the day, *nefastus* in the morning and evening.

The reconstruction of the Calendar of Numa is based on the calendar discovered at Anzio in 1915. It is the only extant pre-Julian *fasti,* belonging to the early first century B.C.[25] Only five months are included in this selection.

---

25. A portion of the text with English translation and commentary may be found in *ROL,* 4:450–465.

THE CALENDAR OF NUMA

MARCH[a]

B	Kalends	NP	
C		F	
D		C	
E		C	
F		C	
G		C?	
H	Nones	F	
A		F	
B		C	
C		C	
D		C	
E		C	
F		EN	
G		NP	Equirria[b]
H	Ides	NP	
A		F	
B		NP	Liberalia
C		C	
D		NP	Quinquatrus
E		C	
F		C	
G		N	
H		NP	Tubilustrium
A	Q R C	F[c]	
B		C	
C		C	
D		C?	
E		C	
F		C	
G		C	
H		C	

31 [days]

QUINTILIS[d]

B	Kalends	N	
C		N	
D		N	
E		N	
F		NP	Poplifugia
G		N	
H	Nones	N	
A		N	
B		N	
C		C	
D		C	
E		C	
F		C	
G		C	
H	Ides	NP	
A		F	
B		C	
C		C	
D		NP	Lucaria
E		C	
F		NP	Lucaria
G		C	
H		NP	Neptunalia
A		N	
B		NP	Furrinalia
C		C	
D		C	
E		C	
F		C	
G		C	
H		C	

31 [days]

SEXTILIS[e]

A	Kalends	F	
B		F	
C		C	
D		C	
E	Nones	F	

F		F	
G		C	
H		C	
A		F	
B		C	
C		C	
D		C	
E	Ides	NP	
F		F	
G		C	
H		C	
A		NP	Portunalia
B		C	
C		F	Vinalia
D		C	
E		NP	Consualia
F		EN	
G		NP	Volcanalia
H		C	
A		NP	Opiconsivia
B		C	
C		NP	Volturnalia
D		C	
E		C	

29 [days]

DECEMBER

G	Kalends	N	
H		N	
A		N	
B		C	
C	Nones	F	
D		F	
E		C	
F		C	
G		C	
H		C	
A		NP	Agonia

B		EN	
C	Ides	NP	
D		F	
E		EN	Consualia
F		C	
G		EN	Saturnalia
H		C	
A		N	Opalia
B		C	
C		NP	Divalia
D		C	
E		NP	Larentalia
F		C	
G		C	
H		C	
A		C	
B		C	
C		C	

29 [days]

FEBRUARY

F	Kalends	N	
G		N	
H		N	
A		N	
B	Nones	N	
C		N	
D		N	
E		N	
F		N	
G		N	
H		N	
A		N	
B	Ides	NP	
C		N	
D		NP	Lupercalia
E		EN	
F		NP	Quirinalia

G	C		E	N	Regifugium	
H	C		F	C		
A	C		G	EN		
B	F	Feralia	H	NP	Equirria	
C	C		A	C		
D	NP	Terminalia		28 [days]		

Source: Accademia Nazionale dei Lincei, *Notizie degli Scavi* (1921), pp. 73–126

[a] The calendar of Anzio begins with January, but there is no doubt that the early Roman year began with March. For the shift to January, see introduction to §193.

[b] An idea of the life of the primitive Roman community can be gained from the content of some of the festivals listed in the calendar: Equirria = horse races in honor of Mars; Liberalia = festival of Liber, god of vegetation; Quinquatrus = sacred to Mars, purification of the sacred shields by the Salian priests; Tubilustrium = purification of trumpets used in summoning *comitia;* Fordicidia = sacrifice of pregnant cows to Tellus (Earth); Cerialia = festival of Ceres, goddess of grain; Parilia = festival of Pales, god of the pasture lands; Vinalia = wine festival; Robigalia = festival of the god of mildew; Lemuria = laying of hostile ghosts of dead; Vestalia = festival of Vesta, goddess of sacred fire; Matralia = festival of Mater Matuta, deity of matrons; Neptunalia = festival of Neptune, ancient Italic deity; Portunalia = festival of the harbor(?); Consualia = festival of Consus, god of sowing; Volcanalia = festival of Vulcan; Opiconsivia = festival of the goddess of good sowing (or of stored harvest); Volturnalia = festival of Volturnus (Tiber?); Meditrinalia = tasting of new wine: Fontinalia = festival of wells and springs; Armilustrium = purification of weapons and sacred shields by the Salian priests; Saturnalia = festival of Saturn, god of agriculture; Opalia = festival of Ops, goddess of agriculture; Divalia = festival of Angerona, primitive deity; Carmentalia = festival of Carmenta, primitive deity; Lupercalia = wolf-festival, fertility ceremony; Quirinalia = festival of Quirinus (Mars); Terminalia = festival of the god of boundaries.

[c] *Quando Rex Comitiavit Fas*—when the king has dissolved the assembly, the day is *fastus.*

[d] Later renamed July, in honor of Julius Caesar.

[e] Later renamed August, in honor of Augustus.

10. The Religion of Numa

The oldest Roman religion possessed a well-defined Italic substratum compounded of magic, taboo, and animism. Characterized by scrupulous exactness in ritual and by elaborate legalistic ceremonial, this "kernel of Roman religion" was directed toward propitiating vague, undefined divine powers known as *numina*. The administration of *ius divinum* (the body of divine regulations) and the preservation of the traditional ritual and formulae of the state-cult were in the hands of a number of priestly colleges, the flamens, Salians, Vestals, pontiffs, fetials, and augurs. All of these priestly organs had their origin in the regal period. The foundation of this highly systematized state-cult was unanimously assigned by Roman tradition to Numa, the second king of Rome.

Livy, *History of Rome* I. xix. 4–xx. 7; From *LCL*

And fearing lest relief from anxiety on the score of foreign perils might lead men who had hitherto been held back by fear of their enemies and by military discipline into extravagance and idleness, Numa thought the very first thing to do, as being the most efficacious with a populace which was ignorant and, in these early days, uncivilized, was to imbue them with the fear of Heaven. As he could not instil this into their hearts without inventing some marvelous story, he pretended to have nocturnal meetings with the goddess Egeria, and that hers was the advice which guided him in the establishment of rites most approved by the gods, and in the appointment of special priests for the service of each.

And first of all he divided the year into twelve months, according to the revolutions of the moon. But since the moon does not give months of quite thirty days each, and eleven days are wanting to the full complement of a year as marked by the sun's revolution, he inserted intercalary months in such a way that in the twentieth year the days should fall in with the same position from which they had started and the period of twenty years be rounded out. He also appointed days when public business might not be carried on, and others when it might, since it would sometimes be desirable that nothing should be brought before the public. [For the Calendar of Numa, see § 9.]

He then turned his attention to the appointments of priests, although he performed very many priestly duties himself, especially those which now belong to the *flamen Dialis* [for the *flamen Dialis,* see § 49]. But inasmuch as he thought that in a warlike nation there would be more kings like Romulus than like Numa, and that they would take the field in person, he did not wish the sacrificial duties of the kingly office to be neglected, and so appointed a flamen for Jupiter, as his perpetual priest, and provided him with a conspicuous dress and the royal curule chair. To him he added two other flamens, one for Mars and the other for Quirinus. In like manner he designated virgins for Vesta's service—a priesthood, this, that derived from Alba and so was not unsuited to the founder's stock. That they might be perpetual priestesses of the temple, he assigned them a stipend from the public treasury, and by the rule of virginity and other observances invested them with awe and sanctity. He likewise chose twelve Salians for Mars Gradivus and granted them the distinction of wearing the embroidered tunic and over it a bronze breastplate and of bearing the divine shields which are called *ancilia* while they proceed through the city, chanting their hymns to the triple beat of their solemn dance. He next chose as pontifex Numa Marcius, son of Marcus, one of the senators, and to him he entrusted written directions, full and accurate, for performing the rites of worship; with what victims, on what days, in what temple sacrifices should be offered, and from what sources money was to be disbursed to pay their costs. All other public and private rituals he likewise made subject to the decrees of the pontifex, that there might be someone to whom the commons could come for advice, lest any confusion should arise in the religious law through the neglect of ancestral rites and the adoption of strange ones. And not merely ceremonies relating to the gods above, but also proper funeral observances and the propitiation of the spirits of the dead were to be taught by the pontifex as well, and also what prodigies manifested by lightning or other visible sign were to be taken in hand and averted.

11. HYMN OF THE ARVAL PRIESTS

The Arvals were an ancient priestly college of twelve members devoted to the cult of the agricultural divinity Dea Dia. The extant records of the proceedings of the brotherhood in A.D. 218 have preserved this archaic litany, one of the oldest documents of Roman religion.

CIL, vol. I, 2d ed., no. 2. The same hymn also appears in CIL, vol. VI, no. 2104, and in ROL, 4: 250–253; From LCL

Oh! Help us, ye Household Gods! Oh! help us, ye Household Gods! Oh! help us, ye Household Gods!

And let not bane and bale, O Marmar,[26] assail more folk. And let not bane and bale, O Marmar, assail more folk. And let not bane and bale, O Marmar, assail more folk.

Be full satisfied, fierce Mars. Leap the threshold! Halt! Beat the ground! Be full satisfied, fierce Mars. Leap the threshold! Halt! Beat the ground! Be full satisfied, fierce Mars. Leap the threshold! Halt! Beat the ground!

By turns address ye all the Half-Gods. By turns address ye all the Half-Gods. By turns address ye all the Half-Gods.

Oh! Help us, Marmor! Oh! Help us, Marmor! Oh! Help us, Marmor! Bound, bound, and bound again, bound and bound again!

26. Marmar (Marmor, Mavors, Mamers), primitive Italic spirit of vegetation; later, under the name Mars, the Roman god of war.

12. The Latin League and Latin Festival

Dionysius of Halicarnassus, *Roman Antiquities* IV. xlix; From *LCL*

After Tarquinius Superbus had obtained the supremacy over the Latins, he sent ambassadors to the cities of the Hernicans and to those of the Volscians to invite them also to enter into a treaty of friendship and alliance with him. The Hernicans unanimously voted in favor of the alliance, but of the Volscians only two cities, Ecetra and Antium, accepted the invitation. And as a means of providing that the treaties made with those cities might endure forever, Tarquinius resolved to designate a temple for the joint use of the Romans, the Latins, the Hernicans, and such of the Volscians as had entered into the alliance, in order that, by coming together each year at the appointed place, they might celebrate a general festival, feast together, and share in common sacrifices. This proposal being cheerfully accepted by all of them, he appointed for their place of assembly a high mountain situated almost at the center of these peoples and commanding the city of the Albans; and he made a law that upon this mountain an annual festival should be celebrated, during which they should all abstain from acts of hostility against any of the others and should perform common sacrifices to Jupiter Latiaris, as he is called,[27] and feast together, and he appointed the share of each city was to contribute to these sacrifices and the portion each of them was to receive. The cities that shared in this festival and sacrifice were forty-seven. These festivals and sacrifices the Romans celebrate to this day,[28] calling them the Latin Festivals; and some of the cities that take part in them bring lambs, some cheeses, others a certain measure of milk, and others something of like nature. And one bull is sacrificed in common by all of them, each city receiving its appointed share of the meat. The sacrifices they offer are on behalf of all, and the Romans have the superintendence of them.

27. "Jupiter [the protector] of Latium."
28. That is, in the early part of the principate of Augustus.

2

THE CONQUEST AND ORGANIZATION OF ITALY TO 264 B.C.

13. TREATIES BETWEEN ROME AND CARTHAGE, 509–279 B.C.

According to R. L. Beaumont, *Journal of Roman Studies* (1939), 29:74–86, "The first treaty between Rome and Carthage seems then to be one of a series concluded by Carthage with the Etruscan cities, and where possible, with Greeks, about the year 500, to secure the acquisitions of the wars of the latter half of the sixth century. It was not until 348 that Carthage felt the need for another agreement with Rome, and then she naturally added a clause closing Spain."

Polybius does not mention the date of the second treaty. It is now generally agreed to belong to the fourth century B.C. The year 348, given by Beaumont, is based on Livy VII. xxvii. 2 and Diodorus XVI. lxix, whereas the year 306 is suggested by others on the authority of Livy IX. xliii.26. The third treaty was drawn up in 279 B.C.

Polybius, Histories III. xxii.1–xxvi.1

The first treaty between Rome and Carthage was made in the year of Lucius Junius Brutus and Marcus Horatius [509 B.C.], the first consuls appointed after the expulsion of the kings, by whom also the temple of Jupiter Capitolinus was consecrated. This was twenty-eight years before the invasion of Greece by Xerxes. Of this treaty I append a translation, as accurate as I could make it—for the fact is that the ancient language differs so much from that at present in use that the best scholars among the Romans themselves have great difficulty in interpreting some points in it, even after much study. The treaty is substantially as follows:

"There shall be friendship between the Romans and their allies, and the Carthaginians and their allies, on these terms:

"Neither the Romans nor their allies are to sail beyond the Fair Promontory, unless compelled by storm or enemies. If any one of them be driven ashore he shall not buy or take away anything save what is needed for the repair of his ship or for ritual purposes, and he shall depart within five days.[1]

"Men landing for trade shall conclude no business save in the presence of a herald or town clerk. Whatever is sold in the presence of these, let the price be secured to the seller on the credit of the state, if it is sold in Libya or Sardinia. If any Roman comes to the Carthaginian province in Sicily he shall enjoy all the rights of Romans.

"The Carthaginians shall do no injury to the people of Ardea, Antium, Laurentium, Circei, Tarracina; or to any other people of the Latins that are subject to Rome. As to those which are not subject to Rome, they [the Carthaginians] shall keep their hands off their cities, and if they take one they shall deliver it unharmed to the Romans. They shall build no fort in Latium; and if they enter the country in arms they shall not pass a night therein."

The "Fair Promontory" here referred to is that which lies immediately in front of Carthage to the north;[2] south of which the Carthaginians absolutely forbade the Romans to sail with ships of war because, I imagine, they did not wish them to become acquainted with either the area around Byssatis or that near the Lesser Syrtis—the region they call Emporia—owing to the productiveness of the country. If any one (the treaty then goes on to say) is driven thither by storm or enemies and requires anything necessary for the worship of the gods and the repair of his vessel, this and no more may he take; and those who touch there must depart within five days. To Carthage, to all of Libya on this side of the Fair Promontory, to Sardinia, and to the Carthaginian province of Sicily, the Romans may sail for trading purposes; and the Carthaginians engage their public credit to guarantee such persons just treatment.

It is clear from this treaty that the Carthaginians speak of Sardinia and Libya as belonging to them entirely; but about Sicily they distinctly express themselves otherwise, and stipulate only for that part of it which falls under Carthaginian rule. Similarly, the Romans also stipulate only

---

1. The last clause, omitted at this point in the MSS, is supplied from Polybius' commentary which follows the text of the treaty.

2. The Fair Promontory is apparently either the present-day Cap Bon (Ras Adder, Promunturium Mercurii), to the northeast of Carthage, or Cap Farina (Ras Sidi Ali Mekki, Promunturium Pulchri).

concerning Latium, making no mention of the rest of Italy, as not being under their authority.

After this treaty they made another, in which the Carthaginians included Tyre and Utica, and to the Fair Promontory they added Mastia in Tarseum as the point beyond which the Romans were not to make marauding expeditions or found cities. The treaty is substantially as follows:

"There shall be friendship between the Romans and their allies, and the people of Carthage, Tyre, and Utica and their allies, on these terms:

"The Romans shall not maraud, trade, or found a city beyond the Fair Promontory, or beyond Mastia in Tarseum.[3]

"If the Carthaginians take any city in Latium which is not subject to Rome, they shall keep the booty and the men but shall deliver up the town. If any of the Carthaginians take captive any of a people who are not subject to Rome, but with whom the Romans have a written treaty of peace, they shall not bring them into Roman harbors; if such a one is brought ashore and a Roman claims him as a slave, he shall be released. The Romans shall be similarly obligated.

"If a Roman takes water or provisions from any region under Carthaginian rule, he shall not use these provisions to injure any one with whom the Carthaginians enjoy peace and friendship. A Carthaginian shall be similarly obligated. If any one shall do so, he shall not be punished by private vengeance, but it shall be a public offense.

"In Sardinia and Libya no Roman shall trade or found a city; he shall do no more than take on provisions or repair his ship. If a storm drives him upon these coasts, he shall depart within five days. In the Carthaginian province of Sicily and in Carthage he may transact any business and sell whatsoever it is lawful for a citizen to do. The same applies to a Carthaginian in Rome."

Once more in this treaty the Carthaginians emphasize the fact of their entire possession of Libya and Sardinia, and close all approaches to the Romans; but of Sicily, on the other hand, they clearly distinguish the part subject to themselves. So too the Romans, in regard to Latium, stipulate that the Carthaginians shall do no wrong to the people of Ardea, Antium, Circei, and Tarracina, the cities that are located on the seaboard of the Latin country with which the treaty is concerned.[4]

---

3. The point of this clause apparently is that by fixing Mastia (modern Cartagena) in Tarshish (the Phoenician name for Spain) as the limit of Roman influence, Carthage effectively excluded the Romans from her preserve in the western Mediterranean.

4. This remark is obviously misplaced; it concerns the first treaty.

A final treaty with Carthage was made by the Romans at the time of Pyrrhus' invasion, before the Carthaginians had undertaken the war for the possession of Sicily. In this they maintained all the existing agreements and added the following:

"If the parties make an alliance with Pyrrhus, both shall make it an express condition that they may go to each other's aid in the country of the one attacked. Whichever one needs the help, the Carthaginians shall provide the ships, both for transport and for war; but each people shall supply the pay for its own men. The Carthaginians shall lend aid to the Romans also on the sea if need be; but no one shall compel the crews to disembark against their will."

These treaties were sworn to as follows: In the case of the first, the Carthaginians swore by their ancestral gods; the Romans, following ancient custom, by Jupiter Lapis, but in the case of the last treaty by Mars and Quirinus. The oath by Jupiter Lapis is as follows. The man swearing to the treaty takes a stone in his hand and, after taking the oath in the name of the state, adds these words, "If I abide by this oath may good things be mine; but if I do otherwise in thought or act, may all other men be kept safe in their own countries, under their own laws, in enjoyment of their own goods, gods and tombs, and may I alone be cast out even as this stone is now." And so saying he throws the stone from his hand.

Such are the treaties that exist, preserved to this day on bronze tablets in the treasury of the aediles[5] next to the temple of Jupiter Capitolinus.

14. The Gallic Catastrophe

The Gauls, or more properly the Celts,[6] left their homeland in the basin of the upper Danube c. 400 B.C. in a great westward and southward migratory movement. Unchecked because of the declining power of the

---

5. In Polybius' time the aediles shared with the quaestors the care of the state archives. The "treasury of the aediles" is perhaps the same as the Atrium Publicum on the Capitoline Hill. In the late Republic a repository for state archives, the Tabularium, was built on the southeastern slope of the Capitoline.

6. Diodorus, *Historical Library* v. xxxii. 1: "And now it will be useful to draw a distinction which is unknown to many. The peoples who dwell in the interior above Massilia, those on the slopes of the Alps, and those on this side of the Pyrenees Mountains are called Celts, whereas the peoples who are established above this land of Celtica in the parts which stretch to the north, both along the Ocean and along the Hercynian Mountain, and all the peoples who come after these, as far as Scythia, are known as Gauls; the Romans, however, include all these nations together under a single name, calling them one and all Gauls." (Quoted from the Loeb Classical Library.)

Etruscans, marauding Celtic tribes, under the leadership of the Senonian chieftain Brennus, sacked and burned the city of Rome in 390 B.C., after inflicting a stunning defeat on the Roman army at the River Allia on July 18, one of the "black days" of Roman history. The receding wave of the migration concentrated itself in the Po valley, which was henceforth known by the Romans as "Cisalpine Gaul" until it became Romanized and was incorporated into Italy proper at the end of the Republic. Roman tradition created many legends of Roman patriotism and fortitude to counterbalance the stigma of the Gallic invasion.

THE CELTS

Polybius, *Histories* II. xvii. 2–xviii. 3; From *LCL*

The Celts, being close neighbors of the Etruscans and associating much with them, cast covetous eyes on their beautiful country and, on a small pretext, suddenly attacked them with a large army and, expelling them from the plain of the Po, occupied it themselves. . . .

They lived in unwalled villages, without any superfluous furniture; for, as they slept on beds of leaves and fed on meat and were exclusively occupied with war and agriculture, their lives were very simple, and they had no knowledge whatever of any art or science. Their possessions consisted of cattle and gold, because these were the only things they could carry about with them everywhere according to circumstances and shift where they chose. They treated comradeship as of the greatest importance, those among them being the most feared and most powerful who were thought to have the largest number of attendants and associates.

On their first invasion they not only conquered this country but reduced to subjection many of the neighboring peoples, striking terror into them by their audacity. Not long afterwards they defeated the Romans and their allies in a pitched battle and, pursuing the fugitives, occupied, three days after the battle, the whole of Rome with the exception of the Capitol; but being diverted by an invasion of their own country by the Veneti,[7] they made on this occasion a treaty with the Romans and, evacuating the city, returned home.

7. This tribe occupied the eastern extremity of the Po valley, on the Adriatic coast.

THE ASSAULT ON THE CAPITOL

Livy, *History of Rome* v. xlvii; From *LCL*

While this was going on at Veii, the citadel of Rome and the Capitol were in very great danger. For the Gauls had noticed the tracks of a man, where the messenger from Veii had got through, or perhaps had observed for themselves that the cliff near the shrine of Carmentis afforded an easy ascent. So on a starlit night they first sent forward an unarmed man to try the way; then, handing up their weapons where there was a steep place and supporting themselves by their fellows or affording support in their turn, they pulled one another up, as the ground required, and reached the summit, in such silence that not only the sentries but even the dogs . . . were not aroused. But they could not elude the vigilance of the geese, which being sacred to Juno had, notwithstanding the dearth of provisions, not been killed. This was the salvation of them all; for the geese with their cackling and the flapping of their wings woke Marcus Manlius, consul of three years before and a distinguished soldier,[8] who, catching up his weapons and at the same time calling the rest to arms, strode past his bewildered comrades to a Gaul who had already got a foothold on the crest and dislodged him with a blow from the boss of his shield. As he slipped and fell, he overturned those who were next to him, and the others in alarm let go their weapons and, grasping the rocks to which they were clinging, were slain by Manlius. And by now the rest had come together and were assailing the invaders with javelins and stones, and presently the whole company lost their footing and were flung down headlong to destruction. Then after the din was hushed, the rest of the night . . . was given up to sleep. At dawn the trumpet summoned the soldiers to assemble before the tribunes. Good conduct and bad had both to be requited. First Manlius was praised for his courage and presented with gifts, not only by the tribunes of the soldiers, but by agreement amongst the troops, who brought each half a pound of spelt and a gill of wine to his house, which stood on the citadel.

---

8. Marcus Manlius Capitolinus, consul 392 B.C. According to tradition he was later, in 384 B.C., condemned to death for treason as the result of the internal struggle over the debtor problem (cf. § 39).

VAE VICTIS!

Livy, *History of Rome* v. xlviii. 8–9; From *LCL*

Thereupon, the senate met and instructed the tribunes of the soldiers to arrange the terms. Then, at a conference between Quintus Sulpicius, the tribune, and the Gallic chieftain Brennus, the affair was settled and a thousand pounds of gold was agreed on as the price of a people that was destined presently to rule the world. The transaction was a foul disgrace in itself, but an insult was added thereto: the weights brought by the Gauls were dishonest and, on the tribunes objecting, the insolent Gaul added his sword to the weight, and a saying intolerable to Roman ears was heard—"Woe to the conquered!"

15. ROMAN STRENGTH *c.* 320 B.C.

Livy, *History of Rome* ix. xix. 1–4

It remains for us to [record] . . . the numbers and types of troops and the strength of the allied forces. The census records put the population of that period at 250,000 persons. Earlier, whenever the Latin allies revolted, ten legions were raised, almost entirely from the city; often during those years four or five armies were engaged simultaneously in Etruria, in Umbria (where they had to meet the Gauls as well), in Samnium, and in Lucania. But now the whole of Latium, including the Sabines, Volscians, and Aequians; the whole of Campania; parts of Umbria and Etruria; the Picentines, Marsians, and Paelignians; and the Vestinians and Apulians, together with the entire coast of the Tyrrhenian Sea (both the Greek-inhabited part from Thurii to Naples and Cumae and the part beyond up to Antium and Ostia)—all these peoples . . . [were] either powerful allies of the Romans or reduced to impotence by their arms.

16. THE SAMNITE WARS: CAUSES

The Samnites, a powerful Italic people settled in cantons in the uplands of the southern Apennines, began to expand in the fourth century B.C. Driven by overpopulation, they turned toward the fertile plains and rich cities of Campania. When the Romans set up a colony at Fregellae, to block one of the Samnite points of entry into Campania, and intervened in the affairs of Naples, the long and disastrous Samnite Wars broke out (327–290 B.C.). "The brutal truth is that from the political, military, and economic standpoint the intervention in Campania promised substantial advantages. . . . Stripped of pious words and phrases, intervention in Campania meant to Rome politically the encirclement of the Latins, militarily cavalry, and economically wheat" (L. Homo, *Primitive Italy and the Beginnings of Roman Imperialism*, pp. 181–182).

SAMNITE OVERPOPULATION AND EXPANSION

Dionysius of Halicarnassus, *Roman Antiquities* I. xvi. 1–4; From *LCL*

First a sacred band of young men [of the Samnites] went forth, consisting of a few who were sent by their parents to seek a livelihood. . . . For whenever the population of any of their cities increased to such a degree that the produce of their lands no longer sufficed for them all, or whenever the earth, injured by unseasonable changes of the weather, brought forth her fruits in less abundance than usual, or whenever any other occurrence of like nature, either good or bad, introduced a necessity of lessening their numbers, they would dedicate to some god or other all the men born within a certain year, and, providing them with arms, would send them out of their country. If, indeed, this was done by way of thanksgiving for populousness or for victory in war, they would first offer the usual sacrifices and then send forth their colonies under happy auspices; but if, having incurred the wrath of Heaven, they were seeking deliverance from the evils that beset them, they would perform much the same ceremony, but sorrowfully and begging forgiveness of the youths they were sending away. And those who departed, feeling that henceforth they would have no share in the land of their fathers but must acquire another, looked upon any land that received them in friendship or that they conquered in war as their country.

SAMNITE INTERVENTION IN CAMPANIA

Livy, *History of Rome* VII. xxix

The history will now be occupied with wars of greater magnitude in respect to the forces of the enemies or the distance of the countries or the length of time they lasted. For it was in this year[9] that hostilities

9. 343 B.C. The so-called first Samnite War (343–341 B.C.) is probably a fiction of the annalistic tradition.

commenced with the Samnites, a people strong in material resources and military power. Our war with the Samnites, waged with varying fortunes, was followed by the war with Pyrrhus, and that again by the war with Carthage. What a chapter of great events! How often had we to pass through the very extremity of danger in order that our empire might be exalted to its present greatness, a greatness which is with difficulty maintained!

The cause of the war between the Romans and the Samnites, who had been our friends and allies,[10] came, however, from without; it did not arise between the two peoples themselves. The Samnites, simply because they were stronger, made an unprovoked attack upon the Sidicines;[11] the weaker side was compelled to fly for succor to those who were more powerful and attached themselves to the Campanians. . . . The Samnites, dropping operations against the Sidicines, attacked the Campanians as being the stronghold of their neighbors; they saw, too, that while victory would be just as easily won, it would bring more glory and spoils. They seized the Tifata hills which overlook Capua and left a strong force to hold them; then they descended in battle order into the plain which lies between the Tifata hills and Capua. Here a second battle took place, in which the Campanians were defeated and driven within their walls. They had lost the flower of their army, and as there was no hope of any assistance near, they were compelled to ask for help from Rome.

SAMNITE COUNTERCHARGES AGAINST ROME

Livy, *History of Rome* VIII. xxiii. 1–7

Both consuls[12] informed the senate that there were very slender hopes of peace with the Samnites. Publilius informed them that 2,000 troops from Nola and 4,000 Samnites had been admitted into Palaeopolis, more under pressure from Nola than by the desire of the Greeks; Cornelius sent the additional information that the Samnite magistrates had ordered a levy, that all Samnium was in motion, and that attempts were being openly made to induce the neighboring communities of Privernum, Fundi, and Formiae to join.

---

10. The Romans and Samnites had signed a treaty of friendship in 354 B.C., perhaps under pressure of Gallic incursions.

11. An Oscan canton in northern Campania.

12. The consuls for the year 327 B.C.

Under these circumstances it was decided to send ambassadors to the Samnites before declaring war. The Samnites sent an insolent reply. They actually accused the Romans of aggression and did not neglect to attempt to refute the charges made against themselves; they declared that the counsel or assistance which the Greeks had received was not furnished by their government, nor had they tampered with Fundi and Formiae, for they had no reason to distrust their own strength if they resolved to fight. Moreover, it was impossible to disguise the deep irritation which the Samnite people felt at the conduct of the Roman people in restoring Fregellae after they had taken it from the Volscians and destroyed it, and placing a colony on Samnite territory which the colonists called Fregellae. If this insult and injury were not removed by those responsible for it, they would themselves exert all their strength to get rid of it.

17. Samnite Levy and Military Oath

Livy, *History of Rome* x. xxxviii

The following year [293 B.C.] Lucius Papirius Cursor, distinguished for his father's glory and his own, was consul. That year brought with it a great war and a victory over the Samnites such as no one up to that day had obtained except Lucius Papirius, the consul's father. As on that occasion, the Samnites had made their preparations for war with equal effort and splendor and with lavish provision of superior weapons. They had also called in the aid of the gods by submitting the soldiers to a kind of initiation in accordance with a certain ancient form of oath. A levy was conducted through all Samnium under this novel regulation: any man of military age who did not report in response to the general's proclamation or any one who departed without permission was devoted to Jupiter and his life was forfeited. Then the whole of the army was summoned to Aquilonia, and some 40,000 men, the full strength of Samnium, assembled.

There a space, about 200 feet square, almost in the center of their camp, was enclosed with wicker hurdles and covered all over with linen cloth. In this enclosure a sacrificial service was conducted, the words being read from an old linen book by an aged priest, a certain Ovius Paccius, who claimed to derive this ceremony from an old ritual of the

Samnite religion. It was the form which their ancestors once used when they formed their secret design of wresting Capua from the Etruscans. When the sacrifice was completed the general sent a messenger to summon all those who were of noble birth or who were distinguished for their military achievements. They were admitted into the enclosure one by one. Besides other ceremonial pomp such as might overwhelm the mind with religious awe, there were altars in the middle of an enclosure, and dead victims lying about, and centurions standing around with drawn swords. As each was admitted he was led up to the altar, more like a victim than like one who was taking part in the ceremony, and he was bound on oath not to divulge what he saw and heard in that place. Then they compelled him to take an oath in accordance with a certain dreadful formula, whereby he imprecated a curse on himself, his household, and his family if he did not go into battle where the commanders should lead him or if he either himself fled from battle or did not at once slay any one whom he saw fleeing. At first there were some who refused to take this oath; they were beheaded beside the altars and they lay amongst the scattered remains of the victims as a warning to the rest not to refuse. After the foremost men among the Samnites had been bound by the dread formula, ten were named by the general and told each to choose another man, and these again to choose others until they had made up the number of 16,000. These were called the Linen Legion, from the material with which the place where the nobles had been sworn was covered. They were provided with resplendent armor and plumed helmets to distinguish them from the others. The rest of the army consisted of something over 20,000 men, but they were not inferior to the Linen Legion either in their personal appearance or in their military renown or in their equipment. This was the number of troops encamped at Aquilonia, forming their total strength.

18. THE WAR WITH PYRRHUS, 280–279 B.C.

When, after the Samnite War, Roman armies remained in southern Italy and began to extend Roman domination there, Tarentum, the leading Greek city of the region, invoked the aid of King Pyrrhus of Epirus, a relative of Alexander the Great, to repel the Roman threat to her independence. Pyrrhus, who dreamed of conquests in the West to rival those of Alexander in the East, seized upon the Tarentine appeal with alacrity. In

280 B.C. he landed at Tarentum with a large army and a contingent of 20 elephants. The ensuing battle, fought near Heraclea in Lucania, marked the first occasion on which the Romans faced these pachydermous "tanks of ancient warfare."

ROME REJECTS PYRRHUS' PEACE OFFER

Appian, *Roman History* III. Fragment 10 (abridged); From *LCL*

Pyrrhus, king of Epirus, having gained a victory over the Romans and desiring to recuperate after the severe engagement, and expecting that the Romans would then be particularly desirous of coming to terms, sent to the city Cineas, a Thessalian, who was so renowned for eloquence that he had been compared to Demosthenes. When he was admitted to the senate chamber, Cineas extolled the king for a variety of reasons, laying stress on his moderation after the victory, in that he had neither marched directly against the city nor attacked the camp of the vanquished. He offered them peace, friendship, and an alliance with Pyrrhus, provided they included the Tarentines in the same treaty, left the other Greeks dwelling in Italy free under their own laws, and restored to the Lucanians, Samnites, Daunians, and Bruttians whatever they had taken from them in war. If they would do this, he said that Pyrrhus would restore all his prisoners without ransom.

The Romans hesitated a long time, being much intimidated by the prestige of Pyrrhus and by the calamity that had befallen them. Finally Appius Claudius, surnamed the Blind (because he had lost his eyesight from old age), commanded his sons to lead him into the senate chamber, where he said: "I was grieved at the loss of my sight; now I regret that I did not lose my hearing also, for never did I expect to see or hear deliberations of this kind from you. Has a single misfortune made you all at once so forget yourselves as to take the man who brought it upon you, and those who called him hither, for friends instead of enemies, and to give the heritage of your fathers to the Lucanians and Bruttians? What is this but making the Romans servants of the Macedonians? And some of you dare to call this peace instead of servitude!" Many other things in the like sense did Appius urge to arouse their spirit. If Pyrrhus wanted the friendship and alliance of the Romans, let him withdraw from Italy and then send his embassy. As long as he remained, let him be considered neither friend nor ally, neither judge nor arbiter of the Romans.

The senate made answer to Cineas in the very words of Appius. They

decreed the levying of two new legions for Laevinus and made proclamation that whoever would volunteer in place of those who had been
lost should put his name on the army roll. Cineas, who was still present
and saw the multitude jostling each other in their eagerness to be enrolled, is reported to have said to Pyrrhus on his return: "We are waging
war against a hydra. . . ."

PYRRHIC VICTORY

Plutarch, Life of Pyrrhus xxi. 5–10

Pyrrhus thus found himself obliged to fight another battle. After refresh-
ing his army he decamped and engaged the Romans about the city of
Asculum. There he was forced onto ground disadvantageous for his
horse and over to a swift river with wooded banks, so that his elephants
could not charge and engage the Roman infantry. After many had been
wounded and many killed, night put an end to the engagement. Next
day, his strategy being to do battle on level ground and get his elephants
among the ranks of the enemy, he first had a detachment seize the
unfavorable ground; then, mixing many slingers and archers among
the elephants, he led a close and well-ordered force in a mighty attack.
The Romans, unable to maneuver backward and forward as on the
previous day, were obliged to fight man to man on level ground; and
being anxious to drive back the infantry before the elephants could come
up, they fought fiercely with swords among the Macedonian spears, not
sparing themselves and looking only to wound and kill, without regard
to what they suffered. It is reported that the Romans first yielded
ground, after long fighting, in the sector where Pyrrhus himself was
leading the attack. But the greatest rout was effected by the overwhelming force of the elephants, since the Romans, unable to make use
of their valor, deemed it imperative to give way as if before an advancing flood or a crushing earthquake and not to stand their ground and die
in vain, suffering all that is most grievous without gaining the least
advantage.

After a short flight they reached their camp. Hieronymus says that
6,000 of the Romans died and that Pyrrhus in his royal memoirs reported 3,505 of his men killed. Dionysius, however, tells neither of two
engagements at Asculum nor of an admitted reverse of the Romans, but
says that they fought but once, till sunset, when they separated; that
Pyrrhus was wounded in the arm by a javelin and that his baggage was

plundered by the Samnites;[13] and that there died on each side more than 15,000 men.

The armies separated; and, it is said, Pyrrhus replied to one who rejoiced with him in his victory, "If we win one more battle against the Romans, we shall be completely ruined."[14] For he had lost a great part of the force he had brought with him and almost all his friends and commanders. There were no others he could summon from home, and he saw his allies in Italy losing their enthusiasm while, as from a fountain continually flowing out of the city, the Roman army was quickly and plentifully filled up with fresh men who did not lose courage because of their defeats, but who even from their very anger gained new force and resolution to go on with the war.

The Roman Organization of Italy

Sources on the Roman organization of Italy are relatively few, consisting mostly of brief mentions of specific treatment accorded individual states. When the available material is collected, however, two general principles can be discerned—annexation and alliance.

The system of annexation was the older; its origin was, in fact, attributed to Romulus. Under this system the conquered population became Roman citizens, but one half or more of their territory was usually confiscated and colonists were sent from Rome to settle on these lands. This practice had two fairly obvious advantages. First, Rome thereby increased in numbers and power. The second advantage was strategic and is succinctly stated by Cicero (*On the Agrarian Law* II. xxvii. 73): "Our ancestors . . . established colonies in places so suitable for guaranteeing them against even the suspicion of danger that they appeared to be not so much towns of Italy as outposts of empire."

The most important fact to be noted about Rome's Italian alliances (*foedera*) is that they did not create an Italian federation. Rome bound each allied state to herself, and herself alone, by a separate treaty. While these treaties varied considerably in their specific details according to cases and circumstances, two major types can be discerned. The most generous treatment was reserved for those states which entered into alliance with Rome voluntarily; these were granted a *foedus aequum,* or "equal alliance"

13. Dionysius of Halicarnassus' text (xx. iii) reads "Daunians."

14. This is, of course, the famous statement of the "Pyrrhic victory," one of the best known epigrams from Roman history.

(see § 20). The other pacts—the majority—were imposed by Rome upon vanquished foes (see § 21). These allies-by-compulsion were bound "to uphold with due propriety the majesty of the Roman people"—a deliberately vague clause which, since it could be interpreted by the Romans to fit practically any circumstances, effectively placed the "ally" completely under Rome's thumb. In addition, each treaty usually contained precise clauses stipulating the number of men to be contributed to the Roman army and the amount of money to be contributed annually in the form of direct and indirect taxes.

19. THE ROMAN FORMULA OF UNCONDITIONAL SURRENDER

The event described next, Rome's annexation of nearby Collatia, belongs to the legendary time of the kings, but the formula of surrender here recorded remained essentially the same throughout republican times, as may be seen from Livy XXVIII. xxxiv. 7 (206 B.C.): "With regard to a people with whom they were not joined by a treaty of friendship or equal alliance, it was the practice of the Romans, observed from very early times, not to treat such people as pacified nor to exercise authority over them until they had surrendered all they possessed, sacred and profane, and until they, the Romans, had received hostages, taken away their arms, and placed garrisons in their towns."

Livy, *History of Rome* I. xxxviii. 1–2

Collatia and the land this side of it were taken from the Sabines, and Egerius, son of the king's brother, was left in the town with a garrison. This was the manner, as I understand, in which the people of Collatia surrendered to the Romans, and this the formula of the surrender:

The king asked, "Are ye ambassadors and spokesmen sent by the Collatine people to surrender yourselves and the Collatine people?"

"We are."

"Has the Collatine people power to dispose of itself?"

"It has."

"Do ye surrender yourselves and the Collatine people, city, lands, water, boundary marks, shrines, utensils, all property sacred and profane, into my power and that of the Roman people?"

"We do."

"Then I receive the surrender."

Polybius, *Histories* XXXVI. iv. 1–3; From *LCL*

I have previously explained about the form of surrender to Rome, but it is necessary here again to remind my readers of it briefly. Those who commit themselves to the charge of the Romans surrender in the first place the land belonging to them and the cities in it, together with all the men and women in the land and cities; and likewise all rivers, harbors, sacred places, and tombs, so that, in a word, the Romans become masters of everything and those who surrender remain masters of absolutely nothing.[15]

20. Treaty of Alliance with the Latin League, 493 b.c.

The authenticity of the Treaty of Alliance with the Latin League has often been questioned, but without good reason. It is notable that in this alliance the two contracting parties are on a footing of equality: the young Republic had apparently been compelled to abandon its claim, which it had still asserted in the first treaty with Carthage (see § 13), to continue the domination that its Etruscan kings had established over the cities of Latium. The text given in the following selection is a summary of the treaty rather than a transcript *in extenso*. From other sources it would appear that the treaty also included a clause concerning money and security and a provision that the command of the allied armies should be alternated annually between Roman and Latin generals. This treaty remained officially in force until all the peoples of Latium were granted full Roman citizenship in 90–89 b.c. (see § 103).

Dionysius of Halicarnassus, *Roman Antiquities* VI. xcv. 1–3; Adapted from *LCL*

At the same time a new treaty of peace and friendship was made with all the Latin cities and confirmed by oaths, inasmuch as they had not attempted to create any disturbance during the sedition,[16] had openly

15. Cf. Livy XXXIV. lvii. 7: "Now there were three kinds of treaties by which kings and states formed friendships with each other: one, when terms were dictated to a people vanquished in war; for, after all their possessions have been surrendered to him who has proved superior in war, he has the sole power of judging and determining what portion of them the vanquished shall retain and what they shall forfeit. . . ."

16. The reference is to the first of the three secessions to which the plebs is said to have resorted during the "struggle of the orders" as the ultimate means of pressing its demands for political rights and economic redress. These secessions are traditionally dated 494, 449, and 287 b.c. Only the last is certainly historical. See §§ 28, 31, 42.

rejoiced at the return of the plebs, and were deemed to have lent ready assistance in the war against those who had seceded.[17] The provisions of the treaty were as follows:

"Let there be peace between the Romans and all the Latin cities as long as heaven and earth shall stay in the same position.[18] Let them neither make war upon one another themselves nor call in foreign enemies, nor grant safe passage to those who shall make war upon either, but let them assist one another with all their might when warred upon, and let each have an equal share of the spoils and booty taken in their common wars. Let suits relating to private contracts be judged within ten days and among the people where the contract was made. And let it not be permitted to add anything to, or take anything away from, this treaty except by the consent of both the Romans and all the Latins."

This was the treaty entered into by the Romans and the Latins with each other, and confirmed by their oaths sworn over sacrificial victims.

21. TREATY OF ALLIANCE WITH THE AEQUIANS, 467 B.C.

The following is an early example of a pact based on Roman mastery.

Dionysius of Halicarnassus, *Roman Antiquities* IX. lix. 3–5

The Aequians sent ambassadors to Fabius to negotiate a reconciliation and friendship before they were compelled to either by defeat of their army or by the loss of their towns. The consul, after exacting from them two months' provisions for his army, two garments for every man, six months' pay, and whatever else he thought necessary, concluded a truce with them till they could go to Rome and obtain a peace from the senate. The senate, however, learning what had happened, gave to Fabius full power to make peace with the Aequians upon such terms as he himself thought fit. After that the two peoples entered into an alliance, by the interposition of the consul, on these conditions: that the Aequians should be subject to the Romans without being dispos-

---

17. That is, the Volscians, Aequians, Hernicans, and Sabines, the non-Latin neighbors of Rome.
18. "Let there be sacred and perpetual peace" was, according to Cicero (*In Defense of Balbus* xvi. 35), a standard clause of Roman treaties of alliance.

sessed either from their cities or from their territories; and that they should not be obliged to send anything to the Romans except troops, when ordered, to be maintained at their own expense.[19]

22. THE ABSORPTION OF LATIUM, 338 B.C.

Livy, *History of Rome* VIII. xi. 12–16, xii. 5, xiii. 8–10, xiv

The Latins all surrendered and the Campanians followed their example [in 340 B.C.]. Latium and Capua were deprived of territory. The Latin territory, including that of Privernum, and the Falernian (which had belonged to the Campanian people) as far as the River Volturnus, were distributed among the Roman plebs. In Latium they received two *iugera* a head, plus three fourths of a *iugerum* in the territory of Privernum; in the Falernian district three *iugera,* the extra fourth being added to compensate for the greater distance from Rome. The people of Laurentum among the Latins and the aristocracy of the Campanians were exempted from this punishment because they had not revolted. It was ordered that the treaty with the Laurentines be renewed, and it has since then been renewed annually on the tenth day after the Latin Festival. The Campanian aristocracy was granted Roman citizenship, in commemoration of which they fastened up a bronze tablet in the temple of Castor at Rome; in addition, the Campanian people were ordered to pay to each of them —they numbered 1,600—the sum of 450 *denarii* annually. . . .

Incensed at the confiscation of their land, the Latins took up arms again [the following year, 339 B.C.]. . . .

The consuls then resolved . . . to lead their victorious army on with a greater and bolder effort to the complete subjugation of Latium.[20] They did not rest until, by storming or accepting the surrender of one city after another, they had reduced all Latium. Then, after placing garrisons in the recovered towns, they returned to Rome and to a triumph accorded them by universal consent. They also received the additional honor—a rare one in those days—of equestrian statues erected in the Forum. Before the consular elections for the following year were held, Camillus placed before the senate the question of the Latin peoples. . . .

The leading senators praised the consul's motion on the general wel-

19. This last was a usual stipulation in Rome's treaties with the Italian "allies."
20. 338 B.C. The consuls were Lucius Furius Camillus and Gaius Maenius.

fare, but as the circumstances differed in different cases, they thought that each case ought to be decided on its merits and that it would facilitate discussion if the consul would make a separate proposal concerning each people by name. They were therefore taken up and disposed of one by one.

The people of Lanuvium received full citizenship and the restoration of their religion, with the proviso that the temple and grove of June Sospita ["Savior Juno"] should belong in common to the Roman people and to the townsmen of Lanuvium. The people of Aricia, Nomentum, and Pedum were admitted to citizenship with the same rights as Lanuvium. The Tusculans retained the citizenship which they had had before, and the responsibility for their revolt was transferred from the whole community to a few ringleaders. The Veliternians, Roman citizens of old, were severely dealt with because they had revolted so often: their walls were thrown down, and their senate was deported and ordered to live on the other side of the Tiber, with the stipulation that if any one of them were caught on this side of the river his fine was to be 1,000 *asses,* and the man who had caught him was not to release his prisoner from confinement until the money was paid. Colonists were settled on the senators' lands, and the addition of their numbers made Velitrae look as populous as before. To Antium also a new colony was dispatched, but the Antiates were permitted to enroll themselves as colonists if they wished; their warships were then taken away, and the Antiate people was forbidden the sea; and they were granted citizenship. Tibur and Praeneste were deprived of territory, not so much because of the part which they, in common with the other Latins, had taken in the recent war, as because some time before, irked by the power of Rome, they had joined arms with the barbarous nation of the Gauls. The rest of the Latin cities were deprived of the rights of intermarriage, trade, and common councils with each other. Capua, as a reward for the refusal of its aristocracy to join the Latins in revolt, was granted citizenship without the suffrage, as were also Fundi and Formiae because they had always allowed a safe and peaceful passage through their territories. It was decided that Cumae and Suessula should enjoy the same rights and terms as Capua. Some of the ships of Antium were removed to the Roman dockyards, the others were burned, and it was voted to erect a platform in the Forum and adorn it with their beaks *(rostra);* and this monument was accordingly called the Rostra.[21]

21. This was henceforth the platform from which orators addressed the Roman people. It stood in the northwest part of the Forum.

3

DOMESTIC AFFAIRS TO 264 B.C.

The Struggle of the Orders

23. THE NEW REPUBLIC

Livy, *History of Rome* II. i. i, 7–10

Henceforward my theme will be the affairs, civil and military, of a free people, for such the Romans had now become; it will concern annual magistrates, and the authority of laws exalted above that of men. . . .

Moreover, you may reckon the beginning of liberty as stemming from the limitation of the consuls' authority to one year[1] rather than from any diminution of the power which the kings had possessed. The earliest consuls enjoyed all their rights and all their insignia of authority; but care was taken only not to cause double terror by giving *fasces* to both consuls. Brutus, with the consent of his colleague, was first honored with the *fasces,* and the zeal which he had displayed as the champion of liberty was not greater than that which he afterwards displayed as its guardian. First of all, while the people were still eager for their newly acquired freedom, lest they might later be swayed by the entreaties or presents of princes, he made them swear an oath that they would permit no man to be king in Rome. Next, in order that the size of its body might give greater weight to the senate, he filled up the number of the

---

1. The principle of annuality involved counterbalancing disadvantages, the most obvious being lack of continuity, especially in military command. Zonaras, for example, remarks on this (*Epitome* VIII. xvi): "The Romans owed the majority of their reverses to the fact that they kept sending out from year to year different and ever different leaders, and took away their offices from them when they were just learning the art of generalship. It looked as if they were choosing them for practice instead of for service." (Quoted from the Loeb Classical Library.)

senators, which had been diminished by the king's murders, to the total of three hundred by appointing to that body the leading men of the equestrian rank.

24. THE RIGHT OF APPEAL

Dionysius of Halicarnassus, *Roman Antiquities* v. xix. 3–5; From *LCL*

Desiring to give the plebeians a definite pledge of their liberty, Publius Valerius[2] took the axes from the rods of the *fasces* and established it as a precedent for his successors in the consulship—a precedent which continued to be followed down to my day—that when they were outside the city they should use the axes, but inside the city they should be distinguished by the rods only. He also introduced most beneficent laws which gave relief to the plebians. By one of these laws he expressly forbade that anyone should be a magistrate among the Romans who did not receive the office from the people; and he fixed death as the penalty for transgressing this law and granted impunity to the one who should kill any such transgressor. In a second law it is provided: "If a magistrate shall desire to have any Roman put to death, scourged, or fined a sum of money, the private citizen may appeal to the judgment of the people, and in the meantime he shall suffer no punishment at the hands of the magistrate until the people have given their vote concerning this." These measures gained him the esteem of the plebeians, who gave him the cognomen *Publicola,* which means "friend of the people."

Livy, *History of Rome* x. ix. 3–6; Adapted from Everyman's Library

In this year [299 B.C.] the consul Marcus Valerius carried a proposal to strengthen the provisions of the law touching the right of appeal. This was the third time since the expulsion of the kings that such a law was enacted, and always on the initiative of the same family.[3] I think that the reason for renewing it so often was simply the fact that the power exercised by a few men was stronger than the liberty of the plebs. The Porcian Law [passed c. 200 B.C.], however, seems to have been the only one concerned with the life and limb of the citizens, for it imposed the

2. According to tradition Publius Valerius was chosen consul in 509 B.C. after Lucius Tarquinius Collatinus had been forced to resign because, although he had been a leader in the overthrow of the monarchy, he was related to the exiled royal family.

3. On the two earlier Valerian laws, of 509 and 449 B.C., see the preceding paragraph and § 33.

severest penalties on anyone who scourged or put to death a Roman citizen. The Valerian law, it is true, forbade anyone who had exercised his right of appeal to be scourged or beheaded, but it provided no penalty for violation, merely declaring such violation a "wicked act." Such was the modesty of men in those days that, I imagine, this seemed a sufficiently strong barrier against violation of the law.

25. DEVELOPMENT OF ROMAN MAGISTRACIES, 509–242 B.C.

Pomponius'[4] *Manual,* cited in Justinian's *Digest* I. ii. 2, 16–28

After the kings were expelled, two consuls were established, and it was provided by statute[5] that they should exercise supreme authority. They were so called from the fact that they above all others "consulted" the interest of the commonwealth. Lest, however, they should lay claim in all respects to the power that had been wielded by the kings, a statute was passed which provided that there should be an appeal from their decisions and that they should not be able to inflict capital punishment on a Roman citizen without the order of the people. All that was left them was the power of summary coercion and of ordering persons to be imprisoned in the name of the state. After this, as the business of conducting the census required a longer time, and the consuls were not equal to this in addition to their other duties, censors were established. Then, as the people increased in numbers and frequent wars arose, including some of considerable severity waged against Rome by bordering tribes, it was sometimes resolved, when the case required it, that a magistrate should be appointed endowed with exceptional powers. Accordingly, dictators were instituted from whom there was no appeal, and who even had conferred upon them the right of inflicting capital punishment [see § 37]. But it was not held right that such a magistrate, wielding as he did supreme power, should be retained in office for more than six months. And to these dictators were joined masters of the horse. . . .

About the same time the plebeians, who had seceded from the patricians some sixteen years after the expulsion of the kings [see § 28],

---

4. A juristic writer during the time of the Emperor Hadrian (A.D. 117–138).
5. That is, by the *lex curiata de imperio,* the "law on *imperium* passed by the *comitia curiata.*"

created tribunes for themselves on the Sacred Mount, who were to be plebeian magistrates. They were called tribunes because at one time the whole body of citizens was divided into three parts, and one tribune was elected from each part, or because they were elected by the votes of the tribes. Moreover, in order that there should be officers to superintend the temples in which the plebeians used to deposit all their enactments, two members of the plebeians were appointed who were called aediles. Afterwards, when the national finance had come to be on a large scale, in order to provide officers to preside over it, quaestors were appointed to superintend money matters, so called because they were created for the purpose of inquiring into [the state of the treasury] and guarding the money. And whereas, as has been mentioned, the consuls were not permitted by law to hold a court for trying a Roman citizen in a capital case without the approval of the people, for this reason quaestors were appointed by the people to preside in capital cases. These were called *quaestores parricidii;* they are in fact mentioned in the statute of the Twelve Tables. It being also resolved that a code of laws should be drafted, it was proposed to the people that all the magistrates should resign from office in order that decemvirs [should be created for the purpose of drawing up statutes. Accordingly the decemvirs] were appointed [see § 31]. . . .

Next, several years having elapsed after the passing of the Twelve Tables, a contest arose between the plebeians and the patricians, the former desiring that the consuls should be chosen out of their own body as well as from the patricians, to which the latter refused to consent. Whereupon it was resolved that military tribunes with consular power should be created, to be chosen partly from the plebeians and partly from the patricians. The number of these officers varied from time to time; sometimes there were twenty, sometimes more, occasionally fewer. Afterwards, it having been resolved that the consuls might be elected from the plebeians themselves, they began to be appointed from both bodies. Whereupon, in order to allow the patricians some kind of precedence, it was resolved that two officers should be appointed from their number [to superintend the games], and this was the origin of the curule aediles. Again, as the consuls were called away by wars on the border and there was no one left to administer justice in the city, the result was that in addition to them a praetor was elected, who was called the *praetor urbanus* because he administered justice in the city. Some years after this, [actually, about 125 years later], as this praetor was not equal to the

discharge of his duties in consequence of the excessive crowding of
foreigners into the city, another praetor was created in addition, called
the *praetor peregrinus,* because his chief duty was to administer justice to
peregrini (foreigners).

26. THE REPUBLICAN MAGISTRATES

In the following selection the etymologies given by Varro for the names
of the different Roman magistrates are linguistically correct, or nearly so,
except for the words *consul* and *praetor,* the real origin of which is uncertain.

Varro, *The Latin Language* v. lxxx–lxxxii; Adapted from *LCL*

The *consul* was so named as the one who should "consult" the people
and senate; unless it is derived, rather, as Accius says in his *Brutus:* "Let
him who counsels rightly become the consul."

The *praetor* was so named as the one who should "head" *(praeire)* the
law and the army; or as Lucilius said: "Therefore it is the duty of the
praetors to go out in front and before."

The *censor* was so named as the one by whose "rating" *(censio),* or
judgment, the people should be rated. The *aedile,* as the one who was to
look after "buildings" *(aedes)* sacred and private. The *quaestors,* from
"inquiring," because they were to inquire into the public moneys and
also into the illegal doings which the three-man board on capital crimes
now investigates;[6] from them, afterwards, those who pronounce judgment in investigations were named "inquisitors." The *military tribunes,*
because in the old days there were sent to the army three each on behalf
of the three "tribes" of Ramnes, Luceres, and Tities. The *tribunes of the
plebs,* because they were first created, in the secession to Crustumerium,
from among the military tribunes for the purpose of defending the
plebs.[7] The *dictator,* because he was named by the consul as the one to
whose "dictum" all should be obedient. The *master of the horse,* because
he has supreme authority over the cavalry and the replacement troops,
just as the dictator has over the people, from which fact the latter is also
called "master of the people." The remaining officials, because they are
inferior to these "masters" *(magistri),* are called "magistrates."

6. The quaestor's functions were apparently originally judicial, later financial. Cf. §§ 25, 34.
7. For a different view, see § 25.

27. THE COMITIA CENTURIATA

The classification of the Roman citizen body according to wealth, and the creation of the centuriate assembly based on this classification, were ascribed by Roman tradition to Servius Tullius, the last but one of the Roman kings. The reorganization, however, actually belongs to the early decades of the young Republic. As will be seen from the following text, this assembly was a political institution based on a military muster designed to regulate and strengthen Rome's armed forces by classifying the citizens according to the equipment each could provide for himself in the field.

The fullest account of the "Servian Constitution" as it is sometimes called, is found in Dionysius' *Roman Antiquities* IV. xvi–xxi (cf. Livy I. xlii–xliii), from which space permits the inclusion here of only part of the last chapter. In these passages Livy and Dionysius give the following minimum property qualifications for eligibility to the different census classes: 1st class, a capital worth of 100,000 *asses;* 2d class, 75,000; 3d class, 50,000; 4th class, 25,000; 5th class, 11,000; 6th class, less than 11,000 (12,500 in Dionysius, 15,000 according to Aulus Gellius XVI. x. 10 and Cicero, *Republic* II. xxii. 40). The men of the sixth class were known as *proletarii,* "offspring givers" (since they were regarded as contributing nothing else to the state), or as *capite censi,* "men enrolled by name alone."

Cicero, in his *Republic* (II. xxii. 39), aptly summarizes the timocratic spirit and purpose of the "Servian" reform: "He made this division in such a way that the greatest number of votes belonged not to the common people but to the rich, and put into effect the principle which ought always to be adhered to in the commonwealth, that the greatest number should not have the greatest power."

Dionysius of Halicarnassus, *Roman Antiquities* VII. lix. 2–8; From *LCL*

In earlier times, whenever the people were to give their votes upon any point referred to them by the senate, the consuls had summoned the centuriate assembly, after first offering up the sacrifices required by law, some of which are still performed down to our own time. The populace was wont to assemble in the Field of Mars before the city, drawn up under their centurions and their standards as in war. They did not give their votes all at the same time, but each by their respective centuries, when these were called upon by the consuls. And there being in all 193 centuries, and these distributed into six classes, that class was first called and gave its vote which consisted of those citizens who had the highest property rating and who stood in the foremost rank in battle; in this were comprised eighteen centuries of horse and eighty of foot. The class that voted in the second place was composed of those of smaller fortunes who occupied an inferior position in battle and had not the same armor as the frontline fighters, but less; this multitude formed twenty centuries, and to them were added two centuries of carpenters, armorers, and other artisans employed in making engines of war. Those who were called to vote in the third class made up twenty centuries; they had a lower property rating than those of the second class and were posted behind them, and the arms they carried were not equal to those of the men in front of them. Those next called had a still lower property rating and had a safer post in battle and their armor was lighter; these also were divided into twenty centuries, and arrayed with them were two centuries of hornblowers and trumpeters.[8] The class which was called in the fifth place consisted of those whose property was rated very low, and their arms were javelins and slings; these had no fixed place in the battle line, but being light-armed men and mobile, they attended the heavy-armed men and were distributed into thirty centuries. The poorest of the citizens, who were not less numerous than all the rest, voted last and made but one century; they were exempt from the military levies and from the war taxes paid by the rest of the citizens in proportion to their ratings, and for both these reasons were given the least honor in voting.[9]

If, therefore, in the case of the first centuries, which consisted of the horse and of such of the foot as stood in the foremost rank in battle, ninety-seven centuries were of the same opinion, the voting was at an end and the remaining ninety-six centuries were not called upon to give their votes. But if this was not the case, the second class, composed of

---

8. Livy's account of the distribution of the centuries among the classes agrees with this, except that he places the two centuries of artisans in the first class and those of the trumpeters in the fifth.

9. Dionysius (*Roman Antiquities* IV. xix. 3) comments: "Tullius made none of these regulations without reason, but from the conviction that all men look upon their possessions as the prizes at stake in war and that it is for the sake of retaining these that they endure all its hardships; he thought it right, therefore, that those who had greater prizes at stake should suffer greater hardships, both with their persons and with their possessions, that those who had less at stake should be less burdened in respect to both, and that those who had no loss to fear should endure no hardships but be exempt from taxes by reason of their poverty and from military service because they paid no tax. For at that time the Romans received no pay as soldiers from the public treasury but served at their own expense." (Quoted from the Loeb Classical Library.) According to Livy (I. xliii. 9), the state did help defray the expenses of the cavalry: "For the purchase of horses they were allowed 10,000 *asses* each from the state treasury, and for the maintenance of these horses unmarried women were designated, who had to pay 2,000 *asses* each, every year." (Quoted from the Loeb Classical Library.)

twenty-two centuries, was called, and then the third and so on, until ninety-seven centuries were of the same opinion. Generally the points in dispute were determined by the classes first summoned, so that it was then needless to poll the later classes. It seldom happened that a matter was so doubtful that the voting went on till the last class was reached, consisting of the poorest citizens; and it was in the nature of a miracle when, in consequence of the first 192 centuries being equally divided, the addition of this last vote to the rest turned the scale one way or the other.

Dionysius of Halicarnassus, *Roman Antiquities* IV. xxi, 1, 3; From *LCL*

In establishing this political system, which gave so great an advantage to the rich, Tullius outwitted the people without their noticing it and excluded the poor from any part in public affairs. For they all thought that they had an equal share in the government because every man was asked his opinion, each in his own century; but they were deceived in this, that the whole century, whether it consisted of a small or a very large number of citizens, had but one vote; and also in that the centuries which voted first, consisting of men of the highest rating, though they were more in number than all the rest, yet contained fewer citizens; but above all, in that the poor, who were very numerous, had but one vote and were the last called. . . .

This form of government was maintained by the Romans for many generations, but it is altered in our times and changed to a more democratic form, some urgent needs having forced the change, which was effected not by abolishing the centuries but by no longer observing the strict ancient manner of calling them—a fact which I myself have noted, having often been present at the elections of their magistrates.[10]

10. Another factor was the gradual supersession of the *comitia centuriata* by the *comitia tributa* for general legislation and for the election of magistrates not holding the *imperium;* and, as Dionysius remarks elsewhere (*Roman Antiquities* XI. xlv. 3), "In the assembly by tribes the plebeians and the poorer sort were superior to the patricians; but in the assembly by centuries the patricians, though far less numerous, were superior to the plebeians." In the later Republic the *comitia centuriata* continued to function only in certain areas traditionally associated with it, such as the election of consuls, praetors, and censors and voting on war, peace and alliances, and appeals in capital cases.

28. Creation of the Tribunate

The creation of the tribunate is recorded in the Roman tradition as the result of the so-called First Secession of the plebs, an event of doubtful authenticity. The traditional date of the first tribunes, 494–493 B.C., is now widely regarded as being too early; many scholars prefer 471 B.C. (cf. note 11).

Dionysius of Halicarnassus, *Roman Antiquities* VI. lxxxix; From *LCL*

The people, dividing themselves into the clans of that day, or whatever one wishes to term the divisions which the Romans call *curiae,* chose for their annual magistrates the following persons: Lucius Junius Brutus and Gaius Sicinius Bellutus, whom they had had as their leaders up to that time, and, in addition to these, Gaius and Publius Licinius and Gaius Visellius Ruga. These five persons,[11] the first tribunes of the plebs, assumed the tribunician power on the fourth day before the Ides of December [December 10th], as is done even in our time. The election being over, the envoys of the senate considered that everything for which they had been sent was now properly settled. But Brutus, calling the plebeians together, advised them to render this magistracy sacred and inviolable, ensuring its security by both a law and an oath. This was approved by all, and a law was drawn up by him and his colleagues, as follows: "Let no one compel a tribune of the people, as if he were an ordinary person, to do anything against his will; let no one whip him or order another to whip him; and let no one kill him or order another to kill him. If anybody shall do any of these forbidden things, let him be accursed and let his goods be consecrated to Ceres; and if anybody shall kill one who has done any of these things, let him be guiltless of murder." And to the end that the people might not even in the future be at liberty to repeal this law, but that it might forever remain unalterable, it was ordained that all the Romans should solemnly swear over the sacrificial victims to observe it for all time, both they and their posterity; and a prayer was added to the oath that the heavenly gods and the divinities of the lower world might be propitious to those who observed it, and that the wrath of those gods and divinities might be visited upon

11. According to another tradition, the number of the tribunes was only two at first and was raised to five in 471 B.C., when they began to be elected by tribal instead of curiate voting (Livy II. lviii. 1).

those who violated it, as being guilty of the greatest sacrilege. From this the custom arose among the Romans of considering the persons of the tribunes as holy and sacrosanct, and this custom continues to this day.

29. POWERS AND DUTIES OF TRIBUNES

Valerius Maximus, *Memorable Deeds and Sayings* II. ii. 7

Tribunes of the plebs were not allowed to enter the senate house; however, seating themselves in front of the door, they scrutinized the senate's decisions with most diligent attention, and vetoed any of which they disapproved. Therefore, it was customary in the old days for the letter *C* to be subscribed to decrees of the senate, signifying that the tribunes too had "confirmed" them. And although the tribunes kept watch for the benefit of the plebs and were occupied in curbing the magistrates, they nevertheless allowed them to appear in public with silver equipment and gold rings, so that by the use of such accoutrements the authority of the magistrates might be the more imposing.

Plutarch, *Roman Questions* lxxxi; From *LCL*

Why does the tribune not wear a *toga praetexta,* although the other magistrates wear it?

Is it because he is not a magistrate at all? For tribunes have no lictors, nor do they transact business seated on the curule chair, nor do they enter their office at the beginning of the year as all the other magistrates do, [but on December 10th]; nor do they cease from their functions when a dictator is chosen, but although he transfers every other office to himself, the tribunes alone remain, as not being officials but as holding some other position. Even as some advocates will not have it that a demurrer is a suit, but hold that its effect is the opposite of a suit—for a suit brings a case into court and obtains a judgment, while a demurrer takes it out of court and quashes it—in the same way they believe that the tribuneship is a check on officialdom and a position to offer opposition to magistracy rather than a magistracy. For its authority and power consist in blocking the power of a magistrate and in the abrogation of excessive authority. . . .

Since the tribunate derives its origin from the people, the popular element in it is strong; and of much importance is the fact that the tribune does not pride himself above the rest of the people, but conforms in appearance, dress, and manner of life to ordinary citizens. Pomp and circumstance become the consul and the praetor; but the tribune, as Gaius Curio used to say, must allow himself to be trodden upon; he must not be proud of mien, nor difficult of access, nor harsh to the multitude, but indefatigable on behalf of others and easy for the multitude to deal with. Wherefore it is the custom that not even the door of his house shall be closed, but it remains open both night and day as a haven of refuge for such as need it. The more humble he is in outward appearance, the more he is increased in power. They think it meet that he shall be available for the common need and be accessible to all, even as an altar; and by the honor paid to him they make his person holy, sacred, and inviolable.

30. THE AEDILES

The aediles, originally two officers of the plebs, were involved in certain aspects of municipal administration affecting plebeians. The aedileship was ultimately elevated to a magistracy of the state, in 367 B.C., with the creation of two curule aedileships, at first solely patrician, but soon open also to plebeians. Thenceforth the four aediles had similar duties, summed up by Cicero, *Laws* III. iii. 7: "There shall be aediles, who shall be curators of the city, of the markets, and of the customary games."

Dionysius of Halicarnassus, *Roman Antiquities* VI. xc. 2–3; From *LCL*

After this they also returned thanks to the gods worshiped in the city, and prevailed upon the patricians to pass a vote for the confirmation of their new magistracy [the tribunate]. And having obtained this also, they asked further that the senate should allow them to appoint every year two plebeians to act as assistants to the tribunes in everything the latter should require, to decide such cases as the others should refer to them, to have the oversight of public places, both sacred and profane, and to scc that the market was supplied with plenty of provisions. Having obtained this concession also from the senate, they chose men whom they called assistants and colleagues of the tribunes, and judges. Now, however, they are called in their own language, from one of their functions, overseers of sacred places or aediles, and their power is no longer subordinate to that of other magistrates, as formerly; but many affairs of great importance are entrusted to them, and in most respects they resemble more or less the *agoranomoi,* or "market overseers," among the Greeks.

31. THE DECEMVIRATE, 451–449 B.C.

Livy, *History of Rome* III. xxxii. 5–7; From *LCL*

The next consuls were Gaius Menenius and Publius Sestius Capitolinus [452 B.C.]. In this year likewise there was no foreign war, but disturbances arose at home. The commissioners had now returned with the laws from Athens [see introduction to § 32]. The tribunes were therefore the most insistent that a beginning should be made at last towards codification. It was resolved to appoint decemvirs,[12] subject to no appeal, and to have no other magistrates for that year. Whether plebeians should be permitted a share in the work was for some time disputed; in the end they yielded to the patricians, only bargaining that the Icilian Law about the Aventine and the other sacred laws[13] should not be abrogated.

Dionysius of Halicarnassus, *Roman Antiquities* x. lvii. 5–lviii. 1

These decemvirs drafted a body of laws, both from those of the Greeks and from their own unwritten customs, and exposed them on ten tablets to the scrutiny of any who wished; and, welcoming every amendment suggested by private individuals, they endeavored to correct them to the satisfaction of all. And for a long time they also had many public conferences with the best men concerning these laws and examined them with the greatest care. And when they were satisfied with their formulation, they first assembled the senate and, no further objections being made to the laws, procured its ratification of them. Then they convened the people in the centuriate assembly; and after the pontiffs, augurs, and other priests present had conducted the performance of the customary rites, they took the votes of the centuries. When the people too had confirmed these laws, they caused them to be engraved on bronze tablets and arranged in sequence in the most conspicuous place in the Forum.

Then, as the time remaining of their magistracy was short, they

---

12. Their official title was *decemviri consulari imperio legibus scribundis,* "board of ten with consular power for the formulation of laws."

13. Particularly the law establishing the tribunate.

assembled the senate and proposed for their consideration the question of what kind of magistrates should be chosen for the next year. After a long debate it was carried that a decemvirate should again be designated to rule the state. For the collection of laws seemed to be incomplete, since it had been compiled in a short time, and some absolute magistracy seemed necessary to compel the unwilling as well as the willing to observe those laws that were already approved. But the chief motive that induced the senators to prefer the decemvirate was the suppression of the tribunate, which they desired above all things.

Livy, *History of Rome* III. xxxvi–xxxviii (abridged); From *LCL*

Appius now threw off the mask he had been wearing and began from that moment to live as his true nature prompted him. His new colleagues too he commenced, even before they entered upon office, to fashion after his own character. Every day they met together in closed session. The violent designs which they there adopted they matured in secret. . . . They seemed like ten kings; and the terror they inspired, not only in the humblest citizens but in the leaders of the senate, was intensified by the belief that the decemvirs were merely seeking a pretext and an opening for bloodshed, so that if anybody should pronounce a word in praise of liberty, either in the senate or before the people, the rods and axes might instantly be made ready, were it only to frighten the rest. For besides the fact that there was no help in the people, the right of appeal having been taken away, they had further agreed not to interfere with each other's decisions; whereas their predecessors had allowed their judgments to be revised upon appeal to one of their colleagues, and certain cases which might have been held to be within their own competence they had referred to the people. For a brief period the terror was shared equally by all; but little by little its full force began to fall upon the plebs. The patricians were left unmolested; humbler folk were dealt with arbitrarily and cruelly. It was all a question of persons, not of causes, with the decemvirs, since influence held with them the place of right. They concocted their judgments in private and pronounced them in the Forum. If anybody sought redress from another decemvir, he came away regretting that he had not accepted the decision of the first. Moreover a report had got out, though it was not vouched for, that they had not only conspired for present wrongdoing, but had ratified with an oath a secret agreement among themselves not to call an election but by means of a perpetual decemvirate to hold the power they had once for all acquired. . . .

The Ides of May came. Without causing any magistrates to be elected, the decemvirs, now private citizens, appeared in public with no abatement either of the spirit with which they exercised their power or the insignia which proclaimed their office. But this was unmistakable tyranny. Men mourned for liberty as forever lost. . . .

[The decemvirate was brought to an end shortly afterward by a plebeian revolt (the so-called Second Secession), touched off, according to tradition, by Appius Claudius' ruthless attempt to secure possession of a beautiful young maiden, Virginia, and the slaying of the girl by her own father as the only way to keep her out of Appius' clutches.[14]]

32. THE TWELVE TABLES, 449 B.C.

The recording of the Twelve Tables (or the Law of the Twelve Tables) was a momentous step in the "struggle of the orders." The story of the decemviral commission appointed to formulate the laws, of its administration, and of its attempt to perpetuate its power illegally, is told in § 31. Plebeian agitation for a written compilation of the law was motivated by a desire not only to curb the arbitrary power of the patrician magistrates, but also to achieve *aequatio iuris* (equality before the law) for both classes. While some reforms were introduced by the decemvirs, the Law of the Twelve Tables is essentially a codification into statutory law of existing customs, and as such it reflects clearly the preponderantly agricultural and pastoral character of the Roman community of small landowners in the first century of the Republic. It is, in fact, our primary source for the social and economic conditions of the fifth century B.C. Recent efforts to date the code c. 300 B.C. or even as late as c 200 B.C. are now generally rejected.

The code is genuinely Roman in content, and the tradition that a three-man commission was sent to Athens in 454 B.C. to study the legislation of Solon is fanciful, although there is evidence of influences emanating from the law codes of the Greek cities of southern Italy. It is mainly a code of private law, with some provisions of sacred and public law (Livy's statement that it was "the fountainhead of all public and private law" [III.

14. Cf. the similar political role in Roman tradition of the rape of Lucretia (§ 7), and note 49.

xxxiv] is an exaggeration). Noteworthy are the formalism, the archaic survivals of primitive severity, the generally secular character, and the significant separation that emerges between sacral and civil law.

The first landmark in the history of Roman law, this code was of fundamental importance in its further development. The code was never formally repealed, though many provisions became antiquated, and in theory it remained the foundation of Roman law for 1,000 years, until it was superseded by the *Corpus Juris Civilis* of Justinian. Until Cicero's time it was one of the basic texts of Roman education; Cicero says (*Laws* II. xxiii. 59) that in his youth Roman boys were still required to memorize it.

Various sources, collected in *ROL*, 3:424–515[15]; Adapted from *LCL*

TABLE I: *Preliminaries to and Rules for a Trial*

If plaintiff summons defendant to court,[16] he shall go. If he does not go, plaintiff shall call witness thereto. Then only shall he take defendant by force.

If defendant shirks or takes to his heels, plaintiff shall lay hands on him.

If disease or age is an impediment, he [who summons defendant to court] shall grant him a team; he shall not spread with cushions the covered carriage if he does not so desire.

For a landowner, a landowner shall be surety; but for a proletarian person, let any one who is willing be his protector.[17]

There shall be the same right of bond and conveyance with the Roman people for a person restored to allegiance as for a loyal person.[18]

When parties make a settlement of the case, the judge[19] shall announce it. If they do not reach a settlement, they shall state the outline of their case in the meeting place or Forum before noon.

They shall plead it out together in person. After noon, the judge shall

---

15. For commentaries on this important text, see for example H. F. Jolowicz and B. Nicholas, *Historical Introduction to the Study of Roman Law*, 3d ed. (Cambridge, 1972), 108–90; T. Frank, ed., *Economic Survey of Ancient Rome*, 1:13–19.

16. That is, into the presence of the consuls at the time of the Twelve Tables. Subpoena was oral and was accompanied by touching the tip of the ear of the defendant.

17. The *vindex*, or surety, was required to appear before the magistrate in place of the defendant at a preliminary trial before an action could begin.

18. Apparently the right of making contracts and conveyances with Roman citizens was guaranteed to Latin allies even in the case of formerly rebellious peoples.

19. The *iudex*, or judge, agreed upon by both parties at the preliminary trial.

adjudge the case to the party present. If both be present, sunset shall be the time limit [of proceedings].

TABLE II: *Further Enactments on Trials*

Action under solemn deposit:[20] 500 *as* pieces[21] is the sum when the object of dispute under solemn deposit is valued at 1,000 in bronze or more, fifty pieces when less. Where the controversy concerns the liberty of a human being, fifty pieces shall be the solemn deposit under which the dispute should be undertaken.

If any of these be impediment for judge, referee,[22] or party, on that account the day of trial shall be broken off.

Whoever is in need of evidence, he shall go on every third day to call out loudly before witness' doorway.

TABLE III: *Execution; Law of Debt*

When a debt has been acknowledged, or judgment about the matter has been pronounced in court, thirty days must be the legitimate time of grace. After that, the debtor may be arrested by laying on of hands. Bring him into court. If he does not satisfy the judgment, or no one in court offers himself as surety in his behalf, the creditor may take the defaulter with him. He may bind him either in stocks or in fetters; he may bind him with a weight no more than fifteen pounds, or with less if he shall so desire. The debtor, if he wishes, may live on his own. If he does not live on his own, the person [who shall hold him in bonds] shall give him one pound of grits for each day. He may give more if he so desires.

Unless they make a settlement, debtors shall be held in bonds for sixty days. During that time they shall be brought before the praetor's[23] court in the meeting place on three successive market days, and the amount for which they are judged liable shall be announced; on the third market day they shall suffer capital punishment or be delivered up for sale abroad, across the Tiber.

20. The *sacramentum,* or "solemn deposit," was a legal action in civil cases, whereby both parties to the litigation deposited a stake which was forfeited to the state by the loser.

21. The *as* was the Roman bronze monetary unit, originally a pound ingot of copper divided into 12 *unciae.* By the Aternian-Tarpeian Law of 454 B.C. the following official equation of values was laid down: 1 ox = 10 sheep = 100 pounds bronze.

22. An *arbiter,* or "referee," for complicated cases.

23. Consul's court. In the time of the Twelve Tables the consul may still have retained his original title of *praetor.*

On the third market day creditors shall cut pieces.[24] Should they have cut more or less than their due, it shall be with impunity.

Against a stranger, title of ownership shall hold good forever.[25]

TABLE IV: *Patria Potestas: Rights of Head of Family*

Quickly kill . . . a dreadfully deformed child.

If a father thrice surrender a son for sale, the son shall be free from the father.

A child born ten months after the father's death will not be admitted into a legal inheritance.

TABLE V: *Guardianship; Succession*

Females shall remain in guardianship even when they have attained their majority . . . except Vestal Virgins.

Conveyable possessions of a woman under guardianship of agnates cannot be rightfully acquired by *usucapio* [see note 25], save such possessions as have been delivered up by her with a guardian's sanction.

According as a person shall will regarding his [household], chattels, or guardianship of his estate, this shall be binding.

If a person dies intestate, and has no self-successor,[26] the nearest agnate kinsman shall have possession of deceased's household.

If there is no agnate kinsman, deceased's clansmen shall have possession of his household.

To persons for whom a guardian has not been appointed by will, to them agnates are guardians.

If a man is raving mad, rightful authority over his person and chattels shall belong to his agnates or to his clansmen.

A spendthrift is forbidden to exercise administration over his own goods. . . . A person who, being insane or a spendthrift, is prohibited from administering his own goods shall be under trusteeship of agnates.

The inheritance of a Roman citizen-freedman shall be made over to his patron if the freedman has died intestate and without self-successor.

Items which are in the category of debts are not included in the

---

24. The majority of modern authorities agree with ancient commentators' literal interpretation that the Twelve Tables authorized actual cutting up of the debtor's body, though in customary practice the debtor's estate may have been divided.

25. This probably means that if a thing is stolen or captured by an enemy, *usucapio* (long-term possession) never validates ownership.

26. A person under the legal power of the head of the household.

division when they have with automatic right been divided into portions of an inheritance.

Debt bequeathed by inheritance is divided proportionally amongst each heir with automatic liability when the details have been investigated.

TABLE VI: *Acquisition and Possession*

When a party shall make bond [27] or conveyance, [28] the terms of the verbal declaration are to be held binding.

Articles which have been sold and handed over are not acquired by a buyer otherwise than when he has paid the price to the seller or has satisfied him in some other way, that is, by providing a guarantor or a security.

A person who has been ordained a free man [in a will, on condition] that he bestow a sum of 10,000 pieces on the heir, though he has been sold by the heir, shall win his freedom by giving the money to the purchaser.

It is sufficient to make good such faults as have been named by word of mouth, and that for any flaws which the vendor had expressly denied, he shall undergo penalty of double damage.

Usucapio of movable things requires one year's possession for its completion; but *usucapio* of an estate and buildings, two years.

Any woman who does not wish to be subjected in this manner to the hand of her husband should be absent three nights in succession every year, and so interrupt the *usucapio* of each year. [29]

A person shall not dislodge from a framework a [stolen] beam which has been fixed in buildings or a vineyard. . . . Action [is granted] for double damages against a person found guilty of fixing such [stolen] beam.

---

27. The *nexum* contract was a form of loan in which the creditor enjoyed the right of execution against the person of the debtor, and through which the defaulting debtor became the bond-slave of the creditor until the debt was paid. Cf. note 50.

28. *Mancipatio*, a method of acquiring ownership through a symbolical sale *per aes et libram*, "by copper and scales." The conveyance took place in the presence of five Roman citizens. The buyer grasped the property, or part of it, claimed ownership, and struck with a piece of bronze or copper a scale held by a *libripens*, "scale-balancer." Finally he handed over to the seller the piece of metal as symbolical of the price.

29. This limitation on the *patria potestas* introduced a form of civil marriage without *manus*, the legal power of a husband over his wife.

TABLE VII: *Rights concerning Land*

Ownership within a five-foot strip [between two pieces of land] shall not be acquired by long usage.

The width of a road [extends] to eight feet where it runs straight ahead, sixteen round a bend. . . .

Persons shall mend roadways. If they do not keep them laid with stone, a person may drive his beasts where he wishes.

If rainwater does damage . . . this must be restrained according to an arbitrator's order.

If a water course directed through a public place shall do damage to a private person, he shall have right of suit to the effect that damage shall be repaired for the owner.

Branches of a tree may be lopped off all round to a height of more than 15 feet. . . . Should a tree on a neighbor's farm be bent crooked by a wind and lean over your farm, action may be taken for removal of that tree.

It is permitted to gather up fruit falling down on another man's farm.

TABLE VIII: *Torts or Delicts*

If any person has sung or composed against another person a song such as was causing slander or insult to another, he shall be clubbed to death.

If a person has maimed another's limb, let there be retaliation in kind unless he makes agreement for settlement with him.

If he has broken or bruised a freeman's bone with his hand or a club, he shall undergo penalty of 300 *as* pieces; if a slave's, 150.

If he has done simple harm [to another], penalties shall be 25 *as* pieces.

If a four-footed animal shall be said to have caused loss, legal action . . . shall be either the surrender of the thing which damaged, or else the offer of assessment for the damage.

For pasturing on, or cutting secretly by night, another's crops acquired by tillage, there shall be capital punishment in the case of an adult malefactor . . . he shall be hanged and put to death as a sacrifice to Ceres. In the case of a person under the age of puberty, at the discretion of the praetor [see note 23] either he shall be scourged or settlement shall be made for the harm done by paying double damages.

Any person who destroys by burning any building or heap of corn deposited alongside a house shall be bound, scourged, and put to death by burning at the stake, provided that he has committed the said misdeed with malice aforethought; but if he shall have committed it by accident, that is, by negligence, it is ordained that he repair the damage, or, if he be too poor to be competent for such punishment, he shall receive a lighter chastisement.

Any person who has cut down another person's trees with harmful intent shall pay 25 *as* pieces for every tree.

If theft has been done by night, if the owner kill the thief, the thief shall be held lawfully killed.

It is forbidden that a thief be killed by day . . . unless he defend himself with a weapon; even though he has come with a weapon, unless he use his weapon and fight back, you shall not kill him. And even if he resists, first call out.

In the case of all other thieves caught in the act, if they are freemen, they should be flogged and adjudged to the person against whom the theft has been committed, provided that the malefactors have committed it by day and have not defended themselves with a weapon; slaves caught in the act of theft should be flogged and thrown from the Rock;[30] boys under the age of puberty should, at the praetor's [see note 23] discretion, be flogged, and the damage done by them should be repaired.

If a person pleads on a case of theft in which the thief has not been caught in the act, the thief must compound for the loss by paying double damages.

A stolen thing is debarred from *usucapio.*

No person shall practice usury at a rate more than one twelfth . . .[31] A usurer is condemned for quadruple amount.

Arising out of a case concerning an article deposited . . . action for double damages.

Guardians and trustees . . . the right to accuse on suspicion . . . action . . . against guardians for double damages.

If a patron shall have defrauded his client, he must be solemnly forfeited.[32]

Whosoever shall have allowed himself to be called as witness or shall have been scales-balancer [see note 28], if he do not as witness pro-

---

30. The Tarpeian Rock on the Capitoline Hill, commonly used as a place of execution in Rome.

31. The first reference to interest rates at Rome. *Unciarium foenus* was probably 8.33 percent, possibly 10 percent, per annum.

32. The man thus judged *sacer* was placed outside human law by being dedicated to a divinity for destruction. This original death by sacrifice was later transformed into outlawry and confiscation of property.

nounce his testimony, he must be deemed dishonored and incapable of acting as witness.

Penalty . . . for false witness . . . a person who has been found guilty of giving false witness shall be hurled down from the Tarpeian Rock. . . .

No person shall hold meetings by night in the city.

Members [of associations] . . . are granted . . . the right to pass any binding rule they like for themselves provided that they cause no violation of public law.

TABLE IX: *Public Law*

Laws of personal exception [i.e., bills of attainder] must not be proposed; cases in which the penalty affects the person of a citizen must not be decided except through the greatest assembly[33] and through those whom the censors[34] have placed upon the register of citizens.

The penalty shall be capital punishment for a judge or arbiter legally appointed who has been found guilty of receiving a bribe for giving a decision.

He who shall have roused up a public enemy, or handed over a citizen to a public enemy, must suffer capital punishment.

Putting to death . . . of any man who has not been convicted, whosoever he might be, is forbidden.

TABLE X: *Sacred Law*

A dead man shall not be buried or burned within the city.

One must not do more than this [at funerals]; one must not smooth the pyre with an axe.

. . . three veils, one small purple tunic, and ten flute-players. . . .

Women must not tear cheeks or hold chorus of "Alas!" on account of funeral.

When a man is dead one must not gather his bones in order to make a second funeral.[35] An exception [in the case of] death in war or in a foreign land. . . .

Anointing by slaves is abolished, and every kind of drinking bout.

---

33. The right of appeal to the *comitia centuriata*.
34. In the time of the Twelve Tables, the consuls (cf. § 36).
35. This provision forbids prolonged mourning through the device of second funerals.

Let there be no costly sprinkling . . . no long garlands . . . no incense boxes. . . .

When a man wins a crown himself or through a chattel or by dint of valor, the crown bestowed on him . . . [may be laid in the grave] with impunity [on the man who won it] or on his father.

To make more than one funeral for one man and to make and spread more than one bier for him . . . this should not occur . . . and a person must not add gold. . . .

But him whose teeth shall have been fastened together with gold, if a person shall bury or burn him along with that gold, it shall be with impunity.

No new pyre or personal burning-mound must be erected nearer than sixty feet to another person's buildings without consent of the owner . . . the entrance chamber [of a tomb] and burning place cannot be acquired by *usucapio*.

TABLE XI: *Supplementary Laws*

Intermarriage shall not take place between plebeians and patricians.

TABLE XII: *Supplementary Laws*

Levying of distress [is granted] against a person who has bought an animal for sacrifice and is a defaulter by non-payment; likewise against a person who is a defaulter by non-payment of fee for yokebeast which any one has hired out for the purpose of raising therefrom money to spend on a sacred banquet.[36]

If a slave shall have committed theft or done damage . . . with his master's knowledge . . . the action for damages is in the slave's name.

Arising from delicts committed by children and slaves of a household establishment . . . actions for damages are appointed whereby the father or master could be allowed either to undergo "assessment for damages," or hand over the delinquent to punishment. . . .

If a person has taken a thing by false claim, if he should wish . . . official must grant three arbitrators; by their arbitration . . . defendant must make good the damage by paying double the usufruct of the article.

---

36. In such cases seizure of some articles of property by *pignoris capio*, "seizure of pledge," to induce payment was permitted.

It is prohibited to dedicate for consecrated use anything about which there is a controversy; otherwise the penalty is double the amount involved. . . .

Whatever the people has last ordained shall be held as binding by law.

33. THE VALERIO–HORATIAN LAWS

The year 449 B.C. was a landmark in the advance of popular liberties not only because of the publication of the Twelve Tables, but also because of the passage of the Valerio–Horatian Laws, promulgated by the first consuls after the abolition of the decemvirate. Though rejected by many authorities as a fiction of the democratic annalists, the legislation of 449 B.C. as recorded in the traditional accounts seems to contain a substratum of truth. The most debated problem concerns the force of plebiscites. It has been suggested that the first of the laws mentioned in the following selection merely recognized the right of the plebs to pass resolutions binding upon itself, or that plebiscites were accorded validity in areas not covered by statutes.

Livy, *History of Rome* III. IV. 1–7, 13–15; From *LCL*

Lucius Valerius and Marcus Horatius were elected to the consulship and at once assumed office. Their administration was favorable to the people without in any way wronging the patricians, though not without offending them; for whatever was done to protect the liberty of the plebs they regarded as a diminution of their own power. To begin with, since it was virtually an undecided question whether the patricians were legally bound by *plebiscita,* they carried a statute in the centuriate assembly, enacting that what the plebs should order in its tribal organization should be binding on the people—a law which provided the motions of the tribunes with a very sharp weapon. Next, they not only restored a consular law about appeal—that unique defense of liberty which had been overthrown by the decemviral power—but they also safeguarded it for the future by the solemn enactment of a new law, that no one should declare the election of any magistrate from whom there was no appeal, and that he who should so declare might be put to death without offense to law or religion, and that such a homicide should not be held a capital crime. And having sufficiently strengthened the plebs by means of the appeal on the one hand and the help of the tribunes on the other, they restored to the tribunes themselves their privilege of sacrosanctity (a thing that had come to be well-nigh forgotten) by reviving certain long-neglected ceremonies and they rendered them inviolate not merely by religious sanction, but also by a statute, solemnly enacting that if anyone should harm the tribunes of the plebs, their aediles, or the decemviral judges,[37] he should forfeit his head to Jupiter, and his property should be sold at the temple of Ceres, Liber, and Libera. . . . The practice was also instituted by the same consuls that the decrees of the senate should be delivered to the aediles of the plebs at the temple of Ceres. Up to that time they were wont to be suppressed or falsified at the pleasure of the consuls. Marcus Duillius, a tribune of the plebs, then proposed to the plebs, and they so decreed, that whosoever should leave the plebs without tribunes and whosoever should declare the election of a magistrate not subject to appeal should be scourged and beheaded. All these measures, though disagreeable to the patricians, were passed without opposition from them because no one person had yet been singled out for attack.

34. The Quaestorship

Zonaras, *Epitome* VII. xiii; From *LCL*

And the management of the funds he[38] assigned to others, in order that the men holding the consulship might not possess the great influence that would spring from their having the revenues in their power. Now for the first time treasurers began to be appointed, and they called them quaestors. These officials in the first place used to try capital cases, from which they have obtained this title—on account of their questionings and their search for truth as the result of questionings [cf. §§ 25, 26]. Later they acquired also the management of the public funds. . . . After a time the courts were put in charge of others, while these officials continued to manage the funds.

Tacitus, *Annals* XI. xxii

The quaestors, indeed, were appointed while the kings still ruled. . . . The consuls retained the power of selecting them until the people took over the bestowal of this office too. The first elected quaestors, sixty-

---

37. This ten-man court judged cases involving personal freedom or citizenship.
38. Publius Valerius Publicola, on whom see § 24.

three years after the expulsion of the Tarquins,[39] were Valerius Potitus and Aemilius Mamercus, and they were attached to military operations. As the public business increased, two more were added to attend to affairs at Rome.[40] This number was again doubled when Italy was already tributary and the tribute of the provinces began to be added.[41]

35. The Canuleian Law on Intermarriage; the Creation of Military Tribunes, 445 B.C.

Livy, *History of Rome* IV. i, vi. 3–12; From *LCL*

Marcus Genucius and Gaius Curtius succeeded these men as consuls. It was a year of quarrels both at home and abroad. For at its commencement Gaius Canuleius, a tribune of the plebs, proposed a bill regarding the intermarriage of patricians and plebeians which the former looked upon as involving the debasement of their blood and the subversion of the principles inhering in the *gentes,* or families. And a suggestion, cautiously put forward at first by the tribunes, that it should be lawful for one of the consuls to be chosen from the plebs, was afterwards carried so far that nine tribunes proposed a bill giving the people power to choose consuls as they might see fit, from either the plebeians or the patricians; to carry out this proposal would be, in the estimation of the patricians, not just sharing the supreme authority with the lowest of the citizens, but actually transferring it from the nobles to the plebs. The senators therefore rejoiced to hear that the people of Ardea had revolted . . . so decidedly did they prefer even an unfortunate war to an ignominious peace. Accordingly they made the most of these threats, that the proposals of the tribunes might be silenced amid the din of so many wars, and ordered levies to be held and military preparations be made with the utmost energy. . . . Thereupon Gaius Canuleius curtly proclaimed in the senate that it was in vain the consuls sought to frighten the plebs out of their concern for the new laws; and he declared that they should never hold the levy while he lived until the plebs had voted the measures which he and his colleagues had brought forward. . . .

---

39. 447 B.C. This was probably one of the measures associated with the Valerio–Horatian Laws (see § 33).

40. 421 B.C., when the office was also thrown open to plebeians; the first plebeian quaestor was not elected, however, till 409 B.C.

41. Actually in 267 B.C., when Rome had no provinces as yet.

At last the patricians were beaten and allowed the law regarding intermarriage to be passed, chiefly because they thought that the tribunes would now either wholly abandon their demand for plebeian consuls or would postpone it until after the war, and that the plebeians meantime, contented with the right to intermarry, would be ready to submit to the levy.

And since Canuleius was grown so great through his victory over the patricians and the favor of the plebeians, the other tribunes were encouraged to take up the quarrel; and they fought for their measure with the utmost violence, hindering the levy, though the rumors of war increased daily. Since nothing could be accomplished through the senate because of the tribunes' veto, the consuls held councils of their leading men in private. It was clear that they must submit to be conquered either by the enemy or by their fellow citizens. . . . The upshot of these consultations was this, that they permitted military tribunes with consular authority to be chosen indifferently from the patricians and the plebeians, but made no change in the election of consuls. With this decision both tribunes and commons were content. An election was called for choosing three tribunes with consular power. No sooner was it proclaimed than everybody who had ever spoken or acted in a seditious manner, especially those who had been tribunes, fell to canvassing voters and bustling all over the Forum in the white robes of candidates; so that the patricians, what with despair of obtaining office now that the plebs were so wrought up, and what with scorn if they must share its administration with these fellows, were deterred from standing. At last, however, they were compelled by their leaders to compete, lest they might seem to have surrendered control of the commonwealth. The outcome of this election showed how different are men's minds when struggling for liberty and station from what they are when they have laid aside their animosities and their judgment is unbiased; for the people chose all the tribunes from among the patricians, quite satisfied that plebeians should have been allowed to stand. Where shall you now find in one single man that moderation, fairness, and loftiness of mind which at that time characterized the entire people?

In the 310th year from the founding of Rome military tribunes for the first time took office in place of consuls.[42]

---

42. In subsequent years military tribunes (three or more in number) were chosen in preference to consuls about two-thirds of the time until 367 B.C., when the definitive admission of plebeians to the consulship under the Licinio-Sextian Laws (§ 38) put an end to this compromise institution.

36. The Censors

Two officials, the censors, were created in 443 B.C., who were at first concerned basically with the registration of the citizens and their property for classification in the *comitia centuriata* (see § 27). To their original duty of taking the census were gradually added the supervision of morals (which gave them the important power of reviewing the membership of the senate) and the leasing of contracts for public works, the collection of public revenues, and the maintenance of state properties. At the end of their term of office the censors performed the solemn ceremony of purification of the citizen body, the *lustratio* (see § 56). The great era of this office, the apex of a senator's political career, was the fourth and third centuries B.C.

POWERS AND DUTIES OF THE CENSORS

Livy, *History of Rome* IV. viii. 2; From *LCL*

This same year [443 B.C.] saw the adoption of the censorship, an institution which originated in a small way but afterwards grew up to such dimensions that it was invested with the regulation of the morals and discipline of the Romans. The distribution of honor and ignominy amongst the senate and the centuries of the knights was controlled by this magistracy, while jurisdiction over public and private sites, together with the revenues of the Roman people, were entirely subject to its discretion.

Cicero, *Laws* III. iii. 7; From *LCL*

Censors shall make a list of the citizens, recording their ages, families, and slaves and other property. They shall have charge of the temples, streets, and aqueducts within the city, and of the public treasury and the revenues. They shall make a division of the citizens into tribes, and other divisions according to wealth, age, and class. They shall enroll the recruits for the cavalry and infantry; they shall prohibit celibacy; they shall regulate the morals of the people; they shall allow no one guilty of dishonorable conduct to remain in the senate. They shall be two in number, and shall hold office for five years. The other magistrates shall hold office for one year. The office of censor shall never be vacant.[43]

43. These were Cicero's proposals for his "ideal state." In Republican Rome two censors were

CENSORIAL SEVERITY

Aulus Gellius, *Attic Nights* IV. xii, xx. 7–10; From *LCL*

Instances of disgrace and punishment inflicted by the censors, found in ancient records and worthy of notice:

If anyone had allowed his land to run to waste and was not giving it sufficient attention, if he had neither plowed nor weeded it, or if anyone had neglected his orchard or vineyard, such conduct did not go unpunished, but it was taken up by the censors, who reduced such a man to the lowest class of citizens.[44] So too, any Roman knight, if his horse seemed to be skinny or not well groomed, was charged with *inpolitia,* a word which means the same thing as negligence. There are authorities for both these punishments, and Marcus Cato has cited frequent instances. . . .

Here is another instance of the sternness of the same officials. The censors deliberated about the punishment of a man who had been brought before them by a friend as his advocate, and who had yawned in court very clearly and loudly. He was on the point of being condemned for his lapse, on the ground that it was an indication of a wandering and trifling mind and of wanton and undisguised indifference. But when the man had sworn that the yawn had overcome him much against his will and in spite of his resistance, and that he was afflicted with the disorder known as *oscedo,* or a tendency to yawning, he was excused from the penalty which had already been determined upon. Publius Scipio Africanus, son of Paullus, included both these stories in a speech which he made when censor, urging the people to follow the customs of their forefathers.

CONTRACTS FOR PUBLIC WORKS

Livy, *History of Rome* XLI. xxvii

Quintus Fulvius Flaccus and Aulus Postumius Albinus were elected censors this year [174 B.C.] and revised the roll of the senate. Marcus Aemilius Lepidus, the *pontifex maximus,* was chosen as *princeps senatus*

---

elected every five years, but in accordance with the Aemilian Law (date unknown) the duration of the office was limited to eighteen months.

44. The class of *aerarii,* who were at first citizens without landed property, but later technically citizens relegated by the censors for improper conduct to one of the four city tribes.

(ranking senator). They expelled nine from the senate, the most important being Marcus Cornelius Maluginensis, who had been praetor in Spain two years before, Lucius Cornelius Scipio, who at the time exercised jurisdiction in cases between citizens and aliens, and Lucius Fulvius, the censor's own brother. . . .

These censors were the first to let contracts for paving the streets of the city with flint, for laying the foundations of roads outside the city with gravel and constructing footpaths at the sides, and also for the construction of bridges in many places. They furnished the aediles and praetors with a stage, placed the stalls in the Circus, and provided such equipment as egg-shaped balls to mark the number of laps, turnposts for the race course, and iron cages through which the animals might be let out. . . . . They also undertook the paving of the ascent from the Forum to the Capitol with flint, and the construction of a portico from the temple of Saturn to the Capitol and then on to . . . the senate house. The market place outside the Porta Trigemina was paved with stone and enclosed with paling; they also contracted for the repairing of the Aemilian portico and made a flight of steps from the Tiber to the market place.[45] Inside the same gate they paved the portico leading to the Aventine with flint. . . . These censors also let contracts for the erection of walls at Calatia and Auximium, and the money they received from the sale of the state domain there was spent in building shops around the forums in both these places. Postumius announced that without the orders of the Roman senate or people he would let no contract. So Fulvius Flaccus with the money allotted them contracted for a temple to Jupiter at Pisaurum and at Fundi, for bringing water to Potentia, for paving a street at Pisaurum with flint, and, at Sinuessa, for the construction of suburbs . . . sewers, and a surrounding wall, for the building of porticoes and shops all around the forum, and for setting up three statues of Janus. These works contracted for by one of the censors were greatly appreciated by the colonists.

The censors were strict and painstaking in the regulation of morals; many of the knights were deprived of their horses.

---

45. A market place along the Tiber, southwest of the Aventine Hill.

37. THE DICTATORSHIP

An integral part of the early republican constitution was the office of dictator, derived and adapted to Roman needs from the similar institution of the Latin League. This extraordinary magistracy for military emergencies concentrated almost unlimited military, executive, and judicial power in one person for a period not exceeding six months (the length of the fighting season). It is possible that the office was also employed by the patricians, after the creation of the military tribunate (§ 35), as a class weapon against the plebeians. At any rate, the historicity of all traditional dictatorships before c. 430 B.C. is suspect. In 356 B.C. plebeians were admitted to the office, shortly after the consulship was opened to them. This early dictatorship went out of practice at the end of the third century B.C., when the "struggle of the orders" was over and the supremacy of the senate was assured during the crisis of the Second Punic War. The late republican dictatorships of Sulla and Caesar, held for life, differ from this office, being extraconstitutional.

Zonaras, *Epitome* VII. xiii; From *LCL*

When a new war was stirred up on the part of the Latins against Rome [about 500 B.C.], the populace demanded that there should be a cancellation of debts and refused to take up arms. Therefore the nobles then for the first time established a new office to have jurisdiction over both classes. Dictator was the name given to the man honored with this position, and he possessed power equal in all respects to that of the kings. People hated the name of king on account of the Tarquins, but desiring the benefit to be derived from sole leadership, which seemed to exert a potent influence amid conditions of war and revolution, they chose it under another name. Hence the dictatorship was, as has been said, so far as its authority went, equivalent to the kingship, except that the dictator might not ride on horseback unless he were about to set out on a campaign and was not permitted to make any expenditure from the public funds unless the right were specifically voted. He might try men and put them to death at home as well as on campaigns, and not merely such as belonged to the populace, but also men from the knights, and from the senate itself. No one, not even the tribunes, had the power to make any complaint against him or to take any action hostile to him, and no appeal could be taken from him.[46] The office of dictator extended

46. The dictator's exemption from the right of appeal *(provocatio)* was abolished in 300 B.C.

for a period of not more than six months, in order that no such official by lingering on in the midst of so great power and unhampered authority should become haughty and be carried away by a passion for sole leadership.

38. THE LICINIO–SEXTIAN LAWS, 367 B.C.

After the establishment of their office, the tribunes became the natural leaders of the plebeians in the "struggle of the orders." There ensued a seesaw political battle, in which the tribunes quickly found that their most effective weapon to wring concessions from an obdurate senate was to veto the military levies until their demands were met (cf. § 35), while the patricians devised ways of controlling this office to which they were ineligible. In turn, the wealthy sector of the plebeian class conducted a steadily increasing agitation for admission to the jealously guarded office of consul.

Livy, *History of Rome* VI. xxxv; From *LCL*

An opportunity for innovation was presented by the enormous load of debt, which the plebs could have no hope of lightening but by placing their representatives in the highest offices. . . . It was resolved that Gaius Licinius and Lucius Sextius should be elected tribunes of the plebs [for the year 376 B.C.], a magistracy in which they might open for themselves a way to other offices. Once elected, they proposed only such measures as abated the influence of the patricians, while forwarding the interests of the plebs. One of these had to do with debt, providing that what had been paid as interest should be deducted from the principal, and the balance discharged in three annual installments of equal size. A second set a limit on [public] lands, prohibiting anyone from holding more than 500 *iugera*. A third did away with the election of military tribunes [see § 35] and prescribed that of the consuls one, at any rate, should be chosen from the plebs. These were all matters of great moment, and it would not be possible to carry them without a tremendous struggle. . . .

The patricians became thoroughly alarmed; and . . . they primed colleagues of the tribunes to oppose their measures. These men, seeing Licinius and Sextius summon the tribes to vote, came up in the midst of a bodyguard of patricians and refused to permit the bills to be recited or anything else to be done that was usual in passing a resolution of the plebs. And now the plebeian assembly had been summoned repeatedly without avail, and the bills were as dead as if they had been voted down, when Sextius cried out, "So be it! Since it is your pleasure that the veto should be so powerful, we will use that very weapon for the protection of the plebs. Come now, senators, and proclaim an assembly for the choice of military tribunes; I warrant you shall have no joy of that word *veto,* which you now hear with such satisfaction from the chorus of our colleagues." His threats were no idle ones: except for the aediles and tribunes of the plebs, there was not an election held. Licinius and Sextius, chosen tribunes of the plebs again, permitted no curule magistrates to be elected; and this dearth of magistrates continued in the city for five years, while the plebs continued to reelect the two men tribunes, and they to prevent the election of military tribunes.

Livy, *History of Rome* VI. xxxviii–xlii (abridged); From *LCL*

At the very outset of the year [368 B.C.] came a final struggle over the laws; and when the tribes were summoned to vote, and the proposers of the measures would not yield to the vetoes of their colleagues, the frightened patricians were put to their last resources—the greatest office and the greatest of the citizens. They voted to name a dictator, and appointed Marcus Furius Camillus, who chose Lucius Aemilius as his master of the horse. To meet these formidable preparations of their adversaries, the proposers of the laws on their side armed the commons with tremendous enthusiasm for the cause, and, proclaiming an assembly of the plebs, called up the tribes to vote.

Attended by a body of patricians and breathing wrath and menaces, the dictator took his seat, and the affair began with the usual skirmish among the tribunes of the plebs, some of whom urged the passing of the law while others interposed their vetoes. But powerful as the veto was from the legal point of view, it was being overcome by the popularity of the bills themselves and of their proposers, and the tribes which had been summoned first were voting "Aye," when Camillus . . . in high dudgeon sent his lictors to turn the plebeians out and threatened that if they continued in their course, he would administer the oath to all of military age and forthwith lead the army out of the city.

The plebs were greatly dismayed; but the courage of their leaders was rather kindled than damped by his vehemence. Yet before the matter had been decided either way, Camillus resigned his office. . . .

In the interval between the abdication of the earlier dictator and the entrance into office of Manlius, the new one, the tribunes—as though there were an *interregnum*—held an assembly of the plebs, and it became evident which of the measures proposed were more gratifying to the mass of the plebeians, and which to their introducers. For they were on the point of passing the bills relating to interest and land and rejecting the one about the plebeian consul, and both matters would have been finally disposed of, if the tribunes had not said that they were putting all these questions to the plebs collectively. . . .

Returned to office for the tenth time [367 B.C.], the tribunes Sextius and Licinius obtained the enactment of a law requiring that half of the board of ten who had charge of sacred rites should be plebeians. Having elected five patricians and five plebeians, the people felt that they had set a precedent for the consulship. . . .

After desperate struggles the senate and the dictator were beaten, and the measures advocated by the tribunes were adopted. An election of consuls was held, against the wishes of the nobles, and resulted in the choice of Lucius Sextius, the first of the plebeians to attain that honor. Even this did not end their disputes. The patricians declared that they would not ratify the election, and the affair almost led to a secession of the plebs and the other terrible menaces of civil strife, when the dictator finally proposed a compromise which allayed the discord: the nobles gave way to the plebs in regard to the plebeian consul, and the plebs conceded to the nobles that there should be elected from the patricians one praetor to administer justice in the city. Thus after their long quarrel the orders were reconciled at last.[47]

39. THE DEBTOR QUESTION

Much that is recorded in the Roman historians concerning the issue of debts in the fifth and fourth centuries B.C. is an invention of the annalists, who projected backward into the early period the debtor agitation and debt legislation of the later Republic. The basic difficulties which weighed

47. It was not until some years later (traditional date 348 B.C.) that the law on the consulship became firmly established and scrupulously observed; until then the patricians still managed in some years to hold both consulships. The creation of the praetorship, although justified on the ground that the two consuls could no longer cope with all the administrative duties of the expanding Roman state, was a maneuver by the patricians to salvage something for themselves by reducing the powers of the consulship. However, once the plebeians were admitted to the consulship, it was difficult to maintain the new barrier for long, and the first plebeian praetor was elected in 337 B.C.

heavily on the mass of the plebeian small landowners were the harsh debtor laws and the high interest rates. Imprisonment was one form of execution available to creditors against insolvent debtors; in addition, debt-slavery resulted from the *nexum* contract, by which loans were secured by the persons of the borrowers, who agreed to enslavement in case of default. It is not unlikely that the difficulties of small landowners in this period stemmed in part from survivals of family ownership of land, which prevented real property from being offered as security for loans, and in part from neglect of farms and property, because of long absence in war. The following selections describe various measures for relieving distress. The Poetelian–Papirian Law of 326 B.C. virtually eliminated personal execution against insolvent debtors.

REDUCTION OF THE INTEREST RATE

Livy, *History of Rome* VII. xvi. 1, xxvii. 3–4; From *LCL*

Less agreeable to the senate was a measure which came up in the following year, in the consulship of Gaius Marcius and Gnaeus Manlius [357 B.C.]. It fixed the rate of interest at 8⅓ percent,[48] and was carried through by Marcus Duillius and Lucius Menenius, tribunes of the plebs. The commons ratified it . . . eagerly.

The same peaceful conditions continued at home and abroad during the consulship of Titus Manlius Torquatus and Gaius Plautius [347 B.C.]. But the rate of interest was reduced from 8⅓ to 4⅙ percent, and debts were made payable one fourth down and the remainder in three annual installments; even so, many of the plebeians were distressed, but the public credit was of greater concern to the senate than were the hardships of single persons. What did the most to lighten the burden was the omission of the war tax and of the military levy.

THE POETELIAN–PAPIRIAN LAW, 326 B.C.

Livy, *History of Rome* VIII. xxviii

This year was marked by the dawn, as it were, of a new era of liberty for the plebs; for they ceased to be enslaved for debt. This change in the law was brought about by the great lust and cruelty of one usurer,

---

48. This was probably a reenactment of the provision on maximum interest in the Twelve Tables (§ 32, table VIII).

Lucius Papirius, to whom Gaius Publilius had pledged his person for a debt which his father had contracted. The youth and beauty of the debtor, which ought to have called forth feelings of compassion, only acted as incentives to lust and insult. Regarding the boy's youthful bloom as added interest on his loan, he at first tried to seduce him with lewd talk. Then, when he turned a deaf ear to the disgraceful proposal, he sought to terrify him with threats, and reminded him constantly of his status. Finally, when he saw that the boy had more regard for his honorable birth than his present status, he ordered him to be stripped and beaten. Mangled by the blows, the boy rushed into the street and complained loudly of the usurer's lust and brutality. A vast crowd gathered, inflamed with pity for his youth and outrage for the wrong, and considering too the conditions under which they and their children were living, and they ran into the Forum and from there in a compact body to the senate house. Forced by this sudden outbreak, the consuls convened a meeting of the senate, and as the members entered the senate house the crowd exhibited the lacerated back of the youth and flung themselves at the feet of the senators. The strong bond of credit was on that day overthrown through the mad excesses of one individual.[49] The consuls were instructed by the senate to lay before the people a proposal "that no man be kept in shackles or in the stocks, except such as, having been guilty of some crime, were waiting to pay the penalty; and that the goods but not the person of the debtor should be the security for money lent." So the *nexi* were released, and it was forbidden for any to become *nexi* in the future.[50]

---

49. With this stereotyped climactic incident in the Roman annalists' treatment of major events, cf. the rape of Lucretia (§ 7) and the affair of Virginia (§ 31).

50. Cf. Varro, *The Latin Language* VII. CV: "A free man who, for money which he owed, *nectebat* [bound] his labor in slavery until he should pay, is called a *nexus* [bond-slave], just as a man is called *obaeratus* [indebted] from *aes* [money debt]. When Gaius Poetelius Libo Visulus was dictator, this method of dealing with debtors was done away with, and all who took oath by the Good Goddess of Plenty were freed from being bond-slaves." (Quoted from the Loeb Classical Library.) Varro, in dating the Poetelian-Papirian Law some years after 326 B.C., is probably not as accurate as Livy. Though it is not likely that personal execution for debt was completely abolished by this "ancient Magna Charta," the provisions that all types of property, including land, could be offered as security for debt; that only the property of the debtor, not his person, might be offered as security; and that judgment in a court had to be obtained before execution by the creditor, all undermined the *nexum* contract and led to its disappearance.

40. AGRARIAN DISCONTENT

The tradition concerning plebeian agitation in the early centuries of the Republic for allotments from the *ager publicus* ("public land," i.e., territory annexed to the state domain from conquered peoples), is too strong to be rejected as merely a retrojection of the agrarian discontent of the late Republic. The details, however, are not to be accepted at face value. Though numerous bills were put forth, there seems to have been no general distribution of public land until the Licinio-Sextian legislation of 367 B.C. (§ 38), which attempted to put a ceiling on holdings of public land. Although this provision was only loosely enforced, it initiated an era of land allotments to impoverished citizen-soldiers, as the ruling aristocracy came to realize that it could use the recurrent wars with the various peoples of Italy not only to divert attention from the domestic struggle but also, by establishing military colonies in the conquered territories, to siphon off some of the malcontents from Rome.

Livy, *History of Rome,* II. xli. 1–5; From *LCL*

Spurius Cassius and Proculus Verginius were then made consuls [486 B.C.]. A treaty was concluded with the Hernicans, and two thirds of their land was taken from them. Of this the consul Cassius proposed to divide one half among the Latins and the other half among the plebeians. To this gift he wished to add some part of that land which, he charged, was held by individuals although it belonged to the state. Whereupon many of the senators, being themselves in possession of the land, took fright at the danger which threatened their interests. But the senators were also concerned on political grounds, namely, that the consul by his largess should be building up an influence perilous to liberty. This was the first proposal for agrarian legislation, and from that day to within living memory such proposals have never been brought up without occasioning the most serious disturbances. The other consul resisted the largess, and the senators supported him; nor were the commons solidly against him, for to begin with, they had taken offense that the bounty had been made general, being extended to include allies as well as citizens; and again, they often heard the consul Verginius declare in his speeches, as though he read the future, that destruction lurked in the gift proposed by his colleague; that those lands would bring servitude to the men who should receive them, and were being made a road to monarchy.

Dionysius of Halicarnassus, *Roman Antiquities* x. xxxiii

The following year [455 B.C.], in which Titus Romilius and Gaius
Veturius had succeeded to the consulship and Lucius Icilius and his
colleagues were chosen tribunes for the second time in succession, was
not of an even tenor but was varied and fraught with great events. For
the internal struggles, which seemed to be already extinguished, were
again stirred up by the tribunes; and some foreign wars sprang up,
which, without being able to harm the commonwealth at all, did her a
great service by banishing these struggles. For it had by now become a
regular and customary thing for the city to be harmonious in war and to
be at odds in peace. When all who assumed the consulship observed
this, they regarded the appearance of any foreign war as an answer to
prayer. And when the enemies were quiet, they themselves invented
grievances and pretenses for wars, since they saw that wars made the
commonwealth great and flourishing, and seditions humiliated and weak.
Having come to this same conclusion, the consuls of that year resolved
to lead an expedition against the enemy, apprehensive that idle and poor
men might, because of peace, begin to raise disturbances. In this
they judged right, that the people ought to be kept employed in foreign
wars.

Dionysius of Halicarnassus, *Roman Antiquities* VII. xiii. 1–2

As to the city of Velitrae, the Romans thought proper to accept it and to
send a large colony thither, in consideration of the many advantages that
would result to them from that measure. For the place itself, if occupied
by an adequate garrison, seemed capable of proving a serious check and
hindrance to the designs of any who might be disposed to begin a
rebellion or to create any disturbance, and it was expected that the
scarcity of provisions under which Rome then labored would be far less
serious if a considerable part of the citizens were removed elsewhere.
But, above all other considerations, the sedition which was now flaring
up again, before the former one was as yet satisfactorily appeased,
induced them to vote to send out the colony.

41. THE OGULNIAN LAW, 300 B.C.

The Ogulnian Law granted the upper stratum of the plebeians admission
to the highest, and politically important, priestly colleges, those of the
pontiffs and the augurs. The elimination of this age-old patrician privilege
cleared the last significant obstacle to the merger of the patricians with the
rich plebeians into a new patrician–plebeian ruling class, the *nobiles*.

Livy, *History of Rome* x. vi. 3–11, ix. 1–2

A conflict between the most prominent men of the state, both plebeians
and patricians, was stirred up by the tribunes of the plebs, Quintus and
Gnaeus Ogulnius. These men had sought everywhere for opportunities
of maligning the patricians before the plebs, and after all other attempts
had failed, they adopted a policy which was calculated to inflame the
minds, not of the dregs of the populace, but of the very leaders of the
plebs, plebeians who had been consuls and enjoyed triumphs, and to
whose official distinctions nothing was lacking but priesthoods. These
were not yet open to all.

The Ogulnii accordingly proposed a measure providing that, whereas
there were at that time four augurs and four pontiffs, and it was desired
that the number of priests should be augmented, the four additional
pontiffs and five augurs should all be coopted from among the plebs.
. . . The proposal to coopt the additional priests from among the plebs
created almost as much distress among the patricians as when they saw
the consulship thrown open. They pretended that the matter concerned
the gods more than it concerned them; the gods would see to it themselves that their rites were not polluted; they only hoped that no disaster
might befall the state. Their opposition, however, was not so keen,
because they had become habituated to defeat in struggles of this kind,
and they saw that their opponents in striving for the highest honors
were not, as formerly, aiming at what they had little hopes of winning;
everything for which they had striven, though with doubtful hopes of
success, they had hitherto gained—numberless consulships, censor-
ships, triumphs. . . .

The people was on the point of ordering the voting to proceed, and it
was evident that the measure would be adopted, when, on account of a
veto, all further business was adjourned for that day. On the following

day the tribunes were cowed, and the law was passed amid great enthusiasm. . . . So the number of the pontiffs was raised to eight and that of
the augurs to nine.[51]

42. THE HORTENSIAN LAW, 287 B.C.

After the admission of plebeians to all the highest offices, the principal
issue that remained outstanding in the "struggle of the orders" was the
validity of *plebiscita,* enactments of the plebeian assembly. The "Third
Secession" of the plebs led to the dictatorship of Quintus Hortensius,
whose famous law on *plebiscita* marked the end of the struggle.

Gaius, *Institutes* I. iii

A law is what the people orders and establishes. A plebiscite is what the
plebs orders and establishes. Now the plebs differs from the people in
this, that by the term "people" the whole citizenry is meant, including
all the patricians, whereas the term "plebs" designates all the citizens
excepting the patricians. Therefore, in former times the patricians used
to maintain that they were not bound by plebiscites, since these had
been enacted without their authority. But afterwards the Hortensian
Law was passed, by which it was provided that plebiscites were to
bind the whole people, and in this way they were placed on a par with
laws.

Aulus Gellius, *Attic Nights* XV. xxvii. 4

He who summons not the whole people, but only some part, should
not call that assembly *comitia,* but *concilium.*[52] Tribunes can neither summon patricians nor lay any proposal before them. Thus, measures approved on motions by tribunes of the plebs are not properly called *laws,*
but *plebiscites.* Formerly the patricians were not bound by such measures,
until the dictator Quintus Hortensius passed a law that all citizens be
bound by any bill that the plebs enacted.

51. It is probable that after this date the number of colleagues in each body was nine, the patricians
enjoying a majority among the pontiffs, the plebeians among the augurs.

52. The point of this sentence is that plebiscites were enacted in a special assembly of plebeians
only, the *concilium plebis.* After the passage of the Hortensian Law plebiscites were enacted by the *comitia
tributa.*

Society and Culture

43. SOLIDARITY OF THE GENS

LIVY, *History of Rome* II. xlviii. 7–xlix. 4; From *LCL*

The enmity of Veii, persistent rather than perilous and resulting in insults oftener than in danger, kept the Romans in suspense, for they were never permitted to forget it or turn their attention elsewhere. Then the Fabian clan went before the senate, and the consul said, speaking for the clan: "A standing body of defenders rather than a large one is required, Conscript Fathers, as you know, for the war with Veii. Do you attend to the other wars, and assign to the Fabii the task of opposing the Veientines. We undertake that the majesty of the Roman name shall be safe in that quarter. It is our purpose to wage this war as if it were our own family feud, at our private costs; the state may dispense with furnishing men and money for this cause."

Thanks were voted with enthusiasm. The consul came out from the senate house and was escorted home by a column of Fabii who had waited in the vestibule of the senate house for the senate's decision. After receiving the command to present themselves armed next day at the consul's threshold, they dispersed to their homes.

The news spreads to every part of the city and the Fabii are lauded to the skies. Men tell how a single family has taken upon its shoulders the burden of a state, how the war with Veii has been turned over to private citizens and private arms. If there were two other clans of equal strength in the city, the one might take on the Volscians, the other the Aequians, and the Roman people might enjoy the tranquillity of peace while all the neighboring nations were being subdued. On the following day the Fabii arm and assemble at the designated place. The consul, coming forth in his crimson general's cloak, sees his entire clan drawn up in marching column in his vestibule, and being received into their midst gives the order to advance. Never did an army march through the city less in number or more distinguished by the applause and wonder of men: 306 soldiers, all patricians, all of one *gens,* no one of whom you would have rejected as a leader, and who would have made an admirable senate in any period, were going out to threaten destruction to the Veientine people with the resources of a single family.[53]

53. The traditional date of this episode is 479 B.C.

44. ASPECTS OF THE AGRICULTURAL ECONOMY OF THE EARLY REPUBLIC

Pliny, *Natural History* XVIII. iii. 9–12

That portion of land used to be known as a *iugerum* which was capable of being plowed by a single yoke of oxen *(iugum)* in one day, and an *actus* was as much as the oxen could plow in a single uninterrupted pull. This last was 120 feet long, and doubled in length made a *iugerum*. The most considerable recompense that could be bestowed upon generals and valiant citizens was the utmost land around which a person could trace a furrow with a plow in a single day; the whole population, too, used to contribute a *quartarius*[54] (or half that) of spelt per person.

The earliest surnames were also derived from agriculture. Thus, the cognomen Pilumnus was given to him who invented the pestle *(pilum)* for the mills; that of Piso was derived from grinding *(piso)* corn; and those of Fabius, Lentulus, and Cicero, from these respective legumes, as each excelled in their cultivation.[55] One member of the family of the Junii received the surname of Bubulcus from his skill in handling oxen *(bubus)*. Among the sacred ceremonials, too, there was nothing more holy than the marriage bond by *confarreatio* [cf. § 8], in which the bride used to present a cake made of spelt *(farreum)*.

Careless cultivation of the land was an offense that came under the cognizance of the censors; and, as we learn from Cato,[56] when it was said of a man that he was a good farmer or a good husbandman, it was looked upon as the very highest compliment. Hence also the rich came to be called *locupletes,* from being well supplied with land *(loci pleni)*. Why, even money received its name *(pecunia)* from cattle *(pecus)*. Even now in the censors' registers we find everything from which the public revenues are derived entered under the heading of "pastures" *(pascua)*, because for a long time those were the only sources of public revenue. Fines, too, were imposed only in amounts of sheep and oxen — not to overlook the benevolent spirit of the ancient laws, which enjoined that the magistrate, when he inflicted a penalty, should start with a sheep, never an ox. Those who conducted the public games celebrated on behalf of the oxen were called the *Bubetii*. King Servius was the first to

54. A fourth of a *sextarius* (see Glossary).
55. *Faba* = bean, *lens* = lentil, *cicer* = chickpea.
56. *On Agriculture*, Preface (see § 166).

stamp our copper money with the figures of sheep and oxen.[57] To go secretly by night and reap the crop on plowland or to pasture cattle there was in the Twelve Tables a capital crime for an adult, and a person convicted of such an act was condemned to be hanged as an offering to Ceres—a punishment more severe than that for murder; if the offender was not an adult, he was scourged at the discretion of the praetor and a penalty double the amount of the damage was exacted [cf. § 32, Table VIII].

45. THE ROMAN ARMY

The early Republican army was organized as a Greek phalanx, fighting as a compact body of heavy-armed infantry. During the fourth century, under the impact of either the Gallic invasion or the Samnite Wars, there occurred a fundamental reform of the Roman military forces. The rigid phalanx was abandoned for the more elastic legionary formation composed of separate tactical units called maniples; and the timocratic principle of the "Servian Constitution" (§ 27) was replaced by cadres based upon skill, experience, and age. This system lasted until the reform of Marius in 107 B.C. (see introduction to § 106).

Livy, *History of Rome* VIII. viii

At first the Romans used the small round shield *(clipeus)*; afterwards, when they began to receive pay for military service, the oblong shield *(scutum)* was adopted. The earlier phalanx formation, similar to the Macedonian one, came afterwards to be a line of battle formed by companies *(manipuli)*, the rear portion being drawn up in a number of units. The foremost line consisted of the *hastati*, forming fifteen maniples stationed a short distance from each other. The maniple had twenty light-armed soldiers, the remainder being equipped with oblong shields; moreover, those were called light-armed who carried only a spear *(hasta)* and javelins.

This front line in the battle consisted of the flower of the young men who were growing ripe for service. Behind them were stationed an equal number of maniples, called *principes,* made up of men of a more stalwart age, all carrying oblong shields and furnished with superior

57. An unfounded tradition. The earliest Roman coins do not antedate *c.* 300 B.C. But uncoined bronze, in the form of ingots stamped with figures of oxen and other animals, was used as a medium of exchange before the introduction of coinage.

weapons. This body of thirty maniples was called the *antepilani* because behind the standards there were stationed fifteen other companies, each of which was divided into three sections, the first section in each being called the *pilus*. The company consisted of three *vexilla* (banners). A single *vexillum* had sixty soldiers, two centurions, and one *vexillarius*, or "color-bearer"; the company numbered 186 men. The first *vexillum* led the *triarii*, veterans of proved courage; the second the *rorarii*, or "skirmishers," younger men and less distinguished men; the third the *accensi*, who were least to be depended upon and were therefore assigned to the rearmost line.

When an army had been drawn up in these ranks, the *hastati* were the first of all to engage. If the *hastati* failed to repulse the enemy, they slowly retired through the intervals between the companies of the *principes,* who then took up the fight, the *hastati* following in their rear. The *triarii,* meantime, were kneeling under their standards with left leg advanced, their shields leaning against their shoulders, and their spears planted in the ground with points obliquely upwards, as if their battle line were fortified by a bristling palisade. If the *principes* were also unsuccessful, they slowly retired from the battle line to the *triarii* (which has given rise to the proverbial saying, when people are in great difficulty, "matters have come down to the *triarii*"). When the *triarii* had admitted the *hastati* and *principes* through the intervals between their companies, they rose up and, instantly closing their companies up, blocked the lanes, as it were, and in one compact mass fell on the enemy, there being no more reserves left behind them. The enemy, who had pursued the others as though they had defeated them, saw with the greatest dread a new line suddenly rising up with increased numbers.

There were generally four legions enrolled, consisting each of 5,000 men, and 300 cavalry were assigned to each legion.[58]

46. EARLY ROMAN RELIGION

The native Roman religion possessed no cult images, cult buildings, or mythology. It was characterized by animism, a belief in vague spirits (*numina*). At the end of the regal period, under the influence of the Etruscan dynasty, occurred one of the great revolutions in Roman religion, the

---

58. The cavalry forces were largely supplied by Rome's allies.

naturalization on Roman soil of anthropomorphic deities, temple structures, and cult statues. The primitive animistic cult survived long after, especially in remote rural areas.

ANIMISTIC SPIRITS

Saint Augustine, *City of God* IV. viii

But how is it possible to mention in one part of this book all the names of gods or goddesses, which the Romans scarcely could comprise in great volumes, distributing among these divine powers their peculiar functions concerning separate things? They did not even think that the care of their lands should be entrusted to any one god; but they entrusted their farms to the goddess Rumina, and the ridges of the mountains to the god Jugatinus; over the hills they placed the goddess Collatina, over the valleys, Vallonia. Nor could they even find one Segetia so potent that they could commend their cereal crops entirely to her care; but so long as their seed grain was still under the ground, they desired to have the goddess Seia watch over it; then, when it was already above ground and formed standing grain, they set over it the goddess Segetia; and when the grain was collected and stored, they entrusted it to the goddess Tutilina, that it might be kept safe. Who would not have thought the goddess Segetia sufficient to protect the standing grain until it had passed from the first green blades to the dry ears? Yet she was not enough for men who loved a multitude of gods. . . . Therefore they set Proserpina over the germinating seeds; over the joints and knobs of the stems, the god Nodutus; over the sheaths enfolding the ears, the goddess Volutina; when the sheaths opened and the spikes emerged, it was ascribed to the goddess Patelana; when the stems were of the same height as new ears, because the ancients described this equalizing by the term *hostire,* it was ascribed to the goddess Hostilina; when the grain was in flower, it was dedicated to the goddess Flora; when full of milk, to the god Lacturnus; when maturing, to the goddess Matuta; when the crop was "runcated"—that is, removed from the soil—to the goddess Runcina.[59]

---

59. All of these divinities are *numina,* divine spirits of the indigenous animistic religion. Cf. § 10.

RELIGIOUS FORMALISM

Valerius Maximus, *Memorable Deeds and Sayings* I. i

Our ancestors desired their religious institutions to be regulated by the following practices: the fixed and customary ceremonies, by the knowledge of the pontiffs; the assurance of successfully conducting affairs, by the observations of the augurs; the prophecies of Apollo, by the books of the seers; the warding off of portents, by the Etruscan system. Also, in the ancient religious institutions, prayer was used when something was entrusted to the gods, the vow when some entreaty was made of them, the public thanksgiving when a vow was repaid, the favorable omen when divination was practiced either by examination of entrails or by oracular lots, the sacrifice when a customary rite was to be fulfilled. By sacrifice also the evil significance of portents and lightning is expiated.

47. THE COLLEGE OF PONTIFFS

The general administration of the state-cult, in particular the cult of the native deities, was in the hands of the college of pontiffs. The nine pontiffs (increased to fifteen in Sulla's time and to sixteen by Caesar) were the sole repository of *ius divinum,* "the sacral law" governing relations between divinities and humans. Charged with the preservation and interpretation of the religious traditions, the calendar, and the sacred formulae and rules of sacrifice, the pontiffs were in effect the earliest Roman jurists, exercising a powerful influence in private and criminal law (see p. 42). Under the jurisdiction of the pontiffs were the flamens and the Vestal Virgins. At the head of the college was the *pontifex maximus* (chief pontiff), "the judge and arbiter of divine and human affairs."

Dionysius of Halicarnassus, *Roman Antiquities* II. lxxiii; From *LCL*

The last branch of the ordinances of Numa [see § 10] related to the sacred offices allotted to those who held the highest priesthood and the greatest power among the Romans. These, from one of the duties they perform—namely, the repairing of wooden bridges[60]—are in their own language called *pontifices;* but they have jurisdiction over the most weighty

---

60. The literal meaning of *pontifex* is "bridgemaker."

matters. For they are the judges in all religious cases wherein private citizens, magistrates, or the ministers of the gods are concerned; they make laws for the observance of any religious rites not established by written law or by custom which may seem to them worthy of receiving the sanction of law and custom; they inquire into the conduct of all magistrates to whom the performance of any sacrifice or other religious duty is committed, and also into that of all the priests; they take care that their servants and ministers whom they employ in religious rites commit no error in the matter of the sacred laws; to the laymen who are unacquainted with such matters they are the expounders and interpreters of everything relating to the worship of the gods and divine spirits; and if they find that any disobey their orders, they inflict punishment upon them with due regard to every offense; moreover, they are not liable to any prosecution or punishment, nor are they accountable to the senate or to the people, at least concerning religious matters.[61]

48. AUGURS AND AUSPICES

Every important act of state, both in civil administration and in military affairs, was preceded by the taking of the auspices by a magistrate possessing *imperium*. The purpose of this act was to obtain from Jupiter, through omens, the assurance that the sanction of the gods attended the business in hand. While the right of taking the auspices was reserved for official representatives of the state, the sacral preparation for and the interpretation of the omens was entrusted to one of the most ancient and important priestly bodies, the college of augurs, who interpreted the will of the gods according to fixed, secretly preserved rules. Originally denoting the observation of birds in flight, *auspices* gradually came to include other methods of divination, summed up by Festus, *On the Significance of Words,* under "quinque genera": "The augurs observe five types of signs: from lightning, from birds, from the feeding of the sacred chickens, from four-footed animals, and from portents."

---

61. Cf. W. W. Fowler, *The Religious Experience of the Roman People,* 226–227: "In no other ancient State that we know of did the citizen so entirely resign the regulation of all his dealings with the State's gods to the constituted authorities set over him. His obligatory part in the religious ritual of the State was simply *nil,* and all his religious duty on days of religious importance was to abstain from civil business and to make no disturbance."

Livy, *History of Rome* I. xviii. 6–10; From *LCL*

Being summoned to Rome, Numa commanded that, just as Romulus had obeyed the augural omens in building his city and assuming royal power, so too in his own case the gods should be consulted. Accordingly an augur (who thereafter, as a mark of honor, was made a priest of the state in permanent charge of that function) conducted him to the citadel and caused him to sit down on a stone, facing the south. The augur seated himself on Numa's left, having his head covered, and holding in his right hand the crooked staff without a knot which they call a *lituus*. Then, looking out over the city and the country beyond, he prayed to the gods, and marked off the heavens by a line from east to west, designating as "right" the regions to the south, as "left" those to the north, and fixing in his mind a landmark opposite to him and as far away as the eye could reach; next shifting the crook to his left hand, and laying his right on Numa's head, he uttered the following prayer: "Father Jupiter, if it is divine will that this man, Numa Pompilius, whose head I am touching, be king in Rome, do thou exhibit to us unmistakable signs within those limits which I have set." He then specified the auspices which he desired should be sent, and upon their appearance Numa was declared king, and so descended from the augural station.

Varro, *The Latin Language* VII. viii; From *LCL*

On the earth, *templum* is the name given to a place set aside and limited by certain formulaic words for the purpose of augury or the taking of the auspices. The words of the ceremony are not the same everywhere; on the citadel they are as follows:[62]

"Temples and wild lands be mine in this manner, up to where I have named them with my tongue in proper fashion.

"Of whatever kind that truthful tree is, which I consider that I have mentioned, temple and wild land be mine to that point on the left.

"Of whatever kind that truthful tree is, which I consider that I have mentioned, temple and wild land be mine to that point on the right.

"Between these points, temples and wild lands be mine for direction, for viewing, and for interpreting, and just as I have felt assured that I have mentioned them in proper fashion."

62. The text of this augural formula is very corrupt. The translation is based on an attempt to reconstruct it.

Cicero, *Laws* II. *xii. 31; From LCL*

But the highest and most important authority in the state is that of the augurs, to whom is accorded great influence. But it is not because I myself am an augur that I have this opinion, but because the facts compel us to think so. For if we consider their legal rights, what power is greater than that of adjourning assemblies and meetings convened by the highest officials, with or without *imperium,* or that of declaring null and void the acts of assemblies presided over by such officials? What is of greater import than the abandonment of any business already begun, if a single augur says, "On another day"? What power is more impressive than that of forcing the consuls to resign their offices? What right is more sacred than that of giving or refusing permission to hold an assembly of the people or of the plebeians, or that of abrogating laws illegally passed? Thus the Titian Law was annulled by a decree of the college of augurs, and the Livian Laws by the wise direction of Philippus, a consul and augur. Indeed, no act of any magistrate at home or in the field can have any validity for any person without their authority.

49. THE FLAMENS

The specialized priests of individual gods of the early native religion were the flamens, the principal task of each of whom was to sacrifice to the god to whom he was consecrated. There were fifteen in all, three *flamines maiores* (those of Jupiter, Mars, and Quirinus) and twelve *flamines minores.* The following selection reveals the survival of primitive taboos in connection with the flamen of Jupiter (*flamen Dialis*).

Aulus Gellius, *Attic Nights* x. xv. 1–25; From *LCL*

Ceremonies in great number are imposed upon the priest of Jupiter and also many abstentions. . . . It is unlawful for the priest of Jupiter to ride upon a horse; it is unlawful for him to see the "classes arrayed"[63] outside the *pomerium,* that is, the army in battle array; hence the priest of Jupiter is rarely made consul, since wars were entrusted to the consuls; also it is always unlawful for the priest to take an oath; likewise to wear a ring, unless it be perforated and without a gem. It is against the law for fire to

---

63. The review of the citizen body as the *comitia centuriata* in the Campus Martius (see § 27).

be taken from the *flaminia,* that is, from the home of the *flamen Dialis,* except for a sacred rite; if a person in fetters enter his house, he must be loosed, the bonds must be drawn up through the *impluvium*[64] to the roof and from there let down into the street. He has no knot in his headdress, girdle, or any other part of his dress; if anyone is being taken to be flogged and falls at his feet as a suppliant, it is unlawful for the man to be flogged on that day. Only a free man may cut the hair of the Dialis. It is not customary for the Dialis to touch, or even name a she-goat, raw flesh, ivy, and beans.

The priest of Jupiter must not pass under an arbor of vines. The feet of the couch on which he sleeps must be smeared with a thin coating of clay, and he must not sleep away from his bed for three nights in succession, and no other person must sleep in that bed. At the foot of his bed there should be a box with sacrificial cakes. The cuttings of the nails and hair of the Dialis must be buried in the earth under a fruitful tree. Every day is a holy day for the Dialis. He must not be in the open air without his cap; that he might go without it in the house has only recently been decided by the pontiffs. . . .

The priest of Jupiter must not touch any bread fermented with yeast. He does not lay off his inner tunic except under cover, in order that he may not be naked in the open air, as it were under the eyes of Jupiter. No other has a place at the table above the *flamen Dialis,* except the *rex sacrificulus.*[65] If the Dialis has lost his wife he abdicates his office. The marriage of the priest cannot be dissolved except by death. He never enters a place of burial, he never touches a dead body; but he is not forbidden to attend a funeral.

50. THE VESTAL VIRGINS

Dionysius of Halicarnassus, *Roman Antiquities* II. lxvii; From *LCL*

The virgins who serve the goddess [Vesta, goddess of the hearth] were originally four and were chosen by the kings according to the principles established by Numa, but afterwards, from the multiplicity of the sacred rites they perform, their number was increased to six, and has so remained to our time. They live in the temple of the goddess, into which

64. The opening in the roof of the reception room *(atrium)* of a Roman house (see § 190).
65. The priest who, at the beginning of the Republic, inherited the religious prerogatives of the early kings.

none who wish are hindered from entering in the daytime, whereas it is not lawful for any man to remain there at night. They were required to remain undefiled by marriage for the space of thirty years, devoting themselves to offering sacrifices and performing the other rites ordained by law. During the first ten years their duty was to learn their functions, in the second ten to perform them, and during the remaining ten to teach others. After the expiration of the term of thirty years nothing hindered those who so desired from marrying, upon laying aside their fillets and the other insignia of their priesthood. . . . And severe penalties have been established for their misdeeds. It is the pontiffs who by law both inquire into and punish these offenses; those Vestals who are guilty of lesser misdemeanors they scourge with rods, but those who have suffered defilement they deliver up to the most shameful and the most miserable death. For while they are yet alive they are carried upon a bier with all the formality of a funeral, their friends and relations attending them with lamentations, and after being brought as far as the Colline Gate, they are placed in an underground cell prepared within the walls, clad in their funeral attire; but they are not given a monument or funeral rites or any other customary solemnities. There are many indications, it seems, when a priestess is not performing her holy functions with purity, but the principal one is the extinction of the fire, which the Romans dread above all misfortunes, looking upon it, from whatever cause it proceeds, as an omen which portends the destruction of the city; and they bring the fire again into the temple with many supplicatory rites.

51. WAR AND PEACE: THE FETIALS AND FETIAL LAW

The ancient priestly college of fetials, consisting of twenty members, was the guardian and interpreter of the *ius fetiale* (fetial law), the traditional rites and formulae of international relations. As representatives of the Roman people, with functions at once religious, political, and judicial, these sacerdotal officials functioned especially in rituals attending the declaration of war, conclusion of treaties, protection of foreign ambassadors at Rome, and extradition.

DUTIES OF THE FETIALS

Dionysius of Halicarnassus, *Roman Antiquities* II lxxii. 4–9; From *LCL*

The multitude of duties, to be sure, that fall within the province of these *fetiales* makes it no easy matter to enumerate them all; but to indicate them by a summary outline, they are as follows. It is their duty to take care that the Romans do not enter upon an unjust war against any city in alliance with them, and if others begin the violation of treaties against them, to go as ambassadors and first make formal demand for justice, and then, if the others refuse to comply with their demands, to sanction war. In like manner, if any people in alliance with the Romans complain of having been injured by them and demand justice, these men are to determine whether they have suffered anything in violation of their alliance; and if they find their complaints well grounded, they are to seize the accused and deliver them up to the injured parties. They are also to take cognizance of the crimes committed against ambassadors, to take care that treaties are religiously observed, to make peace, and if they find that peace has been made otherwise than is prescribed by the holy laws, to set it aside; and to inquire into and expiate the transgressions of the generals in so far as they relate to oaths and treaties. . . .

As to the functions they performed in the quality of heralds when they went to demand justice of any city thought to have injured the Romans . . . I have received the following account. One of the *fetiales,* chosen by his colleagues, wearing his sacred robes and insignia to distinguish him from all others,[66] proceeded towards the city whose inhabitants had done the injury; and, stopping at the border, he called upon Jupiter and the rest of the gods to witness that he was come to demand justice on behalf of the Roman state. Thereupon he took an oath that he was going to a city that had done an injury; and having uttered the most dreadful imprecations against himself and Rome if what he averred was not true, he then entered their borders. Afterwards, he called to witness the first person he met, whether it was one of the countrymen or one of the townspeople, and having repeated the same imprecations, he advanced towards the city. And before he entered it he called to witness in the same manner the gatekeeper or the first person he met at the gates, after which he proceeded to the forum; and taking his stand there, he

---

66. The spokesman of the delegation of fetials assigned to a particular mission was called the *pater patratus* of the Roman people.

discussed with the magistrates the reasons for his coming, adding everywhere the same oaths and imprecations. If, then, they were disposed to
offer satisfaction by delivering up the guilty, he departed as a friend
taking leave of friends, carrying the prisoners with him. Or, if they
desired time to deliberate, he allowed them ten days, after which he
returned and waited till they had made this request three times. But after
the expiration of thirty days, if the city still persisted in refusing to grant
him justice, he called both the celestial and infernal gods to witness and
went away, saying no more than this, that the Roman state would
deliberate at its leisure concerning these people. Afterwards he, together
with the other *fetiales,* appeared before the senate and declared that they
had done everything that was ordained by the holy laws and that, if the
senators wished to vote for war, there would be no obstacle on the part
of the gods. But if any of these things were omitted, neither the senate
nor the people had the power to vote for war.

FORMULA FOR DECLARING WAR

Livy, *History of Rome* I. xxxii; From *LCL*

When the [fetial] envoy has arrived at the frontiers of the people from
whom satisfaction is sought, he covers his head with a bonnet—the
covering is of wool—and says: "Hear, Jupiter; hear, ye boundaries of"
—naming whatever nation they belong to—"let righteousness hear! I
am the public herald of the Roman people; I come duly and religiously
commissioned; let my words be credited." Then he recites his demands,
after which he takes Jupiter to witness: "If I demand unjustly and against
religion that these men and these things be surrendered to me, then let
me never enjoy my native land." These words he repeats when he
crosses the boundary line, and the same to whatever man first meets
him, the same when he enters the city gates, the same when he has come
into the marketplace, with only a few changes in the form and wording
of the oath. If those whom he demands are not surrendered, at the end
of thirty-three days—for such is the conventional number—he declares
war thus: "Hear, Jupiter, and thou, Janus Quirinus, and hear all heavenly gods, and ye, gods of earth, and ye of the lower world; I call ye to
witness that this people"—naming whatever people it is—"is unjust
and does not make just reparation. But of these matters we will take
counsel of the elders in our country, how we may obtain our right."
Then the messenger returns to Rome for the consultation.

Immediately the king[67] would consult the senate, in some such words as these: "Touching the things, the suits, the causes, concerning which the *pater patratus* [see note 66] of the Roman people, the Quirites, has made demands on the *pater patratus* of the ancient Latins, and upon the men of the ancient Latins, which things they have not delivered, nor fulfilled, nor satisfied, speak,"—turning to the man whose opinion he was wont to ask first—"what think you?" Then the other would reply: "I hold that those things ought to be sought in warfare just and righteous; and so I consent and vote." The others were then asked the question, in their order, and when the majority of those present went over to the same opinion, war had been agreed upon. It was customary for the fetial then to carry to the confines of the other nation a bloody spear, iron-pointed or hardened in the fire, and in the presence of not less than three grown men to say: "Whereas the tribes of the ancient Latins and men of the ancient Latins have been guilty of acts and offenses against the Roman people, the Quirites; and whereas the Roman people, the Quirites, has commanded that war be made on the ancient Latins, and the senate of the Roman people has approved, agreed, and voted a war with the ancient Latins; I therefore and the Roman people declare and make war on the tribes of the ancient Latins and the men of the ancient Latins." Having said this, he would hurl his spear into their territory. This is the manner in which at that time redress was sought from the Latins and war was declared, and the custom has been continued by later generations.

FORMULA FOR CONCLUDING A TREATY

Livy, *History of Rome* I. xxiv. 3–9; From *LCL*

One treaty differs from another in its terms, but the same procedure is always employed. On the present occasion we are told that they did as follows, nor has tradition preserved the memory of any more ancient compact. The fetial asked King Tullus,[68] "Dost thou command me, King, to make a treaty with the *pater patratus* of the Alban people?" Being so commanded by the king, he said, "I demand of thee, King, the sacred herb." The king replied, "Thou shalt take it untainted." The fetial brought from the citadel an untainted plant. After this he asked the

---

67. Livy follows the annalistic tradition in assigning the origin of the formula to the regal period, recording it in connection with a war between the Romans and the Latins.

68. Livy records this formula in connection with a war between the Romans and the Albans in the regal period. Cf. note 67.

king, "Dost thou grant me, King, with my emblems and my companions, the royal sanction to speak for the Roman people, the Quirites?" The king made answer, "So far as may be without prejudice to myself and the Roman people, the Quirites, I grant it." The fetial was Marcus Valerius; he made Spurius Fusius *pater patratus,* touching his head and hair with the sacred sprig. The *pater patratus* is appointed to pronounce the oath, that is, to solemnize the pact; and this he accomplishes with many words, expressed in a long metrical formula which it is not worth while to quote. The conditions being then recited, he cries, "Hear, Jupiter; hear *pater patratus* of the Alban people; hear ye, people of Alba: From these terms, as they have been publicly recited from beginning to end, without fraud, from these tablets, or this wax, and as they have been this day clearly understood, the Roman people will not be the first to depart. If they shall first depart from them, by general consent, with malice aforethought, then on that day do thou, great Diespiter [archaic form of the name Jupiter], so smite the Roman people as I shall here today smite this pig: and so much the harder smite them as thy power and thy strength are greater." When Spurius had said these words, he struck the pig with a flint. In like manner the Albans pronounced their own forms and their own oath, by the mouth of their own dictator and priests.

52. THE SIBYLLINE BOOKS

Under the influence of the Sibylline books, the *libri fatales* (Books of Fate), a great influx of Greek gods and Greek rites into the state-cult took place in the early centuries of the Republic. In the fifth century B.C. the practice developed of consulting the oracle of the Sibyl of Cumae, the northernmost Greek city in Campania. Subsequently, the oracular utterances of the Cumaean Sibyl were collected in permanent form and the sacred books, written in the Greek language, were entrusted to one of the four great Roman priestly colleges. This "Board of Ten Men for Performing Sacred Rites" (increased about Sulla's time to fifteen members) Hellenized the Roman state religion. In times of crisis, when they were instructed to consult the secret books, these decemvirs usually ordered the introduction of a new Greek god or Greek religious rite. Their religious innovations came to an end with the introduction of the worship of Magna Mater from Pessinus in Asia Minor in 205 B.C. (see the last selection in § 177). In the last century of the Republic the college became a political tool serving the interests of the party bosses (cf. Cicero, *On Divination* II. liv).

Dionysius of Halicarnassus, *Roman Antiquities* IV. lxii; From *LCL*

Since the expulsion of the kings, the commonwealth, taking upon itself
the guarding of these oracles, entrusts the care of them to persons of
great distinction, who hold this office for life, being exempt from military service and from all civil employment, and it assigns public slaves
to assist them, in whose absence the others are not permitted to inspect
the oracles. In short, there is no possession of the Romans, sacred or
profane, which they guard so carefully as they do the Sibylline oracles.
They consult them, by order of the senate, when the state is in the grip
of party strife or some great misfortune has happened to them in war,
or some important prodigies or apparitions have been seen which are
difficult of interpretation, as has often happened. These oracles till the
time of the Marsian War,[69] as it is called, were kept underground in a
chest under the guard of ten men. But when the temple was burned[70]
after the close of the 173d Olympiad—either purposely, as some think,
or by accident—these oracles together with all the offerings consecrated
to the god were destroyed by the fire. Those which are now extant were
scraped together from many places, some from the cities of Italy, others
from Erythrae in Asia (whither three envoys were sent by vote of the
senate to copy them), and others were brought from other cities, tran-
scribed by private persons. Some of these are found to be interpolations
among the genuine oracles, being recognized as such by means of the
so-called acrostics. In all this I am following the account given by Varro
in his work on religion.[71]

53. INTRODUCTION OF GREEK RITUAL AND GREEK GODS

Under the influence of the Sibylline books (§ 52) the Roman state-cult was
revolutionized. On the cold formalism of the traditional ritual, regulated
and conducted by priestly bodies without the active participation of the
community, there was engrafted a new public emotionalism and elabo-
rateness and novelty in ceremonial. At first restricted to the *Graecus ritus*
(Greek ritual), this new tendency of the fourth and third centuries B.C.

---

69. Part of the Social War, 91–89 B.C.
70. The temple of Jupiter Optimus Maximus on the Capitoline Hill. It was destroyed by fire
in 83 B.C.
71. Part of Varro's lost *Roman Antiquities*.

opened the way for the eventual importation of the Oriental orgiastic cults. The first authentic case of the new Hellenic rites was the introduction, in 399 B.C., of the *lectisternium,* the public offering of a sacred meal to images of Greek deities placed on couches. Closely connected with this was another ritual of Greek origin, the *supplicatio,* a public processional ceremony to propitiate or render thanks to the gods. The first Greek gods had entered the Roman pantheon in the early part of the fifth century B.C., but with the entry of Aesculapius, the Greek god of medicine, in 293 B.C., a new wave of importations began, until by the end of the third century the amalgamation of Greek and Roman religion was completed.

THE LECTISTERNIUM

Livy, *History of Rome* v. xiii. 4–5; From *LCL*

The severe winter [of 399 B.C.] was succeeded, whether in consequence of the sudden change from such inclement weather to the opposite extreme, or for some other reason, by a summer that was noxious and baleful to all living creatures. Unable to discover what caused the incurable ravages of this distemper, or would put an end to them, the senate voted to consult the Sibylline books. The duovirs in charge of the sacred rites then celebrated the first *lectisternium* ever held in Rome, and for the space of eight days sacrificed to Apollo, to Latona and Diana, to Hercules, to Mercury, and to Neptune, spreading couches for them with all the splendor then attainable. They also observed the rite in their homes. All through the city, they say, doors stood wide open, all kinds of foods were set out for general consumption, all comers were welcomed, whether known or not, and men even exchanged kind and courteous words with personal enemies; there was a truce to quarreling and litigation; even prisoners were loosed from their chains for those days, and they scrupled thenceforth to imprison men whom the gods had thus befriended.

Livy, *History of Rome* XXII. x. 9; From *LCL*

A *lectisternium* was then celebrated during three days under the supervision of the decemvirs who had charge of sacrifices. Six couches were displayed: one for Jupiter and Juno, a second for Neptune and Minerva, a third for Mars and Venus, a fourth for Apollo and Diana, a fifth for Vulcan and Vesta, a sixth for Mercury and Ceres.[72]

72. The *lectisternium* of 217 B.C. marks the first appearance of the twelve Olympian gods in the Roman religion and the fusion of the native and the Greek gods.

THE CULT OF AESCULAPIUS

Anonymous, *On Famous Men* xxii. 1–3

The Romans on account of a pestilence, at the instructions of the Sibylline books, sent ten envoys under the leadership of Quintus Ogulnius to bring Aesculapius from Epidaurus.[73] When they had arrived there and were marveling at the huge statue of the god, a serpent glided from the temple, an object of veneration rather than of horror, and to the astonishment of all made its way through the midst of the city to the Roman ship, and curled itself up in the tent of Ogulnius. The envoys sailed to Antium, carrying the god, where through the calm sea the serpent made its way to a nearby temple of Aesculapius,[74] and after a few days returned to the ship. And when the ship was sailing up the Tiber, the serpent leaped on the nearby island, where a temple was established to him. The pestilence subsided with astonishing speed.[75]

54. Prayer and Sacrifice

Though Cato's manual *On Agriculture* was written about the middle of the second century B.C., the formulaic prayers and rituals contained therein are probably traditional ones, derived from the official books of the pontiffs.

PRAYERS AND SACRIFICES FOR OXEN

Cato, *On Agriculture* lxxxiii, cxxxii; From Ernest Brehaut, *Cato the Censor on Farming*
(New York, 1933)

Make an offering in this way for your work oxen to keep them in good health. Make an offering to Mars Silvanus in the wood in the daytime for each head of work oxen. Three pounds of spelt grits, four and one half of lard, four and one half of meat, three *sextarii* of wine. The former

---

73. This is the first instance of the importation of an Hellenic god directly from Greece. The cult of Greek gods had previously reached Rome indirectly through the cults of the Latin cities and the Greek cities of southern Italy.

74. There is no evidence of a temple of Aesculapius at Antium until the second century B.C.

75. The importation of Aesculapius in 293–291 B.C. is the first known fact in the history of medicine at Rome. The legend of the serpent-god of Epidaurus was much embellished in Roman literature.

ingredients you may place together in one dish and the wine likewise in one dish. Either slave or freeman may offer this sacrifice. When it is offered, eat it at once in the same place. No woman should be present at this sacrifice or see how it is offered. If you wish, you are permitted to make this sacrifice every year.

. . . .

The sacrifice [for the work oxen] should be made in this way. Offer to Jupiter Dapalis a dish of wine as large as you wish. The day is a festival for the work oxen and their drivers and those who make the sacrifice. When it is time to make the offering you shall use these words:

"Jupiter Dapalis, inasmuch as it is fitting that a dish of wine be offered to thee as a sacrifice in my house and amid my household, for this reason be honored with the offering of this sacrifice."

Then wash your hands and after that take the wine [and say]:

"Jupiter Dapalis, be honored with the offering of this sacrifice, be honored with this sacrificial wine."

Make an offering to Vesta, if you wish. The feast for Jupiter is roast meat and a half-*amphora* of wine. Make the offering to Jupiter with pious avoidance and without uncleanliness. When the offering has been made, sow millet, Italian millet, garlic, and lentils.

SACRIFICE PRELIMINARY TO A HARVEST

Cato, *On Agriculture* cxxxiv; From Ernest Brehaut, *Cato the Censor on Farming*
(New York, 1933)

Before you make the harvest you should offer a preliminary sacrifice of a sow pig in the following way. Offer a sow pig to Ceres before you store away these crops: spelt, wheat, barley, beans, rape seed. First address Janus, Jupiter, and Juno with incense and wine before you sacrifice the sow pig.

Offer a sacrificial cake to Janus with these words:

"Father Janus, in offering to thee this sacrificial cake I make good prayers that thou be kind and favorable to me, my children, and my house and household."

Offer an oblation cake to Jupiter and worship him in these words:

"Jupiter, in offering thee this oblation cake I make good prayers that thou be kind and favorable to me, my children, and my house and household, being worshiped with this offering."

Afterward offer wine to Janus thus:

"Father Janus, as I besought thee with good prayers in offering the sacrificial cake, let me honor thee for the same purpose with the sacrificial wine."

And then in these words to Jupiter:

"'Jupiter, as thou wert worshiped with the cake, so be worshiped with this sacrificial wine."

Then slaughter the preliminary sow pig. When the internal organs have been taken out, offer a sacrificial cake to Janus and worship him in the same terms as before when you offered the cake. Offer an oblation cake to Jupiter and worship him in the same terms as before. Likewise offer wine to Janus and offer wine to Jupiter in the same terms as it was offered before in the offering of the sacrificial cake and the oblation cake. Then sacrifice the internal organs and wine to Ceres.

55. PUBLIC VOWS

Public vows, involving covenants made with divinities by magistrates with *imperium* in the name of the state according to ancient formulas supplied by the pontiffs, were one of the rituals of the indigenous Roman religion. One form was the *evocatio,* an invitation to the gods of a besieged city to abandon it and move to Rome; another was the *devotio,* the consecration of a besieged city to the infernal gods before its destruction. Though both of these are here recorded in connection with the siege of Carthage, the formulas are of remote antiquity. The self-devotion of Decius, recounted by Livy in connection with the Latin War in 340 B.C., is based on an authentic formula. Another example of a public vow, though of later development, is the vow for victory, illustrated here by the vow taken in 191 B.C., before the war with Antiochus.

EVOCATIO AND DEVOTIO

Macrobius, *Saturnalia* III. ix

Now it is well known that all cities are under the protection of some god, and that it was a secret custom of the Romans, unknown to many, that when they were besieging a city of an enemy, and had reached the point when they were confident that it could be taken, they summoned out the tutelary gods by a certain formula. Otherwise, they believed, either the city would not be able to be taken or, in case it could, it would be a sacrilege to make captives of the gods. This is the reason why the

Romans themselves wished both the god under whose protection the city of Rome is and the Latin name of the city to be secret. . . . But one must be careful not to make the same mistake as some have made in thinking that the gods are summoned out of a city and that the community itself is "devoted" by one and the same formula. For I have found in the Fifth Book of Sammonicus Serenus'[76] *Secret Matters* both formulas, which he himself claims to have found in a very ancient book of a certain Furius.

The following is the formula by which the gods are summoned out when a city is surrounded by siegeworks:

"O thou, whether thou art a god or a goddess, under whose protection the people and the city of Carthage are, and thou, O greatest one, who hast taken under thy protection this city and people, I pray and entreat ye, and ask this indulgence of ye, that ye desert the people and the city of Carthage, and abandon the places, temples, sacred spots, and their city, and that ye depart from them. And cast on that people and city fear, terror, and forgetfulness, and, abandoned by them, come ye to Rome to me and my people. And may our places, temples, sacred spots, city be more acceptable and agreeable to ye. And may ye be propitious to me, the Roman people, and my soldiers, so that we may know and understand. If ye accomplish these things, I vow that temples and games will be established in your honor." . . .

Now once the divine beings have been summoned out, cities and armies are "devoted" in the following way; but only dictators and commanders can pronounce the formula, as follows:

"O Dis pater, Veiovis, Manes,[77] or by whatever names it is proper to name ye, fill ye that city of Carthage and her army, of which I deem myself to be speaking, with flight, fear, and terror. And whoever carries arms and weapons against our legions and army, may ye impede them, and deprive of the light of the sun that army, those enemies, and those men, their cities, and their fields, and whoever dwells in those places, regions, fields, and cities. And as for the army of the enemy, their cities and fields, of which I deem myself to be speaking, may ye possess those cities and fields, their persons and lives as devoted and consecrated to ye, according to the conditions which are stipulated when enemies are especially devoted. I give and devote them as substitutes for me, my honor, and my magistracy, for the Roman people, our armies and

---

76. A scholar of the late second and early third centuries A.D., otherwise unknown.
77. Gods and spirits of the infernal regions.

legions; so that I, my honor, and my *imperium,* and our legions and our army who are involved in this enterprise, may be kept by ye safe and sound. If ye do these things in such a way that I may know, perceive, and understand, then whoever has made this vow, where he has made it, let it be duly fulfilled with three black sheep. O Mother Earth, and thou, Jupiter, I summon ye to witness."

THE SELF-DEVOTION OF DECIUS

Livy, *History of Rome* VIII. ix. 4–10, x. 11–12; From *LCL*

In the confusion of this movement Decius the consul called out to Marcus Valerius in a loud voice: "We have need of the gods' help, Marcus Valerius. Come therefore, state pontiff of the Roman people, dictate the words, that I may devote myself to save the legions." The pontiff bade him don the purple-bordered toga and, with veiled head and one hand thrust out from the toga and touching his chin, stand upon a spear that was laid under his feet and say as follows: "Janus, Jupiter, Father Mars, Quirinus, Bellona, Lares, divine Novensiles, divine Indigites,[78] ye gods in whose power are both we and our enemies, and ye, divine Manes, I invoke and worship you, I beseech and crave your favor, that you may prosper the might and the victory of the Roman people, the Quirites, and visit the foes of the Roman people, the Quirites, with fear, shuddering and death. As I have pronounced the words, even so in behalf of the Republic of the Roman people, the Quirites, and of the army, the legions, the auxiliaries of the Roman people, the Quirites, do I devote the legions and auxiliaries of the enemy, together with myself to the divine Manes and to the Earth."

Having uttered this prayer he bade the lictors go to Titus Manlius and lose no time in announcing to his colleague that he had devoted himself for the good of the army. He then girded himself with the Gabinian cincture,[79] and vaulting, armed, upon his horse, plunged into the thick of the enemy—conspicuous to both armies and of an aspect more august than a man's, as though sent from heaven to expiate all the anger of the gods, and to turn aside destruction from his people and to bring it on their adversaries. . . .

It seems proper to add here that the consul, dictator, or praetor who

---

78. *Novensiles* = imported gods; *Indigites* = native gods.
79. That is, with a part of the toga covering the head and a part tucked up.

devotes the legions of the enemy need not devote himself, but may designate any citizen he likes from a regularly enlisted Roman legion; if the man who has been devoted dies, it is deemed that all is well; if he does not die, then an image of him is buried seven feet or more under the ground and a sin-offering is slain; where the image has been buried, thither a Roman magistrate may not go.

A VOW FOR VICTORY

Livy, *History of Rome* XXXVI. ii. 1–5; From *LCL*

These decrees having been enacted in the senate, and it being up to this time uncertain which province would be assigned to which consul, it was then at length decided that the consuls should cast lots. To Acilius fell Greece, to Cornelius Italy. The drawing being concluded, a decree of the senate was then passed that, since the Roman people had at this time ordered that there be war with King Antiochus and those who were under his authority, the consuls should proclaim a period of prayer for the success of the undertaking, and that the consul Manius Acilius should vow the Great Games to Jupiter and gifts at all the banquet tables of the gods. This vow, at the dictation of Publius Licinius, the *pontifex maximus,* the consul made in the following form: "If the war which the people has ordered to be undertaken with King Antiochus shall have been finished to the satisfaction of the senate and the Roman people, then in your honor, Jupiter, the Roman people will perform the Great Games for ten consecutive days, and gifts will be offered at all the banquet tables, of whatever value the senate shall determine. Whatever magistrates shall celebrate these games, at whatever time and place, let these games be regarded as duly celebrated and the gifts as duly offered." Then the period of prayer was proclaimed by both consuls, to continue for two days.

56. PURIFICATION CEREMONIES

The most impressive ritual of the Roman state-cult was the *lustratio,* the purification ceremony, involving a procession and the sacrifice of a pig, a ram, and a bull *(suovetaurilia).* The procession traced a "magic circle" about the group or territory being lustrated, purifying it from all previous lapses from proper religious form and protecting it from future external dangers. It was the solemn religious act by which the censors closed the census every five years. Varro's description of the formalities preparatory to the *lustratio* that terminated the census is taken verbatim from the official censors' records. The passage from Cato, while it deals with the purification of a private estate, contains, *mutatis mutandis,* the essential formula of the *lustratio.*

LUSTRATION

Dionysius of Halicarnassus, *Roman Antiquities* IV. xxii. 1–2; From *LCL*

Thereupon [Servius] Tullius, having completed the business of the census, commanded all the citizens to assemble in arms in the largest field before the city;[80] and having drawn up the cavalry in their respective squadrons and the infantry in their massed ranks, and having placed the light-armed troops each in their own centuries, he performed an expiatory sacrifice for them with a bull, a ram, and a boar.[81] These victims he ordered to be led three times round the army and then sacrificed them to Mars, to whom that field is consecrated. The Romans are to this day purified by this same expiatory sacrifice, after the completion of each census, by those who are invested with the most sacred magistracy;[82] they call the purification a *lustrum.*

Varro, *The Latin Language* VI. lxxxvi–lxxxvii; From *LCL*

When by night the censor has gone into the sacred precinct to take the auspices, and a message has come from the sky, he shall thus command the herald to call the men: "May this be good, fortunate, happy, and salutary to the Roman people, the Quirites, to the state of the Roman people, the Quirites, and to me and my colleague, and to our probity and our office. All the citizen soldiers under arms and private citizens as spokesmen of all the tribes call hither to me with an *inlicium* [invitation], in case any one for himself or for another wishes a reckoning[83] to be given."

The herald calls them first in the sacred precinct; afterwards he calls them likewise from the walls. When it is dawn, the censors, the clerks,

---

80. The Campus Martius, "Field of Mars."
81. Dionysius is in error here. The sacrifice of the *suovetaurilia* required a pig, not a boar.
82. The censors are meant.
83. That is, wishes to protest the census rating assigned to a citizen.

and the magistrates are anointed with myrrh and ointments. When the praetors and the tribunes of the people and those who have been called to the invitation meeting have come, the censors cast lots between them, to determine which one of them shall conduct the ceremony of purification. When the sacred precinct has been determined, then after that he who is to perform the purification conducts the assembly.

PURIFICATION OF A PRIVATE ESTATE

Cato, *On Agriculture* cxli; From Ernest Brehaut, *Cato the Censor on Framing*
(New York, 1933)

It is necessary to go in procession about the land in this way: Give orders for the swine-sheep-bull procession to be led around, [using this form of words], "With the favor of the gods and the wish for a happy outcome I bid you, Manius, see to it that the swine-sheep-bull procession pass around my farm, fields, and land, in whatever part you order the victims to be led or decide they should be carried around."

First address Janus and Jupiter with wine. Then say: "Father Mars, I beg and entreat thee to be of good will and favorable to me and to our house and household, for which purpose I have ordered the swine-sheep-bull procession to be led around my land and fields and farm. And I beg that thou wilt check, thrust back, and avert diseases seen and unseen, crop failure and crop destruction, sudden losses and storms, and that thou wilt permit the annual crops, the grain crops, the vineyards, and tree and vine slips to grow and turn out well. And that thou keep safe the shepherds and the flocks and give good health and strength to me and to our house and household: with these purposes in view and in consideration of the purifying procession about my estate, land, and fields, and the making of the purifying sacrifice—according to the words as I have spoken them—receive the honor of this suckling swine-sheep-bull sacrifice. Father Mars, with the same purpose in view, receive the honor of this suckling swine-sheep-bull offering."

At the same time move near with the knife the sacrificial cake and the oblation cake, and offer them. When you sacrifice the pig, lamb, and calf, this form of words is necessary: "And with this purpose in view, be honored by the swine-sheep-bull sacrifice." [Here] it is forbidden to name Mars or to say that it is [only] a lamb and a calf.

In case the offering shall be at fault as to all the victims, use these words: "Father Mars, if [there has been some flaw] in the former suckling swine-sheep-bull sacrifice, and sufficient has not been done, I offer thee this swine-sheep-bull sacrifice as an atonement."

If there shall be doubt in case of only one or two victims, use these words: "Father Mars, inasmuch as the former offering of a pig was not satisfactory to thee, I offer thee this pig as an atonement."

4

OVERSEAS CONQUESTS, 264–27 B.C.

57. THE FIRST PUNIC WAR: NAVAL VICTORY AT MYLAE, 260 B.C.

The events here described mark the beginning of Roman maritime supremacy in the Mediterranean.

Polybius, *Histories* I. xx. 5–xxi. 1; From *LCL*

As the Carthaginians maintained without any trouble the command of the sea the fortunes of the war continued to hang in the balance. For in the period that followed, now that Agrigentum was in their hands, while many inland cities joined the Romans from dread of their infantry forces, still more seaboard cities deserted their cause in terror of the Carthaginian fleet. Hence, when they saw that the balance of the war tended more and more to shift to this side or that for the above reasons and that, while Italy was frequently ravaged by the fleet, Libya remained entirely free from damage, they took urgent steps to get on the sea like the Carthaginians. And one of the reasons which induced me to narrate the history of this war at some length is just this, that my readers should, in this case too, not be kept in ignorance of the beginning of how, when, and for what reasons the Romans first took to the sea.

When they saw that the war was dragging on, they undertook for the first time to build ships, a hundred quinqueremes and twenty triremes. As their shipwrights were absolutely inexperienced in building quinqueremes, such ships never having been in use in Italy, the matter caused them much difficulty, and this fact shows us better than anything else how spirited and daring was the Roman policy. It was not that they had good resources for it, rather they had none whatever, nor had they ever given a thought to the sea; yet when they once had conceived the project, they took it in hand so boldly that before gaining any experience in the matter they at once engaged the Carthaginians who had held for generations undisputed command of the sea. Evidence of the truth of what I am saying and of their incredible pluck is this. When they first undertook to send their forces across to Messana not only had they not any decked ships, but no warships at all, not even a single boat, and borrowing fifty-oared boats and triremes from the Tarentines and Locrians, and also from the people of Elea and Naples, they took their troops across in these at great hazard. On this occasion the Carthaginians put to sea to attack them as they were crossing, and one of their decked ships advanced too far in its eagerness to overtake them and running aground fell into the hands of the Romans. This ship they now used as a model and built their whole fleet on its pattern; so that it is evident that if that had not occurred they would have been entirely prevented from carrying out their design by lack of practical knowledge. Now, however, those to whom the construction of the ships was committed were busy in getting them ready, and those who had collected the crews were teaching them to row on shore.

Livy, History of Rome XVII (Résumé); From LCL

The consul Gaius Duilius [260 B.C.; cf. § 90, third selection] fought a successful engagement with the fleet of the Carthaginians and was the first of all Roman leaders to triumph for a naval victory. For this reason he was granted a perpetual honor—that a wax torch should be borne before him and a flautist should make music when he returned from dining out.

CIL, vol. I, 2d ed., no. 25 (=ROL, 4:128–31); From LCL

. . . and the Segestaeans . . . he [Duilius] delivered from blockade; and all the Carthaginian hosts and their most mighty chief after nine days fled in broad daylight from their camp; and he took their town Macela by storm. And in the same command he as consul performed an exploit in ships at sea, the first Roman to do so; the first he was to equip and train crews and fleets of fighting ships; and with these ships he defeated in battle on the high seas the Punic fleets and likewise all the most mighty troops of the Carthaginians in the presence of Hannibal their commander-in-chief.[1] And by main force he captured ships with their

---

1. Not, of course, the famous Hannibal who commanded the Carthaginians in the Second Punic War.

crews, to wit: one septireme, thirty quinqueremes and triremes; thirteen he sank. Gold taken: 3,600 [plus] pieces. Silver taken, together with that derived from booty: 100,000 [plus] pieces. Total sum taken, reduced to Roman money . . . [2,100,000 (plus) sesterces]. . . . He also was the first to bestow on the people a gift of booty from a sea battle, and the first to lead native free-born Carthaginians in triumph. . . . [The rest is lost.]

58. PEACE TREATY WITH CARTHAGE, 241 B.C.; ANNEXATION OF SICILY AND SARDINIA

Polybius, *Histories* I. lxii. 3–lxiii. 4; From *LCL*

Hamilcar[2] acted thoroughly like the good and prudent leader he was. As long as there had been some reasonable hope in the situation he had left no means, however perilous and venturesome it seemed, unemployed, and if there ever was a general who put to proof in a war every chance of success, it was he. But now that fortunes were reversed and there was no reasonable prospect left of saving the troops under his command, he showed his practical good sense in yielding to circumstances and sending an embassy to treat for cessation of hostilities and a treaty. . . .

Lutatius[3] readily consented to negotiate, conscious as he was that the Roman resources were by this time exhausted and enfeebled by the war, and he succeeded in putting an end to the contest by a treaty the terms of which were more or less as follows: "There shall be friendship between the Carthaginians and Romans on the following terms, if approved by the Roman people. The Carthaginians to evacuate the whole of Sicily and not to make war on Hiero or bear arms against the Syracusans or the allies of the Syracusans. The Carthaginians to give up to the Romans all prisoners without ransom. The Carthaginians to pay to the Romans by installments in twenty years 2,200 Euboean talents." But when these terms were referred to Rome, the people did not accept the treaty, but sent ten commissioners to examine the matter. On their arrival they made no substantial changes in the terms, but only slight

2. Hamilcar Barca, the father of Hannibal, had been commander of the Carthaginian forces since 247 B.C.

3. The decisive naval victory was won in 242 B.C. at the Aegatae Islands, off the west coast of Sicily; the Roman commander was the consul Gaius Lutatius Catulus.

modifications rendering them more severe for Carthage: for they reduced the time of the payment by one half, added 1,000 talents to the indemnity, and demanded the evacuation by the Carthaginians of all islands lying between Sicily and Italy.

Such then was the end of the war between the Romans and Carthaginians for the possession of Sicily, and such were the terms of peace.

Polybius, *Histories* I. lxxxviii. 8–12; From *LCL*

The Romans about the same time, on the invitation of the mercenaries who had deserted to them from Sardinia, undertook an expedition to that island.[4] When the Carthaginians objected on the ground that the sovereignty of Sardinia was rather their own than Rome's, and began preparations for punishing those who were the cause of the revolt of the island, the Romans made this the pretext for declaring war on them, alleging that the preparations were not against Sardinia, but against themselves. The Carthaginians, who had barely escaped destruction in this last war, were in every respect ill-fitted at this moment to resume hostilities with Rome. Yielding therefore to circumstances, they not only gave up Sardinia, but agreed to pay a further sum of 1,200 talents to the Romans to avoid going to war for the present.

Polybius, *Histories* III. xxvii. 1–xxviii. 2; From *LCL*

At the close of the war for Sicily, then, they made another treaty,[5] the clauses of which run as follows: "The Carthaginians are to evacuate the whole of Sicily and all the islands lying between Italy and Sicily. The allies of both parties are to be secure from attack by the other. Neither party is entitled to impose any contributions, to build constructions for public purposes, or to enroll soldiers in the dominions of the other, nor to form alliances with the allies of the other. The Carthaginians are to pay 1,200 talents within ten years, and a sum of 1,000 talents at once. The Carthaginians are to give up to the Romans all prisoners without ransom." Later, at the end of the Libyan War[6] after the Romans had actually passed a decree declaring war on Carthage, they added the

4. In 238 B.C., after a revolt of Carthaginian mercenaries on the island. The Romans had put an occupation force ashore on Corsica before the end of the war.
5. For the three earlier treaties with Carthage, see § 13.
6. The war of Carthage against her mutinous mercenaries, which ended in 238 B.C.

following clause, as I stated above: "The Carthaginians are to evacuate Sardinia and pay a further sum of 1,200 talents." The very last of this series, addition to the aforesaid, is the agreement made with Hasdrubal in Spain [in 226 B.C.], that "The Carthaginians are not to cross the Ebro in arms." Such is the diplomatic history of the relations between Rome and Carthage . . . up to the time of Hannibal.

While therefore we find that the crossing of the Romans to Sicily was not contrary to treaty, for the next war, that in which they made the treaty about Sardinia, it is impossible to discover any reasonable pretext or cause. In this case everyone would agree that the Carthaginians, contrary to all justice, and merely because the occasion permitted it, were forced to evacuate Sardinia and pay the additional sum I mentioned.

59. SECOND PUNIC WAR: HANNIBAL'S OATH

"The 'wrath of the house of Barca' and 'the revenge of Hannibal' belong mainly to a Roman tradition which obscures, and was meant to obscure, the extent to which the Roman seizure of Sardinia and her interference in Spain drove Carthage to war" (*Cambridge Ancient History*, 8:31). Soon after Hannibal was proclaimed commander-in-chief of the Punic forces in Spain, he launched his anti-Roman offensive in 219 B.C., by besieging and sacking Saguntum, a Spanish city which, though south of the Ebro River, enjoyed an alliance with Rome.

Livy, *History of Rome* XXI. i. 4–5; From *LCL*

It is said moreover that when Hannibal, then about nine years old, was childishly teasing his father Hamilcar to take him into Spain, his father, who had finished the African war and was sacrificing, before crossing over with his army, led the boy up to the altar and made him touch the offerings and bind himself with an oath that so soon as he should be able he would be the declared enemy of the Roman people. The loss of Sicily and Sardinia was a continual torture to the proud spirit of Hamilcar. For he maintained that they had surrendered Sicily in premature despair, and that the Romans had wrongfully appropriated Sardinia—and even imposed an indemnity on them besides—in the midst of their African disturbances.

60. A Comparison of the Strength and Resources of Rome and Carthage

Polybius, *Histories* VI. li–lii; From *LCL*

The constitution of Carthage seems to me to have been originally well contrived as regards its most distinctive points. For there were kings,[7] and the house of elders was an aristocratic force, and the people were supreme in matters proper to them, the entire frame of the state much resembling that of Rome and Sparta. But at the time when they entered on the Hannibalic War, the Carthaginian constitution had degenerated, and that of Rome was better. . . . For by as much as the power and prosperity of Carthage had been earlier than that of Rome, by so much had Carthage already begun to decline, while Rome was exactly at her prime, as far at least as her system of government was concerned. Consequently the multitude of Carthage had already acquired the chief voice in deliberations; while at Rome the senate still retained this; and hence, as in one case the masses deliberated and in the other the most eminent men, the Roman decisions on public affairs were superior, so that although they met with complete disaster, they were finally by the wisdom of their counsels victorious over the Carthaginians in the war.

But to pass to differences of detail, such as, to begin with, the conduct of the war, the Carthaginians naturally are superior at sea both in efficiency and equipment, because seamanship has long been their national craft, and they busy themselves with the sea more than any other people; but as regards infantry services the Romans are much more efficient. They indeed devote their whole energies to this matter, whereas the Carthaginians entirely neglect their infantry, though they do pay some slight attention to their cavalry. The reason for this is that the troops they employ are foreign and mercenary, whereas those of the Romans are natives of the soil and citizens.[8] So that in this respect also we must pronounce the political system of Rome to be superior to that of Carthage, the Carthaginians continuing to depend for the maintenance of their freedom on the courage of a mercenary force but the Romans on their own valor and on the aid of their allies. Consequently even if they happen to be worsted at the outset, the Romans redeem

---

7. The chief officials of Carthage were not kings but annually elected *shofetim,* or "judges."

8. In addition, however, Rome drew on the great manpower reservoir of her allied communities. Cf. § 61.

defeat by final success, while it is the contrary with the Carthaginians. For the Romans, fighting as they are for their country and their children, never can abate their fury but continue to throw their whole hearts into the struggle until they get the better of their enemies. It follows that though the Romans are, as I said, much less skilled in naval matters, they are on the whole successful at sea, owing to the gallantry of their men; for although skill in seamanship is of no small importance in naval battles, it is chiefly the courage of the marines that turns the scale in favor of victory. Now not only do Italians in general naturally excel Phoenicians and Africans in bodily strength and personal courage, but by their institutions also they do much to foster a spirit of bravery in the young men.

61. ROMAN MANPOWER RESOURCES ON THE EVE OF THE SECOND PUNIC WAR

Polybuis, *Histories* II. xxiv; From *LCL*

But, that it may appear from actual facts what a great power it was that Hannibal ventured to attack, and how mighty was that empire boldly confronting which he came so near his purpose as to bring great disasters on Rome, I must state what were their [the Romans'] resources and the actual number of their forces at this time. The consuls were in command of four legions of Roman citizens, each consisting of 5,200 foot and 300 horse. The allied forces in each consular army numbered 30,000 foot and 2,000 horse. The cavalry of the Sabines and Etruscans, who had come to the temporary assistance of Rome, were 4,000 strong, their infantry more than 50,000. The Romans massed these forces and posted them on the frontier of Etruria under the command of a praetor. The levy of the Umbrians and Sarsinatians inhabiting the Apennines amounted to about 20,000, and with these were 20,000 Veneti and Cenomani. These they stationed on the frontier of Gaul, to invade the territory of the Boii and divert the invaders. These were the armies protecting the Roman territory. In Rome itself there was a reserve force, ready for any contingency, consisting of 20,0000 foot and 1,500 horse, all Roman citizens, and 30,000 foot and 2,000 horse furnished by the allies. The roll of soldiers that had been reported was as follows: Latins, 80,000 foot and 5,000 horse; Samnites, 70,000 foot and 7,000 horse; Iapygians and Messapians, 50,000 foot and 16,000 horse; Lucanians, 30,000 foot and 3,000 horse; Marsi, Marrucini, Frentani, and Vestini, 20,000 foot and 4,000 horse. In Sicily and Tarentum were two reserve legions, each consisting of 4,200 foot and 200 horse. Of Romans and Campanians there were on the roll 250,000 foot and about 23,000 horse. Thus, the total number of Romans and allies able to bear arms was more than 700,000 foot and 70,000 horse, while Hannibal invaded Italy with an army of less than 20,000 men.

62. HANNIBAL'S ARMY

Though the following selection records Hannibal's arrangements for the military security of Africa and Spain, it gives a vivid picture of the motley character of the mercenary troops with which Hannibal invaded Italy in 218 B.C.

Polybius, *Histories* III. xxxiii. 5–18; From *LCL*

Hannibal, who was wintering in New Carthage,[9] in the first place dismissed the Iberians to their own cities hoping thus to make them readily disposed to help in the future; next he instructed his brother Hasdrubal how to manage the government of Spain and prepare to resist the Romans if he himself happened to be absent; in the third place he took precautions for the security of Africa, adopting the very sensible and wise policy of sending soldiers from Africa to Spain and *vice versa,* binding by this measure the two provinces to reciprocal loyalty. The troops who had crossed to Africa were supplied by the Thersitae, Mastiani, Iberian Oretes, and Olcades, and numbered 1,200 horse and 13,850 foot, besides which there were 870 Balearians, a popular appellation, derived from *ballein,* "to throw," and meaning slingers,[10] given to them owing to their skill with this weapon and extended to their people and islands. He stationed most of these troops at Metagonia in Libya and some in Carthage itself. From the so-called Metagonian towns he sent 4,000 foot to Carthage to serve both as reinforcements and as hostages. In Spain he left with his brother Hasdrubal fifty quinqueremes, two quadriremes and five triremes, thirty-two of the quinqueremes and all the triremes being fully manned. He also gave him as cavalry Libyo-Phoenicians and Libyans to the number of 450, 300 Ilergetes, and 1,800

9. Modern Cartagena; the winter was that of 219–218 B.C.
10. This is a case of ancient popular but inaccurate etymology.

Numidians drawn from the Masylii, Masaesylii, Maccoei, and Maurusi, who dwell by the Ocean; and as infantry 11,850 Libyans, 300 Ligurians, and 500 Balearians, as well as twenty-one elephants.

No one need be surprised at the accuracy of the information I give here about Hannibal's arrangements in Spain, an accuracy which even the actual organizer of the details would have some difficulty in attaining, and I need not be condemned offhand with the idea that I am acting like those authors who try to make their misstatements plausible. The fact is that I found on the Lacinian promontory a bronze tablet on which Hannibal himself had made out these lists during the time he was in Italy, and thinking this an absolutely first-rate authority I decided to follow the document.

63. HANNIBAL CROSSES THE ALPS, 218 B.C.

Hannibal's dash across the Alps is one of the most spectacular and best-known events of ancient history. Polybius' account is not as picturesque as Livy's (XXI. xxx–xxxviii) but more accurate and freer from rhetorical flourishes.

Polybius, *Histories* III. l. 1–4, liii. 6–lvi. 4; From *LCL*

After a ten days' march of 800 stades along the bank of the Isère Hannibal began the ascent of the Alps and now found himself involved in very great difficulties. For as long as they had been in flat country, the various chiefs of the Allobroges had left them alone, being afraid both of the cavalry and of the barbarians who were escorting them. But when the latter had set off on their return home, and Hannibal's troops began to advance into the difficult region, the Allobrogian chieftains got together a considerable force and occupied advantageous positions on the road by which the Carthaginians would be obliged to ascend. Had they only kept their project secret, they would have utterly annihilated the Carthaginian army, but, as it was, it was discovered, and though they inflicted a good deal of damage on Hannibal, they did more injury to themselves. . . .

[The ascending columns were harassed by the mountaineer tribes as they made their way up the steep and precipitous road, and Hannibal lost many men, horses, and pack animals.]

The enemy having taken their departure, he joined the cavalry and pack animals and advanced toward the summit of the pass[11] of the Alps, encountering no longer any massed force of barbarians, but molested from time to time and in certain places by some of them who took advantage of the ground to attack him either from the rear or from the front and carry off some of the pack animals. In these circumstances the elephants were of the greatest service to him; for the enemy never dared to approach that part of the column in which these animals were, being terrified by the strangeness of their appearance. After an ascent of nine days Hannibal reached the summit and, encamping there, remained for two days to rest the survivors of his army and wait for stragglers. During this interval a good many of the horses which had broken away in terror and a number of those pack animals which had thrown off their packs returned strangely enough, having followed the track of the march, and came into the camp. As it was now close on the setting of the Pleiads, snow had already gathered on the summit, and noticing that the men were in bad spirits owing to all they had suffered up to now and expected to suffer, he summoned them to a meeting and attempted to cheer them up, relying chiefly for this purpose on the actual view of Italy, which lies so close under these mountains that when both are viewed together the Alps stand to the whole of Italy in the relation of a citadel to a city. Showing them, therefore, the plain of the Po, and reminding them of the friendly feelings of the Gauls inhabiting it, while at the same time pointing out the situation of Rome itself, he to some extent restored their spirits. Next day he broke up his camp and began the descent. During this he encountered no enemy, except a few skulking marauders, but owing to the difficulties of the ground and the snow his losses were nearly as heavy as on the ascent. The descending path was very narrow and steep, and as both men and beasts could not tell on what they were treading owing to the snow, all that stepped wide of the path or stumbled were dashed down the precipice. This trial, however, they put up with, being by this time familiar with such sufferings, but they at length reached a place where it was impossible for either the elephants or the pack animals to pass owing to the extreme narrowness of the path, a previous landslip having carried away about one and a half stades of the face of the mountain and a further landslip having recently

---

11. It is not certain which Alpine pass Hannibal's army took. The literature on the subject is enormous. One widely accepted view is that it was one of the central passes of the Western Alps, Mont Cenis or Mont Genèvre.

occurred, and here the soldiers once more became disheartened and discouraged.

The Carthaginian general at first thought of avoiding the difficult part by a detour, but as a fresh fall of snow made progress impossible he had to abandon this project. The state of matters was altogether peculiar and unusual. The new snow which had fallen on the top of the old snow remaining since the previous winter was itself yielding, both owing to its softness, being a fresh fall, and because it was not very deep, but when they had trodden through it and set foot on the congealed snow beneath it, they no longer sank in it, but slid along it with both feet, as happens to those who walk on ground with a coat of mud on it. But what followed on this was even more trying. As for the men, when, unable to pierce the lower layer of snow, they fell and then tried to help themselves to rise by the support of their knees and hands, they slid along still more rapidly on these, the slope being exceedingly steep. But the animals, when they fell, broke through the lower layer of snow in their efforts to rise, and remained there with their packs as if frozen into it, owing to their weight and the congealed condition of this old snow. Giving up this project, then, Hannibal encamped on the ridge, sweeping it clear of snow, and next set the soldiers to work to build up the path along the cliff, a most toilsome task. In one day he made a passage sufficiently wide for the pack train and horses; so he at once took these across on ground free of snow, sent them to pasture, and then took the Numidians in relays to work at building up the path, so that with great difficulty in three days he managed to get the elephants across, but in a wretched condition from hunger; for the summits of the Alps and the parts near the top of the passes are all quite treeless and bare, owing to the snow lying there continuously both winter and summer, but the slopes halfway up on both sides are grassy and wooded and on the whole inhabitable.

Hannibal having now got all his forces together continued the descent and in three days' march from the precipice just described reached flat country. He had lost many of his men by the hands of the enemy in the crossings of rivers and on the march in general, and the precipices and difficulties of the Alps had cost him not only many men, but a far greater number of horses and pack animals. The whole march from New Carthage had taken him five months, and he had spent fifteen days in crossing the Alps, and now, when he thus boldly descended into the plain of the Po and the territory of the Insubres, his surviving forces numbered 12,000 African and 8,000 Iberian foot, and not more than 6,000 horse in all, as he himself states in the inscription on the column at Lacinium relating to the number of his forces.[12]

64. DEFECTION OF ROMAN ALLIES AFTER CANNAE

The key to Hannibal's strategy in Italy was the bold plan of detaching Rome's allies from her, thereby striking at the main reserve strength of Rome. Despite his efforts, all of central Italy remained monolithically loyal to Rome. But after the battle of Cannae (216 B.C.), the most disastrous defeat in Roman history, almost all of southern Italy seceded to Hannibal. Here, as in the Greek East (see § 72), it was the common people who sought to liberate their communities from subjection to Rome, while the nobility generally found their interests bound to the power of Rome. The worst blow was the defection of Capua; and the Romans meted out a ferocious punishment to the Campanians after they recaptured Capua in 211 B.C.

SOUTHERN ITALY REVOLTS

Livy, *History of Rome* XXII. lxi. 10–14, XXIII. vi. i–vii. 3, xiv. 5–12; From *LCL*

For the rest, how greatly this disaster exceeded those that had gone before is plain from this: the loyalty of the allies, which had held firm until the day of Cannae, now began to waver, assuredly for no other reason than because they had lost all hope of the empire. Now these are the peoples that revolted and went over to the Carthaginians: the Campanians, the Atellani, the Calatini, the Hirpini, a part of the Apulians, all the Samnites but the Pentri, all the Bruttians, the Lucanians, and besides these the Uzentini and almost all the Greeks on the coast (the Tarentines, the Metapontines, the Crotoniates, and the Locrians), together with all the Cisalpine Gauls. Yet these disasters and the falling away of the allies could not induce the Romans anywhere to mention peace, either before the consul came to Rome or after his coming had turned men's thoughts anew to the calamity which they had suffered. In that very hour there was such courage in the hearts of the citizens that when the consul was returning from that defeat for which he himself had been chiefly responsible, a crowd of all classes went out to meet him

---

12. For Hannibal's inscription at Lacinium see § 62. Polybius states elsewhere (III. lx. 5) that Hannibal's losses from the crossing of the Rhone to the arrival in the Po Valley were 50 percent.

on the way and gave him thanks because he had not despaired of the state.

.   .   .   .

The time had come when the Campanians could not only recover the territory formerly taken from them unjustly by the Romans, but could also gain authority over Italy. For they would make a treaty with Hannibal on their own terms. And there would be no doubt that, when Hannibal, upon the completion of the war, retired as victor to Africa and removed his army, authority over Italy would be left to the Campanians. Having agreed unanimously with these words of Virrius,[13] they made such a report of their embassy that the Roman name seemed to all to have been blotted out. At once the populace and a majority of the senate were aiming to revolt. But action was postponed for a few days by the weighty advice of the elder men. Finally the view of the majority prevailed, that the same legates who had gone to the Roman consul should be sent to Hannibal. . . .

The legates came to Hannibal and made an alliance with him on these terms: that no general or magistrate of the Carthaginians should have any authority over a Campanian citizen, and that no Campanian citizen should be a soldier or perform any service against his will; that Capua should have its own laws, its own magistrates; that the Carthaginians should give the Campanians three hundred of the Roman captives of their own choosing, whom they could exchange for the Campanian horsemen who were serving in Sicily.[14] Such were the terms. In addition to what was agreed upon, the Campanians perpetrated these misdeeds: the populace suddenly seized prefects of the allies and other Roman citizens, some of them employed in military duty, some engaged in private business, and with the pretense of guarding them ordered them all to be confined in the baths, that there they might die a terrible death, being suffocated by the extreme heat.

.   .   .   .

Hannibal, after gaining possession of Capua and vainly trying, partly by hope, partly by fear, to work for the second time upon the feelings of the Neapolitans, led his army over into the territory of Nola. . . .

---

13. One of the Capuan envoys sent to the Roman consul to negotiate about the status of Capua.

14. The meaning of this appears in Livy XXIII. iv. 7–8: "All that held them back from at once revolting was that the long-established right of intermarriage had united many distinguished and powerful families with the Romans, and that although a considerable number were serving on the Roman side, the strongest bond was the 3,000 horsemen, noblest of the Campanians, who had been chosen to garrison Sicilian cities by the Romans." (Quoted from the Loeb Classical Library.)

The senate and especially its leading members stood loyally by the alliance with Rome. But the common people, as usual, were all for a change of government and for Hannibal; and they called to mind the fear of devastation of their lands and the many hardships and indignities they must suffer in case of a siege. And men were not lacking to propose revolt. Accordingly the senators, now obsessed by the fear that, if they should move openly, there could be no resisting the excited crowd, found a way to postpone the evil by pretending agreement. For they pretend that they favor revolt to Hannibal, but that there is no agreement as to the terms on which they may go over to a new alliance and friendship. Thus gaining time, they send emissaries in haste to the Roman praetor, Claudius Marcellus, who was at Casilinum with his army, and inform him in what danger the Nolan state is placed; that its territory is in the hands of Hannibal and the Carthaginians, and that the city will be so at once, if help is not given; that the senate, by conceding to the common people that they would revolt whenever the people wished, had prevented their making haste to revolt. Marcellus, after warmly praising the men of Nola, bade them postpone matters by the same pretense until his arrival; in the meantime to conceal the dealings they had had with him and all hope of Roman aid.

ROMAN REPRISALS IN CAMPANIA

Livy, *History of Rome* XXVI. xvi. 5–13, xxxiv; Adapted from *LCL*

From Cales they returned to Capua, and the surrender of Atella and Calatia was received. There also punishment was inflicted on the responsible leaders. Thus about seventy prominent senators were put to death. Some three hundred Campanian aristocrats who were put in prison, and others who were placed in custody among cities of the Latin allies, met death in different ways. The remaining mass of Campanian citizens were sold. In regard to the city and its territory discussion continued, some holding that a city which was very powerful, near, and unfriendly should be destroyed. But immediate advantage prevailed. For on account of the land, which was well known to be the foremost in Italy in general fertility of the soil, the city was preserved, that the tillers of the land might have some dwelling place. To people the city the multitude of resident aliens and freedmen and petty tradesmen and artisans was retained. The whole territory and the buildings became the property of the Roman people. But it was decreed that Capua, as a nominal city, should be only a dwelling place and a center of population, but should have no political body nor senate nor council of the plebs nor magistrates. They thought that the multitude, without a public council, without military authority, having nothing in common amongst them, would be incapable of agreement. The Romans would send out every year a prefect to administer justice. Thus matters concerning Capua were settled according to a plan that was in every respect praiseworthy. Stern and prompt was the punishment of the most guilty; the mass of the citizens were scattered with no hope of return; no rage was vented upon innocent buildings and city walls by burning and demolition. And along with profit they sought a reputation among the allies as well for clemency, by saving a very famous and very rich city, over whose ruins all Campania, all the neighboring peoples on every side of Campania, would have mourned. . . .

For the Campanians, family by family, decrees were passed which it is not worthwhile to recount in full. In the case of some, their property was to be confiscated, themselves and their children and wives sold, with the exception of the daughters who, before they became subject to the authority of the Roman people, had married into other communities. Others were to be put in chains, and action concerning them was to be considered later. In the case of other Campanians they also specified a property-rating level, to determine whether their property should be confiscated or not. Captured animals, except horses, and slaves, except adult males, also everything which was not attached to the soil they decreed should be restored to their owners. All Capuans, Atellans, Calatines, and Sabatines, except such of them as had been with the enemy, either themselves or their fathers, were to be free men, it was ordered, with the reservation that no one of them should be a Roman citizen or be reckoned a Latin, and that no one of them who had been at Capua while the gates were closed should remain in the city or in the territory of Capua beyond a certain date; a region across the Tiber [i.e., in Etruria], but not touching the Tiber, was to be assigned to them as a dwelling place. As for those who during the war had not been in Capua nor in a Campanian city which had revolted from the Roman people, it was voted that these should be removed this side of the Liris River in the direction of Rome; and that those who had come over to the Romans before Hannibal came to Capua should be removed this side of the Volturnus, no one of them to have land or building nearer the sea than fifteen miles. Those of them who were removed across the Tiber were not themselves nor their descendants to acquire or hold land anywhere except in the districts of Veii, Sutrium, or Nepet, with the provision that no one was to possess a larger amount of land than fifty *iugera*. The property of all senators and those who had held office at Capua, Atella, or Calatia they ordered to be sold at Capua; that the free persons who, it had been voted, should be offered for sale be sent the Rome, and sold at Rome. Images, statues of bronze, which were said to have been captured from the enemy, they referred to the college of pontiffs, to decide which of them were sacred and which profane.

65. The Roman War Effort after Cannae

THE SENATE REFUSES TO RANSOM PRISONERS OF WAR

Livy, *History of Rome* XXII. lx. 2–4, lxi. 1–3; From *LCL*

The senate was cleared of strangers and the debate began. Opinions differed. Some were for ransoming the prisoners at the public cost; others would have no money disbursed by the state, but would not prohibit ransoming at the expense of individuals, and to such as might not have the money in hand proposed to grant loans from the treasury, guarding the state against loss by taking sureties and mortgages. . . .

Though most of the senators, too, had relatives amongst the prisoners, yet, besides the example of a state which had shown from of old the scantiest consideration for prisoners of war, they were also moved by the greatness of the sum required, not wishing either to exhaust the treasury, on which they had already made a heavy draft to purchase slaves and arm them for service, or to furnish Hannibal with money — the one thing of which he was rumored to stand most in need. When the stern reply, that the prisoners would not be ransomed, had been given, and fresh sorrow had been added to the old at the loss of so many of their fellow citizens, the crowd attended the envoys to the gate with many tears and lamentations.[15]

15. The Roman war prisoners were sold into slavery by Hannibal, and in 194 B.C., at the request of Flamininus, those enslaved to Greeks were bought up, to the number of about 2,000, and liberated by the Greek states; cf. § 68, third selection.

THE ROMAN RANKS ARE REPLENISHED WITH SLAVES

Valerius Maximus, *Memorable Deeds and Sayings* VII. vi. i

For during the Second Punic War the Roman youth of military age having been drained by several unfavorable battles, the senate, on motion of the consul Tiberius Gracchus, decreed that slaves should be bought up out of public moneys for use in repulsing the enemy. After a plebiscite was passed on this matter by the people through the intervention of the tribunes of the plebs, a commission of three men was chosen to purchase 24,000 slaves,[16] and, having administered an oath to them that they would give zealous and courageous service and that they would bear arms as long as the Carthaginians were in Italy, they sent them to the camp. From Apulia and the Paediculi were also bought 270 slaves for replacements in the cavalry. . . . The city which up to this time had disdained to have as soldiers even free men without property added to its army as almost its chief support persons taken from slave lodgings and slaves gathered from shepherd huts.

NEW FLEETS ARE MOBILIZED

Livy, *History of Rome* XXIV. xi. 7–9; From *LCL*

As the rumor that there was a war in Sicily [214 B.C.] spread more widely, Titus Otacilius was ordered to set sail thither with his fleet. Owing to the lack of sailors [i.e., rowers] the consuls in accordance with a decree of the senate issued an edict that a man who in the censorship of Lucius Aemilius and Gaius Flaminius [220 B.C.] had been rated— either he or his father—at from 50,000 to 100,000 *asses,* or if his property had since increased to that amount, should furnish one sailor provided with six months' pay; that one who had more than 100,000 and up to 300,000 should furnish three sailors and a year's pay; and he who had over 300,000 and up to a million *asses,* five sailors; he who had over a million, seven; that senators should furnish eight sailors and a year's pay. The sailors furnished in accordance with this edict went on board armed and equipped by their masters, and with cooked rations for thirty days. It was the first time that a Roman fleet was manned with crews secured at private expense.

16. The number is exaggerated. Livy (XXII. lvii. 11) states 8,000.

Livy, *History of Rome* XXVIII. xlv. 13–21

As Scipio[17] had stated that his fleet would not be an expense to the state, he was given liberty to accept whatever was contributed by the allies for the construction of new ships. The peoples of Etruria were the first to promise assistance to the consul, each according to its means. Caere contributed grain and provisions of all kinds for the crews; Populonia, iron; Tarquinii, cloth for the sails; Volaterrae, timber for the ships and grain; Arretium, 3,000 shields and as many helmets, while they were ready to supply 50,000 each of darts, javelins, and long spears. They also offered to furnish all the axes, hooks, basins, and millstones required for forty warships as well as 120,000 pecks of wheat and provision for the rowing-masters and the rowers on the voyage. Perusia, Clusium, and Rusellae sent pine wood for the timbers of the ships and a large quantity of grain. . . . The Umbrian communities as well as the inhabitants of Nursia, Reate, and Amiternum, and the whole of the Sabine country promised to furnish soldiers. Numerous contingents from the Marsi, the Paeligni, and the Marrucini volunteered to serve on board the fleet. The people of Camerinum, a city which had a treaty of equal alliance with Rome, sent a cohort of six hundred men under arms. The keels of thirty ships—twenty quinqueremes and ten quadriremes—were laid down, and Scipio pressed on the work so rapidly that on the forty-fifth day after the timber had been brought from the forests the ships were launched with their tackle and armament complete.

ROME STRIKES BACK

This inscription preserves a fragment of a eulogy of Quintus Fabius Maximus, who was given the sobriquet of Cunctator, "the Delayer," in tribute to his successful strategy of aggravating Hannibal's logistical problems by withdrawing ever deeper into Italy without risking open combat. Although only seventeen Latin words are preserved, some additional sense is restorable. The consulship mentioned is that of 230 B.C.

17. In 205 B.C., when the course of the war had already turned in Rome's favor.

AE, 1954, no. 216; c. 205 B.C.

. . . [as censor] he conducted the first revision of the senate membership and held comitial elections in the consulship of Marcus Junius Pera and Marcus Barbula; he besieged and recaptured Tarentum and the stronghold of Hannibal, and [obtained enormous booty?]; he won surpassing glory by his military [exploits?].

66. SECOND PUNIC WAR: THE BALKAN FRONT

In 214 B.C., when it was clear that his brilliant initial successes in Italy fell far short of final victory, Hannibal signed a treaty of mutual assistance with Philip V, king of Macedon, who regarded the Balkan Peninsula as his own sphere of domination and was eager to dislodge the Romans from the toehold they had established there fifteen years earlier. E. J. Bickerman, in *Transactions of the American Philological Association* (1944), 75:87–102, has shown that the Greek version of this treaty given by Polybius is an official translation from the Punic text prepared in Hannibal's chancellery.

The Romans countered by quickly mounting a combined military and diplomatic offensive in Epirus and Greece. They at once dispatched a force across the Adriatic under the praetor Marcus Valerius Laevinus, and three years later they gained the assistance of the Aetolian League. By these means they tied Philip down at home and prevented him from rendering any effective aid to Hannibal.

TREATY BETWEEN CARTHAGE AND MACEDON

Polybius, *Histories* VII. ix; From *LCL*

This is a sworn treaty made between us, Hannibal the general, Mago, Myrcan, Barmocar, and all the other Carthaginian senators present with him, and all the Carthaginians serving with him, on the one side, and Xenophanes the Athenian, son of Cleomachus, the envoy whom King Philip, son of Demetrius, sent to us on behalf of himself, the Macedonians, and their allies, on the other side.

In the presence of Zeus, Hera, and Apollo; in the presence of the *genius* of Carthage, of Heracles, and Iolaus; in the presence of Ares, Triton, and Poseidon; in the presence of the gods who battled for us and of the Sun, Moon, and Earth; in the presence of Rivers, Lakes, and Waters; in the presence of all the gods who possess Carthage; in the presence of all the gods who possess Macedonia and the rest of Greece; in the presence of all the gods of the army who preside over this oath. Thus saith Hannibal the general, and all the Carthaginian senators with him, and all Carthaginians serving with him, that as seemeth good to you and to us, so should we bind ourselves, even as friends, kinsmen, and brothers, by this oath of friendship and good will on the following conditions:

That King Philip and the Macedonians and the rest of the Greeks who are their allies shall protect the Carthaginians, the supreme lords, and Hannibal their general and those with him, and all under the dominion of Carthage who live under the same laws; and the people of Utica, and all cities and peoples that are subject to Carthage; and our soldiers and allies; and all cities and peoples in Italy, Gaul, and Liguria with whom we are in alliance or with whomsoever in that country we may hereafter enter into friendship and alliance.

King Philip and the Macedonians and such of the Greeks as are their allies shall be protected and guarded by the Carthaginians who are serving with us, by the people of Utica and by all cities and peoples that are subject to Carthage, by our allies and soldiers, and by all peoples and cities in Italy, Gaul, and Liguria who are our allies, and by such others as many hereafter become our allies in Italy and the adjacent regions.

We will enter into no plot against each other, nor lie in ambush for each other, but with all zeal and good fellowship, without deceit or secret design, we will be enemies of such as war against the Carthaginians, excepting the kings, cities, and ports with which we have sworn treaties of alliance.

And we, too, will be the enemies of such as war against King Philip, excepting the kings, cities, and peoples with whom we have sworn treaties of alliance.

. And you will render assistance to us in the war in which we are engaged with the Romans until the gods vouchsafe the victory to us and to you, and you will give us such help as we have need of or as we agree upon.

When the gods have been propitious to you and to us in the war against the Romans and their allies, if the Romans ask us to come to terms of peace, we will make a peace that will include you, on the following conditions: that the Romans may never make war upon you;

that the Romans shall no longer be masters of Corcyra, Apollonia, Epidamnus, Pharos, Dimale, Parthini, or Atitania; and that they shall return to Demetrius of Pharos all his friends who are in the dominions of Rome.

If ever the Romans make war on you or on us, we will help each other in the war as may be required on either side. In like manner if others do so, excepting the kings, cities, and peoples with whom we have sworn treaties of alliance.

If we decide to withdraw any clauses from, or add any to, this sworn treaty, we will make such withdrawals or additions by mutual agreement.

ROMAN ALLIANCE WITH THE AETOLIAN LEAGUE

Livy, *History of Rome* XXVI. xxiv

Marcus Valerius Laevinus, having first sounded the attitude of the leading men through secret conferences, came with some swift units of his fleet to a council of the Aetolians which had been previously appointed to meet especially for this purpose. There he first pointed proudly to the capture of Syracuse and Capua as proofs of the success of Roman arms in Sicily and Italy. He then went on to say that it was a custom with the Romans, handed down to them from their ancestors, to take good care of their allies, some of whom they had admitted to citizenship and to equal rights with themselves, while others they treated so favorably that they preferred to be allies rather than citizens; that the Aetolians would be honored by them all the more because they would be the first of the nations across the sea to have entered into friendship with them; that as for Philip and the Macedonians, their troublesome neighbors, he had already broken their might and spirit, and would still further reduce them to such a pass that they would not only evacuate the cities which they had forcibly taken from the Aetolians, but would find Macedonia itself constantly endangered; and that he would place the Acarnanians, whose forcible separation from their league the Aetolians resented, once again under their former jurisdiction and dominion.

These assertions and promises of the Roman general were strengthened by Scopas, who was then *strategus* of the league, and by Dorymachus, a leading man among the Aetolians, both of whom extolled the power and greatness of the Roman people in a manner which, being less restrained, carried greater conviction. But it was the hope of recovering Acarnania that chiefly moved them. The terms, therefore, on which they should enter into friendship and alliance with the Roman people were reduced to writing, and it was added that, if it were agreeable to them and they wished it, the Eleans and Spartans ass well as Attalus, Pleuratus, and Scerdilaedus should have the same right of friendship (Attalus was king of Pergamum, the latter two, kings of the Thracians and Illyrians).

The terms of the treaty were that the Aetolians should immediately make war on Philip by land, and the Romans should assist with not less than twenty-five quinqueremes; that the ground and buildings, together with the walls and lands, of the cities from the Aetolian border as far as Corcyra[18] should belong to the Aetolians, every other kind of booty[19] to the Roman people; that the Romans should see to it that the Aetolians should hold Acarnania. If the Aetolians should make peace with Philip, they should insert a stipulation that the peace would be valid only if Philip abstained from hostilities against the Romans, their allies, and those subject to them; in like manner, if the Roman people should sign a treaty with the king, they should provide that he not have the right to make war upon the Aetolians and their allies.

Such were the terms agreed upon, and copies were posted two years later by the Aetolians at Olympia and by the Romans in the Capitol, that they might be attested by consecrated records. The delay occurred because the Aetolian envoys were detained for a long time in Rome; it did not, however, impede military action. The Aetolians moved at once against Philip. Laevinus captured Zacynthus (this is a small island near Aetolia, with one city with the same name as the island; it was this city he took, all but the citadel) as well as the Acarnanian cities of Oeniadae and Nasus and annexed them to Aetolia; then, considering that Philip was sufficiently engaged by the war with his neighbors to prevent his thinking of Italy, the Carthaginians, and his compact with Hannibal, he retired to Corcyra.

18. The territory here defined would include Acarnania and a large part of Epirus (which Philip coveted). The Romans, in effect, set no limits on Aetolian conquests in Greece but excluded them from Illyria to the north, where the Romans had protectorates.

19. That is, movable property (cf. Livy XXXIII. xiii. 10).

ROME'S TREATY WITH THE AETOLIAN LEAGUE

This inscription, the earliest surviving original of its kind, preserves a portion of the Greek version of the treaty allying the Aetolian League with Rome against Philip V of Macedon—Rome's first alliance in the eastern Mediterranean. The inscription is especially valuable for the details it adds to the accounts of Livy (see earlier) and Polybius (xviii.xxxviii).

SEG, vol. XIII, no. 382; 212 or 211 B.C.

. . . If any cities of those [enemy] nations are seized by force by the Romans, as far as the Roman people are concerned the Aetolian people may take possession of those cities and their territories; whatever [movable property] the Romans capture the Romans shall possess. If any of those cities are captured by the Romans and the Aetolians jointly, as far as the Roman people are concerned the Aetolians may take possession of those cities and their territories; whatever they [jointly] capture besides the city, they shall share it equally. If any of those cities capitulates or surrenders [without resistance] to the Romans or the Aetolians, as far as the Roman people are concerned those men and cities and their territories may be admitted by the Aetolians into their league. [The rest is lost.]

67. PEACE TREATY WITH CARTHAGE, 201 B.C.

Polybius, *Histories* xv. xviii; From *LCL*

The principal points of the conditions proposed were as follows: Carthage was to retain all the cities she formerly possessed in Africa[20] before entering on the last war with Rome, all her former territory, all flocks and herds, slaves, and other property. From that day onward the Carthaginians were to suffer no injury, they were to be governed by their own laws and customs and to receive no garrison. These were the lenient conditions; the others of a contrary kind were as follows: reparations were to be made to the Romans for all acts of injustice committed by the Carthaginians during the truce;[21] prisoners of war and deserters

---

20. Carthage thus agreed to cede its possessions in Spain to Rome.

21. This has reference especially to transports and cargoes seized by Carthage during the abortive truce of 203 B.C. (Livy xxx. xxxvii).

who had fallen into their hands at any date were to be delivered up; they were to surrender their ships of war, with the exception of ten triremes, and all their elephants; they were not to make war at all on any nation outside Africa, nor on any nation in Africa without consulting Rome; they were to restore to King Masinissa,[22] within boundaries that should subsequently be assigned, all houses, lands, and cities, and other property which had belonged to him or to his ancestors; they were to furnish the Roman army with sufficient grain for three months and pay the soldiers until a reply arrived from Rome regarding the treaty; they were to contribute 10,000 talents in fifty years, paying 200 Euboeic talents each year; finally, they were to give as surety 100 hostages chosen by the Roman general among their men between the ages of fourteen and thirty.[23]

68. The Settlement with Macedon and Greece

THE PEACE TREATY WITH PHILIP V, 196 B.C.

Livy, *History of Rome* XXXIII. xii–xiii, xxiv. 5–7, xxx; Adapted in part from *LCL*

The enemy had been granted a fifteen days' armistice, and arrangements made for a conference with the king.[24] Before the date fixed for it Quinctius[25] called his allies into consultation and invited their opinions as to the conditions of peace which ought to be imposed. Amynander, king of the Athamanes, briefly stated his view, which was that the terms should be such that Greece should be strong enough, even in the absence of the Romans, to maintain her peace and liberty. The language of the Aetolians was more vindictive. After a brief allusion to the correctness of the Roman commander's action in consulting with those who had been his allies in the war on the question of peace, they went on to aver that he was totally mistaken if he thought he would leave either peace for the Romans or liberty for Greece on a firm footing unless Philip

---

22. King of Numidia in North Africa, ally of the Romans.

23. Other conditions are given in Appian, *Roman History* VIII. liv: Liguria to be evacuated; all garrisons outside the territory left to Carthage to be withdrawn within sixty days; no mercenaries to be recruited from Celts or Ligurians; Africa to be evacuated by the Romans within 150 days; Carthaginian hostages to be released when the treaty is ratified at Rome.

24. The time is 197 B.C., just after Philip's defeat at Cynoscephalae.

25. Titus Quinctius Flamininus, the Roman commander in Greece.

were either put to death or dethroned, either of which alternatives was easy for him if he but chose to make full use of his success.

Quinctius replied that in uttering these sentiments the Aetolians were losing sight of the settled policy of Rome, and were themselves inconsistent. For they, in all previous councils and conferences, had always spoken of conditions for peace and not of waging a war of extermination; and the Romans, in addition to a policy from the earliest times of sparing the conquered, had recently furnished a conspicuous proof of their mercifulness in the peace granted to Hannibal and the Carthaginians. And, the Carthaginians aside, how often had conferences been held with Philip himself? Never had the question of abdication been raised. Because he had been defeated in battle, did that make war an inexpiable offense? An armed enemy one was bound to meet with ruthless hostility; toward the conquered, the mildest possible attitude was the most effective. They deemed the kings of Macedon a menace to the liberty of Greece; but if that kingdom and people were eliminated, the Thracians, the Illyrians, and then the Gauls, fierce and untamed peoples, would pour into Macedonia and into Greece. Let them not, by destroying the closest states, open the way to themselves for greater and more menacing ones.

Here he was interrupted by Phaeneas, the *strategus* of the Aetolian League, who solemnly declared that if Philip escaped this time he would soon start a more serious war. "Stop making a disturbance," snapped Quinctius, "when we should be deliberating. The king will be bound by such terms that he will not be able to start a war."

This council was adjourned, and on the next day Philip came to the spot fixed for the conference, the pass leading to Tempe; and on the following day he was met by a full council of the Romans and their allies. There Philip showed great discretion, and conceding voluntarily those points without which peace could not be obtained, rather than have them wrung from him after argument, he said that he accepted all the conditions commanded by the Romans or demanded by the allies in the previous conference, and would submit everything else to the decision of the senate. . . . It was agreed with Philip that he should hand over his son Demetrius and some of his "king's friends"[26] as hostages, and pay an indemnity of two hundred talents. With regard to other matters, he was to send ambassadors to Rome, and a four months' truce

26. "The king's friends" and "the king's first friends" were honorific titles of the Hellenistic royal courts.

was arranged for this purpose. If peace was not obtained from the senate, it was stipulated that the hostages and money were to be returned to Philip. . . .

About the end of the year . . . envoys arrived both from Titus Quinctius and from King Philip. The Macedonians were conducted outside the city to the *villa publica*[27] and were there furnished quarters and hospitality, and were granted an audience before the senate in the temple of Bellona. Their message was brief, to the effect that the king promised to do whatever the senate ordered. In the traditional manner, a commission of ten was created, with whose advice the commander in the field, Titus Quinctius, should determine the conditions of peace for Philip, and a clause was inserted providing that Publius Sulpicius and Publius Villius, who had been assigned Macedonia as their sphere of action when they were consuls, should be members of the commission. . . .

The ten commissioners arrived from Rome, and on their advice peace was granted to Philip on the following terms:[28] that all the Greek cities which were in Europe and in Asia should have liberty and their own laws; that Philip should withdraw his garrisons from those cities among them which had been under Philip's rule and should hand them over to the Romans, with his troops evacuated, before the time of the Isthmian Games; that he should withdraw also from those cities which were in Asia, namely, Euromum, Pedasa, Bargylia, Iasus, Myrina, Abydus, Thasos, and Perinthus (for it was decided that these too should be free); that, regarding the liberation of the Ciani, Quinctius should communicate to King Prusias of Bithynia the decisions of the senate and of the ten commissioners; that Philip should return to the Romans the prisoners of war and deserters and surrender all his warships with the exception of five and one royal galley of almost unmanageable size, which was propelled by sixteen banks of oars; that he should have a maximum army of 5,000 men, and no elephants at all; that he should wage no war outside Macedonia without the permission of the senate; that he should pay to the Roman people an indemnity of 1,000 talents, half at once and the other half in ten annual installments. Valerius Antias states that a tribute of 4,000 pounds of silver annually for ten years was

27. This building in the Campus Martius was set aside for various state purposes, including the housing of foreign ambassadors.

28. The time is now 196 B.C. What follows is not actually the text of the treaty, but a number of clauses regulating its application.

imposed on the king; Claudius[29] fixes the payments at 4,200 pounds annually for thirty years and 20,000 pounds immediately. The same writer mentions an explicit provision that Philip should not wage war against Eumenes, son of Attalus—he was the new king of Pergamum. Hostages were taken to insure performance, among them Demetrius, the son of Philip. Valerius Antias adds that the island of Aegina and the elephants were presented as a gift to Attalus, who was absent; that the Rhodians were given Stratonicea and other cities in Caria which Philip had held; and that the Athenians received the islands of Paros, Imbros, Delos, and Scyros.[30]

THE "LIBERATION" OF GREECE, 196 B.C.

Livy, *History of Rome* XXXIII. xxxi. i–xxxiii.9; Adapted in part from *LCL*

All the Greek cities approved this settlement. Only the Aetolians grumbled (but not openly) and criticized the decision of the ten commissioners. Empty words, they said, had been gotten up into a delusive semblance of liberty; for why were some cities to be delivered to the Romans without being named, and others specifically named to be free without such delivery, unless the purpose was that those which were in Asia were to be set free, being more secure by reason of their remoteness, while those which were in Greece, not being similarly named, were to become Roman property, namely, Corinth, Chalcis, and Oreus, together with Eretria and Demetrias?[31] This charge was not altogether groundless. For there was some uncertainty with respect to Corinth, Chalcis, and Demetrias, because in the decree of the senate, under which the ten commissioners had been sent from Rome, the other cities of Greece and Asia were unequivocally set free, but regarding these three cities the commissioners were instructed to make such decisions and take such action as the circumstances warranted, in keeping with the interests of the state and with their own good faith. It was King Antiochus they had in mind; they had no doubt that he would invade Europe

29. Claudius Quadrigarius and Valerius Antias were early Roman annalists.

30. The terms of the treaty as stated by Livy should be compared with Polybius XVIII. xliv. Clauses found in Livy but not contained in Polybius are generally regarded as unreliable. This applies to the clauses on permissible armed forces and wars outside Macedonia, and to the versions of Claudius and Antias.

31. This marks the beginning of the disaffection of the Aetolians, Rome's first ally in the Hellenistic world. Considering their legitimate aspirations flouted in the peace imposed by the Romans, the Aetolians sought to vindicate their claims by an alliance with Antiochus against Rome. See § 69.

as soon as he deemed his forces adequate, and they did not wish to leave such strategically located cities open for him to occupy.

Quinctius with the ten commissioners moved from Elatea to Anticyra and thence to Corinth. There plans for the liberation of Greece were discussed almost every day at meetings of the ten commissioners. Quinctius urged repeatedly that all Greece should be set free if they wished to stop the tongues of the Aetolians, create genuine affection and respect for the Roman name among all the Greeks, and convince them that they had crossed the sea to liberate Greece and not to transfer dominion from Philip to themselves. The others said nothing opposed to this as regards the freedom of the cities, but they believed it safer for the Greeks themselves to remain for a while under the protection of Roman garrisons than to receive Antiochus as lord in place of Philip. Finally, this decision was reached. Corinth was to be given back to the Achaeans, but a garrison would remain in Acrocorinth; Chalcis and Demetrias were to be held until the anxiety about Antiochus had passed.

The appointed time of the Isthmian Games was now at hand. . . . On this occasion it was not the usual attractions alone which drew the people from every part of Greece; they were in a keen state of expectancy, wondering what the future status of the country would be and what fortune awaited themselves. All sorts of conjectures were silently formed and openly expressed as to what the Romans would do, but hardly anyone was persuaded that they would withdraw from Greece altogether.

When the spectators had taken their seats, the herald, as is the custom, stepped forward accompanied by a trumpeter into the middle of the arena where the games are regularly opened with a customary ritual chant. A blast of the trumpet produced silence, and the herald made the following announcement:

"The Roman senate and Titus Quinctius their general, having conquered King Philip and the Macedonians, decree that the Corinthians, the Phocians, all the Locrians, the island of Euboea, the Magnesians, the Thessalians, the Perrhaebians, and the Achaeans of Phthiotis shall be free, exempt from tribute, and subject to their own laws." This list comprised all the states which had been subject to King Philip.

When the herald had finished his proclamation the feeling of joy was too great for men to take it all in. They could scarce believe they had heard aright and gazed wonderingly at one another, as though it were an empty dream. Hardly trusting their ears, they asked those nearest how their own interests were affected, and as every one was eager not only to hear but also to see the announcer of their freedom, the herald was recalled and he read the same announcement again. Then they realized that the joyful news was true, and from the storm of applause and repeated cheers that arose it was perfectly evident that none of life's blessings is dearer to the masses than liberty.

THE ROMANS EVACUATE GREECE, 194 B.C.

Livy, *History of Rome* XXXIV. xlviii. 3, xlix. 4–lii. 1; Adapted from *LCL*

In the beginning of the spring [194 B.C.] Quinctius summoned a council and went to Corinth. There he addressed the embassies of all the states, gathered around as for an assembly. . . . After reviewing the past he added that it was his intention to leave for Italy and take his entire army with him; within ten days they would hear that the garrisons had been evacuated from Demetrias and Chalcis, and under their very own eyes he would turn over Acrocorinth to the Achaeans free from troops, that all might know whether the habit of lying belonged to the Romans or the Aetolians, who in all their talk had spread abroad the notion that the cause of liberty had been unwisely entrusted to the Roman people, and that the Greeks had only changed their Macedonian for Roman masters. . . .[32]

When they heard these words, as from a father's lips, tears of joy dropped from every eye, so that they even interrupted him in the midst of his speech. . . . Then, when they had become silent, he asked them that any Roman citizens who might be in slavery in their states should be sought out and sent to him in Thessaly within two months; it was unbecoming even for themselves that the liberators should be slaves in the land they had set free. All cried out that they owed him thanks for this too, among other things, because he had reminded them to perform so just and necessary an obligation. There was a great number of captives of the Punic War, whom Hannibal had sold when they were not ransomed by their relatives [see § 65, first selection]. An indication of their number is Polybius' statement that freeing them cost the Achaeans alone one hundred talents, even though they had fixed the price per head to be paid the owners at only five hundred *denarii*. On this reckoning

---

32. This was, of course, the case (see, e.g., § 69 and chapter 6), and the fact is given frequent and varied expression in ancient literature. Thus Plutarch writes (*Life of Flamininus* x. 2) that the Aetolians "asked the Greeks whether they were happy to have a heavier but smoother fetter than their former one, and whether they admired Titus [Flamininus] as a benefactor because he had removed the shackle from the foot of Greece and put it around her neck."

Achaea had 1,200 of them, and you can calculate proportionally how many there probably were in all Greece.[33]

The meeting had not been dismissed when they saw the garrison coming down from Acrocorinth, marching towards the gate, and departing. The general followed the column with all the assembly attending him and acclaiming him their savior and liberator; and when he had taken leave of them and dismissed them, he returned to Elatea over the same route by which he had come. Thence he sent his lieutenant Appius Claudius away with all his troops, with orders to march through Thessaly and Epirus to Oricum and await him there, for it was his intention to transport the army thence to Italy. He also wrote to his brother Lucius Quinctius, his lieutenant and fleet commander, to assemble transports there from all the coast of Greece. . . .

He continued his journey to Thessaly, where the states needed not only to be set free but also to be brought into some reasonable form of government after all the chaos and confusion. For they had been thrown into confusion by the faults of the times and the king's lawless and violent behavior as well as by the restless character of the people, which from the earliest times down to the present day has never conducted a meeting or an assembly or a council without dissension and rioting. He chose the senate and magistrates chiefly from the propertied classes, thus placing power in the hands of that element in the states to whose interest it was to have everything peaceful and quiet.

When he had thus completed the organization of Thessaly, he came through Epirus to Oricum, whence he planned to sail for Italy.

69. The Peace Treaty with the Aetolian League, 189 B.C.

In 191 B.C. King Antiochus of Syria was defeated by the Romans at Thermopylae and driven from Greece, and shortly thereafter the Aetolians, his principal supporters in Greece, surrendered unconditionally. The treaty with the Aetolian League was concluded two years later. The peace terms are recited also by Livy (XXXVIII. xi), whose account, though possibly approximating the actual language of the treaty more closely, is slightly less complete. Polybius' version is therefore given here, even though it is broken by two short lacunae; the wording for these, indicated below by

---

33. In the triumph later celebrated by Flamininus at Rome these liberated men followed the commander's chariot, displaying shaven heads as a symbol of their rescue.

brackets, is supplied from Livy. The terms of this treaty should be compared with those of the Treaty of Apamea concluded with Antiochus the following year (§ 70).

Polybius, *Histories* XXI. xxxii; Adapted from *LCL*

When the senate had passed its decree and the people also had approved, the peace was ratified. The terms of the treaty were as follows:

"The people of Aetolia [shall uphold in good faith] the empire and majesty of the Roman people.[34] They shall not permit to pass through their territories and cities, or furnish with any supplies by public consent, any army being led against the Romans or their allies and friends. [They shall count the enemies of the Roman people their enemies], and on whomsoever the Romans make war the people of Aetolia shall likewise make war. The Aetolians shall restore the deserters, fugitives, and prisoners belonging to the Romans and their allies, excepting such as after being made prisoners of war returned to their own country and were later recaptured a second time, and such as were enemies of the Romans during the time when the Aetolians were fighting in alliance with Rome; the above are to be surrendered to the prefect [i.e., the Roman official] in Corcyra within a hundred days of the peace being sworn; but if some are not found within that time, they shall be surrendered without fraud whenever they are discovered, and they shall not be permitted to return to Aetolia after the peace has been sworn.

"The Aetolians shall pay at once to the consul in Greece two hundred Euboeic talents of silver not inferior to the Attic (they may, if they wish, pay a third of the sum in gold at the rate of one gold *mina* for ten silver *minae*), and for the first six years after the treaty is sworn fifty talents annually, this sum to be delivered in Rome. The Aetolians shall surrender to the consul forty hostages for six years, none less than twelve nor more than forty years of age, whomever the Romans select,[35] but they shall not include a *strategus*, hipparch, public secretary, or any one who has previously served as hostage in Rome; these hostages, too, are to be delivered in Rome, and any one of them who dies is to be replaced.

"Cephallenia shall be excepted from the terms of the treaty. The Aetolians shall recover none of the territories, cities, or populations which were formerly under their jurisdiction but were conquered by, or

---

34. On this traditional opening clause of Roman treaties with conquered peoples, see pp. 88–89.

35. "By the consul," according to Livy, who is here no doubt more precise. Cf. Scipio's speech in § 70.

voluntarily submitted to, the Romans during or subsequent to the consulship of Lucius Quinctius and Gnaeus Domitius [192 B.C.]. The city and territory of Oeniadae shall belong to the Acarnanians."

After the oaths had been taken, peace was established on these conditions, and such was the seal finally set on the affairs of Aetolia and of Greece in general.

70. The Peace Treaty with Antiochus III of Syria, 188 B.C.

Antiochus, defeated at Magnesia near the coast of Asia Minor in 190 B.C., fled inland to Apamea, whence he sent envoys to sue for peace. The following selection recites the course of the peace negotiations and the terms of the resultant Treaty of Apamea. The terms of this treaty are preserved in Polybius (XXI. xlii) as well as in Livy. Neither text purports to be an exact copy of the document. Polybius' version was fuller, but the manuscript of this part of his *Histories* is extraordinarily marred by lucunae and omissions. The treaty is therefore given below in the Livian text, with supplements from Polybius inserted in *italics*.

Perhaps the most troublesome problem faced by the Roman senate in the settlement of Asiatic affairs was that of reconciling the conflicting demands of Rome's two leading allies in the eastern Mediterranean, Pergamum and Rhodes, for the cities and lands to be taken from Antiochus in Asia Minor. The decision reached was a compromise division of territory between them according to geographic proximity and certain historic claims. It is worth noting, too, that in order to arrive at this compromise to satisfy the aspirations of Roman allies the senate had to break with the policy of granting freedom and autonomy to all liberated Greek cities, a policy it had publicly espoused less than a decade before (see § 68).

Livy, *History of Rome* XXXVII, xlv. 10–21, lv. 1–lvi. 1, XXXVIII. xxxviii

It had been decided even before the king's envoys arrived what reply should be given them. Scipio Africanus was to be the spokesman,[36] and he is reported to have spoken to the following effect:

"Out of the things which were in the power of the immortal gods, we Romans have such as they have given us; but our souls, which are subject to the will of our minds we have kept and still keep unchanged

---

36. He was serving as lieutenant to his brother Lucius, the commander in this campaign.

in every kind of fortune: prosperity has not puffed them up nor has adversity depressed them. To mention no others, I would offer you your Hannibal[37] as a proof of this if I could not cite yourselves as an example. After we had crossed the Hellespont, before we saw the king's camp, before we saw his battle line, while the contest was still undecided and the outcome of the war undetermined, when you came to treat of peace we offered you conditions as between equal powers. Now that we are the victors and you the vanquished, we still offer you the same terms —stay out of Europe and withdraw from all of Asia on this side of the Taurus Mountains. In addition, for the expenses incurred in this war you will pay us 15,000 Euboeic talents, 500 down, 2,500 when the Roman senate and people have confirmed the peace, and then 1,000 talents annually for twelve years. It is our will that 400 talents be paid also to Eumenes [king of Pergamum], as well as the balance of the grain which was due his father. When we have agreed on these conditions, it will be some guarantee to us that you will carry them out if you will give us twenty hostages, to be selected by us; but never will it be quite clear to us that the Roman people is at peace in any place where Hannibal shall be, and before all else we demand his surrender. You will also give up Thoas the Aetolian, the provoker of the Aetolian War, who instigated both you and the Aetolians, in reliance upon each other to take up arms against us; and with him you will hand over Mnasilochus the Acarnanian, and Philo and Eubulidas of Chalcis. The king will make peace with his fortunes at a lower ebb, because he does so later than he could have done. If he delays now, let him be assured that it is harder to drag the majesty of monarchs down from its topmost pinnacle to a moderate position than to hurl it from that stage to the lowest depths."

The envoys had been sent by the king with instructions to accept any terms of peace. Arrangements were accordingly made for the dispatch of ambassadors to Rome. The consul distributed his army in winter quarters at Magnesia on the Maeander, at Tralles, and at Ephesus. A few days later the hostages from the king were delivered to the consul at Ephesus, and the envoys who were to go to Rome arrived. Eumenes also left for Rome, at the same time as the ambassadors of the king. They were followed by delegations from all the peoples of Asia . . .

37. Hannibal, forced to flee from Carthage, had taken refuge with Antiochus and lent him some assistance in his war against Rome. After Antiochus' defeat he fled to the court of King Prusias of Bithynia, where he committed suicide when the Romans once again demanded that he be surrendered (183 B.C.).

[The envoys reached Rome early in 189 B.C. The senate met and heard first the Roman legate representing Lucius Scipio, then Eumenes, and next the Rhodians.]

After the Rhodians, the envoys from Antiochus were called in. They took the usual line of those who asked for pardon and, after acknowledging that the king was in the wrong, implored the senators to let their decision be guided more by their own clemency than by the fault of the king, for he had suffered punishment enough, and even more than enough. They concluded by begging the senate to confirm by their authority the peace granted by the general Lucius Scipio, on the terms which he had imposed. The senate voted that this peace should stand, and a few days later it was ratified by order of the assembly. The formal treaty ceremonies were concluded in the Capitol with Antipater, son of the king's brother, who was the head of the delegation.

After this, audience was given to other deputations from Asia. To all of these the same reply was given, namely that the senate, in accordance with long-standing custom, would send ten commissioners who would act as referees and settle affairs in Asia along the following general lines: the territory on this side of the Taurus Mountains which had been within the limits of Antiochus' kingdom would be assigned to Eumenes, except for Lycia and Caria as far as the Maeander River, which were to be annexed to the Rhodian state; the other cities of Asia which had been tributary to Attalus were to continue to pay tribute to Eumenes, but those which had been tributary to Antiochus were to be free and exempt from tribute.[38]

The ten commissioners chosen were: Quintus Minucius Rufus, Lucius Furius Purpurio, Quintus Minucius Thermus, Appius Claudius Nero, Gnaeus Cornelius Merula, Marcus Junius Brutus, Lucius Aurunculeius, Lucius Aemilius Paullus, Publius Cornelius Lentulus, and Publius Aelius Tubero. They were given full authority over questions of detail which had to be settled on the spot; the overall settlement was determined by the senate. . . .

In accordance with the decision of the ten commissioners the treaty with Antiochus was drawn up in language approximately as follows.

38. This provision, here somewhat elliptical, is put more precisely in Livy's description (*History of Rome* XXXVIII. xxxix. 7–8) of the final dispositions made by the ten commissioners in 188 B.C.: "The cities which had been tributary to King Antiochus but had sided with the Roman people were granted freedom from taxation; those which had been partisans of Antiochus or tributaries of King Attalus were all ordered to pay tribute to Eumenes."

"There shall be *perpetual* friendship between King Antiochus and the Roman people on these terms and conditions:

"The king shall not permit any army intending to wage war on the Roman people or their allies to pass through the territories of his kingdom or of those who are subject to him, nor aid it with provisions or any other assistance; the Romans and their allies shall provide the same guarantee to Antiochus and those under his sway. Antiochus shall not have the right to wage war upon those who dwell in the islands, or to cross over into Europe. He shall withdraw from the cities, villages, and forts on this side of the Taurus Mountains as far as the Halys river and from all between the Taurus valley and the mountain ridges that descend to Lycaonia.[39] From these towns, lands, and forts he shall not carry away anything except the arms *borne by his soldiers*; if he has carried anything away he shall duly restore each object to the place where it belongs. He shall not receive any soldier or any other person from the kingdom of Eumenes. If there are with King Antiochus *in his army* or within the boundaries of his realm any citizens of those cities which are passing from his rule, they shall all return to Apamea before a designated day; if any of Antiochus' subjects are with the Romans and their allies, they shall be at liberty to depart or remain. He shall restore to the Romans and their allies their slaves, whether fugitives or prisoners of war, and whatever free men he may have, whether captives or deserters. He shall surrender all his elephants *now in Apamea* and acquire no others. He shall likewise surrender his ships of war and their gear, and shall possess not more than ten decked ships and ten(?) merchant vessels, none of which shall be propelled by more than thirty oars, and no moneres[40] for any war which he may wish to begin. He shall not sail west of Cape Calycadnum and Cape Sarpedonium, except for ships carrying payments of tribute, or envoys, or hostages. King Antiochus shall not have the right to hire mercenary troops from those nations which are under Roman rule, nor even to accept volunteers[41] therefrom.

"Such houses and buildings as the Rhodians and their allies own within the kingdom of Antiochus shall belong to the Rhodians and their

---

39. On the boundaries here stipulated, Livy's text is uncertain, that of Polybius lost. The version given here—which seems to us the most generally satisfactory—is the rendering of the text of Livy supplied by W. R. Paton in his translation of Polybius (Loeb Classical Library, 5:335).

40. A vessel with one man to each oar.

41. Polybius says "fugitives."

allies by the same right as before *he made* war *on them;* if any moneys are due them, they shall have the right to exact payment; if anything has been taken away from them, they shall likewise have the right of search, identification, and recovery; *merchandise being shipped to Rhodes shall be free from duties, as before the war.* If any of the cities which are to be surrendered are held by persons to whom they were given by Antiochus, he shall withdraw the garrisons from them also, and shall see to it that they are duly surrendered; *and if any cities afterwards wish to desert to him, he shall not receive them.* He shall pay 12,000 Attic talents of prime silver in equal installments over twelve years—the talent to weigh not less than 80 Roman pounds—and 540,000 modii of wheat. To King Eumenes he shall pay 350 talents within five years, *paying 70 talents a year at the same time that is fixed for his payments to Rome,* and in lieu of the grain its value in money *by his own estimation,* namely, 127 talents *and 1,208 drachmas, which Eumenes has agreed to accept as a sum satisfactory to himself. If any moneys paid by him do not correspond to the above stipulations, he shall make good the discrepancy in the following year.*

"Antiochus shall give the Romans twenty hostages, none less than eighteen nor more than forty-five years of age, and he shall exchange them for others every three years. If any of the allies of the Roman people, *against whom Antiochus is forbidden by this treaty to make war,* shall without provocation launch a war against Antiochus, he shall have the right to resist their attack by force of arms, provided that he neither hold any city by the laws of war nor receive any into friendship. Disputes shall be settled by legal procedures or, if both parties shall so desire, by war."

Also included in this treaty were a clause calling for the surrender of Hannibal the Carthaginian, Thoas the Aetolian, Mnasilochus the Acarnanian, and Eubulidas and Philo the Chalcidians;[42] and a provision allowing additions, deletions, and changes that might seem desirable in the future to be made without invalidating the treaty.[43]

---

42. In Polybius' text this clause appears immediately following that calling for the surrender of captives and deserters and includes, in addition to the men here named, "all Aetolians who have held public office."

43. This concluding clause, as given by Polybius, reads as follows: "If both parties desire by joint decision to add any clauses to this treaty or to delete any, they may do so."

71. THE CHARGES AGAINST PERSEUS

In 172 B.C. the Romans sent five envoys to Genthius, the Illyrian king, and the cities of Greece to exhort them to active participation on the Roman side in the war that now clearly impended with Macedon. The inscription given below, though incomplete at the top and bottom and otherwise badly mutilated, can nevertheless be clearly recognized as part of a letter sent by Roman officials—presumably Quintus Marcius Philippus and Aulus Atilius Serranus, the legates assigned to cover central Greece—to the Amphictyons at Delphi, who inscribed and set it up in 171 B.C. The extant portion of the document is a kind of bill of particulars, charging King Perseus with fifteen separate infractions of the peace and acts of preparation for war. The purpose of this letter was obviously to counteract Perseus' attempts in previous years to win popularity in Greece, especially among the lower classes; accordingly, the accusations against Perseus are skillfully calculated for maximum propaganda effect on the Greeks. The inscription affords confirmation of Livy's record of charges against Perseus (XLII. xi–xiii, xxx, xl).

Dittenberger, no. 643 (=RDGE, no. 40)

Contrary to what is proper, Perseus came to Delphi with his army during the Pythian truce; and it was altogether wrong to permit him to enter or to participate in the oracular rituals, the sacrifices, the games, and the Amphictyonic Council of the League of the Hellenes. He called in the barbarians who dwell across the Danube[44]—those who also on an earlier occasion [279 B.C.], massing for no good purpose but in order to enslave all the Greeks, invaded Greece and marched against the shrine of the Pythian Apollo at Delphi, intending to plunder and destroy it; but they received a fitting punishment from the god and most of them perished. He broke the sworn treaty concluded between us and his father, and renewed by him. He made war on the Thracians, our friends and allies, and drove them from their homes. Abrupolis, whom we included in the treaty with him as our friend and ally, he expelled from his kingdom. Of the ambassadors sent to Rome by the Greeks and the kings concerning an alliance, he drowned the Thebans and attempted to put others out of the way by other means. Indeed, he came to such a point of madness that he planned to get rid of our senate by poison. The Dolopians were deprived of their freedom through his attacks. In Aeto-

---

44. That is, the Bastarnians (cf. Livy XLI. xix. 4–6, xxiii. 12).

lia he plotted war and murder and threw the whole people into internal strife and disorder. Throughout Greece he went on committing the foulest deeds, taking back those exiled from the cities, and planning other evils. He undermined the leading men and cultivated the masses, promising cancellation of debts and launching revolutions, thus making perfectly plain his policy toward the Greeks and the Romans.[45] As a result the Perrhaebians, the Thessalians, and the Aetolians fell into irremediable misfortunes, and the barbarians became an even more terrifying threat to the Greeks. Being long since desirous of a war against us, so that while we were thus rendered helpless, he might enslave all the Greek cities with no one to oppose him, he bribed Genthius, king of the Illyrians, to rise against us. King Eumenes, our friend and ally, when he visited Delphi to fulfill a vow, he plotted to kill through the agency of Evander, recking naught of the protection vouchsafed by the god to all who come to his sanctuary and disregarding the fact that the sanctity and inviolability of the city of Delphi have been acknowledged by all men, Greeks and barbarians, since the beginning of time.

72. THE MEDITERRANEAN WORLD ON THE EVE OF THE WAR WITH PERSEUS

In this passage Livy vividly depicts how the Third Macedonian War involved not merely the two contending powers but, directly or indirectly, the entire Hellenistic world. Particularly noteworthy is the statement on the social situation in the Greek cities, where a sharp cleavage prevailed. The propertied ruling classes naturally favored Rome, their supporter and protector, while the lower classes and have-nots in general, who consistently favored Rome's enemies, enthusiastically sided with

---

45. Cf. Polybius xxv. iii. 1–4: "Perseus, immediately after renewing his alliance with Rome, began to aim at popularity in Greece, calling back to Macedonia fugitive debtors and those who had been banished from the country either by sentence of the courts or for offenses against the king. He posted up lists of these men at Delos, Delphi, and the temple of Itonian Athena [in Thessaly], promising not only safety to such as returned, but the recovery of the property they had left behind them. In Macedonia itself he relieved all who were in debt to the crown and released those who had been imprisoned for offenses against the crown. By these actions he aroused the expectations of many, as he seemed to hold out good hopes to all the Greeks." Similarly, Livy XLII. xiii. 8–9: "He traversed Thessaly and Doris with his army, in order that he might in their civil war aid the worse cause and crush the better, he threw everything in Thessaly and Perrhaebia into confusion and turmoil by the prospect of abolition of debts, in order that with the band of debtors bound to him he might overthrow the ruling nobility." (Both quotations from the Loeb Classical Library.)

Perseus, who in recent years had been cultivating their support by championing revolutionary measures for the relief of economic and social distress (see § 71).

Livy, *History of Rome* XLII. xxix. 1–xxx. 7

As Publius Licinius and Gaius Cassius began their consulship [171 B.C.], not only the city of Rome and the land of Italy, but all kings and states throughout Europe and Asia as well were preoccupied with the approaching war between Rome and Macedonia. Eumenes, in addition to his long-standing enmity toward Macedonia, now had a fresh incentive to his hostility in his narrow escape from being slaughtered like a sacrificial victim at Delphi through Perseus' foul treachery [cf. § 71]. Prusias, the king of Bithynia, had decided to take no part in the conflict, but await the outcome; he felt sure that the Romans could not think it right that he should bear arms against his brother-in-law, and that if Perseus were victorious he would secure forgiveness through his sister. Ariarathes, king of Cappadocia, had already promised to assist the Romans on his own account, and now that he was connected with Eumenes by marriage he associated himself with all his policies, both in peace and in war.

Antiochus was threatening the kingdom of Egypt, contemptuous of the boy-king[46] and his inept guardians. He thought that, by asserting his claim to Coele-Syria, he would have a good pretext for war, and that he would wage it without hindrance while the Romans were occupied with the Macedonian war—for which, however, he had zealously promised all assistance both to the senate through his own envoys and personally to the envoys of the senate. Ptolemy, because of his youth, was under the tutelage of others; his guardians were preparing war with Antiochus in order to retain possession of Coele-Syria, and were at the same time promising to give the Romans all assistance in their war with Macedonia.

Masinissa was helping the Romans with grain, and was preparing to send to the war a force of elephants, under the command of his son, Misagenes. He had, however, laid his plans to meet any turn of fortune: if victory fell to the Romans, his own situation would remain as it was, and he would not be able to make any move to expand farther, for the Romans would not allow any aggression against the Carthaginians; if the power of Rome, which then protected the Carthaginians, was bro-

46. Ptolemy VI Philometor, who was about sixteen years old at this time.

ken, all Africa would be his. Genthius, king of the Illyrians, had made
the Romans suspicious of him, though he had not actually decided
which side he would support, and he seemed likely to align himself with
one side or the other from impulse rather than calculation. The Thracian
Cotys, king of the Odrysae, secretly sided with Macedonia.

Such were the views which the monarchs took of the war. Among
the free nations and peoples the masses everywhere were almost all, as
usual, for the worse side, and favored the king and the Macedonians [cf.
§ 71 and note 45]; among the ruling classes one could discern conflicting
sympathies. One group went so far in their admiration of the Romans
that they impaired their influence by their excessive partiality; a few of
these were attracted by the justice of Roman rule, but most were motivated by the prospect of being made powerful in their own cities if they
rendered the Romans zealous and conspicuous service. A second group
were toadies of the king; some were driven headlong into revolutionary
projects by the pressure of debt and the hopelessness of their condition
if things should remain as they were, others by sheer caprice, simply
because the breeze of popular favor was blowing in Perseus' direction.
A third group, comprising the worthiest and most sensible men, if
merely a choice of masters were given them, preferred to be ruled by
the Romans rather than by Perseus; but if they had a free choice of
circumstances, they wished neither side to become the more powerful
through crushing the other, but rather that, with the strength of both
undiminished, a lasting peace might be established through a balance of
power; for the cities, placed between the two, this would be the opti-
mum situation, since one power would always protect the weak from
injury at the hands of the other. Holding these sentiments, they watched
silently from a safe position the rivalries of the partisans of both sides.[47]

73. DECLARATION OF WAR AGAINST PERSEUS,
171 B.C.

Livy, *History of Rome* XLII. xxx. 8–11

On the day they entered office the consuls, in accordance with a decree
of the senate, offered sacrifices of larger victims at all the shrines in
which banquets for the gods were customarily spread during the greater

47. Livy's lack of pro-Roman bias in describing this "neutral" group is probably due to his having
taken this material from Polybius, who was an advocate of the balance-of-power policy.

part of the year; then, interpreting the omens as signifying that their prayers had been accepted by the immortal gods, they reported to the senate that the sacrifices and prayers for the war had been duly made. The *haruspices* advised that if any new enterprise was to be begun it should be speeded on, for all the portents pointed to victory, triumph, and expansion of empire. With the prayer that it might be good, auspicious, and propitious to the Roman people, the senate ordered the consuls to summon a meeting of the centuriate assembly on the first possible day and submit the following resolution to the people:

"Whereas Perseus, son of Philip, king of Macedonia, contrary to the treaty concluded with his father Philip, and renewed with himself after the death of his father, has taken up arms against allies of the Roman people, has devastated their fields and seized their cities;

"And whereas he has initiated plans for preparing war against the Roman people, and has to this end gotten together arms, soldiers, and ships:

"Therefore be it resolved that, unless he gives satisfaction for these things, war be undertaken against him."

74. THE POLITICAL SETTLEMENT OF MACEDONIA

To prevent another resurgence of Macedon as a first-rate power, the Romans in 167 B.C. made a new application of their long-effective method of "divide and rule" by abolishing the monarchy and breaking the country up into four autonomous republics sealed off from one another by rigid social and economic barriers.

Livy, *History of Rome* XLV. xxix

Aemilius [Paullus] had ordered ten leaders from each community to assemble at Amphipolis, and all archives and documents wherever deposited and all money belonging to the realm to be brought thither on a given day. When the day arrived he took his seat on the tribunal, together with the ten commissioners. . . .

After the herald had called for silence, Paullus, speaking in Latin, explained the arrangements decided upon by the senate and by himself on the advice of the ten commissioners; the praetor Gnaeus Octavius, who was also present, translated the address into Greek.

First of all it was laid down that the Macedonians were to be a free people, possessing their cities and fields as before, enjoying their own laws, and electing annual magistrates; and they were to pay to the Roman people half the tribute which they had been paying to the king. Secondly, Macedonia was to be broken up into four separate cantons.

[The boundaries of the four cantons, defined in what follows, are here omitted.]

Aemilius then designated the capital cities of the cantons, where the councils were to be held: Amphipolis in the first canton, Thessalonica in the second, Pella in the third, and Pelagonia in the fourth. There, by his order, the councils of the several cantons were to be convoked, the public moneys deposited, and the magistrates elected. He announced next that no one was permitted to marry or to purchase land or buildings outside the boundaries of his own canton. The gold and silver mines were not to be worked,[48] but the iron and copper mines might; those working the mines would have to pay one half the tax which they had paid to the king. The use of imported salt was also forbidden. To the Dardanians, who claimed Paeonia on the ground that it had once been theirs and bordered on their territory, the consul announced that he was granting liberty to all who had been under the rule of Perseus. But after refusing them Paeonia, he granted them the right to purchase salt: he ordered the third canton to carry it down to Stobi in Paeonia, and he fixed the price. He forbade the Macedonians either to cut timber for shipbuilding themselves, or to allow others to do so. He granted permission to those cantons which bordered on the barbarians—which meant all but the third canton—to maintain armed garrisons on their frontiers.[49]

75. Rome Commands the Entire Mediterranean World

With Syria subdued twenty years earlier and Egypt virtually a Roman protectorate, the final defeat of Macedon in 168 B.C. established beyond question Roman domination of the eastern half of the Mediterranean, as the wars with Carthage had previously established it in the western half.

48. The gold and silver mines were reopened in 158 B.C. All the mines and royal estates of Macedonia became the property of the Roman state in 167 B.C.

49. In the terms of the settlement originally laid down by the Senate (Livy XLV. xvii. 7–xviii. 8) the leasing of crown lands was abolished. A settlement similar to that described in this selection was made in Illyria.

Nothing illustrates this fact in sharper relief than the famous story of the circle of Popilius Laenas, given below. This event, which occurred a few weeks after the defeat of the Macedonians at Pydna, understandably enjoyed a great vogue among the Romans (cf. Livy XLV. xii). For further details, see the analysis of the events here involved by J. W. Swain, in *Classical Philology* (1944), 39:73–94.

Polybius, *Histories* XXIX. xxvii

When Antiochus had advanced to attack Ptolemy in order to possess himself of Pelusium, he was met by the Roman commander Gaius Popilius Laenas. Upon the king greeting him orally from some distance and holding out his right hand to him, Popilius answered by holding out the tablet which contained the decree of the senate and bade Antiochus read that first—not thinking it right, I suppose, to give the usual sign of friendship until he knew the attitude of the recipient, whether he was to be regarded as friend or foe. But when the king, after reading it, said that he desired to consult with his friends on the situation, Popilius did a thing which was looked upon as offensive and exceedingly arrogant. Happening to have a vine stick in his hand, he drew a circle around Antiochus with it, and ordered him to give his answer to the letter before he stepped out of that ring. The king was taken aback by this haughty proceeding, but after a few moments' hesitation he replied that he would do whatever the Romans demanded. Then Popilius and his aides shook him by the hand, and one and all greeted him warmly.

The contents of the despatch was an order to put an end to the war with Ptolemy at once. Accordingly a stated number of days was allowed him, within which he withdrew his army into Syria, in high dudgeon indeed, and complaining, but yielding to the necessities of the existing circumstances. Popilius and his aides then restored order in Alexandria; and after exhorting the two kings[50] to live in harmony and ordering them at the same time to send Polyaratus to Rome, they sailed to Cyprus, wishing to lose no time in expelling the Syrian troops that were in the island. When they arrived they found that Ptolemy's generals had already sustained a defeat and that things generally in Cyprus were in a turmoil. They quickly made the invading army evacuate the country, remaining there on watch until the forces had sailed off for Syria.

In this way did the Romans save the kingdom of Ptolemy when it

---

50. The two brothers Ptolemy, Philometor and Physcon, on whose rivalry for the Egyptian throne Antiochus had tried to capitalize.

was all but sinking under its disasters, fortune having so disposed the matter of Perseus and Macedonia that when the position of Alexandria and the whole of Egypt had become almost desperate, it was reversed and set right again simply because the fate of Perseus had just been decided. For had this not been so, and had Antiochus not been certain of it, he would never, I think, have obeyed the Roman orders.

76. THE NEW ROMAN DIPLOMACY

In 187 B.C. control over Roman policy was wrested from the hands of the more liberal wing of the senate by the conservative forces led by Cato. The hardening of this new trend in foreign affairs into ever harsher methods during the course of the second century was caused by many factors: the ambitions of members of the senate for lucrative foreign commands, spoils of war, and triumphs; the contact with the intrigues of Hellenistic diplomacy; impatience with and fear of the persistently recur- ring nationalist and revolutionary uprisings; the need for an abundant supply of slave labor on the growing landed estates of the senatorial aristocracy (see § 166); and, finally, the influence of nonsenatorial business interests seeking new fields of exploitation. It was especially with the victory over Perseus, which left the Romans undisputed masters of the Hellenistic world, that this tendency emerged as a policy of terror and cruelty. The final crystallization of this development was the almost fre- netic exploitation that characterized Roman provincial administration in the last century of the Republic. For further manifestations of this ruthless foreign policy see § § 77–80.

Livy, *History of Rome* XLII. xlvii. 1–9

On their return to Rome, Marcius and Atilius[51] reported the results of their mission to the senate in the Capitol. They prided themselves on nothing so much as the way in which they had hoodwinked the king [Perseus] by agreeing on a truce and holding out hopes of peace. He was so fully provided with all the means of war, while they themselves had nothing ready, that all the strategic positions could have been occupied by him before an army was sent over into Greece. The interval of the armistice, however, would make the war an equal combat; he would no longer have the advantage of preparation, and the Romans would begin the war better equipped in every way. In addition, they had succeeded

---

51. On the identity of these men, see § 71. The year is 172 B.C.

by a clever stroke in disrupting the Boeotian League, so that it could never again be united in support of the Macedonians.

A good many of the senators approved of these actions as showing very skillful management. The elder senators, however, and others who had not forgotten the moral standards of earlier days, said that they failed to recognize the traditional Roman character in these negotiations. "Our ancestors," they said, "did not conduct their wars by lurking in ambush and attacking by night, nor by feigning flight and then turning back unexpectedly upon the enemy when he was off guard, and they did not pride themselves on cunning more than on true valor. It was their custom to declare war before waging it, sometimes even giving the enemy notice of the time and place where they would fight. . . . This is the Roman scrupulousness, unlike the cunning of the Carthaginians or the cleverness of the Greeks, who pride themselves more on deceiving an enemy than on overcoming him by force. Occasionally more can be gained for the time being by craft than by courage, but an enemy's spirit is broken for good only when you have compelled him to confess that he has been overcome not by tricks nor by accident, but after a hand-to-hand trial of strength in a just and righteous war."

Such were the views of the older senators, who were not well-pleased with the new overcunning diplomacy; but that portion of the senate which preferred expediency to honor won out, with the result that the previous mission of Marcius was approved.

77. THE SACK OF EPIRUS, 167 B.C.

The incident described in this passage, which took place on the return of Paullus from Greece, is a striking example of the new rapacious and brutal foreign policy of Rome (cf. introduction to § 76). The event is reported also in Plutarch's *Life of Aemilius Paullus* xxix.

Livy, *History of Rome* XLV. xxxiii. 8–xxxiv. 6

Paullus made for Epirus, reaching Passaro on his fifteenth encampment. Anicius' camp was not far, and Paullus sent him a letter telling him not to be disturbed at what was going on, for the senate had granted his army the plunder of the cities of Epirus which had gone over to Perseus. He despatched centurions to each of the cities to say that they had come to lead away the garrisons, so that the Epirots, like the Macedonians, might be free. He summoned ten leaders from each city and ordered them to have the gold and silver brought out into the public square. He then sent cohorts to all the cities, those going to more distant places setting out before those going to nearer ones, so that they might all arrive on the same day. The tribunes and centurions had been instructed as to what they were to do.

Early in the morning all the gold and silver had been brought together, and at the fourth hour the signal was given the soldiers to sack the cities. So great was the booty that 400 *denarii* were appointed to each cavalryman and 200 to each foot soldier, and 150,000 human beings were led away into slavery. Then the walls of the plundered cities were razed; these cities numbered about seventy. The booty was sold, and the soldiers' shares paid out of the proceeds.[52]

78. THE PUNISHMENT OF RHODES, 167 B.C.

The struggle between Rome and Perseus had brought severe distress resulting from the economic dislocations of wartime to Rhodes, Rome's faithful ally of long standing in the Hellenistic world. A popular movement ousted the pro-Roman oligarchy, and the new government proposed in 169 B.C. to negotiate a peace between the warring powers. By thus daring to place their own welfare before unquestioning obedience to Roman wishes, the Rhodians alienated the Roman Senate. When the war had ended in Roman victory, the Rhodians, in fear of reprisals, hastily restored their pro-Roman government and sent an embassy to Rome in 167 B.C. to plead for a return to their old status as Roman allies. The story of this embassy, part of which is given below, is another reflection of the absolute mastery which the Romans now held in the Mediterranean. The Senate's final disposition of the matter was to strip the Rhodians of the territories in Asia Minor granted them after the war with Antiochus (see § 70) and to declare Delos a free port. This last move was the deathblow to Rhodes, as it was intended to be, for it siphoned away to Delos the rich East–West trade that had formerly centered in Rhodes. But in the end this vindictive act boomeranged upon the Romans, for Rhodes no longer possessed the economic resources to maintain the large navy with which she had policed the eastern Mediterranean. As a result piracy once again

---

52. Plutarch (*Life of Aemilius Paullus* xxix. 3) reports the share per soldier as much smaller: "Yet what was given to each soldier, out of so vast a destruction and utter ruin, amounted to no more than eleven drachmas; so that all men could only shudder at the issue of a war where the wealth of a whole people thus divided turned to so little advantage and profit to each particular man."

became rife, and in the course of the next 100 years Rome herself suffered direly at the hands of the pirates and had repeatedly to mount expeditions to drive them from the seas (see § 131).

Livy, *History of Rome* XLV. xxiv. 9–xxv. 4

"You, senators, are now the judges of whether Rhodes is to exist in the world or to be utterly blotted out. The question before you is not one of war, senators; you can begin one, but you cannot continue it, since not a single Rhodian is going to bear arms against you. If you persist in nursing your wrath against us, we shall ask you for time to carry home the tidings of this fatal embassy. All of us, every free person, every man and woman in Rhodes, will then go on board our ships with all the money we possess, and bidding farewell to our national and household gods we shall come to Rome. All the gold and silver, public and private property alike, will be placed in a heap in the Comitium, at the entrance of your senate house, and we shall deliver up to you our persons and those of our wives and children, prepared to suffer here whatever may be in store for us. Far removed from our eyes let our city be sacked and burned. The Romans have it in their power to judge the Rhodians to be enemies; but we too can pass some judgment on ourselves, and we shall never judge ourselves to be your enemies, nor will we commit any hostile act, even if we have to suffer every extremity."

Such was the speech of the Rhodian envoys. At its close they all again prostrated themselves, waving their suppliant olive branches to and fro. At last they rose and left the senate house.

The senators were then asked to state their views. The bitterest opponents of the Rhodians were those who had served in the war in Macedonia as consuls, praetors, or lieutenants. The foremost advocate of the Rhodian cause was Marcus Porcius Cato, who, though naturally stern and inflexible, showed himself on this occasion a lenient and conciliatory senator. I shall not insert here a specimen of his eloquence by reporting what he said, since his written speech is extant, included in the Fifth Book of his *Origins*. The following reply was made to the Rhodians: that they were neither declared to be enemies nor allowed to remain allies.

79. A Roman Atrocity in Spain, 150 B.C.

Servius Sulpicius Galba was praetor of Farther Spain during part of the
war with the Lusitanians that began in 154 B.C. His treacherous annihilation of a disarmed populace, for which he escaped without so much as a
reprimand at Rome (see note 53), is another evidence of the increasing
tendency of Roman foreign policy toward ruthless suppression (see § 76).
A similar atrocity was committed the year before in the Spanish city of
Cauca by the consul Lucius Licinius Lucullus. But the Spaniards, instead
of being crushed by these outrages, were infuriated and for years offered a
tenacious resistance under the leadership of their brilliant guerilla leader
Viriathus. This phase of Spanish opposition to Roman rule came to an end
only in 133 B.C., when their stronghold of Numantia was starved into
submission and destroyed. But there were sporadic outbreaks for the next
century, and it was not until the time of Augustus that Spain could be
declared *provincia pacata,* "a peaceful province."

Appian, Roman History VI. x. 59–60; From LCL

Lucullus, who had made war on the Vaccaei without authority, was
wintering in Turditania. When he discovered that the Lusitanians were
making incursions in his neighborhood he sent out his best lieutenants
and slew about 4,000 of them. He killed about 1,500 others while they
were crossing the straits near Gades. The remainder took refuge on a
hill, and he drew a line of circumvallation around it and captured an
immense number of them. Then he invaded Lusitania, and gradually
devastated it. Galba did the same on the other side. When some of their
ambassadors came to him desiring to renew the very treaty which they
had made with Atilius (his predecessor in the command) and then trans-
gressed, he received them favorably and made a truce, and pretended
even to sympathize with them because they had been compelled by
poverty to rob, make war, and break treaties. "For," said he, "poorness
of soil and penury force you to do these things. But I will give my poor
friends good land, and settle them in fertile country, in three divisions."

Beguiled by these promises they left their own habitations and came
together at the place appointed by Galba. He divided them into three
parts and, showing to each division a certain plain, he commanded them
to remain in this open country until he should come and assign them
their places. When he came to the first division he told them as friends
to lay down their arms. When they had done so he surrounded them

with a ditch and sent in soldiers with swords who slew them all, while they lamented and invoked the names of the gods and the pledges which they had received. In like manner he hastened to the second and third divisions and destroyed them while they were still ignorant of the fate of the first. Thus he avenged treachery with treachery, imitating barbarians in a way unworthy of a Roman. A few escaped, among them Viriathus, who not long afterward became the leader of the Lusitanians and killed many Romans and performed great exploits. But these things happened at a later time, and I shall not relate them now. Galba, being even more greedy than Lucullus, distributed a little of the plunger to the army and a little to his friends, but kept the rest himself, although he was already one of the richest of the Romans. But not even in time of peace, they say, did he abstain from lying and perjury to get gain. Although generally hated, and called to account for his rascalities, he escaped punishment by means of his wealth.[53]

80. THE DESTRUCTION OF CARTHAGE AND CORINTH, 146 B.C.

The "mailed-fist" foreign policy of Rome (see § 76) is strikingly evidenced by the complete destruction, within three months of each other, of two major commercial cities of the Mediterranean, Carthage in the west and Corinth in the east. Carthage was razed because of panicky fear of the military revival of Rome's most deadly enemy of the past. According to Livy (*Résumé* LII), the senate decreed the destruction of Corinth because of the outrage done there to Roman envoys. It is more likely that the act was a brutal warning to the ever-troublesome Achaeans.

"DELENDA EST CARTHAGO!"

Plutarch, *Life of Cato* xxv. 1–xxvi. 1

The last of Cato's acts of state is thought to have been the destruction of Carthage. Indeed, it was Scipio the Younger who gave it its deathblow, but it was chiefly on the counsel and advice of Cato that the Romans undertook the war, for the following reason. Cato was sent to the

53. The news of Galba's treachery caused a great stir at Rome. The following year, when Galba returned to the city, the tribune Lucius Scribonius Libo moved to indict him; but though this proposal had the support of the elder statesman Cato, then in the last year of his life, Galba's wealth and influence with the *nobiles* prevailed, and he escaped scot free.

Carthaginians and to Masinissa the Numidian, who were at war with each other, to investigate the causes of their dispute. Masinissa had been a friend of the Roman people from the beginning; and the Carthaginians had entered into treaty relations with Rome after their defeat by Scipio [the Elder], having been deprived of their empire and burdened with a heavy tribute of money. Cato found the city not (as the Romans thought) in distress and low estate but rather possessing an abundance of men of fighting age, overflowing with great wealth, and filled with arms of all kinds and military equipment, and not a little proud of all this. He therefore thought that it was not a time for the Romans to adjust the affairs of Masinissa and the Numidians, but rather that they themselves would again be involved in the same dangers unless they repressed the city which had been Rome's ancient irreconcilable enemy, now so unbelievably grown. Therefore, returning speedily to Rome, he advised the senate that the former defeats and calamities of the Carthaginians had diminished not so much their power as their foolhardiness and were likely to render them not weaker but more experienced in war; that they were but skirmishing with the Numidians to prepare themselves for a contest with the Romans; that the peace and treaty were but names to disguise their postponement of war until a proper occasion presented itself.

Moreover, they say that, shaking his toga, he purposely let drop some African figs in the senate. And then, on their admiring their size and beauty, he said that the country that produced them was only three days' sail from Rome. And he was even more violent in this, that whenever he declared his opinion in the senate on any matter whatsoever he added the following: "And I also think that Carthage must be destroyed."

THE RAZING OF CARTHAGE

Zonaras, *Epitome* IX. xxx (in part); From *LCL*

Thus Scipio took Carthage; and he sent to the senate the following message: "Carthage is taken. What are your orders now?" When these words had been read, they took counsel as to what should be done. Cato expressed the opinion that they ought to raze the city and blot out the Carthaginians, whereas Scipio Nasica still advised sparing the Carthaginians. And thereupon the senate became involved in a great dispute and contention, until some one declared that for the Romans' own sake, if for no other reason, it must be considered necessary to spare them. With this nation for antagonists they would be sure to practice valor instead of turning aside to pleasures and luxury; whereas, if those who were able to compel them to practice warlike pursuits should be removed from the scene, they might deteriorate from want of practice, through a lack of worthy competitors.[54] As a result of the discussion all became unanimous in favor of destroying Carthage, since they felt sure that its inhabitants would never remain entirely at peace. The whole city was therefore utterly blotted out of existence, and it was decreed that for any person to settle upon its site should be an accursed act. The majority of the men captured were thrown into prison and there perished, and some few were sold. But the very foremost men together with the hostages and Hasdrubal and Bithias spent the rest of their lives in different parts of Italy in honorable confinement. Scipio secured both glory and honor and was called Africanus, not after his grandfather but because of his own achievements.

THE SACK OF CORINTH

Pausanias, *Description of Greece* VII. xvi. 7–10; Adapted from *LCL*

As soon as night fell the Achaeans who had escaped to Corinth after the battle fled from the city, and most of the Corinthians fled with them. At first, although the gates were open, Mummius hesitated to enter Corinth, suspecting that some ambush had been laid within the walls. But on the third day after the battle he proceeded to storm Corinth and set it on fire. The majority of those found in it were put to the sword by the Romans, but the women and children Mummius sold into slavery. He also sold all the slaves who had been set free and had fought on the side of the Achaeans but had not fallen at once on the field of battle. The most admired votive offerings and works of art were carried off by Mummius;[55] the less valuable he gave to Philopoemen, the general sent

54. The moralistic concept here attributed to 146 B.C. really developed about a century later. See introduction to § 91.

55. The conquering general, Lucius Mummius, had vowed a temple to Hercules, which he dedicated in Rome a few years later. The dedicatory inscription is extant (*CIL*, vol. I, 2d ed., no. 626 = Dessau, no. 20): "Lucius Mummius son of Lucius, consul. Under his leadership, his auspices, and his command Achaea was taken and Corinth destroyed. He then returned to Rome and was granted a triumph. In recompense for these exploits prosperously achieved, he the commander is the dedicator of this temple and statue of Hercules the Conqueror, which he had vowed in the war."

by Attalus, and even in my day[56] there were Corinthian spoils in Pergamum. In all the cities that had made war against Rome Mummius demolished the walls and disarmed the inhabitants before commissioners were sent from Rome;[57] and when these arrived, he proceeded to put down democracies and establish governments based on property qualifications. Tribute was imposed upon Greece, and those who had money were forbidden to acquire property outside their own state.[58] Ethnic leagues, whether of Achaeans or Phocians or Boeotians or anywhere else in Greece, were likewise all dissolved.[59] A few years later the Romans, taking pity on Greece, restored the old ethnic leagues and the right to acquire property abroad and canceled the fines imposed by Mummius. For he had ordered the Boeotians to pay 100 talents to the people of Heraclea and Euboea, and the Achaeans to pay 200 to the Lacedaemonians. The Greeks obtained from the Romans a remission of these payments, but down to my day a governor continues to be sent to the country.[60]

81. First Mithridatic War: Massacre of Romans and Italians in Asia, 88 B.C.

Appian, *Roman History*, XII. iv. 22–23; From *LCL*

In the meantime Mithridates built a large number of ships for an attack on Rhodes and wrote secretly to all his satraps and the magistrates of the cities that on the thirteenth day thereafter they should set upon all Romans and Italians in their towns, and upon their wives and children and their freedmen of Italian birth, kill them and throw their bodies out

---

56. Latter half of the second century A.D. On the removal of works of art from Greek cities by conquering Romans, see also § 188. Additional details about the art plunder of Corinth are found in Strabo, *Geography* VIII. vi. 23; Velleius Paterculus, *Compendium of Roman History* I. xiii. 4; Pseudo-Dio Chrysostom, *Discourses* XXXVII. xlii.

57. To assist him in planning the political settlement.

58. The same provision is found in the political settlement imposed by the Romans on Macedonia in 167 B.C. (cf. § 74).

59. Pausanias' statement is too sweeping. It is not likely that the Romans dissolved leagues that remained loyal to them.

60. The senatorial commission sent to reorganize Greece at this time made it into a province, but Greece was placed under the administrative authority of the governor of Macedonia, which had been transformed into a province in 148 B.C. Greece retained this status until 27 B.C., when it became a separate province under the name of Achaea.

unburied, and share their goods with King Mithridates. He threatened to punish any who should bury the dead or conceal the living, and proclaimed rewards to informers and to those who should kill persons in hiding. To slaves who killed or betrayed their masters he offered freedom, to debtors who did the same to their creditors, the remission of half of their debt. These secret orders Mithridates sent to all the cities at the same time. When the appointed day came, disasters of the most varied kinds occurred throughout Asia, among which were the following:

The Ephesians tore away the fugitives, who had taken refuge in the sanctuary of Artemis and were clasping the images of the goddess, and slew them. The Pergamenes shot with arrows those who had fled to the sanctuary of Aesculapius, without removing them from the statues to which they were clinging. The people of Adramyttium followed into the sea those who sought to escape by swimming, and killed them and drowned their children. The Caunians, who had been made subject to Rhodes after the war against Antiochus and had been lately liberated by the Romans, pursued the Italians who had taken refuge about the statue of Vesta in the senate house, tore them from the shrine, first killed the children before their mothers' eyes, and then killed the mothers themselves and their husbands after them. The citizens of Tralles, in order to avoid personal responsibility for the crime, hired a savage monster named Theophilus, of Paphlagonia, to do the work. He conducted the victims to the temple of Concord and there murdered them, chopping off the hands of some who were embracing the sacred images. Such was the awful fate that befell the Romans and Italians in Asia, men, women, and children, their freedmen and slaves, all who were of Italian origin.[61] Thus it was made very plain that it was quite as much hatred of the Romans as fear of Mithridates that impelled the Asiatics to commit these atrocities. But they paid a double penalty for their crime — one at the hands of Mithridates himself, who ill-treated them perfidiously not long afterward, and the other at the hands of Cornelius Sulla [see § 83].

61. According to Valerius Maximus, *Memorable Deeds and Sayings* IX. ii, 80,000 Roman citizens lost their lives in the massacre.

82. First Mithridatic War: Roman Supporters in Asia

Dittenberger, no. 741 (= *RDGE*, no. 48)

King Mithridates to the satrap Leonippus, greeting. Whereas Chaeremo, son of Pythodorus, a man most hatefully and belligerently disposed to our state, has always consorted with our most hated enemies, and now learning of my arrival has gotten his sons Pythodorus and Pythio away and has himself fled, do you proclaim that if anyone brings Chaeremo or Pythodorus or Pythio in alive he will receive forty staters, and if anyone brings in the head of any of them he will receive twenty talents.

King Mithridates to Leonippus, greeting, Chaeremo, son of Pytho-dorus, before this got the fugitive Romans away with his sons to Rhodes, and now, learning of my arrival, he has taken refuge in the sanctuary of the Ephesian Artemis, and from there he sends communications to the Romans, the common enemy of all. His impunity for the offenses he has committed is a stimulus for the actions against us. Think how you may, preferably, bring him to us, or how he may be kept under guard in confinement until I am rid of the enemy.

> The city of Ephesus was at first an enthusiastic supporter of Mithridates (see § 81). But after Sulla's initial victories and her experience with the tyranny of Mithridates' rule, Ephesus in 87/86 B.C. returned to the Roman fold and declared war on the king. Despite her action, Sulla imposed a heavy fine on Ephesus in 84 B.C. (see § 83). The following decree of the city carefully avoids reference to her original support of Mithridates.

Dittenberger, no. 742

. . . the people preserving their long-standing good will towards the Romans, the saviors of all, and eagerly agreeing to all their orders. Mithridates, the king of Cappadocia, infringing his treaties with the Romans and mobilizing his forces, attempted to become master of our territory, which in no way belonged to him. And occupying first the cities situated before us, he seized them by treachery, and then also our city, overwhelmed by the size of his forces and the unexpectedness of the attack. But our people, preserving from the beginning its good will towards the Romans, and having seized the opportunity to come to the aid of our common interests, has decided to declare war against Mithridates in behalf of the hegemony of the Romans and the common freedom, all the citizens having, with one accord, consecrated themselves to the struggles for these. Therefore, it was decreed by the people that, since it is a matter of war and the protection, security, and safety of the temple of Artemis and of the city and its territory, the generals and the secretary and the presiding officers of the council should bring in a decree at once, and should make proposals, as are expedient, concerning privileges; and the people acted on this matter. . . .

[The remainder of the inscription contains the decree announcing economic and political privileges of various kinds intended to unify the people —amnesty, extension of citizenship, manumissions, abolition of debts.]

. . . . .

In the war against Mithridates the city of Plarasa-Aphrodisias honored its obligation to assist the Romans. The first of the following inscriptions records the city's decision to send help; the second is the letter of thanks which the Roman general sent to the city after the war's end and his release from captivity. Both documents were inscribed on the theater at Aphrodisias.

J. M. Reynolds, *Aphrodisias and Rome*. no. 2; 88 B.C.

It was decreed by the council and people, on motion by _____:

Whereas Quintus Oppius son of Quintus, praetor proconsul of the Romans, has sent word that Laodicea and he himself are besieged, and the people decided to come to the rescue in force and also to have the non-citizens(?) and slaves join the expedition, and they have also chosen in the assembly a man to serve as leader; and [whereas] it is necessary also to despatch envoys to inform the proconsul regarding the policy which our people has towards the Romans who are [our] saviors and benefactors, and to arrange that any other order which the governor may issue to our city is made clear and carried out;

It has been decreed by the people to chose as envoys men from among those who have been honored [with public office], are men of good faith, and are favorably disposed towards the Romans, and proceeding to Quintus Oppius the proconsul they will inform him of the policy which our people has towards him and towards all Romans, and they will report that not only have we decided to help him in force but have also chosen as the man in charge of our assistance Artemidorus our garlanded magistrate, a man from among those who have been honored and are of good faith, a man outstanding for his skill at arms; and they will inform him that our whole people, together with our wives and children and our whole means of livelihood, is ready to undergo the risk on behalf of Quintus [Oppius] and the Roman cause, and that without the governance of the Romans we prefer even not to live.

J. M. Reynolds, *Aphrodisias and Rome,* no. 3; 85 or 84 B.C.

Quintus Oppius son of Quintus, proconsul of the Romans, praetor, to the magistrates, council and people of Plarasa-Aphrodisias, greeting. _____ son of _____, Antipater son of Adrastus(?), Pereitas son of Apollonius, Artemidorus son of Myon, Dionysius son of Menis and Timocles son of Zeno, your envoys, gentlemen of character, met me in Cos and congratulated me and gave me the decree which plainly showed that you rejoice greatly at my return [from captivity]—which, in view of your good will towards me and our state, I firmly believe, for at the time when I wrote you from Laodicea to send me soldiers you were among the first to send them, and you did that just as it was incumbent upon good allies and friends of the Roman people to do, and I enjoyed the fine and fullest cooperation of the envoys you sent. For these reasons I will exert myself, both in my public office and in my private capacity, in whatever I can, consistent with my bona fides, to be of service and always to be responsible for some good to your city; and I will inform the senate and the people, when I am back in Rome, of the actions you have taken. The same envoys begged that you too be allowed to enjoy my patronage, and I acceded to them and, because of my regard for your city, I will be your people's patron.

83. First Mithridatic War: The Ruin of Greece and Asia

The revolt of the Greeks who followed the banner of Mithridates in 88–86 B.C. left Greece and Asia Minor in ruins, for their support of the king led to such staggering reprisals at the hands of the Romans that the Aegean area never effectively recovered from the ensuing economic stagnation and demoralization.

Appian, *Roman History* xii. ix. 61–63; From *LCL*

Having settled the affairs of Asia, Sulla bestowed freedom on the inhabitants of Ilium, Chios, Lycia, Rhodes, Magnesia, and some others, either as a reward for their cooperation, or a recompense for what they had suffered from their loyalty to him, and inscribed them as friends of the Roman people. Then he distributed his army among all the remaining places and issued a proclamation that the slaves who had been freed by Mithridates should at once return to their masters. As many disobeyed and some of the cities revolted, numerous massacres ensued, of both free men and slaves, on various pretexts. The walls of many towns were demolished. Many others were plundered and their inhabitants sold into slavery. The pro-Cappadocian faction, both men and cities, were severely punished, and especially the Ephesians, who with servile adulation of the king had treated the Roman offerings in their temples with indignity. After this a proclamation was sent around commanding the principal citizens of each city to come to Ephesus on a certain day to meet Sulla. When they had assembled, Sulla addressed them from the tribunal as follows:

"We first came to Asia with an army when Antiochus, king of Syria, was despoiling you. We drove him out and fixed the boundaries of his dominions beyond the Halys river and Mount Taurus. We did not retain possession of you when you had become our subjects instead of his, but made you free and autonomous, except that we awarded a few places to Eumenes and the Rhodians, our allies in the war [see § 70], not as tributaries, but as clients. A proof of this is that when the Lycians complained of the Rhodians we freed them from the authority of Rhodes. Such was our conduct toward you. You, on the other hand, when Attalus Philometor left his kingdom to us in his will, gave aid to Aristonicus against us for four years [see §§ 128, 129], until he was captured and most of you, under the impulse of necessity and fear, returned to your duty. Notwithstanding all this, after a period of twenty-four years, during which you had attained to great prosperity and magnificence, public and private, you again became insolent through peace and luxury and took the opportunity, while we were preoccupied in Italy, some of you to call in Mithridates and others to join him when he came. Most infamous of all, you obeyed the order he gave to kill all the Italians in your communities, including women and children, in one day. You did not even spare those who fled to the temples dedicated to your own gods. You have received some punishment for this crime from Mithridates himself, who broke faith with you and gave you your fill of rapine and slaughter, redistributed your lands, canceled your debts, freed your slaves, appointed tyrants over some of you, and committed robberies everywhere by land and sea; so that you learned immediately by experience and comparison what kind of patron you had chosen instead of your former one. The instigators of these crimes paid some penalty to us also. But it is necessary, too, that some punishment should be inflicted upon you in common for doing such things; and it is reasonable that it should be one corresponding to your crimes. But may the Romans never dream of impious slaughter, indiscriminate confiscation, servile insurrections, or other acts of barbarism. From a desire to spare even now the Greek people and name, so celebrated throughout Asia, and for the sake of that fair repute that is ever dear to the Romans, I shall only impose upon you the taxes of five years, to be paid at once, together with what the war has cost me, and whatever else may be spent in settling the affairs of the province. I will apportion these charges to each of you according to cities and will fix the time of payment. Upon the disobedient I shall visit punishment as upon enemies."

After he had thus spoken Sulla apportioned the fine to the delegates and sent men to collect the money. The cities, being in financial straits, borrowed it at high rates of interest and mortgaged their theaters, their gymnasia, their walls, their harbors, and every other scrap of public property, being urged on by the soldiers with contumely. Thus was the money collected and brought to Sulla, and the province of Asia had her fill of misery.

84. Caesar's First Campaign in Gaul, 58 b.c.

This selection from the opening pages of Caesar's *Commentaries* on his wars in Gaul is especially interesting for giving us a Roman view of one of the great migratory movements, which, beginning centuries earlier, began to hammer at the northern frontiers of the Roman Empire about 100 b.c. and created for the Romans in subsequent centuries a frontier problem of steadily growing intensity.

Caesar, *Gallic War* I. i–vi. (abridged), xxix

All Gaul is divided into three parts, one of which the Belgians inhabit, another the Aquitanians, and the third those who in their own language are called Celts, in ours Gauls.[62] All these differ from each other in language, customs, and laws. The River Garonne separates the Gauls from the Aquitanians; the Marne and the Seine separated the Gauls from the Belgians. Of all these the Belgians are the bravest, because they are farthest from the civilization and refinement of our province,[63] and traders least frequently come to them and import those things which tend to enervate their spirit; and they are the nearest to the Germans, who dwell across the Rhine, with whom they are continually waging war. For this reason the Helvetians also surpass the rest of the Gauls in courage, as they contend with the Germans in almost daily battles, when they either repel them from their own territories or themselves wage war in the territories of the Germans. . . .[64]

Among the Helvetians Orgetorix was by far the most famous and wealthy. He, in the consulship of Marcus Messala and Marcus Pupius Piso [61 B.C.], consumed by ambition for royal power, formed a conspiracy among the nobility, and persuaded the people to emigrate from their territories with all their possessions, saying that it would be very easy, since they excelled all in courage, to acquire the supremacy of the whole of Gaul. It was all the easier for him to persuade them to do this because the Helvetians are confined on every side by the nature of the terrain; on the one side by the Rhine, a very broad and deep river, which separates the Helvetian territory from the Germans; on a second side by the Jura, a very high mountain which lies between the Sequanians and the Helvetians; on a third by Lake Geneva and by the River Rhone, which separates our province from the Helvetians. As a result of these circumstances, they did not have much room for movement, and were hampered in making war upon their neighbors. For this reason, fond of war as they were, they were very much grieved. Considering the extent of their population and their renown for warfare and bravery, they thought that their territory was small, although it extended in length 240, and in breadth 180 [Roman] miles.

Induced by these considerations and influenced by the prestige of Orgetorix, they determined to provide such things as were necessary for

62. Caesar does not include the Roman province of Gallia Narbonensis (Provence); cf. note 63.
63. That is, Transalpine (or Narbonese) Gaul.
64. The Helvetians occupied what is now Switzerland.

their expedition: to buy up as great a number as possible of beasts of burden and wagons, to make their sowings as large as possible, so that on their trek they might have an adequate supply of grain, and to establish peace and friendship with the neighboring peoples. They reckoned that a period of two years would be sufficient for them to execute their designs; they fixed by law their departure for the third year. Orgetorix was chosen to complete these arrangements. . . .

[Orgetorix, however, died shortly afterward.]

After his death the Helvetians nevertheless attempted to do what they had resolved upon, namely to emigrate from their territories. When they thought that they were at length prepared for this undertaking, they set fire to all their towns, about twelve in number, to the villages, about four hundred in number, and to the private dwellings that remained; they burned up all the grain except what they intended to carry with them, so that with all hope of returning home destroyed they might be more ready to undergo all dangers. They ordered every one to carry forth from home for himself ready-ground provisions for three months. They persuaded the Raurici, the Tulingi, and the Latovici, their neighbors, to adopt the same plan—to burn down their towns and villages and to set out with them. And they admitted and joined to themselves as allies the Boii, who had lived across the Rhine and had crossed into the Norican territory and assaulted Noreia.

There were in all two routes by which they could go forth from their country: one through the Sequanians, a narrow and difficult one, between Mount Jura and the River Rhone (by which scarcely one wagon at a time could be led; there was, moreover, a very high mountain overhanging, so that a small force could easily stop them); the other through our province, much easier and freer from obstacles, because the Rhone flows between the boundaries of the Helvetians and those of the Allobroges, who had lately been pacified, and is in some places crossed by fords. The farthest town of the Allobroges, and the nearest to the territories of the Helvetians, is Geneva. From this town a bridge extends to the Helvetians. They thought that they would either persuade the Allobroges, because they did not seem as yet well disposed towards the Roman people, or compel them by force to allow them to pass through their territories. Having provided everything for the expedition, they announced a day on which they should all assemble on the bank of the Rhone. This day was the 28th of March, in the consulship of Lucius Piso and Aulus Gabinius [58 B.C.].

[Caesar, regarding the Helvetians as a buffer protecting Roman Gaul and Italy against the Germans, refused to permit them to migrate across the Roman province. When they persisted in their attempt, he attacked them, defeated them swiftly and disastrously, and ordered them back to their homeland.]

In the camp of the Helvetians records were found, drawn up in Greek letters, and were brought to Caesar. In these records a reckoning had been drawn up, name by name, of the number which had gone forth from their country, of those who were able to bear arms, and likewise separately the boys, the old men, and the women.

The total of these items was:

Helvetians	263,000
Tulingi	36,000
Latovici	14,000
Raurici	23,000
Boii	32,000
Total	368,000

Out of these such as could bear arms amounted to about 92,000. When a census of those who returned home was taken, as Caesar had commanded, the number was found to be 110,000.

85. CAESAR'S CONQUEST OF GAUL: AN APPRAISAL

Cicero, *On the Consular Provinces* xii. 30, xiii. 32–xiv. 34

It is my view, members of the senate, that at this time [June, 56 B.C.] in assigning the provinces we ought to take into account a lasting peace. For who does not perceive that all other regions are free from every danger and even a suspicion of war. . . .[65]

The Gallic War, members of the senate, has been prosecuted by the general Gaius Caesar, not merely checked as before. Our generals always thought that those peoples should be repulsed rather than punished in war. The famous Gaius Marius himself, whose divine and extraordinary ability relieved the great affliction and destruction visited upon the Roman people, checked the enormous forces of the Gauls flowing into

65. This is a rhetorical exaggeration.

Italy but did not himself penetrate to their cities and abodes. Recently my colleague in labors, dangers, and plans, Gaius Pomptinus, a very courageous man, smashed by military action a war suddenly started by the Allobroges—a war stimulated by that criminal conspiracy[66]—and he subdued those who had taken aggressive action; and content with this victory, once the state was freed from fear, he abstained from further action.

Gaius Caesar's strategy I see to be far different; for he believed not only that it was necessary to wage war against those who he saw were already in arms against the Roman people, but also that all Gaul must be subjected to our sway. And so he has fought with the fiercest peoples, in gigantic battles against the Germans and Helvetians, with the greatest success. He has terrified, confined, and subdued the rest, and accustomed them to obey the empire of the Roman people; and regions and peoples which no books, no voice, no rumor had made known to us previously were penetrated by our general, our army, and the arms of the Roman people.

Previously, we possessed merely a path through Gaul, members of the senate; the other parts were held by peoples either unfriendly to this empire, or untrustworthy, or unknown, or certainly savage, uncivilized, and warlike—peoples which everyone always desired to be smashed and subdued. Everyone who thought wisely about our state, even from the beginning of this empire, regarded Gaul as a prime danger to this empire, but because of the vigor and great numbers of those peoples war has never been waged previously against all of them. Always we resisted when we had been attacked; now finally this has been accomplished, that the terminus of our empire will coincide with those lands. Previously, nature, not without some divine aid, had fortified Italy with the Alps; for had that avenue of approach lain open to the savage hordes of Gauls, never would this city have provided a home and seat for the greatest of empires. Let the Alps now sink into the earth! For there is nothing beyond those lofty mountains up to the Atlantic Ocean that Italy needs to fear. But one or two more summer campaigns[67] can bind all of Gaul with eternal chains, either through fear or threat of punishment or rewards or arms or laws.

---

66. Cicero is referring to the conspiracy of Catiline, 63–62 B.C. (see § 105). The connection between this revolt and the conspiracy is farfetched.

67. Caesar's Gallic campaigns were not concluded until 50 B.C.

86. The Customs of the Gauls and the Germans

This ethnological digression interpolated by Caesar in his *Commentaries* on his Gallic War should be compared with the more extensive account of the Germans composed by Tacitus some 150 years later. Such descriptions of the life and manners of foreign peoples formed part of ancient historiography from its inception, as may be seen in the work of the "father of history," Herodotus.

Caesar, *Gallic War* VI. xiii–xxiii (abridged)

In all Gaul there are two classes of those men who are of any account and distinction. For the common people are held almost in a condition of slavery and dare undertake nothing by themselves and are admitted to no public deliberations. Most of them, when they are burdened by debt or the size of taxes or the oppression of the more powerful attach themselves in vassalage to the nobles, who possess the same rights over these as masters over slaves. Now of those two classes, one is the druids, the other the knights. The former are engaged in sacred matters, attend to the public and private sacrifices, and interpret religious matters. A great number of young men flock to these for instruction and they are highly honored among them. For they give decisions in almost all disputes, both public and private, and if any crime has been committed, if any murder has occurred, if there is a dispute about an inheritance or about boundaries, the druids decide it, and they make awards and determine penalties. If anyone, either a private individual or a people, does not abide by their decision, they exclude them from sacrifices. This is the severest punishment among them. Those who have been thus excluded are regarded as impious and criminal; all shun them and avoid association and conversation with them, so as not to receive any harm from contact with them. Nor is justice administered to them when they seek it, nor is any honor bestowed upon them. One druid presides over all of them, and he has the highest authority among them. When he dies, if any one of the rest excels in prestige he succeeds, but if there are several of equal prestige, one is elected by the druids; sometimes they even fight for the leadership with weapons. At a fixed time of the year the druids hold meetings in a consecrated place in the territory of the Carnutes, which is considered the central region of all Gaul. Here all who have disputes assemble from all parts and abide by their decisions and judgments. This institution is thought to have originated in Britain and to have been brought over from there to Gaul,[68] and now those who desire to obtain a more precise understanding of it generally go there to study it.

It is the custom of the druids to abstain from war, and they do not pay taxes along with the rest; they are exempt from military service and are free from taxation in respect to all their property. Spurred on by these great privileges, many come together of their own accord to receive the training, and many are sent by their parents and relatives. They are said there to learn by heart a great number of verses. Thus, some remain in training for twenty years. Nor do they regard it as right to record these in writing, although in almost all other matters, in their public and private transactions, they employ the Greek alphabet. This seems to me to have been established for two reasons: because they do not want either their doctrine to be divulged to the common people or their pupils to devote less effort to memory work by relying on writing. . . . They wish especially to inculcate the following, that souls are immortal and pass after death from one body to another, and they regard this as a special incentive to courage, once the fear of death is disregarded. In addition, they discuss and transmit to the youth many things about the stars and their movements, about the size of the world and the earth, about natural science, and about the might and power of the immortal gods.

The other class is the knights. All these, when there is need and some war breaks out (before Caesar's arrival this used to happen almost every year, as they either themselves inflicted wrongs or repelled those being inflicted on them), are engaged in warfare. And the more distinguished in birth and resources one of them is, the greater the number of vassals and clients he has about him. This is the only kind of influence and power they know.

The people of all the Gauls are exceedingly devoted to religious rites. And for this reason those who are afflicted with rather severe diseases or who are engaged in battles and dangers either sacrifice human beings as victims or vow that they will sacrifice them, and they employ the druids to officiate at these sacrifices. Because they think that unless the life of a human being be offered for the life of another they cannot appease the power of the immortal gods, they have sacrifices of this kind established for public purposes. Some have images of immense size woven out of

68. Tacitus (*Agricola* xi) says that druidism was introduced into Britain from Gaul.

twigs, which they fill with living human beings. When these are set on fire, the men perish enveloped in flames. They regard the offering of those who have been apprehended in theft, brigandage, or some other offense as more acceptable to the immortal gods, but when a supply of this kind is lacking, they even resort to offerings of innocent persons. . . .

When they have determined to engage in battle, they generally vow [to their war god] what they capture in war. They sacrifice all captured living beings that may have survived the conflict, and collect the remaining things in one place. In many states one may see mounds of these things heaped up in consecrated places; and it rarely happens that anyone, in disregard of religious obligations, dares either to conceal captured objects in his home or to remove any that have been thus deposited. The most severe punishment, with torture, has been established for this offense. . . .

Whatever sum husbands have received from their wives as dowries, they add to it a like amount from their own property, after making an appraisal. A joint accounting is kept of all this money, and the profits are saved. To the survivor revert the shares of both, together with the profits of the preceding period. Husbands have the power of life and death over their wives as well as over their children; and when the head of a household of a rather distinguished status dies, his relatives assemble and, if the circumstances of his death are suspicious, they hold an investigation of his wives, in the manner of questioning slaves, and if proof is obtained, kill them after subjecting them to fire and every other kind of torture. Their funerals, if one considers the level of culture among the Gauls, are magnificent and costly; and they cast into the fire all the things which they think were dear to their hearts when they were alive, including animals; and a little before our time slaves and clients who were ascertained to have been beloved by them were cremated with them after the regular funeral service was concluded. . . .

The Germans differ much from this mode of life. For they neither have druids to preside over sacred matters nor do they pay much attention to sacrifices. They consider as gods only those whom they perceive and by whose assistance they are obviously benefited, namely, the sun, fire, and the moon. Of the remaining divinities they have not even heard. Their whole life consists of hunting and the pursuit of warfare. From childhood they devote themselves to toil and austerity. Those who have remained chaste the longest have the greatest respect among their people. Some think that the height is increased in this way, others that the physical powers and sinews are thus strengthened. Indeed, they regard it as very disgraceful to have had familiarity with a woman before the twentieth year. There is no concealment in this matter, for they bathe promiscuously in the rivers, and they wear skins or small coverings made of deerskin, a great part of their bodies being nude.

They do not pay attention to agriculture, and a large part of their food consists of milk, cheese, and meat. Nor does anyone possess a fixed amount of land or private fields. But the magistrates and the chiefs assign for a year at a time to the families and clans that have banded together the quantity of land and the location they see fit, and the following year they compel them to move elsewhere. They advance many reasons for this practice: that they should not be attracted by a permanent mode of living and exchange the pursuit of war for agriculture; that they should not be eager to acquire large landed estates, the more powerful driving the weaker from their possessions; that they should not build houses too carefully in order to avoid cold and heat; that the desire for wealth should not develop, from which arise factions and internal disorder; and that they may keep the common people in check through the contentment they feel when each sees his own property equal to that of the most powerful.

The greatest glory to the various states is to have as wide an area of wilderness as possible around them along their frontiers, which they themselves devastate. They consider this a sign of courage, that their neighbors be driven from their fields and abandon them, and that no one dares to settle near them. At the same time they think that they will thus be safer if the fear of sudden incursion has been removed. When a state defends itself from an aggressive war or commits aggression against another, magistrates are chosen to be in charge of that war with the power of life and death. In peacetime there is no common magistrate, but the chiefs of the districts and cantons administer justice and settle disputes among their peoples. Brigandage beyond the frontiers of each state entails no disgrace, and they declare that such acts are committed to train their youth and to reduce idleness. And whenever any of the chiefs declares in an assembly that he will be a leader of such an expedition and that those who wish to follow him should so declare, those who approve of the enterprise and the leader arise and promise aid, and they are applauded by the multitude. Those of them who do not accompany him are regarded as deserters and traitors, and confidence is afterwards withheld from them in all matters. They consider it sacrilegious to injure a guest; those who have come to them for any reason whatsoever they protect from injury and consider inviolable; the homes of all are open to these and food is shared with them.

87. CAESAR INVADES BRITAIN, 55–54 B.C.

Caesar's two expeditions into the south of Britain, the first (55 B.C.) exploratory, the second (54 B.C.) in strength, were undertaken not only to cut off British assistance to the Gauls but also with one eye on the political reaction in Rome to his spectacular exploit, and another on the rumored, but exaggerated, wealth of the little-known island. Though his legions fought their way across the Thames, and Caesar received the formal submission of the British tribes united under King Cassivellaunus, the invasion must be considered an abortive adventure.

THE FIRST EXPEDITION

Caesar, *Gallic War* IV. xx–xxiii (abridged), xxxvi

During the short part of the summer which remained, Caesar, although in these regions—all Gaul lies toward the north—the winters are early, nevertheless hastened to proceed into Britain, because he discovered that in almost all the wars with the Gauls assistance had been furnished to our enemy from that country. And even if the time of the year should be insufficient for carrying on the war, yet he thought it would be of great service to him if he only approached the island, investigated the character of the people, and obtained knowledge of the terrain, harbors, and landing places, all of which were for the most part unknown to the Gauls. For none except traders go there voluntarily, and even to them the only portion of it that is known is the seacoast and those parts which are opposite Gaul. Therefore, although he summoned traders from all parts, he could learn neither what was the size of the island, nor what peoples inhabited it, nor how numerous they were, nor what method of warfare they used, nor what customs they had, nor what harbors were suitable for a great number of large ships. . . .

Having gathered and brought together about eighty transports, the number he thought necessary for transporting the two legions, he assigned the supporting warships to his quaestor, lieutenants, and cavalry officers. There were, in addition to these, eighteen transports which were prevented by winds, eight miles from that place, from being able to reach the same port.[69] These he assigned to the cavalry; the rest of the army he turned over to Quintus Titurius Sabinus and Lucius Aurunculeius Cotta, his lieutenants, to lead into the territories of the Menapii[70] and into those cantons of the Morini from which ambassadors had not come to him. He ordered Publius Sulpicius Rufus, his lieutenant, to hold the harbor with such a garrison as he thought sufficient.

Having disposed of these matters and finding the weather favorable for the voyage, he set sail about the third watch, and ordered the cavalry to march forward to the farther port, to embark there and follow him. As this was executed rather tardily by them, he himself reached Britain with the first squadron of ships about the fourth hour of the day, and there saw the forces of the enemy arrayed in arms on all the hills. The nature of this place [the cliffs of Dover] was as follows—the sea was bordered by mountains so close to it that a dart could be thrown from the heights upon the shore. Considering this by no means a suitable place for disembarking, he waited at anchor till the ninth hour for the other ships to arrive. Having in the meantime assembled the lieutenants and military tribunes, he briefed them both on what he had learned . . . and on what he wished to have done. . . . Having dismissed them and finding both wind and tide simultaneously favorable, he gave the signal and anchors were weighed. He advanced about seven miles from that place and stationed his fleet at an open and level stretch of shore.

[The Romans effect a landing and encamp. A few days later they defeat the Britons in pitched battle and lay waste the surrounding countryside.]

Ambassadors sent by the enemy came to Caesar to negotiate a peace. Caesar doubled the number of hostages which he had before demanded and ordered them to be brought over to the Continent because, since the time of the equinox was near, he did not consider that, with his ships out of repair, his return should be deferred till winter. Finding the weather favorable, he set sail a little before midnight, and his whole fleet arrived safely at the Continent.

---

69. It is probable that Caesar used Boulogne as his port of embarcation and that he landed on the Kentish coast, at Walmer.

70. A Belgian tribe northeast of the Morini and bordering on the Rhine.

BRITAIN AND ITS INHABITANTS

Caesar, *Gallic War* v. viii, xii–xiv, xxii

When these things were done, he left Labienus on the Continent with three legions and 2,000 horse to defend the harbors and provide for the grain supply, and to learn what was going on in Gaul, and to take measures according to occasion and circumstance. Caesar himself, with five legions and a number of horse equal to that which he had left on the Continent, set sail at sunset. . . . All the ships reached Britain nearly at midday.[71] Not a single enemy was seen in that place, but, as Caesar afterwards learned from prisoners, though large bodies of troops had assembled there, yet being alarmed by the great number of our ships (more than eight hundred of which had appeared at one time, including those of the preceding year and the private vessels which some had built for their own convenience), they had withdrawn from the coast and concealed themselves on the heights. . . .

The interior of Britain is inhabited by those who, according to their oral tradition, are indigenous to the island; the maritime portion, by those who had crossed over from the land of he Belgians for booty and making war. Almost all of the latter are called by the names of those peoples from whom they have their origin and whence they came to Britain, where, after waging war, they remained and began to cultivate the land. The number of the people is countless, and their buildings exceedingly numerous, for the most part very like those of the Gauls. The number of cattle is large. They use either bronze or gold coins or iron bars of a definite weight in place of coined money. Tin is found in the midland regions [i.e., Cornwall], iron in the maritime regions, but the quantity of it is small. They use imported bronze. As in Gaul, there is timber of every description, except beech and fir. They do not regard it lawful to eat the hare, hen, or goose; they breed them, however, for amusement and pleasure. The climate is more temperate than in Gaul, the cold weather being less severe. . . .

The most civilized of all these peoples are those who inhabit Kent, which is entirely a maritime district, and they do not differ much from the Gauls in customs. Most of the inland inhabitants do not sow grain, but live on milk and flesh and are dressed in skins. All the Britons,

---

71. Caesar's second expedition sailed probably from Wissant and landed between Sandown and Sandwich, on the Kentish coast.

indeed, dye themselves with woad, which produces a bluish color, and thereby have a more terrible appearance in battle. They wear their hair long and have every part of their body shaved except their head and upper lip. Groups of ten and twelve have wives in common, and especially brothers with brothers, and parents with children; but whatever issue there is by these wives are considered to be the children of those to whom each respectively was first espoused when a virgin. . . .

Caesar, since he had determined to pass the winter on the Continent, on account of the sudden revolts in Gaul, and since little of the summer was left and he perceived that not much could be gained by remaining, demanded hostages and prescribed what tribute Britain should pay annually to the Roman people.[72]

88. Enrichment of the Roman Treasury

Pliny, *Natural History* XXXIII. xvii

In the consulship of Sextus Julius and Lucius Aurelius [157 B.C.], seven years before the beginning of the Third Punic War, there were in the treasury of the Roman people 17,410 pounds' weight of uncoined gold, 22,070 pounds' weight of silver, and in specie 6,133,400 sesterces. In the consulship of Sextus Julius and Lucius Marcius [91 B.C.], i.e., at the beginning of the Social War, there were 1,620,831 sesterces in the public treasury.[73] Gaius Caesar, at his first entry into Rome during the Civil War which bears his name [49 B.C.], withdrew from the treasury 15,000 pounds' weight of gold bullion, 30,000 pounds' weight in uncoined silver and[74] 30,000,000 sesterces in specie: indeed, at no period was the Republic more wealthy. Aemilius Paullus, too, after the defeat of King Perseus, paid into the public treasury from the spoils obtained in Macedonia 300,000,000[75] sesterces, and from that time the Roman people ceased to pay the *tributum*.[76]

72. It is doubtful whether Caesar ever received the hostages and tribute from the Britons.

73. The figures for uncoined gold and silver in this year, if they were given by Pliny, have dropped out of the MSS. Cf. T. Frank, ed., *An Economic Survey of Ancient Rome*, 1:266.

74. Frank, ed., *Economic Survey*, 1:338, suggests that "and" may be a mistake for "i.e."—in other words, that 30,000,000 sesterces is the equivalent of the preceding 30,000 silver bars.

75. Frank, ed., *Economic Survey*, 1:137, suggests that the MS reading is a copyist's error for the numeral 120,000,000, the figure given by Livy XLV. xl. 1.

76. This direct tax to defray war costs, which was thus abolished in 167 B.C., was first reimposed in 43 B.C. to pay for the war of the Senate and Octavian against Mark Antony (see § 114). J. A. O. Larsen, in Frank, ed., *Economic Survey*, 4:323, has estimated that the total value of the booty and

89. DIVISION OF SPOILS

Polybius, *Histories* x. xvi; From *LCL*

Such was the manner in which the Romans gained possession of Spanish Carthage [i.e., Nova Carthago (modern Cartagena)]. Next day the booty, both the baggage of the troops in the Carthaginian service and the household stuff of the townsmen and the working classes, having been collected in the market, was divided by the tribunes among their own legions on the usual system. The Romans after the capture of a city manage matters more or less as follows: according to the size of the town sometimes a certain number of men from each maniple, at other times certain whole maniples, are told off to collect booty, but they never thus employ more than half their total force, the rest remaining in their ranks at times outside and at times inside the city, ready for any emergency. As their armies are usually composed of two Roman legions and two legions of allies, the whole four legions being rarely massed, all those who are told off to spoil bring the booty back, each man to his own legion, and after it has been sold the tribunes distribute the profits equally among all, including not only those who were left behind in the protecting force, but also the men who are guarding the tents, the sick, and those absent on any special service.[77] I have already stated at some length in my chapters on the Roman state how it is that no one appropriates any part of the loot, but that all keep the oath they make when first assembled in camp on setting out for a campaign. So that when half of the army disperse to pillage and the other half keep their ranks and afford them protection, there is never any chance of the Romans suffering disaster owing to individual covetousness. For as all, both the spoilers and those who remain to safeguard them, have equal confidence that they will get their share of the booty, no one leaves the ranks, a thing which usually does injury to other armies.

---

indemnities secured in Macedonia and Greece alone from *c.* 200 to 149 B.C. amounted to 73,229,336 denarii (=292,917,344 sesterces).

77. All booty was legally the property of the Roman state, but the general had the right to retain part of the booty for various purposes, among them the distribution of a portion to his troops. See further § 90.

90. ROMAN TRIUMPHS

The first of the following selections is a general description of a Roman triumph; the second and third comprise an account of one of the most magnificent of Roman triumphal processions—that of Aemilius Paullus for his victory over Perseus of Macedon at Pydna in 168 B.C.—and two excerpts from the *Fasti Triumphales* (Calendar of Triumphs), a part of the *Fasti Capitolini* (see Introduction, note 1).

Zonaras, *Epitome* VII. xxi; From *LCL*

Now the celebration of a military victory which they call a triumph was somewhat as follows. When any great success worthy of a triumph had been gained, the general was immediately saluted as *imperator* by the soldiers, and he would bind sprigs of laurel upon the *fasces* and deliver them to the messengers who announced the victory to the city. On arriving home he would assemble the senate and ask to have the triumph voted him.[78] And if he obtained a vote from the senate and from the people, his title of *imperator* was confirmed. If he still occupied the office which he had held when he won his victory, he continued to hold it while celebrating the festival; but if his term of office had expired he received some other title appropriate to the office, since it was forbidden for a private individual to hold a triumph.

Arrayed in the triumphal dress and wearing armlets,[79] with a laurel crown upon his head, and holding a branch in his right hand, he called together the people. After praising collectively the troops who had served with him, and some of them individually, he presented them with money and honored them also with decorations. Upon some he bestowed armlets and spears without the iron; to others he gave crowns, sometimes of gold, sometimes of silver, bearing the name of each man and the representation of his particular feat. . . . And these rewards were

78. Valerius Maximus, *Memorable Deeds and Sayings* II. viii. 1, states that there was a law—of very questionable authenticity—that forbade triumphs unless 5,000 of the enemy had been killed in one battle; that during the tribuneship of Cato the Younger (62 B.C.) a law was passed which imposed penalties on generals who falsified, in their dispatches to the Senate, the number of the enemy killed and of citizens lost in battle; and that "however distinguished and useful to the state successes in civil war may have been, no one was proclaimed *imperator* on that account, nor have any thanksgivings been decreed, nor has anyone triumphed . . . because, however necessary these victories may have been, they have always been considered occasions of mourning, inasmuch as they were gained by the shedding not of foreign blood but of the blood of citizens."

79. As amulets to ward off the evil eye.

not only given to men singly, as the result of individual deeds of prowess, but were also bestowed upon whole companies and legions. A large part of the spoils also was assigned to the soldiers who had taken part in the campaign; but some victors have distributed the spoils even among the entire populace and have devoted them toward the expenses of the festival or turned them over to the treasury; if anything was left over, they would spend it for temples, porticoes, or some other public work.

After these ceremonies the triumphant general would mount his chariot. Now this chariot did not resemble one used in games or in the war, but was fashioned in the shape of a round tower. And he would not be alone in the chariot, but if he had children or relatives, he would make the girls and the infant male children get up beside him in it and place the older ones upon the horses. . . . If there were many of them, they would accompany the procession on chargers, riding along beside the victor. None of the rest rode, but all went on foot wearing laurel wreaths. A public slave, however, rode with the victor in the chariot itself, holding over him the crown of precious stones set in gold, and kept saying to him, "Look behind!" . . .[80] Both a bell and a whip were fastened to the chariot, signifying that it was possible for him to meet with misfortune also, to the extent even of being scourged or condemned to death. . . . Thus arrayed, they entered the city, having at the head of the procession the spoils and trophies and figures representing the captured forts, cities, mountains, rivers, lakes, and seas—everything, in fact, that they had taken. If one day did not suffice for the exhibition of these things in procession, the celebration was held during a second and a third day. When these adjuncts had gone on their way, the victorious general arrived at the Roman Forum, and after commanding that some of the captives be led to prison and put to death, he rode up to the Capitol. There he performed certain rites and made offerings and dined in the porticoes up there, after which he departed homeward towards evening, accompanied by flutes and pipes. Such were the triumphs in olden [i.e., Republican] times.

Plutarch, *Life of Aemilius Paullus* xxxii–xxxiv (abridged)

All the tribes decreed a triumph for Aemilius. He is reported to have triumphed in the following manner. . . .

This triumph lasted three days. On the first . . . were to be seen the

---

80. This saying is more commonly given in the sources as "Remember that you are a mortal."

captured statues, paintings, and colossal images drawn upon 250 chariots. On the second was carried on many wagons the finest and richest
armor of the Macedonians, both of bronze and iron, all newly polished
and gleaming, the pieces of which were artistically arranged so as to
seem to be tumbled in heaps carelessly and by chance. . . . After these
wagons bearing the armor there proceeded 3,000 men who carried
the coined silver in 750 vessels, each holding three talents and each
carried by four men. Others brought silver bowls and drinking horns
and flat bowls and wine cups, each well arranged for display and all
extraordinary as well for the size as for the thickness of their embossed
work.

On the third day, early in the morning, first proceeded the trumpeters, who did not sound as they were wont in a solemn procession, but
blew such a call as the Romans use when they encourage themselves in
battle. Next followed young men wearing tunics with purple borders,
who led to the sacrifice 120 stalled oxen with gilded horns and heads
adorned with ribbons and garlands; and with these were boys that
carried basins for libations, of silver and gold. Then after these came
those carrying the gold coin, which was divided into vessels each holding three talents, like those that contained the silver; the number of the
vessels was seventy-seven. These were followed by those that brought
the consecrated bowl which Aemilius had caused to be made of ten
talents of gold set with precious stones. Then were exposed to view the
bowls of Antigonus, Seleucus, and Thericles, and all the gold plate that
was used at Perseus' table. Next to these came Perseus' chariot, and his
armor, and lying on that his diadem. And, after a little intermission, the
king's children were led as captives, and with them a train of their
personal attendants and teachers, all shedding tears and stretching out
their hands to the spectators, and showing the children also how to beg
and entreat their compassion. . . .

After his children and their attendants came Perseus himself, wearing
a dark garment and the boots of his country, and looking like one
altogether stunned and deprived of reason through the greatness of his
misfortunes. Next followed a great company of his friends and inti-
mates, whose countenances were disfigured with grief. . . . After these
were carried 400 golden crowns sent from the cities by embassies to
Aemilius in honor of his victory. Then he himself came, mounted on a
chariot magnificently adorned . . . dressed in a purple robe interwoven
with gold and holding a laurel branch in his right hand. All the army, in
like manner, carried branches of laurel, and divided into centuries and

cohorts followed the chariot of their commander, some singing verses, according to the ancestral custom, mingled with raillery, others songs of triumph and praise of Aemilius' deeds.

Inscriptiones Italiae, vol. XIII, part I, pp.77, 87

[260 B.C.]Gaius Duilius, son of Marcus, grandson of Marcus, consul; year 493;[81] first to celebrate a naval victory, over the Sicilians and the Punic fleet; Kalends of the intercalary month.[82]

[259 B.C.] Lucius Cornelius Scipio, son of Lucius, grandson of Gnaeus, consul; year 494; over the Carthaginians, Sardinia, and Corsica; 5 days before the Ides of March.

[258 B.C.] Gaius Aquillius Florus, son of Marcus, grandson of Gaius, proconsul; year 495; over the Carthaginians; 4 days before the Nones of October.

[258 B.C.] Gaius Atilius Paterculus, son of Quintus, grandson of Quintus, consul; year 495; over the Carthaginians and Sardinia; 3 days before the Nones of October.

[257 B.C.] Aulus Atilius Caiatinus, son of Aulus, grandson of Gaius, praetor; year 496; over Sicily and the Carthaginians; 14 days before the Kalends of February.

[257 B.C.] Gaius Atilius Regulus, son of Marcus, grandson of Marcus, consul; year 496; naval victory over the Carthaginians; 8 days before. . . .

[256 B.C.]Lucius Manlius Vulso Longus, son of Aulus, grandson of Publius, consul; year 497; naval victory over the Carthaginians; 8 days before. . . .

[254 B.C.]Servius Fulvius Paetinus Nobilior, son of Marcus, grandson of Marcus, proconsul; year 499; over the Cossurenses, and naval victory over the Carthaginians; 13 days before the Kalends of February.

[254 B.C.] Marcus Aemilius Paullus, son of Marcus, grandson of Lucius, proconsul; year 499; over the Cossurenses, and naval victory over the Carthaginians; 12 days before the Kalends of February.

[45 B.C.] Quintus Fabius Maximus, son of Quintus, grandson of Quintus, consul; year 708; over Spain; 3 days before the Ides of October.

[45 B.C.] Quintus Pedius, son of Marcus, proconsul; year 708; over Spain; Ides of December.

81. Calculated from the traditional date of the founding of Rome, which is taken here as 752 B.C.

82. This notation here and in the following indicates the date of the triumph. For the intercalary month, see the introduction to § 9.

[44 B.C.] Gaius Julius Caesar, son of Gaius, grandson of Gaius, hailed *imperator* for the sixth time, dictator for the fourth year; year 709; ovation from the Alban Mount;[83] 7 days before the Kalends of February.

[43 B.C.] Lucius Munatius Plancus, son of Lucius, grandson of Lucius, proconsul; year 710; over Gaul; 4 days before the Kalends of January.

[43 B.C.] Marcus Aemilius Lepidus, son of Marcus, grandson of Quintus, hailed *imperator* for the second time, trumvir for reestablishing the state, proconsul; year 710; over Spain; day before the Kalends of January.

[42 B.C.] Publius Vatinius, son of Publius, proconsul; year 711; over Illyria; day before the Kalends of Sextilis.

[41 B.C.] Lucius Antonius, son of Marcus, grandson of Marcus, consul; year 712; over the peoples of the Alps; Kalends of January.

[40 B.C.] Imperator Caesar, son of a god, grandson of Gaius, triumvir for reestablishing the state; year 713; ovation because he had made peace with Marcus Antonius. . . .

[40 B.C.] Marcus Antonius, son of Marcus, grandson of Marcus, triumvir for reestablishing the state; year 713; ovation because he had made peace with Imperator Caesar. . . .

91. ROME'S CONQUEST OF THE HELLENISTIC WORLD: "DIVIDE AND CONQUER"

In the summer of 72 B.C. the Roman armies under Lucullus forced Mithridates, king of Pontus, to flee from his kingdom and seek refuge with his son-in-law, King Tigranes of Armenia. Under these circumstances Sallust pictures Mithridates as writing this letter in 69 B.C. to King Arsaces of Parthia, proposing a military alliance against Rome. In the words of M. L. W. Laistner, this Sallustian epistle is on the face of it "a rhetorical fiction and not without absurdity. Can we seriously believe that the king of Pontus, in order to win over Arsaces of Parthia as an active ally against Rome, would send him a historical disquisition on Roman imperialism?" (*The Greater Roman Historians,* p. 52).

Nevertheless, the document is not without value in reflecting Roman self-criticism. Sallust's purpose in introducing this "letter" into his work is to preach a sermon on the corruption of Roman public morality—a theme that figured prominently in contemporary and subsequent Roman

---

83. An ovation was a minor triumph. Traditionally, the general so honored walked in the procession. Caesar was granted the privilege of parading on horseback, and that remained the norm thereafter.

literature (cf. § 96). By the end of the Republic the Romans had developed an ambivalence in their views on the growth of their empire. First came nationalistic glorification, whereby the Romans explained their world supremacy as a just reward vouchsafed them by the gods for the unique combination of sterling traits that characterized the Roman people. But in the declining days of the Republic when Sallust wrote, the glamor of Roman domination had been dimmed even for the Romans themselves by an unsavory history of provincial administration, and even more by the century-long domestic revolution, which was nearing its climax. Thus there arose in the literature of the time an opposing attitude of breast-beating anti-imperialism, which decried the moral decadence and political troubles of the times as products of a lust for power and riches that their vast conquests had fostered in the Romans.

Sallust, Histories IV Fragment 69 (abridged); Adapted from *LCL*

King Mithridates to King Arsaces, greeting. All those who in the time of their prosperity are asked to form a military alliance ought to consider, first, whether it is possible for them to keep peace at that time; and secondly, whether what is asked of them is wholly right and safe, honorable or dishonorable. If it were possible for you to enjoy lasting peace, if you were not exposed to most treacherous foes at hand, if to crush the Roman power would not bring you glorious fame, I should not venture to sue for your alliance, and it would be vain for me to hope to unite my misfortunes with your prosperity. . . .

The Romans have one inveterate motive for making war upon all nations, peoples, and kings, namely, a deep-seated desire for dominion and riches. Therefore they first began a war with Philip, king of Macedon, after pretending to be his friends as long as they were hard pressed by the Carthaginians. When Antiochus came to his aid, they craftily diverted him by conceding Asia to him, and then, after Philip's power had been broken, Antiochus was stripped of all the territory this side of Taurus and of 10,000 talents. Next Perseus, Philip's son, after many battles with varying results, they took under their protection in the presence of the Samothracian gods, and then those masters of craft and artists in treachery caused his death from want of sleep, since they had compacted not to kill him. Eumenes, whose friendship they boastfully parade, they first betrayed to Antiochus as the price of peace; later, after making him the guardian of a conquered territory, they burdened him with expenses and insults, thus transforming him from a king into the most wretched of slaves. Then, having forged an unnatural will, they led his son Aristonicus in triumph like an enemy because he had sought to occupy his father's throne, and took possession of Asia [see § 128]. Finally, on the death of Nicomedes, they snatched away Bithynia, although Nysa, whom Nicomedes had called queen, unquestionably had a son. . . .

I pray you, now, consider whether you believe that when we have been crushed you will be better able to resist the Romans, or that there will be an end to the war. I know well that you have great resources of men, arms, and gold, and it is for that reason that I seek your alliance and the Romans your spoils. Yet my advice is that, while the kingdom of Tigranes is entire and I have soldiers who have been trained in warfare with the Romans, you at the expense of *our* bodies finish far from *your* homes and with little labor on *your* part a war in which we cannot conquer or be conquered without danger to you. Do you not know that the Romans turned their arms in this direction only after the Ocean had terminated their westward progress? and that from their very beginning they have possessed nothing except what they have stolen—their homes, their wives, their lands, their empire? Once vagabonds without fatherland or parents, created to be the scourge of the whole world, no laws, human or divine, prevent them from seizing and destroying allies and friends, those near them and those far off, the weak and the powerful, and from considering every government not subject to them, especially monarchies, as their enemies.

Of a truth, few men desire freedom, the greater part are content if they have just masters; we are suspected of being rivals of the Romans and future avengers [of those they have subjugated]. But you, who possess Seleucea, greatest of cities, and the realm of Persia, famed for its riches, what can you expect from them except deceit in the present and war in the future? The Romans have weapons against all men, the sharpest ones for those whose defeat will yield the greatest spoils; it is by audacity, by treachery, and by constant warfare that they have grown great, and following this custom they will blot out everything or perish in the attempt.

5

THE DECLINE AND FALL OF
THE ROMAN REPUBLIC:
THE "ROMAN REVOLUTION"

Domestic Changes to 133 B.C.

92. EMERGENCY WAR FINANCING AND PROVISIONING

During the "total war" against Hannibal, the Roman state, plagued repeatedly by critical shortages of supplies and funds, resorted to a series of extraordinary measures, some of which are recounted here (cf. also § 65). In addition to these, recourse was had to such expedients as currency inflation, patriotic appeals for voluntary contributions of metals and valuables, and deferment "for the duration" of payment on state contracts. Particularly noteworthy is the emergence of the *equites* as the new commercial and financial class of the Republic (cf. also introduction to § 94). For further details and commentary, see T. Frank, ed., *An Economic Survey of Ancient Rome,* 1:81–97.

Livy, *History of Rome* XXIII. xxi.1–6, xlviii.4–xlix. 3, XXVIII. xlvi.4–6, XXXI. xiii

[216 B.C.] About the same time letters were brought from Sicily and Sardinia. That of Titus Otacilius, the propraetor, was read first in the senate. It stated that Publius Furius, the praetor, had arrived at Lilybaeum from Africa with his fleet; that he himself, severely wounded, was in imminent danger of his life; that neither pay nor grain was punctually supplied to the soldiers or the naval forces, nor were there any resources from which they could be supplied; that he earnestly advised that such supplies should be sent with all possible expedition;

and that, if it was thought proper, they should send one of the new praetors to succeed him. Nearly the same intelligence respecting grain and pay was conveyed in a letter from Aulus Cornelius Mammula, the propraetor in Sardinia. The answer to both was that there were no resources whence they could be supplied, and orders were given to them that they should themselves provide for their fleets and armies. Titus Otacilius sent envoys to Hiero,[1] the only source of assistance the Romans had, and received as much money as was needed to pay the troops and a supply of grain for six months. In Sardinia the allied states contributed liberally to Cornelius. The scarcity of money at Rome also was so great that, on the proposal of Marcus Minucius, a tribune of the plebs, a three-man financial commission was appointed,[2] consisting of Lucius Aemilius Papus, who had been consul and censor, Marcus Atilius Regulus, who had been twice consul, and Lucius Scribonius Libo, who was then plebeian tribune.

[215 B.C.] At the close of the summer . . . letters arrived from Publius and Gnaeus Scipio, stating the magnitude and success of their operations in Spain, but adding that the army was in want of pay, clothing, and grain, and that their crews were in want of everything. With regard to the pay, they said that if the treasury was low they would adopt some plan by which they might procure it from the Spaniards; but that the other supplies must certainly be sent from Rome, for otherwise neither could the army be maintained nor the province held. When the letters were read, all to a man admitted that the statement was correct and the request reasonable. . . . It was resolved that Fulvius, the praetor, should present himself to the public assembly of the people, point out the exigencies of the state, and exhort those persons who had increased their patrimonies by farming the public revenues to furnish loans to the state from which they had derived their wealth, and to contract to supply what was needed for the army in Spain on the condition of being first to be paid when there was money in the treasury. This the praetor laid before the assembly, and fixed a day on which he would let the contract for furnishing the army in Spain with clothes and grain, and with such other things as were necessary for the crews.

1. The ruler of Syracuse (270–216 B.C.).

2. This was an extraordinary measure resorted to only once before in a financial crisis (351 B.C.). These commissioners (called *triumviri mensarii*) were empowered to lend state funds on security to individuals who needed ready cash to discharge private debts. In addition, they made and received payments for the treasury.

When the day arrived, three companies, composed of nineteen persons, came forward to enter into the contract; but they made two requests: one was that they should be exempt from military service while employed in that public business, the second, that their shipments should be at the state's risk against attacks of the enemy or storms. On obtaining both their requests, they entered into the contracts, and the affairs of the state were conducted with private funds.

[205 B.C.] As there was a scarcity of money for carrying on the war, the quaestors were ordered to sell a district of the Campanian territory extending from the Grecian Trench to the sea.[3] They were also permitted to receive information as to what land belonged to native Campanians, so that it could be expropriated by the Roman people, and the reward fixed for informers was a tenth of the value of the lands so discovered. Gnaeus Servilius, the urban praetor, was charged with seeing that the Campanians dwelt where they were permitted by the decree of the senate, and ordered such as dwelt anywhere else to be punished.[4]

[200 B.C.] When the consuls were ready to set out to their provinces, a number of private persons, to whom there was due that year the third payment of the money which they had lent to the state in the consulship of Marcus Valerius and Marcus Claudius,[5] applied to the senate; for the consuls had declared that, since the treasury was scarcely sufficient for the new war, in which a great fleet and great armies must be employed, there were no means of paying them at present. The senate could not stand against them when they complained that if the state intended to use for the Macedonian war the money which had been lent for the Punic war, as one war constantly arose after another, what would be the result but that, in return for their generosity, their property would be confiscated as if for some crime? The demands of the private creditors being equitable, and the state being in no capacity of discharging the debt, the senate decreed a middle course between equity and expediency, resolving that, since many of them spoke of the lands for sale that they wished to purchase, they should therefore have the opportunity to pur-

---

3. This was a most unusual procedure. State land was normally let to tenants, who paid the state a rent (*vectigal:* see Glossary); this recourse to outright sale of Campanian land, which was very fertile and desirable, bespeaks a most desperate shortage of state funds.

4. Cf. the punishment of the Campanians in § 64.

5. This refers to the voluntary contributions made in 210 B.C., the story of which is told by Livy XXVI. xxxvi. In 204 B.C. it was decided to begin paying back this money in three biennial instalments.

chase any public land located within fifty miles of the city. The consuls would make a valuation and impose a nominal rental of one *as* per *iugerum* in attestation of its being public land, in order that, when the people should become able to pay, if anyone chose to have his money rather than the land, he might restore the land to the state. The private creditors accepted the terms with joy; and that land was called *Trientabulum* because it was given in lieu of the third part of their money.[6]

93. A War-Contract Fraud, 212 b.c.

One of the results of Hannibal's initial victories in Italy was a wave of disillusionment at Rome with the conduct of affairs by the senatorial class, and vociferous demands were heard for the infusion of new blood into that ruling body of patrician and plebeian wealthy families. In the third and second centuries b.c. the popular assemblies on several occasions took matters into their own hands in defiance of the ruling nobility. These "revolts" were, as in the case described below, popular reactions to specific situations, not attempts to effect a revolutionary change in the control of the Roman state; they were, nevertheless, the first harbingers of the storm that was eventually to overwhelm the senatorial order.

Livy, *History of Rome* xxv. iii. 9–iv. 11

Postumius was a tax farmer who, for knavery and rapacity practiced over many years, had no equal except Titus Pomponius Veientanus, who had been taken prisoner by the Carthaginians the year before, when Hanno was carelessly ravaging the lands in Lucania. As the state had taken upon itself the risk of any loss that might arise from storms to the commodities conveyed to the armies [see § 92], not only had these two men fabricated false accounts of shipwrecks, but even those which had really occurred were occasioned by their own knavery and not by accident. Their practice was to put a few goods of little value into old, battered hulls, which they sank in the deep, taking off the sailors in boats prepared for the purpose, and then falsely to bill the cargo at many times its actual value. This fraudulent practice had been pointed out the year before to Marcus Atilius, the praetor, who had communicated it to the senate; no decree, however, had been passed censuring it, because

6. Livy reports (*History of Rome* xxxiii. xlii. 2) that the third payment was made in money in 195 b.c., after the war with Philp V had been brought to an end and the treasury replenished by the war indemnity.

the senators were anxious that no offense should be given to the class of the tax farmers in such a critical time. The people were severer avengers of the fraud: two tribunes of the plebs, Spurius and Lucius Carvilius, aroused at length and taking cognizance of this detestable and notorious affair, proposed that a fine of 2,000 *asses* be imposed on Marcus Postumius. . . .

[In desperation, a group of publicans forcibly prevented a vote from being taken, and the assembly was dismissed to avoid an armed clash.]

The senate [assembled and] passed a decree to the effect that the violence offered was prejudicial to the state and a precedent of pernicious tendency. Immediately the Carvilii, tribunes of the plebs, giving up their demand of a fine, appointed a day for Postumius to be tried on a capital charge and ordered that unless he gave bail he should be apprehended by the apparitor and led away to prison. Postumius posted bail but did not appear for trial. The tribunes then proposed to the commons, and the commons resolved, that if Marcus Postumius did not appear before the Kalends of May, and if on being cited on that day he did not answer and sufficient cause were not shown why he did not, he would be adjudged to be an exile, his goods would be sold, and he would be interdicted from fire and water. They then proceeded to fix capital trials for, and demand bail of, each of those who had been responsible for the disorder and the riot. At first they threw into prison those who did not post bail, and afterwards even such as could; upon which the greater part of them went into exile, to avoid the danger to which this proceeding exposed them.

94. THE CHANGING ECONOMY

These selections highlight two new sources of wealth opened up to the Romans by their overseas conquests—an abundance of cheap slaves for latifundist operations, and lucrative opportunities in money-lending and trade. Members of the senatorial class, disbarred from commercial activities by a law of *c.* 218 B.C., participated in the equestrian corporations as silent partners, investing in the name of a freedman or other client. According to the following account even Cato—despite his vigorous opposition to the new economic, political, and cultural influences emanating from the conquest, and despite his express declaration that agriculture was the only honorable source of income for a gentleman (see § 166) — did not disdain to increase his wealth through the economic activities he condemned.

THE RISE OF THE LATIFUNDIA

Appian, *Civil Wars* I. i. 7; From *LCL*

The Romans, as they subdued the Italian peoples successively in war, used to seize a part of their lands and build towns there, or enroll colonists of their own to occupy those already existing, with the idea of using these as outposts; but of the land acquired by war they assigned the cultivated part forthwith to the colonists, or sold or leased it. Since they had no leisure as yet to allot the part which then lay desolated by war (this was generally the greater part), they made proclamation that in the meantime those who were willing to work it might do so for a toll of the yearly crops, namely a tenth of the grain and a fifth of the fruit. From those who kept flocks was required a toll of the animals, both oxen and small cattle. They did these things in order to multiply the Italian people, whom they considered very hardy, so that they might have plenty of allies at home. But the very opposite thing happened; for the rich, taking possession of the greater part of the undistributed lands and being emboldened by the lapse of time to believe that they would never be dispossessed, absorbing any adjacent strips and their poor neighbors' allotments partly by purchase under persuasion and partly by force, came to cultivate vast tracts instead of single estates, using purchased slaves as agricultural laborers and herdsmen, since free laborers could be drawn from agriculture into the army. At the same time the ownership of slaves brought them great gain from the multitude of their progeny, who increased free from danger because they were exempt from military service. Thus certain powerful men became extremely rich and the class of slaves multiplied throughout the country, while the Italian people dwindled in numbers and strength, oppressed by penury, taxes, and military service. If they had any respite from these evils, they passed their time in idleness, because the land was held by the rich, who employed slaves instead of freemen as cultivators.

Pliny, *Natural History* XVIII. iv

When Roman manners were such as these,[7] not only did Italy produce sufficient for its needs without relying on any of the provinces for its

7. Pliny refers to the early Roman simplicity and austerity. The whole passage is written from the

food, but also the price of provisions was incredibly cheap. . . . In the year in which the Mother of the Gods was brought to Rome [204 B.C., see the last selection in § 177], the harvest of that summer, it is said, was more abundant than it had been for ten years before. Marcus Varro informs us that in the year in which Lucius Metellus exhibited so many elephants in his triumphal procession,[8] *a modius* of spelt sold for one *as,* which was the price likewise of a *congius* of wine, thirty pounds' weight of dried figs, ten pounds of olive oil, or twelve pounds of meat. Nor did this cheapness originate in the latifundia of individuals encroaching continually upon their neighbors, for by the law of Licinius Stolo the landed property of each individual was limited to 500 *iugera*[9] (he himself was convicted under his own law of possessing more than that amount by registering some in his son's name). Such was the size of estates when the state was growing apace. Well-known, too, is the remark uttered by Manius Curius [consul in 290 B.C.] after his triumphs that added an immense extent of territory to the Roman sway: "Any man for whom seven *iugera* of land are not enough must be regarded as a dangerous citizen"—for that was the amount of land that was allotted to the plebs after the expulsion of the kings [cf § 40].

What, then, was the cause of this great fertility? Why, the fact that in those days the lands were tilled by the hands of the very generals, the soil exulting beneath the plowshare crowned with wreaths of laurel and guided by a husbandman graced with triumphs. . . . But today these same lands are tilled by slaves whose legs are in chains, by the hands of malefactors and men with branded countenance. . . . And we are surprised that the yields from the labor of workhouse slaves are not the same as from the honest toil of warriors!

NEW BUSINESS VENTURES: THE EXAMPLE OF CATO

Plutarch, *Life of Cato the Elder* xxi

Cato purchased a great many slaves out of the captives taken in war, but chiefly brought up the young ones, who, like whelps and colts, were still capable of being reared and trained. None of these ever entered into another man's house unless sent either by Cato himself or his wife. If anyone of them were asked what Cato did, he answered only that he did

---

point of view of a moralist, not an economist. Particularly noteworthy is his attribution of the rise in prices and decline in productivity to the inefficiency of slave labor.

8. 150 B.C. The prices are apparently garbled but are intended to indicate cheapness.

9. The Licinio-Sextian Law of 367 B.C., limiting holdings of public land, is meant; see § 38.

not know. When at home, a slave had to be either at work or asleep. Indeed Cato greatly favored the sleepy ones, accounting them more docile than those who were wakeful, and more fit for anything when refreshed with slumber than those who lacked it. Being also of the opinion that the greatest cause of misbehavior in slaves was their sexual passions, he arranged for the males to consort with the females at a fixed price and permitted none to approach a woman outside the household.

At first, when he was but a poor soldier, he was not difficult in anything which related to his eating, declaring it was shameful to quarrel with a slave for the belly's sake. But afterwards, when he grew richer and gave feasts for his friends and colleagues in office, as soon as dinner was over he used to go with a leather thong and flog those who had been at all remiss in preparing or serving it. He always contrived, too, that his slaves should have some dissension and difference among themselves, always suspecting and fearing harmony among them. Those who were thought to have committed an offense worthy of death he had judged by the entire body of slaves, and put to death if convicted.

But being much given to the desire of gain, he looked upon agriculture as a pleasure rather than a profit, and invested his money in safe and sure things. He purchased ponds, hot springs, grounds full of fuller's earth, pitch works, and lands containing natural pastures and woods— all of which yielded him large returns and could not, as he used to say, be damaged even by Jupiter himself. He also engaged in the most odious form of money-lending, namely, bottomry loans. His method was the following: he required his borrowers to take numerous partners; when they and their ships numbered fifty, he himself took one share through his freedman Quintio, who sailed with the borrowers and worked with them. Thus the risk was not his entirely, but only in small part, and at great profit. He also lent money to those of his slaves who wished it; they would buy boys and, after training and teaching them at Cato's expense, would sell them again after a year. Many of these Cato would keep for himself, crediting the trainer-slave with the price offered by the highest bidder. To incline his son to such procedures, he used to tell him that it was not like a man, but rather like a widow woman, to lessen an estate. But the strongest indication of Cato's avaricious nature was when he went so far as to affirm that that man was most wonderful, nay godlike, who left more behind in his final accounting than he had inherited.

95. THE GREAT SLAVE UPRISINGS

The overseas conquests of the Roman Republic brought huge numbers of slaves to Italy, where they were employed on latifundia and, to a lesser extent, in industry and commerce. The bulk of these slaves were war captives, but considerable numbers were enslaved also by pirates preying on the shipping lanes (see § 131) and by slave traders who raided "barbarian" regions to help supply the demands of the slave markets of the Roman empire. We have no way of estimating even approximately the total slave population of the Roman world, but some idea of the numbers involved can be obtained from statistics such as the following. We read of 5,000 prisoners taken in Macedonia in 197 B.C. and over 5,000 in Illyria in 177; 80,000 slain and captured that same year in Sardinia; 150,000 Epirotes enslaved in 167 (§ 77); some 60,000 taken at Carthage in 146; 140,000 Teutons and Cimbrians captured by Marius in 102–1 B.C. Caesar is said to have taken nearly half a million captives in his nine years in Gaul.

"Every slave we own is an enemy we harbor." So ran a Roman proverb born of the series of bloody uprisings that marked the last two centuries of the Republic. "There were many of these revolts," says one ancient writer, "and more than a million slaves were killed in them" (Athenaeus, *Savants at Dinner* VI. 272f). Three of these revolts attained the proportions of full-fledged wars, for which the Romans were compelled to mount major military efforts. The Great Slave War, described next, erupted on the latifundia of Sicily in 134 B.C.; before it was finally ended in 131 the slave army in Sicily had swollen to 70,000 or more and their successes had provided the signal for sporadic outbreaks in various parts of the empire. The threatened invasion of Italy by Germanic tribes at the end of the second century B.C. was accompanied by a second great slave uprising in Sicily (*c.* 104–100 B.C.) and by other lesser flare-ups elsewhere. The last of this series was the revolt of the gladiators led by Spartacus, who terrorized the entire Italian peninsula for over two years (73–71 B.C.); more than 100,000 slaves were killed in the fighting, and the 6,000 who were captured were crucified along the Appian Way from Capua to Rome.

Diodorus of Sicily, *Historical Library* XXXIV. Fragments

Never had there been such an uprising of slaves as now occurred in Sicily. In it many cities experienced terrible misfortunes, and untold numbers of men, women, and children suffered most grievous calamities; and the whole island was on the point of falling into the power of the runaways, who set the complete destruction of their masters as the goal of their power.

To most people these events came to pass unlooked for and unexpectedly; but to men of competent political judgment their occurrence did not seem unreasonable. For on account of the immense wealth of those exploiting this rich island, practically all the very wealthy reveled in luxury, arrogance, and insolence. Consequently, as the slaves' hatred of their masters increased *pari passu* with the masters' cruelty towards their slaves, the hatred burst forth one day at an opportune moment. Then, without prearrangement, many thousands of slaves quickly gathered together to destroy their masters.

A similar thing happened in Asia about the same time, when Aristonicus claimed the kingdom not belonging to him, and slaves, because of their masters' cruelty, joined his desperate struggle and involved many cities in great calamities [see introduction to § 128].

The Servile War broke out from the following cause. The Sicilians, being grown very rich and elegant in their manner of living, bought up large numbers of slaves. They brought them in droves from the places where they were reared, and immediately branded them with marks on their bodies. Those that were young they used as shepherds, and the others as need required. . . . Oppressed by the grinding toil and beatings, maltreated for the most part beyond all reason, the slaves could endure it no longer. Therefore, meeting together at suitable opportunities they discussed revolt, until at last they put their plan into effect. There was a Syrian from Apamea named Eunus, a slave of Antigenes of Enna. A kind of magician and conjurer, he claimed to foretell future events from divine revelations in his dreams, and he imposed upon many by his cleverness in this. . . . Before the revolt he used to boast that the Syrian goddess had appeared to him and told him that he would be king; and he repeated this not only to others but even to his own master. . . .

The whole revolt began in the following manner. There was a man in Enna named Damophilus, magnanimous in his wealth but arrogant in disposition. This man was exceedingly cruel to his slaves, and his wife Megallis strove to outdo her husband in torture and general inhumanity toward them. As a result, those who were thus cruelly abused were enraged like wild beasts and plotted together to rise in arms and kill their masters. They applied to Eunus and asked whether the gods would speed them in their design. Performing some of his usual mumbo-jumbo, he concluded that the gods granted it, and urged them to begin at once. Thereupon they forthwith collected 400 of their fellow-slaves and, when the opportunity presented itself, they burst fully armed into the city of Enna with Eunus leading them and performing tricks with flames of fire for them. They stole into the houses and wrought great slaughter. They spared not even the suckling babes, but tore them from the breast and dashed them upon the ground. It cannot be expressed with what wanton outrage they treated wives before the very eyes of their husbands. They were joined by a large throng of the slaves in the city, who first visited the extreme penalty upon their masters and then turned to murdering others. . . .

Then they chose Eunus king, not for his valor nor for his generalship, but only on account of his conjuring power and the fact that he had led the revolt; also, his name seemed like a good omen, portending kindness to his subjects.[10] After being appointed absolute ruler by the rebels, he summoned an assembly and ordered all the inhabitants of Enna that had been taken prisoner put to death except such as were skilled in the manufacture of arms; these he put to work. . . . Eunus himself killed his own master Antigenes and his wife Pytho. Then, wearing a crown and adorned with all the other insignia of royalty, he designated his wife, a Syrian from the same city as himself, as queen, and formed a council of those reputed to be outstanding in intelligence. . . . After arming over 6,000 men as best he could in the space of three days and collecting in addition others equipped with axes, hatchets, slings, sickles, stakes burnt and sharpened at one end, or cooks' spits, he went about plundering the whole country. He attracted a boundless number of slaves, and was emboldened to engage in war even with Roman generals; and in these encounters he overpowered them many times by force of numbers, for he had over 10,000 soldiers.

In the meantime one Cleon, a Cilician, began another revolt of slaves. This fellow . . . hearing of the success of Eunus and the good luck of his followers, persuaded some of the slaves nearby to join with him in revolt, and overran the city of Agrigentum and the countryside round about. Now all were in high hopes that the two groups would make war upon each other, that the rebels would thus destroy themselves and free Sicily of the revolt. But contrary to expectation, they joined forces. Cleon was observant to Eunus' every command and discharged the function of a general serving his king, even though he had 5,000 soldiers of his own.

10. Eunus is a Greek word meaning "well-intentioned," "benevolent."

It was now nearly thirty days since the beginning of the revolt. Shortly thereafter the praetor Lucius Hypsaeus arrived from Rome and met them in battle at the head of 8,000 soldiers mobilized in Sicily. The rebels, now 20,000 in number, were victorious, and before long their army increased to 200,000 men.[11] And they won renown in many battles with the Romans and made few false steps. Upon this being noised abroad, slave revolts flared up in Rome (where 150 conspired against the government), in Athens (over 1,000 involved), in Delos, and in many other places. But these the government officials in the several places quickly suppressed with prompt action and terrible torture as punishment, so that others who were hovering on the point of revolt were recalled to their senses.[12] But in Sicily the evil kept increasing—cities were taken and their inhabitants enslaved, and many armies were cut to pieces by the rebels—until the Roman general Rupilius recovered Tauromenium for the Romans after besieging it tightly and reducing the rebels to such indescribable famine and suffering that they began to eat the children, then the women, and were finally even driven to eating one another. There he captured Comanus, the brother of Cleon, as he was endeavoring to escape out of the besieged city. Finally, a Syrian named Sarapion betrayed the citadel, and the general seized all the runaways in the city, whom he scourged and then crucified. Thence he marched to Enna, and by a like siege reduced the hopes of the rebels to the last extremity. Their general Cleon sallied forth from the city and fought heroically, but before long collapsed beneath his wounds, and his corpse was exposed to open view. Then this city too was betrayed into Rupilius' hands, for its strong natural position made it impregnable. Eunus gathered up his 600 bodyguards and fled like a coward to the top of an abrupt cliff, where those with him, realizing that their doom was

11. This number seems exaggerated. According to Orosius (*History Against the Pagans* v. vi), "70,000 slaves were in the army of the conspirators. This number did not include slaves from the city of Messina, which kept its slaves peaceful by treating them with kindness." Diodorus himself (*Historical Library* xxxvi) gives the number of rebels in the final battle of the Second Sicilian Slave War as 40,000.

12. "The contagion of the Slave War that had arisen in Sicily infected many provinces far and wide. At Minturnae the Romans crucified 500 slaves, at Sinuessa Quintus Metellus and Gnaeus Servilius Caepio overwhelmed about 4,000. In the mines of the Athenians the *strategus* Heraclitus broke up a slave uprising of like character. At Delos citizens, anticipating the movement, crushed the slaves when they arose in another rebellion. These riots, if I may so express myself, represented but additional sparks which, set ablaze by that trouble in Sicily, leaped forth and started all these different fires" (Orosius, *History Against the Pagans* v. ix). Similarly, the Second Sicilian Slave War, thirty years later, also touched off a revolt of the slaves who worked the Athenian mines at Laurium (Athenaeus, *Savants at Dinner* vi. 272f).

inevitable (for already Rupilius was coming after them), cut one another's throats. . . . After that Rupilius overran all Sicily with a few picked companies of men and cleared it of all brigandage more quickly than anyone had hoped.

From *The Gracchi to Octavian, 133–27 B.C.*

96. THE INTERNAL EFFECTS OF FOREIGN CONQUESTS: THE "ROMAN REVOLUTION"

Florus, *Epitome of Roman History* I. xlvii. 1–13; Adapted from *LCL*

Such are the events overseas of the third period[13] of the history of the Roman people, during which, having once ventured to advance outside Italy, they carried their arms over the whole world. The first hundred years of this period were pure and righteous and, as we have said, a golden age, free from vice and crime, while the innocence of the old pastoral life was still untainted and uncorrupted, and the imminent threat of our Carthaginian foes kept alive the ancient discipline. The following hundred years, which we have traced from the destruction of Carthage, Corinth, and Numantia and the inheritance of the Asiatic kingdom of Attalus down to the time of Caesar and Pompey and of their successor Augustus, with whose history we still have to deal, were as unhappy and deplorable owing to internal calamities as they were illustrious for the glory of their military achievements. For, just as it was honorable and glorious to have won the rich and powerful provinces of Gaul, Thrace, Cilicia, and Cappadocia as well as the territory of the Armenians and Britons, which, though they brought no material benefit,[14] constituted important titles to imperial greatness; so it was disgraceful and deplorable at the same time to have fought at home with fellow citizens and allies, with slaves and gladiators, and the whole senate divided against itself. Indeed, I know not whether it would not have been better for the Roman people to have been content with Sicily and Africa, or even to have been without these and to have held domin-

---

13. About 264–30 B.C. The primitivistic nostalgia for the "innocence" of the Romans during their first period of overseas conquests is a convention of late Republican and later literature (cf. above pp. 7–8, the second selection in § 80, and the introduction to § 91).

14. Another of the virtuous pretenses of the post-conquest period; its unreality is obvious.

ion only over their own land of Italy, than to increase to such greatness that they were ruined by their own strength. For what else produced those outbursts of domestic strife but excessive prosperity? It was the conquest of Syria which first corrupted us, followed by the Asiatic inheritance bequeathed by the king of Pergamum. The resources and wealth thus acquired spoiled the morals of the age and ruined the state, which was engulfed in its own vices as in a common sewer. For what else caused the Roman people to demand land and food from their tribunes, except the scarcity which luxury had produced? Hence arose the first and second Gracchan revolutions and the third raised by Appuleius.[15] What was the cause of the violent division between the equestrian order and the senate on the subject of the judiciary laws except avarice, in order that the revenues of the state and the law courts themselves might be exploited for private profit? Hence arose the attempt of Drusus and the promise of citizenship to the Latins, which resulted in war with our allies. Again, what brought the Servile Wars upon us except the excessive size of our slave establishments? How else could those armies of gladiators have arisen against their masters, save that a profuse expenditure, which aimed at winning the favor of the common people by indulging their love of shows, had turned what was originally a method of punishing enemies into a competition of skill? Again, to touch upon less ugly vices, was not ambition for office also stimulated by this wealth? Why, it was from such ambition that the Marian and Sullan disturbances arose. Again, were not the sumptuous extravagances of banquets and profuse largess due to a wealth which was bound soon to produce want? That was what brought Catiline into collision with his country. Finally, whence did the lust for personal power and domination arise save from excessive wealth? It was this lust which armed Caesar and Pompey with the raging torches that destroyed the state.

---

15. Lucius Appuleius Saturninus, tribune of the plebs in 103 and 100 B.C., followed in the Gracchan tradition and met a similar violent death.

97. AGRARIAN REFORM: TIBERIUS GRACCHUS, 133 B.C.

See introduction to § 166.

Plutarch, *Life of Tiberius Gracchus* viii.7–ix. 5, xiv. 1–2

His brother Gaius recorded in one of his writings that when Tiberius on his way to Numantia passed through Etruria and found the country almost depopulated and its husbandmen and shepherds imported barbarian slaves, he [Tiberius] first conceived the policy which was to be the source of countless ills to himself and to his brother. But it was the people themselves who chiefly excited his zeal and determination with writings on the porticoes, walls, and monuments, calling on him to retrieve the public land for the poor.

However, he did not draw up this law by himself, but sought the advice of the citizens who were the most eminent for their virtue and authority; among these were Crassus the *pontifex maximus,* Mucius Scaevola the jurist, who was then consul, and Appius Claudius his father-in-law. Never, it seems, was a law directed against such great injustice and avarice drafted in milder and gentler terms. For men who should have been punished as lawbreakers,[16] who should have been fined and made to surrender the land which they were illegally exploiting, were granted compensation for quitting their unlawful acquisitions so that citizens in need of assistance could have them. But though the terms of the reform were so favorable and the people were willing to let bygones be bygones if they could be secure from such wrong in the future, yet the men of wealth and property were led by their greed to hate the law and by their anger and party spirit to hate the lawgiver. They endeavored to dissuade the people by charging that Tiberius was introducing a redistribution of lands in order to cause dissension in the state, and was starting a general revolution.

But they had no success. For Tiberius, fighting for an honorable and just cause with an eloquence that would have dignified even a meaner cause, was formidable and invincible whenever, with the people crowding around the Rostra, he took his place and spoke in behalf of the poor.

16. That is, violators of the Licinio-Sextian Law of 367 B.C. on maximum holdings of public land (see § 38).

"The wild beasts that roam over Italy," he said, "have their dens, each has a place of repose and refuge. But the men who fight and die for Italy enjoy nothing but the air and light; without house or home they wander about with their wives and children.[17] Their commanders lie when they exhort the soldiers in battle to defend sepulchers and shrines from the enemy, for not one of these many Romans has either hereditary altar or ancestral tomb; they fight and die to protect the wealth and luxury of others; they are styled masters of the world, and have not a clod of earth they can call their own." . . .

About this time King Attalus Philometor died, and Eudemus of Pergamum brought to Rome his last will, in which the Roman people was named the king's heir [see § 128]. Tiberius promptly proposed a law of popular appeal providing that the king's money, when brought to Rome, should be distributed among those of the citizens receiving allotments of public land, to provide them with equipment and give them a start in farming. As for the cities that were in the kingdom of Attalus, he declared that the disposal of them was not the senate's business, but that he himself would put a resolution before the people. By this he offended the senate more than ever.

Appian, Civil Wars i.i. 9–ii. 16 (abridged); Adapted from LCL

Tiberius Sempronius Gracchus, an illustrious man, eager for glory, a most powerful speaker, and for these reasons well known to all, delivered an eloquent discourse while serving as tribune, lamenting the fact that the Italians, a people so valiant in war and related in blood to the Romans, were declining little by little into pauperism and paucity of numbers without any hope of remedy. He inveighed against the multitude of slaves as useless in war and never faithful to their masters, and adduced the recent calamity brought upon the masters by their slaves in Sicily [see § 95], where the demands of agriculture had greatly increased the number of the latter; recalling also that the war waged against them by the Romans was neither easy nor short, but long-protracted and full of vicissitudes and dangers. After speaking thus he again brought forward the law providing that nobody should hold more than 500 *iugera* of public domain [see note 16]. But he added a provision to the former law, that [two] sons of the occupiers might each hold one half that

---

17. One is reminded of the similar Scriptural protest (Luke 9:58): "The foxes have holes, and the birds of the air nests, but the Son of Man hath not where to lay his head."

amount and that the remainder should be divided among the poor by three elected commissioners, who should be changed annually.

This was extremely disturbing to the rich because, on account of the commissioners, they could no longer disregard the law as they had done before; nor could they buy from those receiving allotments, because Gracchus had provided against this by forbidding such sales. They collected together in groups, and made lamentation, and accused the poor of appropriating their fields of long standing, their vineyards, and their buildings. Some said they had paid the price of the land to their neighbors. Were they to lose the money with the land? Others said the graves of their ancestors were in the ground, which had been allotted to them in the division of their fathers' estates. Others said that their wives' dowries had been expended on these estates, or that the land had been given to their own daughters as dowry. Moneylenders could show loans made on this security. All kinds of wailing and expressions of indignation were heard at once. On the other side were heard the lamentations of the poor—that they were being reduced from competence to extreme poverty, and from that to childlessness, because they were unable to rear their offspring. They recounted the military services they had rendered, by which this very land had been acquired, and were angry that they should be robbed of their share of the common property. They reproached the rich for employing slaves, who were always faithless and ill-disposed and for that reason exempted from military service, instead of freemen, citizens, and soldiers. While these classes were thus lamenting and indulging in mutual recrimination, a great number of others— colonists or inhabitants of municipalities or persons otherwise interested in this land—who were under like apprehensions, flocked in and took sides with their respective factions. Emboldened by numbers and exasperated against each other they kindled incessant disturbances, and waited eagerly for the voting of the new law, some intending to prevent its enactment by all means, and others to enact it at all costs. . . .

What Gracchus had in mind in proposing the measure was not wealth of money, but wealth of men. Inspired greatly by the usefulness of the work, and believing that nothing more advantageous or admirable could ever happen to Italy, he took no account of the difficulties surrounding it. When the time for voting came, he advanced many other arguments at considerable length, but asked them especially whether it was not just to divide the common property among the commons; whether a citizen was not worthy of more consideration at all times than a slave; whether a man who served in the army was not more useful than one who did not; and whether one who had a share in the country was not more likely to be devoted to the public interests. He did not dwell long on this comparison between freemen and slaves, which he considered degrading, but proceeded at once to a review of their hopes and fears for the country, saying that the Romans possessed most of their territory by conquest, and that they had hopes of occupying the rest of the habitable world; but now the question of greatest hazard was whether they should gain the rest by having plenty of brave men or, through their weakness and mutual jealousy, lose to their enemies what they already possessed. After exaggerating the glory and riches on the one side and the danger and fear on the other, he admonished the rich to take heed, and said that for the realization of these hopes they ought to bestow this land as a free gift, if necessary, on men who would rear children and not, by quarreling about small things, overlook larger ones; especially since they were receiving ample compensation for any improvements they had made by obtaining without cost absolute title, guaranteed forever, to 500 *iugera* apiece and half as much more for each son [up to two] in the case of those who had sons. After saying much more to the same purport and exciting the poor, as well as others who were moved by reason rather than by the desire for gain, he ordered the clerk to read the proposed law.

> [When, under pressure from the senate, Marcus Octavius, one of the ten tribunes, vetoed the law, Gracchus had him deposed from office by a vote of the assembly—an act without precedent in Roman constitutional history. The agrarian law was then enacted.]

The first commissioners elected to divide the land were Gracchus himself, the proposer of the law, his brother of the same name [Gaius Gracchus (see § 98)], and his father-in-law Appius Claudius, since the people still feared that the law might fail of execution unless Gracchus together with his whole family took the lead. Gracchus, immensely popular by reason of the law, was escorted home by the multitude as though he were the founder, not of a single city or people, but of all the nations of Italy. After this the victorious party returned to the fields from which they had come to attend to this business. The defeated ones remained in the city and talked the matter over, feeling aggrieved and saying that as soon as Gracchus should become a private citizen he would be sorry that he had done outrage to the sacred and inviolable office of tribune, and had sown in Italy so many seeds of future strife.

It was now summer, and the election of tribunes was imminent. As the day for the voting approached it was evident that the rich had earnestly promoted the election of those most inimical to Gracchus. The latter, fearing that evil would befall if he should not be reelected for the following year, summoned his friends from the fields to the election; but as they were occupied with the harvest, he was obliged, when the day fixed for the voting drew near, to have recourse to the plebeians of the city. So he went around asking each one in turn to elect him tribune for the ensuing year, in view of the danger he was incurring for their sake. When the voting took place the first two tribes pronounced for Gracchus. The rich thereupon objected that it was unconstitutional for the same man to hold the office twice in succession [but cf. §§ 38–40].

[Because of parliamentary maneuvering over the chairmanship of the *comitia* the election was postponed to the following day.]

Gracchus assembled his partisans before daybreak and communicated to them a signal to be displayed if there was need for fighting. He then took possession of the Capitol, where the voting was to take place, and occupied the middle of the assembly. As he was obstructed by the other tribunes and by the rich, who would not allow the votes to be taken on this question, he gave the signal. There was a sudden shout from those who knew of it, and violence followed. Some of the partisans of Gracchus took position around him like bodyguards. Others, girding up their cloaks, seized the *fasces* and staves in the hands of the lictors and broke them in pieces. They drove the rich out of the assembly with such disorder and wounds that the tribunes fled from their places in terror, and the priests closed the doors of the temple. Many ran away pell-mell and scattered wild rumors. Some said that Gracchus had deposed all the other tribunes, conjecturing this because none of them could be seen. Others said that he had declared himself tribune for the ensuing year without an election.

In these circumstances the senate assembled at the temple of Fides. . . . After reaching such decision as they did reach, they marched up to the Capitol, Cornelius Scipio Nasica, the *pontifex maximus,* leading the way. . . . When he arrived at the temple and advanced against the partisans of Gracchus they yielded out of regard for so distinguished a citizen, and because they observed the senators following with him. The latter, wresting the clubs out of the hands of the Gracchans themselves, and breaking up benches and other furniture that had been brought for the use of the assembly, began beating them, pursued them, and drove them over the precipice. In the tumult many of the Gracchans perished, and Gracchus himself, vainly circling around the temple, was slain at the door close to the statues of the kings. All the bodies were thrown by night into the Tiber.

98. GAIUS GRACCHUS' REFORM PROGRAM, 123–121 B.C.

Plutarch, *Life of Gaius Gracchus* iii–ix (abridged)

Gaius now came forward to ask for the tribuneship. Though he was universally opposed by all persons of distinction, yet there came such infinite numbers of people from all parts of Italy to vote for him that lodgings for many could not be provided in the city; and the Campus Martius not being large enough to contain the assembly, there were many who climbed upon the roofs and tilings of the houses to use their voices in his favor. However, the nobility so far forced the people to their will and disappointed Gaius' hopes, that he was not returned the first, as he expected, but the fourth tribune. But when he came to the execution of his office, it was quickly seen who was really first tribune, as he was a more powerful orator than any of his contemporaries, and his affliction gave him greater boldness in speaking as he lamented his brother's death. . . .

Having moved the people's passion with such addresses . . . he proposed two laws. The first provided that any magistrate deprived of his office should be thereby disbarred from holding any future office; the second made liable to prosecution before the people any magistrate who had condemned a citizen to be banished without trial. The first of these laws was manifestly leveled at Marcus Octavius, who had been deposed from the tribuneship at Tiberius' instigation. The second affected Popilius, who in his consulship had banished Tiberius' friends [see introduction to § 99]; whereupon Popilius, being unwilling to risk a trial, fled out of Italy. . . . As for the former law, it was withdrawn by Gaius himself, who said he spared Octavius at the request of his mother, Cornelia. . . .

Of the laws which he now proposed with the object of gratifying the people and destroying the power of the senate, the first concerned public lands, which were to be divided among the poor citizens; another provided that the common soldiers should be clothed at public expense without any reduction in pay, and that no one under seventeen years of age should be conscripted for military service; another concerned the allies, giving the Italians equal suffrage rights with the citizens of Rome; a fourth related to grain, lowering the market price for the poor;[18] a fifth, dealing with the courts of justice, was the greatest blow to the power of the senators, for hitherto they alone could sit on the juries, and they were therefore much dreaded by the plebs and *equites*. But Gaius joined 300 citizens of equestrian rank with the senators, who were also 300 in number, and made jury service the common prerogative of the 600. . . .[19] When the people not only ratified this law but gave him power to select those of the *equites* who were to serve as jurors, he was invested with almost kingly power, and even the senate submitted to receiving his counsel. Nor did he advise any measure that might derogate from the honor of that body. For example, the decree about the grain which the propraetor Fabius sent from Spain was very equitable and honorable; for he persuaded the senate to sell the grain and send the money back to the Spanish cities, and also to censure Fabius for rendering his government of the province odious and intolerable to the inhabitants. This earned him great respect and good will in the provinces.

He also proposed measures for sending out colonies, for constructing roads, and for building public granaries. He himself undertook the management and superintendence of all these works and was never too busy to attend to the execution of all these different and great undertakings. . . . His most especial exertions were given to road construction, in which he had an eye to beauty and grace as well as to utility. For the roads were carried through the country in a perfectly straight line, and were paved with hewn stone and reinforced with banks of tight-rammed sand. Depressions were filled up, all intersecting torrents or ravines were bridged, and both sides were of equal and corresponding height, so that the work presented everywhere an even and beautiful appearance. Besides all this, he measured off all the roads by miles . . . and planted stone pillars as distance markers.[20] He also placed other stones at shorter

18. The law set up a state granary from which Roman citizens could purchase one bushel of grain a month. Since this grain was sold at a price approximately equivalent to the market price in the grain-producing area, it can hardly be said that the law was exhausting the treasury, as the nobility charged (see § 101). However, since the threshing-floor price would be only a fraction of the market price in Rome, it is easy to see why the Gracchan law aroused the outraged opposition of large landowners, grain speculators, and others who profited from the grain trade.

19. This is not quite accurate. See further below, and § 100.

20. For a milestone of this period, see § 99.

intervals on both sides of the way, by the help of which travelers might easily mount their horses without needing a groom. . . .

Gaius was elected tribune a second time on a wave of popular enthusiasm, without his announcing candidacy or campaigning. And when he realized that the senators were his avowed enemies, and that Fannius'[21] good will toward him was only lukewarm, he began again to rally the people with other laws. He proposed that colonies be sent to Tarentum and Capua, and summoned the Latins to equal partnership in Roman citizenship. But the senate, fearing that he would become altogether invincible, made a new and unusual attempt to alienate the people from him by competing with him in playing the demagogue and gratifying the people contrary to the best interests of the state. One of Gaius' colleagues was Livius Drusus, a man of as good family and breeding as any of the Romans, and the equal in eloquence and wealth of the men most honored and most powerful in these respects. To him, then, the nobles turned, urging him to join them and attack Gaius—not by resorting to violence or clashing with the common people, but by exercising his office so as to gratify and oblige them, even in matters where sound policy would have incurred their hatred.

Livius accordingly offered the senate the services of his office in this matter, and proceeded to bring forward laws neither honorable nor advantageous: his one purpose was to outdo Gaius in pleasing and cajoling the populace. . . . The senate thus made it perfectly clear that it was not angry with Gaius' public measures, but only anxious to destroy the man himself, or at least to humble him. For when Gaius proposed two colonies, to which he would admit only the soberest of citizens, they accused him of truckling to the mob; but when Drusus proposed to found twelve colonies, and to send out to each 3,000 of the poor citizens, they supported him. When Gaius divided public land among the needy and charged each of them a small rental to be paid into the treasury, they were angry at him, accusing him of seeking to curry favor with the populace; but they commended Livius when he proposed to abolish the rental altogether. And when Gaius was for offering the Latins equal suffrage rights, they were incensed; but when Livius proposed that it be made unlawful for a Latin to be scourged with rods even during military service, they supported his law.

---

21. One of the consuls of 122 B.C., elected with Gaius Gracchus' backing.

Appian, *Civil Wars* I. iii. 22–26; Adapted from *LCL*

Thus Gaius Gracchus was tribune a second time. Having bought the plebeians, as it were, be began by another like political maneuver to court the equestrian order, which holds the middle rank between senate and plebs. He transferred the courts of justice, which had become discredited by bribery, from the senators to the *equites,* reproaching the former especially with [three] recent examples of . . . notorious extortioners who had been acquitted by their juries (the envoys sent to complain of the conduct of these men were still present in Rome, going about uttering bitter accusations against them). The senate was extremely ashamed of these things and yielded to the law, and the people ratified it. In this way the courts of justice were transferred from the senate to the *equites.* It is said that soon after the passage of this law Gracchus remarked that he had broken the power of the senate once and for all, and the truth of his remark was progressively revealed by the course of events. For this power of sitting in judgment on all Romans and Italians, including the senators themselves, in all matters concerning property, civil rights, and banishment, exalted the *equites* to be rulers over them, as it were, and reduced the senators to the level of subjects. Moreover, as the *equites* voted in the election to sustain the power of the tribunes and obtained from them whatever they wanted in return, they became more and more formidable to the senators. Thus it shortly came about that the political mastery was reversed, the *equites* wielding the power while the senate was left with honor alone. The *equites* indeed went so far that they not only held the whip hand over the senators but openly flouted them beyond their right: they too became addicted to bribe-taking, and when they had tasted these enormous gains they indulged in them even more basely and immoderately than the senators had done; they suborned accusers against the rich and did away with prosecutions for bribe-taking altogether, partly by agreement among themselves and partly by open violence, so that this kind of inquiry ceased entirely. Thus the judiciary law gave rise to another struggle of factions, which lasted a long time and was not less baneful than the former ones. . . .

After losing the favor of the rabble, Gracchus sailed for Africa together with Fulvius Flaccus, who had been chosen tribune after his consulship for the same reasons as Gracchus himself. It had been decided to send a colony to Africa on account of its famed fertility, and these men had been expressly chosen the founders of it in order to get them out of the way for a while, so that the senate might have a respite from their demagogy. They marked out the city for the colony on the site where Carthage had previously stood, disregarding the fact that Scipio, when he destroyed it, had devoted it with solemn imprecations to sheep pasture forever. They marked out lands for 6,000 colonists instead of the smaller number fixed by the law, in order to curry favor with the people [cf. § 102]. When they returned to Rome they invited the 6,000 from the whole of Italy. The functionaries who were still in Africa laying out the city wrote home that wolves had pulled up and scattered the boundary markers of Gracchus and Fulvius. The soothsayers considered this an ill omen for the colony, and the senate summoned the assembly to propose the repeal of the law concerning this colony. When Gracchus and Fulvius saw their failure in this matter they were furious, and declared that the senate had lied about the wolves. The boldest of the plebeians joined them, carrying daggers, and proceeded to the Capitol, where the assembly was to be held in reference to the colony. . . .

Gracchus went into the Forum anxious to exculpate himself of the killing, but no one would listen to him; all turned away from him as from one stained with blood. Both he and Flaccus were at their wits' end and, having lost by this rash act the chance of accomplishing what they desired, they hastened to their homes, accompanied by their supporters. After midnight the rest of the crowd occupied the Forum as though some calamity were impending, and the consul Opimius, who was staying in the city, ordered an armed force to gather at the Capitol at daybreak and sent heralds to convoke the senate. He took his own station in the temple of Castor and Pollux in the center of the city, and there awaited developments.

When these arrangements had been made, the senate summoned Gracchus and Fulvius from their homes to defend themselves. But they fled, armed, to the Aventine Hill, hoping that if they could seize it first the senate would agree to some terms with them. As they ran through the city they summoned the slaves to freedom, but none listened to them. With such forces as they had, however, they occupied and fortified the temple of Diana and sent Quintus, Flaccus' son, to the senate with an offer to reach an accommodation and live in harmony. The senate replied that they should lay down their arms, come to the senate house and tell what they wanted, or else send no more messengers.

When they sent Quintus a second time the consul Opimius arrested him (on the ground that he was no longer an ambassador after the above warning), and sent his soldiers against the Gracchans.[22]

Gracchus fled with one slave by the wooden bridge across the river to a grove, and there, when on the point of capture, he presented his throat to the slave. Flaccus took refuge in the shop of an acquaintance. As his pursuers did not know which house he was in, they threatened to burn the whole row. The man who had given him shelter scrupled to point him out, but directed another to do so. Flaccus was seized and put to death. The heads of Gracchus and Flaccus were carried to Opimius, who gave their weight in gold to those who brought them, and people plundered their houses. Opimius arrested their fellow conspirators, cast them into prison, and ordered them to be strangled; but he allowed Quintus, Flaccus' son, to choose his own manner of death. After this he performed a lustration of the city for the bloodshed, and the senate ordered him to erect a temple of Concord in the Forum.

99. DISTRIBUTION OF PUBLIC LAND

The violent removal of each of the Gracchus brothers was followed by a decade of senatorial reaction. Nevertheless, the reforms they had championed could not be entirely or immediately undone. In particular, the land commissions continued to function until 118 B.C., and the land assignments made by them remained in force (cf. § 102); concrete evidence is afforded by a series of extant inscribed boundary stones attesting their activity, a few of which are reproduced here (technical surveying marks are here omitted). It is especially striking to find Popillius Laenas, who as consul in 132 presided over the bloody purge of Tiberius Gracchus' followers, publicly proclaiming that he was the first to carry out the provisions of Gracchus' land law.

---

22. The senate authorized the consul to take military action within the city limits by passing its "ultimate decree" *(senatus consultum ultimum)*, the first such in Roman history. Cicero gives the actual text of the decree *(Philippics* VIII. iv. 14): "Whereas Lucius Opimius the consul spoke on a matter touching the state, concerning this matter the Senate decreed that Lucius Opimius the consul should defend the state." On this Roman approximation of martial law, see further § 157.

CIL, vol.I, 2d ed., no. 638 (=ROL, 4:150–151)

[Near Forum Popilii in Lucania. 132 B.C.] Publius Popillius son of Gaius, consul. I built the road[23] from Regium to Capua, and on that road I placed all the bridges, milestones, and signposts. From here it is 51 miles to Nuceria, 84 to Capua, 74 to Muranum, 123 to Cosentia, 180 to Valentia, 231 to the strait [of Messina] at the Statue, 237 to Regium; total from Capua to Regium, 321. I also, as praetor in Sicily [during the Great Slave War (§ 95)]: hunted down the runaway slaves belonging to men from Italy and handed back 917 to their owners. Further, I was the first to make cattle breeders retire from public state land in favor of plowmen. Here I erected a market and public buildings.

CIL, vol. I, 2d ed., nos. 640, 643, 719 (=ROL, 4:170–175); From LCL

[Near St. Angelo in Formis. 131 B.C.] Gaius Sempronius Gracchus son of Tiberius, Appius Claudius Pulcher son of Gaius, Publius Licinius Crassus son of Publius, Board of Three for adjudging and assigning lands.

[Near ancient Aeclanum. 123 B.C.] Marcus Fulvius Flaccus son of Marcus, Gaius Sempronius Gracchus son of Tiberius, Gaius Papirius Carbo son of Gaius, Board of Three for adjudging and assigning lands. Estate allowed to established occupier free of charge.[24]

[Between ancient Pisanum and Fanum. 82 or 81 B.C.] Marcus Terentius Varro Lucullus son of Marcus, propraetor, by decree of the senate superintended the reestablishment of boundary stones where Publius Licinius, Appius Claudius, and Gaius Gracchus, Board of Three for granting, assigning, and adjudging lands, established them.

100. LAWS ON EXTORTION

THE ACILIAN LAW ON EXTORTION

The eleven surviving pieces of this inscription comprise a precious record of one of the most significant phases of Gaius Gracchus' [123 or 122 B.C.] program—uniting the *equites* with the plebs against the senate. By this

---

23. A continuation of the Appian Way, the greatest highway in southern Italy.
24. The last phrase is a conjecture.

law the nobility were excluded from the juries of the extortion court and replaced by *equites* (cf. §§ 98, 158), thus opening an era in which control of this criminal court became a political football (the Acilian Law itself was superseded by 111 B.C.). It is noteworthy that no such measures were taken in the Gracchan program to put teeth into the prosecution of extortion perpetrated by publicans, who were members of the equestrian order. Only selected sections of this long document are given here.

CIL, vol. I, 2d ed., no. 583 (= *ROL,* 4:316–371)

. . . Acilius Glabrio, tribune of the plebs, duly proposed, and the plebs duly approved . . . the . . . tribe voted first, the first tribesman to vote was. . . .

From any person who has been dictator, consul, praetor, master of the horse, censor, aedile, tribune of the plebs, quaestor, member of the three-man board on capital crimes [see chapter 7, note 1] or the three-man board for granting or assigning lands, military tribune in any one of the first four legions, or from a son of any of the foregoing, or from . . . any person who, or whose father, is a senator, for a sum of money, the amount of which for any particular year shall exceed . . . sesterces[25] . . . such sum having been, in the exercise of an *imperium* or magisterial office, carried off, taken away, exacted, embezzled or misappropriated from the said person himself or his king or his people or his parent, or from any person who is or shall be subject to him or his parent as head of a family, husband or owner, or from any person to whom he or his parent or his son shall stand as heir. In such case the said person shall have the right to sue and to summon the defendant, the inquiry shall fall to a praetor, and the trial, adjudication, and assessment of damages shall by this law belong to those persons who by this law shall constitute the court. . . .

In the case of any defendant under this law who, after adjudication of his case, shall be alleged to have acted in violation of this law, or against whom a summons shall have been taken out by way of collusion, or whose name in accordance with this law shall have been stricken from the list of defendants, if any person shall desire a second time to summon such party before a praetor, in such matter the said person shall have the right to sue and to summon such party; the inquiry shall fall to the said praetor, and the trial, adjudication, and assessment of damages shall by

---

25. It is a safe guess that the figure here lost was a large one; the law does not concern itself with small amounts.

this law belong to those persons who by this law shall constitute the court. If any person shall desire in accordance with this law . . . to sue or to bring a summons in the name of another person, such person shall have the right to sue and to summon the defendant, the inquiry shall fall to the said praetor, and the trial, adjudication and assessment of damages shall by this law belong to those persons who by this law shall constitute the court.

Such person shall bring the defendant into court before the praetor, to whom in accordance with this law the inquiry shall for that year belong, before September 1st of that year, and shall take out his summons. . . .[26] In the case of a summons being taken out after September 1st the praetor shall, if the petitioner so desire, grant *recuperatores.* . . . Any person summoned in accordance with this law later than September 1st in any year and condemned by such board of *recuperatores,* shall pay the amount of money at which the damages for such matter shall be assessed, to the person who brought about his conviction . . . and the said money shall belong to the person who brought the suit. The praetor to whom in accordance with this law the inquiry shall belong, shall see that whatever sum . . . has been so adjudged shall be paid to the private individual who brings the suit.

THE FOLLOWING PERSONS NOT TO BE TRIED AS LONG AS THEY SHALL HOLD A MAGISTRACY OR AN IMPERIUM. A dictator, consul, praetor, master of the horse, censor, aedile, tribune of the plebs, quaestor, member of the three-man board on capital crimes or of the three-man board for granting or assigning land, military tribune of any of the first four legions, shall not be summoned to undergo trial as long as he shall hold his magistracy or his *imperium.* It is not the intention of this law to prevent any one of the said persons from being summoned to undergo trial after he has laid down his magistracy or *imperium.* . . .

CONCERNING THE 450 PERSONS TO BE SELECTED ANNUALLY. A praetor who after the passage of this law shall in accordance with this law be appointed to preside over the court[27] . . . shall within the ten days next following the commencement of the said magistracy take steps

---

26. Sufficient time had to be allowed for the praetor to dispose of the case before the end of his year of office. If the case was tried before the praetor and the defendant was convicted, restitution was for double the amount involved; if summary judgment was given by *recuperatores,* the case was treated as a private action and restitution was for the simple amount.

27. A special "praetor for extortion cases" *(praetor de repetundis)* was apparently created by this law.

to select [a jury panel of] 450 persons who, being citizens within this state, possess or have possessed a ratable property of 400,000 sesterces or more[28]. . . . provided that he selects no person who is or shall have been tribune of the plebs, quaestor, member of the three-man board on capital crimes, military tribune of any of the first four legions, member of the three-man board for granting or assigning lands, or who is or shall have been in the senate, or who has fought or shall have fought as a hired gladiator . . . or who has been condemned in a criminal inquiry or public court, thereby becoming disqualified for election to the senate, or who is less than 30 or more than 60 years of age, or who does not possess a domicile in or within one mile of the city of Rome, or who is the father, brother, or son of any magistrate mentioned above, or is the father, brother, or son of any person who is or shall have been in the senate, or who shall be beyond the sea. . . .

CONCERNING THE HOLDING OF AN INVESTIGATION FOR EVIDENCE. The praetor, after the summons has been brought before him, shall cause the court to be constituted on the first possible day and shall, without prejudice, assign to the summoner under this law as many days as he thinks fit for holding the investigation for evidence, provided that nothing be done contrary to this law; nor, after the passage of this law . . . and he shall order evidence to be collected within Italy in the towns, *fora,* and *conciliabula* [see chapter 7, note 38] where prefects are customarily sent for jurisdiction, or outside Italy in the towns, *fora,* and *conciliabula* where prefects are customarily sent for jurisdiction. . . .

CONCERNING THE MANNER OF GIVING A VERDICT ON THE ACCUSED. As soon as two thirds of the jurors present shall have declared that their minds are made up on the case . . . the praetor conducting the inquiry shall cause those jurors who have refused to give any verdict to be removed . . . and shall proceed with the case. Then the praetor shall, with the assistance of his attendants and apparitors, see that no juror shall leave the court . . . and shall cause a box . . . digits broad and 20 digits high to be set in place, into which the jurors may cast their voting tablets . . . and the said praetor shall publicly place in the hand of each several juror one voting tablet of box wood, 4 digits long and . . . digits wide, waxed on both sides, with the letter *A* written on one side and the

28. The minimum property qualification for the equestrian order, from which the jurors were to be selected.

letter *C* on the other,[29] and shall order the said juror to obliterate whichever one he wishes . . . The juror shall in such manner obliterate the same and shall bring forward the said tablet, clearly visible in accordance with this law—i.e., with his arm open to view but the letter covered by his fingers—towards the said box, shall display the said tablet towards the public . . . and in like manner towards the other jurors severally, and shall in such manner cast the same into the said box.

CONCERNING THE ACQUITTAL OF THE DEFENDANT. Unless the majority of the said votes shall be for condemnation, the praetor conducting the inquiry in accordance with this law shall pronounce the said defendant not guilty. A defendant in respect of whom the praetor shall have so pronounced shall then, save as regards any later act or any act of collusion or conspiracy, be acquitted of the charge in accordance with this law.

CONCERNING THE CONDEMNATION OF THE DEFENDANT. If the majority of the said votes shall be for condemnation, the praetor conducting the inquiry in accordance with this law shall pronounce the said defendant guilty.

THE SAME CASE NOT TO BE TRIED TWICE. As respecting any defendant condemned or acquitted in accordance with this law, no further proceedings shall be taken against such person save in respect to any later act or any act of collusion or conspiracy, or in respect to assessment of damages. . . .

CONCERNING THE GRANT OF THE CITIZENSHIP. If any person, not being a Roman citizen, shall summon another person in accordance with this law before the praetor to whom such inquiry shall belong, and the said person shall be condemned in such trial under this law, then the person who brought the summons, and by whose agency it shall appear that the said person was chiefly condemned . . . shall, if he so will, both himself and the sons who shall have been born to him, be made Roman citizens by this law, and the grandsons afterward born to such a son shall be full Roman citizens, and in whatever tribe the person summoned

29. A = "I acquit," C = "I condemn."

by him in accordance with this law shall have voted, the said persons shall vote in that tribe and be registered by the censor therein; and the said persons shall have exemption from military service. . . .

UPDATED LEGISLATION

The continuing serious problems of official corruption in the administration of the empire were addressed some time in the last decade of the second century B.C. by the following new law, parts of which are preserved in this fragmentary, much restored, bronze inscription found in Tarentum in southern Italy.

Zeitschrift für Papyrologie und Epigraphik (1982), 45:127–138

If anyone who is not a Roman citizen has reported the name of another person to the praetor who in accordance with this law is in charge of the investigation, and that person is found guilty through this judicial procedure, then he who reported his name and through whose efforts especially he has been found guilty, each such one who in his own community is not a dictator, praetor or aedile, if he does not wish in accordance with this law to become a Roman citizen, he, his sons, and grandsons born of such a son, shall in their own community be immune in every respect including payment of tribute, and have the right of appeal to Roman magistrates or promagistrates as if they were Roman citizens, and all obligations of military and public service and all military payments and stipends shall be considered as absolved by them.

If in a lawsuit he himself, his sons and grandsons by such a son shall summon another, or if they are subpoenaed by another for a legal proceeding, let the matter be tried in Rome if they so desire, before any magistrate before whom it is lawful for Roman citizens to appear in such a matter. And no magistrate or promagistrate shall cause the judicial procedure in his case to be lessened or worsened. And that magistrate to whom there is access in his lawsuit shall not proceed otherwise in his case than is proper in accordance with this law. And if any decision is made in this matter contrary to this law without his consent, it shall be lawful that that judgment be restrained in the case of that magistrate, provided it results from the latter's deceit.

A Roman citizen who in accordance with this law has reported the name of another person, if that person is found guilty in that legal proceeding, then the one among those by whose efforts especially he was found guilty, he himself, his sons and grandsons born of such a son, it shall be lawful for those of them who so desire it to cast their votes in the tribe of the one who was convicted, and to be enrolled in that tribe in the census. And for them a summons to military and public service and military pay and stipends shall be considered satisfied. With regard to a summons to public or military service, present or future, in accordance with this law, no magistrate or promagistrate shall cause him in his community to perform such service against his will, nor order him to do so, nor exercise restraint contrary to the right of appeal, nor enrol him as a soldier, nor administer the military oath, nor ask for an oath of allegiance, nor order him to be so asked, nor lead him into military action, nor cause him to do so without his consent, except in the case of a Gallic or Italian uprising. . . .

The praetor who has jurisdiction in cases involving foreigners shall see to it that copies of this law be given to envoys of the allies, of all of the Latin name, and of foreign peoples and client kings if they desire it. And he shall see to it that this law is read at a public assembly and in the senate annually six months before and six months after [such distribution].

The quaestor whose competence is the treasury shall look after the posting in the Forum where it can be read at eye level, of a bronze tablet inscribed with this law and made with inscribed letters. When this tablet has been so posted, all the magistrates shall see to it that this tablet not be thrown down nor suffer detriment at the hands of those who drafted it and were present at the writing, and those who for any other reason handled it.

The praetor under whose jurisdiction this will fall shall see to it that a complete register is posted in the Forum on a white tablet of the names of the informers during his year from every ally, people, or community or kingdom. And when judgment in accordance with this law has been made, with regard to this register he shall see to it that the decision is recorded of those who were jurors in the matter concerning him who in accordance with this law will be acquitted or who in accordance with this law will be found guilty.

If anyone has been found guilty in accordance with this law and it is proposed that the one among those by whose efforts especially he was found guilty shall receive a reward, concerning that matter with regard to those who reported his name each juror openly and separately in court shall cast a ballot, and the praetor shall honor the one who is seen to have a majority of the votes of the jurors with a reward as written above, and the name of the one so rewarded he shall cause to be inscribed on a bronze tablet and affixed to the base of the Rostra.

The magistrate or promagistrate and the jurors impaneled in accordance with this law shall swear by Jupiter and the Penates gods that they will do what is required by this law and that they will not act contrary to this law with malice aforethought nor interfere in a manner whereby this law will be lessened or worsened. A person who has not sworn in accordance with this law shall not be a candidate for a magistracy nor receive the *imperium,* nor act or declare views in the senate nor shall any censor permit him in or select him for the senate.

Whoever has so sworn in accordance with this law shall see to it that his name be recorded with the quaestor who has received the treasury as his competence, and this quaestor shall receive those names, and the persons who have sworn before him in accordance with this law he shall cause their names to be recorded in the public records.

For those required to swear in accordance with this law the praetor who has jurisdiction in cases involving foreigners when he has announced the deadline date before which it will be required to swear in accordance with this law on each of three market days in a row shall openly summon them to the oath. Thereafter the names of those who have sworn in accordance with this law shall be inscribed on a tablet and set up in the Forum. When cases are brought forth . . . the praetor under whose jurisdiction it lies in accordance with this law shall see to it that that tablet be cited in its entirety.

No one shall perpetrate any fraud against this law with malice aforethought, nor make decisions so that what is required to be done in accordance with this law is lessened or worsened. If anyone acts contrary to this law, the praetor shall fine each one . . . sesterces for each separate matter.

If anything of a sacral nature has not been properly enacted, nothing shall be enacted in this respect by this law. The tribunes of the plebs of the year in which they are bound by this law or in which they swear by this law shall enact nothing of that kind by this law.

101. "OPTIMATES" AND "POPULARES"

One of the results of the Gracchan movement was the crystallization of an antisenatorial movement *(populares)*. The senate's recourse to lynch law against the Gracchans established a precedent of violence which ultimately brought about its own undoing: in the first century B.C. armed force became the regular arbiter of political differences in republican Rome, and the final result was the overthrow of the senatorial regime and the establishment of the Principate (cf. introduction to § 106).

The opinions and attitudes expressed by Cicero in the second and third of the following selections are, as so often in his speeches and writings, not his alone, but those held by most of the Roman nobility in the last decades of the Republic (these selections date, respectively, from 56 B.C. and 44 B.C.). Thus, the *optimates,* or senatorial bloc, are equated with the honest, good, sober, respectable, and important citizens *(integri, boni, sani, bene constituti, graves);* and, with the lack of penetration that characterized senatorial policy in its ultimate days, the ferment of the century-long Roman Revolution is dismissed as the work of professional demagogues and "agitators." Characteristically, since the existence of deep-seated economic and political maladjustments is thus blandly denied, there are no proposals for reform but merely a reaffirmation of the sanctity of property rights and the necessity of firmly maintaining the status quo.

THE INCREASING RESORT TO VIOLENCE IN ROMAN POLITICS

Appian, *Civil Wars* 1, Introduction. 2; Adapted from *LCL*

The sword was never carried into the assembly and there was no civil slaughter until Tiberius Gracchus, tribune and lawbringer, was the first to fall a victim to internal commotion; and with him many others, who were crowded together at the Capitol around the temple, were also slain. Sedition did not end with that abominable deed. Repeatedly the parties came into open conflict, often carrying daggers, and from time to time in the temples, the assemblies, or the Forum some tribune, praetor, consul, or candidate for these offices, or some person otherwise undistinguished, would be slain. Unseemly violence prevailed almost constantly, together with shameful contempt for law and justice. As the evil gained in magnitude, open insurrections against the government and large warlike expeditions against their country were undertaken by exiles, criminals, or persons vying with one another for some office or military command. Factions arose repeatedly, with chiefs aspiring to sole rule, some of them refusing to disband the troops entrusted to them by the state, others even hiring forces against each other on their own account, without public authority. Whenever either side got possession of the city, the opposing side made war, ostensibly against their adversaries, but actually against their country. They assailed it like an enemy's capital: those on hand were ruthlessly and indiscriminately massacred, others suffered proscription to death, banishment, confiscation of property; some were even subjected to excruciating tortures.

THE CONSERVATIVE ARGUMENT

Cicero, *In Defense of Sestius* xliv. 96-xlvi. 100, xlviii

You asked me in your speech for the prosecution what our "breed of *optimates*" is—those were your very words. What you ask is an excellent thing for our youth to learn, and an easy lesson for me to teach. . . .

There have always been in this state two classes of men eager to participate and predominate in public affairs: one group wished to be, and to be known as, *populares,* the other, *optimates.* The *populares* were those who wanted their actions and words to be pleasing to the people at large; the *optimates* acted so as to recommend their policies to all the best people. And who are these "best people"? Their number is legion (and we should go under otherwise); they are the leaders of public opinion, and those who support them; they are the men of the upper classes, who are eligible for the senate; they are Romans in municipalities, on farms, in business; even freedmen are *optimates.* The number of this group, as I have said, is spread far and wide, but the whole group can be briefly described and defined, so as to leave no room for error. All who are neither pernicious, nor base in character, nor mad, nor embarrassed by domestic troubles are *optimates.* In other words, this "breed," as you called it, comprises those who are honest, sober, and respectable family men. Those who, in governing the state, cater to the wishes interests, and expectations of this group, being defenders of the *optimates,* are themselves accounted most important *optimates,* most distinguished citizens and civic leaders. What, then, is the aim which these pilots of the state ought to observe and toward which they ought to direct their course? Why, that which is finest and most desirable for all sober, good, and prosperous men—peace with honor. Those who want this are all *optimates,* those who bring it about gain the reputation of being outstanding citizens and preservers of the state. Indeed, men should neither be so far carried away by the honor of governing as to disregard peace, nor embrace any peace that is inconsistent with honor.

The bases and elements of this honorable peace, which must be guarded by our leaders and defended at the risk of their lives if necessary, are the following: religious obligations, auspices, powers of the magistrates, authority of the senate, laws, mores, judicial process, administration of justice, the pledged word, provinces, allies, glory of empire, army, treasury. To be the defender and protector of so many and such great interests bespeaks a great soul, a great mind, and a great constancy. For in so numerous a citizenry there is no lack of men who, conscious of their transgressions and in fear of punishment, aim at renewal of agitation and revolution; nor of men who, because of some innate madness, feed on civil discord and insurrection; nor of men who, in the throes of financial embarrassment, prefer to be destroyed in a common rather than a private conflagration. When these men have found leaders to take in hand and direct their desires and vices, disturbances are aroused in the state, and those who have asked to be given the helm of the ship of state must be on their watch and must strive with all their knowledge and diligence so that they may, without harm to those things which I just now called bases and elements, be able to hold their course and reach that safe harbor of peace and honor. Should I attempt to deny that this public career is hard, laborious, full of dangers and traps, I should be lying, the more so as I have not only always understood it, but have even experienced it more than others. . . .

The task is hard, I deny it not, the dangers many, I admit it freely. Truly has it been said, "Many traps await the virtuous." . . . An electoral law was introduced by Lucius Cassius [137 B.C.; cf. § 154]; the people thought its liberty was at stake, but the leading men disagreed, fearing how the rashness of the populace, given the secret ballot, would affect the safety of the *optimates*. Tiberius Gracchus carried an agrarian law [133 B.C.; see § 97]; the people acclaimed it, for it seemed to restore the fortunes of the impoverished; but the *optimates* vigorously opposed it, because they saw it breeding disorders and felt that to dispossess the wealthy from holdings of long standing was to strip the state of its first line of defense. Gaius Gracchus passed a grain law: this delighted the plebs, for an abundance of food could now be had without working for it; but good men opposed it, because they held that the plebs was being seduced from industriousness to sloth, and they saw the treasury being drained.[30]

---

30. Here too Cicero echoes a traditional senatorial position, as similar statements in other authors show. These strictures on the Gracchan grain law of 123 B.C. are a characteristically partisan and unfair attack on a realistic effort to alleviate misery and reduce discontent; cf. note 18.

Cicero, *On Duties* I. xxxiv. 124–125, II. xxi. 73–xxiv. 85 (abridged); From *LCL*

It is peculiarly the place of a magistrate to bear in mind that he represents the state and that it is his duty to uphold its honor and its dignity, to enforce the law, to dispense to all their constitutional rights, and to remember that all this has been committed to him as a sacred trust.

The private individual ought first, in private relations, to live on fair and equal terms with his fellow citizens, with a spirit neither servile and groveling nor yet domineering; and second, in matters pertaining to the state, to labor for her peace and honor; for such a man we are accustomed to esteem and call a good citizen. As for the foreigner or resident alien, it is his duty to attend strictly to his own concerns, not to pry into other people's business, and under no circumstances to meddle in the politics of a country not his own. . . .

The man in administrative office, however, must make it his first care that everyone shall have what belongs to him and that private citizens shall suffer no invasion of their property rights by act of the state. It was a ruinous policy that Philippus proposed when in his tribuneship he introduced his agrarian bill.[31] However, when his law was rejected, he took his defeat with good grace and displayed extraordinary moderation. But in his public speeches on the measure he often played the demagogue, and particularly viciously when he said that there were not in the entire state two thousand people who owned any property. That speech deserves unqualified condemnation, for it favored an equal distribution of property; and what more ruinous policy than that could be conceived? For the chief purpose of the establishment of constitutional state and municipal governments was that individual property rights might be secured. For although it was by nature's guidance that men were drawn together into communities, it was in the hope of safeguarding their possessions that they sought the protection of cities.

The administration should also put forth every effort to prevent the levying of a property tax, and to this end precautions should be taken long in advance. Such a tax [the *tributum;* see Glossary and chapter 4, note 76] was often levied in the time of our forefathers on account of the depleted state of their treasury and their incessant wars. But if any state . . . ever has to face a crisis requiring the imposition of such a burden, every effort must be made to let all the people realize that they must bow to the inevitable if they wish to be saved. . . .

31. Lucius Marcius Philippus was tribune in 104 B.C.

But they who pose as friends of the people *[populares]*, and who for that reason either attempt to have agrarian laws passed in order that the occupants may be driven out of their established places, or propose that money loaned should be remitted to the borrowers—these are undermining the foundations of the commonwealth. First of all, they are destroying harmony, which cannot exist when money is taken away from one party and bestowed upon another; and second, they do away with equity, which is utterly subverted if the rights of property are not respected. For as I said above, it is the peculiar function of the state and the city to guarantee every man the free and untroubled control of his own particular property. . . . And how is it fair that a man who has never had any property should take possession of lands that had been occupied for many years or even generations, and that he who had them before should lose possession of them?[32] It was on account of just this sort of wrongdoing that the Spartans banished their ephor Lysander, and put their king Agis to death. . . . What shall we say of our own Gracchi, the sons of the famous Tiberius Gracchus and grandsons of Scipio Africanus? Was it not strife over the agrarian issue that caused their downfall and death?

And this is the highest statesmanship and the soundest wisdom on the part of a good citizen, not to divide the interests of the citizens but to unite all on the basis of impartial justice. "Let them live in their neighbor's house rent-free."[33] Why so? In order that, when I have bought, built, kept up, and spent my money on a place, you may without my consent enjoy what belongs to me? What else is that but to rob one man of what belongs to him and give to another what does not belong to him? And what is the meaning of an abolition of debts, except that you buy a farm with my money? You have the farm, and I have not my money.

We must, therefore, take measures that there shall be no indebtedness of a nature to endanger the public safety. It is a menace that can be averted in many ways;[34] but should a serious debt situation arise, we are

32. Cicero is speaking here of public lands held by private individuals. In treating them in practically the same breath as private property he is not simply disingenuous, but again faithfully reflects the attitude of the senatorial class. On the history of the public lands in Italy after the Gracchi, see §§ 102, 106.

33. This sarcastic proposal is the *reductio ad absurdum* of an actual edict of Caesar's dictatorship; see § 110.

34. But Cicero does not supply any way to solve this "menace" (which had become chronic and was one of the most urgent problems of his day) other than to insist, below, on the payment of all debts in full.

not to allow the rich to lose their property while the debtors profit by what is their neighbors'. For there is nothing that upholds a government more powerfully than its credit; and it can have no credit unless the payment of debts is enforced by law.[35] Never were measures for the repudiation of debts more strenuously agitated than in my consulship. Men of every sort and rank attempted with arms and armies to bring it about.[36] But I opposed them with such energy that this plague was wholly eradicated from the body politic. Indebtedness was never greater, yet debts were never liquidated more easily or more fully; for the hope of defrauding the creditor was cut off and payment was enforced by law. . . .

Those, then, whose office it is to look after the interests of the state will refrain from that form of liberality which robs one man to enrich another. Above all they will use their best endeavors that everyone shall be protected in the possession of his own property by the fair administration of the law and the courts, that the poorer classes shall not be oppressed because of their helplessness, and that envy shall not stand in the way of the rich to prevent them from keeping or recovering possession of what is theirs.

102. THE END OF THE GRACCHAN LAND LAW

The land commission established by the Gracchan legislation was discontinued by the Thorian Law of 118 B.C. This was followed by the Agrarian Law of 111 B.C., which marked the end of another epoch in the long struggle over the distribution and possession of public land. Its aim was to reduce to order the chaotic legal status of public and private land in Italy and to stabilize land tenure in the recently acquired African and Corinthian territory (see § 80). Accepting as *faits accomplis* the results of all agrarian legislation since 133 B.C., the law declared all occupied public domain the private property of the existing holders and reserved to the state in perpetuity all public land as yet unoccupied. Thus this law was, in effect, the death knell of the Gracchan attempt to revive a class of peasant smallholders and a major victory for the latifundists in Italy and the provinces, since it removed all obstacles to the expansion of large private holdings.

35. The allusion is to Caesar's law of 49 B.C. remitting all interest in arrears and reducing the principal of outstanding loans by the amount of the interest already paid: see § 110.

36. The reference is, of course, to the Catilinarian affair; see § 105.

THE THORIAN LAW, 118 B.C.

Appian, *Civil Wars* I. iv. 27; From *LCL*

Not long after [the death of Gaius Gracchus] a law was enacted to permit holders to sell the land about which they had quarreled; for even this had been forbidden by the law of the elder Gracchus. At once the rich began to buy the allotments of the poor, or found pretexts for seizing them by force. So the condition of the poor became even worse than before, until Spurius Thorius, a tribune of the plebs, brought in a law providing that the distribution of public domain should be discontinued, that the land should belong to those in possession who should pay rent for it to the state, and that the money so received should be distributed; and this distribution was a kind of solace to the poor, but it did not help to increase the population. By these devices the law of Gracchus—a most excellent and useful one if it could have been carried out—was once for all frustrated, and a little later the rent itself was abolished at the instance of another tribune.[37] So the plebeians lost everything, and hence resulted a still further decline in the numbers of both citizens and soldiers, and in the revenue from the land and the distributions thereof and in the allotments themselves.

THE AGRARIAN LAW OF 111 B.C.

CIL, vol. I, 2d ed., no. 585 (= *ROL,* 4:370–437)

[Part I: Land in Italy]

. . . tribunes of the plebs, duly proposed, and the plebs duly approved . . . the . . . tribe voted first, the first to vote in the name of his tribe was Quintus Fabius, son of Quintus.

With respect to the public land belonging to the Roman people within Italy in the consulship of Publius Mucius and Lucius Calpurnius,[38] excluding that land which by the law or plebiscite of Gaius Sempronius [Gracchus] son of Tiberius, tribune of the plebs, was by special enactment excepted from division[39] . . . whatever land or ground each several original occupier in accordance with the law or plebiscite took or

37. Probably meant is the Agrarian Law of 111 B.C., given immediately below.

38. 133 B.C., the year when Tiberius Gracchus was tribune.

39. For instance, the very fertile Campanian territory, which yielded a high revenue to the state. Cf. above, note 3.

retained for himself out of the said land or ground, provided that the measure be not greater than the amount which by the law or plebiscite one man was permitted to take or retain for himself;

With respect to the public land belonging to the Roman people within Italy in the consulship of Publius Mucius and Lucius Calpurnius, excluding that land which by the law or plebiscite of Gaius Sempronius son of Tiberius, tribune of the plebs, was by special enactment excepted from division . . . whatever land or ground a land commissioner[40] has in accordance with the law or plebiscite granted or assigned to any Roman citizen allotted to a colony, provided that it be not in the said land or ground lying beyond . . . ;

With respect to the public land belonging to the Roman people within Italy in the consulship of Publius Mucius and Lucius Calpurnius, excluding that land which by the law or plebiscite of Gaius Sempronius son of Tiberius, tribune of the plebs, was by special enactment excepted from division . . . whatever such land or ground has been granted, exchanged, or confirmed by a land commissioner to an individual in return for private land exchanged for public; ·

With respect to the public land belonging to the Roman people within Italy in the consulship of Publius Mucius and Lucius Calpurnius, excluding that land which by the law or plebiscite of Gaius Sempronius son of Tiberius, tribune of the plebs, was by special enactment excepted from division . . . whatever portion of such public land or ground within Italy, or outside the city of Rome, or in a city, town, or village a land commissioner has granted or assigned and any individual shall hold or possess at the time when this measure becomes law;

With respect to the public land belonging to the Roman people within Italy in the consulship of Publius Mucius and Lucius Calpurnius, excluding that land or ground which by the law or plebiscite of Gaius Sempronius son of Tiberius, tribune of the plebs, was by special enactment excepted from division . . . out of such land or ground whatever portion of land, ground, or building within Italy a land commissioner has granted or assigned or left to any individual, or has entered or caused to be entered in the land lists and schedules;

All land, ground, or buildings above mentioned, excluding such land or ground specially excepted as aforesaid, shall be private land, and for all such land, ground, or buildings there shall be the same right of

40. That is, a member of the three-man board established to carry out the Gracchan land law; cf. § 99.

purchase and sale as for other private lands, grounds, or buildings; and the incumbent censor shall see that such land, ground, or building made private by this law shall be entered in the census in the same way as other lands, grounds, or buildings . . . and in the matter of the said land, ground, or buildings he shall order the person to whom the said land, ground, or building shall belong to make the same kind of declaration which in the matter of other lands, grounds, or buildings he shall have ordered the several owners to make . . . nor shall any person take steps whereby an individual who rightfully holds or shall hold the said land, ground, or building in accordance with law or plebiscite shall be prevented from using, enjoying, holding, and possessing the said land, ground, or building . . . nor shall any person make a proposal to that effect in the senate, . . . nor shall anyone by virtue of a magistracy or *imperium* express or bring forward any proposal whereby any person of those who rightfully possess or shall possess such land, ground, or building . . . shall be prevented from using, enjoying, holding, or possessing the said land, ground, or building, or whereby its possession shall be taken away without his consent or that of his heirs if he be deceased.

> [The next two clauses, omitted here, except from this grant of private ownership certain lands, probably those fronting on public roads, whose tenants had undertaken the maintenance of the roads in lieu of rent.]

With respect to the public land belonging to the Roman people within Italy in the consulship of Publius Mucius and Lucius Calpurnius, excluding that land which by the law or plebiscite of Gaius Sempronius son of Tiberius, tribune of the plebs, was by special enactment excepted from division, and excluding that land which in accordance with the law or plebiscite an original occupier took or retained for himself, provided that the measure be not greater than the amount which one man was permitted to take or retain for himself, whatever portion of such land, not exceeding 30 *iugera,* any individual shall have entered upon for the purpose of tillage and shall hold or possess, all such shall be private land.[41]

> [Five clauses, omitted here, provide for free grazing of herds on common pasture land and for the confirmation of titles by a competent court, and abolish on all state land in Italy made private by this law the rent and pasture fees previously charged.]

41. That is, illegal occupation of public land after 133 B.C. is hereby recognized up to thirty *iugera* under cultivation.

With respect to the public land or ground belonging to the Roman people within Italy in the consulship of Publius Mucius and Lucius Calpurnius . . . excluding all that land which the censors Lucius Caecilius and Gnaeus Domitius let on lease on the 20th of September [115 B.C.], together with the territory beyond Curio, in the case of a Roman citizen on the said land or ground, or a member of the allies or of the Latin name[42] from whom soldiers are customarily requisitioned in Italy according to the military roll, who, as an original occupier or person recognized as such, has given up out of his own possession public land or ground belonging to the Roman people to the end that on the said land or ground a town or colony might in accordance with a law or plebiscite be established, planted, or placed, and in which land or ground a land commissioner has so established, planted, or placed such town or colony in accordance with a law or plebiscite, whatever land or ground a land commissioner has granted, confirmed, or assigned in place of the said land or ground out of the said public land or ground belonging to the Roman people within Italy in the consulship of Publius Mucius and Lucius Calpurnius, always excepting that land or ground which by the law or plebiscite of Gaius Sempronius son of Tiberius, tribune of the plebs, was by special enactment excepted from division—such land shall be the private property of the person to whom the same has been granted, confirmed, or assigned, or of any person who has or shall have succeeded to such land from him or his heir by inheritance, testament, or gift, or any person who has or shall have purchased from him, or any person who has or shall have purchased from the first purchaser.

With respect to such public land, ground, or building belonging to the Roman people as a land commissioner has granted, confirmed, or assigned out of the said land or ground in return for land or ground on which he has planted a colony as aforesaid, the praetor or consul who shall have jurisdiction concerning such land under this law, to whose court application shall have been made concerning such land before the Ides of March next following,[43] shall so adjudicate the said matter and so decree as to grant legal possession to that person, or to his heir, to whom a land commissioner has granted, confirmed, or assigned such land in return for land or ground on which he has planted a colony; and the said praetor or consul, to whose court application on such matter shall have been made, shall take steps. . . .

---

42. That is, members of Latin towns and Latin colonies; cf. introduction to § 40.
43. The beginning of the Roman financial year.

With respect to any part of the land or ground above mentioned which after the passage of this law shall be public land belonging to the Roman people, excluding that land or ground which has been reserved for public purposes or has been let by public authority, in such land anyone who wishes may graze cattle, . . . nor shall such land be community pasture land,[44] nor shall any person occupy, hold, or fence off land within the same and thereby prevent anyone who wishes from grazing cattle thereon. Should anyone do so, he shall for every such act be required to pay 50 sesterces for every *iugerum* concerned to whatever person holds the usufruct or the right of purchase or lease of rent charges for the said land.

Upon the land or ground which after the passage of this law shall be public land belonging to the Roman people, it shall be lawful to graze oxen, horses, mules, or asses up to the number of animals prescribed in this law, and no person shall be required to pay rent or fee for such purpose.

No person driving cattle into the public lanes or roads for convenience of travel and pasturing them there shall be required to pay anything to the people or to a tax farmer for such cattle which have been pastured or let loose on the public lanes or roads for travel purposes.

[The next six clauses deal with other public lands made private, rent collection by publicans, road maintenance, and enforcement of this law.]

With respect to land given for usufruct by the people or by decree of the senate to colonies or municipalities, or to towns in the status of municipalities or colonies, inhabited by Roman citizens or members of the Latin name, or land among the *Trientabula;*[45] and with respect to colonists or inhabitants of a municipality or town in the status of a municipality, enjoying such usufruct, or persons enjoying such usufruct on behalf of a colony or municipality or town in the status of a municipality, or persons enjoying such usufruct among the *Trientabula* . . . any such land held by colonists or members of a municipality or town in the status of a municipality, or by persons deriving their holding from a colony or municipality or town in the status of a municipality, and any such land which has or shall have been acquired by the said persons among the *Trientabula* by testament, inheritance, or gift, assuming the

---

44. That is, pasture lands belonging to a local community or district to whose inhabitants its use was restricted.

45. For this land, assigned in partial repayment of loans made to the state during the Second Punic War, see § 92. It paid a nominal rent to the state.

said persons to have had the right before the passage of this law to hold on lease, enjoy, possess, or lay claim to the said land or ground, and excluding such land or ground as may in accordance with this law properly be sold, granted or confirmed . . . of all such land, whatever was permitted to each several person before the passage of this law, it shall be lawful in like manner after the passage of this law for such person to hold, use, enjoy, possess, or lay claim to.

[The remaining five clauses of this part of the law deal with the adjudication of disputes about land made private since 133 B.C., judgments on money due to publicans, and the invalidation of laws conflicting with this law.]

[Part II: Land in Africa]

[One long but badly mutilated clause is omitted here; it is uncertain whether it refers to Africa.]

With respect to land or ground situate in Africa, whatever portion of such land . . . he shall hold, possess, and enjoy in like manner as if the said land or ground was sold by the Roman people. . . .

[The next clause provides that claims concerning land are to be made by colonists to a *duovir* of the colony.]

A *duovir* appointed or created under this law . . . shall in such wise institute inquiry concerning the said lands . . . nor, with respect to land situate in Africa, which in accordance with the Rubrian Law, since repealed, might properly or lawfully have been granted to a person who was a colonist or registered as a colonist, shall he adjudge . . . to have been granted or assigned; nor with respect to land situate in Africa which in accordance with the aforesaid law, since repealed, might properly or lawfully have been granted to an individual who was a colonist or registered as a colonist shall he adjudge more than 200 *iugera* to have been granted or assigned to any individual . . . nor shall he adjudge a larger number of persons to be or to have been conducted to the colony or colonies in Africa than the number which under the Rubrian Law, since repealed, was specified as proper and lawful to be conducted to the colony or colonies by the three-man commission appointed to conduct colonies. . . .[46]

46. The *Lex Rubria* was the law which authorized the founding of a colony, called Junonia, on the site of Carthage. It was passed in 122 B.C., during the second tribunate of Gaius Gracchus, but was repealed shortly thereafter. On the reference to a larger number of colonists than authorized, cf. p. 260. Though the colony was soon abandoned, the rights of the original colonists are here confirmed.

[The next seven clauses of the law deal with confirmation of land purchased, compensation in certain cases of dual claim to title, rights of publicans with respect to certain land purchasers, and sureties and securities to be given by purchasers in default 120 days after the sale.]

The praetor who has jurisdiction over Roman citizens . . . unless before that time landed security shall have been pledged to the state on account of the said land or ground or a surety provided to the state, shall sell for cash any land or any ground for which, in the praetor's judgment, adequate security has not in accordance with this law been registered. . . .

With respect to land or ground situate in Africa which has or shall have been sold by the people at Rome, if any portion of such land or ground has been held by the free communities in Africa, namely those which in the last Punic war remained firm in the friendship of the Roman people or those which in the said war deserted from the enemy to a general of the Roman people,[47] to which for that reason land has been granted or assigned by decree of the senate . . . then in place of such land or ground in that of every free community or in that land or ground granted or assigned to deserters which shall have been made the property of Roman citizens under this law, provided that other land instead thereof has not under this law been granted, confirmed, or given in compensation to the said Roman citizen, a *duovir* appointed or created under this law shall, within . . . days of his appointment, cause land or ground of the same amount to be granted or assigned to such free community or deserters. . . .

[The next clause, omitted here, deals with conflicting claims to certain African land.]

With respect to all land situate in Africa with the exception of:
land or ground granted or assigned in accordance with the Rubrian Law, since repealed, to a colonist or person registered as a colonist . . . in exchange for which other land or ground has not been given in compensation or confirmed;
land situated within the territories of the free communities of Utica, Hadrumetum, Tampsus, Leptis, Aquilea, Usalis, and Teudalis at the time when they lately entered into friendship with the Roman people;
land or ground . . . granted or assigned by decree of the senate to

47. These were the seven towns named in the clause following.

those persons who in the last Punic war deserted from the enemy to a general of the Roman people;

land made private by this law, in exchange for which other land or ground has not been given in compensation or confirmed;

land or ground granted or assigned by a *duovir* in accordance with this law to payers of tribute, to the extent that such land has in accordance with this law been entered in the public schedules;

land which . . . the general Publius Cornelius [Scipio] granted to the children of King Masinissa, or gave orders for them to hold or enjoy;

the land or ground where the city of Carthage formerly stood;

the land or ground left or assigned to the people of Utica by the ten-man commission appointed or created under the Livian Law—

With respect to all other land situate in Africa, a *duovir* appointed or created under this law shall, within the next 250 days after the ratification of this law by the people or plebs, see to it that those persons who shall be required to pay rent, tithes, or pasture fee for such land to the people or to a tax farmer, shall hold, possess, or enjoy the land granted, confirmed, or given them in compensation under this law, and that for such land or ground as they may enjoy subsequent to this law they shall in fact pay rent, tithes, or pasture fee to the people or to a tax farmer. . . .

[The remaining eleven clauses of this part of the law deal with public revenues, publicans, public roads, penalties for false claims, and compensation for justified claimants whose land has been sold.]

[Part III: The Corinthian Land]

[The remainder of the law, except for one badly mutilated clause and a few small fragments, is lost.]

103. THE ITALIC, OR "SOCIAL," WAR

The agitation of the Italian allies for Roman citizenship, which had been growing ever since the death of Gaius Gracchus, flamed into armed rebellion upon the assassination of their latest champion, the tribune Livius Drusus. The establishment of an Italian Confederacy in the mountainous districts of central and southern Italy and the mobilization of a large, well-trained force initiated a fierce struggle which exposed Rome to her greatest peril since Hannibal. Although most of Etruria, Umbria, Latium, Campania, and the Greek towns to the south remained loyal, the Romans were forced to call on auxiliary troops from the provinces. In 90 B.C., after several reverses, the Romans passed the Julian Law granting full citizenship *en masse* to all communities in Italy which had not revolted, and probably authorizing commanders in the field to bestow the franchise on provincial auxiliaries as a reward for valor.[48] Early in 89 B.C. the Plautian–Papirian Law offered citizenship to individuals even in rebellious Italian communities. Except for a few die-hard Samnite bands, the revolt collapsed after two years; but out of the crucible of the struggle there emerged for all Italy south of the Po Valley a uniform citizenship which, in the next two generations, was to weld the peninsula into a common culture.

THE COURSE OF THE WAR

Velleius Paterculus, *Compendium of Roman History* II. xv. I–xvii. I (abridged);
From LCL

The long smoldering fires of an Italian war were now fanned into flame by the death of Drusus. . . . In the consulship of Lucius Caesar and Publius Rutilius [91 B.C.] all Italy took up arms against the Romans. The rebellion began with the people of Asculum, who had put to death the praetor Servilius and his deputy Fonteius; it was next taken up by the Marsians, and then made its way into all the districts of Italy. The fortune of the Italians was as cruel as their cause was just, for they were seeking citizenship in the state whose power they were defending by their arms: every year and in every war they were furnishing a double number of men, both of cavalry and of infantry, and yet were not admitted to the rights of citizens in the state which through their efforts had reached so high a position that it could look down upon men of the same stock and blood as foreigners and aliens.

The war carried off more than 300,000 of the youth of Italy. On the Roman side in this war the most illustrious commanders were Gnaeus Pompeius, father of Pompey the Great, Gaius Marius, already mentioned, Lucius Sulla, who in the previous year had held the praetorship, and Quintus Metellus, son of Metellus Numidicus. . . . On the Italian side the most celebrated generals were Silo Popaedius, Herius Asinius, Insteius Cato, Gaius Pontidius, Telesinus Pontius, Marcus Egnatius, and Papius Mutilus. . . .

---

48. Plutarch (*Moralia* 202C–D) reports that Marius had made similar grants on his own authority some ten years earlier; but the story may be apocryphal. In the Empire, granting of citizenship to provincials after military service in the Roman army became a regular practice.

So bitter was this Italian war, and such its vicissitudes, that in two successive years two Roman consuls, first Rutilius and subsequently Porcius Cato, were slain by the enemy, the armies of the Roman people were routed in many places, and the Romans were compelled to resort to military garb and to remain long in that garb. The Italians chose Corfinium as their capital and named it Italica. Then little by little the strength of the Romans was recruited by admitting to citizenship those who had not taken up arms or had not been slow to lay them down again, and Pompeius, Sulla, and Marius restored the tottering power of the Roman people.

Except for the remnants of hostility which lingered at Nola, the Italian war was now in large measure ended, the Romans, themselves exhausted, consenting to grant citizenship to the conquered and humbled in preference to giving it to them as a body when their own strength was still unimpaired.

Appian, *Civil Wars* I. vi. 49; *From LCL*

While these events were occurring on the Adriatic side of Italy, the inhabitants of Etruria and Umbria and other neighboring peoples on the other side of Rome heard of them and were all excited to revolt. The senate, fearing lest they should be surrounded by war and be unable to protect themselves, garrisoned the seacoast from Cumae to the city with freedmen, who were then for the first time enrolled in the army on account of the scarcity of soldiers. The senate also decreed that those of the Italians who had adhered to their alliance should be admitted to citizenship, which they practically all most desired and gladly accepted. By this favor the senate made the faithful more faithful, secured the wavering, and mollified those at war by the hope of similar treatment. The Romans did not enroll these new citizens in the thirty-five existing tribes, lest they should outvote the old citizens in the elections, but incorporated them in ten new tribes, which voted last. So it often happened that their vote was useless, since a majority was obtained from the thirty-five tribes that voted first.[49]

---

49. It is not clear from the various sources whether the newly enfranchised allies were enrolled in ten new tribes, in eight of the existing tribes, or in ten of the existing tribes.

DECREE OF GNAEUS POMPEIUS STRABO, 90 B.C.

CIL, vol. I, 2d ed., no. 709 (=ROL, 4:272–275)

Gnaeus Pompeius son of Sextus, commander-in-chief, in reward for valor made Spanish horsemen Roman citizens in camp at Asculum on the 17th day of November, in accordance with the Julian Law. On the general's staff were: Lucius Gellius son of Lucius, of the Tromentine tribe, Gnaeus Octavius son of Quintus, [etc.][50]

The Salluitan squadron:[51] Sanibelser son of Adingibas, Illurtibas son of Bilustibas, Estopeles son of Ordennas, Tersinno son of Austinco . . . Gnaeus Cornelius son of Nesille, Publius Fabius son of Enasagin.

Gnaeus Pompeius son of Sextus, commander-in-chief, in reward for valor presented the Salluitan squadron in camp at Asculum with a helmet-horn and plate, a necklace, a bracelet, breast-pieces, and a double ration of grain.

THE PLAUTIAN-PAPIRIAN LAW, 89 B.C.

Cicero, *In Defense of Archias* iv.7

Roman citizenship was granted by the law of Silvanus and Carbo to "all whose names are listed in the citizen rolls of allied communities, if they have a permanent residence in Italy at the time of the passage of this law and if they make application before a praetor within sixty days."

THE LAST FLARE-UP OF ITALIC RESISTANCE

Velleius Paterculus, *Compendium of Roman History* ii. xxvii. 1–2; From *LCL*

While Carbo and Marius were still consuls,[52] 109 years ago, on the Kalends of November, Pontius Telesinus, a Samnite chief, brave in spirit and in action and hating to the core the very name of Rome, collected about 40,000 of the bravest and most steadfast youth who still persisted in retaining arms, and fought with Sulla near the Colline Gate a battle so critical as to bring both Sulla and the city into gravest peril. Rome had not faced a greater danger when she saw the camp of Hanni-

---

50. The decree lists here sixty members of the general's *consilium*.

51. The thirty members of the squadron are listed in the decree; only a sampling is given here. Note that the last two Spaniards in the list already have Romanized names.

52. Gnaeus Papirius Carbo and Gaius Marius the Younger, consuls in 82 B.C.

bal within the third milestone than on this day when Telesinus sped about from rank to rank exclaiming, "The last day is at hand for the Romans!" and in a loud voice exhorted his men to overthrow and destroy their city, adding: "These wolves that have made such ravages upon Italian liberty will never vanish until we have cut down the forest that harbors them."

THREE GREEK PROVINCIALS REWARDED FOR THEIR SERVICES, 78 B.C.

CIL, vol. I, 2d ed., no. 588 (= *IGRR*, I, no. 118 = ROL, 4:444–51 = *RDGE*, no. 22)

In the consulship of Quintus Lutatius Catulus son of Quintus, and Marcus Aemilius Lepidus son of Quintus, grandson of Marcus, in the urban and peregrine praetorship[53] of Lucius Cornelius Sisenna son of . . . in the month of May.

Quintus Lutatius Catulus son of Quintus, consul, consulted the senate on the 22d day of May, in the Comitium. Present at the writing [of this decree] were Lucius Faberius son of Lucius, of the Sergian tribe, Gaius . . . son of Lucius, of the Poblilian tribe, and Quintus Petillius son of Titus, of the Sergian tribe.

Whereas Quintus Lutatius Catulus son of Quintus, consul, declared in a speech that Asclepiades of Clazomenae, son of Philinus, and Polystratus of Carystus, son of Polyarchus, and Meniscus of Miletus, son of Irenaeus, born the son of Thargelius,[54] had stood by in their ships at the outbreak of the Italic War, that they had rendered valiant and faithful service to our state, and that he wished, if it were the senators' pleasure, to send them back to their homelands in accordance with a decree of the senate, so that public acknowledgment might be accorded them in return for the good services and valiant deeds performed by them on behalf of our state;

Concerning this matter it was decreed as follows: that Asclepiades of Clazomenae, son of Philinus, and Polystratus of Carystus, son of Polyarchus, and Meniscus of Miletus, son of Irenaeus, born the son of Thargelius, be proclaimed gentlemen of character and friends [of Rome].

That the Roman senate and people judge that their services were good, valiant, and faithful to our state, for which reason the senate

---

53. This combined praetorship is rare.

54. All three are Greeks, the first and last named from Asia Minor, the second from Euboea in Greece.

decrees: that these men, their children and their descendants be exempt in their own homelands from all compulsory public services and taxes; if any taxes have been exacted on their property since these men left their homes on behalf of our state, that these be given back and restored to them; if any fields, houses, or possessions of theirs have been sold since they left their homes on behalf of our state, that all these be restored to them in full; and if any due date [for meeting obligations] has passed since they left their homes on behalf of our state, that this circumstance shall not be damaging to them in any way, no indebtedness to them shall on this account be any less valid, and their right to sue and exact payment shall not be in any way impaired; whatever inheritances have fallen to them or their children, that they may have, possess, and enjoy them; in whatever suits they, their children, descendants, or wives may bring against another, and whatever suits others may bring against them, their children, descendants, or wives, that they, their children, descendants, and wives shall have the right to choose whether they wish to have the case tried at home according to their own laws, or by an Italian jury before our magistrates, or in some one of the free cities which have remained uninterruptedly in the friendship of the Roman people, and that, wherever they prefer, the trial be held there on the said matters; if any judgments have been rendered concerning them in their absence since they left their homes, that these revert to their previous status and judgment be given anew, in accordance with the decree of the senate; if their cities owe any public debts, that they shall not be obligated to make any contribution toward those debts; that our magistrates, when they lease out the public land in Asia and Euboea or impose revenue taxes on Asia and Euboea, shall see to it that these persons be not required to pay anything.

And that Quintus Lutatius and Marcus Aemilius, the consuls, one or both, if they see fit, shall see to it that these men are entered on the official roll of friends, shall permit them to set up a bronze tablet of friendship and offer sacrifice in the Capitol, and shall order the urban quaestor to send them gifts in accordance with the official schedule [see chapter 6, note 37] and to contract for quarters and supplies for them; and if they desire to send envoys to the senate concerning their own affairs, or prefer to come themselves, that they, their children, and their descendants shall have the right to come as envoys or to send such; and that the consuls Quintus Lutatius and Marcus Aemilius, one or both, if they see fit, shall send letters to our magistrates who govern the provinces of Asia and Macedonia, as well as to their magistrates, informing them that the senate desires and considers it just that these matters be carried out as they deem best in keeping with the interests of the state and with their own good faith.[55]

Adopted.

104. THE DICTATORSHIP OF SULLA, 82–79 B.C.

Appian, Civil Wars I. xi. 95–xii 103 (abridged); From *LCL*

After thus crushing Italy by war, fire, and murder, Sulla's generals visited the several cities and established garrisons at the suspected places. . . . Sulla himself called the Roman people together in an assembly and made them a speech, vaunting his own exploits and making other menacing statements in order to inspire terror. He finished by saying that he would bring about a change which would be beneficial to the people if they would obey him, but of his enemies he would spare none but would visit them with the utmost severity. He would take vengeance by strong measures on the praetors, quaestors, military tribunes, and everybody else who had committed any hostile act after the day when the consul Scipio violated the agreement with him. After saying this, he forthwith proscribed about forty senators and 1,600 *equites*. He seems to have been the first to make such a formal list of those whom he condemned to death, to offer prizes to assassins and rewards to informers, and to threaten with punishment those who concealed the proscribed. Shortly afterward he added the names of other senators to the proscription. Some of these, taken unawares, were killed where they were caught, in their homes, in the streets, or in the temples. Others were hurled through mid-air and thrown at Sulla's feet. Others were dragged through the city and trampled on, none of the spectators daring to utter a word of remonstrance against these horrors. Banishment was inflicted upon some, and confiscation upon others. Spies were searching everywhere for those who had fled from the city, and those whom they caught they killed.

There was much massacre, banishment, and confiscation also among those Italians who had obeyed Carbo, Norbanus, Marius, or their lieutenants. Severe judgments of the courts were rendered against them throughout all Italy on various charges—for exercising military command, for serving in the army, for contributing money, for rendering

---

55. With this whole document cf. the similar grants of privileges in chapter 6.

other service, or even for giving counsel against Sulla. Hospitality, private friendship, the borrowing or lending of money, were alike accounted crimes. Now and then one would be arrested for doing a kindness to a suspect or merely for being his companion on a journey. These accusations abounded mostly against the rich. When charges against individuals were exhausted, Sulla took vengeance on whole communities. He punished some of them by demolishing their citadels or destroying their walls, or by imposing collective fines and crushing them under heavy contributions. Among most of them he placed colonies of his troops in order to hold Italy under garrisons, sequestrating their lands and houses and dividing them among his soldiers, whom he thus made true to him even after his death. . . .

When everything had been accomplished against his enemies as he desired, and there was no longer any hostile force except that of Sertorius, Sulla sent Metellus into Spain against him and arranged everything in the city to suit himself. There was no longer any occasion for laws or elections or casting lots, because everybody was shivering with fear and in hiding, or mute. Everything that Sulla had done as consul or as proconsul was confirmed and ratified, and his gilded equestrian statue was erected in front of the Rostra with the inscription: "Cornelius Sulla, Commander Ever Fortunate". . . .

Thus Sulla became a king, or tyrant, *de facto*—not elected but holding power by force and violence. . . . There had been autocratic rule before —that of the dictators—but it was limited to short periods; under Sulla it first became unlimited, and so an absolute tyranny. But this much was added for propriety's sake, that they chose him dictator for the enactment of such laws as he himself might deem best and for the settlement of the commonwealth. . . .

By way of keeping up the form of the Republic, he allowed them to elect consuls. Marcus Tullius and Cornelius Dolabella were chosen. But Sulla, like a reigning sovereign, was dictator over the consuls. Twenty-four axes [the *fasces;* see Glossary] were borne in front of him as dictator, the same number that had been borne before the ancient kings, and he had also a large bodyguard. He repealed laws and enacted others. He forbade anybody to hold the office of praetor until he had held that of quaestor, or to be consul before he had been praetor, and he prohibited any man from holding the same office a second time till after a lapse of ten years. He reduced the tribunes' power to such impotence as practically to destroy it, and he curtailed it by a law which provided that one holding the office of tribune should never afterward hold any other office; for which reason all men of reputation or family, who formerly had contended for this office, shunned it thereafter. . . . To the senate, which had been much thinned by the sedition and the wars, he added about 300 members from the best of the *equites,* taking the vote of the tribes on each one. To the plebeians he added more than 10,000 slaves of the men who had been killed, choosing the youngest and strongest, to whom he gave freedom and Roman citizenship, and he called them Cornelii after himself. In this way he made sure of having 10,000 men among the plebeians always ready to obey his commands. In order to provide the same kind of safeguard throughout Italy, he distributed to the twenty-three legions [about 120,000 men] that had served under him a great deal of land in the various communities . . . some of which was public property and some taken from the communities by way of penalty. . . .

The following year [80 B.C.] Sulla, although he was dictator, undertook the consulship a second time, with Metellus Pius for his colleague, in order to preserve the pretense and form of democratic government. . . . The next year the people, in order to pay court to Sulla chose him consul again, but he refused the office and nominated Servilius Isauricus and Claudius Pulcher, and voluntarily laid down the supreme power, although nobody interfered with him.

105. ROME IN 63 B.C.: THE POLITICAL AND SOCIAL SCENE

With this description may be compared Cicero, *Against Catiline* II. viii. 17–x. 23, which, though spoken in the heat of crisis and much more rhetorical, emphasizes that Catiline's appeal was essentially to the debt-ridden and the bankrupt. Catiline based his electoral campaign in 63 B.C. on the promise of a general cancellation of debts, and when defeated at the polls he went on to attempt the *coup d'état* rendered famous by Cicero's oratory. His revolutionary-sounding program—even though its chief beneficiaries would be among the nobility, many of whom in this period squandered fortunes to maintain their political and social positions (cf. *Cambridge Ancient History,* 9:491–494)—must have aroused considerable sympathy, if not active support, among the city plebs. For the following year, even after the suppression of the conspiracy, Caesar and his adherents were able to keep popular agitation alive and demonstrative until "Cato, seeing that the people was being greatly stirred up by Caesar in the affair of Catiline and was dangerously inclined toward a revolution,

persuaded the senate to vote a dole to the poor, and the giving of this
halted the disturbance and checked the insurrection" (Plutarch, *Moralia*
818D).

Sallust, *Catiline* xxxvi. 4–xxxix. 3; From *LCL*

At no other time has the condition of imperial Rome, as it seems to me,
been more pitiable. The whole world, from the rising of the sun to its
setting, subdued by her arms, rendered obedience to her; at home there
was peace and an abundance of wealth, which mortal men deem the
chiefest of blessings. Yet there were citizens who from sheer perversity
were bent upon their own ruin and that of their country. For in spite of
the two decrees of the senate not one man of all that great number was
led by the promised reward to betray the conspiracy, and not a single
one deserted Catiline's camp; such was the potency of the malady which
like a plague had infected the minds of a great many citizens.

This insanity was not confined to those who were implicated in the
plot, but the whole body of the commons through desire for change
favored the designs of Catiline. In this very particular they seemed to act
as the populace usually does; for in every community those who have
no means envy the good, exalt the base, hate what is old and established,
long for something new, and from disgust with their own lot desire a
general upheaval. Amid turmoil and rebellion they maintain themselves
without difficulty, since poverty is easily provided for and can suffer no
loss. But the city populace in particular acted with desperation for many
reasons. To begin with, all who were easily conspicuous for their
shamelessness and impudence, those, too, who had squandered their
patrimony in riotous living, finally all whom disgrace or crime had
forced to leave home, had all flowed into Rome as into a cesspool.
Many, too, who recalled Sulla's victory, when they saw common soldiers risen to the rank of senator, and others become so rich that they
feasted and lived like kings, hoped each for himself for like fruits of
victory if he took the field. Besides this, the young men who had
maintained a wretched existence by manual labor in the country, tempted
by public and private doles, had come to prefer idleness in the city to
their unprofitable toil; these, like all the others, battened on the public
ills. Therefore it is not surprising that men who were beggars and
without character, with illimitable hopes, should respect their country
as little as they did themselves. Moreover, those to whom Sulla's victory
had meant the proscription of their parents, loss of property, and cur-
tailment of their rights, looked forward in a similar spirit to the outcome

of a war. Finally, all who belonged to another party than that of the senate preferred to see the government overthrown rather than be out of power themselves. Such then was the evil which after many years had returned upon the state.

For after the tribunician power had been restored in the consulship of Gnaeus Pompey and Marcus Crassus,[56] various young men, whose age and disposition made them aggressive, attained that high authority; they thereupon began to excite the commons by attacks upon the senate and then to inflame their passions still more by doles and promises, thus making themselves conspicuous and influential. Against these men the greater part of the nobles strove with might and main, ostensibly in behalf of the senate but really for their own aggrandizement. For, to tell the truth in a few words, after that time all who took part in politics used specious pretexts, some maintaining that they were defending the rights of the commons, others that they were upholding the prestige of the senate; but under pretense of the public welfare each in reality was striving for personal power. Such men showed neither self-restraint nor moderation in their strife, and both parties used their victory ruthlessly. When, however, Gnaeus Pompey had been dispatched to wage war against the pirates and against Mithridates, the power of the commons was lessened, while that of the few increased. These possessed the magistracies, the provinces, and everything else; being themselves rich and secure against attack, they lived without fear and by resort to the courts terrified the others, in order that they might manage the commons with less friction under their magistracy. But as soon as the political situation became doubtful and offered hope of revolution, then the old controversy aroused their passions anew.

106. Agrarian Legislation in the First Century b.c.

In 107 b.c. Marius, to augment his forces for the completion of the Jugurthine War, ignored the property qualifications until then in force and opened the legions to all citizens willing and able to serve. The senatorial class, unwilling to relinquish any of its holdings of public land, was compelled to acquiesce in this recruitment reform, hoping that it would siphon off large numbers of landless discontents from Rome and abate the

---

56. 70 B.C. The Sullan restrictions on tribunes were repealed in that year.

agrarian agitation. But the senate thereby signed its own eventual death warrant: for thereafter the conscript army of Roman landholders gave way to professional armies composed almost entirely of propertyless volunteers, who signed on for the promise of booty during, and of land after, military service (sixteen, later twenty, years); and as the senate continued to obstruct land reform, the soldiers came to look for their rewards to a succession of generals, the last of whom (Caesar) by his army, ended the senatorial regime of the Republic.

Thus the agrarian issue took a new turn, and agrarian legislation in the first century B.C was no longer directed primarily toward the restoration of an independent peasantry, but was chiefly concerned with satisfying the demands of the veterans. But after the law of 111 B.C. had made practically all public land in Italy private property (see § 102), the land hunger could be satisfied only through confiscation (such as that practiced by Sulla; cf. § 104), through government purchase in Italy, or through overseas colonization. At the same time the agrarian issue continued to afford the *populares* their chief political weapon against the ruling oligarchy. Thus the Rullan bill, which Cicero began his consulship by attacking with the most unscrupulous demagogy, combined agrarian reform with political maneuvering. Though bearing the name of the tribune who introduced it, the bill's real author and backer was generally understood to be Caesar. It aimed at the disposal of most of the public land remaining in Italy, included provisions for selling large tracts of public domain in the provinces, and enunciated for the first time the idea of using state funds to buy private land in Italy for redistribution; and it was so worded that the administration of the law would fall almost automatically into the hands of Caesar and his associates. Possibly because of the brashness of this attempted political grab, the Rullan Bill was defeated, as was a bill of 60 B.C. to provide land for Pompey's veterans. This last setback was one of the events which precipitated the formation of the First Triumvirate (see § 107). In the following year, when Caesar was consul, land was provided for the veterans by the Julian Agrarian Law and, apparently, by a supplementary measure concerning Campania, by which Caesar disposed of all the remnants of public domain in Italy. After the Civil War Caesar settled some of his veterans in overseas colonies (see § 110). Octavian after Philippi sanctioned outright confiscation to meet his veterans' demands for land in Italy (see § 117); later, as Augustus ruling a stabilized Principate, he initiated a large-scale program of overseas colonization as a regular means of providing for veterans.

THE RULLAN BILL, 63 B.C.

Cicero, *On the Agrarian Law,* First Speech, Chapter ii, and Second Speech, Chapters
xxv–xxvii (abridged); From *LCL*

Rullus is selling all the public property in Italy item by item. No doubt
he is busy about that, for he does not let a single item pass. He searches
through the whole of Sicily in the censors' registers; he leaves no building, no land unnoticed. You have heard the sale of what belongs to the
Roman people publicly advertised by a tribune of the plebs, arranged
for the month of January, and you have no doubt, I imagine, that the
reason why those who won it by the valor of their arms did not sell it
for the sake of the treasury was that we might have something that we
could sell for the sake of bribery.

Now mark what they would be at more openly than before. . . .
They order the lands of the inhabitants of Attalia and Olympus[57] to be
sold, towns which the victory of the gallant Publius Servilius added to
the dominion of the Roman people; next, the royal territories in Macedonia, acquired by the valor partly of Titus Flamininus, partly of Lucius
Paullus who conquered Perseus; next, the most excellent and fruitful
land of Corinth, which the successful campaign of Lucius Mummius
added to the revenues of the Roman people; and afterwards the land in
Spain near New Carthage, which became Roman possessions by the
distinguished valor of the two Scipios; then they sell old Carthage itself,
which Publius Africanus consecrated to be eternally remembered, stripped
of its buildings and walls, either to mark the disaster to the Carthaginians, or as evidence of our victory, or pursuant to some religious sign
vouchsafed to him. After the sale of these distinctions and jewels of our
imperial crown, which adorned this commonwealth that our ancestors
have handed down to us, they order those lands to be sold which King
Mithridates possessed in Paphlagonia, Pontus, and Cappadocia. . . .

Here I do not even argue a point which is absolutely clear, O Romans
—that our ancestors left us no such custom as that of buying lands from
private persons, on which to settle the common people as colonists; that
by all laws it was on public lands that private persons were settled. I
confess that I expected some such statement from this boorish and
truculent tribune of the plebs, but I have always considered this most

57. Towns in Pamphylia, in Asia Minor; the area was subdued by the consul Publius Servilius
Vatia in 79 B.C.

lucrative and most disgraceful traffic in buying and selling inconsistent with the functions of a tribune, inconsistent with the dignity of the Roman people. He orders land to be bought. I first ask, what lands and where? I do not wish the Roman people to hang in suspense and uncertainty with obscure hopes and blind expectation. . . . "The reason," says he, "why I cannot mention any particular lands is because I shall not touch any land belonging to anyone who does not want to sell." . . .

For two kinds of lands, O Romans, are concerned in these purchases. Of one of them the owners wish to get rid because of the unpopularity they cause, of the other because of their desolate condition. The lands which come from Sulla, very largely extended beyond their limits by certain persons, arouse such odium that they cannot endure it if a genuine and courageous tribune of the plebs gives but one hiss; whatever price is paid for any such land, it will be too much. The other kind of lands, uncultivated owing to their barrenness, waste and abandoned owing to their pestilential unhealthiness, will be purchased from those who see that they must abandon them if they cannot sell them. And beyond doubt this is the meaning of what was said by this tribune of the plebs in the senate, that the common people of the city had too much power in the state, and they they ought to be drained off—that is the word he used, as if he were speaking of sewage instead of a class of excellent citizens. But do you, Romans, if you will be guided by me, keep possession of the influence you enjoy, of your liberty, of your votes, of your dignity, of your city, of your Forum, of your games, of your festivals and all your other enjoyments; unless perhaps you prefer to abandon these privileges and this brilliant Republic, and to settle in the dry sands of Sipontum or in the pestilential swamps of Salapia[58] with Rullus for your leader. . . .

THE FLAVIAN BILL, 60 B.C.

Cicero, *Letters to Atticus* book 1, no. 19 (abridged); Adapted from *LCL*

Cicero to Atticus, greeting.   *Rome, March 15, 60 B.C.*
The agrarian law was zealously pushed by the tribune Flavius with the support of Pompey, though its only claim to popularity was its supporter. I was favorably received by a public meeting when I proposed to delete from the law all provisions which encroached on private rights: to exempt land that was public in the consulship of Publius

---

58. These places were in Apulia, the most desolate part of Italy, and the remotest from Rome.

Mucius and Lucius Calpurnius,[59] to confirm Sulla's veterans in their possessions, to allow the people of Volaterrae and Arretium to retain in their possession their lands which Sulla had confiscated but not distributed. The only provision I did not reject was that land be purchased with the windfall which will come in from the new foreign revenues in the next five years [i.e., from the recent eastern conquests of Pompey]. The senate was opposed to this whole agrarian scheme, suspecting that Pompey was aiming at getting some new powers. Pompey had set his heart on carrying the law through. I, with the full approval of the applicants for land, was for confirming the holdings of all private persons—for, as you know, our strength lies in the rich landed gentry; at the same time I satisfied Pompey and the populace—which I also wanted to do—by supporting the purchase of land, thinking that if it were faithfully carried out, the dregs of the city populace could be drained off and the deserted parts of Italy peopled.[60]

107. THE FIRST TRIUMVIRATE, 60–55 B.C.

Plutarch, *Life of Crassus* xiv–xv

Caesar now returned from his province,[61] designing to obtain the consulship, and saw that Crassus and Pompey were again at variance. He was unwilling to make one his enemy by applying to the other, and he had no hope of success if neither helped him. He therefore made it his business to reconcile them, showing them that by ruining each other they would only increase the power of such men as Cicero, Catulus, and Cato, who would be really powerless if they united their friends and adherents and directed public affairs with one power and one policy. And so reconciling them by his persuasions, he brought them together, and out of the three he constituted an irresistible power, with which he overthrew the government of senate and people. Nor did he make either Pompey or Crassus greater through each other, but through them he made himself greatest of all. For with the support of both he was at once triumphantly elected consul, and when he was consul they voted him the command of armies and allotted him the province of Gaul, and so

59. 133 B.C. This land had been made private by the Gracchan and subsequent agrarian legislation; see introduction to § 102.

60. Note how, when writing in confidence to a friend, Cicero really approves what he denounced in public in order to defeat the Rullan Bill.

61. In 61 B.C. Caesar was propraetor of Farther Spain.

placed him as it were in a citadel, not doubting but they would divide the rest at their pleasure between themselves when they had confirmed him in his allotted command. Pompey was actuated in all this by an unbounded love of power; and Crassus now added to his old disease of covetousness a new and ardent passion for trophies and triumphs. Emulous of Caesar's exploits, not content to be beneath him in these though surpassing him in all else, he could not rest or let up till it ended in his ignominious death and in public calamities.[62]

When Caesar came down from Gaul to the city of Luca, many Romans came there to meet him, among them Pompey and Crassus. The latter two held conferences with him in private, and they decided to proceed to still more decisive steps and to take the entire conduct of the state into their hands. Caesar was to keep his army, and Pompey and Crassus were to obtain other provinces and armies. The one way to achieve all this was to stand for a second consulship: they would be candidates and Caesar was to cooperate with them by writing his friends and sending many of his soldiers to support them in the election.[63] With this understanding they returned to Rome, where their design was at once suspected, and report was rife that their meeting had been for no good. . . . "Why should these men want a second consulship?" many asked. "And why once again together? why not with other colleagues? We have many men not unworthy, surely, to be fellow consuls with Crassus and Pompey." Alarmed at this opposition, Pompey's partisans resorted to the greatest disorder and violence and capped it all by waylaying Domitius[64] as he was coming down to the polls before daybreak with his attendants, killing his torchbearer and wounding many, Cato among them. After these had been routed and shut up at home, Pompey and Crassus were proclaimed consuls. Not long after, they once more surrounded the Rostra with armed men, ejected Cato from the Forum, killed some that offered resistance, and then had Caesar granted his command for another five-year period and the provinces of Syria and both the Spains voted to themselves. When the lot was cast, Syria fell to Crassus and the Spains to Pompey.

---

62. Crassus lost his life and most of his army of 44,000 to the Parthians in 53 B.C.

63. This conference at Luca, at which it was agreed to renew the Triumvirate for five years more, took place in 56 B.C. Pompey and Crassus were consuls again in 55.

64. The rival candidates put up by the Catonian bloc.

108. CIVIL WAR: THE "IRREPRESSIBLE CONFLICT"

The death of Crassus in 53 B.C. precipitated the rupture of the already strained Triumvirate, as both Caesar and Pompey sought to gain predominance by winning the support of the important body of Crassus' adherents. When it became apparent that Caesar, even though away in Gaul, was winning in this contest, Pompey and Cato were impelled to combine their factions against him. The crisis came in the twelvemonth preceding March 1, 49 B.C., on which date Caesar's proconsular power, extended after the conference at Luca (§ 107), was to expire. The conquest of Gaul completed, Caesar was ready to return to Rome; but to revert to private-citizen status would be to expose himself to easy prosecution by his political enemies for illegal conduct in Gaul. He therefore decided to stand in the election of 49, while he still had his army, for the consulship of the following year. His adherents in Rome had already secured the passage of a *plebiscitum* specifically authorizing Caesar to stand for the consulship *in absentia,* a procedure for which there was ample precedent. Thereafter various anti-Caesarian motions were put through the Senate, but they were usually vetoed by pro-Caesarian tribunes. Then, on December 1, 50 B.C., a resolution in the Senate, calling on both Pompey and Caesar to resign their commands in the interest of avoiding civil war, was carried by an overwhelming vote. Caesar, who had meanwhile stationed himself with one legion at Ravenna, offered to comply if Pompey did likewise. Instead, the violently anti-Caesarian consuls of the following year, flouting more moderate counsels, rammed a resolution through the Senate declaring Caesar a public enemy if he refused to lay down his command by March 1. Two tribunes, Mark Antony and Quintus Cassius, vetoed the Senate's motion. A few days later (January 7, 49 B.C.) they were warned by the consuls to leave the senate house if they wished to escape violence. The Senate passed its "ultimate decree" instituting martial law (see § 157), and the two tribunes fled in the night to deliver the news to Caesar. Thereupon Caesar harangued his troops and led them (January 11) across the little Rubicon River, which was the boundary between Italy and Cisalpine Gaul. "Caesar could brook no superior, Pompey no equal" (Lucan, *Pharsalia* I. 125–126). The Civil War was on.

The following letters from Cicero's correspondence reveal vividly the varying emotions of the anti-Caesarians in the months preceding and immediately following the outbreak of hostilities. There stand out in particular the senatorial leaders' obdurate rejection of widely held moderate counsels as the crisis drew to a head, and the wild panic that overwhelmed Pompey's supporters when Caesar, after crossing the Rubicon, began to sweep down through Italy, with one town after another opening its gates to him.

Cicero, *Letters to Friends* book VIII, nos. 8.4–9, 14.2–3, *Letters to Atticus* book VII, nos. 6, 8, 13, 22, book VIII, no. 13 (all abridged); From *LCL*

Rome, October, 51 B.C.[65]

As for politics, absolutely nothing has been done for many days past, because people are waiting to see what happens about the Gallic provinces. At last, however, after several postponements and grave discussions, and when it had been definitely ascertained that Pompey's inclinations were in the direction of having a decree passed that Caesar should quit his province after March 1, a decree of the senate was passed, which I send you, and the following resolutions were entered in the minutes.

"Decrees and resolutions[66] of the senate.

"September 29, in the temple of Apollo. Present at the writing [of the decree] were [eight names follow].

"Whereas the consul Marcus Marcellus opened the question of the provinces to be assigned to the consulars, concerning this matter the senate voted as follows:

"The consuls Lucius Paullus and Gaius Marcellus [the consuls of 50 B.C.], when they have entered upon their office, after the first day of the month of March that shall fall within their year of office, shall bring the matter of the consular provinces before the senate and shall not after the first of March give precedence to any other motion, nor shall any other motion be brought before the senate in combination with that one; and they shall hold a meeting of the senate for that purpose even on comitial days,[67] and shall pass a decree of the senate. And when that matter is being brought before the senate by the consuls, then it shall be lawful to call in such of the senators as are on the roll of the 300 jurors without their incurring a penalty. If it be necessary to bring that matter before the people or the plebs, Servius Sulpicius and Marcus Marcellus, the

65. This letter and the next were written not by Cicero but by Marcus Caelius to Cicero, who was then serving as governor of Cilicia (see § 145); the remaining letters in this group were written by Cicero to his friend Atticus.

66. The distinction in these technical terms is that the resolutions *(auctoritates)* were motions carried in the Senate but vetoed by one or more tribunes of the plebs.

67. It was not customary for the Senate to meet on days on which assemblies *(comitia)* could be held.

present consuls, and the praetors and tribunes of the plebs, whosoever of them sees fit, shall bring it before the people or plebs. But if the aforesaid have not so brought it, their successors in their several offices shall so bring it before the people or plebs. No veto was interposed."[68]

"September 29, in the temple of Apollo. Present at the writing [of this decree] were [the same eight persons as above].

"Whereas the consul Marcus Marcellus opened the question of the provinces, concerning this matter the senate voted as follows:

"That in the opinion of the senate it is inexpedient that any of those who have the right of veto or of obstruction should cause any such delay as could prevent a motion concerning the Republic of the Roman people being brought before the senate at the earliest possible opportunity, or a decree of the senate being passed thereon. That in the opinion of the senate, the man who so obstructs or forbids the debate will have acted against the interests of the state. That if anyone shall veto this decree of the senate, it is the pleasure of the senate that a resolution to the same effect be drafted and the matter at the earliest opportunity brought before the senate and the people.

"The above decree was vetoed by Gaius Caelius, Lucius Vinucius, Publius Cornelius, and Gaius Vibius Pansa, tribunes of the plebs.[69]

"That it is further resolved by the senate in reference to the soldiers now in the army of Gaius Caesar, that those of them who have served their full time or have pleas to advance, which pleas would entitle them to a discharge, shall have their cases brought before this body in order that they may be considered and their pleas investigated. That, if anyone shall veto this decree of the senate, it is the pleasure of the senate that a resolution to the same effect be drafted and the matter brought before the senate at the earliest opportunity.

"The above decree was vetoed by Gaius Caelius and Gaius Pansa, tribunes of the plebs.". . .[70]

The following remarks, moreover, of Gnaeus Pompey attracted attention and gave people the greatest confidence, when he stated that he could not with any justice decide about Caesar's provinces before March

68. No tribune vetoed this motion since it did not call for the supersession of Caesar in Gaul on March 1, 50 B.C., but merely instructed the incoming consuls to take up on that date—one year before the expiry of Caesar's command—the question of appointing his successor.

69. The veto of this measure by pro-Caesarian tribunes was a foregone conclusion, since it declared any magistrate who on March 1 blocked settlement of the question of Caesar's command to be guilty of high treason.

70. Since the measure was plainly motivated not by a sudden solicitude for the soldiers on the part of the Senate, but was an attempt to embarrass Caesar and draw off as many of his men as possible.

1, but that after that date he would not hesitate to do so. When he was asked, "What if there were any vetoes interposed on that day?" he replied that "It made no difference whether Caesar was going to refuse to obey the senate or would put someone up to obstruct its decrees." "What if he is minded," somebody else asked, "to be consul and keep his army at the same time?" and he replied with the utmost suavity, "What if my own son should be minded to lay his stick across my back?" By such expressions he had led people to suspect that there is some trouble between him and Caesar. So now, as far as I can see, Caesar means to have recourse to one or the other of these alternatives —either to remain in Gaul, so that his candidature may not be considered this year, or else, if he can carry his election, to quit his province.

Rome, August, 50 B.C.

With regard to the general political situation, I have repeatedly told you in my letters that I foresee no peace that can last a year; and the nearer the struggle—and there is bound to be a struggle—approaches, the more clearly do we see the danger of it. The point at issue, on which those who are at the head of affairs are going to fight, is this: Gnaeus Pompey is determined not to allow Gaius Caesar to be elected consul unless he has handed over his army and his provinces; Caesar on the other hand is convinced that there is no safety for him if he once quits his army. He proposes, however, this compromise—that both should deliver up their armies. So it is that their vaunted mutual attachment and detestable alliance is not merely degenerating into private bickering, but is breaking out into war. . . .

Amid all this discord I see that Pompey will have on his side the senate and the body of jurors; all who live a life of fear, or but little hope, will join Caesar, for his army is altogether above comparison. Only may we have time enough to consider the resources of each and choose our side!

Formiae, December 17, 50 B.C.

My fears as to the political situation are great. And so far I have found hardly a man who would not yield to Caesar's demand[71] sooner than fight. That demand is shameless, it is true, but stronger in its appeal than we thought. But why should we choose this occasion to begin resisting? "No greater evil threatens now"[72] than when we prolonged

---

71. That Caesar and Pompey should surrender their commands simultaneously.

his office for another five years, or when we agreed to let him stand as a candidate in his absence. But perhaps we were then giving him these weapons to turn against us now. You will say, "What then will your view be?" [i.e., when asked to speak it in the senate]. My view will be not what I shall say; for my view will be that every step should be taken to avoid a conflict, but I shall say the same as Pompey.

Formiae, December 25 or 26, 50 B.C.

Your guess that I should meet Pompey before coming to Rome has come true. On the 25th he overtook me near the Lavernium. We reached Formiae together, and were closeted together from two o'clock until evening. As to your query whether there is any hope of a peaceful settlement, so far as I could tell from Pompey's full and detailed discourse, he does not even wish it. He thinks that the constitution will be subverted if Caesar is elected consul even after disbanding his army; and he reckons that when Caesar hears of the energetic preparations against him, he will give up the idea of the consulship this year and prefer to keep his army and his province. Still, if Caesar should play the fool, Pompey has an utter contempt for him and firm confidence in his own and the state's resources. Well, although the "uncertainty of war"[73] came constantly to my mind, I was relieved of anxiety as I listened to a soldier, a strategist, and a man of the greatest influence discoursing in a statesmanlike manner on the risks of a hollow peace. We had before us a speech of Antony made on December 21, which attacked Pompey's entire life, complained about the condemnation of certain people, and threatened war. Pompey's comment was, "What do you suppose Caesar will do, if he becomes master of the state, when a wretched, insignificant subordinate dares to talk like that?" In a word, Pompey appeared not only not to seek peace, but even to fear it. But I fancy the idea of leaving the city shakes his resolution. What annoys me most is that I have to pay up to Caesar. . . . It is bad form to owe money to a political opponent.[74]

Menturnae, January 22, 49 B.C.

It is civil war, though it has not sprung from division among our citizens but from the daring of one abandoned citizen. He is strong in

72. A quotation from Homer's *Odyssey* (XII. 209).

73. A quotation from the *Iliad* (XVIII. 309).

74. This is an interesting sidelight on the wealth acquired by Caesar in Gaul; cf. also Cicero, *Letters to Friends* book I, no. 9.21.

military forces, he attracts adherents by hopes and promises, he covets the whole universe. Rome is delivered to him stripped of defenders, stocked with supplies:[75] one may fear anything from one who regards her temples and her homes not as his native land but as his loot. What he will do, and how he will do it, in the absence of senate and magistrates, I do not know. He will be unable even to pretend constitutional methods. But where can our party raise its head, or when? You too remark how poor a general our leader is: why, he did not even know how things were in Picenum;[76] and the crisis shows his lack of plan. Pass over other faults of the last ten years: what compromise were not better than this flight? I do not know what he is thinking of doing now, though I inquire by constant letters. It is agreed that his alarm and confusion have reached the limit. He was kept in Italy to garrison Rome, but no garrison or place to post a garrison can I see. We depend entirely upon two legions that were kept here by a trick and are practically disloyal.[77] For so far the levy has found unwilling recruits, disinclined to fight. But the time of compromise is past. The future is obscure. We, or our leaders, have brought things to such a pass that, having put to sea without a rudder, we must trust to the mercy of the storm.

Formiae, February 8 or 9, 49 B.C.

I see there is not a foot of ground in Italy which is not in Caesar's power. I have no news of Pompey, and I imagine he will be captured unless he has taken to the sea. . . . What can I do? In what land or on what sea can I follow a man when I don't know where he is? In fact, on land, how can I follow, and by sea whither? Shall I then surrender to Caesar? Suppose I could surrender with safety, as many advise, could I do so with honor? By no means. I will ask your advice as usual. The problem is insoluble.

75. Pompey had decided to withdraw from Rome to avoid being trapped there by Caesar's rapid southward sweep through Italy. A large number of the nobility, including the two consuls and most of the senators, followed him. In their haste the consuls removed the keys of the treasury, but left the treasure behind. In another letter (*To Atticus* book VIII, no. 1), written from Formiae on February 16, Cicero remarks: "I saw I was writing [to Pompey] in vain, but wanted to put on record my opinion about not abandoning Italy, as I had done before about holding Rome."

76. Pompey's home territory, which Caesar quickly seized.

77. In the spring of 50 B.C. two legions had been withdrawn from Caesar on the pretext that they were needed in Syria. Arrived in Italy, these legions were retained there and placed under the command of Pompey, to whom, however, they were a dubious asset, since Caesar had taken the precaution of giving each man a farewell gift equivalent to a year's pay.

Formiae, March 1, 49 B.C.

I depend entirely on news from Brundisium. If Caesar has caught up with our friend Pompey, there is some slight hope of peace: but if Pompey has crossed the sea, we must look for war and massacre. Do you see the kind of man into whose hands the state has fallen? What foresight, what energy, what readiness! Upon my word, if he refrain from murder and rapine he will be the darling of those who dreaded him most. The people of the country towns and the farmers talk to me a great deal. They care for nothing at all but their lands, their little homesteads, and their tiny fortunes. And see how public opinion has changed: they fear the man they once trusted and adore the man they once dreaded. It pains me to think of the mistakes and wrongs of ours that are responsible for this reaction.

109. POMPEY THE GREAT

Pliny, *Natural History* VII. xxvi; From *LCL*

But it concerns the glory of the Roman Empire, and not that of one man, to mention in this place all the records of the victories of Pompey the Great and all his triumphs, which equal the brilliance of the exploits not only of Alexander the Great but even almost of Hercules and Father Liber [the god Bacchus]. After the recovery of Sicily, which inaugurated his emergence as a champion of the commonwealth in the party of Sulla, and after the conquest of the whole of Africa and its reduction under our sway and the acquirement as a trophy therefrom of the title of *the Great,* he rode back in a triumphal chariot though only of equestrian rank, a thing which had never occurred before. Immediately afterwards he crossed over to the West, and after erecting trophies in the Pyrenees he added to the record of his victorious career the reduction under our sway of 876 towns from the Alps to the frontiers of Farther Spain, and with greater magnanimity refrained from mentioning Sertorius,[78] and after crushing that civil war which threatened to stir up our foreign relations, a second time led into Rome a procession of triumphal chariots as an *eques,* having twice been commander-in-chief before ever having served in the ranks.

78. Writing about a century after the end of the Republic, Pliny was apparently unaware that it was the practice of the Republic never to declare war against a Roman citizen—in other words, never officially to admit the existence of civil war; cf. chapter 4, note 78.

Subsequently he was dispatched to the whole of the seas and then to the far East, and he brought back titles without limit for his country, after the manner of those who conquer in the sacred contests [at Olympia, Nemea, etc.]—for these are not crowned with wreaths themselves but crown their native land. Consequently he bestowed these honors on the city in the shrine of Minerva that he was dedicating out of the proceeds of the spoils of war: "Gnaeus Pompeius Magnus, commander-in-chief, having completed a thirty years' war, routed, scattered, slain, or received the surrender of 12,183,000 people, sunk or taken 846 ships, received the capitulation of 1,538 towns and forts, subdued the lands from the Maeotians [on the sea of Azov] to the Red Sea, duly dedicates his offering vowed to Minerva."

This is his summary of his exploits in the East. But the announcement of the triumphal procession that he led on September 28 in the consulship of Marcus Piso and Marcus Messala [61 B.C.] was as follows: "After having rescued the seacoast from pirates and restored to the Roman people the command of the sea, he celebrated a triumph over Asia, Pontus, Armenia, Paphlagonia, Cappadocia, Cilicia, Syria, the Scythians, Jews and Albanians, Iberia, the Island of Crete, the Bastarnians, and, in addition to these, over King Mithridates and Tigranes."

The crowning pinnacle of this glorious record was (as he himself declared in assembly when discoursing on his achievements) to have found Asia the remotest of the provinces and then to have made her a central dominion of his country. If anybody on the other side desires to review in similar manner the achievements of Caesar, who showed himself greater than Pompey, he must assuredly roll off the entire world, and this it will be agreed is a task without limit.

110. CAESAR'S DICTATORSHIP

Suetonius, *Life of Caesar* xxxvii–xxxviii, xl–xliv; From *LCL*

Having ended the wars, he celebrated five triumphs—four in one month (at intervals of a few days) after vanquishing Scipio,[79] and another after defeating Pompey's sons.[80] The first and most splendid was the Gallic triumph, the next the Alexandrian, then the Pontic, after that the African, and finally the Spanish, each differing from the rest in its equipment

79. At Thapsus in North Africa, April 6, 46 B.C.
80. At Munda in Spain, March 17, 45 B.C.

and display of spoils. As he rode through the Velabrum on the day of his Gallic triumph, the axle of his chariot broke and he was all but thrown out; and he mounted the Capitol by torchlight, with forty elephants bearing lamps on his right and left. In his Pontic triumph he displayed among the showpieces of the procession an inscription of but three words: "I came, I saw, I conquered"—not indicating the events of the war, as others did, but the speed with which it was finished.

To each and every foot soldier of his veteran legions he gave 24,000 sesterces by way of booty, over and above the 2,000 apiece which he had paid them at the beginning of the civil strife. He also assigned them lands, but not side by side, to avoid dispossessing any of the former owners. To every man of the people, besides 10 *modii* of grain and the same number of pounds of oil, he distributed the 300 sesterces which he had promised at first, and 100 apiece to boot because of the delay. He also remitted a year's rent to tenants who paid 2,000 sesterces or less in Rome, 500 or less in Italy. He added a banquet and a dole of meat, and after his Spanish victory two dinners. For, deeming that the former of these had not been served with a liberality creditable to his generosity, he gave another five days later on a most lavish scale. . . .

Then turning his attention to the reorganization of the state, he reformed the calendar, which the pontiffs had long since so disordered, by neglecting to order the necessary intercalations, that the harvest festivals did not come in summer nor those of the vintage in the autumn. He adjusted the year to the sun's course by making it consist of 365 days, abolishing the intercalary month and adding one day every fourth year. Furthermore, that the correct reckoning of time might begin with the next Kalends of January, he inserted two additional months between November and December.[81] Hence the year in which these arrangements were made was one of fifteen months, including the intercalary month which belonged to that year according to the former custom.

He filled the vacancies in the senate, enrolled additional patricians, and increased the number of praetors, aediles, and quaestors as well as of minor officials. He reinstated those who had been degraded by official action of the censors or found guilty of electoral bribery by verdict of the jurors. He shared the elections with the people on this basis: that except in the case of the consulship, half of the magistrates should be appointed by the people's choice while the rest should be those whom

81. Of 46 B.C., which was thus lengthened to 445 days. For further details on the Julian Calendar, see § 193.

he personally had nominated. And these he announced in brief notes like the following, circulated among the tribes: "Caesar the Dictator to this or that tribe: I commend to you So and So, to hold their positions by your votes." He admitted to office even sons of those who had been proscribed. He limited the right of serving as juror to the two classes, the equestrian and senatorial orders, disqualifying the third group, the tribunes of the treasury.

He made the enumeration of the people neither in the usual manner nor place, but from street to street aided by the owners of blocks of houses. He then reduced the number of those who received grain at public expense from 320,000 to 150,000 [cf. § 161] and to prevent the calling of additional meetings at any future time for purposes of enroll-ment, he provided that the places of such as died should be filled by lot each year by the praetor from those who were not on the list. Moreover, to keep up the population of the city, depleted as it was by the assign-ment of 80,000 citizens to colonies across the sea,[82] he enacted a law that no citizen older than twenty or younger than forty, unless detained by service in the army, should be absent from Italy for more than three successive years; that no senator's son should go abroad except as the companion of a magistrate or on his staff; and that those who made a business of grazing should have among their herdsmen at least one third who were men of free birth.[83] He conferred citizenship on all who practiced medicine at Rome, and on all teachers of the liberal arts, to make them more desirous of living in the city and to induce others to resort to it.

As to debts, he disappointed those who looked for their cancellation, which was often agitated, but finally decreed that the debtors should satisfy their creditors according to a valuation of their possessions at the price which they had paid for them before the Civil War, deducting from the principal any interest that had been paid in cash or assigned in writing—an arrangement which wiped out about a fourth part of their indebtedness. He dissolved all associations, except those of ancient foun-dation.[84] He increased the penalties for crimes; and inasmuch as the rich

82. The most notable of these colonies were at Carthage and Corinth, which Caesar refounded; for a charter of a Caesarian colony, see § 162.

83. This was clearly an attempt to restore a free, if hired, peasantry on the latifundia. It may have been motivated further by a desire to break up the solidity of the slave gangs on the large estates.

84. In the charged political atmosphere of 64 B.C. the jittery Senate outlawed all clubs *(collegia)* except a few artisan associations of long standing that had kept to their original purposes of common worship and recreation. When tribune in 58, Publius Clodius restored complete freedom of association, and proceeded by this means to create a highly organized private army of political supporters. The

involved themselves in guilt with less hesitation because they merely suffered exile without any loss of property, he punished murderers of freemen by the confiscation of all their goods, and murderers of others by the loss of half.

He administered justice with the utmost conscientiousness and strictness. Those convicted of extortion he even expelled from the senatorial order. He annulled the marriage of an ex-praetor who had married a woman the very day after her divorce, although there was no suspicion of adultery. He imposed duties on foreign wares. He denied the use of litters and the wearing of scarlet robes or pearls to all except those of a designated position or age, and then only on fixed days. In particular he enforced the law against extravagance, setting watchmen in various parts of the market to seize and bring to him dainties which were exposed for sale in violation of the law; and sometimes he sent his lictors and soldiers to take from a dining room any articles which had escaped the vigilance of his watchmen, even after they had been served.[85]

In particular, for the beautification and convenience of the city, as well as for guarding and extending the bounds of the empire, he formed more projects and more extensive ones every day: first of all, to raise a temple to Mars, greater than any in existence, filling up and leveling the pool in which he had exhibited the sea fight, and to build a theater of vast size over by the Tarpeian Rock; to reduce the civil law to fixed limits, and of the vast and prolix mass of statutes to include only the best and most essential in a limited number of volumes; to open to the public the greatest possible libraries of Greek and Latin books, assigning to Marcus Varro the charge of procuring and classifying them; to drain the Pomptine Marshes; to let out the water from Lake Fucinus; to make a highway from the Adriatic across the summit of the Apennines to the Tiber; to cut a canal through the Isthmus of Corinth; to check the Dacians, who had poured into Pontus and Thrace; then to make war on the Parthians by way of Lesser Armenia, but not to risk a battle with them until he had first tested their mettle. All these enterprises and plans were cut short by his death.

---

senatorial faction was not slow to answer in kind, and the ensuing decade was marked by frequent bloody clashes between hoodlum bands supporting rival political figures. Caesar in effect reimposed, with some variations apparently, the ban of 64; and his law, strengthened and extended by Augustus, prevailed through the centuries of the Principate.

85. On luxury and sumptuary legislation, see further §§ 170, 171.

111. The Assassination of Caesar, 44 B.C.

In addition to this passage and sections in Suetonius' *Life of Caesar* and Plutarch's *Life of Brutus,* there is a lengthy and valuable account of Caesar's assassination, particularly full on the motives of the conspirators and on the events leading up to the deed, in Nicolaus of Damascus' *Life of Augustus* xix–xxvi. The number of the conspirators is variously given as between sixty and eighty. Some twenty can be identified by name, and of these six were Caesarians, ten Pompeians, and the party affiliation of the other four is uncertain.

Plutarch, *Life of Caesar* lvii, lxiii–lxvii (abridged)

Nevertheless his countrymen, bowing to his good fortune and accepting the bit in the expectation that the government of a single person would give them some respite from the civil wars and calamities, appointed him dictator for life.[86] This was indeed a tyranny avowed, since his power was now not only absolute, but permanent as well. His first honors, which at least did not exceed the limits of ordinary human moderation, were proposed to the senate by Cicero; but others vied with one another and carried them so excessively high that they rendered Caesar odious to the most moderate sort of men because of the pretension and extravagance of the honors voted. His enemies too, no less than his flatterers, are thought to have taken a hand in this, so as to have as many pretexts as possible against him and appear to have the greatest justification for an attempt upon him. . . .

Fate, however, is to all appearances not so much unexpected as unavoidable, for many amazing prodigies and apparitions are said to have been observed [shortly before the assassination]. . . . It is also related by many that a soothsayer warned him to be on his guard against a great danger on the day of the month of March which the Romans call the Ides. When this day was come Caesar, on his way to the senate, greeted the soothsayer and said by way of raillery, "Well, the Ides of March are come." And the soothsayer said to him quietly, "Aye, they are come, but they are not gone.". . .

All these things might have happened by chance. But the place which was the scene of that murder and action, the place in which the senate

---

86. This was early in 44 B.C., probably some time in February.

was then assembled, contained a statue of Pompey, as it was one of the public adornments dedicated by Pompey in addition to his theater— showing quite clearly that it was the work of some heavenly power guiding and calling the deed to that place. Indeed, it is also said that Cassius, just before the onslaught, looked across to Pompey's statue and silently implored his assistance, even though he was an adherent of the doctrines of Epicurus;[87] but the crisis, it would seem, with the awful deed now close at hand, replaced his former reasoning with inspired emotion.

As for Antony, who was faithful to Caesar and a strong man, Brutus Albinus[88] detained him outside, engaging him purposely in a lengthy conversation. When Caesar entered, the senate arose obsequiously, and some of Brutus' confederates came and stood around behind his chair while others went to meet him, as if to add their entreaties to Tillius Cimber's petition in behalf of his exiled brother, and accompanied him to his chair with their joint entreaties. After taking his seat, he continued to repulse their beseechings and, as they pressed upon him with greater importunity, he began to be angry at one after another. Thereupon Tillius, laying hold of Caesar's toga with both hands, pulled it down from his neck, and this was the signal for the assault.[89] Casca struck the first blow in his neck, not a mortal wound nor even a deep one, since he was probably very nervous at the beginning of a great venture. Caesar turned about, seized the dagger and held it fast. And almost at the same instant both of them cried out, the smitten man in Latin, "Vile Casca, what does this mean?" and the smiter in Greek to his brother, "Brother, help!"

Such was the beginning, and those who were not privy to the plot were filled with consternation and horror at what was going on: they durst not fly, nor go to Caesar's aid, nor so much as utter a word. But those who had come prepared for the murder bared each of them his dagger and closed in on Caesar in a circle. Whichever way he turned he encountered blows and weapons leveled at his face and eyes, and driven hither and thither like a wild beast he was entangled in the hands of all; for it had been agreed that they should all strike him and taste of the

87. And as such might be expected to disdain such superstition.
88. This is an error. The man who detained Antony was Gaius Trebonius, as stated by Cicero, Appian, and Plutarch himself in his *Life of Brutus* xvii. 1.
89. According to Nicolaus of Damascus (*Life of Augustus* xxiv), the purpose of Cimber's grabbing Caesar's toga in this way was to prevent him from standing up or using his hands.

slaughter, for which reason Brutus also gave him one stab in the groin. Some say that he fought and resisted all the rest, tossing this way and that and crying aloud, but when he saw that Brutus had drawn his dagger he pulled his toga down over his head and sank, whether by chance or because pushed there by his murderers, against the pedestal on which Pompey's statue stood. And the pedestal was drenched with his blood, so that Pompey himself seemed to be presiding over the vengeance upon his enemy, who lay here at his feet quivering from a multitude of wounds. For they say he received twenty-three, and many of the conspirators were wounded by one another as they directed so many blows against one body.

When Caesar had been dispatched, Brutus came forward as if to say something about what had been done. The senate would not hear him, but burst out of doors and in its flight filled the people with confusion and helpless fear, so that some shut up their houses, while others left their counters and shops, and all were running about, some to the place to see the sad spectacle, others away from there when they had seen. Antony and Lepidus, Caesar's most faithful friends, stole away and took refuge in some friends' houses. But Brutus and his followers, just as they were, still hot from the murder, displaying their naked daggers, marched in a body from the senate house to the Capitol, not like fugitives, but full of joy and confidence, summoning the people to liberty and welcoming into their ranks the most distinguished of those they encountered. Some of these did join and go along with them, acting as if they had shared in the deed and laying claim to the glory. . . . The next day Brutus, accompanied by the others, came down from the Capitol and made a speech to the people, who listened to what was said without either expressing resentment at what had been done or appearing to approve; but they showed by their complete silence that they pitied Caesar but respected Brutus. The senate attempted to effect a general amnesty and reconciliation. It voted that Caesar should be honored as a divinity, and that not even the most insignificant measure which he had enacted during his dictatorship should be changed. To Brutus and his followers it distributed provinces and other suitable offices. Thus, all thought matters were brought to the best possible settlement and compromise.

112. THE WILL AND FUNERAL OF CAESAR

Suetonius, *Life of Caesar* lxxxiii–lxxxv; From *LCL*

At the request of his father-in-law, Lucius Piso, his will was opened and read in Antony's house. He had made it on the Ides of the preceding September at his villa near Lavicum, and committed it to the care of the chief Vestal Virgin. Quintus Tubero states that from his first consulship until the beginning of the Civil War [59–49 B.C.] it was his wont to write down Gnaeus Pompey as his heir and to read this to the assembled soldiers. In his last will, however, he named three heirs, the grandsons of his sisters, namely, Gaius Octavius[90] to three fourths of his estate, and Lucius Pinarius and Quintus Pedius to share the remainder. At the end of the will he also adopted Gaius Octavius into his family and gave him his name. Several of his assassins were named among the guardians of his son in case one should be born to him, and Decimus Brutus even among his alternate heirs. To the people he left his gardens near the Tiber for their common use, and 300 sesterces to each man.

When the funeral was announced, a pyre was erected in the Campus Martius near the tomb of Julia. Before the platform was placed a gilded shrine, made after the model of the temple of Venus Genetrix.[91] Within was a bier of ivory with coverlets of purple and gold, and at its head a pillar hung with the robe in which he was slain. Since it was clear that the day would not be long enough for those who offered gifts, they were directed to bring them to the Campus by whatsoever streets of the city they wished, regardless of any order of precedence. . . . Instead of a eulogy the consul Antony caused a herald to recite the decree of the senate in which it had voted Caesar all divine and human honors at once, and likewise the oath with which they had all pledged themselves to watch over his personal safety; to which he added a few words of his own. The bier before the platform was carried to the Forum by magistrates and ex-magistrates. While some were urging that it be burned in the temple of Jupiter Capitolinus, and others in the Curia of Pompey, on a sudden two beings with swords by their sides and brandishing a

---

90. The later Emperor Augustus. From 44 to 27 B.C. his name as adoptive son of Caesar was Gaius Julius Caesar Octavianus (whence Octavian, the name most commonly used in English). From 38 B.C. he regularly styled himself Imperator Caesar Divi Filius ("Commander Caesar, son of the deified [Julius]").

91. This was the temple erected by Julius Caesar in his Forum to the goddess whom the Julian family claimed as its ancestress.

pair of darts set fire to it with blazing torches, and at once the throng of bystanders heaped upon it dry branches, the judgment seats with the benches, and whatever else could serve as an offering. Then the musicians and actors tore off their robes, which they had taken from the equipment of his triumphs and put on for the occasion, rent them to bits, and threw them into the flames; the veterans of the legions threw in the arms with which they had adorned themselves for the funeral; many of the women, too, offered up the trinkets which they wore and the amulets and robes of their children. At the height of the public grief a throng of foreigners went about lamenting each after the fashion of his country, above all the Jews, who even flocked to the place for several successive nights.

The populace, with torches in their hands, ran from the funeral to the houses of Brutus and Cassius, and after being repelled with difficulty they slew Helvius Cinna when they met him, through a mistake in the name, supposing that he was Cornelius Cinna, who the day before had made a bitter indictment of Caesar and for whom they were looking; and they set his head upon a spear and paraded it about the streets. Afterwards they set up in the Forum a solid column of Numidian marble almost twenty feet high, and inscribed upon it: "To the Father of his Country." At the foot of this they continued for a long time to sacrifice, make vows, and settle some of their disputes by an oath in the name of Caesar.

113. CAESAR: TWO OPPOSING VIEWS

In the first two selections that follow, both written after the assassination of Caesar, Cicero expresses without mincing words an estimate of the late dictator that was undoubtedly shared by a large segment, if not a large majority, of the senatorial nobility. Of the third selection, Matius' reply to Cicero's letter the eminent historian T. Rice Holmes has written (*The Roman Republic,* 3:349): "The funeral oration of Mark Antony . . . Shakespeare has transmuted into a possession for all time; but Gaius Matius left a tribute to the memory of Caesar, which, although it is at present known only to the few who are versed in Latin literature, may eventually be recognized as of greater worth. Matius had offended the assassins and their sympathizers by helping to defray the cost of the games which Caesar had instituted in connection with the foundation of the temple of Venus; and Cicero had made remarks about this and other matters which were repeated to Matius and wounded him. Cicero composed an apology which did honor to Matius if not to himself; and Matius, gladly accepting his explanation, replied in a letter which seems to me the noblest that has come from antiquity."

Cicero, *On Duties* III. xxi. 82–83; From *LCL*

Caesar used to have constantly upon his lips the Greek verses from the *Phoenissae*,[92] which I will reproduce as well as I can—awkwardly, it may be, but still so that the meaning can be understood:

> "If wrong may e'er be right, for a throne's sake
> Were wrong most right—be God in all else feared!"

Our tyrant deserved his death for having made an exception of the one thing that was the blackest crime of all. Why do we gather instances of petty crime—legacies criminally obtained and fraudulent buying and selling? Behold, here you have a man who was ambitious to be king of the Roman people and master of the whole world; and he achieved it! The man who maintains that such an ambition is morally right is a madman, for he justifies the destruction of law and liberty and thinks their hideous and detestable suppression glorious. But if anyone agrees that it is not morally right to be king in a state that once was free and that ought to be free now, and yet imagines that it is advantageous for him who can reach that position, with what remonstrance or rather with what appeal should I try to tear him away from so strange a delusion? For, O ye immortal gods! can the most horrible and hideous of all murders—that of fatherland—bring advantage to anybody, even though he who has committed such a crime receives from his enslaved fellow citizens the title of "Father of his Country"?

Cicero, *Letters to Friends* book XI, no. 27.8; From *LCL*

Rome, August, 44 B.C.

Cicero to Gaius Matius, greeting. . . .

It must be obvious to so clever a man as yourself that if Caesar was a king (and it seems to me that he was), two opposite views may be taken of the morality of your attitude—either the one I generally take myself, that your loyalty and kindly feeling in showing your esteem for a friend even after his death is worthy of all praise, or the other, which some people take, that our country's freedom should be preferred to a friend's life. . . .

92. Of Euripides; the verses are 524–525.

Cicero, *Letters to Friends* book XI, no. 28

Rome, August, 44 B.C.

Gaius Matius to Cicero, greeting.

Your letter gave me great pleasure, because I learned that your opinion of me was what I had hoped and prayed for. . . .

I know the charges made against me since Caesar's death. People blame me for lamenting the death of a dear friend and expressing my indignation that the man whom I loved has perished. They say that country should be preferred to friendship, as though they had proved that his death has been good for the state. I will not enter any subtle plea: I confess that I have not attained that height of philosophy. I was not a partisan of Caesar in the political controversy (though I did not abandon a friend, however much I disapproved of what he was doing); nor did I ever approve of the civil war or of the motive for the quarrel, which in fact I did my utmost to get nipped in the bud. So, when my friend was victorious, I was not caught by the charm of office or of money—prizes which others, though they had less influence with him than I, clutched at with unrestrained avidity. Indeed, my own property was actually curtailed by Caesar's law,[93] thanks to which most of those who are now exulting in his death maintained their position in the state. That my vanquished countrymen should be spared was as much an object to me as my own safety.

Can I, then, who desired that all should be left unharmed, help being indignant that the man by whom that boon was bestowed has perished? Especially as the same men were responsible both for his unpopularity and for his death? "You shall smart then," they say, "for daring to condemn what we have done." What unheard-of insolence! One man may glory in crime, yet another may not even lament it with impunity! Why, even slaves have always been free to indulge their fears and joys and sorrows without anyone's dictation; but from what your "champions of liberty" keep saying, they are trying to wrest this right from us by terrorism. But they will try in vain. No dread of danger shall ever turn me from gratitude or from humanity; for never have I thought that an honorable death should be shirked, often that it should even be welcomed. But why this indignation against me, if my only wish is that they should regret what they have done? My desire is that all the world should feel the bitterness of Caesar's death. Ah but, as a loyal citizen, it

93. Probably Caesar's law on debts or on rents; see § 110.

is my duty to desire the safety of the constitution! Well, unless my past life, as well as my hopes for the future, prove without a word of mine that such is my earnest wish, I make no claim to demonstrate it by speechifying. . . .

Am I then, in the evening of my life, to effect a radical change in the principles I maintained in the heyday of my youth, when even a serious error might have been excused, and with my own hands unweave the texture of my life? That I will not do. Nor will I do anything to give offense, except that I do grieve at the hard fate of one who was to me the dearest of friends and withal the most illustrious of men. But even if I were otherwise minded, I should never disavow my own actions and thereby get the reputation of being a rogue in wrongdoing, and a coward and hypocrite in concealing it.

Ah, but I undertook the management of the games celebrated by the young Caesar [Octavian] in honor of the elder Caesar's victory! Well, that is a matter of private obligation and has nothing to do with the constitution of the Republic; anyhow, it was a duty I was bound to perform as a tribute to the memory and eminence of one very dear to me, even though he was dead, and a favor I could not refuse, when he claimed it, to a youth of such brilliant promise and so entirely worthy of his namesake.

I have also often visited the house of Antony, the consul, to pay him my respects; but you will find that those very men who consider me lacking in patriotism are constantly going to him in crowds, with the intention of asking him for something or of carrying something away with them. Is this not the height of presumption, that, while Caesar never interfered to prevent my having friends of my own choice—even those whom he himself disliked—those who have robbed me of my friend should now captiously endeavor to prevent my bestowing my affection on whom I choose? I have no fear, however, that the moderation of my life will hereafter prove an inadequate protection against slander, or that even those who dislike me for my steadfast loyalty to Caesar will not prefer friends of my stamp rather than of their own.

If my prayers are granted me, I shall pass what remains to me of life in retirement at Rhodes; if any accident intervenes to prevent it, I shall live at Rome, but only as one whose lifelong desire is to maintain the right.

114. OCTAVIAN AND THE SENATE
AGAINST ANTONY
(JANUARY–APRIL, 43 B.C.)

The transitory coalition of convenience between the Senate and young Octavian against Antony, of which Cicero was the chief architect, lasted until the defeat of Antony at Mutina in April, 43 B.C., after which the Senate erroneously expected that young Caesar could be "praised, honored, and removed" (the epigram is Cicero's [*Letters to Friends* book XI, no. 20.1]). The following are two out of a larger number of similar resolutions proposed (but mostly not passed) in the senate by Cicero during this period. Particularly significant are the proposals in favor of veterans (cf. introduction to § 106).

Cicero, *Fifth Philippic* xvii. 46, xix. 53; Adapted from *LCL*

Whereas Gaius Caesar son of Gaius, *pontifex,* propraetor, at a serious crisis of the state has exhorted the veteran soldiers to defend the liberty of the Roman people, and has enrolled them; and whereas the Martian and Fourth Legions, with the utmost zeal and the most admirable unanimity in serving the state, under the instigation and leadership of Gaius Caesar are defending and have defended the state and the liberty of the Roman people; and whereas Gaius Caesar, propraetor, has with an army set out for the relief of the province of [Cisalpine] Gaul, has brought under his own obedience and that of the Roman people cavalry, archers, and elephants, and has at a most difficult crisis of the state come to the assistance of the safety and dignity of the Roman people;

Therefore for these reasons it is the pleasure of the senate that Gaius Caesar son of Gaius, *pontifex,* propraetor, shall be a senator and shall express his opinion on the praetorian benches; and that for whatever office he seeks the same account shall be taken of his candidacy as would be legally permissible if he had been quaestor last year.[94]

.   .   .   .

It is the pleasure of the senate that the veteran soldiers who, attaching themselves to the leadership of Caesar, *pontifex,* propraetor, have defended and are defending the liberty of the Roman people and the authority of this our order, shall have, they and their children, exemp-

94. Octavian (Gaius Caesar) was at this time only nineteen years old, and thus ineligible to run for office.

tion from military service; that the consuls, Gaius Pansa and Aulus Hirtius, one or both, if they see fit, shall investigate what land there is in those colonies in which the veteran soldiers have been settled, which is held in violation of the Julian Law,[95] so that it may be divided among the veteran soldiers, and that they shall make a separate investigation concerning the Campanian land and devise a plan for increasing the benefits of the veteran soldiers; that the Martian and Fourth Legions, and those soldiers of the Second and Thirty-fifth legions who joined the consuls, Gaius Pansa and Aulus Hirtius, and enlisted because the authority of the senate and the liberty of the Roman people is and has been most dear to them, shall have, for themselves and their children, exemption from military service, except in case of insurrection in Gaul or Italy; that these legions at the end of the war shall be discharged; that whatever sum of money Gaius Caesar, *pontifex,* propraetor, has promised the soldiers of these legions per man, such shall be given them; that the consuls, Gaius Pansa and Aulus Hirtius, one or both, if they see fit, shall keep an account of what land can, without injury to private individuals, be divided; and that to these soldiers of the Martian and Fourth Legions lands shall be granted and assigned in the fullest measure ever granted or assigned to soldiers.

115. OCTAVIAN AND ANTONY RECONCILED

FORMATION OF THE SECOND TRIUMVIRATE
(OCTOBER, 43 B.C.)

Appian, *Civil Wars* IV. i. 2–3; From *LCL*

Octavian and Antony composed their differences on a small, depressed islet in the Lavinius River, near the city of Mutina. Each had five legions of soldiers whom they stationed opposite each other, after which each proceeded with 300 men to the bridges over the river. Lepidus by himself went before them, searched the island, and waved his military cloak as a signal to them to come. Then each left his 300 men in charge of friends on the bridges and advanced to the middle of the island in plain sight, and there the three sat together in council, Octavian in the center because he was consul. They were in conference from morning till night for two days, and came to these decisions: that Octavian should

---

95. The Julian Agrarian Law of 59 B.C.: see § 106.

resign the consulship and Ventidius take it for the remainder of the year; that a new magistracy for settling the civil dissensions should be created by law, which Lepidus, Antony, and Octavian should hold for five years with consular power[96] (for this name seemed preferable to that of dictator, perhaps because of Antony's decree abolishing the dictatorship); that these three should at once designate the yearly magistrates of the city for the next five years; that a distribution of the provinces should be made, giving Antony the whole of Gaul except the part bordering the Pyrenees mountains, which was called Old Gaul—this, together with Spain, was assigned to Lepidus—while Octavian was to have Africa, Sardinia, Sicily, and the other islands in the vicinity thereof.

Thus was the dominion of the Romans divided by the triumvirate among themselves. Only the assignment of the parts beyond the Adriatic was postponed, since these were still under the control of Brutus and Cassius, against whom Antony and Octavian were to wage war. Lepidus was to be consul the following year and to remain in the city to do what was needful there, meanwhile governing Spain by proxy. He was to retain three of his legions to guard the city, and to divide the other seven between Octavian and Antony, three to the former and four to the latter, so that each of them might lead twenty legions to war. To encourage the army with expectation of booty they promised them, besides other gifts, eighteen cities of Italy as colonies—cities which excelled in wealth, in the splendor of their estates and houses, which were to be divided among them (land, buildings, and all) just as though they had been captured from an enemy in war. The most renowned among these were Capua, Regium, Venusia, Beneventum, Nuceria, Ariminum, and Vibo. Thus were the most beautiful parts of Italy marked out for the soldiers. But they decided to destroy their personal enemies beforehand, so that the latter should not interfere with their arrangements while they were carrying on war abroad. Having come to these decisions, they reduced them to writing, and Octavian as consul communicated them to the soldiers—all except the list of proscriptions. When the soldiers heard them they applauded and embraced each other in token of mutual reconciliation.

---

96. The official title of the group was "triumvirs for the settlement of the commonwealth" *(triumviri rei publicae constituendae)*. Unlike the First Triumvirate, they had their office formally legalized (November, 43 B.C.; see § 116). Their powers apparently went into effect officially in January of 42 B.C. and were renewed in 37 for another five years.

THE PROSCRIPTIONS OF THE SECOND TRIUMVIRATE,
43 B.C.

Appian, *Civil Wars* IV. ii. 5–iv. 20 (abridged); From *LCL*

As soon as the triumvirs were by themselves [at Mutina; see above], they joined in making a list of those who were to be put to death. They put on the list those whom they suspected because of their power, and also their personal enemies, and they exchanged their own relatives and friends with each other for death, both then and later. For they made additions to the catalogue from time to time, in some cases on the ground of enmity, in others for a grudge merely, or because the victims were friends of their enemies or enemies of their friends, or on account of their exceptional wealth, for the triumvirs needed a great deal of money to carry on the war, since the revenue from Asia had been paid to Brutus and Cassius, who were still collecting it, and the kings and satraps were also contributing to them. So the triumvirs were short of money because Europe, and especially Italy, were exhausted by wars and exactions; for which reason they levied very heavy contributions from the plebeians and finally even from women, and contemplated taxes on sales and rents. By now, too, some were proscribed because they had handsome villas or city residences. The number of senators who were sentenced to death was about 300, and of *equites* about 2,000. There were brothers and uncles of the triumvirs in the list of the proscribed, and also some of the officers serving under them who had had some difficulty with the leaders or with their fellow officers. . . .

The triumvirs entered the city separately on three successive days, Octavian, Antony, and Lepidus, each with his praetorian cohort and one legion. As they arrived, the city was speedily filled with arms and military standards, disposed in the most advantageous places. A public assembly was forthwith convened in the midst of these armed men, and a tribune, Publius Titius, proposed a law providing for a new magistracy for settling the present disorders, to consist of three men, namely Lepidus, Antony, and Octavian, to hold office for five years with the same power as consuls. . . . No time was given for scrutiny of this measure nor was a day fixed for voting on it, but it was passed forthwith. That same night the proscription of 130 men . . . was proclaimed in various parts of the city, and a little later 150 more, and additions to the lists were constantly made of those who were condemned later or previously killed by mistake, so that they might seem to have perished justly. It was ordered that the heads of all the victims should be brought to the triumvirs for a fixed reward, which to a free person was payable in money and to a slave in both money and freedom. All persons were required to afford opportunity for searching their houses. Those who received fugitives, or concealed them, or refused to allow search to be made, were liable to the same penalties as the proscribed, and those who informed against such were allowed the same rewards [as above].

The proscription edict was in the following words: "Marcus Lepidus, Marcus Antonius, and Octavius Caesar, chosen by the people to set in order and regulate the Republic, declare as follows:

"Had not perfidious traitors begged for mercy and when they had obtained it become the enemies of their benefactors and conspired against them, neither would Gaius Caesar have been slain by those whom he saved by his clemency after capturing them in war, whom he admitted to his friendship, and upon whom he heaped offices, honors, and gifts, nor should we have been compelled to use this widespread severity against those who have insulted us and declared us public enemies. Now, seeing that the malice of those who have conspired against us and by whose hands Gaius Caesar perished cannot be mollified by kindness, we prefer to anticipate our enemies rather than suffer at their hands. Let no one who sees what both Caesar and we ourselves have suffered consider our action unjust, cruel, or immoderate. Although Caesar was clothed with supreme power, although he was *pontifex maximus,* although he had overthrown and added to our sway the nations most formidable to the Romans, although he was the first man to attempt the untried sea beyond the Pillars of Hercules and was the discoverer of a country hitherto unknown to the Romans, [97] this man was slain in the middle of the senate house, which is designated as sacred, under the eyes of the gods, with twenty-three dastardly wounds, by men whom he had taken prisoner in war and had spared, while some of them he had named co-heirs of his wealth. After this execrable crime, instead of arresting the guilty wretches, the rest sent them forth as commanders and governors, in which capacity they seized upon the public money, with which they are collecting an army against us and are seeking reinforcements from barbarians ever hostile to Roman rule. Cities subject to Rome that would not obey them they have burned, ravaged, or leveled to the ground; other cities they have forced by terror to bear arms against the country and against us.

97. Britain is meant (see § 87); the statement, is of course, exaggerated.

"Some of them we have punished already; and by the aid of divine providence you shall presently see the rest punished. Although the chief part of this work has been finished by us or is well under control, namely the settlement of Spain and Gaul as well as matters here in Italy, one task still remains, and that is to march against Caesar's assassins beyond the sea. On the eve of undertaking this foreign war for you, we do not consider it safe, either for you or for us, to leave other enemies behind to take advantage of our absence and watch for opportunities during the war; nor again do we think that in such great urgency we should delay on their account, but that we ought rather to sweep them out of our pathway once for all, seeing that they began the war against us when they voted us and the armies under us public enemies.

"What vast numbers of citizens have they, on their part, doomed to destruction with us, disregarding the vengeance of the gods and the reprobation of mankind! We shall not deal harshly with any multitude of men, nor shall we count as enemies all who have opposed or plotted against us, or those distinguished for their riches merely, their abundance or their high position, or as many as another man slew who held the supreme power before us when he too was regulating the commonwealth in civil convulsions, and whom you named the Fortunate on account of his success;[98] and yet necessarily three persons will have more enemies than one. We shall take vengeance only on the worst and most guilty. This we shall do for your interest no less than for our own, for while we keep up our conflicts you will all be involved necessarily in great dangers, and it is necessary for us also to do something to quiet the army, which has been insulted, irritated, and decreed a public enemy by our common foes. Although we might arrest on the spot whomsoever we had determined on, we prefer to proscribe rather than seize them unawares—and this too on your account, so that it may not be in the power of enraged soldiers to exceed their orders against persons not responsible, but that they may be restricted to a certain number designated by name and spare the others according to order.

"So be it then! Let no one harbor anyone of those whose names are appended to this edict, or conceal them, or send them away anywhere, or be corrupted by their money. Whoever shall be detected in saving, aiding, or conniving with them we will put on the list of the proscribed without allowing any excuse or pardon. Let those who kill the proscribed bring us their heads and receive the following rewards: to a free

98. The reference is to Sulla's proscriptions (see § 104).

man 25,000 Attic drachmas per head, to a slave his freedom and 10,000 Attic drachmas and his master's right of citizenship. Informers shall receive the same rewards. In order that they may remain unknown the names of those who receive the rewards shall not be inscribed in our records." Such was the language of the proscription edict of the triumvirs as nearly as it can be rendered from Latin into Greek. . . .

Cicero, who had held supreme power after Caesar's death as much as a public speaker could, was proscribed together with his son, his brother, his brother's son, and all his household, faction, and friends. He fled in a small boat, but as he could not endure the seasickness he landed and went to a country place of his own—which I visited to gain knowledge of this lamentable affair—near Caieta [modern Gaeta], a town of Italy, and here he remained quiet. While the searchers were approaching (for of all others Antony sought for him most eagerly, and the rest did so for Antony's sake), ravens flew into his chamber and awakened him from sleep by their croaking, and pulled off his bed covering, until his servants, divining that this was a warning from one of the gods, put him in a litter and again conveyed him toward the sea, going cautiously through a dense thicket. Many soldiers were hurrying around in squads, inquiring if Cicero had been seen anywhere. Some people, moved by good will and pity, said that he had already put to sea. But a shoemaker, a client of Clodius, who had been a most bitter enemy of Cicero, pointed out the path to Laena, the centurion, who was pursuing with a small force. The latter ran after him, and seeing slaves mustering for the defense in much larger number than the force under his command, he called out by way of stratagem, "Centurions in the rear, to the front!"

Thereupon the slaves, thinking that more soldiers were coming, were terror-stricken and Laena, although he had once been saved by Cicero when under trial, drew his head out of the litter and cut it off, striking it three times, or rather sawing it off because of his inexperience. He also cut off the hand with which Cicero had written the speeches against Antony as tyrant, which he had entitled *Philippics* in imitation of Demosthenes. Then some of the soldiers hastened on horseback and others by ship to bring the good news quickly to Antony. The latter was sitting in front of the tribunal in the Forum when Laena, a long distance off, showed him the head and hand by lifting them up and shaking them. Antony was delighted beyond measure. He crowned the centurion and gave him 25,000 Attic drachmas in addition to the stipulated reward, for killing the man who had been his greatest and bitterest enemy. The head and hand of Cicero were suspended for a long time from the Rostra in the Forum where formerly he had been accustomed to make public speeches, and more people came together to behold this spectacle than had previously come to listen to him. It is said that even at his meals Antony placed Cicero's head before his table, until he became satiated with the horrible sight. Thus was Cicero, a man famous for his eloquence and one who had rendered the greatest service to his country when he held the office of consul, slain and insulted after his death.

116. LAND FOR THE VETERANS, 41 B.C.

See introduction to § 106.

Appian, *Civil Wars* v. ii. 12–13, 17; From *LCL*

The task of assigning the soldiers to their colonies and dividing the land was one of exceeding difficulty. For the soldiers demanded the cities which had been selected for them before the war as prizes for their valor [see § 115], and the cities demanded that the whole of Italy should share the burden, or that lots should be cast with the other cities; they asked that the recipients pay the value of the land, and there was no money. They came to Rome in turns, young and old, women and children, to the Forum and the temples, uttering lamentations, saying that they had done no wrong for which they, Italians, should be driven from their fields and their hearthstones like people conquered in war. The Romans mourned and wept with them, especially when they reflected that the war had been waged and the rewards of victory given not in behalf of the commonwealth but against themselves and for a change in the form of government; that the colonies were being established to the end that democracy should never again lift its head—colonies composed of hirelings settled there by the triumvirs to be in readiness for whatever purpose they might be wanted.

Octavian explained to the cities the necessities of the case, but he knew that it would not satisfy them—and it did not. The soldiers encroached upon their neighbors in an insolent manner, seizing more than had been given them and choosing the best lands;[99] nor did they cease even when Octavian rebuked them and made them numerous

99. Among those evicted in this land confiscation was the poet Vergil; but unlike most of the victims he was successful in his appeal to Octavian to have his property restored to him.

other presents, since they were contemptuous of their rulers in the knowledge that they needed them to confirm their power, for the five-year term of the Triumvirate was passing away, and army and rulers needed the services of each other for mutual security. The chiefs depended on the soldiers for the continuance of their government while, for the possession of what they had received, the soldiers depended on the permanence of the government of those who had given it. Believing that they would not be secure in their possession unless the givers were secure in their rule, they fought for them, from necessity, with good will. Octavian made many other gifts to the indigent soldiers, borrowing from the temples for that purpose, for which reason the affections of the army were turned toward him, and the greater thanks were bestowed upon him both as the giver of the land, the cities, the money, and the houses, and as the object of hostile denunciation (on the part of the despoiled) who bore this contumely for the army's sake. . . .

Let these two instances out of many serve as examples of the prevailing insubordination. The cause was that the generals for the most part, as is usually the case in civil wars, were not regularly chosen; that their armies were not drawn from the enrollment according to the ancestral custom nor for the benefit of their country; that they did not serve the public, but rather those alone who brought them together; and that they served these not by the force of laws, but by reason of private promises, not against the common enemy, but against private foes, not against foreigners, but against fellow citizens, their equals in rank. All this relaxed military discipline, and the soldiers thought that they were not so much serving in the army as lending assistance, by their own favor and judgment, to leaders who needed them for their own personal ends. Desertion, which had formerly been unpardonable to Romans, was now actually rewarded with gifts; whole armies resorted to it,[100] and also a number of illustrious men, who did not consider it desertion to change to a like cause, for all parties were alike, since neither of them could be distinguished as battling against a common enemy of the Roman people. The common pretense of the generals that they were all striving for the good of the country made desertion easier, in the thought that one could serve his country in any party. Understanding these facts, the generals tolerated this behavior, for they knew that their authority over their armies depended on donatives rather than on law.

---

100. In 44 B.C., for example, two legions (the Martian and the Fourth: cf. § 114) went over *en masse* from Antony to Octavian. In 42, Brutus' army promptly joined the victors after the battle of Philippi.

117. REPAIRING THE RAVAGES OF CIVIL WAR

J. M. Reynolds, *Aphrodisias and Rome,* no. 12; c. 38 B.C.

Imperator Caesar, son of the deified Julius [Caesar], to the magistrates, council and people of Ephesus, greeting. If you are well it would be well; I myself am in good health together with my army. Solon son of Demetrius, envoy of Plarasa-Aphrodisias, has reported to me how much their city suffered in the war against Labienus[101] and how much property both public and private was looted, concerning all of which I have given a mandate to my colleague [Marcus] Antonius that, as far as possible, he should restore to them whatever he finds; and I decided to write to you, since you have a city well placed to assist them if they lay claim to a slave or any other piece of private property.

I was also informed that out of the loot a golden Eros, which had been dedicated by my father to Aphrodite, has been turned over to you and set up as an offering to Artemis. You will act properly and worthily of yourselves by restoring the offering given by my father to Aphrodite; besides, an Eros is an unsuitable offering to Artemis.

It is necessary that I show care for the people of Aphrodisias, upon whom I have conferred such great benefactions, about which I think you have also heard. [102]

118. THE FINAL VICTORY OF OCTAVIAN

Velleius Paterculus, *Compendium of Roman History* II. lxxxiv–lxxxix (abridged); From *LCL*

Then, in the consulship of Caesar and Messala Corvinus [31 B.C.], the decisive battle took place at Actium. The victory of the Caesarian party was a certainty long before the battle. On this side commander and soldiers alike were full of ardor, on the other was general dejection; on the one side the rowers were strong and sturdy, on the other weakened by privations; on the one side ships of moderate size, not too large for

101. Titus Labienus was a lieutenant of Julius Caesar in Gaul, but he went over to the anti-Caesarian side in the Civil War.

102. In addition to the political considerations, Octavian would also be motivated in part by the fact that Aphrodite corresponded to the Roman Venus, the legendary progenitor of the Julian family, of which Octavian was now a member by virtue of his adoption by his great-uncle, Julius Caesar.

speed, on the other vessels of a size that made them formidable in appearance only; no one was deserting from Caesar to Antony, while from Antony to Caesar someone or other deserted daily. . . .

Then came the day of the great conflict, on which Caesar and Antony led out their fleets and fought, the one for the safety of the world, the other for its ruin. . . . When the conflict began, on the one side was everything—commander, rowers, and soldiers; on the other, soldiers alone. Cleopatra took the initiative in the flight; Antony chose to be the companion of the fleeing queen rather than of his fighting soldiers, and the commander, whose duty it would have been to deal severely with deserters, now became a deserter from his own army. Even without their chief his men long continued to fight bravely, and despairing of victory they fought to the death. Caesar, desiring to win over by words those whom he might have slain with the sword, kept shouting and pointing out to them that Antony had fled, and kept asking them for whom and with whom they were fighting. But they, after fighting long for their truant commander, reluctantly surrendered their arms and yielded the victory, Caesar having promised them pardon and their lives before they could bring themselves to sue for these. . . .

The following year Caesar followed Cleopatra and Antony to Alexandria and there put the finishing touch to the civil wars. Antony promptly ended his life, thus by his death redeeming himself from the many charges of lack of manliness. As for Cleopatra, eluding the vigilance of her guards she caused an asp to be smuggled in to her, and ended her life by its venomous sting. . . .

As for Caesar's return to Italy and to Rome—the procession which met him, the enthusiasm and magnificence of his triumphs and of the spectacles which he gave—all this it would be impossible adequately to describe even within the compass of a formal history, to say nothing of a work so condensed as this. There is nothing that man can desire from the gods, nothing that the gods can grant to a man, nothing that wish can conceive or good fortune bring to pass, which Augustus on his return to the city did not bestow upon the state, the Roman people, and the world. The civil wars were ended after twenty years, foreign wars suppressed, peace restored, the frenzy of arms everywhere lulled to rest.

> At the scene of his decisive victory over Antony and Cleopatra at Actium Octavian soon after commemorated the event by building a temple to his favorite god, Apollo, on one arm of the Ambracian Gulf, and on the other, where his camp had been, he erected a victory monument, "a platform of squared stones adorned with the beaks of the captured ships"

(Cassius Dio, *Roman History* LI, chapter 1.3). Remains of that vainglorious monument are still to be seen *in situ*. Its dedicatory inscription has been reconstructed from twenty-six small, incomplete fragments.

AE, 1977, no. 778; 29 B.C.

To Neptune and Mars, Imperator Caesar son of the deified Julius [Caesar], having attained a naval victory in the war which he waged for the Republic in this vicinity, adorned with spoils the camp from which he set out to pursue the enemy and dedicated it when he was consul for the fifth time, hailed *imperator* seven times, peace having been won on land and sea.

Orosius, *History against the Pagans* VI. xx. 1–2

In the 725th year after the founding of the city, in the consulship of the Emperor Augustus Caesar (for the fifth time) and Sextus Appuleius [29 B.C.], Caesar returned from the East as a conqueror. On the 6th of January he entered the city in a triple triumph, and it was at this time, when all the civil wars had been lulled to sleep and brought to an end, that he first ordered the gates of Janus to be closed.[103] On this day Caesar was first saluted as Augustus.[104] This title, which everyone up to that time had held inviolate, and one to which other rulers theretofore had not presumed, signified that the assumption of the supreme power to rule the world was legitimate, and from that same day on the highest power of the state began to be, and remained, reposed in one man. This type of government the Greeks call monarchy.

103. The closing of the gates of the temple of Janus symbolized that "peace with victory" reigned throughout the Roman empire.

104. This is an error. The title of Augustus was conferred on Octavian on January 16, 27 B.C.

6

THE ADMINISTRATION OF THE IMPERIAL REPUBLIC: FOREIGN DOMINATION AND PROVINCES

119. ROME AND HER COLONIES IN THE SECOND PUNIC WAR

Rome was saved during the crisis after Cannae by the fundamental loyalty of her colonies and allies, despite the temporary defection of southern Italy (§ 64). In the gigantic effort mounted by the Romans after 210 B.C. most of the colonies met their military and financial obligations despite the continuous drain on their resources. In 204, as this selection tells, twelve colonies which had until then pleaded inability to furnish troops and money were penalized and whipped into line.

Livy, *History of Rome* XXIX. XV. 1–10

When the reinforcement of the legions in the combat theaters was under consideration, it was suggested by some senators that now, when at last by the favor of the gods their fears had been dissipated, was the time to put a stop to certain practices which they had somehow or other tolerated in perilous circumstances. As the senate listened in intent expectation, they added that the twelve Latin colonies which had refused to furnish soldiers to the consuls Quintus Fabius and Quintus Fulvius were now for the sixth year enjoying exemption from military service, as though it had been granted them as a mark of honor and favor, while in the meantime their good and dutiful allies, in return for their fidelity and obedience to the Roman people, had been exhausted by continual levies every year. These words reminded the senators of a matter now almost forgotten and aroused their indignation. Accordingly, granting the consuls priority for no other business, they decreed that the consuls should summon to Rome the magistrates and the ten leading citizens from Nepet, Sutrium, Ardea, Cales, Alba, Carseoli, Sora, Suessa, Setis, Circeii, Narnia, and Interamna (for these were the colonies involved), and command them that each of these colonies should furnish double the greatest number of foot soldiers that they had ever provided for the Roman people since the enemy had been in Italy, and 120 horsemen each; if any of them was unable to make up that number of horsemen, it should be allowed to furnish three foot soldiers in place of one horseman; both the foot and horse soldiers should be chosen from the wealthiest inhabitants and should be sent out of Italy wherever there was need of reinforcements. If any of them refused to comply, it was the senate's pleasure that the magistrates and envoys of that colony be detained, and not be granted an audience in the senate if they requested it, until they had obeyed these orders. Furthermore, an annual tax should be imposed upon and collected from these colonies at the rate of one *as* per thousand; a census should be taken in these colonies in a form assigned by the Roman censors, which should be the same as that used for the Roman people; and a return should be made at Rome by sworn censors of the colonies before they retired from office.

120. THE BEGINNINGS OF ROMAN DOMINATION IN THE GREEK WORLD, 196–193 B.C.

The first selection, dating from 194 (possibly 196) B.C., is the earliest extant inscription bearing on the relations of Rome and the Greek states. Its text is a letter from Titus Quinctius Flamininus, turning over to the town of Chyretiae all the property in its territory which the Romans after their recent victory had confiscated from the townspeople who had supported Philip V of Macedon, and ordering this property restored to the former owners under certain conditions. While instancing the oft-repeated disclaimer of political or territorial ambitions in Greece that was Rome's officially proclaimed policy at this time, Flamininus' letter in itself constitutes an example of Roman dictation in local Greek affairs and demonstrates in addition the Roman practice of supporting the propertied classes in the Greek cities. This gesture of conciliation toward the recently pro-Macedonian faction must be understood as part of an attempt to solidify the ruling and propertied classes behind Rome in the years preceding the war with Antiochus, when, under the leadership of the disaffected Aetolians, the masses in the Greek cities were being won to the support of the Syrian king. On these matters see further § 68. In the second selection we see the Romans, in 193 B.C., mending other fences in preparation for the conflict brewing with Antiochus: Here they confirm the privileges of the city of Teos in Asia Minor, an important center of the cult of Dionysus.

IG, vol. IX, part 2, no. 338 (= Dittenberger, no. 593 = *RDGE,* no. 33)

Titus Quinctius, consul[1] of the Romans, to the chief magistrates and the city of Chyretiae, greeting. Whereas on all other occasions we have made manifest the policy which I personally and the Roman people pursue toward you, we have decided also in what follows to prove ourselves in every respect champions of what is honorable, so that those who are not accustomed to conduct themselves in accordance with the best principles may not be able to calumniate us in this matter. Now therefore, all landed property and buildings belonging to the public domain of the Roman state which are still in its possession we give to your city, so that in this too you may learn our character and the fact that we are determined to seek absolutely no financial profit, esteeming good will and reputation above all else. With respect to all those, moreover, who have not recovered what belongs to them, explore their cases in accordance with my written judgments, and if they give you proof and appear to have a reasonable claim, I judge it just that the property be restored to them.[2]

Dittenberger, no. 601 (= *IGRR,* vol. IV, no. 1557 = *RDGE,* no. 34)

Marcus Valerius son of Marcus, praetor, and the tribunes and the senate to the council and the people of Teos, greeting. Menippus, who was sent as envoy to us by King Antiochus and also chosen by you to serve as envoy for your city, transmitted your decree and himself spoke with all zeal in accordance with it. We received the man kindly, because of his previous reputation and his inherent character, and gave a full and favorable hearing to his requests. And that we are people who set quite the highest store on reverence toward the gods, one might surmise especially from the favor vouchsafed us by the divine power on that

---

1. Flamininus, consul in 198 B.C., was proconsul when this letter was written, but at that time no distinction was yet made in Greek documents between the two titles.

2. The proconsul here instructs the local authorities to follow his precedents and honor the claims of persons who have appealed for restoration of their property on the grounds of innocence of pro-Macedonian partisanship or other error in the confiscation.

account; indeed, we are persuaded also by many other considerations that our high regard for the divine power has been manifest. Therefore, both for these reasons and because of our good will toward you, and because of the envoy who has made the request, we adjudge your city and territory to be sacred, as it even now is, inviolate, and exempt from taxation by the Roman people; and we shall endeavor to increase our honors to the god and our kindnesses to you commensurately, if you faithfully maintain in the future as well your good will toward us. Farewell.

121. DECREE OF LUCIUS AEMILIUS PAULLUS IN SPAIN, 189 B.C.

CIL, vol. II, no. 5041 (= *ROL,* 4:254); *Adapted from LCL*

Lucius Aemilius son of Lucius, commander-in-chief,[3] decreed that the slaves of the Hastensians dwelling in Lascuta Tower should be free. The land and the town which they had possessed at that time he ordered that they should possess and hold as heretofore, so long as the Roman people and senate are so minded.[4] Done in camp on the 19th of January.

122. THE DE FACTO ROMAN PROTECTORATE OVER "LIBERATED" GREECE AND THE EAST

The following texts reveal the growth of the Roman hegemony and protectorate over the Greek East as a result of the wars with Philip V of Macedon and Antiochus III of Syria. The first three selections are Greek inscriptions, all from 189 B.C. The fourth selection is from a speech put by Livy in the mouth of Lycortas, *strategus* of the Achaean League; it is addressed to Appius Claudius, head of a Roman ten-man commission sent to Greece in 184 B.C. in answer to Sparta's complaint against the Achaeans' attack.

3. Lucius Aemilius Paullus, proconsul of Farther Spain at this time, later the conqueror of Perseus, king of Macedon (see § 74 and § 90, second selection). The Hastensians are the inhabitants of Hasta Regia, near Gades (Cadiz).

4. The freed slaves were thus transferred from the domination of the Hastensians to that of Rome; they did not, however, acquire full ownership of the land. Note the use here of *populus senatusque Romanus,* the reverse of the later and more familiar formula S.P.Q.R. *(senatus populusque Romanus),* in which the Senate is given precedence.

DELPHI GRANTED AUTONOMY BY THE
ROMAN SENATE

Dittenberger, no. 612 (= *RDGE*, no. 1)

. . . concerning the freedom of the city and the inviolability of the temple. . . .

Spurius Postumius son of Lucius, praetor of the Romans, to the commonwealth of Delphi, greeting. Boulo, Thrasycles, and Orestas, the envoys sent by you, spoke about the inviolability of your sanctuary and city, acquitting themselves with complete honor; and concerning freedom and exemption from tribute they requested that the city and territory of Delphi should be autonomous and tax-free. Know, then, that it has been decreed by the senate that both the sanctuary of Apollo and the city be inviolate, that both the city and the territory of Delphi be exempt from taxation, and that its citizens be forever[?] autonomous . . . enjoying freedom and governing themselves according to their own wishes . . . and exercising control over the sanctuary and sacred precinct, as has been their ancestral right from the beginning. For your information we append a copy [of the senate's decree].

Spurius Postumius son of Lucius consulted the senate on the 6th of May in the Comitium[?]. Present at the writing [of this decree] were . . . Gaius Aterius son of Gaius, Tiberius Claudius. . . .

Whereas the Delphians spoke concerning the inviolability of their sanctuary, the freedom of their city, and the autonomy and exemption from tribute of their territory, concerning this matter it was decreed as follows: Just as these rights belonged to the Delphians in the past and were reaffirmed by Manius Acilius,[5] it is our pleasure to abide by this decision. . . .

FURTHER BENEFITS GRANTED DELPHI

Dittenberger, no. 611 (= *RDGE*, no. 38)

Gaius Livius son of Marcus, consul of the Romans, and the tribunes and the senate, to the chief magistrates and the city of Delphi, greeting. Herus son of Eudorus, and Damosthenes son of Archelaus, the envoys sent by you, transmitted the documents and themselves spoke with all

---

5. Manius Acilius Glabrio was the consul who in 191 B.C. defeated Antiochus at Thermopylae and drove him from Greece.

zeal in accordance with what was therein recorded, acquitting themselves with complete honor; and they explained also why you instituted
the gymnastic games and the sacrifice in our honor. The senate directed
its attention to this, and also concerning the previous envoys, Boulo,
Thrasycles, and Orestas, who reached us but perished on their homeward journey, [6] it decreed to write to our proconsul Marcus Fulvius to
take steps, as soon as the affair of Samos is under control, [7] to track
down the guilty and see to it that they receive condign punishment and
that the property of the envoys is all restored to their relatives. It also
decreed to write to the Aetolians concerning the injuries suffered by you
at their hands, so that they shall now search out and restore to you all
that has been looted, and that this shall never again happen in the future.
And concerning the [Aetolian and Locrian] settlers in Delphi, the senate
ordered that you should have the power to expropriate whomever you
wish, and to permit to settle among you those who are acceptable to the
commonwealth of Delphi.

The answers given to the envoys who previously came to us from
you, we have transmitted to these, as they requested. [8] And for the
future we shall endeavor always to be the authors of some good to the
Delphians, on account both of the god [the Delphian Apollo] and of
yourselves, and because it is our ancestral practice to reverence the gods
and to honor them as being the authors of all blessings.

HERACLEA GRANTED AUTONOMY BY ROMAN
COMMANDERS IN THE FIELD

This letter was sent by Lucius and Publius Scipio (Africanus) in response
to a formal surrender *(deditio)* brought by envoys from the city of Hera-
clea-near-Latmos in Asia Minor. There is extant a similar letter from these
generals to the city of Colophon (*SEG*, vol. I, no. 440).

Dittenberger, no. 618 (= *RDGE*, no. 35)

Lucius Cornelius Scipio, consul of the Romans, and Publius Cornelius
his brother, to the council and people of Heraclea, greeting. We have
met with your envoys, Dias, Dies, Dionysius, Anaximander, Eudemus,
Moschus, Aristides, and Menes, gentlemen of character, who transmit-

6. They were presumably killed by the Aetolians; cf. the following sentence.
7. Samos was at this time under Roman siege.
8. That is, they requested a copy of the Senate's earlier ruling (given in the preceding selection).

ted your decree and themselves spoke in accordance with what was recorded in the decree, acquitting themselves with complete honor. It happens that we are kindly disposed towards all the Greeks, and we shall endeavor, now that you have come under our protection, to take the best possible care of you and be ever the authors of some good. To you, just as to all the other cities which have placed themselves in our care, we grant freedom, with the right to administer all your affairs yourselves, under your own laws; and in other matters we shall endeavor to be of service to you and to be ever the authors of some good. We accept the gifts and the pledges sent by you, and we for our part shall endeavor to omit nothing in requiting your kindness. And we have sent to you Lucius Orbius, who will take care of your city and territory, so that no one may trouble you. Farewell.

A CLARIFICATION OF GREEK FREEDOM

Livy, *History of Rome* xxxix. xxxvii. 9–21

"I am quite aware, Appius Claudius, that the language I have so far used in not the language that allies should hold toward allies, nor does it befit a nation of free men; it is really appropriate to the bickerings of slaves before their masters. For if those were not just empty words of the herald in which you Romans ordered the Achaeans first of all the Greeks to be free, [9] if our treaty is still in force, if our friendship and alliance are to be equally observed on both sides, why do you demand an accounting for what we Achaeans did to the Spartans after we had conquered them in war, when I do not ask what you Romans did when you took Capua? Grant that some of them were killed by us, what of it? Did you not behead Campanian senators? We tore down their walls; you deprived the Campanians not only of their walls, but of their city and their fields. [10] Our treaty, you say, is ostensibly one between equal partners; in fact, however, the Achaeans enjoy a precarious freedom, the supreme power rests with the Romans. . . ."

His speech was received with approbation by most, and all recognized that he had spoken as befitted the dignity of his office, so that it was quite clear that the Romans could not maintain their authority with mild procedures. Appius thereupon said that he would strongly advise

9. Actually, the first named was not Achaea but Corinth (see § 68), which was, however, reincorporated into Achaea by Flamininus.

10. For the episode referred to, see § 64, last selection.

the Achaeans to court the favor of the Romans while there was yet time to do so of their own free will, lest they be compelled later to act against their will. These words evoked a general groan, but made them afraid to reject the Roman demands.

123. DECREE OF THE SENATE CONCERNING THISBAE, 170 B.C.

In 172 B.C., when war with Perseus was imminent, a senatorial commission was sent to neutralize through alliances the pro-Macedonian Boeotian League (cf. § 76). All members of the League succumbed to the Roman pressure except three—Coronea, Thisbae, and Haliartus. When Haliartus was taken by Roman troops and razed, Thisbae was surrendered by the pro-Roman oligarchical party. The following year an embassy was sent to Rome for a settlement of Thisbaean affairs by the senate.

IG, vol. VII, no. 2225 (=Dittenberger, no. 646=*RDGE*, no. 2)

Quintus Maenius son to Titus, praetor, consulted the senate on the 9th of October in the Comitium. Present at the writing [of this decree] were Manius Acilius son of Manius, of the Voltinian tribe, and Titus Numisius son of Titus.

Whereas the Thisbaeans spoke about the matters affecting them, requesting that they, who had remained firm in our friendship, be granted an opportunity to explain the matters affecting them; concerning this matter it was decreed as follows: That the praetor Quintus Maenius should delegate five members of the senate, as he deemed best in keeping with the interests of the state and with his own good faith. Adopted.

October 14. Present at the writing were Publius Mucius son of Quintus, Marcus Claudius son of Marcus, and Manius Sergius son of Manius.

Likewise, whereas they also spoke concerning territory, harbors and revenues, and mountains,[11] it was decreed that it be permitted them, as far as we are concerned, to possess those which had been theirs.[12]

---

11. The word "mountains" is here generally understood in the sense of "upland pastures;" another suggestion is that the reference is to "mines."

12. In this and the following sections of the decree, since Thisbae had been unconditionally surrendered to the Romans with all its possessions, public and private (cf. § 19), the Senate restores the independence of the city, places the administration exclusively in the hands of the pro-Roman party, and restores to the latter their private property.

Concerning magistracies, and shrines and revenues, that they themselves might control them, concerning this matter it was decreed as follows: Whoever had entered into our friendship before Gaius Lucretius led his army against the city of Thisbae, that these should control them for the next ten years. Adopted. Concerning land, buildings, and goods belonging to them it was decreed that whoever own any of these should be permitted to possess their own property.

Likewise, whereas they also requested that those of them who had deserted [to the Roman lines] and were exiles there [i.e., during the siege] be permitted to wall the citadel and settle there, it was decreed as follows: That they settle there and wall it. Adopted. It was decreed that the city should not be fortified.

Likewise, whereas they also spoke about the gold which they had contributed for a crown in order to dedicate a crown in the Capitol, requesting that it be restored to these, [13] as indicated, in order that they might dedicate this crown in the Capitol, it was decreed that it be restored on these terms.

Likewise, whereas they also requested that all the men who are opposed to our government and theirs be arrested, concerning this matter it was decreed to do as the praetor Quintus Maenius deemed best in keeping with the interests of the state and with his own good faith. As for their request that all those who had gone away to other cities and had not presented themselves before our praetor should not be restored to citizenship, concerning this matter it was decreed to send a letter to the consul Aulus Hostilius, instructing him to give his attention to this matter as he deemed best in keeping with the interests of the state and with his own good faith. Adopted.

[Four additional clauses, specific to certain individuals or incidents, are here omitted.]

124. Decree of the Senate Concerning Delos, 164 B.C.

After the defeat of Perseus, the Roman senate declared Delos a free port (see introduction to § 78) and placed the island under the administration of Athens, with which Rome maintained an alliance. But the senate did

13. That is, those who had deserted to the Romans. The gold had been forfeited in the unconditional surrender.

not hesitate, as this document strikingly reveals, to intervene directly in the internal affairs of Delos over the heads of the Athenian officials.

Dittenberger, no. 664

The *strategoi* [of Athens] to Charmides, superintendent of Delos, greeting. After prolonged debate in the council concerning the decree of the senate which Demetrius of Rhenea brought from Rome regarding the affair of the Serapeum,[14] it was voted not to prevent him from opening and maintaining the sanctuary as before, and also to write you concerning these matters, so that you might be informed. We have also appended for your information a copy of the decree brought by him.

Quintus Minucius son of Quintus, praetor, consulted the senate in the Comitium on the 13th of the intercalary month. Present at the writing [of this decree] were Publius Porcius son of Publius, Tiberius Claudius son of Tiberius, of the Crustumine tribe, and Manius Fonteius son of Gaius. Whereas Demetrius of Rhenea spoke, requesting that he be permitted to maintain his sanctuary of Sarapis at Delos and complaining that the Delians and the governor sent from Athens are preventing him from maintaining it, concerning this matter it was decreed as follows: As far as we are concerned he is permitted to maintain it just as he used to in the past, so long as nothing is done contrary to the decree of the senate. Adopted.

125. PERGAMUM THE PUPPET OF ROME

To prevent King Eumenes of Pergamum, their ally, from becoming too powerful, the Romans had adopted a policy of supporting the Galatians and the kingdom of Bithynia to the east. Attalus II, who succeeded his brother Eumenes in 159 B.C., conferred with Attis, the priest of the celebrated shrine of Cybele at Pessinus (cf. the third selection in § 177), and they decided on a joint military campaign, probably against the Galatians. But upon his return to Pergamum Attalus was persuaded by his state council not to engage in aggressive action contrary to Roman policy, and he wrote this letter to Attis, withdrawing his promise of cooperation. This document is to be dated 159–156 B.C.; after that Pergamum was in effect a vassal state of Rome until it was willed to the western colossus by its last ruler (see § 128).

---

14. Demetrius had a private shrine of the Egyptian god Sarapis, which the Athenian governor of Delos had closed to prevent its interference with the public worship of the god.

OGIS, no. 315: Adapted from C. B. Welles, *Royal Correspondence in the Hellenistic Period*
(New Haven, 1934)

King Attalus to Priest Attis, greeting. If you are well, it would be as I
wish; I myself am also in good health. When we came to Pergamum
and I assembled not only Athenaeus and Sosander and Menogenes but
many others also of my relatives,[15] and when I laid before them what
we discussed in Apamea and told them our decision, there was a very
long discussion, and at first all inclined to the same opinion with us, but
Chlorus kept bringing up forcefully the question of Rome and coun-
selled us by no means to do anything without them. In this at first few
concurred, but afterwards, as day after day we kept deliberating, it
appealed more and more, and to launch an undertaking without their
participation began to seem fraught with great danger; if we were successful the attempt promised to bring us envy and detraction and baneful
suspicion—which they felt also toward my brother—while if we failed
we should meet certain destruction. For they would not, it seemed to
us, regard our disaster with sympathy but would rather be delighted to
see it, because we had undertaken such projects without them. As things
are now, however, if—may Heaven forbid—we suffer any defeats,
having acted entirely with their approval we receive help and may
recover our losses, if the gods favor us. I decided therefore to send men
to Rome on every occasion to make constant report of cases where we
are in doubt, while we ourselves make thorough preparation so that we
may protect ourselves should it be necessary. [The rest is lost].

126. Cyrene Bequeathed to Rome, 155 b.c.

In 163 B.C. Ptolemy VIII Euergetes II was ousted by his co-rulers in Egypt
(his elder brother Ptolemy VIII Philometor and his sister Cleopatra II) and
relegated to the position of ruler of Cyrene. Eight years later, fearing that
the dynastic intrigues in which he was involved might cost his life, he
drew up this will bequeathing his kingdom of Cyrene to Rome, in order
to prevent its falling into his brother's hands. The will was never executed
because Ptolemy regained the throne of Egypt upon his brother's death in
145 B.C. Cyrene eventually came into Rome's possession through bequest
from his son, Ptolemy Apion, in 96 B.C. See further introduction to § 128.

15. This term does not necessarily denote members of the king's family but is an honorific court
title awarded, for example, to members of his advisory council; cf. chapter 8, note 20.

SEG, vol. IX, no. 7

Year 15, month of Loios. May Good Fortune attend.

Following is the last will and testament of King Ptolemy, the younger son of King Ptolemy and Queen Cleopatra, Gods Manifest, a copy of which has also been sent to Rome.

May it be granted me with the gods' favor to take vengeance in fitting manner upon those who have set on foot the unholy plot against me and have undertaken to deprive me not only of my kingdom but even of my life. But if anything happens to me before I leave successors to my throne, I bequeath the kingdom which belongs to me[16] to the Romans, with whom I have from the beginning faithfully[17] maintained my friendship and alliance; and to the same I entrust the protection of my interests, beseeching them by all the gods and by their own honor, if any persons attack my cities or countryside, to render aid with all their might, in accordance with justice and with the mutual treaty of friendship and alliance existing between us.[18]

As witnesses of these dispositions I will appoint Jupiter Capitolinus, and the Great Gods, and Helius, and Apollo the Founder [of Cyrene], in whose safekeeping also the original of this document has been consecrated.

May Good Fortune attend.

127. LETTER TO DYMAE, C. 139 B.C.

In the city of Dymae a popular revolution had attempted to overthrow the pro-Roman party and replace the oligarchic constitution established by the Romans with a democratic one. The proconsul of Macedonia, under whose jurisdiction Greece stood in this period, promptly suppressed the uprising and took vigorous measures to punish the leaders of the insurgents.

16. By this carefully chosen wording Ptolemy tacitly includes in his legacy his as yet unfulfilled claim to Cyprus (see note 18).

17. In contrast with his brother; cf. note 18.

18. A treaty of friendship with Rome was first concluded by Ptolemy II Philadelphus (285–246 B.C.) and renewed by his successors. In 162 the Roman Senate supported the younger Ptolemy's claim to Cyprus, and when the elder brother (Ptolemy VI) refused to cede the island, the Senate denounced the alliance with him and sent envoys to the younger Ptolemy in Cyrene. It was then, no doubt, that the treaty here referred to was signed (or renewed?).

Dittenberger, no. 684 (= *RDGE*, no. 43)

Quintus Fabius Maximus son of Quintus, proconsul of the Romans, to the chief magistrates, councilmen and city of Dymae, greeting. The councilmen of the party of Cyllanius informed me of the crimes committed amongst you—to wit, the burning and destruction of the town hall and of the public records,[19] the leader in which was Sosus son of Tauromenes, who fomented the entire upheaval and also enacted laws contrary to the constitution granted to the Achaeans by the Romans— the particulars of which we went over in Patrae together with my council. Therefore, since it was clear to me that those who brought these things to pass were establishing the worst kind of conditions and political confusion for all the Hellenes (not only involving a lack of harmonious relations with one another and cancellation of debts, but also incompatible with the freedom granted in common to all the Hellenes and with our policy), and since his accusers produced substantiated proofs, I adjudged Sosus to be guilty and condemned him to death for having been the leader of what was done and the drafter of the laws for the destruction of the constitution granted; and likewise Phormiscus son of Echesthenes, one of the magistrates, who assisted him in the burning of the town hall and the public records, as he himself confessed. Timotheus son of Nicias, who drafted the laws in conjunction with Sosus, since he appeared to have committed a lesser offense, I ordered to proceed to Rome, after having him take an oath to be there on the first day of the ninth month, and sending instructions to the urban praetor that he is not to return home until. . . . [The rest is lost.]

128. THE LEGACY OF ATTALUS, 133 B.C.

Attalus III, the last of the kings of Pergamum, died in 133 B.C. Being without an heir, he left a will bequeathing his kingdom to Rome. While the rest of the kingdom was to pass directly under Roman control, Attalus granted Pergamum itself, subject to confirmation by Rome, the status of a free and autonomous city. Roman confirmation of the will was extended in due course by a decree of the senate some time between 133 and 129 B.C.

19. The purpose was no doubt to destroy both the census lists forming the basis of the oligarchic constitution and the official records of private debts.

Meanwhile Aristonicus, who like Attalus was a son of Eumenes II by a concubine, challenged the genuineness of the will and raised a revolt to assert his claim to the throne.[20] To his banner flocked large numbers of slaves and poverty-stricken malcontents from all over the Pergamene kingdom. In an attempt to conciliate large sections of the population and prevent further defections, the city of Pergamum hurriedly granted citizenship to noncitizen residents, mercenary soldiers, and royal freedmen, and penalized those who left the city with loss of rights. The Romans had to call on their client kings and on the Greek cities all the way from Byzantium to Halicarnassus for aid (cf. § 129), and it was not until 129 B.C. that they had completely suppressed the uprising and could proceed to organize Attalus' legacy into the Roman province of Asia.

These and other bits of information suggest that, although in the last half-century Pergamum had become more and more an only nominally independent Roman protectorate (cf. § 125), Attalus' bequest was motivated only partly by reasons of political expediency. In addition, a troubled socioeconomic situation made him anxious to entrust his kingdom to the western colossus, which had so long clearly demonstrated its intention and ability to maintain law and order in the Hellenistic world in the interest of the propertied classes.

Other similar bequests followed that of Attalus. In this way Rome in 96 B.C. acquired Cyrene from Ptolemy Apion, who, like Attalus, apparently liberated his cities and left Rome his lands; the country was locally administered under the senate's supervision until 75 B.C., when it was made a Roman province. The bequest of Egypt by Ptolemy XI Alexander II in 80 B.C. went unfulfilled, but six years later Bithynia became a Roman province on the death of Nicomedes III. The senate's procedure when annexing such royal domains seems to have been to issue a decree confirming the monarch's acts up to the day of his death, and to dispatch a ten-man commission or other administrators to set up the new provincial machinery on the spot.

OGIS, no. 338 (= *IGRR*, vol. IV, no. 289)

In the priesthood of Menestratus son of Apollodorus, on the 19th day of the month Eumeneus. On motion of the *strategoi*, the assembly decreed:

Whereas King Attalus Philometor Euergetes has departed from among men and left our city — including the surrounding countryside which he

---

20. Aristonicus' claim that the will was fraudulent apparently became a standard item of anti-Roman propaganda; cf. § 91.

allocated to the city—free, and whereas this will must still be ratified by the Romans, therefore it is necessary in the interest of the common safety that the categories of persons listed below be granted citizenship in view of the complete good will they have manifested the city.

[The rest of the text, mainly a list of classes of people affected by the decree, is summarized in the preceding introduction.]

OGIS, no. 435 (=*IGRR*, vol. IV, no. 301 = *RDGE*, no. 11)

Decree of the Senate

Gaius Popillius son of Gaius, praetor, consulted the senate on the. . . . Whereas discussion was held concerning the affairs in Pergamum and the instructions to be given to the praetors setting out for Asia so that all the amendments, gifts, exemptions, and penalties that had been decreed by the kings down to the death of Attalus should remain valid, concerning this matter the senate decreed as follows:

In the matter on which the praetor Gaius Popillius son of Gaius spoke, concerning this matter it was decreed as follows—that whatever amendments, penalties, exemptions, or gifts were decreed by King Attalus and the other kings, that all those which were in effect on the day before Attalus died are to be valid; and that the praetors setting out for Asia are not to upset the will but are to allow all its terms to remain valid, as the senate decreed.[21]

Orosius, *History against the Pagans* v. x. 1–5; From I. W. Raymond's translation
(New York, 1936)

In the 622d year of the city [131 B.C.], Publius Licinius Crassus, consul and *pontifex maximus,* was dispatched with a well-equipped army against Aristonicus, the brother of Attalus. Aristonicus had invaded the province of Asia, which had been left as a legacy to the Romans. The consul was also supported by powerful kings, Nicomedes of Bithynia, Mithridates of Pontus and Armenia, Ariarathes of Cappadocia, and Pylaemenes of Paphlagonia, all of whom contributed great forces. Neverthe-

---

21. This became the standard procedure and formula of the Senate in such cases. In return for his services in the war against Aristonicus the Romans made Mithridates V of Pontus a gift of Phrygia Major. After he died (120 B.C.) the Senate repossessed the territory and added it to the province of Asia; the pertinent decree of the Senate (*OGIS*, no. 436 = *IGRR*, vol. IV, no. 752) reads: "The Senate decreed that whatever laws King Mithridates decreed, whatever gifts or exemptions he granted to anyone, that these should remain valid just as he granted them to his last day, and that the ten envoys crossing over to Asia should make whatever other decisions might be necessary."

less, he was defeated in a pitched battle and his army was compelled to flee after suffering heavy losses. When Crassus himself was surrounded by the enemy and was about to be captured, he thrust the whip which he had used for his horse into the eye of a Thracian. The barbarian, smarting from the pain and burning with rage, stabbed him through the side with a sword. Thus Crassus escaped both dishonor and slavery by meeting death in the way he had chosen to die. Upon hearing of the death of Crassus and the slaughter of the Roman army, the consul Perperna, who had succeeded Crassus, speedily marched over into Asia and surprised Aristonicus, who was resting after his recent victory. Perperna annihilated his army and forced him to flee. Next he besieged the city of Stratonicea, to which Aristonicus had fled for refuge, reduced him to starvation, and compelled him to surrender. The consul was taken ill at Pergamum and died. Aristonicus, by order of the senate, was strangled in a prison at Rome.

129. Decree of Elaea or Pergamum, 129 B.C.

This decree celebrates the fact that the city was granted the status of a Roman ally as a reward for its help to the Romans in their war against Aristonicus (cf. § 128).

Dittenberger, no. 694 (= *IGRR*, vol. IV, no. 1692)

It was decreed by the council and the people. . . . son of Nicanor . . . son of Dionysius . . . son of Archias . . . son of Menander and Polystratus son of Menon, *strategi,* spoke to the motion.

Whereas our people, preserving from the beginning its good will and friendship towards the Roman people, has given many other evidences of its policy in the most pressing circumstances, and likewise also in the war against Aristonicus made most zealous contribution and underwent great dangers both by land and by sea, wherefore the Roman people, observing the policy of our people and acknowledging our good will, has received our people into friendship and alliance; and since a bronze tablet has been dedicated in the temple of Jupiter Capitolinus reciting both the decree passed by the senate concerning the alliance and also the treaty, and it is fitting that among us too these be inscribed on two bronze tablets and placed in the temple of Demeter and in the council chamber beside the statue of Democracy;

The council and the people have decreed that the auditors of public accounts shall through the proper agency let out the contract for the preparation of the tablets and the inscription on them, and likewise also of the two marble stelae into which the bronze tablets, when they have been completed, shall be fitted; that there shall be recorded on the stelae a copy of this decree in full; that, when the setting up of them has been completed, the crown-wearer, [22] the priests and priestesses, and the chief magistrates shall open the temples of the gods and offer incense and pray in the name of the citizens that the friendship and alliance with the Romans may endure for us forever, to the good fortune and safety both of our people and of the Roman people and of the guild "The Theatrical Artists of Dionysus Our Leader;" that the most elegant possible sacrifice shall be offered to Demeter and Kore, tutelary goddesses of our city, and likewise to the goddess Roma [23] and to all the gods and goddesses; that the day shall be a holy day, and the children released from their studies and the slaves from their labors; that after the sacrifice a parade shall be performed by the boys and young men, under the supervision of the superintendents of education and athletic training; and that the expenses incurred for the preparation of the tablets and the rest shall be met by the treasurers Eucles and Dionysius from the revenues which they administer.

130. A ROMAN SENATOR VISITS EGYPT, 112 B.C.

Ptolemaic Egypt remained nominally an independent kingdom until it was annexed by Octavian in 30 B.C. More than a century before that, however, it had become in effect a Roman protectorate (cf. §§ 75, 126, 131), and Roman and Italian businessmen enjoyed the protective solicitude of the royal house (see § 169). This document not only reflects the senate's growing interest in that strategically situated country, but also affords an insight into the kind of reception expected and received by representatives of all-powerful Rome when they traveled abroad on official or even private business. With this document may be compared the swing around the eastern Mediterranean made in 141 B.C. by the Younger Scipio, Mum-

22. The title of an official in many Greek cities.
23. The cult of the goddess Roma, developed under Hellenistic influence in the Greek East, is known as early as 195 B.C., the city of Smyrna being the first to establish a temple in her honor. Also of Greek origin was a widespread festival in honor of the Roman people, the *Romaea,* frequently mentioned in inscriptions (e.g., § 137); the oldest known is that established by Alabanda in 170 B.C.

mius, and Metellus; an incident of their visit to Egypt is related in Plutarch, *Moralia* 200E–F and 777A, and in Athenaeus, *Savants at Dinner* XII. 549D.

Tebtunis Papyrus No. 33 (= *Select Papyri*, vol. II, no. 416); Adapted from *LCL*

Hermias to Horus, greeting. Below is a copy of the letter to Asclepiades. Take care that its instructions are followed. Goodbye. Year 5, Xandicus 17, Mecheir 17.[24]

To Asclepiades.[25] Lucius Memmius, a Roman senator, who occupies a position of great dignity and honor, is sailing up from Alexandria to the Arsinoite Nome to see the sights.[26] Let him be received with special magnificence: see to it that the guestchambers are prepared at the proper spots and the riverbank landing places to them completed, that the gifts mentioned below[27] are presented to him at the landing place, and that the furniture of the guestchamber, the tidbits for Petesuchus[28] and the crocodiles, the conveniences for viewing the Labyrinth,[29] and the requisite sacrificial offerings and supplies are provided; and in general take the greatest pains in everything to see that the visitor is satisfied, and display the utmost zeal. . . . [The rest is mutilated or lost.]

131. SUPPRESSION OF PIRACY

Piracy, always endemic in the Mediterranean, developed into a phenomenon of overwhelming proportions in the last century of the Republic as a result of the foreign policy of the Roman senate in the second century B.C. Rome destroyed the sea power of Rhodes (see § 78), which had successfully policed the eastern Mediterranean for a century, and then maintained no standing navy of her own to take over the patrolling of the seas, thus

24. The date, which is given by the Macedonian calendar followed by the Egyptian month, is equivalent to March 5, 112 B.C.

25. Asclepiades was obviously a regional official of the royal administration (perhaps the superintendent of revenues?). The letter to him was sent from Alexandria, clearly by someone in high office, and copies, preceded by brief covering letters (as here), were in turn dispatched from his office to the communities affected.

26. The Arsinoite nome corresponds to the present-day Fayum, which lies west and south of Cairo and contains such famous sights as the pyramids and the Sphinx.

27. The list is hopelessly mutilated, but we know from other examples of visiting dignitaries that the gifts would consist largely, if not exclusively, of foodstuffs.

28. The crocodile god of the Arsinoite nome.

29. The temple beside the pyramid of the Pharaoh Amenemhet III at Hawara.

opening the floodgates to organized piracy. This early Roman indifference toward the pirates is to be explained in part also by the economic function they served, for their kidnappings supplied large numbers of slaves, which the Roman ruling classes bought up for use on their latifundia and in their town houses.

From their headquarters in Cilicia, on the southern coast of Asia Minor, the pirates swarmed all over the Mediterranean in great fleets, dominating the sea. No direct military action was taken against them by the Romans until 102 B.C., under Marcus Antonius; this campaign was supplemented c. 100 B.C. by an order closing all the ports of the empire and of allied states to pirate vessels. The pirate war may be said to have lasted intermittently from 102 to 67 B.C. and involved such leading generals as Sulla, Lucullus, and Pompey. [30] By 69 B.C. the seas were almost closed to trade and travel, and the pirates were able to strike at any point of the Italian coast, even at Ostia, the harbor of Rome. Decisive action was finally taken under the threat of famine and financial disaster: in 67 B.C. the Gabinian Law was passed, granting to Pompey the most extraordinary powers ever granted to any Roman—almost unlimited powers over the entire Mediterranean for dealing with the pirate menace. In a brilliant campaign Pompey swept the pirates out of the sea within three months. Though there were sporadic outbreaks of piracy thereafter, freebooting ceased to be a menace in the Roman Empire.

MEASURES TAKEN AGAINST PIRACY, 101 OR 100 B.C.

Three limestone blocks excavated on the island of Cnidus in 1970 were found to contain extensive portions of the Greek version of a Roman law akin to, or perhaps identical with, the so-called piracy law found 100 years earlier at Delphi. Actually, the law was more extensive, dealing also with various other aspects of Roman administration in the eastern Mediterranean. The new fragments are given first, followed by the Delphi text.

Journal of Roman Studies (1974), 64:201–209

. . . to act in good faith so that the citizens of Rome and the allies of the Latin name and likewise those of the nations which are in the friendship of the Roman people may be able to sail the seas in safety and obtain justice. . . .

As for the peoples and nations which, at the time when this law is

30. Julius Caesar's brush with pirates in his youth (c. 80 B.C.) was of a private character. Captured by pirates in the eastern Mediterranean, he, after being ransomed, returned to their hideout, took some of them captive, and crucified them.

ratified by the Roman people, contribute taxes or revenues to a king or kings or peoples who have friendship and alliance with the Roman people, nothing in this law relates to them. . . .[31]

The ranking consul shall send letters to the peoples and states as he thinks fit, announcing that the Roman people has acted to assure that the citizens of Rome and the Latin allies and those of the nations outside [Italy] who are in the friendship of the Roman people may be able to sail the seas in safety, and for this reason Cilicia has by this law been made a praetorian province.[32] And likewise he shall write to the king holding sway in Cyprus and to the king ruling in Alexandria and Egypt and to the king ruling in Cyrene and to the king ruling[33] in Syria who all have friendship and alliance with the Roman people, and he shall make clear also that it is just that they see to it that no pirate sets out from their kingdom, land, or territories and that no officials or commanders appointed by them harbors the pirates under their protection, and that they see to it as far as is in their power that the Roman people have in them zealous collaborators for the safety of all. . . . Whatever the senate decrees concerning this matter every magistrate and promagistrate shall take thought and see to it that such decree is implemented as seems best to him.

[The remaining clauses related to the authority of Roman officials in Macedonia and Asia.]

SEG, vol. III, no. 378 (=*FIRA*, vol. I, no. 9)

Only parts of this long law are given here.

. . . The ranking consul shall dispatch to all peoples who have friendship and alliance with the Roman people letters in which he shall order them to see to it that Roman citizens and Latin allies from Italy can conduct without peril whatever business they require in the eastern cities and islands, and are able to sail the sea securely; and he shall remind them that it was for these very reasons that the proconsul Marcus Antonius occupied Cilicia. Likewise he shall write to the king ruling in the island of Cyprus, and to the king ruling in Alexandria and Egypt, and to the king ruling in Cyrene, and to the kings ruling in Syria, all of whom

---

31. That is, this law does not interfere in their internal affairs.

32. The praetor, a holder of *imperium,* could command a Roman army, and ex-praetors could have their *imperium* extended as governors of provinces.

33. From this word to the end of the paragraph the text is supplied from the Delphi inscription.

have friendship and alliance with the Roman people, and declare to them that it is just that they see to it that no pirate shall use their kingdom, land, or territories as a base of operations and that no officials or garrison commanders appointed by them shall harbor the pirates, and see to it, as far as is in their power, that the Roman people shall have in them zealous collaborators for the safety of all. The letters addressed to the kings in accordance with this law he shall deliver [for transmittal] to the envoys from Rhodes, who are about to return to their homeland.

The consul who is charged with these matters shall see to their security in conformity with law and justice; and if also subsequently embassies are appointed by one of the allies and it is necessary, he shall present[?] them before the senate in whatever manner they prefer, and the senate shall decree as it deems best in keeping with the interests of the state and with its own good faith; and whatever the senate decrees concerning this matter, every magistrate or promagistrate shall bend his efforts and see to it that it is put into effect just as decreed. . . .

The praetor, consul, or proconsul who goes to the province of Asia in the consulship of Gaius Marius and Lucius Valerius [100 B.C.] . . . shall dispatch letters to the peoples who are our friends and allies, to the above-mentioned kings, and likewise to those to whom the consul also, in accordance with this law, shall desire him to write, according as he deems advisable; and he shall dispatch a copy of this law to the cities and states to which he is to write in accordance with this law, seeing to it and taking care, as far as lies in his power, that whatever letters he dispatches anywhere in accordance with this are delivered in accordance with this law; and, in conformity with the customs of each of those to whom a letter is sent in accordance with this law, the letter shall be engraved on a bronze tablet or, failing that, on a marble stele or even on a whitewashed bulletin board,[34] so that it may be plainly exposed to public view in the cities, in a sanctuary or market place, where those who wish may stand and read it at eye level. . . .

The praetor, consul, or proconsul who has either Asia or Macedonia as his province shall, within the ten days next following his learning that this law has been ratified by the people in the assembly, take an oath to do everything he is charged with in this law, and shall not do anything contrary to its provisions with malice aforethought.

The magistrates now in office, excepting the tribunes and prefects, within the five days next following the ratification of this law by the

---

34. The equivalent of the Roman *album*, a whitened wall or board for public notices.

people, and all who shall subsequently hold a magistracy, excepting [tribunes and] prefects, within the five days next following their induction into office, shall, those of them who are in Rome, take an oath by Jupiter and the ancestral gods to do all the things which have been recorded in this law and see to it that they are put into effect, and not to act contrary to this law, and not to act so as to make it possible for anyone else to do so, and not to act otherwise than prescribed in this law. . . .

[The remainder of the inscription deals with fines and prosecution for those who violate the provisions of the law.]

THE PIRATES DOMINATE THE MEDITERRANEAN

Plutarch, *Life of Pompey* xxiv. 1–6

The power of the pirates first started in Cilicia from precarious and unnoticed beginnings, but gained arrogance and boldness in the Mithridatic War, when they manned the king's crews. Then, while the Romans were clashing in civil war with one another about the gates of Rome, the seas lay unguarded and they were little by little enticed and led on no longer merely to fall upon those plying the seas, but even to ravage islands and seacoast towns. And now even men of great wealth, of noble birth, of outstanding reputation for good sense, embarked on and shared in these freebooting adventures as if this occupation brought honor and distinction. The pirates had anchorages and fortified beacon-towers in many places, and the fleets encountered there were fitted for their special task with excellent crews, skilled pilots, and swift, light vessels. But the envy they aroused and their ostentation were even more irksome than the dread they caused. Their ships had gilded flagmasts at the stern, purple hangings, and silvered oars, as if they reveled and gloried in their evildoing. There was music and dancing and carousal along every shore, generals were kidnaped, and cities were captured and freed on payment of ransom, to the disgrace of the Roman Empire. The pirate ships numbered over 1,000, and the cities taken by them, 400. They attacked and pillaged sanctuaries previously inviolate and unentered. . . .

Thus, in a very short time, they increased in number to tens of thousands. They dominated now not only the eastern waters, but the whole Mediterranean to the Pillars of Hercules. They now even vanquished some of the Roman generals in naval engagements, and among others the praetor of Sicily on the Sicilian coast itself. No sea could be navigated in safety, and land remained untilled for want of commercial intercourse. The city of Rome felt this evil most keenly, her subjects being distressed and herself suffering grievously from hunger by reason of her populousness. But it appeared to her to be a great and difficult task to destroy such large forces of seafaring men scattered everywhither on land and sea, with no heavy tackle to encumber their flight, sallying out from no particular country or visible places, having no property or anything to call their own, but only what they might chance to light upon. Thus the unexampled nature of this war, which was subject to no laws and had nothing tangible or visible about it, caused perplexity and fear. Murena had attacked them [in 84–83 B.C.] but accomplished nothing much, nor had Servilius Isauricus, who succeeded him [77–75 B.C.]. And now the pirates contemptuously assailed the very coasts of Italy, around Brundisium and Etruria, and seized and carried off some women of noble families who were traveling, and also two praetors with their very insignia of office.

Who sailed the seas without exposing himself to the risk either of death or of slavery, sailing as he did either in winter or when the sea was infested with pirates? Who ever supposed that a war of such dimensions, so inglorious and so long-standing, so widespread and so extensive, could be brought to an end either by any number of generals in a single year or by a single general in any number of years? What province did you keep free from the pirates during those years? What source of revenue was secure for you? What ally did you protect? To whom did your navy prove a defense? How many islands do you suppose were deserted, how many of your allies' cities either abandoned through fear or captured by the pirates?

But why do I remind you of events in distant places? Time was, long since, when it was Rome's particular boast that the wars she fought were far from home and that the outposts of her empire were defending the prosperity of her allies, not the homes of her own citizens. Need I mention that the sea during those years was closed to our allies, when your own armies never made the crossing from Brundisium save in the depth of winter? Need I lament the capture of envoys on their way to Rome from foreign countries, when ransom has been paid for the ambassadors of Rome? Need I mention that the sea was unsafe for merchantmen, when twelve lictors fell into the hands of pirates? Need I record the capture of the noble cities of Cnidus and Colophon and Samos and countless others, when you well know that your own harbors—and those, too, through which you draw the very breath of your life—have been in the hands of the pirates? Are you indeed unaware that the famous port of Caieta,[35] when crowded with shipping, was plundered by the pirates under the eyes of a praetor, and that from Misenum the children of the very man [Marcus Antonius; cf. introduction to this section] who had previously waged war against the pirates were kidnaped by the pirates? Why should I lament the reverse at Ostia, that shameful blot upon our commonwealth, when almost before your own eyes the very fleet which had been entrusted to the command of a Roman consul was captured and destroyed by the pirates?

POMPEY CRUSHES THE PIRATES

Appian, *Roman History* XII. xiv. 94–96; From *LCL*

When the Romans could no longer endure the damage and disgrace they made Gnaeus Pompey, who was then their man of greatest reputation, commander by law for three years, with absolute power over the whole sea within the Pillars of Hercules, and of the land for a distance of 400 stadia from the coast. They sent letters to all kings, rulers, peoples, and cities, instructing them to aid Pompey in everything, and they gave him power to raise troops and collect money there. And they furnished a large army from their own muster roll, and all the ships they had, and money to the amount of 6,000 Attic talents—so great and difficult did they consider the task of overcoming such great forces, dispersed over so wide a sea, hiding easily in so many coves, retreating quickly and darting out again unexpectedly. Never did any man before Pompey set forth with such great authority conferred upon him by the Romans.

35. Present-day Gaeta, c. 70 miles southeast of Rome.

Presently he had an army of 120,000 foot and 4,000 horse, and 270 ships including *hemiolii*.[36] He had twenty-five assistants of senatorial rank, whom the Romans call legates, among whom he divided the sea, giving ships, cavalry, and infantry to each, and investing them with the insignia of praetors, in order that each one might have absolute authority over the part entrusted to him, while he, Pompey, like a king of kings, should move to and fro among them to see that they remained where they were stationed so that, while he was pursuing the pirates in one place, he should not be drawn to something else before his work was finished, but that there might be forces to encounter them everywhere and to prevent them from forming junctions with each other. . . .

Thus were the commands of the praetors arranged for the purpose of attacking, defending, and guarding their respective assignments, so that each might catch the pirates put to flight by others, and not be drawn a long distance from their own stations by the pursuit, nor carried round and round as in a race, thus dragging out the task. Pompey himself made a tour of the whole. He first inspected the western stations, accomplishing the task in forty days, and passing through Rome on his return. Thence he went to Brundisium, and proceeding from this place he occupied an equal time in visiting the eastern stations. He astonished all by the rapidity of his movement, the magnitude of his preparations, and his formidable reputation, so that the pirates, who had expected to attack him first, or at least to show that the task he had undertaken against them was no easy one, became straightway alarmed, abandoned their assaults upon the towns they were besieging, and fled to their accustomed peaks and inlets. Thus the sea was cleared by Pompey forthwith without a fight, and the pirates were everywhere subdued by the praetors at their several stations.

Pompey himself hastened to Cilicia with forces of various kinds and many engines, as he expected that there would be need of every kind of fighting and siege against their precipitous peaks; but he needed nothing. His fame and preparations had produced a panic among the pirates, and they hoped that if they did not resist they might receive lenient treatment. First, those who held Cragus and Anticragus, their largest citadels, surrendered themselves, and after them the mountaineers of Cilicia, and finally all, one after another. They gave up at the same time a great quantity of arms, some completed, others in the workshops; also their ships, some still on the stocks, others already afloat; also brass and

36. These were swift vessels, lightly manned.

iron collected for building them, and sailcloth, rope, and timber of all kinds; and finally, a multitude of captives either held for ransom or chained to their tasks. Pompey burned the timber, carried away the ships, and sent the captives back to their respective countries. Many of them found there their own cenotaphs, for they were supposed to be dead. Those pirates who had evidently fallen into this way of life not from wickedness, but from poverty consequent upon the war, Pompey settled in Mallus, Adana, and Epiphania, or any other uninhabited or thinly peopled town in Cilicia Trachea. Some of them, too, he sent to Dymae in Achaea. Thus the war against the pirates, which it was supposed would prove very difficult, was brought to an end by Pompey in a few days. He took 71 ships by capture and 306 by surrender from the pirates, and about 120 of their cities, fortresses, and other places of rendezvous. About 10,000 of the pirates were slain in battle.

132. A Treaty of Alliance

This inscription of 105 B.C. records the treaty of "equal alliance" by which the little island of Astypalaea in the Aegean Sea, off the southwest coast of Asia Minor, became a "free allied state" *(civitas libera et foederata)* of the Roman Republic. There are extant (but less well preserved) several other such treaties from this era of Roman expansion; see for example, Dittenberger, nos. 693 and 732; *OGIS*, no. 762; and *ROL*, 4:292–295 (with English translation). For earlier examples of this type, see p. 88–89.

IG, vol. XII, part 3, no. 173 (= *IGRR*, vol. IV, no. 1028 = *RDGE*, no. 16)

. . . concerning this matter the senate decreed as follows: To renew peace, friendship, and alliance with the people of Astypalaea; to address the envoy as a gentleman of character from an honorable and friendly people, and answer him courteously. Adopted. And that the consul Publius Rutilius see to it that a bronze tablet containing the treaty of alliance is nailed up in the Capitol, as he deems best in keeping with the interests of the state and with his own good faith. Adopted. And that the consul Publius Rutilius order the quaestor to give the envoy gifts according to the schedule;[37] that he be permitted, if he wishes, to offer sacrifice in the Capitol according to the Rubrian-Acilian Law;[38] and that

37. The *formula* which specified the emoluments granted to foreign ambassadors to defray their expenses while in Rome.

38. A *plebiscitum* of 122 B.C. regulating sacrifices made in Rome by foreign envoys.

[in Astypalaea] a copy be set up in a public and easily visible place where most of the citizens pass by, and it be given a public reading each year in the assembly. Adopted.

In the consulship of Publius Rutilius son of Publius, and Gnaeus Mallius son of Gnaeus, the *praetor urbanus* being Lucius . . . onius son of Lucius, the *praetor peregrinus* . . . son of Publius, and, in the dating of Astypalaea, in the magistracy of Philetaerus son of . . . it was decreed that a tablet containing the treaty of alliance negotiated by Rhodocles son of Antimachus be set up, and that a tablet containing this treaty of alliance be given to the people of Astypalaea, according to the decree of the senate.

. . . there shall be peace, friendship, and alliance, both on land and on sea, for all time, between the Roman people and the people of Astypalaea, and there shall be no war.

The people of Astypalaea shall not by public consent permit the enemies and adversaries of the Roman people to pass through its own territory and whatever territory the people of Astypalaea controls, so as to make war upon the Roman people and those subject to the Romans; and it shall not by public resolution and with malice aforethought assist their enemies with either arms, money, or ships. The Roman people shall not by public resolution and with malice aforethought permit the enemies and adversaries of the council and people of Astypalaea to pass through its own territory and whatever territory the Roman people controls, so as to make war upon the people of Astypalaea and those subject to it; and the Roman people shall not with malice aforethought assist the enemies of Astypalaea with arms, money, or ships.

If anyone makes war upon the people of Astypalaea, the Roman people shall assist the people of Astypalaea. And if anyone first makes war upon the Roman people, the people of Astypalaea shall render assistance in accordance with the treaty and oaths existing between the Roman people and the people of Astypalaea.

If the people and senate [of either party] wish by common consent to add to or take away from this treaty, whatever they desire shall be permitted; and whatever they add to or take away from the treaty shall be apart from the terms written in the treaty.

And they shall set up a memorial in the Roman temple of Jupiter on the Capitoline, and in the Astypalaean sanctuary of Athena and Aesculapius, and near the altar . . . of Rome.

REWARDS FOR A LOYAL ALLY

Aphrodisias in Asia Minor enjoyed the status and privileges of a "free allied state." The first of the following inscriptions records a lengthy decree of the Roman senate on the subject; in its present state the inscription comprises a number of fragments, from which it is possible to reconstruct the general sense of the whole document and even its precise details in considerable part. The city's pride in its special status is reflected in its decision to record the second inscription on its archive wall.

J. M. Reynolds, *Aphrodisias and Rome*, no. 8; 39 B.C.

[Date, names of senators present at the writing, the informing considerations], it was decreed by the senate to renew our favor, friendship and alliance with the people of Plarasa-Aphrodisias, and to greet their envoy as a gentleman of character as well as a friend from a fine and noble people, our friend and ally;

. . . and whereas Marcus Antonius and Gaius Caesar, triumvirs for the settlement of the commonwealth, spoke in this body about the outstanding loyalty which the people of Plarasa-Aphrodisias have manifested toward our state, (it was decreed) that it appears to be in the interest of the (Roman) state that the people of Plarasa-Aphrodisias, themselves, their children and descendants, shall be exempt from all taxes and their names removed from all records of revenues of the Roman people, and that they themselves, their wives, children and descendants, shall be enrolled in the number of our allies; and that no magistrate or promagistrate of the Roman people or anyone else shall upon the city or land or territory of Plarasa-Aphrodisias billet a soldier, irregular, cavalryman or anyone else for winter quarters or order such arrangement, or requisition money, soldiers, ships, grain, weapons, rafts or any other thing from the people of Plarasa-Aphrodisias . . . ; and in keeping with the piety of the Roman people the senate decreed . . . its resolution that their temple [of Aphrodite] shall be an asylum also with the same right as the right which the temple of Ephesian Artemis at Ephesus has, and all that the deified Julius [Caesar] ordained regarding such matters shall remain valid . . .; and the senate likewise resolved that with regard to local levies in all matters the people of Plarasa-Aphrodisias shall be exempt from liturgies and taxes . . . and the city of Plarasa-Aphrodisias shall be free and shall enjoy its own laws and courts . . . ; and whatever rewards, honors and privileges Gaius

Caesar or Marcus Antonius, triumvirs for the settlement of the commonwealth, by his own decree has granted or shall grant, has allotted or shall allot, has conceded or shall concede to the people of Plarasa-Aphrodisias, all those are ruled to have been enacted rightly and conformably; and the senate likewise resolved that the people of Plarasa-Aphrodisias, their children and descendants shall have and enjoy freedom and immunity from taxation in all matters with the same right as any state with most advantageous right and law, a state which (by grant) from the Roman senate and the people of Rome has freedom and immunity from taxation and is a friend and ally of the Roman people.

[Further details defining the preceding privileges follow here, poorly preserved.]

And with regard to the proposal of the consuls Gaius Calvisius and Lucius Marcius Censorinus, (it was decreed) . . . and that at games, gladiatorial combats and hunts and at any athletic contests that are held in the city of Rome or within one mile of the city of Rome, the envoys of Plarasa-Aphrodisias shall have the right to sit in the seats of the senators; and that whenever envoys of the people of Plarasa-Aphrodisias arrive in Rome [as a delegation to] the senate, they shall report to the magistrates or promagistrates of the Roman people having the authority to convene the senate, so that they may be given access to the senate, and it was resolved that they be introduced to the senate before their turn, and that they be permitted to speak and report to that body, and that a reply be given to the envoys of Plarasa-Aphrodisias within the next ten days of their appearance and report. . . .

[There follow, only fragmentarily preserved, provisions for the swearing of the oath of alliance by both parties, for the passage of enabling legislation, and for copies of this inscription to be placed on the Capitol in Rome and in the precinct of Aphrodite in Aphrodisias.]

Decreed. In the senate when the decree was passed were [number lost] senators and 340 senators when the oath was taken.

Reynolds, *Aphrodisias and Rome*, no. 13; 31–27 B.C.

The Emperor Caesar Augustus, son of the deified Julius [Caesar], subscribed the petition of Samos: You can see for yourselves that I have given the privilege of freedom to no people except that of Aphrodisias, which took my side in the war [against Antony] and suffered capture because of their devotion to me. For it is not right for the greatest privilege of all to be granted at random and without cause. I view you with favor, and with my wife zealous on your behalf I should like to indulge her, but not to the extent of violating my customary practice. It is not the money that you pay for tribute which concerns me, but I wish the most prized privileges to be given to no one without suitable cause.

AN OATH OF ALLIANCE

This inscription on a marble altar ratifies a treaty of alliance between Rome and three cities in Caria (southern Asia Minor).

Reynolds, *Aphrodisias and Rome*, no. 1; c. 100 B.C.

To Zeus god of friendship, to Concord, and to the goddess Rome, the people of Plarasa-Aphrodisias, of Cibyra, and of Tabae [have dedicated this altar] with oaths taken over freshly burnt offerings and with sacrifices, on behalf of their natural alliance and eternal concord and brotherhood with one another; and to take no action hostile to Rome or to themselves, and not to draft, propose, introduce or record anything contrary to the terms of the sworn treaty; and anyone taking any action contrary to this shall be utterly destroyed, himself and his family, and liable to [punishment by] death, and indictable by anyone who wishes; and in accordance with their joint covenants they shall cooperate with one another for mutual benefits to the fullest extent possible without evasion, and they shall observe what has been jointly agreed.

133. ARBITRATION OF DISPUTES

The Romans inherited from the diplomacy of the Hellenistic world the principles and procedures of international arbitration developed over centuries by the Greeks. Under Roman hegemony Greek cities frequently referred disputes to the senate for authoritative settlement, and the quasi-independent allied states were required to do so. Such appeals were handled in one of three ways. Sometimes the senate itself adjudicated the case after hearing argument from envoys of both disputants (see the first selection); more often it sent a commission of inquiry with power to make awards, subject to ratification by the senate (second selection); or thirdly, the investigation might be assigned to a neutral entity with power to find a verdict in a field of inquiry precisely delimited by the senate or the

Roman provincial governor (third and fourth selections). The second selection, the arbitration of a boundary dispute between the state of Genoa and a tribe subject to her, affords still another of the many instances of Roman intervention in the internal affairs of supposedly sovereign allied states (cf. §§ 120, 124, 176).

DECREE OF THE SENATE CONCERNING NARTHACIUM AND MELITAEA, 150–147 B.C.

IG, vol. IX, part 2, no. 89 (= Dittenberger, no. 674 = *RDGE,* no. 9)

Leon of Larissa, son of Hagesippus, being *strategus* of the Thessalian League, and Crito son of Amenias, Polycles son of Phidippus, and Glaucetas son of Agelaus being the chief magistrates in Narthacium, there was recorded the decree passed by the senate when Thessalus of Pherae, son of Thrasymedes, was *strategus* of the Thessalian League.

Gaius Hostilius Mancinus son of Aulus, praetor, consulted the senate on the . . . of Quintilis[39] in the Comitium. Present at the writing [of this decree] were Quintus Statilienus son of Quintus, of the Cornelian tribe, Gnaeus Lutatius son of Gnaeus, of the A. . .an tribe, and Aulus Sempronius son of Aulus, of the Falernian tribe.

Whereas the envoys of Melitaea in Thessaly, Harmoxenus son of Lysander and Lampromachus son of Politas, gentlemen of character and friends from an honorable people, our friend and ally, gave renewed assurances of their good will, friendship, and alliance and spoke concerning the public land and the deserted region—land which they possessed when they entered into the friendship of the Roman people, and which the Narthacians afterwards unjustly seized as their own—requesting concerning this matter that attention be directed to it, so that they might have this matter restored to its former status as it had been previously adjudicated in their favor by Medeus and . . . of the Thessalians and by Pyllus and his Macedonian associates, and that these decisions might remain valid for them;

Concerning this matter . . .us and the Narthacians . . . decide the present issue in Melitaea . . . in this land. . . .

And whereas the envoys of Narthacium in Thessaly, Nicatas son of . . ., gentlemen of character and friends from an honorable people, our friend and ally, spoke in their presence in the senate, gave renewed assurances of their good will, friendship, and alliance, and discoursed

39. July; the missing day was between the 2d and the 6th.

concerning the matters affecting themselves—the land and sanctuaries, i.e., the land taken away from Melitaean rule by the Narthacians in Achaea [i.e., Achaea Phthiotis, then part of Thessaly]—stating that the Narthacians possessed this land when they entered into the friendship of the Roman people and that they had won judgments concerning the land and the sanctuaries in accordance with the laws of the Thessalian League (laws which the consul Titus Quinctius granted following the advice of the ten commissioners[40] and which are still in force to this day) and in accordance with a decree of the senate, [ratifying Flamininus' acts], and that concerning these matters they had two years before won a decision before three boards of arbitrators, from Samos, Colophon, and Magnesia, and that this decision had been made in accordance with the laws, so that it should be valid, just as it has been in other cases;

Concerning this matter it was decreed as follows: to give renewed assurances of good will, friendship, and alliance, to give a courteous answer to these, and to address them as gentlemen of character; and whatever decisions have been rendered in accordance with laws which the consul Titus Quinctius granted, these, it is deemed, should be valid just as rendered; it is not a light matter to invalidate decisions which have been made in accordance with laws. And the praetor Gaius Hostilius is to order the quaestor to give gifts worth 125 sesterces to each of the two embassies, as he deems best in keeping with the interests of the state and with his own good faith. Adopted.

ARBITRATION OF A DISPUTE BETWEEN GENOA AND THE VETURIANS, 117 B.C.

CIL, vol. I, 2d ed., no. 584 (=*CIL,* vol. V, no. 7749 = *ROL,* 4:262–271); Adapted from *LCL*

Quintus and Marcus Minucius Rufus, sons of Quintus, inquired on the spot into the quarrels between the Genoese and the Veturians and in their hearing settled the quarrels between them and informed them on what conditions they were to hold their land and boundaries were to be fixed. They ordered them to fix the boundaries and to have boundary markers set up; they ordered them to come to them in Rome when these commands had been carried out. At Rome in accordance with a decree of the senate the Minucii reported in person on the 13th of December in

---

40. That is, Flamininus and the ten commissioners assigned to him by the Senate to assist in the settlement of Greek and Macedonian affairs; see § 68.

the consulship of Lucius Caecilius son of Quintus and Quintus Mucius son of Quintus:

"Wherever there is private land belonging to the fortress of the Veturians, land which they may sell and which can pass to an heir, the said land shall not be put under rent charges [i.e., *vectigal;* see Glossary].

"The boundaries of the private land of the Langensians are: [The lengthy boundary specifications of this private land and of the state land held by the Veturians are here omitted.]

"Whatever land we judge to be public state land, that land we think the fort-holders, namely the Langensian Veturians, ought to hold and enjoy. For the said land the Langensian Veturians shall pay into the public treasury of Genoa every year a rent of 400 victoriates.[41] If the Langensians fail to pay the said money and do not give satisfaction according to the will and pleasure of the Genoese (on condition that it is not through the fault of the Genoese that any delay hinders them from receiving the money), in that case the Langensians shall be required to pay into the public treasury of Genoa every year a twentieth part of the grain and a sixth part of the wine which shall have been produced on the said land.

"Any Genoese or Veturian who has come into possession of land within the said boundaries, if he held possession on the 1st of August in the consulship of Lucius Caecilius and Quintus Mucius, may thus remain in possession and till the land. Those who shall possess a holding must pay to the Langensians a rent in the same proportion as the remaining Langensians, such of them as shall possess and enjoy any area within the said land.[42] Furthermore, within the said land no one shall possess a holding except by a majority vote of the Langensian Veturians and on condition that he admit no other onto his holding for the purpose of tilling except a Genoese or a Veturian. If any of the said persons shall, in the majority opinion of the Langensian Veturians, not obey this condition, he shall not keep the land or enjoy it.

"No man shall hinder the Genoese and the Veturians from pasturing cattle on such of the land as is joint pasture land [see chapter 5, note 44] in the way in which it is allowed on the remaining joint pasture land of Genoa, and no man shall use force or hinder them from taking from the said land firewood and building-timber and using the same.

41. A Roman coin, so called from the goddess of Victory depicted on the reverse. It was widely used in Italy. Originally ¾ of a denarius, it was later normally equated with it.

42. The meaning seems to be that holders of long standing must pay their share no less than new holders.

"The Langensian Veturians are required to pay into the public treasury of Genoa a first year's rent on the January 1 after the next. For such land as the Langensians have and shall have enjoyed before the 1st of January next they are not required to pay against their will.

"The meadows which, at the last hay-mowing, in the consulship of Lucius Caecilius and Quintus Mucius, were within the limits of the public state land in the possession of the Langensian Veturians, the Odiates, the Dectunines, the Cavaturines, and the Mentovines—the said meadows no one shall mow or use as pasture against the will of the Langensians and the Odiates and the Dectunines and the Cavaturines and the Mentovines on land which any of the said people shall severally possess. If on the said land the Langensians or the Odiates or the Dectunines or the Cavaturines or the Mentovines prefer to let grow, fence off, and mow other meadows, they shall be allowed to do so provided that they hold no larger measure of meadowland than they held and enjoyed last summer.

"As to the Veturians who have been condemned or found guilty on account of contumelious wrongs in quarrels with the Genoese, if anyone is in prison because of such matters, we think that all such should be released, discharged, and set free before the 13th of August next. If any shall think there is unfairness in this matter, they must come to us on the first possible day and be quit of all quarrels in the public interest[?]."

Commissioners:[43] Mocus Meticanius son of Meticonus, Plaucus Pelianius son of Pelionus.

ARBITRATION OF A DISPUTE BETWEEN MAGNESIA AND PRIENE, 143 B.C.

Dittenberger, no. 679 (=*FIRA*, vol. III, no. 162 = *RDGE*, no. 7)

. . . the decree brought from the Roman senate. . . . Marcus Aemulius son of Marcus, praetor, to the council and people of Mylasa, greeting. Envoys of Magnesia and Priene requested that I should grant them an audience before the senate. I did grant them an audience on the . . . of . . . in the Comitium. Present at the writing [of this decree] were . . . Fonteius son of Quintus, of the Papirian tribe, Titus Maelius Fa. . . .

Whereas the envoys of Magnesia, Pythodorus, Heraclitus . . . gentlemen of character from an honorable people, our friend and ally, spoke in person, and whereas the envoys of Priene, . . .nes, gentlemen of

---

43. Of Genoa; their names are Ligurian.

character from an honorable people, our friend and ally, spoke in person concerning the territory from which the people of Magnesia withdrew, surrendering possession of this territory to the people of Priene, and requested that a tribunal of arbitration be assigned according to a decree of the senate; concerning this matter it was decreed as follows: that Marcus Aemulius son of Marcus, praetor, shall assign as arbitrator some free community agreed upon by both parties; and if they cannot agree between them, that Marcus Aemulius son of Marcus, praetor, shall assign a free community as arbitrator for this dispute as he deems best in keeping with the interests of the state and with his own good faith. Adopted. The arbitrator for Magnesia and Priene concerning this territory, separate from that of Priene, from which territory the Magnesians assert that they have withdrawn, shall award this territory to whichever of these peoples it finds possessed this territory when they entered into the friendship of the Roman people, and shall order boundary stones set up. Adopted.

Likewise, whereas the same envoys of Priene spoke in the presence of the envoys of Magnesia concerning the injuries which the Magnesians had done them, concerning this matter it was decreed as follows: That Marcus Aemulius son of Marcus, praetor, shall order the same community that is assigned as arbitrator concerning the territory to adjudicate concerning these injuries; if they have been committed by the Magnesians, it shall estimate what seems a fair and just penalty. And that Marcus Aemulius son of Marcus, praetor, shall send a letter to the same arbitrator community concerning these matters, indicating by what day the two parties shall appear for each of the two judgments, and on what day they shall render decision. . . . [The rest is lost.]

AN ARBITRATION IN SPAIN

A dispute between two Spanish communities was arbitrated by a third, and the approval of the Roman governor was obtained to render the decision valid. The text is written in the archaic Latin spelling that remained in vogue to the end of the Republic. The Iberian personal names at the end, so different from the Roman, are noteworthy.

AE, 1979, no. 377; May 15, 87 B.C.

Those of the senate of Contrebia who were [assigned] shall be the judges of whether it appears that a field which the Sallviensians bought from the Sosinestans for the purpose of creating a channel and bringing in water—the matter at issue—whether the Sosinestans were within their rights when they sold it to the Sallviensians against the will of the Allovonensians, and then, if it so appears, those judges shall render the decision that the Sosinestans were within their rights when they sold that field—the matter at issue—to the Sallviensians, and if it does not so appear, they shall render the decision that they were not within their rights when they sold. The same who are written above shall be the judges of whether the Sosinestan community then extended to where the Sallviensians recently publicly staked out—the matter at issue— whether within those markers the Sallviensians had the legal right to create a channel through public land of the Sosinestans, or whether the Sallviensians had the legal right to create a channel through private land of the Sosinestans, where it would be permissible for the channel to be created provided that the Sallviensians paid the amount of money at which that field is valued through which the channel was run, and if it so appears, those judges shall render the decision that they did have the legal right to do it; if they decide that the Sallviensians had the right to create the channel then the Sallviensians shall pay publicly for the private land through which the channel is run an amount of money according to the assessment of those five magistrates whom Contrebia assigned from its senate.

Judgment approved by Gaius Valerius Flaccus son of Gaius, commander-in-chief.

They pronounced sentence that it is our judgment in the matter at issue that we render our decision in favor of the Sallviensians.

When this matter was judged the magistrates of Contrebia were the following: Lubbus Urdinocum son of Letondo, praetor [of Contrebia]; Lesso Siriscum son of Lubbus, magistrate; Babpus Bolgondiscum son of Ablo, magistrate; Segilus Annicum son of Lubbus, magistrate; ..atus son of ...ulovicum son of Uxentus, magistrate; Ablo Tindilicum son of Lubbus, magistrate. ...assius son of .eihar, Sallviensian, defended the cause of the Sallviensians, Turibas son of Teitibas, Allavonensian, the cause of the Allavonensians. Done at Contrebia Balaisca on the Ides of May in the consulship of Lucius Cornelius and Gnaeus Octavius.

134. THE PRIVILEGES OF "FREE NONTRIBUTARY" STATES

Of the three categories of communities in the Roman orbit the "free nontributary state" *(civitas libera et immunis)* stood midway between the "free allied state" *(civitas libera et foederata),* which had a formal treaty with Rome (see § 132), and the "tributary state" *(civitas stipendiaria).* How precarious were the freedom and privileges of such quasi sovereign states is reflected, for example, in a statement of Tacitus *(Annals* xii lviii): "Freedom was restored to the Rhodians, a freedom often taken away or confirmed according as they earned it by their services in our foreign wars or lost it through their domestic revolutions [against the pro-Roman ruling oligarchy]"; cf. also § 122, last selection. The inscriptions relating to such states are fairly numerous. The two given here concern two cities of southern Asia Minor, Stratonicea and Termessus Major. The first selection is a decree of the Senate (*c.* 81 B.C.) renewing an earlier grant of autonomy for loyalty and services to the Romans in the Mithridatic War; the second selection is a *plebiscitum* (71 or 70 B.C.) confirming privileges granted twenty years earlier, probably for the same reasons. These reaffirmations of previous grants were no doubt necessitated by infringements of the privileges, perpetrated in the intervening years by Roman officials.

OGIS, no. 441 *(=RDGE,* no. 18)

Lucius Cornelius Sulla Felix son of Lucius, dictator, to the chief magistrates, council, and people of Stratonicea, greeting. We are not ignorant of the fact that you, through your ancestors, have fulfilled all your obligations towards our empire and have on every occasion preserved unbroken your fidelity towards us; and that in the war against Mithridates you were the first of those in Asia to offer resistance, and on that account most zealously took upon yourselves many dangers of all sorts on behalf of our state . . . both public and private, on account of your friendship, benevolence, and good will towards us, and on the occasion of the war sent envoys to the other cities of Asia and to the cities of Greece.

Lucius Cornelius Sulla Felix, dictator, to the chief magistrates, council, and people of Stratonicea, greeting. I have transmitted to your envoys the following decree passed by the senate:

Lucius Cornelius Sulla Felix son of Lucius, dictator, consulted the senate on the 27th of March in the Comitium. Present at the writing [of this decree] were Gaius Fannius son of Gaius . . . Gaius Fundanius son of Gaius. . . .

Whereas the envoys of Stratonicea of the Chrysaoreum,[44] Paeonius son of Hieracles . . . Hecataeus son of Pa ...Dionysius son of He... spoke in accordance and conformity with the decree of the people of Stratonicea, begging to express their joy because the affairs of the Roman people were in better state, and requesting permission to dedicate to the senate a golden crown from their city worth 200 talents, permission to offer sacrifice in the Capitol on behalf of the victory and empire of the Roman people, and, for the rest, that Lucius Cornelius Sulla Felix son of Lucius, dictator, should please to treat the people of Stratonicea generously; and since the city in time of peace preserved its good will, fidelity, and friendship towards the Roman people and was the first of those in Asia that chose to resist when Mithridates was practicing the most ruthless despotism there; and since the king attacked the city, captured it, and held it . . . Lucius Cornelius Sulla son of Lucius, dictator, having ordered . . . and since the city ever preserved its existing good will, fidelity, and alliance toward the Roman people, administering its own affairs in accordance with the policy of the latter, and made war against Mithridates, and revealing its own spirit most zealously opposed the will and might of the king . . .;

And whereas Lucius Cornelius Sulla Felix, dictator, proposed[?] . . . that they employ their own laws and customs which they employed before, and that whatever decrees they made on account of this war which they declared against King Mithridates, that all these remain valid; that they be permitted to retain Pedasus, Themessus, Ceramus, and the territories, villages, harbors, and revenues of the towns which the commander Lucius Cornelius Sulla assigned and granted them in honor of their excellence; that the long-revered sanctuary of Hecate, goddess most manifest and greatest . . . and the sacred precinct be inviolate; concerning what was lost to them in the war, that the senate give orders to the magistrate setting out for Asia to see and attend to it that their actual property be restored to them, that they recover their prisoners of war, and that concerning the rest they receive their due; and that the magistrates grant the earliest possible audience before the senate to any envoys who come to Rome from Stratonicea;

Concerning this matter the senate decreed as follows:

44. This was the general assemblage of Carian cantons, which had its center at the temple of Zeus Chrysaoreus.

It was decreed to give friendly reply in their presence, in the senate, to the envoys of Stratonicea, to give renewed assurances of good will, friendship, and alliance, and to address the envoys as gentlemen of character and our friends and allies from an honorable people, our friend and ally. And whereas these envoys declared and whereas Lucius Cornelius Sulla Felix, dictator, declared that it was well known to the Romans from the letters sent by the governors of Asia and Greece and by the legates who had been in those provinces that the Stratoniceans had always steadfastly preserved their friendship, fidelity, and good will toward the Roman people in time of war and peace, had most zealously protected the public interests of the Roman people with soldiers, grain, and great expenditures . . . had waged joint war with them because of their own high sense of honor, and had most courageously resisted the generals and forces of King Mithridates on behalf of the cities of Asia and Greece; concerning these matters it was decreed as follows: that it is the pleasure of the senate to remember good and just men and to provide that Lucius Cornelius Sulla Felix, dictator, should order the proquaestor to give them gifts according to the schedule [cf. note 37]; and that they should employ those laws and customs of theirs which they employed in the past; and that whatever laws and decrees they passed on account of this war against Mithridates, that all these remain valid for them; and that whatever states, revenues, territories, villages, and harbors the commander Lucius Cornelius Sulla assigned and granted them on the advice of his council in honor of their excellence, that they be permitted to retain these; and that the Roman people . . .; and that Lucius Cornelius Sulla Felix, dictator, if he pleases, investigate the states, villages, territories, and harbors which he as commander assigned to Stratonicea, and arrange how much revenue each shall pay to Stratonicea, and if he so arranges, that he send letters to those states which he assigned to Stratonicea, ordering them to pay a tax of such amount to Stratonicea; and that those who may at any time govern the provinces of Asia and Greece see and attend to it that these things are so carried out; that the sanctuary of Hecate be inviolate; that whatever proconsul may govern the province of Asia investigate the properties they are missing, who carried these off, and who are in possession of them, so that he may see to it that these are returned and restored, that they are able to recover their prisoners of war, and that in the other matters they receive their due, as he deems best in keeping with the interests of the state and with his own good faith. Adopted.

And with regard to the crown sent to the senate by the people [of

Stratonicea], that they be permitted to dedicate it whenever Lucius Cornelius Sulla Felix, dictator, deems it good, and that they be permitted to offer sacrifice in the Capitol if they desire. And to the envoys who may come to Rome from Stratonicea it was decreed that the earliest audience before the senate be granted by the magistrates. Adopted.

CIL, vol. I, 2d ed., no. 589

Concerning the people of Termessus Major in Pisidia.

Gaius Antonius son of Marcus, Gnaeus Cornelius son of . . . and Gaius Fundanius son of Gaius, tribunes of the plebs, in accordance with a decision of the senate, duly proposed to the plebs and the plebs duly approved . . . the . . . tribe voted first, the first to vote in the name of his tribe was. . . .

All persons who were citizens of Termessus Major in Pisidia or who by laws of the said community were made citizens previous to the Kalends of April in the consulship of Lucius Gellius and Gnaeus Lentulus [72 B.C.] and their children, and their posterity, being citizens of Termessus Major in Pisidia, shall be the free allies and friends of the Roman people and shall enjoy their own laws; and it shall hereby be lawful for the said persons, being citizens of Termessus Major in Pisidia, to enjoy their own laws in such manner as shall not be contrary to this law.

All lands, all grounds and buildings, public or private, included within the territory of the people of Termessus Major in Pisidia now or in the consulship of Lucius Marcius and Sextus Julius [91 B.C.], and all blocks of buildings belonging to them under the above-named consuls, and whatever part of such properties the said people under the said consuls held, possessed, used, or enjoyed, such of the said properties as have not been leased out, they shall hold and possess as aforetime; and whatever portion of the said properties, lands, grounds, or buildings have been leased out, notwithstanding the legal prohibition of such leasing out enacted in the consulship of Lucius Gellius and Gnaeus Lentulus, the people of Termessus Major in Pisidia shall nevertheless hold, possess, use, and enjoy all such properties, grounds, lands, and buildings as they held, possessed, used, and enjoyed the same previous to the first Mithridatic War.

The possessions, public or private, of the people of Termessus Major in Pisidia, excepting lands or buildings already leased out, which belong or belonged to the said people previous to the first Mithridatic War, and whatever part of such properties they previously held, possessed, used, or enjoyed, such of the same as they have not themselves of their own free will alienated shall all belong to the people of Termessus Major in Pisidia just as they now do and did; and it shall be lawful for the said people in such manner to hold, possess, use, and enjoy all the same.

Respecting the free men or slaves lost by the people of Termessus Major in Pisidia in the Mithridatic War, the [Roman] magistrate or promagistrate to whom jurisdiction in such matter shall belong, and to whose court application shall be made, shall adjudicate the said matter and shall grant a court and *recuperatores* whereby the said people may recover the same.

No magistrate, promagistrate, legate, or any other person shall introduce soldiers into the town or land of the people of Termessus Major in Pisidia with the object of winter billeting or make it possible for another to introduce soldiers there or for soldiers to winter there, unless the senate shall have expressly declared that soldiers be brought into winter quarters among the people of Termessus Major in Pisidia; and no magistrate, promagistrate, legate, or any other person shall cause or order the said people to render, furnish, or be deprived of anything, save what is or shall be incumbent upon the same to render or furnish in accordance with the Porcian Law.

Between Roman citizens and the people of Termessus Major in Pisidia there shall be the same laws, the same legal rights, and the same customs as existed in the consulship of Lucius Marcius and Sextus Julius; and whatever rights the people of Termessus Major in Pisidia possessed under the above-named consuls in respect to whatever properties, grounds, lands, buildings, and towns—i.e., such of the same, excepting lands or buildings already leased out, as they have not themselves of their own free will alienated—the people of Termessus Major in Pisidia shall possess the same rights in respect to the said properties, grounds, lands, buildings, and towns; and it is nowise intended by this law that the matters specified in this clause shall be otherwise than they now are.

Whatever terms for the collection of customs dues, inland or maritime, within their own territories the people of Termessus Major in Pisidia may have laid down, the same terms for the collection of such dues shall remain in force, provided that no customs duty be collected from those persons who shall farm the public revenues of the Roman people; whatever produce[?] from such revenue the tax farmers shall transport through their territory. . . .[45] [The rest is lost.]

45. The sense of this incomplete sentence was no doubt that such shipments by publicans were to be free from customs duties.

135. A GRANT OF PRIVILEGES TO ACTORS

In the winter of 85–84 B.C. Sulla billeted his troops in the towns of Asia which had supported Mithridates against Rome and imposed an indemnity of 20,000 talents (cf. § 83). When these directives were put into force the actors' guild of the region apparently appealed to Sulla, who confirmed their preexisting exemption from such obligations. In 81 B.C., when Sulla was dictator, he granted a representative of the guild permission to erect a marble stele commemorating and recording these benefactions.

RDGE, no. 49

May Good Fortune Attend!

Lucius Cornelius Sulla Felix son of Lucius, dictator, to the chief magistrates, council, and people of Cos, greeting. I have granted the citharist Alexander of Laodicea, a gentleman of character and our friend, envoy of the Joint Society of "The Theatrical Artists of Ionia and the Hellespont" and "The Theatrical Artists of Dionysus Our Leader,"[46] permission to erect, in the most conspicuous place in your community, a stele on which will be inscribed the privileges granted by me to the artists; and the senate having, in response to his embassy to Rome, passed a decree of approval, I accordingly desire you to take the necessary steps to provide a most conspicuous place, in which the stele concerning the artists may be set up. I append below a copy of my letter [to the artists] and of the decree of the senate. . . .[47]

. . . and also the good will you bear us, I therefore desire you to know that, on the advice of my council, I have made known my decision that you shall retain whatever privileges, offices, and exemptions from compulsory public services our senate, consuls, and proconsuls have given or granted you as kindnesses in honor of Dionysus, the Muses, and your profession; and that, just as in the past, you shall be exempt from all public and military service, you shall not pay any tax or contribution, you shall not be troubled by anyone for provisions[48] or billets, and you shall not be compelled to receive any lodger in your homes against your will. . . .[49] [The rest is lost.]

46. These guilds are known from other sources to have had their centers at Teos and Pergamum, respectively.

47. In what follows, Sulla's earlier letter confirming the artists' privileges is preserved in part; the Senate's decree is completely lost.

48. That is, for visiting Roman officials and their retinues; cf. notes 70, 81.

49. A similar grant by Lucius Mummius in Greece (*IG,* vol. VII, no. 2,413; second century B.C.)

136. THE ROMANS' STAKE IN ASIA

Cicero, *In Favor of the Manilian Law* vi–vii; From LCL

While the revenues of our other provinces, gentlemen, are barely sufficient to make it worth our while to defend them, Asia is so rich and
fertile as easily to surpass all other countries in the productiveness of her
soil, the variety of her crops, the extent of her pastures, and the volume
of her exports. This province, gentlemen, if you wish to retain what
makes either war possible or peace honorable, it is your duty to defend
not only from disaster but from fear of disaster. For in most cases it is at
the moment when disaster occurs that loss is sustained; but in the case
of revenue it is not only the occurrence of a calamity but the mere dread
that brings disaster—for when the enemy's forces are near at hand, even
though they have not crossed the frontier, the pastures are deserted, the
fields are left untilled, and the sea-borne trade comes to an end. Consequently neither from customs duties, tithes, nor grazing dues can the
revenues be maintained; and so a single rumor of danger, a single alarm
of war, often means the loss of a whole year's income. What, pray, do
you suppose to be the state of mind either of those who pay us the taxes
or of those who farm and collect them, when two kings with mighty
armies are near at hand; when a single cavalry raid can in an instant carry
off the revenue of a whole year; when the tax farmers feel that there is
the gravest risk in keeping the large staffs which they maintain on the
pastures and the grain lands, at the harbors and the coastguard stations?
Do you imagine that you can enjoy these advantages unless you preserve
those from whom you derive them and keep them free, as I said before,
not only from disaster but from fear of disaster?

There is still another point which, when setting out to discuss the
nature of the [Mithridatic] War, I decided to keep to the end—a point
of which you must not lose sight: I mean the fact that there are many
Roman citizens whose property is affected by this war; and wise men
like yourselves know that their interests demand your careful consideration. For in the first place the honorable and distinguished men who
farm our revenue have transferred their business and their resources to

---

explicitly includes the wives and minor children of the players as beneficiaries; presumably the same
was the case here.

that province, and their interests and fortunes ought to be your particular concern. For if we have always held that your revenues are the sinews of the commonwealth, then we shall assuredly be right in saying that the class which farms those revenues is the mainstay of the other classes. Moreover, of those other classes there are men of energy and industry who are some of them personally engaged in business in Asia, and you ought to consult their interests in their absence; while others of them have vast sums invested in that province. Your humanity therefore enjoins that you should save this large body of citizens from ruin, and your wisdom shows you that the state cannot but be involved in the ruin of many of its citizens. For in the first place the subsequent recovery of our taxes through the victory makes but little difference once the tax farmers are lost; for the individuals in question will lack the power to buy the contract owing to their ruin, and others will lack the inclination owing to their fear. In the second place we ought assuredly to remember the lesson which we learned from this same Asia and this same Mithridates at the beginning of the Asiatic war, since we were taught it through disaster. For, coinciding with the loss by many people of large fortunes in Asia, we know that there was a collapse of credit at Rome owing to suspension of payments. It is indeed impossible for many individuals in a single state to lose their property and fortunes without involving still greater numbers in their own ruin. Do you defend the commonwealth from this danger; and believe me when I tell you— what you see for yourselves—that this system of credit and finance which operates at Rome, in the Forum, is bound up in and depends on capital invested in Asia; the loss of the one inevitably undermines the other and causes its collapse. Bethink you, therefore, whether you should hesitate to throw yourselves with the utmost enthusiasm into a war to defend the honor of your name, the well-being of your allies, the most important of your revenues and—a thing in which the commonwealth is closely concerned—the fortunes of so many citizens.

137. TAXATION IN THE PROVINCES: PUBLICANS AND TEMPLE LANDS

This inscription records the settlement, in 73 B.C., of a dispute between the sanctuary of the god Amphiaraus at Oropus and the publicans claiming the right to collect taxes from it. The matter was investigated by the consuls, who reported their findings to the Senate (cf. § 133, second selection). The Senate then passed a decree, pursuant to the consuls' recommendations, confirming the tax exemption of the sacred precinct and temple revenues and rejecting the publicans' claim.

IG, vol. VII, no. 413 (= Dittenberger, no. 747 = *RDGE*, no. 23)

Marcus Terentius Varro Lucullus son of Marcus and Gaius Cassius Longinus son of Lucius, consuls, to the chief magistrates, council, and people of Oropus, greeting. If you are well, we are pleased. We wish you to know that, in accordance with the decree of the senate passed in the consulship of Lucius Licinius and Marcus Aurelius [74 B.C.] we have investigated the dispute which arose between the ministrants to the god Amphiaraus and the tax farmers.

October 14, in the Basilica Porcia. Present on our council were [sixteen names follow].

Whereas Hermodorus son of Olympichus, priest of Amphiaraus, who previously was named ally by the senate, and Alexidemus son of Theodorus, and Demaenetus son of Theoteles, envoys of the Oropians, submitted that in the law on tax farming those lands were exempted which Lucius Sulla granted for the sake of maintaining the sacred precincts of the immortal gods, and that these revenues which are under dispute were assigned by Lucius Sulla to the god Amphiaraus, so that no revenue should be paid to the tax farmers for these lands;

And whereas Lucius Domitius Ahenobarbus submitted on behalf of the tax farmers that in the law on tax farming those lands were exempted which Lucius Sulla granted for the sake of maintaining the sacred precincts of the immortal gods, but that Amphiaraus, to whom these lands are said to have been granted, is not a god, so that the tax farmers should have the right to collect taxes on these lands;

On the advice of our council we declared this decision: We shall lay before the senate our findings, which we have recorded also in the minutes [of the consuls' investigation]:

"Concerning the territory of Oropus, about which there was a dispute with the tax farmers, this has been exempted by the law on tax farming, so that the tax farmer may not collect taxes on it. We investigated in accordance with the decree of the senate.

"In the law on tax farming it seems to have been exempted as follows: 'excluding those, which in accordance with a decree of the senate, a commander or commanders of ours, for the sake of honoring the immortal gods and maintaining sacred precincts, granted and relinquished to them to enjoy, and excluding those which the commander Lucius Cornelius Sulla on the advice of his council, for the sake of the immortal gods and the maintenance of sacred precincts, granted to them to enjoy, which same the senate confirmed and which was not subsequently invalidated by a decree of the senate.'

"Lucius Cornelius Sulla seems to have rendered this decision on the advice of his council: 'For the sake of repaying a vow I assign to the sanctuary of Amphiaraus land extending 1,000 feet in all directions, so that this land also may be inviolate.' Similarly for the god Amphiaraus he seems to have consecrated 'all the revenues of the city, the territory, and the harbors of the Oropians to the games and sacrifices which the Oropians perform for the god Amphiaraus, and likewise also all those which they may hereafter perform for the victory and empire of the Roman people, excluding the lands of Hermodorus son of Olympichus, priest of Amphiaraus, who has remained steadfastly in the friendship of the Roman people.'

"Concerning this matter a decree of the senate seems to have been passed in the consulship of Lucius Sulla Felix and Quintus Metellus Pius [80 B.C.]. The decree of the senate was worded as follows: 'Whatever Lucius Cornelius Sulla on the advice of his council assigned or granted to the god Amphiaraus and to his sanctuary, these same the senate deemed should be given and granted to this god.'

"On [Sulla's] council were present the same as in the first record of deliberations, fourteenth page."

The following decree of the senate was passed: October 16 in the Comitium. Present at the writing [of this decree] were Titus Maenius son of Titus, of the Lemonian tribe, Quintus Rancius son of Quintus, of the Claudian tribe, Gaius Visellius Varro son of Gaius, of the Quirine tribe. Whereas the consuls Marcus Lucullus and Gaius Cassius investigated and reported that they had investigated concerning the territory of Oropus and the tax farmers, that the territory of the Oropians too seemed to have been exempted by the law on tax farming, and that it did not seem right that the tax farmers should collect taxes on it, it was so decreed, as they deemed best in keeping with the interests of the state and with their own good faith.

138. THE PROVINCE OF SICILY: ITS IMPORTANCE AND STATUS IN THE EMPIRE

Cicero, *Second Speech Against Verres* II. i. 2–iii.8, xiii. 32; Adapted from *LCL*

But before I speak of Sicily's distresses, I feel that I should say a little of the high position of that province, of its antiquity, and of its practical importance. Your attentive consideration, due to the interests of all our allies and all our provinces, is especially due, gentleman, to those of Sicily for many strong reasons, the first of which is this, that Sicily was the first of all foreign nations to turn to the friendship and protection of the Roman people. She was the first of all to receive the title of province, the first such jewel in our imperial crown. She was the first who made our forefathers perceive how splendid a thing a foreign empire is. No other people has equaled her in loyal good will toward us: once the various states in the island had embraced our friendship, they never thereafter seceded from it, and most of them—and those the most notable—remained without a break our firm friends. From this province therefore it was that our forefathers took that great step in their imperial career, the invasion of Africa; for the great power of Carthage would never have been crushed so readily had not Sicily been at our disposal, supplying us with grain and affording safe harborage to our fleets . . . [cf. § 92].

Accordingly, our relations with this province for all purposes were always such that we looked upon her various products not as growing on her soil, but as already added to our stores at home. When has she failed to pay up punctually her tribute of grain? When has she not spontaneously offered us what she believed we needed? When has she refused to supply what was ordered of her? Cato the Wise called her in consequence "the nation's storehouse, the nurse at whose breast the Roman people is fed." Nay, we in our time have found, in the critical days of the great Italic War, how Sicily has been to us no mere storehouse, but like the ancient and well-filled state treasury of our fathers' days, supplying us with hides and shirts and grain, free of cost to ourselves, to clothe, feed, and equip our great armies. Yes, and she does us services, great services, of which we, gentlemen, are I daresay not even aware. Many of our citizens are the richer for having a profitable field of enterprise in this loyal province close at hand, which they can visit so easily, and where they can carry on their business so freely. To some of these Sicily supplies merchandise, and sends them away enriched with profits; others she keeps with her, to become, according to their preference, farmers or cattlemen or businessmen, and in short, to settle and make their homes there. It is a national advantage of no trifling kind that so large a number of Roman citizens should be kept so near their own country, engaged in occupations so honest and profitable. Our tributes and our provinces constitute, in a sense, our nation's landed estates; and thus, just as you, gentlemen, gain most pleasure from such of your estates as are close to Rome, so to the nation there is something pleasant in the nearness of this province to the capital.

And then again, the character of the inhabitants is such, so hardy and upright and honest, that it really reminds us of the stern old Roman manners rather than of those which have come to prevail among us today. They have none of the failings found elsewhere among Greeks; they are neither slothful nor self-indulgent; on the contrary, they are highly industrious, for their own and for the public good; plain-living and conscientious folk. Such, moreover, is their attachment to our own people that only among them is neither tax collector nor moneylender an object of hatred. Acts of oppression, again, on the part of Roman officials, they have borne so patiently time after time that never before this day have they, as a community, sought refuge in the sanctuary of the law and the stronghold of your protection. . . . It was an inherited tradition of theirs to regard Rome as so great a benefactor of the Sicilians that they must even endure oppression, if the oppressors were Romans. . . .

The legal rights of the Sicilians are as follows. Cases between two citizens of the same city are tried in that city's courts under that city's laws. For cases between two Sicilians of different cities, the praetor chooses jurors by lot, in accordance with the ordinance known in Sicily as the Rupilian Law, which Publius Rupilius[50] decreed on the recommendation of a ten-man commission. When an individual sues a community or a community an individual, the council of some city is named to try the case, each party being entitled to one challenge. When a Roman citizen sues a Sicilian, a Sicilian is appointed to try the case, and when a Sicilian sues a Roman citizen, a Roman citizen is appointed. In all other cases the regular procedure is to nominate the jurors from a

50. Proconsul of Sicily in 131 B.C.; cf § 95.

panel of Roman citizens resident in the district, except that cases between farmers and collectors of the tithe are tried under the provisions of the grain laws known as the laws of Hiero [cf. note 52].

139. TAXATION IN THE PROVINCES: THE GRAIN OF SICILY

Cicero, *Second Speech Against Verres* III. v. 11–vi. 15, lxx. 163; Adapted from *LCL*

Keep before you, gentlemen, the fact that when you investigate the agricultural part of this case you will be investigating the position and welfare of the whole Sicilian people, the property of those Roman citizens who are farmers in Sicily, the revenues we have inherited from our forefathers, the sources of the food and subsistence of the Roman nation. . . .

You must all be aware, gentlemen, that so far as the interests of the Roman nation are concerned, the general utility and advantage of our province of Sicily are mainly derived from the grain which it sends us; its other contributions are useful to us, but this one is the food we live on. This section of the prosecution will fall into three parts. I shall deal first with the grain tithe, then with grain purchase, and finally with grain commutation.

Let me remind this court of the differences in the system of land taxation between Sicily and our other provinces. In the others, either a fixed tax has been imposed, which is called a "tribute," as for example that imposed on the Spaniards and most of the Carthaginians, which may be considered as the reward of victory and penalty of defeat; or else the censors let contracts for the collection, as in Asia under the Sempronian Law. But we received the Sicilian city-states into our friendship and trust under terms whereby their old rights were maintained, and their position as subjects of Rome remained the same as it had been under their own rulers. A very few of them our ancestors subdued by force of arms; though the territory of these few thus became the property of the Roman state, it was restored to their possession, and the collection of taxes on this land is regularly let by the censors. Two cities, Messana and Tauromenium, have special treaties of alliance, and no contracts are made for collecting tithes from them; five others, though not allies by treaty, are free states exempt from taxation, namely, Centuripa, Halaesus, Segesta, Halicyae, Panhormus.[51] With these exceptions, all the lands of the Sicilian cities are subject to payment of tithe, and were so under regulations voluntarily made by their own inhabitants before the days of Roman sovereignty. I would draw your attention to the wise action of our forefathers in this matter. Having secured to our country, by the acquisition of Sicily, a valuable source of strength in peace and war, they were so earnestly resolute to secure and maintain the loyalty of its people that they refrained not only from imposing any new tax upon Sicilian land but even from altering either the conditions of the sale of the right to collect the tithe or the time and place of such sale, so that the Sicilians might continue to sell these rights at the established time of year, right there in Sicily, and as provided by the laws of Hiero. They resolved that the Sicilians should manage their own affairs themselves, and should not be irritated either by new laws or even by the old laws under new names. And so they decided that the collection of tithes should always be sold as provided by the laws of Hiero, desiring to make the discharge of this duty less irksome to the Sicilians by preserving to them, under their new sovereigns, not only the institutions but the name of the most popular of their kings.[52] They enjoyed these rights uninterruptedly until Verres became praetor; he was the first man who dared to uproot and transform an order of things established everywhere, a usage inherited from their ancestors, their constitutional privilege and right as the friends and the allies of Rome. . . .

It was Verres' duty to make purchases of grain in Sicily in accordance with a decree of the senate and the provisions of the Terentian–Cassian grain law.[53] There were two kinds of purchase to be made, the first a tithe, the second an additional purchase distributed fairly among the communities. The amount of the former was to be the same as that yielded by the first tithes;[54] that of the additional requisition was to be 800,000 *modii* of wheat each year. The price fixed was 3 sesterces per *modius* for the tithe grain, and 3½ sesterces for the requisitioned grain. Verres was therefore voted 2,800,000 sesterces a year to pay the farmers

51. On the status of these states, cf. introduction to § 134.

52. Besides the tithe on cultivated lands, the laws of Hiero (chapter 5, note 1) provided also for a tax on pasture land in the form of an annual money impost on each head of grazing stock, and for port dues of 5 percent.

53. Passed in 73 B.C., when Verres began his governorship of Sicily. These purchases of grain were requisitioned in addition to the "first tithe" collected by the tax-farmers.

54. 3,000,000 *modii,* as revealed by the amount of the appropriation four lines below.

for the requisitioned grain, and about 9,000,000 sesterces a year for the second tithe. Thus nearly 12,000,000 sesterces a year were appropriated for three years for this purchase of Sicilian grain.

140. PRECEPTS OF PROVINCIAL GOVERNMENT

This letter was written by Cicero toward the end of 60 B.C. to his brother, who was about to enter upon his third year as propraetor of the province of Asia. Cicero took the opportunity to indulge in a lengthy disquisition on provincial administration, enunciating principles of government which, as he himself remarks, Roman governors generally honored in the breach rather than in the observance. Cicero himself, when governor of Cilicia nine years later, hardly lived up to the lofty precepts here outlined (see § 145).

Cicero, *Letters to his Brother Quintus* book 1, no. 1.8–35 (abridged); Adapted from *LCL*

It is a glorious thought that you should have been three years in Asia in supreme command and not been tempted by the offer of any statue, picture, plate, garment, or slave, by any fascination of human beauty, or by any pecuniary proposals — temptations with which that province of yours abounds — to deviate from the path of strict integrity and sobriety of conduct. . . .

In these matters, however, experience itself has by this time taught you that it is by no means sufficient to possess these virtues yourself, but that you must keep diligent watch around you so that in this guardianship of your province it may appear that you are responsible to the allies, the citizens, and the state not for yourself alone, but for all the officials of your government. You have as legates men who are likely to consider their own reputation [as well as yours]. . . . Your quaestor is not a man of your own deliberate selection, but one assigned you by lot; he ought to be a man of instinctive self-control, and should also comply with your policy and instructions. Among these men, should it happen that anyone could not show a clean record of conduct, you would put up with him so long as he disregarded only the regulations by which he was bound in his capacity as a private individual, but not if he abused for purposes of private lucre the powers you have vouchsafed him for the maintenance of his public position. . . .

As for those, however, whom you have chosen to be about you either in your domestic entourage or on your train of personal attendants

—generally spoken of as a sort of "praetor's retinue"—in *their* case we have to be responsible not only for their every act, but for their every word. . . . Let this third year show the same standard of integrity as the preceding two, but even an increase in caution and in diligence. Let your ears be such as are reputed to hear only what they do hear, and not such as are open to false and interested whispers prompted by the hope of profit. Let not your signet ring be a sort of utensil but, as it were, your very self—not the servant of another's will, but the witness of your own. Let your apparitor[55] hold the rank which he was intended to hold by our ancestors, who, regarding that post not as a lucrative sinecure but as one of work and duty, were slow to confer it upon any but their own freedmen, over whom they exercised much the same authority as over their slaves. Let your lictor be the dispenser not of his own but of your clemency, and let the *fasces* and axes they carry before them be more the symbols of rank than of power. In a word, let it be recognized by the whole province that the welfare, children, reputation, and fortunes of all whom you govern are most precious to you. Finally, let it be the general impression that you will regard with disfavor not only those who have taken a bribe, but also those who have given one, if ever you get to know of it. And, as a matter of fact, there will be no giving of bribes when it is made perfectly clear that, in general, nothing is got out of you through the machinations of persons pretending to have great influence with you. . . .

And further, among the Greeks themselves there are certain intimacies against which you must be strictly on your guard, except intimacy with the very few, if any, who are worthy of ancient Greece. In your province, however, there are a great many who are deceitful and unstable, and trained by a long course of servitude to show an excess of sycophancy. What I say is, that they should all of them be treated as gentlemen, but that only the best of them should be attached to you by ties of hospitality and friendship; unrestricted intimacies with them are not so much to be trusted, for they dare not oppose your wishes, and they are jealous not only of our countrymen, but even of their own. . . .

These and all the other precedents of notable severity you have established in your province we should not easily justify except by the most perfect probity. For that reason be as severe as you please in administering justice, provided that your severity is not varied by partiality but

---

55. The *accensus,* a petty official attached to a magistrate having *imperium;* his function was to summon persons to court, and to act as a sergeant-at-arms during the proceedings.

kept on the same level of consistency. However, it is of little importance that your own administration of justice is consistent and careful, unless it is so administered also by those to whom you have yielded any portion of that duty. And indeed it seems to me that there is no great variety of transactions in the government of Asia, but that the entire government mainly depends upon the administration of justice; and, being thus limited, the theory of government itself, especially in the provinces, presents no difficulty; you only need to show such consistency and firmness as to withstand not only favoritism, but the very suspicion of it. In addition to this there must be civility in hearing, clemency in deciding, and careful discrimination in the satisfactory settlement of disputes. . . .

And my personal opinion is that those who govern others must gauge their every act by this one test—the greatest possible happiness of the governed; and that this principle is and has been from the beginning, from the moment you set foot in Asia, of primary importance in your eyes, is a fact bruited abroad by unvarying report and the conversation of all. And indeed it is the duty not only of one who governs allies and citizens, but also of one who governs slaves and dumb animals, to be himself a slave to the interest and well-being of those he governs. And in this respect I see that there is universal agreement as to the extraordinary pains you are taking; I see that no new debt is being contracted to burden the states, whereas many of them have been relieved by you of a big and heavy debt of long standing; that several cities, demolished and almost deserted (among them Samos and Halicarnassus, the most famous cities of Ionia and Caria, respectively), have been rebuilt through your instrumentality; that there are no insurrections, no civil discords in the towns; that you are providing for the government of the states by councils of their aristocracies; that brigandage has been exterminated in Mysia, murder suppressed in various places, and peace established throughout the province; that thefts and robberies, not only those on the highways and in the country, but also (and these are far more frequent and serious) in towns and temples, have been effectually checked; that the good name, the possessions, and the peace of mind of the wealthy have been delivered from that pernicious instrument of praetorian greed—prosecution on a false charge; that the incidence of expenditure and taxation in the states bears in equal proportion upon all those who dwell within the boundaries of those states; that it is the easiest thing in the world to gain access to you; that your ears are open to the complaints of all; that no man's lack of means or of friends has ever shut him out from approaching you, not only in public and on the tribunal, but even in your very house and bedchamber; in short, that in the whole sphere of your command there is nothing harsh, nothing brutal, nothing but clemency, gentleness, and kindness of heart. . . .

Therefore throw your whole heart and soul into the policy you have hitherto adopted, treating as friends those whom the senate and the people of Rome have committed and entrusted to your care and authority, protecting them in every possible way, and desiring their greatest possible happiness. Why, if the drawing of lots had given you the government of the Africans or the Spaniards or the Gauls, uncouth and barbarous peoples, it would still be incumbent upon a man of your humane character to study their interest and work for their welfare and security. But seeing that we are governing that division of mankind in which not only do we find true humanity, but from which it is also supposed to have spread to the others, it is surely our duty to bestow it especially upon them from whom we received it. . . .

And yet to all your good will and devotion to duty there is a serious obstacle in the publicans; if we oppose them, we shall alienate from ourselves and from the commonwealth a class that has deserved extremely well of us and been brought through our instrumentality into close association with the commonwealth; and yet, if we yield to them in everything, we shall be acquiescing in the utter ruin of those whose security, and indeed whose interests, we are bound to protect. This is the one outstanding difficulty (if we would face the question honestly) in the whole sphere of your command. For as to one's being unselfish, curbing all one's passions, keeping one's staff in check, maintaining a consistently uniform policy in the administration of justice, conducting one's self with kindly courtesy in investigating cases and in giving audience to suitors and not shutting one's door to them—all that is magnificent rather than difficult to do, for it depends not upon any strenuous exertion, but upon making up one's mind and setting one's will in a certain direction.

What bitterness of feeling this question of the publicans causes the allies we have gathered from our own citizens, who recently, on the abolition of port dues in Italy, complained not so much of that impost itself as of certain malpractices on the part of the customs officers.[56] I therefore know pretty well what happens to allies in distant lands from the complaints I have heard from citizens in Italy. So to conduct yourself

56. These were employees of the publicans.

in this connection as to satisfy the publicans, especially when they have taken over the collection of taxes at a loss,[57] and at the same time not to allow the allies to be ruined, seems to demand a sort of divine excellence —in other words, an excellence such as yours. Let us take the Greeks first; their greatest grievance is that they are subject to taxation; but they should not regard that as so very much of a grievance, for the simple reason that they put themselves in that position of their own free will by their own enactment, without any command from the Roman people. Moreover they cannot afford to disdain the name of publican, since without the aid of that publican they themselves could never have paid the assessment imposed by Sulla as a poll tax on all alike [see § 83]. And that the Greek collectors are no more gentle in enforcing the payment of taxes than our own publicans may be inferred from the fact that quite recently the Caunians and all the islands that had been made tributary by Sulla to the Rhodians fled for protection to our senate, begging that they might pay their taxes to us rather than to the Rhodians. . . . Let Asia at the same time bear this in mind, that were she not under our government, there is no disaster in the way of either foreign war or intestine discords that she would have been likely to escape. Seeing, however, that such government cannot possibly be maintained without taxes, she should not resent having to pay for perpetual peace and tranquility with some portion of what her soil produces.

If they will but accept without resentment the mere existence of such a class and the name publican, all else, owing to your counsel and wisdom, may possibly seem to them less oppressive. . . . You too are able to do what you have done, and are doing, in the most admirable way—you can remind everyone of the high responsibility imposed upon the publicans, and of our own great indebtedness to that order, so that, waiving your official command and the power of your authority and *fasces,* you may unite the publicans with the Greeks by means of the regard and respect they have for you personally, and entreat the Greeks, whom you have so admirably served and who owe you everything, to allow us, by showing a compliant temper, to maintain and preserve the intimate connection which subsists between us and the publicans.

---

57. The syndicate of publicans had bid too high for the contract and was trying to recoup its losses.

Aspects of Roman Misrule

141. GENERALS AND ARMIES ABROAD

"No administration in history has ever devoted itself so whole-heartedly to fleecing its subjects for the private benefit of its ruling class as Rome in the last age of the Republic" (E. Badian, *Roman Imperialism in the Late Republic*, 2d ed., p. 87). Throughout the Hellenistic world in the second and first centuries B.C., wherever Roman armies operated, complaints such as these arose from Roman provincials and allies; see also, for example, § 147.

Livy, *History of Rome* XLIII. vii. 5–viii. 9

The Cretans were dismissed and the Chalcidians called in [170 B.C.]. From the very entrance of this deputation it was at once apparent that their business must be of vital importance; for Micython, their leader, was brought in on a litter, as he had lost the use of his feet, yet, afflicted as he was, he either had not thought it right to ask to be excused on the ground of health, or if he had asked his request had not been granted. After remarking by way of introduction that there was nothing left alive in him except his tongue to deplore the calamities of his native land, he went on to enumerate the services that Chalcis had rendered to the Roman generals and their armies in the past and now in the war with Perseus, and then described the tyrannical, rapacious, and brutal way in which the Roman praetor, Gaius Lucretius, had treated his countrymen [the year before], and the way in which Lucius Hortensius was actually behaving at that very moment. Though they thought it better to endure even worse sufferings than they were enduring rather than abandon their allegiance, they were convinced, so far as Lucretius and Hortensius were concerned, that it would have been safer to shut their gates than to admit them into the city. The cities which had shut them out—Emathia, Amphipolis, Maronea, Aenus—were unharmed, but in their own case the temples had been despoiled of all their adornments and the sacrilegious plunder had been carried off by Gaius Lucretius in his ships to Antium; the persons of freemen had been snatched away into slavery; the property of allies of the Roman people had been plundered and was being plundered every day. Following the precedent of Gaius Lucretius, Hortensius too kept his crews in billets winter and summer alike, and their homes were filled with a mob of rowdy sailors, who lived with them, their wives, and their children, and had no scruples about what they said or did.

The senate decided to send for Lucretius, that he might confront his accusers and clear himself of their charges. However, when he put in an appearance he had to listen to many more accusations than those hurled in his absence, and accusers now came forward of greater weight and authority in the persons of two tribunes of the plebs, Manius Juventius and Gnaeus Aufidius. They not only ripped into him in the senate, but also dragged him before the assembly [see note 77], where he was exposed to much vituperation, and fixed a day for his trial.

By order of the senate the praetor Quintus Maenius gave the following reply to the Chalcidians. With regard to the services they say they have rendered to the Roman people both previously and in the war now being waged, the senate is aware that they are stating what is true, and is duly grateful for them. As to the conduct of the Roman praetors, Gaius Lucretius and Lucius Hortensius, about which they complain, who could fail to realize that such conduct was not in accordance with the wish of the senate when everyone knew that the Roman people had made war on Perseus and on his father before him on behalf of the liberty of Greece and not that their friends and allies should suffer such treatment at the hands of their magistrates. They would send a letter to the praetor Lucius Hortensius, informing him that the acts of which the Chalcidians complained were displeasing to the senate; if any freemen had gone into slavery, he was to see to it that they were sought out at the earliest opportunity and restored to freedom; and no member of the crews, excepting captains, was to be billeted in private homes. These instructions, by order of the senate, were sent to Hortensius. A present of 2,000 sesterces was sent to each of the envoys, and carriages were hired at public expense to convey Micythion in comfort to Brundisium.

When the day set for the trial arrived, the tribunes arraigned Lucretius before the people and demanded a fine of 1,000,000 *asses*. After the hearing in the assembly the thirty-five tribes unanimously found him guilty.

Cicero, *In Favor of the Manilian Law* xiii. 37–39; From *LCL*

For what general can we hold in any sort of esteem when in his army the appointment of centurions is for sale and has been sold? How can we attribute a great and lofty conception of patriotism to the sort of man who has been induced, by his ambition to become a governor, to divide among the magistrates the money issued to him from the treasury for the conduct of a campaign or, by his avarice, to leave it on interest at Rome? Your groans, gentlemen, show that you recognize the men who have done these things. For my part, I mention no names, so that no one can feel resentment against me unless he would admit that the shoe fits. Who then does not know how great is the ruin which, owing to this avarice on the part of our generals, is caused by our armies in every place to which they go? Think of the tours which of late years our generals have made in Italy itself through the lands and the towns of Roman citizens, and then you will more easily judge what, it seems, are their practices among foreign peoples. Which do you think have been more frequently destroyed of late years—the cities of your enemies by your soldiers' arms or the communities of your allies by their winter quarters? No commander can control an army who does not control himself, nor can he be a strict judge if he is unwilling that others should judge him strictly. Are we surprised, then, to find Pompey so far superior to other commanders, when they tell of his legions' arrival in Asia that no one who had laid down his arms suffered injury either from any act of violence done by that great army or even from its passage? And further, the way in which his soldiers behave in winter quarters is shown by the tidings and the letters which reach us daily: so far from any man being compelled to incur expense on a soldier's account, no man is allowed to do so even if he would. For our forefathers desired that the roofs of their allies and friends should be a shelter against the winter, not a refuge for avarice.

142. The "Legatio Libera"

A member of the Roman senate who wished to travel abroad for personal reasons could obtain from that body a *legatio libera,* that is, a roving ambassadorship free of all duties. Though not on official business, the traveler thus enjoyed all the advantages of official status and was entitled in particular to demand the lavish reception and entertainment which had to be furnished to traveling Roman dignitaries by the localities on their itinerary (cf § § 130, 141, 145, 147).

Cicero, *Laws* III. viii. 18; From *LCL*

It is obvious at once that nothing can be more disgraceful than the appointment of an ambassador for any other than a public purpose. I will say nothing of the behavior, either at present or in the past, of those who go out as ambassadors to claim legacies or enforce contracts, for perhaps that is due to a weakness of human nature. But I ask only this: what could be more disgraceful than a senator's holding an appointment as ambassador without official duties, without instructions, without any public business whatever to attend to? In fact, when I was consul [63 B.C.], I should have been able to abolish embassies of this kind with the approbation of a full meeting of the senate, in spite of the fact that the custom gave the senate valuable privileges, if it had not been for the intercession of an irresponsible tribune of the plebs; but I did limit the duration of such appointments, which had previously been unrestricted, to one year. And so the disgrace still persists, but with the time allowance limited.

143. PREDATORY GOVERNORS

"Nothing but honor from enemy or ally should be brought home by good and upright officials," wrote Cicero in his *Laws* (III. viii. 18). The implication is clear that in reality Roman officials brought home much more tangible prizes. By the first century B.C. a tour of duty in a province as governor or as a member of a governor's staff had come to be regarded as the quickest and surest way to riches. In fact, many young men of the nobility freely borrowed and squandered vast sums to launch their political careers, confident of more than recouping their expenditures when assigned to provincial office; and creditors were perfectly ready to lend large sums of money on the security of such future prospects. The opportunities for enrichment in the provinces, legal and illegal, were practically limitless; some of the more common practices are illustrated by this and the succeeding selections. The present selection and the one following are from Cicero's prosecution of Gaius Verres, who governed Sicily from 73 to 71 B.C.; the interminable list of crimes, from which these are but the briefest extract, shows Verres to have been thoroughly unscrupulous, yet there is no reason to believe that he was unique.

Cicero, *Second Speech Against Verres* ii. xlix. 122, lvii. 141–lviii. 143; From *LCL*

The people of Halaesus were made independent in recognition of the many valuable services and benefits rendered to Rome by themselves and their ancestors; but not long ago, in the consulship of Lucius Licinius and Quintus Mucius [95 B.C.], owing to an internal dispute regarding the way of filling vacancies in their senate, they asked the Roman senate to legislate for them. The senate honored them by passing a decree appointing the praetor Gaius Claudius Pulcher (son of Appius Claudius) to draw up for them regulations for filling the aforesaid vacancies. Claudius, having secured the help of all the contemporary members of the Marcellus family,[58] in accordance with their advice provided Halaesus with regulations laying down a number of points, such as the age of candidates (those under thirty were excluded), the occupations disqualifying for membership, the property qualification, and all such other points.[59] All these regulations, supported by our magistrates and thoroughly approved by the inhabitants, were faithfully observed until Verres became praetor. Verres was bribed to sell the honor even to an auctioneer who wanted it; from Verres boys of sixteen and seventeen purchased the rank of senator. The right to prohibit such things, even by election, had been granted at Rome to our old and faithful friend and ally, Halaesus; and Verres made such things possible to those who bribed him! . . .

Having referred to the money contributed by the censors for your statue,[60] I think I should also say something of the method of making money whereby you extracted it, ostensibly for providing statues, from the various cities. The total amount is, I observe, very large, not less than 2,000,000 sesterces; the personal and written evidence supplied by the cities will show it to come to fully as much as that. Verres indeed admits so much, nor can he help admitting it; and when the offenses he does not deny are so serious, what are we to think of the offenses he does deny? Why, to what conclusion would you have us come? That all this money was spent on statues? Suppose that true: it remains quite intolerable that our allies should be robbed of enough money to set up a statue of this buccaneering ruffian in every alleyway, in places where

---

58. The traditional patrons of Sicily, going back to the Marcellus who captured Syracuse in 212 B.C.

59. Such regulations were customary in municipal characters; cf. § 162.

60. Cicero is here indulging in an apostrophe to his opponent, a frequent practice in Roman oratory.

one would think it hardly safe to go. But where, on what statues, has all that money of yours in fact been spent? It *will* be spent, you will answer. We are to wait, I take it, for the legal five-year period of grace to elapse; and if he has not so spent it meanwhile, then will come our time to prosecute him for extortion in connection with these statues! He stands here charged now with a great number of serious offenses, and we find that under this *one* count he has illegally exacted 2,000,000 sesterces. . . . Surely, if Verres had simply demanded the sum of 100,000 sesterces from, shall we say, the people of Centuripa and taken that sum away from them, there could really be no doubt that the proof of this fact must lead to his conviction. Well then, now that he has, from those very people, demanded, extracted, and taken away 200,000 sesterces, he will surely not be acquitted simply because a note has been added that this money was given for statues? No, I think not—unless, of course, our object is not to discourage our officials from taking such payments but to encourage our allies to make them.[61]

144. Collusion Between Governor
and Publicans

See introduction to § 143, and cf. § 140.

Cicero, *Second Speech Against Verres* II. lxix. 169–lxxviii. 191 (abridged); Adapted from *LCL*

Perhaps, however, you[62] derive some sort of confidence and comfort from having been popular with the tax farmers? My watchfulness has made it impossible for this popularity to help your case at all; and your cleverness has taken effective steps to make it actually tell against you. Let me, gentlemen, put the whole story before you in a few words.

In the case of the pasture rents of Sicily the tax-collecting company has a local manager named Lucius Carpinatius. This man, both for his own profit and possibly also with an eye to the shareholders' interests, worked his way very thoroughly into intimacy with Verres. He used to

---

61. The story of these statues goes on for many more chapters. A particularly significant detail is this (lix. 146): after Verres' departure the cities of Sicily sent a petition to the Senate in Rome, requesting among other things "that they should not promise statues to any official unless and until he has quit the province." Cf. note 71.

62. Cicero is addressing Verres: cf. note 60.

follow the praetor around from one market town to another, never leaving him; and before long had become so closely connected with him, marketing his decrees and decisions and putting through his pieces of jobbery, that he was looked on as a second Timarchides, but even more deadly, from his custom of lending money at interest to those who wanted to buy something from Verres. And this system of loans was so managed, gentlemen, that the profits from this source came to our friend [Verres] here; for the sums that Carpinatius entered in his accounts as paid to those to whom he made loans, he also debited against himself as received from Verres' secretary, or from Timarchides, or even from Verres himself; besides which he also lent in his own name large sums of Verres' money not entered in the accounts at all. In the early days, before establishing this close connection with Verres, Carpinatius had several times written to the company complaining of wrongs done by Verres; and Canuleius, who saw to the collection of the harbor dues at Syracuse, had sent the company a detailed list of numerous thefts Verres had also committed in the matter of goods exported from Syracuse without paying the export tax (the same company being contractors for harbor dues as for pasture rents). The result was to provide us with a number of points from the company's records to quote and bring up against Verres.

But it so happened that Carpinatius, being before long closely associated with Verres as his regular intimate—and by substantial reasons as well—subsequently wrote a number of letters to the company about the great services that Verres had been good enough to render the company's interests. And indeed, by the time that Verres was regularly doing and ordering whatever Carpinatius asked of him, the latter was writing even more frequently to the company, hoping that, if possible, the effect of his earlier letters would be completely wiped out. Finally, when Verres was about to leave Sicily, he wrote urging them to assemble in force and meet him on his arrival, to express their thanks and to promise to execute zealously any commands he might have for them. The company accordingly observed this traditional practice of tax farmers, not because they thought he deserved any marks of respect, but because they felt it would pay them to seem mindful and grateful; they expressed their thanks to him, and told him that Carpinatius had frequently written to them about his services. He replied that it had been a pleasure to him, and spoke in high terms of the good work of Carpinatius; and then he instructed one of his friends, who was at the time an executive of that company, to take the utmost care and precaution that the company's records should contain nothing that could possibly endanger his civic status[63] or reputation. Accordingly the chairman, when the main body of shareholders was out of the way, called a meeting of the directors and put this before them. This meeting passed a resolution that all records damaging to the reputation of Gaius Verres should be expunged, and that care should be taken to prevent this action from being injurious to the said Gaius Verres.

If I prove that the directors did pass this resolution, if I establish the fact that in accordance with this resolution the records were expunged, what more would this court have? Could I bring forward any issue more clearly decided in advance, or prosecute any defendant more clearly convicted in advance? . . .

So it comes to this: the Roman *equites,* whose own verdict pronounced this man guilty, did not wish to have him pronounced guilty by the verdict of this court; it is now for this court to consider whether it will rather be guided by their verdict or by their wishes.

And now ask yourself, Verres, how much good the devotion of your friends, or your own designs, or the good will of the company can do you. I will speak with some little boldness, for I have now no fear of being thought to have spoken more like a prosecutor than like a fair-minded man. If the directors had not made away with those records, I should be able to accuse you only of such misconduct as I had actually found recorded; as it is, that resolution having been carried and the records made away with, it is open to me to say the worst I can of you, and to each member of this court to suspect the worst he will of you. I assert that you exported from Syracuse a great weight of gold, silver, ivory, and purple fabrics, a great deal of Maltese cloth and tapestries, a quantity of Delian wares, a large number of Corinthian vessels, a large quantity of grain, and an immense amount of honey; and that Lucius Canuleius, the agent for harbor dues, wrote to his company complaining that no export tax had been paid on these goods. . . .

Now I do not ask you where you got those 400 jars of honey, or all that Maltese cloth, or those 50 dining-room couches, or all those chandeliers. I do not, I repeat, at present ask where you got them all; what I do ask is what you wanted them all for. Never mind the honey; but why so much Maltese cloth, as if you meant to equip even your friends'

63. If brought to trial for extortion and condemned, he might have to go into exile and abandon his citizenship; cf. § 151.

wives, and why so many couches, as if you meant to furnish all their country houses? Moreover, the record contained in these papers is for a few months only; so you must allow, gentlemen, for the full three years [of Verres' governorship]. My contention is that, from these brief papers found in the hands of a single executive of the company, you can fairly infer the nature of the man's piratical career in the province, the number and variety and boundless extent of his greedy desires, and the amount of money he secured, not only in cash but also invested in such forms as those here mentioned. The story of all this shall be told in clearer detail later on; for the moment I ask you to note this point. On the export transactions mentioned . . . the writer states that the company lost 60,000 sesterces due from the 5 percent tax on exports from Syracuse. In a few short months, therefore, as these contemptible scraps of paper inform us, our praetor exported contraband goods to the value of 1,200,000 sesterces from one town alone. . . .

We will now go back to the company's accounts of receipts and expenditures, which they had no respectable means of suppressing, and to your friend Carpinatius. I was at Syracuse looking through the company's accounts kept by Carpinatius, in which a number of items showed that persons who had paid sums of money to Verres had borrowed for the purpose from Carpinatius—a fact that will be clearer than daylight to you, gentlemen, the moment I bring forward the actual persons who made these payments; for you will see that the dates at which they bought release from their critical situations by bribery correspond, not only year for year but month for month, with the company's accounts. While noting these particular facts, with the accounts open in my hands, I suddenly caught sight of some erasures that suggested recent injuries to the tablets. As soon as this suspicion struck me, I transferred my eyes and attention to these special items. There were sums entered as received from *Gaius Verrucius son of Gaius;* but whereas up to the second *r* the letters were plainly untouched, all after that were written over an erasure; and there was a second, a third, a fourth, a large number of items of the same character.

Since these erasures on the tablets manifestly indicated some conspicuously villainous and dirty proceeding, I proceeded to ask Carpinatius who this Verrucius was with whom he had such extensive money transactions. The man hesitated, shuffled, went red in the face. As the law exempts the accounts of tax farmers from liability to removal to Rome, and as I wished to have the facts cleared up and corroborated as far as I could, I brought an action against Carpinatius before Metellus,[64] and took the company's accounts along to the courthouse there. A large crowd gathered; and since Carpinatius was notorious as a partner of Governor Verres and as a moneylender, there was great and general curiosity to know what the account books contained. I stated my charge before Metellus, saying that I had inspected the company's accounts; that they included a large one, with a great many entries, under the name of Gaius Verrucius; and that by comparing the months and years I had discovered that this Verrucius had had no account with Carpinatius either before the arrival of Gaius Verres or after his departure. I demanded therefore that Carpinatius should tell me who this Verrucius was, merchant or banker, farmer or cattleman, and whether he was still in Sicily or had left. The whole audience shouted with one accord that there never had been in Sicily anyone called Verrucius. I insisted that he should answer me and say who this man was, where he was, where he came from, and why the company's slave who wrote up the accounts always went wrong at one particular point when he wrote the name Verrucius. And I did not make these demands because I thought it right that he should be forced to answer my questions against his will; my purpose was to make quite plain to everyone the peculation of Verres, the misconduct of Carpinatius, and the audacity of them both. So I left the man there before the praetor, speechless and dazed and half dead with the terrors of his guilty conscience, and proceeded to make a copy of the accounts, there in the market place, with a great crowd looking on. Men of position in the district helped with the writing, and every letter and erasure was transferred, reproduced exactly, from the accounts to my books. The whole thing was then examined and compared with scrupulous care, and signed and sealed by certain gentlemen of high standing.

If Carpinatius would not answer me then, will you answer me now, Verres, and say who you suppose this Verrucius is who is almost one of your own clan?[65] I see the man was in Sicily during your praetorship, and the account is enough to show me that he was rich, so it is out of the question that you in your own province were not acquainted with him. Or rather, for the sake of brevity and clearness, step forward, gentlemen, and unroll this facsimile transcript of the accounts, so that instead of following the tracks of his veracity the world may now see it

---

64. Verres' successor as governor of Sicily.
65. Since the family names Verres and Verrucius are so similar.

at home in its lair. Do you see the word *Verrucius?* Do you see how the first letters are all right? Do you see the last part of the name, the tail-bit of *Verres* there sunk in the erasure like a pig's tail in the mud?[66] Well, gentlemen, the accounts are what you see they are; what are you waiting for, what more would you have? You yourself, Verres, why are you sitting there doing nothing? Either you must show us Verrucius, you know, or you must confess that Verrucius is you.

Cicero, *Second Speech Against Verres* III. xv. 38–xvi. 40; From *LCL*

And then for a thing which violates not only the code of Hiero [see note 52], not only the usage of previous governors, but all the rights which the Sicilians enjoy as the gift of the Roman senate and people, whereby no man may be required to post bond for his appearance in court beyond the limits of his own district. Verres ordained that a farmer must post bond to appear in court wherever the tithe collector might choose, so that Apronius[67] might summon a man to go for this purpose all the way from Leontini to Lilybaeum, and thus make a further profit out of the unhappy farmers by bringing false actions against them.[68]

However, for making profit out of false actions there was another especially ingenious method devised, the regulation that farmers should make returns of their acreage under crops. This, as I will explain, was highly effective for compelling unjust settlements with the collectors, and tended in no way to the public advantage; but, besides that, it was effective in involving all whom Apronius chose to involve in these false accusations. No sooner did a man express opposition to his wishes, than a summons was applied for against him on the charge of making an untrue return of acreage: and fear of prosecution on this charge led to large quantities of grain being carried off, and large sums of money extorted, from a great many people. Not that there was any difficulty

66. There is a play on the word *verrinam,* which means both "belonging to Verres" and "belonging to a pig." The erasure produced a slight trough or depression in the wax surface of the tablet, in which the obliterated final letters were thus "sunk."

67. Apronius was introduced a few chapters earlier in this speech (viii. 21–ix. 22): Verres "appointed certain persons to be nominally tithe collectors but really the servants and ministers of his own greedy passions, by whose agency, as I will show you, gentlemen, the province has for three years been so thoroughly ravaged and devastated that not even after many years and a succession of honest and able governors shall we be able to repair the damage done. Of all the persons thus entitled tithe collectors, the foremost was the notorious Quintus Apronius." (Quoted from the Loeb Classical Library.)

68. The implication is, of course, that the victim, to avoid a long and costly journey, would pay Apronius to withdraw the summons against him.

about reporting the acreage as what it was or even more than it was; that was of course safe enough. No, but the charge alleged in the application for the summons was that the regulation had been disobeyed and no return made at all. You cannot but be aware of what sort of hearing such charges would get when Verres was praetor, if you bear in mind the character of his staff and personal following.

Now, gentlemen, what is the point that I wish to make clear regarding the result of these iniquitous new regulations? The wrong done to our allies? You see that for yourselves. The man's repudiation of the authority of his predecessors' decisions? This he will not dare deny. The vast power, during his governorship, enjoyed by Apronius? He cannot help admitting this. But it may be that in this connection you will ask, as the law bids you ask, whether he had made money himself out of these doings. I will prove that he has made a great deal. I will establish the fact that all the iniquities I have already referred to were devised by him for his personal profit.

145. A Scrupulous Governor

In 51–50 B.C. Cicero served a year as governor of the province of Cilicia, which included the island of Cyprus. Though reluctant to accept his assignment to this remote cultural backwater, once committed to the office he prided himself that he would give his province exemplary government: "I have bound myself to it." he wrote (*To Atticus* book VI, no. 1), "by the principles of government expressed in my six books *[The Republic]*."

Cicero's case is therefore particularly instructive as showing, first, the kinds of established abuses which the occasional honest governor had to eradicate and, second, the limited degree to which he could succeed because of his personal and political ties with the men of the senatorial and equestrian classes who were exploiting the provinces. Foremost among the latter were, of course, the publicans. Of the numerous references in Cicero's voluminous writings to his close relations with the Roman tax farmers and the favors he has done them (and they him), none is so revealing, perhaps, as the letter to his former son-in-law, Publius Furius Crassipes, who was then quaestor in the province of Bithynia.

In the wake of the publicans, to batten on the hapless provincials, came the loan sharks. In addition to *equites,* members of the Roman nobility frequently engaged in this lucrative business, though usually through silent partners. Thus, the city of Salamis in Cyprus was harried by a pair of moneylenders who came with letters of recommendation from Marcus

Brutus to bespeak Cicero's good will and assistance in collecting their loan plus interest at 48 percent. These men were, it seems, agents for Brutus, who had advanced the money: the "idealistic" tyrannicide-to-be was no different from the other gentlemen of the senatorial order in regarding the provinces as fair game for all that the traffic would bear. As for Cicero, he again found himself torn between principle and personal ties, and as usual the former suffered in the conflict. Disapproving thoroughly of such usurious extortion, yet not wishing to offend Brutus by finding in favor of the provincials, he compromised by leaving the matter in abeyance for his successor in office to settle (cf. also § 140).

Cicero, *Letters to Atticus* book v, no. 16; Adapted from *LCL*

Cilicia, c. August 10, 51 B.C.

Cicero to Atticus, greeting.

Though the tax farmers' messengers are actually on their road and I am traveling, still I think I must snatch a moment for fear you may imagine I have forgotten your commission. So I sit down on the high-road to scribble you a summary of what really calls for a long epistle.

My arrival in this province, which is in a state of lasting ruin and desolation, was expected eagerly. I stayed three days at Laodicea, three at Apamea, and as many at Synnas, and got here on July 31. Everywhere I heard the same story: people could not pay the poll tax; they were forced to sell out; the townspeople groaned and lamented—and all the result of the outrages of one who is no man, but rather some kind of savage beast.[69] All the people are, as you may suppose, tired of life. However, the unhappy towns are relieved that they have had to spend nothing on me, my legates, a quaestor, or anyone. For I want you to know that I not only refused to accept money or any proper perquisite under the Julian Law,[70] but none of us will take firewood or anything beyond four beds and a roof; and in many places we do not accept even a roof, but remain mostly under canvas. So, extraordinary throngs of people have come to meet me from farms and villages and every homestead. Upon my word, my very coming seems to revive them. Your friend Cicero has won all hearts by his justice, self-restraint and kind bearing. . . .

69. Appius Claudius Pulcher, Cicero's predecessor as governor of Cilicia.

70. A far-reaching law of Caesar's consulship (59 B.C.) which, among other things, limited the contributions that could be demanded from the provincials by governors and their retinues.

Cicero, *Letters to Friends* book XIII, no. 9; Adapted from *LCL*

Cilicia, toward the end of 51 B.C.

Cicero to Crassipes, greeting.

Although I recommended the Bithynian company to you in person as particularly as I could and understood that not only because of my recommendation, but also because that was your own inclination, you were anxious to accommodate that company in any way you could, still, since those whose interests are in question thought it of paramount importance to them that I should make it plain to you by letter also how I felt towards them, I have not hesitated to write you this note.

I would have you believe that while it has always been the greatest pleasure to me to make much of the class of publicans as a whole—and considering the great services that class has rendered me, I am under obligation to do so—I am in a special sense a friend of this Bithynian company. This company, made up of members from all the other companies, constitutes a most important factor in the state by virtue of the kind of men who compose it and the class to which they belong; and, as it happens, a large proportion of its partners are on very intimate terms with myself, especially the man who is at this moment the executive head, namely Publius Rutilius son of Publius, of the Menenian tribe, who is the manager of that company.

Such being the case, I entreat you with more than usual urgency to support with every kindness and all your generosity Gnaeus Pupius, who is in the company's employ; to see to it that his services (you will find it easy to do so) are as acceptable as possible to the partners; and to exert yourself (and how much power a quaestor has in such matters I am well aware) to protect and augment the property and interests of those partners as much as possible. Not only will you greatly oblige me by so doing, but I can promise and pledge you from my own experience that, if you oblige them, you will find the Bithynian partners neither forgetful nor ungrateful.

Cicero, *Letters to Atticus* book V, no. 21 (abridged); Adapted from *LCL*

Laodicea, February 13, 50 B.C.

Cicero to Atticus, greeting.

. . . During the six months of my administration there have been no requisitions and not a single case of billeting. Before my time this season had been devoted each year to the pursuit of gain. The richer towns used to pay large sums to escape from having soldiers billeted on them for the winter. The people of Cyprus, for example, used to pay 200 Attic talents, but under my administration they will appropriate, in literal truth, not a penny. I will accept no honors except speechifying in return for these kindnesses which have so amazed people. I permit no statues, shrines, or sculptured chariots;[71] and I don't annoy the communities in any other respect—but perhaps I annoy you by my egotism. Bear with it out of your regard for me: it was you who wished me to act as I have. My tour through Asia was such that even the crowning misery of famine, which existed in my province owing to crop failure, gave me a welcome opportunity: wherever I went, without force, without resort to legal process, without harsh words, by my personal influence and exhortations, I induced the Greeks and the Roman citizens who had stored grain to promise a large quantity to the communities. . . .

Now let me tell you about Brutus. Some creditors of the city of Salamis in Cyprus, namely Marcus Scaptius and Publius Matinius, were warmly recommended to me by your friend Brutus as being associates of his. Matinius I have not met; Scaptius came to see me in camp. I promised that I would see to it, for Brutus' sake, that the people of Salamis paid him his money. The fellow thanked me and asked for the post of prefect. I informed him that I always refused to appoint business-men to my staff, as I have told you. This rule Gnaeus Pompey accepted when he made a similar request. So did Torquatus, Marcus Laenius, and many others. However, I told Scaptius that if he wanted the post on account of his loan, I would see that he got paid. He thanked me and took his leave. Our friend Appius [see note 69] had given him some squadrons to put pressure on Salamis, and had also given him the office of prefect. He was causing trouble to the people of Salamis. I gave orders that his cavalry should leave the island. That annoyed him.

In short, to keep faith with him I ordered the people, when they came along with Scaptius to see me at Tarsus, to pay the money. They had a good deal to say about the loan, and about the harm that Scaptius had done them. I refused to listen. I prayed and besought them to settle the business in consideration of the good I had done their city. Finally I threatened to compel them. So far from refusing to settle, the people said that really they would be paying out of my pocket, in the sense that I had refused to take the honorarium usually given to the governor,

---

71. That is, to be erected in his honor. This was one of the practices to which the provinces had recourse in their attempts to win the favor of the all-powerful proconsuls and other officials who came to govern them. The inscribed bases of many such statues are extant today. Cf. also note 61.

which they admitted was more than the amount they owed Scaptius. I praised their attitude. "Very well," said Scaptius, "let us reckon up the total." Now in my traditional edict[72] I had fixed the rate of interest at 12 percent compounded annually. But Scaptius demanded 48 percent in accordance with the terms of the loan. I declared that I could not break the rule laid down in my edict. But he produced a decree of the senate, passed in the consulship of Lentulus and Philippus [56 B.C.], ordering the governor of Cilicia to give judgment according to the terms of this contract!

At first I was horror-stricken, for it spelled ruin to the community. I find, however, that there are two decrees of the senate in the same year about this identical contract. When the people of Salamis wanted to raise a loan at Rome to pay off another, they were hampered by the Gabinian Law. Then these friends of Brutus, depending on his political influence, professed willingness to lend at 48 percent if they were protected by a decree of the senate. Brutus induced the senate to decree that the transaction between the people of Salamis and the moneylenders should be exempt from the provisions of the law. They put up the money. Afterwards it came into the heads of the moneylenders that this decree would be futile, because the Gabinian Law forbade any legal process on the basis of the contract. The senate then passed a decree that the contract should be admissible in court, giving this loan the same validity as others and no more. When I pointed this out, Scaptius took me aside. He said that he had no objection to my ruling; but that the people of Salamis imagined they owed him 200 talents and he wanted to get that sum, although they really owed rather less. He begged me to induce them to fix it at that amount. "Very well," said I. I sent Scaptius away, and summoned the people and asked them the amount of the debt. They replied, "106 talents." I consulted Scaptius again. He was loud in his protests. I said that the only plan was for them to check their accounts. They sat down and made out the account. It agreed to the penny with their statement. They wanted to pay and begged him to accept the money. Again Scaptius led me aside, and asked me to let the matter stand over. The request was impertinent, but I consented. I would not listen to the complaints of the Greeks and their demand to deposit the sum in the temple treasury.[73] The bystanders all declared that the conduct of Scaptius was outrageous in refusing 12 percent compound inter-

---

72. The *edictum tralaticium*, on which see pp. 38–39.
73. Interest would cease to run from the time of such depositing of the money.

est. Others said he was a fool. He seemed to me to be more of a knave than a fool: for either he was not content with 12 percent on good security, or he hoped for 48 percent on very doubtful security.

146. Punishment of Culpable Officials

Roman officials and businessmen operated abroad secure in the knowledge that there was little likelihood of their ever being brought to account for their actions. The creation, in 149 B.C., of a permanent court to try charges of extortion brought against provincial governors marked no great improvement for the complainants. Convictions remained difficult to obtain, for the charges concerned the common practices of an entire class; the likelihood of an accused being convicted by a jury of past or potential perpetrators of similar acts was not great (see further introduction to § 158). Moreover, in the rare cases where a conviction was obtained, the guilty defendant could still keep his loot by going into exile. "Condemned by a futile verdict (for what matters public disgrace if the cash be kept?), the exiled Marius[74] drinks from the eighth hour of the day and revels in the wrath of heaven, while you, poor province, win your case and weep" (Juvenal, *Satires* I. 47–50).

In short, the prosecution of Roman officials for malfeasance in the provinces was generally determined by personal and political enmities (cf. §§ 100, 158) and other extraneous considerations rather than by the demands of impartial justice. The most fully documented of these trials is the successful prosecution of Verres by Cicero (see §§ 143–144). Two other cases of considerable interest figure below. The first selection shows that as late as 140 B.C. the primitive *disciplina domestica,* the judicial competence exercised by the *paterfamilias* (cf. § 8), still survived as an extraordinary procedure. But if it was difficult to obtain the conviction of a provincial administrator, it was infinitely more so to prosecute successfully a general for acts committed in war (cf § 79). One of the rare exceptions is the case of Marcus Aurelius Cotta, who, in the war with Mithridates, burned Heraclea and plundered it for his own enrichment (70 B.C.). Lucullus, the commander-in-chief of the war against Mithridates, was at this time urging a policy of generous treatment for the captured cities of Asia Minor in order to convert them into reliable pro-Roman outposts. The conviction of Cotta was thus politically expedient, and he was brought to trial in 67 B.C. for exceeding his authority. Unwilling, however, to condemn him to the full penalty of exile, the Romans sentenced him to loss of senatorial rank.

74. Marius Priscus, condemned in A.D. 100 for extortion in the province of Africa.

THE DOMESTIC TRIAL OF SILANUS

Valerius Maximus, *Memorable Deeds and Sayings* v. viii. 3

Titus Manlius Torquatus[75] enjoyed a rare reputation because of many outstanding deeds, and was also very learned in civil law and pontifical lore. . . . When the province of Macedonia sent envoys to the senate to complain against the administration of his son, Decimus Silanus, in that province, Torquatus begged the conscript fathers not to make any decision in the matter until he had personally examined the case of the Macedonians and that of his son. With the unanimous consent not only of that honorable body, but also of the plaintiffs themselves, he opened the inquiry, sitting in his house as sole judge. He devoted two whole days to hearing both sides, and on the third day, after listening to the witnesses most carefully to the very end, he pronounced the following sentence:

"It having been proved to my satisfaction that my son Silanus took money from the allies, I judge him unworthy both of the Republic and of my house, and order him forthwith to depart from my sight."

Overcome by this terrible sentence from his father, Silanus could no longer endure to look upon the light and took his life by hanging that very night. Torquatus had now carried out the duties of a severe and scrupulous judge: the Republic had been satisfied and Macedonia had its revenge.

THE CONVICTION OF COTTA

Memnon,[76] *History of Heraclea* Fragment 59

When Cotta returned to Rome he was honored by the senate with the title of Ponticus, because he had captured Heraclea. But when an accusation was brought to Rome charging him with having sacked so great a city for his own private profit, he incurred public odium and his great wealth aroused envy. Therefore, in an attempt to dispel the envy caused by his wealth, he brought many of the spoils into the Roman treasury; but he thereby made them no whit more kindly disposed toward him,

75. Pontiff since 170 B.C., consul in 165.

76. Memnon of Heraclea, who lived after the time of Caesar but before that of Hadrian, was the author of a history of his native city.

since they suspected that he was dispensing with but a few of his many spoils and they voted that the Heraclean captives should at once be set free.

Thrasymedes, one of those from Heraclea, accused Cotta before an assembly.[77] He recalled his city's evidences of good will toward the Romans and remarked that if there had been any decline therein it was not the voluntary doing of the city, but was the result either of treachery on the part of some of their magistrates[78] or of the exigencies imposed by the siege. He bewailed the burning of the city and all the property destroyed by the fire, telling how Cotta pulled down the statues and took them as loot, how he razed the temples, and all the other cruelties he perpetrated, and describing the untold gold and silver of the city and the other wealth of Heraclea that he had appropriated. When Thrasymedes finished his mournful and tearful recital, the leading men burst into tears at the calamity, which was symbolized before their eyes by the throng of captives present—men, women, and children in mourning garb, lamenting and holding forth suppliant branches. Then Cotta in turn came forward, spoke a few words in his native tongue,[79] and sat down. Carbo thereupon arose and said, "We ordered you to capture the city, not destroy it;" and after him others similarly blamed Cotta.[80] Many judged Cotta deserving of exile, but they moderated the sentence and voted to expel him from the senate. To the people of Heraclea they restored their territory, their maritime rights, and their harbors, and decreed that none of them should be a slave.

147. EXPRESSIONS OF ANTI-ROMAN FEELING

It was no secret to the Romans that their economic and political policies had won them the profound hatred of the provincials and "allied" peoples, as the following passages from Cicero clearly show (cf. also §§ 141, 188).

77. Except in cases of extortion and a few other major offenses, for which special courts had been created, the centuriate assembly retained jurisdiction over criminal malfeasance; cf. §§ 141 (first selection), 149, 154, and introduction to 158.

78. That is, those who aligned the city with Mithridates against Rome.

79. A Roman would naturally speak Latin before the assembly at Rome. Memnon is thinking of the arrogance of Roman officials in their dealing with the Greeks, whom they also addressed in Latin (see §§ 74, 185).

80. An interesting footnote is provided by Cassius Dio (*Roman History* XXXVI. xl. 4): "But when Carbo himself later became governor of Bithynia and erred no less than Cotta, he was in turn accused by Cotta's sons and convicted."

This hatred of Rome was expressed in various ways in the Graeco-Oriental world. One was the regularity with which the lower classes aligned themselves with any leader who arose to challenge the Roman power—Philip V, Antiochus, Perseus, Aristonicus, Mithridates (see §§ 71, 72, 120; introduction to § 128). Another was in the composition of a tendentious literature, consisting chiefly of wishful prophecies forecasting a day of reckoning and doom for the proud city on the Tiber that ruled the Mediterranean world.

The selection from Phlegon's *Amazing Stories* is recorded as an extract—probably authentic—from a work by the Peripatetic philosopher Antisthenes, a contemporary of Polybius. The dramatic date of this piece is during the war with Antiochus and the scene is laid in Aetolia, the leading center of Greek hostility to Rome at that time, but it was obviously composed somewhat later, probably about the time when Greek aspirations for the overthrow of Rome centered around Perseus. The last selection dates from the first century B.C., and probably from the period of the Mithridatic Wars. Though preserved in that curious potpourri of Jewish–Christian apocalyptic material known as the *Sibylline Oracles,* it is in its present form merely a reworking, with Messianic overtones, of a prophecy originating among the Greeks of Asia Minor. About 12 B.C. Augustus had over 2,000 anonymous or unauthorized prophetic books confiscated and burned (Suetonius, *Life of August* xxxi. 1), and according to St. Justin (*Apology* I. xx. 1, xliv. 12) the Romans forbade the reading of such oracles on pain of death.

A SOBER WARNING

Cicero, *Second Speech Against Verres* III. lxxxix; Adapted from *LCL*

All the provinces are mourning, all the autonomous communities are complaining, indeed all foreign kingdoms even are protesting over Roman greed and Roman injustice. Within the bounds of Ocean there is no longer any place so distant or so out of the way that the wanton and oppressive deeds of our countrymen have not penetrated there in recent years. Rome can no longer hold out against the whole world—I do not mean against its power and arms in war, but against its groans and tears and lamentations. When such are the facts and such the prevailing moral standards, if any prosecuted person, upon his crimes being clearly demonstrated, shall plead that others have done the like, he will not find himself without precedents; but Rome will find herself without hope of escaping doom if scoundrels are to secure acquittal and impunity on the precedents set by other scoundrels. Are you satisfied with the prevailing moral standards? satisfied that our governors shall govern as they do? satisfied that our allies shall be treated in the future as you have seen them treated in recent years?

Cicero, *In Favor of the Manilian Law* xxii. 65–xxiii. 68 (abridged)

Words cannot express, gentlemen, how bitterly we are hated among foreign nations owing to the wanton and outrageous conduct of the men whom of late years we have sent to govern them. For in those countries what temple do you suppose has been held sacred by our officers, what state inviolable, what home sufficiently guarded by its closed doors? Why, they look about for rich and flourishing cities that they may find an occasion of a war against them to satisfy their lust for plunder. . . . Do you imagine that when you send an army, it is to defend our allies and attack the enemy—or to use the enemy as an excuse for attacking your allies and friends? What state in Asia is sufficient to contain the arrogance and insolence of a single military tribune, let alone a general or his legate?[81] Wherefore, even if you possess a general who seems capable of vanquishing the royal army [of Mithridates] in a pitched battle, still, unless he be also capable of withholding his hands, his eyes, his thoughts from the wealth of our allies, from their wives and children, from the adornments of temples and of cities, from the gold and treasure of kings, he will not be a suitable man to be sent to the war against an Asiatic monarch. . . . Pompey owes his greatness not to his own merits alone but also to the demerits of other men. Then hesitate no longer to entrust supreme command to this one man, the only general found in all these years whom our allies rejoice to receive with his army into their cities.

PROPHECIES OF DOOM

Phlegon,[82] *Amazing Stories* iii (abridged)

In the encounter with Antiochus at Thermopylae most remarkable portents appeared to the Romans. For after Antiochus had made his appearance and fled, on the next day the Romans went about picking up the bodies of those of their army who had fallen and collecting spoils, arms,

81. The higher the Roman official, the greater was his retinue, and the greater, accordingly, would be his demands upon the cities through which he passed for lodgings, food, and entertainment. On the abuses that Roman officers made of this requisitioning power, see also, for example, §§ 141, 145.

82. Publius Aelius Phlegon of Tralles, a freedman of the Emperor Hadrian (A.D. 117–138).

and prisoners of war. Now one Buplagus, a cavalry commander of the Syrian army and a man held in high esteem by King Antiochus, was among those who had fallen after a valiant struggle. At noon, as the Romans were taking up all the booty, Buplagus, bearing the marks of twelve wounds, arose from among the corpses, came to their camp, and in a thin voice uttered the following verses:

"Leave off stripping an army proceeding into the land of Hades,
For already the son of Cronus, Zeus, is displeased at the sight of
    such mischief,
He is wroth at the slaughter of the army and at your works,
And he will send a stout-hearted host into your land,
Who will end your rule and will requite what you have wrought."

Alarmed at these words, the generals quickly summoned the army to an assembly and took counsel concerning the apparition. It was decided first to cremate Buplagus, who had expired immediately after speaking these words, and bury him with due honors, next to cleanse the army and offer sacrifice to Jupiter the Averter of Woe, and then to send to Delphi to ask the god what ought to be done. When the envoys had come to Delphi and made inquiry as to what was to be done, the Pythia uttered this response:

"Now hold! Roman, let the right be abiding,
Lest Pallas rouse against you a much mightier slaughter
And make desolate your market places. And you, senseless one,
    after much toil,
Will come to your land after destroying much wealth."

On hearing this utterance they gave up all intention of marching against any of those dwelling in Europe. Instead, they marched away from the above-mentioned place and came to Naupactus in Aetolia, where there is a common sanctuary of the Greeks; here they made ready public sacrifices and first fruits according to custom.

As these rites were being performed, the general Publius[83] went raving mad and gave voice to a number of inspired utterances, some in verse, others in prose. Word of this happening spread through the ranks, and all came running up to Publius' tent. . . . The words he spoke in verse, while still in his tent, were the following:

---

83. That is, Scipio Africanus. The whole story, it need hardly be added, is fanciful, and Scipio is chosen to utter the prophecies in order to lend them greater weight.

"O my country, what a baneful war Athena is bringing you
When after ravaging very wealthy Asia you return
To the Italian land and its cities circled with towers
And the lovely island of Thrinacia [Sicily] that Zeus created.
For an army far the mightiest will come, stout of heart,
From afar out of Asia, where is the rising of the sun:
A king, crossing the narrow strait of Hellespont,
Will strike a sworn alliance with the lord of Epirus;[84]
Leading an army without number, collected
From all quarters out of Asia and lovely Europe,
He will overpower you, will leave your houses and walls desolate,
And slavery for all, the day of freedom lost,
Will be your lot because of magnanimous Athena's wrath."

After declaring these verses he rushed from his tent in his tunic . . .
and cried out in a loud voice: "I see bronze-breasted forces, kings united
in common purpose, and nations of all sorts crossing from Asia into
Europe, the clatter of horses' hoofs, the crashing of spears, bloody
slaughter, terrible pillage, toppling towers, razing of walls, and an indescribable desolation of the land." After this he resumed in verse:

"When white Nisaean horses with frontlets of gold
Walk upon the divine earth, forsaking their fixed abode . . .
Then, Rome, shall all grievous woes befall you.
For a massive host will come, which will destroy your whole land:
It will make desolate the market places, lay waste cities with fire,
Fill rivers with blood, yea, and fill Hades too,
And establish pitiful, hateful, dark slavery.
Nor shall a woman welcome back her spouse from war
Returning, but Hades, infernal, black-clad,
Will have him among the dead, taking children, too, from their
        mothers,
And war will bring a day of enslavement unto foreign masters."

After uttering these words he fell silent, and marching out of the
camp he climbed up a tree. The throng followed him, and he called to
them and said: "Romans, and other soldiers, I am to die and be devoured
by a big, red wolf this very day. As for you, be assured that all I have

---

84. Probably the king Perseus is meant; cf. introduction to this section. A possible anti-Roman
coalition of two or more Hellenistic monarchs was the constant nightmare under which Roman foreign
policy was shaped in the second century B.C.; cf. § 91.

prophesied for you will come to pass; and you may take the imminent appearance of the wolf and my destruction as proofs that I have spoken the truth at the prompting of some god." He then bade them stand back and not prevent the animal from approaching, adding that it would do them no good to turn it away. The crowd did as he ordered, and presently the wolf arrived. Seeing it, Publius came down from his tree and fell on his back. The wolf rent him asunder and devoured him in the sight of all, and, after consuming the whole body except the head, returned to the mountain. The throng rushed forward, wishing to take up the remains and give them due burial, but the head lying on the ground pronounced the following verses:

"Touch not our head, for it is not meet —
Athena has planted fierce wrath in her heart —
To touch a sacred head. But hold,
And hear the true prophecy I shall tell you.
There will come to this land a great and mighty war
Which will send the armed [Roman] host to Hades beneath the
    shadow,
Will shatter anew stone towers and lofty walls,
And laying hold of our wealth, our helpless children, and our
    wives,
Will carry them away to Asia across the wave.
These unerring truths are vouchsafed you by Phoebus Apollo
The Pythian, who, sending his mighty servant to me,
Led me to the abodes of the blessed and of Persephone."

Sibylline Oracles III. 350–380; From H. N. Bate, *The Sibylline Oracles, Books* III–V
(London, 1937)

For all the wealth that Rome took from tributary Asia, three times as much shall Asia take from Rome, requiting upon her her cursed arrogance: and for all the men from Asia made household slaves in Italy, twenty times so many men of Italy shall serve in Asia as penniless slaves, and a thousandfold shall be the requital.

Daughter of Latin, Rome, clothed in gold and luxury, drunken full oft with thy wedding of many wooers, thou shalt be a slave-bride in dishonor, and oft shall thy mistress cut off thy flowing hair, and do justice on thee and cast thee down from heaven to earth, and yet again lift thee from earth to heaven, because men gave themselves to evil and unrighteous living.

And Samos shall become a sand, Delos be deleted, and Rome a mere roadway; and all that is foretold shall be fulfilled; but none shall take account of the ruin of Smyrna. There shall be an avenger, but through evil counsels and the cowardice of her leaders . . . and calm peace shall make her way to the land of Asia: and Europe then shall be blessed, the air fruitful year after year, healthy, without frost or hail, bringing forth all the beasts and birds and creeping things of the earth. Most blessed shall the man and woman be who live to see that time . . . for the reign of law and justice shall come from the starry heaven upon men, and with them wise concord, best of all gifts for mortals, and love and faith and hospitable ways; and lawlessness, blame, envy, anger, madness, and poverty shall flee from among men, in those days pain too shall flee, and murder and accursed strife and grievous wrangling, and theft by night and every ill.

7

THE ADMINISTRATION OF THE
IMPERIAL REPUBLIC:
THE GOVERNMENT AT ROME

148. THE ADMINISTRATION OF THE REPUBLIC

In imitation of Plato, Cicero sets down here the framework of the Roman political system, mingling ideals with actual institutions and practices.

Cicero, Laws III. iii–iv; Adapted from *LCL*

Commands shall be just, and the citizens shall obey them dutifully and without protest. Upon the disobedient or guilty citizen the magistrate shall use compulsion by means of fines, imprisonment, or lashing, unless an equal or higher authority or the people, to which the citizens shall have the right of appeal, forbids it. After the magistrate has made judicial examination and pronounced sentence, there shall be a trial before the people for the final determination of the fine or other penalty. There shall be no appeal from decisions of the commander in the field; while a magistrate is waging war his commands shall be valid and binding.

There shall be minor magistrates with partial authority, who shall be assigned to special functions. In the army they shall command those over whom they are placed, and be their tribunes; in the city they shall be custodians of public moneys [quaestors]; they shall have charge of the confinement of criminals; they shall inflict capital punishment;[1] they

---

1. *Triumviri capitales* (three-man board for capital cases); they also assisted generally in the maintenance of public order.

shall coin bronze, silver, and gold money;[2] they shall decide lawsuits;[3] they shall do whatsoever the senate decrees.

There shall also be aediles, who shall be caretakers of the city, of the markets, and of the traditional games. This magistracy shall be their first step in the advancement to higher office.

Censors shall make a list of the citizens, recording their ages, families, and slaves and other property. They shall have charge of the temples, streets, and aqueducts within the city, and of the public treasury and the revenues. They shall make a division of the citizens into tribes, and other divisions according to wealth, age, and class. They shall enroll the recruits for the cavalry and infantry; they shall prohibit celibacy; they shall regulate the morals of the people; they shall allow no one guilty of dishonorable conduct to remain in the senate. They shall be two in number and shall hold office for five years. The other magistrates shall hold office for one year. The office of censor shall never be vacant.[4]

The administrator of justice, who shall decide or direct the decision of civil cases, shall be called praetor; he shall be the guardian of the civil law. There shall be as many praetors, with equal powers, as the senate shall decree or the people command.

There shall be two magistrates with royal powers. Since they precede, judge, and consult, from these functions they shall be called praetors, judges, and consuls.[5] In the field they shall hold the supreme military power and shall be subject to no one. The safety of the people shall be their highest law.

No one shall hold the same office a second time except after an interval of ten years. They shall observe the age limits for the several offices, as fixed by the law on the subject.

But when a serious war or civil dissensions arise, one man shall hold, for not longer than six months, the power which ordinarily belongs to the two consuls, if the senate shall so decree. And after being appointed under favorable auspices, he shall be master of the people [dictator; see § 37]. He shall have an assistant to command the cavalry,[6] whose rank shall be equal to that of the administrator of justice.

But when there are neither consuls nor a master of the people, there

---

2. *Triumviri aere argento auro flando feriundo* (three-man board for casting and striking bronze, silver, and gold).

3. *Decemviri litibus iudicandis* (ten-man board for judging cases).

4. This was not actual Roman practice. See chapter 3, note 43.

5. On the etymology of "praetor" and "consul," see § 26.

6. *Magister equitum* (master of the horse); cf. § 26.

shall be no other magistrates, and the auspices shall be in the hands of the senate, which shall appoint one of its number [the *interrex*] to conduct the election of consuls in the customary manner.

Officials with and without *imperium* and ambassadors shall leave the city when the senate shall so decree or the people so command; they shall wage just wars justly; they shall spare the allies; they shall hold themselves and their subordinates in check [cf. § 140]; they shall increase the national renown; they shall return home with honor.

No one shall be made an ambassador for the purpose of attending to his own personal affairs [cf. § 142].

The ten officials whom the plebeians shall elect to protect them from violence shall be their tribunes. Their prohibitions and resolutions passed by the plebeians under their presidency shall be binding. Their persons shall be inviolable. They shall not leave the plebeians without tribunes.

All magistrates shall possess the right of taking the auspices, and the judicial power. The senate shall consist of those who have held magistracies. Its decrees shall be binding. But in case an equal or higher authority than the presiding officer shall veto a decree of the senate, it shall nevertheless be written out and preserved.

The senatorial order shall be free from dishonor, and shall be a model for the rest of the citizens.

When elective, judicial, and legislative acts of the people are performed by vote, the people shall enjoy freedom of the ballot, but shall reveal their votes to *optimates* [cf. § 154].

But if any acts of administration shall be necessary in addition to those done by the regular magistrates, the people shall elect officials to perform them, and give them the authority to do so.

Consuls, praetors, masters of the people, masters of the horse, and those officials whom the senate shall appoint to conduct the election of consuls shall have the right to preside over meetings of the people and the senate. The tribunes chosen by the plebeians shall have the right to preside over the senate and shall also refer whatever is necessary to the plebeians.

Moderation shall be preserved in meetings of the people and the senate.

A senator's absence from a meeting of the senate shall be either for cause or culpable. A senator shall speak in his turn and at moderate length. He shall be conversant with public affairs.

No violence shall be used at meetings of the people. An equal or higher authority than the presiding officer shall have the greater power [i.e., to veto measures passed in a popular assembly]. But the presiding officer shall be responsible for any disorder which may occur. He who vetoes a bad measure shall be deemed a citizen of distinguished service.

Presiding officers shall observe the auspices and obey the state augur [cf. §§ 48, 175]. They shall see that bills, after being read, are filed among the archives in the state treasury. They shall not take the people's vote on more than one question at a time. They shall instruct the people in regard to the matter at hand, and allow them to be instructed by other magistrates and by private citizens.

No law of personal exception shall be proposed. Cases in which the penalty is death or loss of citizenship shall be tried only before the greatest assembly and by those whom the censors have enrolled among the citizens.

No one shall give or receive a present, either during a candidacy[7] or during or after a term of office.

The punishment for violation of any of these laws shall fit the offense.

The censors shall have charge of the official text of the laws. When officials go out of office, they shall report their official acts to censors but shall not receive exemption from prosecution thereby.

149. THE REPUBLICAN CONSTITUTION AT ITS HEIGHT

Polybius, *Histories* VI. xi–xviii; Adapted from *LCL*

[The Roman constitution] was always one of those polities which were objects of special study, and it was at its best and nearest to perfection at the time of the Hannibalic War, the period at which I interrupted my narrative to deal with it. Therefore, now that I have described its growth, I shall try to explain what were the conditions of the time when by their defeat at Cannae the Romans were brought face to face with disaster. . . .

The three kinds of government that I spoke above all shared in the control of the Roman state. And such fairness and propriety in all respects was shown in the use of these three elements for drawing up the constitution and in its subsequent administration that it was impossible even for a native to pronounce with certainty whether the whole system was aristocratic, democratic, or monarchical. This was indeed

7. Cf. the charter of the colony Genetiva Julia (§ 162), XCIII and CXXXII.

only natural. For if one fixed one's eyes on the power of the consuls, the constitution seemed completely monarchical and royal; if on that of the senate, it seemed again to be aristocratic; and when one looked at the power of the masses, it seemed clearly to be a democracy. The parts of the state falling under the control of each element were and with a few modifications still are as follows.

The consuls, previous to leading out their legions, exercise authority in Rome over all public affairs, since all the other magistrates except the tribunes are under them and bound to obey them, and it is they who introduce embassies to the senate. Besides this, it is they who consult the senate on matters of urgency, they who carry out in detail the provisions of its decrees. Again, as concerns all affairs of state performed by the people, it is their duty to take these under their charge, to summon assemblies, to introduce measures, and to preside over the execution of the popular decrees. As for preparation for war and the general conduct of operations in the field, here their power is almost uncontrolled, for they are empowered to make what demands they choose on the allies, to appoint military tribunes, to levy soldiers, and to select those who are fittest for service. They also have the right of inflicting, when on active service, punishment on anyone under their command; and they are authorized to spend any sum they decide upon from the public funds, being accompanied by a quaestor who faithfully executes their instructions. So that if one looks at this part of the administration alone, one may reasonably pronounce the constitution to be a pure monarchy or kingship. . . .

To pass to the senate. In the first place, it has the control of the treasury, all revenue and expenditure being regulated by it. For with the exception of payments made to the consuls, the quaestors are not allowed to make any disbursement for any particular object without a decree of the senate. And even the item of expenditure which is far heavier and more important than any other—the outlay every five years by the censors on public works, whether construction or repairs—is under the control of the senate, which makes a grant to the censors for the purpose. Similarly, crimes committed in Italy which require a public investigation, such as treason, conspiracy, poisoning, and assassination, are under the jurisdiction of the senate. Also if any private person or community in Italy is in need of arbitration or indeed claims damages or requires succor or protection, the senate attends to all such matters. It also occupies itself with the dispatch of all embassies sent to countries outside Italy for the purposes either of settling differences, or of offering friendly advice, or indeed of imposing demands, or of receiving submission, or of declaring war; and in like manner with respect to embassies arriving in Rome it decides what reception and what answer should be given to them. All these matters are in the hands of the senate, nor have the people anything whatever to do with them. So that again, to one residing in Rome during the absence of the consuls, the constitution appears to be entirely aristocratic; and this is the conviction of many Greek states and many of the kings, as the senate manages practically all business connected with them.

After this we are naturally inclined to ask what part in the constitution is left for the people, considering that the senate controls all the particular matters I have mentioned (and most important, manages all matters of revenues and expenditure), and considering too that the consuls have uncontrolled authority as regards preparations for war and operations in the field. But nevertheless there is a part, and a very important part, left for the people too. For it is the people which alone has the right to confer honors and inflict punishment, the only bonds by which kingdoms and states and in a word all human society are held together. . . . It is by the people, then, in many cases, that offenses punishable by a fine are tried, especially when the accused have held the highest office; and they are the only court which may try capital charges. As regards the latter they have a practice which is praiseworthy and should be mentioned. Their usage allows those on trial for their lives when found guilty to depart openly, thus inflicting voluntary exile on themselves, if even only one of the tribes pronouncing the verdict has not yet voted. Such exiles enjoy safety in the territories of Naples, Praeneste, Tibur, and other allied states. Again it is the people who bestow office on the deserving, the noblest reward of virtue in a state; the people have the power of approving or rejecting laws, and what is most important of all, they deliberate on the question of war and peace. Further, in the case of alliances, terms of peace, and treaties, it is the people who ratify all these or the reverse. Thus here again one might plausibly say that the people's share in the government is the greatest, and that the constitution is a democratic one.

Having stated how political power is distributed among the different parts of the state, I will now explain how each of the three parts is enabled, if it wishes, to counteract or cooperate with the others. The consul, when he leaves with his army, invested with the powers I have mentioned, appears indeed to have absolute authority in all matters necessary for carrying out his purpose; but in fact he requires the support of the people and the senate, and is not able to bring his operations to a conclusion without them. For it is obvious that the legions require constant supplies, and without the consent of the senate neither grain, clothing, nor pay can be provided for them; so that the commander's plans come to nothing if the senate chooses to be deliberately negligent and obstructive. It also depends on the senate whether or not a general can carry out completely his conceptions and designs, since it has the right of either superseding him when his year's term of office has expired or of retaining him in command. Again it is in its power to celebrate with pomp and to magnify the successes of a general, or on the other hand to obscure and belittle them. For the processions they call triumphs [see § 90], in which the generals bring the actual spectacle of their achievements before the eye of their fellow citizens, cannot be properly organized and sometimes cannot even be held at all, unless the senate consents and provides the requisite funds. As for the people, it is most indispensable for the consuls to conciliate them, however far away from home they may be; for, as I said above, it is the people which ratifies or annuls terms of peace and treaties, and, what is most important, on laying down office the consuls are obliged to submit to the scrutiny of their actions by the people. So that in no respect is it safe for the consuls to neglect keeping in favor with both the senate and the people.

The senate, again, which possesses such great power, is obliged in the first place to pay attention to the people in public affairs and respect the wishes of the people, and it cannot carry out inquiries into the most grave and important offenses against the state, punishable with death, and their correction, unless the decree of the senate is confirmed by the people. The same is the case in matters which directly affect the senate itself. For if anyone introduces a law meant to deprive the senate of some of its traditional authority, or to abolish the precedence and other distinctions of the senators or even to curtail them of their private fortunes, it is the people alone which has the power of passing or rejecting any such measure. And what is most important is that if a single one of the tribunes interposes a veto, the senate is unable to put any of its resolutions into effect and cannot even meet and hold sittings; and here it is to be observed that the tribunes are always obliged to act as the people decree and to pay every attention to their wishes. Therefore, for all these reasons the senate is afraid of the masses and pays due attention to the popular will.

Similarly, again, the people must be submissive to the senate and respect its members both in public and in private. Through the whole of Italy a vast number of contracts, which it would not be easy to enumerate, are given out by the censors for the construction and repair of public works, and besides this there are many sources of revenue which are farmed out, such as navigable rivers, harbors, gardens, mines, lands, in fact everything that forms part of the Roman public domain. Now all these matters are undertaken by the people, and one may say that almost everyone is interested in these contracts and the work they involve. For certain people are the actual purchasers of the contracts from the censors, others are the partners of these first, others stand surety for them, others pledge their own fortunes to the state for this purpose. But in all these matters the senate is supreme. It can grant extension of time; it can relieve the contractor if any accident occurs; and if the work proves to be absolutely impossible to carry out it can release him from his contract. There are in fact many ways in which the senate can either benefit or injure greatly those who manage public property, as all these matters are referred to it. What is even more important is that the judges in most civil trials, either public or private, are appointed from its members, where the action involves large interests. So that all citizens, being at the mercy of the senate, and looking forward with alarm to the uncertainty of litigation, are very shy of obstructing or resisting its decisions. Similarly, everyone is reluctant to oppose the projects of the consuls, as all are individually and collectively under their authority when in the field.

Such being the power that each part has of hampering the others or of cooperating with them, their union is adequate to all emergencies, so that it is impossible to find a better political system than this. For whenever the menace of some common danger from abroad compels them to act in concord and support each other, so great does the strength of the state become that nothing which is requisite is neglected as all are zealously competing in devising means of meeting the need of the hour, nor is any decision put into effect too late, as all are cooperating both in public and in private to accomplish the task they have set themselves; and consequently this peculiar form of constitution possesses an irresistible power of attaining every object upon which it is resolved.

150. EXTENSION OF CITIZENSHIP

Two factors that made for the growth of the Roman state, namely, the granting of citizenship to manumitted slaves and the establishment of colonies (see pp. 67–68, and introduction to § 40), are paid an interesting tribute in this letter sent in 214 B.C. by Philip V of Macedon to the city of Larissa. Against oligarchic resistance, Philip was attempting to remedy the political and economic weaknesses of the Thessalian communities subject to him by encouraging more democratic constitutions through the extension of citizenship.

IG, vol. IX, no. 517 (=Dittenberger, no. 543)

King Philip to the chief magistrates and the city of Larissa, greeting. I learn that those upon whom citizenship was conferred in accordance with the letter sent by me and with your decree, and whose names were inscribed on the stelae, have been stricken from the list of citizens. If, then, this has indeed happened, those who advised you have erred as to what is profitable for your country and as to my decision. For it is best by far when, with as many as possible sharing in the citizenship, the city is strong and the countryside is not, as now, being shamefully deserted. This I think not even any of you would deny; and it is possible to observe others who similarly enroll citizens, among whom are also the Romans, who admit to citizenship even slaves when they manumit them, and grant them a share in the offices.[8] And in this manner they have not only enlarged their own city, but they have also sent out colonies to nearly seventy places.[9] But yet, I even now exhort you to approach the matter without party prejudice and restore to citizenship those chosen by the citizens; and if any of them have committed a grievous offense against the royal power or the city, or for any other reason are not worthy of sharing this stele, to postpone decision about them until I return from the campaign and hear the cases; but give advance warning to those intending to lodge complaints against such, that they may not prove to be doing this for political reasons. Year 7, Gorpiaeus 13 [July or August, 214 B.C.].

8. This is inaccurate. Not the freedmen themselves, but their descendants enjoyed the right of office-holding, until the time of Augustus, who imposed additional restrictions on freedmen.

9. The number is exaggerated. Less than fifty colonies of Latins and Roman citizens are known to have been established up to 214 B.C.

151. On the Retention and Loss of Roman Citizenship

This is a classic statement of the theory of the citizenship privilege. The salient points are these: liberty and citizenship are concomitants for the Romans; no Roman can be deprived of his liberty or citizenship against his will, but only as the result of a deliberate act on his part expressing or implying renunciation; and, as opposed to Hellenistic practice, no Roman can be a citizen of two states. A briefer statement of the first two of these points occurs in Cicero's oration *On His House* xxix. 77–78.

Cicero, *In Defense of Caecina* xxxiii. 96–xxxv. 101; From *LCL*

I ask you: if the people command me to be your slave or you mine, do you think that command would be binding and valid? You realize and you admit that it would be null and void. And in doing so you first of all concede that not everything which the people command ought to be valid; and in the second place you advance no reason why, if liberty cannot possibly be taken away, citizenship can. For we have inherited the same tradition with regard to both, and if once it is possible to take away citizenship it is impossible to preserve liberty. For how can a man enjoy his rights to the freedom of a Roman citizen if he is not among the number of Roman citizens? . . .

There is certainly one question which, I am well aware, is constantly asked . . . : How is it that, if citizenship cannot be lost, our citizens have often joined Latin colonies?[10] They have done so either of their own free will or to avoid a penalty imposed by law; had they been willing to undergo the penalty, they could have remained within the citizen body. Again, when anyone is surrendered to the enemy by the *pater patratus* [see chapter 3, note 66], or sold as a slave by his own father or by the state, what legal justification is there for the loss of his citizenship? A Roman citizen is surrendered to save the honor of the state: if those to whom he is surrendered accept him, he becomes theirs; if they refuse to accept him, as the Numantines did Mancinus,[11] he retains his original

---

10. Thereby giving up Roman citizenship rights and acquiring the lesser Latin rights.

11. Mancinus was surrendered to the Numantines in 137 B.C. to free Rome from the obligation of ratifying the treaty which he had concluded with them, when military commander in Spain, in order to save his surrounded and demoralized army from annihilation.

status and his rights as a citizen. A father, by selling a son over whom he had assumed authority at birth, frees him from that authority. So too the state, by selling a man who has evaded military service, does not take away his freedom but proclaims that one who has refused to face danger for the sake of freedom is not a free man. By selling a man who has evaded the census the state proclaims that, whereas those who have been slaves in the normal way gain their freedom by being included in the census, one who has refused to be included in it although free has of his own accord repudiated his freedom.

Now if these are the special grounds on which citizenship and liberty can be lost, do those who quote them fail to understand that if our forefathers intended that their loss should be possible in these circumstances, they intended that it should be impossible in any others? For as they have produced these instances from our civil law, I wish they would also produce instances in which citizenship or liberty has been taken away by any statute or proposal. For the position with regard to exile is transparently clear. Exile is not a punishment: it is a harbor of refuge from punishment. Because people want to escape from some punishment or catastrophe, they quit their native soil, i.e., they change their place of abode. And so, in no statute of ours will you find, as you will in the laws of other states, that exile figures as the punishment for any crime at all; but people seeking to avoid imprisonment, death, or dishonor, when imposed upon them by our laws, take refuge in exile as in a sanctuary. Should they consent to remain in the state and submit to the rigor of the law, they would lose their citizenship only with their lives. But they do not consent; and therefore their citizenship is not taken from them, but is by them abandoned and discarded. For as no one under our law can be a citizen of two states, citizenship of Rome is actually lost at the moment when the runaway has been received into a place of exile, i.e., into another citizen body.

Now, gentlemen, though I fail to mention very many points in connection with this right of citizenship, I do not fail to see that I have been led on to speak about it at greater length than consideration for your verdict demanded. But I have done so, not because I thought that in this case you would look for this particular defense, but in order to bring it home to everybody that citizenship has never been and can never be taken away from any man. I wished all men to know this— both those whom Sulla intended to injure and all other citizens as well, whether old or new. For no argument can be advanced to show why, if citizenship could be taken away from any newly created citizen, it cannot be taken away from all patricians, all the citizens of oldest creation.

152. DUAL CITIZENSHIP OF PROVINCIALS: THE PRIVILEGES OF SELEUCUS OF RHOSUS

This Greek inscription sheds important light on the juridical status of newly created Roman citizens from the eastern provinces of the Empire. Here the established Hellenistic practice of multiple citizenship clashed with a fundamental principle of Roman law, which held that Romans could not simultaneously hold another citizenship elsewhere (see § 151). Following their usual policy of accepting existing Hellenistic institutions whenever possible, the Romans permitted these new citizens to retain their original local citizenship in addition to their newly acquired privilege. The inscription contains four related documents, of which two are given here. With these should be compared § 103, last selection; §§ 134, 135, 153, and 202.

FIRA, vol. I, no. 55 (=*RDGE*, no. 58)

[Edict of Octavian, 41 B.C.]

Imperator Caesar, triumvir for the settlement of the commonwealth, in accordance with the Munatian–Aemilian Law[12] granted citizenship and exemption of all property from taxation, as follows:

Whereas Seleucus of Rhosus, [a city in the province of Asia], son of Theodotus, campaigned with us under our command in the wars in . . . and endured many great hardships and dangers on our behalf, not sparing himself at all in enduring suffering, and exhibited complete devotion and fidelity to the Republic, and joined his own fortunes to our safety, and sustained all kinds of damage on behalf of the Republic of the Roman people, and was useful to us both in our presence and absence;

To him and his parents, to his children and his descendants, and to the wife he shall have hereafter, we grant citizenship and exemption of property from taxation, in the same measure as any who are tax-exempt

---

12. This law, passed in 42 B.C., apparently gave the triumvirs the power to grant Roman citizenship and other privileges to provincials who fought in the campaigns against the assassins of Caesar.

citizens with fullest legal right, and exemption from military service and all compulsory public services.

The aforementioned and his parents, children, and descendants shall belong to the Cornelian tribe, and they shall have the right to cast their votes and be enrolled in the census therein; and if they wish to be enrolled *in absentia,* or to belong to some municipality or colony in Italy, they may be so enrolled.

Insofar as the aforementioned—and his wife, parents, children, and descendants—before he became a tax-exempt Roman citizen, enjoyed privileges in any city, if, even after becoming a tax-exempt Roman citizen, he wishes to enjoy these privileges, he shall have legal right to hold priesthoods . . . offices, prerogatives . . . and to possess and enjoy his property, just as anyone who possesses and enjoys such with fullest legal right. . . .

[The next fifteen lines are badly mutilated; they include exemption from billeting and the right of intermarriage.]

. . . to him into a city or district of the provinces of Asia and Europe . . . if he imports or exports for his own needs from a city or a district . . . if he exports from his own possessions, or cattle for his own needs . . . in all these cases no city or tax farmer shall exact a tax from him. If anyone wishes to bring an accusation against them, or lodge a complaint, or bring them to trial and institute proceedings . . . in all such cases, if they wish to be tried at home in accordance with their own laws, or in free cities, or before our magistrates or promagistrates . . . the choice shall be theirs; and no one shall act otherwise than has been set forth in this document, or pass judgment concerning them . . . or pronounce sentence. And if any trial is held concerning them contrary to this document, it shall be invalid.

And if any [magistrate] agrees to entertain an accusation against the aforementioned, his parents, wife, children, or descendants, or to allow prejudgment of a capital crime . . . the aforementioned shall have the right to come as appellants to our senate and our magistrates and promagistrates, or to send envoys concerning their personal affairs. . . .

Any state or any magistrate that does not do what is called for by this document, or acts contrary to this document (either holding an *ex parte*[?] judicial inquiry[13] or acquiescing in such a decision, or exacting security from them), or that with malice aforethought prevents the

13. Possibly the phrase merely means "summoning them and holding judicial inquiry."

aforementioned from enjoying the privileges decreed to them, shall be liable to pay to the Roman people a fine of 100,000 sesterces; they may be prosecuted and sued for this sum by any person at will, and he may present his case and collect in the province before our magistrates and promagistrates, or at Rome; and in such cases [?] the man bringing the suit must provide sufficient sureties.[14] Our magistrates and promagistrates who have jurisdiction shall make the necessary decisions and see to it that the foregoing are put into effect as stated.

[Letter of Octavian to the city of Rhosus, 30 B.C.]

Year . . . , 9th day of the month Apellaeus. Imperator Caesar, son of a god, imperator for the sixth time, consul for the fourth time, to the chief magistrates, council, and people of the sacred, inviolate, and autonomous city of Rhosus, greeting. If you are well, I am pleased; I too, together with my army, am in good health. Seleucus, your fellow citizen and my ship captain, campaigned with me in all the wars and gave many proofs of his good will, loyalty, and valor. As befitted those who campaigned with us and who comported themselves bravely during the war, he has been honored with privileges, exemption from taxation, and [Roman] citizenship. I therefore recommend him to you, for men of this kind also encourage greater good will on our part toward their native cities. With the knowledge therefore that I shall do everything possible for you the more readily out of regard for Seleucus, send to me with confidence concerning any matters you desire. Farewell.

153. EDICT OF OCTAVIAN ON THE PRIVILEGES OF VETERANS, 31 B.C.

Berlin Papyrus no. 628 (= *FIRA*, vol. I, no. 56)

Imperator Caesar, son of a god, triumvir for the second time for the settlement of the commonwealth, declares: I have decided to decree that all veterans be granted exemption from tribute . . . to grant to them, their parents and children, and the wives they have or shall have, exemption of all their property from taxation; and to the end that they may be

---

14. That is, "the prosecutor must put up security. He cannot with impunity drag innocent people into tedious and expensive litigation and expose them to the risk of ruin. If he loses the case, he loses the wager" (J. H. Oliver, *American Journal of Archaeology* [1941], 45:538).

Roman citizens with fullest legal right, they shall be exempt from taxation, exempt from military service, and exempt from the performance of compulsory public services. Likewise, the aforementioned shall have the right to cast their votes and be enrolled in the census in any tribe they wish; and if they wish to be enrolled *in absentia,* it shall be permitted, both to the aforementioned themselves and to their parents, wives, and children. Likewise, just as I desired the veterans to be privileged in the said respects, I grant permission that they possess, use, and enjoy also whatever priesthoods, offices, prerogatives, privileges, and emoluments they possessed. Neither the other magistrates nor a legate nor a procurator nor a farmer of the tribute shall be in their homes for the purpose of lodging or wintering, nor shall anyone be conducted to winter quarters therein[15] against their will.

154. The Secret Ballot

In this selection we have a frank statement of the aristocratic preference for open voting as practiced in the earlier Roman Republic, and a proposal by Cicero to achieve essentially the same result under existing conditions of secret ballot by adding the proviso that each voter, before depositing his ballot, must reveal his vote to a member of the nobility — thereby combining, he argues, all the appearances of freedom of the ballot for the people at large with effective control by the *optimates.*

In the interest of clarity and brevity, the argument of this passage has here been reduced to its essentials. Suspension points, if inserted wherever required by the continuous excerpting, would be unduly frequent and have accordingly been omitted altogether.

Cicero, *Laws* III. xv. 33–xvii. 39 (abridged); Adapted from *LCL*

Marcus Cicero. The next law takes up the matter of voting. According to my proposal, *The people are to enjoy freedom of the ballot, but are to reveal their votes to optimates.* This subject is a difficult one, and has been frequently investigated.. The problem is this: In electing magistrates, judging criminal cases and voting on proposed legislation, is it better for the votes to be recorded openly or secretly?

Quintus Cicero. My dear brother, who does not realize that laws providing for a secret ballot have deprived the nobility of all their

---

15. It is possible that the last phrase is to be construed as "no one is to be dispossessed against his will."

influence? The people should not have been afforded a hiding place where they could conceal a mischievous vote by means of the ballot, and keep the nobility in ignorance of each man's opinion. Accordingly, no adherent of the nobility has ever introduced or supported a measure like yours. There are indeed four such balloting laws in existence. The first, concerning the election of magistrates, is the Gabinian Law, proposed by an unknown man of low degree. It was followed two years later by the Cassian Law concerning trials before the people; Lucius Cassius, who introduced this law, was a noble but—and I say this with all due respect to his family—he dissented from the nobility and was always seeking the fickle applause of the mob by favoring popular measures. The third of these laws, on the adoption or rejection of proposed legislation, was introduced by Carbo, a factious reprobate who later returned to the party of the nobility but even so could not obtain his personal safety from them. Oral voting apparently remained in force only in trials for treason, which even Cassius had excepted from his balloting law. But Gaius Coelius provided the ballot even for such trials—and he regretted to the end of his days that he had done injury to the Republic out of a personal desire to crush Gaius Popilius.[16]

Therefore, if you propose a balloting law, you must take the responsibility for it alone. For I will not approve it, nor will our friend Atticus, as far as I can judge from his expression.

Atticus. Certainly no popular measure has ever received my approval, and I think the best government is the kind that Marcus here established when he was consul—a government under the control of the *optimates*.

Marcus. Well, you have rejected my law, I see, and without a ballot! But let me explain that I am granting the people this freedom you object to in such a way as to ensure that the nobility shall have great influence and the opportunity to exercise it. For the text of my voting law is, *The people are to enjoy freedom of the ballot, but are to reveal their votes to optimates.* This law implies the repeal of all the recent laws which ensure the secrecy of the vote in every way, allowing no one to look at a ballot or question or accost voters. If these provisions are intended, as they usually are, as deterrents to vote buying, I have nothing against them. But since laws have not succeeded in preventing bribery, let the people have their ballots as an assertion of their liberty, but with the provision that these ballots are to be shown and freely exhibited to any one of our

16. The four laws mentioned here were passed in the tribunate of their respective proposers: Aulus Gabinius, tribune 139 B.C.; Lucius Cassius Longinus Ravilla, tribune 137 B.C.; Gaius Papirius Carbo, tribune 131 B.C.; Gaius Coelius Caldus, tribune 107 B.C.

leading and most eminent citizens, so that the people may enjoy freedom of choice also in this very privilege of honorably gaining the favor of the members of the nobility. Thus my law grants the appearance of liberty, preserves the influence of the nobility, and removes the causes of class strife.

155. CAMPAIGNING FOR OFFICE

It is generally held that this long letter on canvassing, about a third of which is given here, was addressed to Cicero in late 65 or early 64 B.C., when he was preparing to stand for the consulship, by his brother Quintus. The reader must be cautioned, however, that the commonly accepted date and authorship have frequently been called into question, some arguing that the work may be a clever literary exercise composed a century or so later.

In any case, this letter is a priceless document for its frank picture of the hard realities of a political campaign in the late Republic. Special stress is laid on the necessity of personal spadework in cultivating valuable friendships, "gladhanding" the voters, keeping one's self constantly in the public eye, and being liberal with campaign promises — in short, trying to be all things to all men. These procedures are deprecated, but are defended as an honest man's only way of contending with the prevalent bribery and corruption, and the hostility of the nobility to "new men," as the frank political parlance of republican Rome called those occasional public figures who attained the consulship (and consequent ennoblement of their families) though not members of noble families by origin. In 63 B.C. Cicero was the first "new man" to attain the consulship in over thirty years.

Quintus Cicero, *On Canvassing for the Consulship* i, viii, ix, xi–xiv (abridged)

Consider these three things: what state this is, what you are seeking and who you are. Then every day, as you descend to the Forum, you must say to yourself, "I am a new man; I am standing for the consulship; this is Rome."

The political newness of your name you will overcome to a large extent by your reputation as a speaker. That is an accomplishment which has always carried with it the highest distinction. The man who is considered a worthy advocate for men of consular rank cannot be reckoned unworthy of the consulship. . . .

Next, let the number and quality of your friends be apparent. For you have in your favor what not many new men have had: all the publicans, nearly all the equestrian order, many faithful municipalities, many individuals of every class who have been defended by you, some private groups, also a large number of young men won over by their pursuit of eloquence, and the diligent daily concourse of your personal friends. Take care to retain all these supporters by reminding them, asking for their votes, and taking all steps to make them understand— those who are under obligation to you—that they will never have another opportunity of showing their gratitude, and those who desire your services, that they will never have another opportunity of placing you in their debt.

Another thing, it seems to me, that can be of great assistance to a new man is the good will of the nobles, especially those of consular rank. It is well to be considered worthy of that rank by those into whose rank and number you wish to enter. You must take pains to solicit the votes of all these men, you must assure and convince them that we have always sided with the *optimates* in politics and have never been supporters of the *populares* [for the *optimates* and *populares* see § 101]; that if we appear to have given utterance to any popular sentiments, we did so with a view to winning the support of Gnaeus Pompey in order to have the most powerful man in the state friendly to our candidacy, or at least not hostile to it. Further, make a special effort to win over the young nobles, and to keep the ones you have won over devoted to you; they will bring you great esteem. You have many such friends; see to it that they know how important you consider them. If you can convert them from passive to active supporters, they will do you the greatest good. . . .

Therefore take care to secure all the centuries[17] by your many varied friendships. First of all, it is obvious you must conciliate the senators and *equites,* and the active and influential men of the other orders. There are many industrious men in the city, many freedmen influential and active in the Forum. Some you can reach in person, some through mutual friends: exercise the greatest diligence, bend every effort to make them your active supporters—court them, assure them, point out that they will be doing you the greatest service. Next, take into account the whole city, all the private groups, country districts, and neighborhoods. If you can win over the leading men in these to your friendship, you will through them easily gain the crowd. After that, see that you imprint on your mind and memory the whole of Italy, divided and catalogued by tribes, so that you may let no municipality, colony, or prefecture, in

17. The consuls were elected by the *comitia centuriata* (§ 27).

short no place at all in Italy exist in which you have not sufficient support. Seek out and discover men in every district, make their acquaintance, solicit them, give them assurances, and see to it that they canvass for you in their neighborhoods and become, as it were, candidates themselves in your cause. They will wish to have you for a friend if they see that their friendship is sought for by you, and you can bring this home to them by suitable address; for men who live in the municipal towns and in the country think themselves friends of ours if they can gain in addition some assistance for themselves from our friendship, they lose no opportunity of earning it. The others, and in particular your rivals, don't even know these men, but you have some acquaintance, and will easily be able to increase it. . . .

The centuries of *equites,* it seems to me, can be much more easily won over by diligence. First, make their acquaintance (they are but few), then court them (they are mostly young men, and youth is much more easily won to friendship), and then you will have with you all of the best of the youth and the most assiduous in kindnesses. . . . And the zeal of the young men in your behalf, in voting, in canvassing, in spreading reports, and in attending you about the city, is of wonderful importance and very honorable.

And speaking of attending you about the city, you must take care to have a daily company of attendants, of every class, order, and age. From their numbers it will be possible to conjecture how much power and support you are likely to have at the election itself. Now, there are three parts to this matter: the first, those who wait upon you at your house in the morning; the second, those who escort you from your house,[18] and the third, those who accompany you about the city. In the case of the first, who are the most ordinary kind of attendants and, in the current fashion, come in great numbers, you must take care to make even this trifling service of theirs appear most acceptable to you. Let those who come to your house know that you notice it: tell it to them often, and to their friends, who will report it to them. In this way, when there are several rival candidates and people see that there is one man who takes especial notice of these acts of attention, they often desert the others and swing over to him. . . . Now as to those who escort you from your house, show them and let them know that you are the more grateful for their attention, since it is greater than that of your morning greeters, and as far as possible come down into the Forum at regular times. A great

18. To the Forum or other place of public business.

company escorting you every day lends great reputation and distinction. The third group of this kind are those who attend you constantly. See to it that those among them who do so of their own volition understand that they are placing you in their perpetual debt by the greatest favor. From those who are under obligation to you, you can simply require this service, that those whose age and business permit be in constant attendance upon you, and those who cannot attend in person assign relatives to this service. . . .

As enough has now been said about contracting friendships, we must proceed to speak of that other branch of a candidate's concerns, his popularity among the common people. That requires calling everyone by his name, flattery, assiduity, courtesy, reputation, and confidence in your political career. As to the first, knowing men's names, let it be evident that you do, and improve so as to be better at it day by day. Nothing seems to me to be so popular or so pleasing. Next, though flattery is not in your nature, convince yourself that you must pretend to practice it naturally, for though character is more important, still in a business of a few months [i.e., an election campaign] pretense can prevail over character. You are not lacking in the complaisance worthy of a good and agreeable person, but you particularly need the gift of flattery, which, though vicious and repulsive in the rest of one's life, is indispensable in an election campaign. Indeed, it is bad only when, by "yessing" a man, it makes him worse; when it renders him more friendly it is not so blamable; but in any case it is indispensable for a candidate, whose expression, countenance, and language must be constantly changed and adapted to the feelings and inclinations of everyone he meets. . . .

Courtesy has a wide range. It appears in a man's family life, which cannot directly reach the multitude, to be sure, but pleases the multitude if praised by his friends. It appears at banquets, which you should take care to have celebrated both by yourself and by your friends on many occasions and for each tribe. It appears in services, which you must offer to all: see that there is ready access to you night and day, and that not only the doors of your house are open, but also your countenance and expression, which are the doors of your mind; and if the latter indicate that your intentions are concealed and hidden, it is little use for your house door to be open. For men like not only to be promised things, especially such things as they ask of a candidate, but to have them promised liberally and honorably. Accordingly, this rule, at least, is easy to practice: always to make it clear that you will be doing eagerly and cheerfully whatever you are going to do. But it is more difficult, and more suited to the requirements of the occasion than to your nature, to promise what you may not be able to perform, instead of refusing politely.[19] The second is the conduct of a good man, the first of a good campaigner. . . . Gaius Cotta, a past master at canvassing, used to say that he would promise his services to all, so long as nothing contrary to his duty was asked of him, but would really render them only to those on whom he thought they were best bestowed; that he would refuse no one, because it often happened that the man to whom he had given a promise did not avail himself of it, or that he himself had more free time than he had expected; and that the man who only promised what he was sure he could perform would never have a house full of well-wishers. . . . If you make a promise, the thing is still uncertain, is a matter for a future day, and concerns but few people; but if you refuse, you alienate many people definitely and at once. . . .

Lastly, see that your whole campaign is full of pomp, illustrious, splendid, and pleasing to the people, that it has the greatest honor and dignity, so that your rivals may reproach you with no wickedness, lust, or bribery such as they practice. And in this campaign it is necessary to take especial care that people shall have confidence in your political career and an honorable opinion of you. A political career is achieved neither in a campaign nor in the senate nor in the assembly; the things that count are that the senate shall judge that you will be a defender of its authority because you have been so hitherto, that the *equites* (and virtuous and wealthy men in general) shall judge from your past life that you will be a lover of peace and tranquillity, and that the multitude shall judge, from the fact that in your speeches at least you have been a supporter of popular causes in the assembly and in the courts, that you will not be unfriendly to its interests.

These are the thoughts which occurred to me with respect to the first two of the morning meditations that I said you ought to ponder every day as you were descending to the Forum: "I am a new man; I am standing for the consulship." The third point remains, "The city is Rome," a state formed of an assemblage of all nations, a state in which many intrigues, much deceit, many vices of every kind abound, in which the arrogance of many, the contumacy of many, the malevolence of many, the pride of many, the hatred and vexation of many must be endured. I see that it requires great prudence and tact for one, living amid so many and such great vices of men of every sort, to avoid giving

---

19. The text is corrupt. The translation attempts to give the sense.

offense, to avoid gossip, to avoid treachery; and that there is but one man adapted to such a variety of manners, talk and dispositions. Wherefore, continue constantly to walk in that path in which you have set out: excel in speaking. This is the means by which men are controlled at Rome, won over and kept from hindering or harming you. And since this is the point in which the state is most at fault, that it is apt to forget virtue and worth when bribery intervenes, in this see that you fully realize your own power, i.e., that you are a man who can cause your rivals the greatest fear of the risks of a trial. Let them know that they are being watched and observed by you, and they will fear not only your diligence, authority, and powerful eloquence, but also the zeal of the equestrian order in your behalf. And I wish you to put this to them, not so as to appear to be actually planning prosecution, but merely in order, by alarming them thus, to attain your goal more easily. In a word, strive in this way with all your strength and ability, so that we may obtain what we seek.

156. PARLIAMENTARY PRACTICES OF THE SENATE

Aulus Gellius, *Attic Nights* xiv. vii

Gnaeus Pompey was elected consul for the first time with Marcus Crassus.[20] When he was on the point of entering upon the office, being unacquainted with the method of convening and consulting the senate, and of city affairs in general, because of his long military service, he asked his friend Marcus Varro to prepare a handbook of parliamentary practice. . . .[21]

Varro tells there first by what magistrates the senate was customarily convened according to the usage of our forefathers, namely: the dictator, consuls, praetors, tribunes of the plebs, *interrex,* and prefect of the city. No others except these, he said, had the right to submit a decree to the senate for passage, and whenever it happened that all these magistrates were in Rome at the same time, then the first in order in the above list had the prior right of consulting the senate. By exceptional privilege, the military tribunes who had served in place of consuls [see §§ 25, 35], the decemvirs [see §§ 25, 31] who had had consular authority in their

---

20. They were consuls together in 70 B.C.

21. This handbook was lost, and Gellius quotes the following from a later treatment of the same material by Varro.

day, and the triumvirs appointed for the settlement of the commonwealth[22] also had the right to consult the senate.

Next he wrote about vetoes, stating that only those had the right to veto a decree of the senate who had equal authority with, or greater authority than, the presiding officer proposing the decree.

He then added a list of the places in which a decree of the senate could legally be passed, demonstrating conclusively that such a decree was not legal unless passed in a place appointed by an augur, called a "temple." Therefore in the Hostilian and Pompeian senate houses, and later in the Julian, since those were unconsecrated places, "temples" were established by the augurs, so that in them legal decrees of the senate might be passed according to the usage of our forefathers. . . .

After this he goes on to say that a decree of the senate passed before sunrise or after sunset was not valid, and that those who put a decree to a vote at such times were deemed to have committed an act worthy of censure.

He continues with instruction on many matters: on what days it is illegal to hold a meeting of the senate; that one who was about to convene the senate had first to offer up a victim and take the auspices; that questions relating to the gods were to be presented to the senate before those concerning men; then further, that resolutions should be presented in general terms when affecting the general welfare, and in definite terms on specific cases; that a decree of the senate was voted in one of two ways—either by a division if there was general agreement, or, if the matter was undecided, by asking the opinion of each member separately;[23] and that these individual opinions should be asked according to rank, beginning with the consular rank. In that rank the one to be called upon first was always in former times the one who had been enrolled in the senate first; but Varro reports that at the time he was writing this a new custom had become established through favoritism and influence of calling first on the one whom the presiding officer wished to call, provided however that he was of consular rank. In addition he treats of the imposition of a fine on a senator absent from a meeting of the senate when it was his duty to attend, and of the lien placed on the property [of such a senator, as security for the fine].

---

22. That is, the Second Triumvirate (§ 114), consisting of Antony, Octavian, and Lepidus. Mention of this triumvirate, created in 43 B.C., could of course not have been contained in Varro's original handbook of 70 B.C.

23. This is rather misleading, since even after the expression of individual opinions a vote would be taken by a formal division of the house.

157. "Martial Law"

In the second century, when all serious external threats to the security of the Roman state had been removed, dictators were no longer chosen in critical emergencies (see § 37). Instead, in the last century of the Republic, when the crises of the state were internal, the Senate had recourse to a new device, the "ultimate decree of the Senate" *(senatus consultum ultimum),* which declared the existence of a state of emergency and ordered the consuls to take appropriate measures for the defense of the constitutional government. Between 121, when it was first invoked against Gaius Gracchus (cf. chapter 5, note 22), and 49 B.C. this decree was passed only ten times; between 49 and 40 B.C., when it was resorted to for the last time, it was employed on about five occasions.

Sallust, *Catiline* xxix; Adapted from *LCL*

When these events were reported to Cicero, he was greatly disturbed by the twofold peril, since he could no longer by his unaided efforts protect the city against these plots and had no exact information as to the size and aim of Manlius' army; he therefore placed the matter, which had already been the subject of much popular discussion, before the senate. Consequently, as is often done in a dangerous emergency, the senate decreed "that the consuls should see to it that the state suffered no harm." In Roman practice the power thus conferred by the senate upon a magistrate is supreme, authorizing him to raise an army, wage war, exert any kind of compulsion upon allies and citizens, and exercise unlimited command and jurisdiction at home and in the field; otherwise the consul has none of these rights except by order of the people.

158. Corruption in the Courts

The corruption of the Roman courts in the last century of the Republic was notorious. In 149 B.C., under the stimulus of the scandalous acquittal of Servius Sulpicius Galba (see § 79), jurisdiction in cases of extortion charged against provincial governors was transferred from the popular assembly to a special court created for the purpose *(quaestio de repetundis);* subsequently, similar tribunals were created to try other criminal offenses. Accused officials were still only rarely convicted, however, since they belonged to the same noble families as the senators, who constituted the juries of the new court. In his endeavor to weld an antisenatorial "united front" of the equestrian and plebeian classes, Gaius Gracchus, by the Acilian Law (see § 100), provided that the extortion-court juries should thenceforth be drawn only from wealthy men of nonsenatorial rank. This gave the equestrian order a powerful weapon against the senate, and thereafter the composition of the juries became a political football. When he restored senatorial domination of the state, Sulla enacted (81 B.C.) that the juries once again be composed exclusively of senators. By 70 B.C., when Cicero delivered his speeches against Verres, much of Sulla's legislation already lay in ruins, and there was considerable agitation to repeal his law on juries too. Several weeks after the condemnation of Verres, a law was passed providing that criminal juries be made up of senators, *equites,* and treasury tribunes (army paymasters) in equal numbers. On the prosecution of Verres see further introduction to § 143.

Cicero, *First Speech Against Verres* i–xiii (abridged); From *LCL*

Gentlemen of the court: At this great political crisis, there seems to have been offered you, not through man's wisdom but almost as the direct gift of heaven, the very thing that was most to be desired; a thing that will help, more than anything else, to mitigate the unpopularity of your order and the discredit attaching to these courts of law. A belief has by this time established itself, as harmful to the whole nation as it is perilous to yourselves, and everywhere expressed not merely by our own people but by foreigners as well—the belief that these courts, as now constituted, will never convict any man, however guilty, if he has money. And now, at the moment of supreme danger for your order and your judicial privileges, when preparations have been made for an attempt, by means of public meetings and proposals for legislation, to fan the flames of senatorial unpopularity, Gaius Verres is brought to trial: a man already condemned, in the world's opinion, by his life and deeds; already acquitted, according to his own confident assertions, by his vast fortune. In this case, gentlemen, I appear as prosecutor, backed by the strong approval and keen interest of the nation; not to increase the unpopularity of your order, but to help in allaying the discredit which is mine as well as yours. The character of the man I am prosecuting is such that you may use him to restore the good name of these courts, to regain favor at home, and to give satisfaction abroad: he has robbed the treasury and plundered Asia and Pamphylia; he behaved like a pirate in his urban praetorship and like a destroying pestilence in his province of Sicily. You have only to pronounce against this man an upright and conscientious verdict, and you will continue to possess that respect which ought always to belong to you. If, however, the vastness of his wealth shatters the conscience and the honesty of the judges of these courts, I shall achieve one thing at least: it will be felt that the nation lacked the right jurors in this case, and not that the jurors lacked the right defendant to convict, or the defendant the right man to prosecute him. . . .

No sooner was Verres back from his province than he offered an agent a large sum of money to buy up this court. The terms of the contract held good as arranged, until the challenging of jurors took place, when . . . the contractor threw up his undertaking completely.[24] Things now looked good. . . . Verres, from looking lively and cheerful, had been plunged suddenly into so gloomy a state of depression that he was looked on as an already condemned man by everyone in Rome, himself included. And now behold, equally suddenly, within these last few days, since the result of the consular elections has been known,[25] the same old methods are being set going again, and more money than before is being spent upon them. . . . When Hortensius, after being declared consul-elect, was being escorted home from the Campus Martius[26] by a large crowd of his supporters, it chanced that they were met by Gaius Curio. . . . Just near the Arch of Fabius he noticed Verres among the crowd, called out to him, and congratulated him loudly. He said not a word to the consul-elect Hortensius himself, nor to the relatives and friends of Hortensius who were there at the time. No, it was Verres with whom he stopped to talk, Verres whom he embraced and told to put aside all anxiety. "I hereby inform you," he said, "that today's election means your acquittal." This remark, being overheard by a number of honest gentlemen, was forthwith repeated to me; or I should rather say, everyone told me of it as soon as he saw me. Some found it outrageous, others absurd: it was absurd to those who regarded the issue of the case as depending on the credit of the witnesses, the methods of the prosecution, and the court's power to decide, not on the consular election; outrageous to those who could look further beneath the surface, and saw that this speech of congratulation pointed to the corruption of the members of the court. For they argued thus, and

24. That is, the jury remaining after the challenging was too honest to be bribed for the sum offered.

25. In this election Quintus Hortensius, Verres' attorney, and Quintus Metellus, a prominent noble in league with Verres, were elected. Shortly after, Metellus' brother Marcus was elected praetor and obtained the presidency of the extortion court.

26. Where the elections were held.

honest gentlemen kept saying so to one another and to me, that it was at last unmistakably plain that our law courts were worthless. An accused man one day regards his own condemnation as an accomplished fact, and the next day is acquitted by the election of his advocate to the consulship? Why, is the presence at Rome of all Sicily and its inhabitants [the plaintiffs], of all its businessmen, of all its public and private records —is all this, then, to count for nothing? Aye, nothing, against the will of the consul-elect. Why, will the court have no regard for the statements of the prosecution, the evidence of the witnesses, the judgment of the Roman nation? No; everything is to be steered and directed by the hand of one powerful man. I will speak frankly, gentlemen. This circumstance disturbed me profoundly. Everywhere *optimates* were telling me, "Verres will certainly escape your clutches, but the law courts will be in our keeping no longer; for who can possibly hesitate about transferring them to other hands, if Verres is acquitted?" . . .

A few days later, when the praetors-elect were casting lots for their respective functions and it fell to Marcus Metellus to be president of the extortion court next year, I received the news that Verres had been so warmly congratulated on this that he even sent off slaves to his house to carry the news to his wife. . . . I now discovered, gentlemen, that the plan of action formed and adopted by Verres and his friends was this: to prolong proceedings by whatever method might be necessary, so that the trial should take place under the presidency of Marcus Metellus as praetor. This would have several advantages. First, the strong friendly support of Marcus Metellus. Next, not only would Hortensius be consul, but Quintus Metellus as well, the strength of whose friendship for Verres I will ask you to note—he had indeed given so clearly a preliminary indication of his good will that Verres feels himself already paid in full for the votes he bought at the election. . . . This second consul-elect sent for the Sicilians, and some of them came, remembering that Lucius Metellus was now praetor in Sicily. He talked to them in this sort of way: "I am consul; one of my brothers is governing Sicily, the other is going to preside over the extortion court; many steps have been taken to assure that no harm can come to Verres." To attempt to intimidate witnesses, especially these timorous and calamity-stricken Sicilians, not merely by your personal influence, but by appealing to their awe of you as consul and to the power of the two praetors—if this is not judicial corruption, Metellus, I should be glad to know what is. What would you do for an innocent kinsman, if you forsake duty and honor for an utter rascal who is no kin of yours at all, and make it possible for anyone who does not know you to believe in the truth of his allegations concerning you? . . .

The whole story shall not only be recalled, but set forth and corroborated in detail, the story of all the judicial crimes and villainies that have been committed during the ten years since the transfer of the law courts to the senate. The people of Rome shall learn from me how it is that, so long as the law courts were in the hands of the equestrian order, for nearly fifty years together not even the faintest suspicion resting upon one single Roman knight, when sitting as juror, of accepting a bribe to give a particular verdict;[27] how it is that, with the courts transferred to the senatorial order and the power of the people over you as individuals destroyed, Quintus Calidius observed, on being convicted, that a man of praetorian rank could not decently be convicted for less than 3,000,000 sesterces.

159. CATO THE CENSOR

Marcus Porcius Cato, a "new man" from Tusculum near Rome, was, in the first half of the second century B.C., the champion of the traditional Roman simplicity and austerity against the rising luxury of the times. As the spokesman of intransigent Roman conservatism, puritanism, and nationalism, he led the opposition to the invasion of Hellenistic influences into Roman public and private life (cf. § 185). His stern censorship (184 B.C.), though famed for its unwonted severity, is a good example of the powers and functions of that office in the last two centuries of the Republic.

Livy, *History of Rome* xxxix. xl–xliv

This election [of a praetor] was stopped through the wisdom and courage of the senate, but a greater contest followed in which more numerous and more influential men competed for a more important prize. This was the election to the censorship. The candidates were Lucius Valerius Flaccus, Publius and Lucius Scipio, Gnaeus Manlius Vulso, and Lucius Furius Purpurio of the patricians, and Marcus Porcius Cato, Marcus Fulvius Nobilior, Tiberius Sempronius Longus, and Marcus Sempronius

---

27. This is, of course, rhetorical exaggeration.

Tuditanus of the plebeians. The rivalry was most intense, but all the patricians and plebeians of the most illustrious families were far excelled by Marcus Porcius. This man possessed such ability and force of character that it seemed certain he would have made his fortune in whatever station he had been born. . . . He was undoubtedly a man of hard temper and bitter and unbridled tongue, but absolute master of his passions, unwavering in integrity, and indifferent alike to wealth and popularity. In his frugality, in his endurance of toil and danger, he had a mind and body almost of iron. . . .

> [Despite the united opposition of the nobility, Cato and Lucius Valerius Flaccus were elected.]

Amid suspense mingled with foreboding the censors Marcus Porcius and Lucius Valerius made up the roll of the senate. They expelled seven, one of them a man of consular rank, distinguished for his high birth and the offices he had held, Lucius Quinctius Flamininus. Long ago, we are told, it became the custom for the censors to note their reasons next to the names of those they expelled from the senate. There are extant bitter speeches of Cato (and others) against those whom he expelled from their places in the senate or removed from the list of *equites,* but by far the most devastating is the one against Lucius Quinctius; indeed, if Cato had delivered this speech as accuser before the expulsion rather than as censor after it, not even his brother Titus Quinctius,[28] had he been censor at the time, could have kept Lucius Quinctius in the senate. Among other charges, he reproached him regarding Philip, a Carthaginian who was a notorious catamite, whom he loved and had attracted by the promise of great gifts from Rome to his province of Gaul. This boy would often in mock petulance reproach the consul for having carried him away from Rome just before the gladiatorial show, in order to put a high price on his favors to his lover. It happened that while they were banqueting and heated with wine a message was brought in that a Boian noble had come as a deserter, together with his children, and wanted to meet the consul in order to obtain a promise of protection from him in person. He was brought into the tent and began to address the consul through an interpreter. In the middle of his speech Quinctius said to his paramour: "Since you have missed the gladiatorial show, would you like to see this Gaul die now?" And when he nodded, though not really

28. Flamininus, the conqueror of Philip V of Macedon. See § 68.

in earnest, the consul seized the sword hanging above his head, struck the Gaul, who was still speaking, on the head, and then as he turned to flee, imploring the protection of the Roman people and of those who were present, ran him through the side. . . . Cato closed his speech by challenging Quinctius, if he denied this deed and the other charges, to post security and defend himself in court; but if he admitted them, did he suppose that any one would grieve over his disgrace when, mad with drink and lust, he had amused himself by shedding a man's blood at a banquet?

In the review of the list of *equites* Lucius Scipio Asiaticus was removed. In fixing assessments the censorship was severe and harsh on all classes. The assessors were ordered to list jewels, feminine apparel, and carriages worth more than 15,000 *asses* at ten times their value; similarly, slaves less than twenty years old who had been purchased since the last *lustrum*[29] for 10,000 *asses* or more were also to be assessed at ten times their value; and on all these items a tax of three *asses* per thousand was to be collected. The censors shut off all public water flowing into private houses or land, and whatever private individuals had built or erected on public ground they demolished on thirty days' notice. They next let contracts for public works from funds appropriated for that purpose: lining reservoirs with stone, cleaning out sewers where necessary, and constructing sewers in the Aventine quarter and in other sections where there were none as yet. Flaccus separately constructed a dike at the Waters of Neptune to provide a public way and also a road over the hill at Formiae; Cato built two auction halls, the Maenian and the Titian, near the Lautumiae,[30] and bought up four shops for the state and on their site he erected the basilica called the Porcian. They farmed the revenues to the highest bidders, and awarded the contracts for public works to the lowest. When the senate, yielding to the prayers and tears of the publicans, ordered these contracts canceled and let anew, the censors let all the same contracts at slightly lower figures but did not allow those who had evaded the original contracts to bid. It was a noteworthy censorship and full of quarrels which occupied Marcus Porcius, to whose severity they were considered due, throughout his life.

---

29. The *lustrum* took place normally every five years. It was the closing purificatory sacrifice performed by the censors. See § 56.

30. A state prison, northeast of the Capitoline Hill.

160. Road Repairs

This inscription, dating from *c.* 90–80 B.C., is a record of public contracts for repairs on a Via Caecilia (unidentified) let by an urban quaestor in his capacity as commissioner of roads.

CIL, vol. I., 2d ed., no. 808 (= *ROL*, 4:180); Adapted from *LCL*

[Works contracted for on the Caecilian Road out of a cash appropriation of . . . thousand sesterces]

At the 35th milestone a bridge over the river: money appropriated, cost to the state . . . sesterces cash; Quintus Pamphilus contractor and labor, with urban quaestor Titus Vibius Temudinus, commissioner of roads.

Road to be paved in gravel from the 78th milestone and laid through the Apennine range for a distance of 20 miles: money appropriated, cost to the state 150,000 sesterces cash; Lucius Rufilius freedman of Lucius, and Lucius . . . contractor, with quaestor Titus Vibius, commissioner of roads.

Road to be paved in gravel[?] from the 98th milestone to the . . .[31] milestone and the branch towards Interamnium to the 120th milestone: money appropriated, cost to the state 600,000 sesterces cash; . . . Titus Sepunius O . . . son of Titus, contractor, with urban quaestor Titus Vibius Temudinus, commissioner of roads.

. . . tumbledown arch . . . money appropriated, cost to the state . . . sesterces cash . . . contractor . . . with urban quaestor Titus Vibius, commissioner of roads.

161. Caesar's Legislation Concerning Rome

See the introduction to the Tablet of Heraclea in § 162.

CIL, vol. I, 2d ed., no. 593, lines 1–82

[Registration for the Grain Dole]

If a person required by this law to declare before a consul [that he has become ineligible for the grain dole] shall be absent from Rome at the time when the declaration ought to be made, then his agent or represen-

---

31. The number is 110 or higher.

tative shall in his behalf make the same declaration before a consul, in the same manner and on the same days as the said person would be required by this law to make the declaration if he were at Rome.

If a person, whether male or female, required by this law to make declaration before a consul shall be under legal wardship, then his or her legal guardian shall in his or her behalf make the said declaration before a consul, in the same manner and on the same days as the said person would be required by this law to make the declaration if he or she were not under legal wardship.

If the consul before whom the said declarations are required by this law to be made shall be absent from Rome, then any person required to make a declaration shall make it before the *praetor urbanus,* or, if he shall be absent from Rome, before the *praetor peregrinus,* in the same manner as he would be required by this law to make the declaration before the consul if he were in Rome.

If neither the consul nor the said praetors, before whom the said declarations are required by this law to be made, shall be in Rome, then a person required to make a declaration shall make it before a tribune of the plebs, in the same manner as he would be required by this law to make the declaration before a consul or the *praetor urbanus* or the *praetor peregrinus* if they were in Rome.

In the case of every declaration required of any person by this law, it shall be the duty of the magistrate before whom the declaration is made to see that the name of the person, his declaration, and its date shall be entered in the public records; he shall further see that the said entries made by him in the records shall be copied in black letters on a white board [cf. chapter 6, note 34] and exposed in the Forum during the greater part of every day at the place in which grain is distributed to the people, so that it may be plainly read from the level of the ground.

Whosoever shall distribute grain or cause others to distribute grain to the people, shall neither give grain nor order nor permit grain to be given to any of those persons whose names shall have been given in to a consul or praetor or tribune of the plebs and in accordance with this law placed on the list upon the notice board. Whosoever, contrary to this law, shall give grain to any such person, shall be condemned to pay a fine to the people of 50,000 sesterces for every *modius* of wheat so given, and may be sued at will by any person for the said sum.

[Maintenance of Roads]

As regards the roads which are or shall be within the city of Rome or within one mile of the city of Rome, up to the limit of continuous habitation it shall be the duty of every person, before whose building any such road shall run, to maintain that road to the satisfaction of the aedile to whom in accordance with this law that portion of the city shall be assigned. And it shall be the duty of the said aedile to see that every such person required by this law to maintain any such road running before his building shall maintain the said road to his satisfaction, and that no water shall stand in such places, whereby the convenient use of the road by the public may be impaired.

It shall be the duty of the aediles, whether curule or plebeian, who are now in office, or who shall be appointed or elected or shall enter on the magistracy after the passage of this law, within the five days next following upon their designation to or their entrance upon the said magistracy, to arrange among themselves, either by agreement or by lot, in which part of the city each of them shall see to the repairing and paving of the public roads within the city of Rome and within one mile of the city of Rome, and shall have the special charge of such business. On every aedile, to whom by this law any such part of the city shall be assigned, shall be laid the special charge of repairing and maintaining the roads in all places within that part in such a manner as this law shall direct.

Where a road lies or shall lie between a sacred temple or a public building or a public place and a private building, it shall be the duty of the aedile to whom that part of the city is assigned in which such sacred temple or public building or public place is situated, to contract for the maintenance of one half of the said road.

If any person required by this law to maintain a public road in front of his building shall fail to maintain such road to the satisfaction of the aedile concerned, then it shall be the duty of the aedile at whose discretion the road ought to be maintained to contract for the maintenance of such road. Furthermore, the said aedile, not less than ten days before he concludes the contract, shall have publicly posted in the Forum in front of his tribunal the description of the road to be maintained, the day on which the contract is to be let, and the name of the persons before whose buildings the said road is situated. He shall further cause due notice to be given to the said persons and to their agents at their respective houses of his intention to contract for the road and of the day on which the contract is to be let. He shall conclude the said contract openly in the Forum through the urban quaestor or the one then in charge of the public treasury. Of the sum paid to the contractor for the said road the urban quaestor or the one then in charge of the public treasury shall cause to be entered in the public records of money owing to the people the proportion of that sum falling on the several persons whose buildings abut on the road, according to the length and breadth of the road in front of their several buildings. For such sums he shall in good faith make the several parties legally responsible to the person contracting for the maintenance of the said road. If the person so liable shall, within the next thirty days after he or his agent is notified of the legal obligation, fail to pay the money to or satisfy the party to whom he is made responsible, he shall be obliged to pay to the party to whom he is made responsible one and a half times the sum for which he is liable, and for such purpose the magistrate to whom application shall be made in the matter shall assign a judge or court in such manner as a judge or court would be assigned in a suit for the recovery of a loan.

Where the maintenance of a road is by this law to be assigned to a contractor, the aedile responsible for the same shall contract for the maintenance of the said road through the urban quaestor or the one then in charge of the public treasury in such manner that the road shall be maintained to the satisfaction of the person who shall have let the said contract. The urban quaestor, or the one then in charge of the public treasury, shall see that the sum thus agreed upon for the contract of each road is given and assigned to the contractor to whom it should be given. according to the terms of the contract.

Nothing in this law is intended to prevent the incumbent aediles, *quattuorviri* for cleaning the streets within the city, and *duoviri* for cleaning the roads outside but within one mile of the city of Rome from seeing to the cleaning of the public roads and having full power in such matter in all respects as they are or shall be required by the laws, plebiscites, or decrees of the senate.

Any person before whose building a footpath shall be situated shall be required to keep such footpath fitly paved along the whole length of the said building with whole stones closely compacted to form a solid surface, to the satisfaction of the aedile to whom by this law the charge of roads in that portion of the city shall appertain.

In the roads which are or shall be within the city of Rome, within the limit of continuous habitation no person, after the first day of January next following, shall be allowed in the daytime, after sunrise or before the tenth hour of the day, to lead or drive any heavy wagon, except where it shall be requisite to bring in or transport material for the sake of building the sacred temples of the immortal gods or for carrying out some public work, or where, in pursuance of a public contract for demolition, it shall be requisite for public ends to carry material out of the city or away from such places, and in cases for which specified persons shall be permitted by this law for specified causes to drive or lead such wagons.

On days when the Vestal Virgins, the *rex sacrorum* [cf. chapter 3, note 65], and the flamens shall be required to ride in wagons in the city for the sake of the public sacrifices of the Roman people; or when wagons shall be required for a triumphal procession on the day fixed for such triumph; or where wagons shall be needed for games publicly celebrated at Rome, or within one mile of the city of Rome, or for the procession at the circus games—for all such causes and on all such days nothing in this law is intended to prevent wagons from being led or driven in the city in the daytime.

Nothing in this law is intended to prevent wagons, brought into the city by night, if returning empty or carrying away refuse, from being drawn by oxen or asses in the city of Rome or within one mile of the city of Rome after sunrise in the first ten hours of the day.

As regards the public places and public porticoes which are or shall be within the city of Rome or within one mile of the city of Rome, the charge of which shall by law appertain to the aedile or to those magistrates who shall superintend the cleaning of the roads and public places within the city of Rome and within one mile of the city of Rome, no person shall in such public places or in such porticoes have any building or construction carried out, or shall occupy such public place or portico, or shall keep any of the said places closed off or blocked, whereby the public shall be deprived of free access to and free use of the said places and porticoes, except in the case of such persons and in such manner as may be allowed and permitted by laws, plebiscites, or decrees of the senate.

[The remainder of the document deals with exceptions to the last clause in the case of those who have contracts for collecting public revenues or performing public services, those celebrating public games, clerks and secretaries of magistrates, and public slaves.]

162. ROMAN MUNICIPALITIES: ADMINISTRATION AND INTERNAL AFFAIRS

THE CHARTER OF BANTIA

This fragment (about one sixth of the original) of the municipal charter of Bantia, a town on the border of Apulia and Lucania, is preserved on a bronze tablet inscribed in the Oscan tongue. Its date is *c.* 150–100 B.C. It is important not only as the earliest preserved municipal charter but also because it reveals the influence of Roman administrative institutions on traditional local practices.

FIRA, vol. I, no. 16; Adapted from C. D. Buck, *A Grammar of Oscan and Umbrian* (Boston, 1904)

. . . he shall take oath with the assent of the majority of the [local] senate, provided that not less than forty are present when the matter is under advisement.

If anyone by right of intercession shall prevent the assembly, before preventing it he shall swear that he prevents this assembly knowingly and in good faith for the sake of the public welfare, rather than out of favor or malice toward anyone, and that he is so doing in accordance with the judgment of the majority of the senate. The presiding magistrate whose assembly is prevented in this way shall not hold the assembly on this day.

Whatever magistrate shall hereafter hold an assembly in a suit involving the death penalty or a fine, let him make the people pronounce judgment after having sworn that they will render such judgment on these matters as they believe to be for the best public good, and let him prevent anyone from swearing in this matter with malice aforethought. If anyone shall act or hold an assembly contrary to this, let the fine be 2,000 sesterces. And if any magistrate prefers to fix the fine he may do so, provided it is for less than half the property of the guilty person.

If any magistrate shall have appointed the day for another in a suit involving the death penalty or a fine, he shall not hold the assembly until he has brought the accusation four times in the presence of the people, knowingly and in good faith, and the people have been advised of the fourth day. Four times, and not more than five, shall he argue the case with the defendant before he pronounces the indictment, and when he has argued for the last time with the defendant, he shall not hold the assembly within thirty days from that day.[32] And if anyone shall have acted contrary to this, if any magistrate wishes to fix the fine he may do so, provided it is for less than half the property of the guilty person.

When the censors shall take the census of the people of Bantia, whoever is a citizen of Bantia shall be rated, himself and his property, according to the regulations under which these censors shall have proposed to take the census. And if anyone fraudulently fails to come to the census, and is convicted of it, let him be scourged [?] in the assembly, under the magistracy of the praetor, in the presence of the people, and let the rest of his household and all his property which is not rated become public property without remuneration to him.[33]

The praetor, or if there shall be a prefect at Bantia after this, in case anyone wishes to go to law with another before him, or to make a forcible seizure as if judgment had been rendered on these matters which are written of in these laws, shall not prevent anyone for more than the ten succeeding days. If anyone contrary to this shall prevent, the fine shall be 1,000 sesterces. And if any magistrate wishes to fix the fine he may do so, provided it is for less than half the property of the guilty person.

No one shall be praetor or censor of Bantia unless he has been quaestor, nor shall anyone be censor unless he has been praetor. And if anyone shall be praetor and . . . he shall not become a tribune of the people after this. And if anyone shall be made tribune contrary to this, he shall be made so wrongfully.

THE CHARTER OF TARENTUM

For about two centuries Tarentum, in southern Italy, had remained an allied state *(civitas foederata)*, retaining its Greek constitution. After the Social War (see § 103) it received the Roman franchise and became a *municipium*. Sometime between 88 and 62 B.C. it was assigned its charter, only the ninth tablet of which, inscribed on bronze, is extant. This charter is the best evidence we possess for the general administrative reorganization of allied communities necessitated by the enfranchisement of Italy.

32. In the Roman procedure there were three preliminary hearings before the thirty-day interval, the fourth taking place on the day of the appeal before the assembly.

33. Personal appearance was required also at Rome, as elsewhere. The penalty at Rome for failure to appear at the census without due cause was death, slavery, or sale or confiscation of property.

CIL, vol. I, 2d ed., no. 590 (= *ROL*, 4:438–445)

. . . nor shall any person seize by fraud or misappropriate any money which does or shall belong to the said municipality, whether public or sacred or employed for religious purposes, or do aught to facilitate the occurrence of such fraud or misappropriation; nor shall he with malice aforethought impair the public property by fraud or mishandling of public accounts. Any person so acting shall be liable to a fine of four times the amount involved, and shall be condemned to pay the said money to the municipality, and may be sued or prosecuted for that amount by any magistrate in the municipality.

As respecting the *quattuorviri* and aediles[34] first created by this charter, whoever of these shall have come to Tarentum[35] shall within the twenty days next following his coming to Tarentum, subsequent to the promulgation of this charter, take steps whereby he shall stand as surety for himself and shall furnish satisfactory sureties and securities before the *quattuorviri* as a guarantee that any money belonging to the said municipality, whether public, sacred, or employed for religious purposes, passing into his hands during his magistracy, shall be properly secured to the municipality of Tarentum, and that he will render an account of the said matter in such manner as the senate shall decree. And the said *quattuorvir*, to whom such surety shall be furnished, shall accept the same and cause the matter to be entered in the public records. Furthermore, whatever person shall hold an assembly for the election of *duoviri* or aediles shall, before any candidate for a magistracy at the said assembly shall be declared elected by a majority of the *curiae*,[36] accept from the said candidates satisfactory sureties, as a guarantee that any money belonging to the said municipality, whether public, sacred, or employed for religious purposes, passing into the hands of any of the said persons during his magistracy, shall be properly secured to the municipality of Tarentum, and that he will render account of such matter in such manner as the senate shall decree, and he shall further see that the said matter is entered in the public records; and respecting any person to whom any business in the municipality has been publicly given by

34. This is inaccurate, for the four-man board *(quattuorviri)*, as in other *municipia*, included the aediles, the others being the higher magistrates known as *duoviri iure dicundo*, "two-man board with judicial power."

35. It is likely that the first *quattuorviri* under the new charter were Roman citizens nominated by the commissioner or commissioners who assigned the charter.

36. Voting units, organized, as at Rome, on a geographical basis.

decree of the senate, or who has performed any public business, or who has expended or received any public money, it shall be the duty of the said person, to whom such business shall be given, or who has publicly transacted such business, or who has expended or received public money, to give and render an account of such matter to the senate in good faith within the ten days next following the decree issued by the senate of the said municipality.

Every person who is or shall be a *decurio* of the municipality of Tarentum, or who shall have declared his vote in the senate of the said municipality, shall in good faith possess a house of his own in the town of Tarentum or within the territory of the said municipality, roofed with not less than 1,500 tiles. Any of these who does not so possess a house of his own, or has bought or received by formal transfer such house in order that this law may be fraudulently evaded, the said person shall be liable to pay to the municipality of Tarentum the sum of 5,000 sesterces for every year of offense.[37]

No person within the town of the said municipality of Tarentum shall unroof or demolish or dismantle any house without a decree of the [local] senate, unless he shall intend to restore such house to its former condition. Any person acting in violation of this ordinance shall be liable to pay to the municipality a sum of money equal to the value of the said house, and may be sued at will by any person for that amount. The magistrate who shall collect such fines shall pay one half into the public treasury; the other half he shall spend on the public games he will give during his magistracy, or if he shall desire to expend the same on some public memorial of himself, it shall be lawful for him to do so without risk of personal penalty.

If any *quattuorvir, duovir,* or aedile shall desire in the public interest of the said municipality, and within the territories belonging to the said municipality, to make, lay down, alter, build, or pave any streets, gutters, or sewers, it shall be lawful for the said person to do the same provided that no injury is done to private persons.

Any person who owes no money to the municipality of Tarentum and is a citizen of the municipality but has not been *duovir* or aedile during the six preceding years shall be permitted to move from the municipality of Tarentum without risk of personal penalty.

37. This clause was intended not so much to guarantee a permanent residence in the municipality as to prevent the wealthy from moving to Rome yet continuing to vote in Tarentum.

THE TABLET OF HERACLEA
(THE "JULIAN MUNICIPAL LAW")

This long bronze inscription, found at Heraclea in southern Italy, was long thought to contain part of a uniform charter for Rome and all Roman municipalities prepared by Julius Caesar. This theory has now been abandoned by most scholars, and the inscription is now believed to embody the drafts of four measures found among the papers of Caesar after his death, and enacted into law, on the motion of Mark Antony, in June 44 B.C. Only the last two laws, dealing with municipal administration, are given here. The first two measures, concerning the distribution of grain to the urban plebs at Rome and the duties of aediles and other public officials in Rome, are given separately under § 161.

CIL, vol. I, 2d ed., no. 593, lines 83–163 (= *FIRA*, vol. I, no. 13)

It shall not be lawful for the *duoviri* or *quattuorviri* in a municipality or colony or prefecture or *forum* or *conciliabulum* of Roman citizens, or for those who under any other title[38] shall hold a magistracy or minor office conferred by the vote of those who belong to such municipality or colony or prefecture or *forum* or *conciliabulum,* to elect directly or in substitution for another, to coopt, or to cause to be enrolled any person as a member of the senate or decurions or *conscripti* within the aforesaid communities respectively, except in the place of a deceased member or one convicted by a court, or of one who has testified that he is prohibited by this law from being a senator or decurion or conscript in such community.[39]

No person who is or shall be less than thirty years of age, shall, after the first day of January in the second year from this date, stand for or accept or hold the office of *duovir* or *quattuorvir* or any other magistracy in a municipality or colony or prefecture, unless he has served three

---

38. In some communities the municipal board of magistrates, which was vested with the judicial and administrative powers of the Roman praetors and aediles, consisted of two members *(duoviri)*. In others titles such as "dictator," "praetor," and "aedile" survived from earlier times. A prefecture was a town that possessed partial Roman citizenship and local administrative apparatus but whose judicial matters were handled by a *praefectus iure dicundo* ("prefect with judicial power") sent from Rome; or a town without magistrates, administered by a perfect sent from Rome. A *forum* and a *conciliabulum* were country towns or meeting centers of Roman citizens possessing a local senate and minor magistrates, but dependent for jurisdiction and census on Rome and the nearest large community. Originally administered from Rome, these communities were granted municipal self-government in the last years of the Republic.

39. The purpose of this provision was to maintain the size of the local senate at about 100 members.

years as a cavalryman in a legion, or six years as an infantryman in a legion, such service to be rendered in a camp or a province during the greater part of each several year, or during two consecutive periods of six months, which may be credited as equivalent to two years, or unless he shall be entitled by laws or plebiscites or by virtue of a treaty to exemption from military duty, whereby he is freed from involuntary service. Furthermore, no person who practices the trade of town crier or master of ceremonies at funerals or undertaker shall, so long as he practices such trade, stand for or accept or have or hold the office of *duovir* or *quattuorvir* or any other magistracy in a municipality or colony or prefecture, or become a senator or decurion or conscript, or declare his vote as such,[40] within such community. Whoever of the aforesaid persons shall act in contravention of this clause shall be liable to pay to the people the sum of 50,000 sesterces and may be sued at will by any person for that amount.

> [The next clause forbids magistrates to declare such persons elected and imposes a fine of 50,000 sesterces for violations.]

In every municipality, colony, prefecture, *forum*, or *conciliabulum* of Roman citizens it shall be unlawful for the following persons within such communities to be in the senate or among the decurions or *conscripti,* or to vote orally or by voting tablet in the said body: such persons as have been convicted of theft committed by themselves or have practiced collusion for the theft with the injured party; or those persons who have been or shall be convicted of breach of trust, partnership, guardianship, contract, or of injurious conduct or fraudulent intent; or those persons who have been or shall be convicted under the Plaetorian Law or for action which they have or shall commit contrary to the said law;[41] or those persons who are, have been or shall be hired to fight as gladiators; or those persons who have or shall have declared their insolvency on oath before a court, or declared their solvency;[42] or those persons who have or shall have given notice to their sureties or creditors to the effect that they are unable to pay in full, or have or shall have practiced collusion to that effect with the said sureties or creditors; or those

---

40. The annual magistrates had a vote in the local senate.

41. The Plaetorian Law (*c.* 191 B.C.) was passed to protect minors under twenty-five years of age. It authorized legal action against those who abused the inexperience of minors, and the rescinding of the transactions involved.

42. To escape summary judgment for debt. Both of these declarations led to *infamia*, "public disgrace."

persons in whose behalf such obligations have been or shall be undertaken or incurred; or those persons whose property has been or shall be
seized or publicly sold in accordance with the edict of those magistrates
who are or shall be invested with judicial authority, except in cases
where the seizure or public sale took place at the time when the said
persons were under legal wardship, or were absent in the public service,
provided that such absence in the public service was not or shall not be
due to malice aforethought; or those persons who have been or shall be
convicted by a criminal court in Rome, whereby their residence in Italy
is rendered unlawful, and are not or shall not be restored to their former
status; or those persons who have been or shall be convicted in a criminal
court within the municipality, colony, prefecture, *forum,* or *conciliabulum*
to which they shall belong; or those persons who have been or shall be
tried for having brought an accusation or done any act for the purpose
of making a false charge or from collusion; or those persons who for
any dishonorable cause have lost or shall lose their rank in the army, or
whom a commander has or shall have dishonorably discharged; or those
persons who have or shall have received money or any reward for
bringing in the head of a Roman citizen,[43] or who have or shall have
prostituted their persons; or those persons who have been or shall be
trainers of gladiators or actors, or who maintain a public brothel.

Whosoever of the aforesaid persons shall in contravention of this law
take his place or declare his vote in the senate or among the decurions or
conscripti within a municipality, colony, prefecture, *forum,* or *conciliabulum,* shall be condemned to pay to the people the sum of 50,000 sesterces
and may be sued at will by any person for that amount.

[The next clause orders the magistrates to enforce the exclusion of such
persons.]

It shall not be lawful for any persons who within a municipality,
colony, prefecture, *forum,* or *conciliabulum* are forbidden by this law to
be senators or decurions or *conscripti* to stand for or to hold the office of
duovir or *quattuorvir* or any other magistracy or minor office from which
they would pass into the said body, nor to sit in or be spectators in the
space assigned to senators, decurions, or *conscripti* at the public games or
gladiatorial contests, nor to be present at a public banquet; nor shall any
person, elected or returned contrary to this law, rank as *duovir* or *quattuorvir,* or hold any magistracy or minor office within such communi-

---

43. This refers to those who had benefited from the proscriptions of Sulla (see § 104).

ties. Whosoever shall act in contravention of this clause shall be condemned to pay to the people the sum of 50,000 sesterces and may be sued at will by any person for that amount.

In all municipalities, colonies, or prefectures of Roman citizens, such as are or shall be within Italy, those persons who shall hold the highest magistracy or office within such communities shall, at the time when the censor or any other magistrate at Rome shall take a census of the people,[44] within the sixty days next following upon their knowledge of such census being taken at Rome, proceed to take a census of all those persons belonging to their respective municipalities, colonies, or prefectures who shall be Roman citizens. From all such persons, duly sworn, they shall receive their family names and given names, their fathers or patrons, their tribes, their surnames, the age of each, and a statement of their property, in accordance with the schedule of the census set forth by the magistrate about to take the census of the people at Rome; all such particulars they shall cause to be entered in the public records of their respective communities, and they shall dispatch the said documents to the officials then taking the census at Rome by the hands of delegates selected to be sent for that purpose by a vote of a majority of the decurions or *conscripti* present at a meeting convened for such purpose; they shall further see that, within sixty days of the date on which the aforesaid magistrates shall have completed the census of the people at Rome, the said delegates shall reach the said magistrates and deliver the documents of their respective municipalities, colonies, or prefectures. Thereupon, the said censor, or whatever magistrate shall take the census of the people at Rome, shall, within the five days next following the arrival of the said delegates from their respective communities, receive in good faith the said census documents delivered by the said delegates; he shall further see that the particulars contained in the said documents shall be entered in the public records, and that such records shall be preserved in the same place as the other public records in which the census of the people is registered and kept.

All persons having a domicile in more than one municipality, colony, or prefecture, and whose census deposition is made at Rome, shall not be included in the census of a municipality, colony, or prefecture, notwithstanding any provisions of this law.

---

44. This took place normally every five years; hence the local magistrates at the time of the taking of the census were known as *quinquennales*.

[The last clause contains advance confirmation of amendments made in the charter of the town of Fundi in Campania by the person assigned to frame the charter.]

THE CHARTER OF THE COLONY GENETIVA JULIA (URSO)

These four bronze tablets, found at Osuna (ancient Urso, in Hispania Baetica) about sixty miles east of Seville, are the best preserved remains of a Roman municipal charter, and the only extant colonial charter. The colony, composed of persons sent from among the urban plebs at Rome, was established by law in 44 B.C., and the charter was granted by Julius Caesar in the same year. Most of it deals with local municipal affairs, but it also touches on the relationship of the municipality to the central government. The influence of Roman administrative institutions is apparent.

CIL, vol. I, 2d ed., no. 594 (=*CIL,* vol. II, supplement, no. 5439)

[The beginning of the charter is lost as far as clause LX.]
LXI. [This clause deals with legal procedures in the execution of judgments against debtors.]

LXII. In respect to all *duoviri,* each *duovir* shall have the right and power to employ two lictors, one attendant, two clerks, two apparitors, a secretary, a herald, a soothsayer, and a flute player.[45] In respect to the aediles in the said colony, each aedile shall have the right and power to employ one clerk, four public slaves in girded aprons,[46] a herald, a soothsayer and a flute player. In this number they shall employ persons who are colonists of the said colony. The said *duoviri* and the said aediles, so long as they shall hold their magistracy, shall have the right and power to use the *toga praetexta,* wax torches, and wax tapers.

In respect to the said clerks, lictors, attendants, apparitors, flute players, soothsayers, and heralds employed by each of the same, all the said persons, during the year in which they shall perform such services, shall have exemption from military service. And no person shall, during the year in which they perform such services for magistrates, make any such person a soldier against his will, or order him to be so made, or use compulsion against him, or administer the oath, or order such oath to

45. The flute player accompanied the magistrate on all public occasions, including sacrifices.
46. The dress of slaves. Slaves were assigned to the aediles because of their duties connected with the care of streets, extinguishing fires, and so on.

be administered, or swear in such person or order such person to be sworn in with the preliminary oath, except on the occasion of sudden military alarms in Italy or Gaul. The following shall be the rate of pay for such persons as perform services for the *duoviri*: for each clerk 1,200 sesterces; for each attendant 700; for each lictor 600; for each apparitor 400; for each secretary 300; for each soothsayer 500; for a herald 300. For persons serving the aediles the pay shall be: for each clerk 800 sesterces; for each soothsayer 500; for each flute player 300; and for each herald 300. And the aforesaid sums it shall be lawful for the said persons to receive without risk of personal penalty.

LXIII. [This clause deals with the prorating of pay for the staff of the *duoviri* who serve until the end of the year 44 B.C.]

LXIV. All *duoviri* holding office after the establishment of the colony shall, within the ten days next following the commencement of their magistracy, bring before the decurions for decision, when not less than two thirds shall be present, the question as to the dates and number of the festal days, the sacrifices to be publicly performed, and the persons to perform such sacrifices. Whatever a majority of the decurions present at such meeting shall have decreed or determined concerning the said matters shall be lawful and valid, and such sacrifices and such festal days shall be observed in the said colony.

LXV. [This clause allocates to sacrificial purposes all fines levied in connection with the collection of municipal taxes.]

LXVI. In respect to pontiffs and augurs appointed from the Colonia Genetiva by Gaius Caesar or the person who by his command shall establish the colony, such persons shall be pontiffs and augurs of the Colonia Genetiva Julia, and shall be members of the colleges of pontiffs and augurs within the said colony with all the rights and privileges appertaining to pontiffs and augurs in every colony. And the said pontiffs and augurs who shall be members of the several colleges, and also their children, shall have exemption from military service and compulsory public services solemnly guaranteed, in such wise as a pontiff in Rome has or shall have the same, and all their military service shall be accounted as discharged. Respecting the auspices and matters appertaining to the same, jurisdiction and adjudication shall belong to the augurs. And the said pontiffs and augurs shall have the right and power to use the *toga praetexta* at all games publicly celebrated by magistrates, and at public sacrifices of the Colonia Genetiva Julia performed by themselves, and the said pontiffs and augurs shall have the right and power to sit among the decurions to witness the games and the gladiatorial combats.

LXVII–LXVIII. [These clauses deal with the election of pontiffs and augurs.]

LXIX. [This clause deals with the payment of moneys due contractors providing the requisites for religious ceremonies.]

LXX. All *duoviri,* except those first appointed after this law, shall during their magistracy at the discretion of the decurions celebrate a gladiatorial show or dramatic spectacles in honor of Jupiter, Juno, Minerva,[47] and the gods and goddesses, as far as possible during four days, for the greater part of each day; and on the said spectacles and the said shows each of the said persons shall expend of his own money not less than 2,000 sesterces, and out of the public money it shall be lawful for each several *duovir* to appropriate and expend a sum not exceeding 2,000 sesterces, and it shall be lawful for the said persons so to do without risk of personal penalty. Always provided that no person shall appropriate or make assignment of any portion of the money which in accordance with this charter shall be properly given or assigned for those religious ceremonies which are publicly performed in the colony or in any other place.

LXXI. [On games to be given by the aediles of the colony.]

LXXII. [On the expenditure of moneys collected for religious purposes.]

LXXIII. No person shall, within the boundaries of the town or colony, within the area marked round by the plow,[48] introduce a dead person, or bury or cremate the same therein,[49] nor build therein a monument to a deceased person. Any person acting in contravention of this shall be condemned to pay to the colonists of the Colonia Genetiva Julia 5,000 sesterces, and may be sued or prosecuted at will by any person for that amount. Any monument so built a *duovir* or aedile shall cause to be demolished, and if, in contravention of this law, a dead person has been introduced and placed therein, they shall make the proper expiation.

47. The Capitoline Triad (see chapter 1, note 15).
48. The *pomerium* is meant (see § 6).
49. Cf. the Twelve Tables (§ 32, table x).

LXXIV. [This clause forbids the building of new crematories within one half mile of the town.]

LXXV. No person shall unroof or demolish or dismantle any building in the town of the Colonia Julia, unless he shall have furnished sureties, at the discretion of the *duoviri,* that he has the intention of rebuilding the same, or unless the decurions have allowed such act by decree, provided that not less than fifty shall be present when the said matter is discussed. Any person acting in contravention of this shall be condemned to pay to the colonists of the Colonia Genetiva Julia a sum of money equal to the value of the said building, and may, in accordance with this charter, be sued or prosecuted at will by any person for that amount.

LXXVI. [Restrictions on the size of pottery and tile works in the town.]

LXXVII. If any *duovir* or aedile shall desire in the public interest to make, lay down, alter, build, or pave any streets, gutters, or sewers within the boundaries belonging to the Colonia Julia, it shall be lawful for the said persons to do the same, provided that no injury be done to private persons.

LXXVIII. Respecting public roads and footpaths which were within the boundaries assigned to the colony, all such thoroughfares, roads, and footpaths which exist or shall exist or have existed in the said territories, shall be public property.

LXXIX. Respecting all rivers, streams, fountains, lakes, springs, ponds, or marshes within the territory divided among the colonists of this colony, the holders and possessors of such land shall have the same right of access, carriage and drawing of water in respect to the said streams, fountains, lakes, springs, ponds, and marshes, as belonged to former holders and possessors. In like manner, the persons who own or possess or shall own or possess the said land shall have legal right of way to the said waters.

LXXX. Whatever public business in the colony is given to any person by decree of the decurions, the person to whom such business shall be given shall produce and render an account of the said matter to the decurions in good faith as far as possible within the 150 days next following his completion of the said business or his ceasing to carry it on.

LXXXI. In respect to all clerks of the *duoviri* and aediles of the Colonia Julia to be employed in making entry of public money and in writing the accounts of the colonists, every *duovir* and every aedile shall, before the said clerks make up or handle public records, administer to each publicly and openly, in the daytime, on a market day in the Forum, an oath by Jupiter and the *Penates* [tutelary gods of the state property] that they will conscientiously and in good faith guard the public money of the said colony and keep true accounts, and that they will not knowingly and with malice aforethought defraud the colony by false entries. As each clerk shall so take the oath, the said magistrate shall cause him to be entered in the public records. Clerks failing to take such oath shall not make up the public accounts, nor shall they receive the money or the pay due attendants for such service. Magistrates failing to administer such oath shall be fined 5,000 sesterces, and may be sued or prosecuted for that amount by any person at will in accordance with this charter.

LXXXII. In respect to all lands or woods or buildings granted or assigned to the colonists of the Colonia Genetiva Julia for public use, no person shall sell the said lands or woods, or lease the same for a longer period than five years, or bring a proposal before the decurions or carry a decree of the decurions whereby the said lands and woods shall be sold or leased otherwise than as aforesaid. Nor, in case they are sold, shall they thereby cease to be the property of the Colonia Genetiva Julia. And any person using the produce of the same on the ground of such purchase shall be condemned to pay to the colonists of the said colony 100 sesterces for every *iugerum* for each year of use, and may be sued or prosecuted by any person at will for that amount in accordance with this charter. [The remainder of this section is lost.]

XCI. Respecting any person in accordance with this charter appointed or elected *decurio,* augur, or pontiff in the Colonia Genetiva Julia, whatsoever *decurio,* augur, or pontiff of the said colony shall fail within the next five years to possess in the colony or town, or within a mile of the town, a domicile whence a sufficient pledge can be taken [i.e., within five years after appointment], the same shall cease to be an augur, pontiff, or *decurio* in the said colony; and the *duoviri* in the said colony shall conscientiously cause the names of such persons to be struck from the public lists of decurions and priests; and it shall be lawful for the said *duoviri* so to do without risk of personal penalty.

XCII. [This clause concerns public embassies dispatched by the colony.]

XCIII. No *duoviri* appointed or elected after the establishment of the colony, and no prefect left in charge by a *duovir* in accordance with the charter of the colony, shall, concerning public ground or for public ground, receive or accept from a contractor or leaseholder or surety any gift or present or remuneration or any other favor; nor shall he cause any such favor to be bestowed upon himself or upon any member of his family. Any person acting in contravention of this shall be condemned to pay to the colonists of the Colonia Genetiva Julia 20,000 sesterces, and may be sued or prosecuted by any person at will for that amount.

XCIV. [This clause limits legal jurisdiction to authorized officials.]

XCV. [Legal procedures in a case involving the collection of fines due to the colony.]

XCVI. [Decurions may vote a public investigation of the administration at any time.]

XCVII. [Limitations on the selection of patrons of the colony by decree of the decurions.]

XCVIII. In the case of any compulsory public service[50] decreed by the decurions of the said colony, a majority of the decurions being present when the said matter is discussed, it shall be lawful for such work to be carried out, provided that in any one year not more than five days' work be decreed for each adult male, nor more than three days' work for each yoke of draught animals. The said public work shall by decree of the decurions be superintended by the incumbent aediles. They shall see that the work is carried out in accordance with the decree of the decurions, provided that no labor be required, without his own consent, from any person less than fourteen or more than sixty years of age. Persons possessing a domicile or land in the said colony, or within the boundaries of the said colony, who are not colonists of the said colony shall be liable to the same amount of labor as a colonist.

XCIX. Respecting any public aqueducts brought into the town of the Colonia Genetiva the incumbent *duoviri* shall make proposal to the decurions, when two thirds of the same are present, as to the lands through which an aqueduct may lawfully be brought. Whatever lands a majority of the decurions then present shall have determined upon, provided that no water be brought through any building not constructed for that purpose, it shall be lawful and right to bring an aqueduct through the said lands, and no person shall do aught to prevent an aqueduct from being so brought.

50. Such as fortification work and, most commonly, road construction and repair.

C. [Concerns the granting by the decurions of permission to private individuals to use public water overflowing from a reservoir.]

CI. [Disqualified persons not to be entered in elections to magistracies.]

CII. [On the amount of time for pleading allotted to accusers and defendants in trials.]

CIII. Whenever a majority of the decurions present at a meeting shall have decreed to call out armed men for the purpose of defending, the territories of the colony, it shall be lawful, without risk of personal penalty, for the responsible *duovir* or prefect invested with judicial power in such manner to call out under arms colonists, resident aliens, and attributed persons.[51] And the said *duovir* or any person placed in command of such armed forces by the *duovir* shall have the same authority and the same power of punishment as belongs to a military tribune of the Roman people in an army of the Roman people; and he shall lawfully and properly exercise such authority and power without risk of personal penalty, provided that this is done in accordance with the decree of a majority of the decurions present at the said meeting.

CIV. [Forbids the blocking up of boundary roads, crossroads, and drainage ditches.]

CV. [Expulsion of disqualified decurions from the local senate.]

CVI. [Forbids unlawful assembly.]

CVII–CXXII. [This section is lost.]

CXXIII and CXXIV. [On procedures connected with accusations of conduct unbecoming a *decurio*.]

CXXV and CXXVI. [On persons permitted to sit in the place assigned to decurions for viewing games in the circus; on places assigned to decurions at theatrical performances.]

CXXVII. Respecting any dramatic spectacles in the Colonia Genetiva Julia, no person shall sit in the orchestra to view the performance, save a magistrate or promagistrate of the Roman people, or a Roman official invested with legal jurisdiction, or one who is or has been a senator of the Roman people, or the sons of such senator, or the *praefectus fabrum*[52] of the magistrate or promagistrate governing the province of Farther Spain or Baetica, or those persons who are or shall be allowed by this law to sit in the place assigned to the decurions. Nor shall any person, acting conscientiously and in good faith, introduce into the said place or allow to sit therein any other persons.

51. These last were Spaniards without Roman citizenship.

52. This officer, of equestrian rank, was appointed by the proconsul to supervise the workmen and engineers attached to the governor's military forces.

CXXVIII. [On the annual appointment by the magistrates of officers in charge of shrines and of the conduct of religious services.]

CXXIX. All *duoviri,* aediles, and prefects of the Colonia Genetiva Julia, and likewise all decurions of the said colony, shall diligently and in good faith observe and obey the decrees of the decurions,[53] and they shall use their diligence to do and perform, conscientiously and in good faith, all things whatsoever it shall be proper for the said persons respectively to do or perform in accordance with the decree of the decurions. Any person failing so to act, or knowingly and with malice aforethought acting in contravention of this, shall for every such act or omission be condemned to pay to the colonists of the Colonia Genetiva Julia 10,000 sesterces, and may be sued or prosecuted for that amount in accordance with this charter through *recuperatores* before a *duovir* or prefect by any person at will.

CXXX. [Additional severe restrictions on the adoption of Roman senators as patrons of the colony.]
CXXXI. [Severe restrictions on the adoption of Roman senators as honorary public guests *(hospites)* of the colony.]

CXXXII. No person in the Colonia Genetiva Julia who is a candidate for election to any magistracy within the said colony shall, after the promulgation of this charter, with a view to seeking such magistracy, or during the year in which he shall be a candidate or shall stand for or intend to stand for such magistracy, knowingly and with malice aforethought provide entertainments, or invite any person to dinner, or hold or provide a banquet, or knowingly and with malice aforethought cause another person to hold a banquet or invite any person to dinner with a view to his candidature, except that the said candidate himself who shall be seeking a magistracy may, if he so desire, in good faith invite during the said year daily any persons not exceeding nine.[54] No candidate seeking office shall knowingly and with malice aforethought give or make largess of any gift or present or any other thing with a view to his candidature. Nor shall any person, with a view to the candidature of another, provide entertainments, or invite any person to dinner, or hold a banquet, or knowingly and with malice aforethought give or make largess of any gift or present or any other thing. Any person acting in

53. Note the continuation by Caesar of the Roman policy, traditional both in Italy and in the provinces, of vesting supreme power in the town council or municipal senate, which was made up of the local aristocracy.
54. The usual number of guests at the formal Roman *cena*, "dinner."

contravention of this shall be condemned to pay to the colonists of the Colonia Genetiva Julia 5,000 sesterces, and may be sued or prosecuted in accordance with this charter for that amount through *recuperatores* before a *duovir* or prefect by any person at will.

CXXXIII. Respecting all persons who, in accordance with this charter, are or shall be colonists of the Colonia Genetiva Julia, the wives of all such persons who are within the colony in accordance with this charter shall obey the laws of the Colonia Genetiva Julia and of their husbands, and shall in good faith enjoy, in accordance with this charter, all such rights as are specified in this charter.

CXXXIV. No *duovir* or aedile or prefect of the Colonia Genetiva shall after the promulgation of this charter make proposal to the decurions of the said colony, or consult the same, or carry a decree of the decurions, or enter such a decree, or order such a decree to be entered in the public records, and no *decurio* when such matter is discussed among the decurions shall declare his vote, or frame a decree of the decurions, or enter such a decree, or cause such a decree to be entered in the public records, whereby any public money or anything else is given or granted to any person as a reward for holding office, or for giving or promising a gladiatorial show, or for the sake of giving or setting up a statue . . . [The rest is lost.]

BENEFACTOR OF AN ITALIAN TOWN

CIL, vol. I, 2d ed., no. 1529 (= *ROL,* 4:146–147); Adapted from *LCL*

Aletrium (Latium); *c.* 135–90 B.C.

Lucius Betilienus Varus son of Lucius, in accordance with a vote of the [municipal] senate superintended the construction of the works which are recorded below: all the street paths in the town, the colonnade along which people walk to the citadel, a playing field, a sundial [or water clock], a meat market, the stuccoing of the townhall, seats, a bathing pool; he constructed a reservoir by the gate, an aqueduct about 340 feet long leading into the city and to the hill of the citadel, also the arches and good sound water pipes. As reward for these works the senate made him censor twice and ordered that his son be exempt from military service; and the people bestowed the gift of a statue on him over the title of Censorinus.

CONTRACT FOR CONSTRUCTION WORK AT
PUTEOLI, 105 B.C.

CIL, vol. I, 2d ed., no. 698 (= *CIL,* vol. X, no. 1781 = *ROL,* 4:274–79); Adapted from
LCL

In the 90th year from the foundation of the colony, in the magistracy of
Numerius Fufidius son of Numerius, and Marcus Pullius, duovirs, and
the consulship of Publius Tutilius and Gnaeus Mallius.

Second Contract Relating to Works

Contract for making a wall in the plot which lies in front of the temple
of Sarapis across the road. The contractor shall provide sureties and
register their estates as securities at the discretion of the duovirs. In the
middle of the party wall which is near the road and which is in the plot
across the road, he shall make an opening for a doorway; he shall make
it 6 ft. wide and 7 ft. high. . . . [Some of the specifications given are
here omitted.] The same person shall also make two latticed folding
doors having posts of winter oak and shall put up and close and pitch
them in the same manner as at the temple of Honor. In regard to the
wall which forms the outermost enclosure, he shall further reconstruct
the said wall 10 ft. high including coping. He shall also block up the
doorway which now forms an entrance into the plot, and also wall up
the windows which are in the wall along the said plot; and on the wall
which is at present along the road he shall put an uninterrupted coping.
And all those walls and copings which will be found uncoated he shall
cause to be well coated with a plaster of lime mortar mixed with sand
and smoothed and whitewashed with wet lime. Material requiring preparation that he will use in this structure he shall make of clay mixed with
one fourth part of slaked lime. And the rough tiles which he shall lay
shall not be larger than such rough tile as weighs 15 lbs. when dry, nor
shall he make the corner tiles more than 4½ inches high. And he shall
clear the site according to the requirements of the work. Likewise the
chapels, altars, and statues which are on the building ground and which
shall be pointed out to him he shall remove, transfer, arrange, and set
up in a place which shall be pointed out to him, at the discretion of the
duovirs. He shall complete the whole of this work at the discretion of
the duovirs and ex-duovirs who customarily sit in council at Puteoli,

provided that no less than twenty members are present when the matter is under discussion. Whatever may be approved by twenty of them on oath shall be legally valid; whatever they may not approve shall be legally invalid. Day for beginning the work: the first day of November next. Day of payment: one half of the sum shall be handed over when the estates have been satisfactorily registered as securities; the other half shall be paid off when the work is completed and approved.

Gaius Blossius son of Quintus; he contracts for 1,500 sesterces; is likewise surety. Quintus Fuficius son of Quintus; Gnaeus Tetteius son of Quintus; Gaius Granius son of Gaius; Tiberius Crassicius.[55]

ELECTION NOTICES AT POMPEII, *c.* 80 B.C.

Painted in red on the walls of the town.

CIL, vol. 1, 2d ed., nos. 1640–79 (= *ROL,* 4:286–289); From *LCL*

1. Lucius Aquitius, a fine man; settlers, I appeal to you to elect him duovir.
2. Numerius Barcha, a fine man; I appeal to you to elect him duovir. So may Venus of Pompeii, holy, hallowed goddess, be kind to you.
3. Numerius Veius Barcha, may you rot!
4. Your best friend—Marcus Marius. Elect him aedile!
5. Marcus Marius; I appeal to you to elect him aedile.
6. Marcus Marius, a fine man; I appeal to you, settlers.
7. Quintus Caecilius, a generous man; to be quaestor—I appeal to you.
8. Publius Carpinius, a fine man; I appeal to you to elect him duovir.
9. Publius Furius, a fine man; I appeal to you to elect him duovir.
10. Lucius Niraemius, a fine man; to be duovir.
11. Marcus Septumius, a fine man; I appeal to you, settlers — duovir.
12. Quinctius; let anyone who votes against him take a seat by an ass.

---

55. The additional sureties for the contractor Blossius.

163. Mobilization of the Roman Army

Livy, *History of Rome* XXII. xxxviii. 1–5; Adapted from *LCL*

After completing the levy [of 216 B.C.], the consuls waited a few days
for the soldiers from the allies and the Latins to arrive. Then the military
tribunes had the soldiers swear a personal oath. This was unprecedented,
for until that day there had been nothing but the oath to assemble at the
bidding of the consuls and not to depart without their orders; and, after
assembling, the cavalry in their decuries and the infantry in their centuries would take a voluntary pledge among themselves that they would
not go off in flight or fear, and would not leave their ranks except to
take up or seek a weapon, or to smite an enemy, or to save a fellow
citizen. This voluntary compact among the men was now replaced by
an individual oath formally administered by the military tribunes.

Aulus Gellius, *Attic Nights* XVI. iv. 2–5; Adapted from *LCL*

In the Fifth Book of . . . Cincius'[56] *On Military Science* the following is
written: "When a levy was made in former times and soldiers were
enrolled, the military tribune administered an oath to them in the following words: 'In the army of the consuls such and such—e.g., Gaius
Laelius son of Gaius and Lucius Cornelius son of Publius—and for ten
miles around it, you will not with malice aforethought steal, alone or
with others, anything worth more than a silver sesterce in any one day;
and excepting a spear, a spearshaft, wood, fruit, fodder, a wineskin, a
purse, or a torch, if you there find or carry off anything which is not
your own and is worth more than one silver sesterce, you will bring it
to the consul Gaius Laelius son of Gaius, or to the consul Lucius Cornelius son of Publius, or to whomever either of them shall designate, or
you will report within the next three days whatever you have found or
carried off with malice aforethought, or you will restore it to the owner
to whom you believe it belongs, acting in good conscience.'

"Moreover, when the soldiers had been enrolled, a day was appointed
on which they should appear and answer to the consul's summons, and
they recited an oath that they would appear, with the following exceptions: 'Except for one of the following causes: a funeral in the family or
purification from a dead body (provided these were not set for that day

56. An antiquarian of the Augustan Age.

to avoid appearing on that day), serious illness, an omen which might not be passed by without propitiation, an anniversary sacrifice which could not be properly celebrated unless he were there present in person on that day, *force majeure* or enemy attack, or a day appointed or agreed upon with a foreigner [for a trial]; if anyone shall have any of these excuses, then on the day after that on which he is excused for these reasons he shall come and render service to the one who held the levy in that district, village, or town.' "[57]

Also in the same book are these words: "When a soldier was absent on the appointed day and had not been excused, he was branded a malingerer."

164. The Roman Military System in the Second Century b.c.

The following selections deal with the enrollment of the legions, the administration of the military oath, the levying of the allies, the tactical organization of the legion, commissioned and noncommissioned officers, the marshaling of the legions and allied troops, encampment arrangements, court-martial and decimation, and pay for soldiers. For the organization of the Roman army, see also § 45.

Polybius, *Histories* vi. xix–xlii (abridged); Adapted from *LCL*

After electing the consuls, they appoint military tribunes, fourteen from those who have seen five years' service and ten from those who have seen ten. As for the rest, a cavalry soldier must serve ten years in all and an infantry soldier for sixteen years before reaching the age of forty-six, with the exception of those whose census is under 400 drachmas, all of whom are employed in naval service. In case of pressing danger twenty years' service is demanded from the infantry. No one is eligible for any political office before he has completed ten years' service. The consuls, when they are about to enroll soldiers, announce at a meeting of the popular assembly the day on which all Roman citizens of military age must present themselves, and this they do annually. On the appointed day, when those liable to service arrive in Rome and assemble at the Capitol, the junior tribunes divide themselves into four groups, as the popular assembly or the consuls determine, since the main and original

57. The sections here preserved obviously do not constitute the whole military oath; cf. § 164.

division of their forces is into four legions. The four tribunes first nominated are appointed to the first legion, the next three to the second, the following four to the third, and the last three to the fourth. Of the senior tribunes the first two are appointed to the first legion, the next three to the second, the next two to the third, and the last three to the fourth. The division and appointment of the tribunes having thus been so made that each legion has the same number of officers, those of each legion take their seats apart, and they draw lots for the tribes, and summon them singly in the order of the lottery. From each tribe they first of all select four lads of more or less the same age and physique. When these are brought forward the officers of the first legion have first choice, those of the second second choice, those of the third third, and those of the fourth last. Another batch of four is now brought forward, and this time the officers of the second legion have first choice and so on, those of the first choosing last. A third batch having been brought forward the tribunes of the third legion choose first, and those of the second last. By thus continuing to give each legion first choice in turn, each gets men of the same standard. When they have chosen the number determined on—that is when the strength of each legion is brought up to 4,200, or in times of exceptional danger to 5,000—the old system was to choose the cavalry after the 4,200 infantry, but they now choose them first, the censor selecting them according to their wealth; and 300 are assigned to each legion.

The enrollment having been completed in this manner, those of the tribunes on whom this duty falls in each legion collect the newly-enrolled soldiers, and picking out of the whole body a single man whom they think the most suitable make him take the oath that he will obey his officers and execute their orders as far as is in his power. Then the others come forward and each in his turn takes the oath simply that he will do the same as the first man.

At the same time the consuls send their orders to the chief magistrates of the allied cities in Italy from which they want allied contingents, stating the numbers required and the day and place at which the men selected must present themselves. The cities, choosing the men and administering the oath in the manner above described, send them off, appointing a commander and a paymaster.

The tribunes in Rome, after administering the oath, fix for each legion a day and place at which the men are to present themselves without arms, and then dismiss them. When they come to the rendez-vous, they choose the youngest and poorest to form the *velites;* those next to them are made *hastati;* those in the prime of life *principes;* and the oldest of all *triarii,* those being the names among the Romans of the four classes in each legion distinct in age and equipment. They divide them so that the senior men known as *triarii* number 600, the *principes* 1,200, the *hastati* 1,200, the rest, consisting of the youngest, being *velites.* If the legion consists of more than 4,000 men, they divide accordingly, except as regards the *triarii,* the number of whom is always the same.

The youngest soldiers or *velites* are ordered to carry a sword, light javelins, and a light shield. This shield is strongly made and sufficiently large to afford protection, being circular and measuring three feet in diameter. They also wear a plain helmet, and sometimes cover it with a wolf's skin or something similar both to protect it and to act as a distinguishing mark by which their officers can recognize them and judge if they fight pluckily or not. . . .

The next older group, called *hastati,* are ordered to wear a complete panoply. The Roman panoply consists firstly of a shield *(scutum),* the convex surface of which measures two and a half feet in width and four feet in length, the thickness at the rim being a palm's breadth. It is made of two planks glued together, the outer surface being then covered first with canvas and then with calfskin. Its upper and lower rims are strengthened by an iron edging which protects it from descending sword blows and from injury when rested on the ground. It also has an iron boss *(umbo)* fixed to it which turns aside the more formidable blows of stones, pikes and heavy missiles in general. Besides the shield they also carry a sword, hanging on the right thigh and called a Spanish sword. This is excellent for thrusting, and both of its edges cut effectively, as the blade is very strong and firm. In addition they have two heavy javelins *(pila),* a bronze helmet, and greaves. . . . Finally, they wear as an ornament a circle of feathers with three upright purple or black feathers about a cubit in height, the addition of which on the head surmounting their other arms makes every man look twice his real height and gives him a fine appearance, such as will strike terror into the enemy. The common soldiers wear in addition a breastplate of bronze a span square, which they place in front of the breast and call a heart-protector *(pectorale),* and this completes their accoutrements; but those who are rated above 10,000 drachmas wear instead of this a coat of chain mail *(lorica).* The *principes* and *triarii* are armed in the same manner except that instead of *pila* the *triarii* carry long spears *(hastae).*

From each of the classes except the youngest they select ten centurions according to merit, and then they select a second ten. All these are called centurions, but the first man chosen also has a seat in the military council. . . . When both centurions are on the spot, the first selected commands the right half of his company (maniple) and the second the left, but if both are not present the one who is commands the whole. They wish the centurions to be not so much venturesome daredevils as natural leaders of a steady and sedate spirit, not so much men who will initiate attacks and open the battle as men who will hold their ground when worsted and hard pressed and be ready to die at their posts.

In like manner they divide the cavalry into ten squadrons *(turmae)*, and from each they select three commanders, who themselves appoint their rear guard officers *(optiones)*. The first commander chosen commands the whole squadron, but the other two also have the rank and title of *decurio,* and if the first of them is not present the second takes command of the squadron. . . .

The tribunes, having thus organized the troops and ordered them to arm themselves in this manner, dismiss them to their homes. When the day comes on which they have all sworn to assemble at the place appointed by the consuls—each consul as a rule appointing a separate rendezvous for his own troops, since each has received his share of the allies and two Roman legions—none of those on the roll ever fail to appear, no excuse whatever being admitted, once they have taken the military oath, except adverse omens or physical disability. The allies having now assembled also at the same places as the Romans, their organization and command are undertaken by the officers appointed by the consuls, known as *praefecti sociorum* (prefects of the allies) and twelve in number. They first of all select for the consuls from the whole force of allies assembled the horsemen and footmen most fitted for actual service, these being known as *extraordinarii,* that is "select." The total number of allied infantry is usually equal to that of the Roman legions, while the cavalry are three times as many. Of these they assign about a third of the cavalry and a fifth of the infantry to the select corps; the rest they divide into two bodies, one known as the right wing and the other as the left.

When these arrangements have been made, the tribunes take both the Romans and the allies and pitch their camp, one simple plan of encampment being adopted at all times and in all places. . . .

The manner in which they form their camp is as follows. When the site for the camp has been chosen, the position in it giving the best general view and most suitable for issuing orders is assigned to the general's tent *(praetorium)*. Fixing an ensign on the spot where they are about to pitch it, they measure off round this ensign a square plot of ground each side of which is 100 feet distant, so that the total area measures four *plethra*.[58] Along one side of this square in the direction which seems to give the greatest facilities for watering and foraging, the Roman legions are disposed as follows. As I have said, there are six tribunes in each legion; and since each consul has always two Roman legions with him, it is evident that there are twelve tribunes in the army of each. They then place the tents of these all in one line parallel to the side of the square selected and fifty feet distant from it, to leave room for the horses, mules, and baggage of the tribunes. These tents are pitched with their backs turned to the *praetorium* and facing the outer side of the camp—a direction which I will always speak of as "the front." The tents of the tribunes are at an equal distance from each other, and at such intervals that they extend along the whole breadth of the space occupied by the Roman legions.

They now measure 100 feet from the front of all these tents, and starting from the line drawn at this distance parallel to the tents of the tribunes they begin to encamp the legions, managing matters as follows. Bisecting the above line, they draw a line from this spot at right angles to the first, and along it they encamp the cavalry of each legion facing each other at a distance of fifty feet from each other, with the bisecting line midway between them. The manner of encamping the cavalry and the infantry is very similar, the whole space occupied by the maniples and squadrons [of each legion] forming a rectangle. This faces one of the through streets *(viae)* and its length is fixed by that of the street, namely, 100 feet; and they usually try to make its depth the same except in the case of the allies. When they employ the larger legions they add proportionately to the length and depth. . . .

The spaces lying behind the tents of the tribunes to right and left of the *praetorium* are used as follows: one for the market and the other for the office of the quaestor and the supplies of which he is in charge. Behind the last tent of the tribunes on either side, and more or less at right angles to these tents, are the quarters of the cavalry picked out of the *extraordinarii,* and a certain number of volunteers serving to oblige the consuls. These are all encamped parallel to the two sides of the circumvallation, facing in the one case the quaestor's depot and in the other the market. As a rule these troops are not only thus encamped right near the consuls, but on the march and on other occasions are in

58. The *plethron,* a Greek measure, equaled 10,000 square feet.

constant attendance on the consul and quaestor. Back to back with them, and looking towards the circumvallation, are the select infantry, who perform the same service as the cavalry just described. . . .

The whole camp thus forms a square, and the way in which the streets are laid out in it and its general arrangement give it the appearance of a town. The circumvallation is on all sides at a distance of 200 feet from the tents, and this empty space is of important service in several respects. To begin with it provides the proper facilities for marching the troops in and out, seeing that they all march out into this empty space by their own streets and thus do not come into one street in a mass and tumble into or trample each other. Again, it is here that they collect the cattle brought into camp and the booty taken from the enemy, and keep them safe during the night. But the most important thing of all is that in night attacks neither fire can reach them nor missiles except a very few, which are practically harmless owing to the distance and the space in front of the tents. . . .

A court-martial composed of the tribunes is convened at once to try him,[59] and if he is found guilty he is punished by the bastinado *(fustuarium)*. This is inflicted as follows: the tribune takes a cudgel and just touches the condemned man with it, after which all in the camp beat or stone him, in most cases dispatching him in the camp itself. But even those who manage to escape are not saved thereby: impossible! for they are not allowed to return to their homes, and none of his relatives would dare to receive such a man in his house. So that those who have once fallen into this misfortune are utterly ruined. . . .

While the soldiers are subject to the tribunes, the latter are subject to the consuls. A tribune, and in the case of the allies a prefect, has the power of inflicting fines, of demanding sureties, and of punishing by flogging. The bastinado is also inflicted on those who steal anything from the camp; on anyone who gives false evidence; on anyone in full manhood caught abusing his person; and finally on anyone who has been punished thrice for the same fault. Those are the offenses which are punished as crimes, while the following are treated as unmanly acts and disgraceful in a soldier: when a man boasts falsely to the tribune of his valor in the field in order to gain distinction; when any men who have been placed in a covering force leave the station assigned to them from fear; likewise when anyone out of fear throws away any of his arms in actual battle. Therefore the men in covering forces often face certain

59. A soldier delinquent in patrol duty.

death, refusing to leave their ranks even when vastly outnumbered, owing to dread of the punishment they would meet with; and again, men who have lost a shield or sword or any of their other arms in battle unexpectedly throw themselves into the midst of the enemy, hoping either to recover the lost object or to escape by death inevitable disgrace and the insults of their relatives.

If the same thing ever happens to large bodies, and if entire maniples desert their posts when exceedingly hard pressed, the officers refrain from inflicting the bastinado or the death penalty on all, but find a solution for the situation which is both salutary and terror-inspiring. Assembling the legion, the tribune brings forward those guilty of leaving their post, denounces them bitterly, and finally chooses by lot sometimes five, sometimes eight, sometimes twenty of the offenders, so adjusting the number thus chosen that they equal as nearly as possible the tenth part of those guilty of cowardice. Those on whom the lot falls are bastinadoed mercilessly in the manner described above; the rest receive rations of barley instead of wheat and are ordered to encamp outside the safety of the camp wall. As therefore the danger and dread of drawing the fatal lot affects all equally, since it is uncertain on whom it will fall, and as the public disgrace of receiving barley rations falls on all alike, this practice is the one best calculated both to inspire fear and to correct the mischief. . . .

As pay the foot soldier receives two obols a day, a centurion twice as much, and a cavalryman a drachma. As his grain ration, a foot soldier receives per month about two thirds of an Attic *medimnus*[60] of wheat, a cavalryman seven *medimni* of barley and two of wheat; of the allies the infantry receive the same, the cavalry one and one third *medimni* of wheat and five of barley. These rations are a free gift to the allies, but in the case of the Romans the quaestor deducts from their pay the price fixed for their grain and clothing and any additional weapon they require.

60. The *medimnus* = 6 *modii* (see Glossary).

8

SOCIETY AND CULTURE,
264–27 B.C.

165. Occupations, Vulgar and Gentlemanly

The upper-class prejudices here expressed parallel the well-known attitude voiced by Greek writers for banausic or socially degrading occupations. (This treatise of Cicero, incidentally, is based on the work of the Greek Stoic, Panaetius.) The inclusion of merchants and tax collectors among the deprecated groups is especially interesting, in view of Cicero's close ties to the equestrian class (see introduction to § 145). This disdain, however, is obviously directed against the freedmen and others among the lower classes who served as publicans' agents or small-scale tradesmen; but, in keeping with the large-scale operations of the *equites,* this attitude is qualified so that the size of the enterprise placed upon the activity the stamp of acceptability or rejection.

Cicero, *On Duties* I. xlii, II. xxiv. 87–xxv. 89; From *LCL*

Now in regard to trade and other means of livelihood, which ones are to be considered becoming to a gentleman and which ones are vulgar, we have been taught, in general, as follows. First, those means of livelihood are to be rejected as undesirable which incur people's ill will, as those of customs collectors and usurers. Unbecoming to a gentleman, too, and vulgar are the means of livelihood of all hired workmen whom we pay for mere manual labor, not for artistic skill; for in their case the very wages they receive is a pledge of their slavery. Vulgar we must consider those also who buy from wholesale merchants to retail immediately; for they would get no profits without a great deal of downright lying; and indeed, there is no action meaner than misrepresentation.

And all mechanics are engaged in vulgar trades; for no workshop can have anything liberal about it. Least respectable of all are those trades which cater to sensual pleasures:

> Fishmongers, butchers, cooks, and poulterers,
> And fishermen,

as Terence says [*Eunuch.* II: ii. 26]. Add to these, if you please, the perfumers, dancers, and the whole *corps de ballet*.

But the professions in which either a higher degree of intelligence is required or from which no small benefit to society is derived—medicine and architecture, for example, and teaching—these are proper for those whose social position they become. Trade, if it is on a small scale, is to be considered vulgar; but if wholesale and on a large scale, importing large quantities from all parts and distributing to many without misrepresentation, it is not to be greatly disparaged. Nay, it even seems to deserve the highest respect, if those who are engaged in it, satiated, or rather, I should say, satisfied with the fortunes they have made, make their way from the port to farmlands and country estates, as they have often made it from the sea into port. But of all the occupations by which gain is secured, none is better than agriculture, none more profitable, none more delightful, none more becoming to a freeman. . . .

As for property, it is a duty to make money, but only by honorable means; it is a duty also to save it and increase it by care and thrift. These principles Xenophon, a pupil of Socrates, has set forth most happily in his book entitled *Oeconomicus*. When I was about your present age, I translated it from Greek into Latin.[1]

But this whole subject of acquiring money, investing money (I wish I could include also spending money) is more profitably discussed by certain worthy gentlemen on the Exchange than could be done by any philosophers of any school. We must, nevertheless, take cognizance of these matters, for they come fitly under the head of expediency, and that is the subject of the present book.

But it is often necessary to weigh one expediency against another. . . . Outward advantages may also be weighted against one another: glory, for example, may be preferred to riches, an income derived from city property to one derived from the farm. To this class of comparison belongs that famous saying of old Cato's; when he was asked what was

---

1. Cicero wrote his treatise *On Duties* in 44 B.C. for his son, then twenty-one-years old.

the most profitable feature of an estate, he replied, "Raising cattle successfully." What next to that? "Raising cattle with fair success." And
next? "Raising cattle with but slight success." And fourth? "Raising
crops." And when his questioner said, "How about moneylending?"
Cato replied, "How about murder?" [cf. § 166, first selection].

166. MANAGEMENT OF A LANDED ESTATE

Pliny the Elder asserts (*Natural History* XVIII. iii. 22) that "to give precepts
on agriculture was an activity of leading men." The separation of the
ruling classes from the ancestral tradition of farm work through the
growth of wealth and large estates in the second century B.C. created new
problems of farm technique and management for the Roman latifundists.
Cato's manual on the operation of a landed estate by an absentee owner is
eloquent witness of the extent to which Italian agriculture had been transformed by the first half of the second century B.C., when it was composed.
In Italy subsistence husbandry by peasant smallholders continued thereafter increasingly to give way to commercial farming on large estates
operated by absentee owners with slave labor—which the Roman overseas conquests had made plentiful and cheap—supplemented where economically advisable by free sharecropping peasants and seasonal contract
labor. While in southern Italy large-scale cattle grazing prevailed, in central Italy the latifundia abandoned the cultivation of cereals—which could
be imported more cheaply from Sicily and other overseas provinces—and
concentrated on the intensive cultivation of the vine and the olive, which
provided readily salable "cash crops." Thus in Varro's treatise, written
about a century after Cato's, we find essentially similar conditions, except
that the large estates have in the intervening century grown markedly in
size through the absorption of additional small holdings.
    Among the concomitants of the spread of latifundist operations were
the emergence in Italy of a large mass of economically displaced peasants;
the growth of a large "Lumpenproletariat" in Rome, to which many of
these peasants flocked; and increased dependence of Italy, especially urban
centers, upon the provinces for cereals (cf. §§ 131, 139).

Cato, *On Agriculture* Preface, i, ii, x, lvi–lix, cxxxv–cxxxvii, clx; From Ernest Brehaut,
Cato the Censor on Farming (New York, 1933)

It is true that it would sometimes be better to seek a fortune in trade if it
were not so subject to risk, or again, to lend money at interest, if it were
an honorable occupation. But our forefathers held this belief and enacted

it into law, that while a thief was compelled to repay double, one who loaned at interest had to repay fourfold. From this one may judge how much worse than a common thief they considered the fellow citizen who lent at interest (cf. § 32, table VIII). And when they were trying to praise a good man they called him a good farmer and a good tiller of the soil, and the one who received this compliment was considered to have received the highest praise.

Now I esteem the merchant as active and keen to make money, but, as I have said before, he is exposed to risk and absolute ruin.

Moreover, it is from among the farmers that the sturdiest men and keenest soldiers come, and the gain they make is the most blameless of all, the most secure, and the least provocative of envy, and the men engaged in this pursuit are least given to disaffection. . . .

When you think of buying a farm, make up your mind not to be eager to buy, and not to spare any exertion on your own part in going to see farms, and not to think it enough to go over them once. The oftener you visit it the more a good farm will please you.

Notice carefully how prosperous the neighbors are; in a good district they should be quite prosperous. And see that you go on a farm and look around it in such a way that you can find your way off it. See that it has a good exposure to the heavens or it may be subject to disaster. It should have a good soil and be valuable for its own worth. If possible, let it be at the foot of a mountain, looking toward the south, in a healthful situation, and where there is plenty of labor. It should have a good water supply.

It should be near a thriving town or near the sea or a river where ships go up or a good and well-traveled highway. It should be in a region where owners do not often change, and where those who do sell their farms repent of having sold them. See that it has good buildings. Beware of hastily disregarding the experience of others. It will be better to buy from an owner who is a good farmer and a good builder.

When you come to the farmstead, notice whether there is much equipment for pressing and many storage jars. If there are not, be sure the profit is in proportion. . . . Take care that it is not a farm requiring the least possible equipment and expense. Be sure that a farm is like a man, that however much it brings in, if it pays much out, not a great deal is left.

If you ask me what sort of farm is best, I will say this: one hundred *iugera* of land consisting of every kind of cultivated field, and in the best situation; the vineyard is of first importance if the wine is good and the yield is great; the irrigated garden is in the second place, the willow plantation in the third, the olive orchard in the fourth, the meadow in the fifth, the grain land in the sixth, forest trees to furnish foilage[2] in the seventh, the vineyard trained on trees in the eighth, the acorn wood[3] in the ninth.

When the head of the household comes to the farmhouse, on the same day, if possible, as soon as he has paid respect to the god of the household, he should make the round of the farm; if not on the same day, at least on the next. When he has learned in what way the farm work has been done and what tasks are finished and what not yet finished, he should next day summon the foreman and inquire how much of the work is done, how much remains, whether the different operations have been completed in good season and whether he can complete what remains, and what is the situation as to wine and grain and all other produce.

After he has been informed on these points he should go into an accounting of the day's work and the days. If the work accomplished is not made clear to him, and the foreman says he has pushed the work hard, but the slaves have not been well, the weather has been bad, the slaves have run away, they have done work on the public account [maintenance of public roads?]—when he has given these and many other excuses, then bring the foreman back to an accounting of the farm tasks and of the day's work spent on them.

When the weather was rainy, [tell him] what work could have been done in spite of the rain: the storage jars could have been washed and tarred, the farm buildings could have been cleaned out, the grain shifted, the manure carried out and a manure pile made, the seed cleaned, the ropes mended and new ones made; the slaves should have mended their patchwork cloaks and hoods.

On festivals they could have cleaned old ditches, repaired the public road, cut briars, dug the garden, weeded the meadow, made bundles of the small wood cut in pruning, dug out thorns [i.e., thorny hedges], broken up the spelt into grits, and made the place neat. When slaves were sick they should not have been given as large an allowance of food. . . .

If anything is needed for the year's supply it should be bought; if there is a surplus of anything it should be sold. What needs to be put out

2. Used as fodder for the sheep and work oxen.
3. This provided food for pigs and oxen.

under contract should be contracted for. The owner should give directions and leave them in writing as to what work he wishes to be done and what he wishes put out on contract.

He should look over the flock. He should hold an auction and, if he gets his price, sell the oil, the wine, and the surplus grain; let him sell the old work oxen, the blemished cattle, the blemished sheep, the wool, the skins, the old wagon, the worn-out tools, the aged slave, the slave that is diseased, and everything else that he does not need. An owner should be a man who is a seller rather than a buyer. . . .

How an olive orchard of two hundred and forty *iugera* [about 150 acres; cf. Glossary] should be equipped:

[It should have] a foreman, a foreman's wife, five laborers, three ox drivers, one ass driver, one swineherd, one shepherd, thirteen persons in all; three teams of oxen, three asses equipped with pack saddles to carry out the manure, one ass for mill work, one hundred sheep.

Five oil presses fully equipped including the pulping mills, a bronze cauldron to hold thirty *amphorae,* a cover for the cauldron, three iron hooks, three water pitchers, two funnels, a bronze cauldron to hold five *amphorae,* a cover for it, three hooks, a small vat for water, two *amphorae* for oil, one half-*amphora* measure holding fifty,[4] three skimming ladles, one well bucket, one wash basin, one water pitcher, one slop pail, one small tray, one chamber pot, one watering pot, one ladle, one lamp stand, one *sextarius* measure.

Three wagons of the larger size, six plows with plowshares, three yokes fitted with rawhide ropes, harness for six oxen; one harrow with iron teeth, four wickerwork baskets for manure, three rush baskets for manure, three packsaddles, three pads for asses.

Implements of iron: eight heavy spades, eight heavy two-pronged hoes, four spades, five shovels, two four-pronged drags, eight scythes for mowing grass, five sickles for harvesting, five billhooks for trimming trees, three axes, three wedges, one mortar for spelt, two fire tongs, one fire shovel, two portable fire pans.

One hundred storage jars for oil, twelve vats, ten storage jars for the wine-press refuse, ten for oil dregs, ten for wine, twenty for grain, one vat for lupins, ten storage jars of the smaller kind, a vat used for washing, one tub for bathing, two vats for water, separate covers for all storage jars large and small.

One mill to be worked by an ass, one hand mill, one Spanish mill,

---

4. A utensil possibly holding 50 *heminae* (about 0.6 pints to the *hemina*).

three harnesses for the mill asses, one kneading table, two round plates of bronze, two tables, three long benches, one stool for the chamber, three low stools, four chairs, two large chairs, one bed in the chamber, four beds with woven thongs and three beds; one wooden mortar, one mortar for fuller's work, one loom for cloaks, two mortars, one pestle for beans and one for spelt, one for [cleaning] spelt for seed, one to separate olive pits, one *modius* measure and one half-*modius* measure.

Eight mattresses, eight spreads, sixteen pillows, ten coverlets, three towels, six cloaks made of patchwork for the slaves. . . .

Bread rations for the slaves. For those who do the field work, four *modii* of wheat in winter, four and one half in summer; for the foreman, the foreman's wife, the overseer,[5] and the shepherd, three *modii;* for the slaves working in chains, four pounds of bread in winter, five when they begin to dig the vineyard, until there begin to be figs [early in summer], then go back to four pounds.

Wine for the slaves. When the vintage is over, let them drink the after wine for three months. In the fourth month a half-*sextarius* daily, i.e., for the month, two and one half *congii;* in the fifth, sixth, seventh, and eighth months, a *sextarius* daily, i.e., for the month, five *congii;* in the ninth, tenth, eleventh, and twelfth months, a *sextarius* and one half daily, i.e., for the month, an *amphora;* in addition to this, on the Saturnalia and the Compitalia,[6] three and a half *congii* for each man; the total of wine for the year for each man, seven *amphorae.* For the slaves working in chains add more in proportion to the work they are doing. It is not too much if they drink ten *amphorae* of wine apiece in a year.

Relishes for the slaves. Preserve as many as possible of the dropped olives. Later, when the olives are ripe, preserve some of those that yield the least oil, and use them sparingly so that they will last as long as possible. After the olives have been eaten, give them fish pickle and vinegar. Give each one per month one *sextarius* of olive oil. A *modius* of salt is enough for each one for a year.

Clothing for the slaves. A tunic weighing three and one half pounds and a cloak in alternate years. Whenever you give a tunic or a cloak to any of them, first get the old one back to make patchwork cloaks of. Good wooden shoes should be given to them every second year. . . .

5. Mentioned only here by Cato, he is to be differentiated from the foreman. He was possibly the representative of the owner during the harvesting season.

6. The Saturnalia was a festival that came at the end of December, when the sowing season was over. It was an occasion for gaiety during which slaves were given special privileges. The Compitalia was a rural community festival conducted at crossroads.

At Rome [buy] tunics, togas, rough cloaks, patched cloaks, wooden shoes; at Cales and Minturnae hoods, iron implements, sickles, spades, grubbing hoes, axes, harness, bridle-bits, and small chains; at Venafrum, spades; at Suessa and in Lucania, wagons; threshing sledges at Alba and Rome; storage jars, vats, and roof tiles at Venafrum.

Plows of the Roman style will be good for stiff land, of the Campanian style for light soil; yokes of the Roman style will be best; the plowshare that slips over will be best.

Olive mills at Pompeii and at the walls of Rufrium near Nola; keys and door bars at Rome; water buckets, half-*amphora* oil measures, water pitchers, half-*amphora* measures for wine and other containers made of bronze, at Capua and Nola. . . .

On what agreement share work in grain growing should be given out:

In the country around Casinum and Venafrum on good soil [the owner] should give [the share worker] the eighth part in the basket; on fairly good soil, the seventh; on third-class soil, the sixth; and if it is threshed grain that is divided by *modius* measure, the fifth part. In Venafrum the best land will give [the share worker] the ninth part in the basket. If spelt is cleaned before it is divided, in so far as there is a share coming to the share worker for this, let him [give it] in return for the use of the pounding mill.

Let [the owner] give [the share worker] the fifth part by *modius* measure of barley and the fifth of beans.

The working of a vineyard by a share tenant:

He is to take good care of the farm, the vineyard trained on trees, and the grainland. The share tenant gets hay and fodder enough for the work oxen that are on the place. All the rest is owned in common. . . .

If any joint is dislocated it will be made well by this incantation. Take a green reed four or five feet long, split it in half, and let two men hold the halves at their hips. Begin to sing a charm: *motas vaeta daries dardares astataries dissunapiter,* until the halves come together. Keep brandishing a sword over them. When they come together and one half-reed touches the other, seize them in the hand and cut them off to right and left, bind them on the dislocation or fracture and it will be cured. However, go through the form of incantation daily over the man who has suffered the dislocation. Or use this form: *huat haut haut istasis tarsis ardannabou dannaustra.*[7]

---

7. The meaning of these magic formulas is unknown.

Varro, *On Landed Estates* I. iv. 1–2, xvi. 1–xvii. 7, II. Preface. 3–4, 6, x; From *LCL*

Equipped with this knowledge, the farmer should aim at two goals, profit and pleasure, the object of the first is material return, and of the second enjoyment. The profitable plays a more important role than the pleasurable; and yet for the most part the methods of cultivation which improve the aspect of the land, such as planting of fruit and olive trees in rows, make it not only more profitable but also more salable, and add to the value of the estate. . . .

It remains to discuss the second topic, the conditions surrounding the farm, for they, too, vitally concern agriculture because of their relation to it. These considerations are the same in number: whether the neighborhood is unsafe; whether it is such that it is not profitable to transport our products to it, or to bring back from it what we need; third, whether roads or streams for transportation are either wanting or inadequate; and fourth, whether conditions on the neighboring farms are such as to benefit or injure our land. Taking up the first of the four: the safety or lack of safety of the neighborhood is important; for there are many excellent farms which it is not advisable to cultivate because of the brigandage in the neighborhood, as in Sardinia certain farms near . . . and in Spain on the borders of Lusitania. Farms which have suitable means near by of transporting their products to market and convenient means of transporting thence those things needed on the farm are for that reason profitable. For many have among their holdings some into which grain or wine or the like which they lack must be brought, and on the other hand not a few have those from which a surplus must be sent away. And so it is profitable near a city to have gardens on a large scale; for instance, of violets and roses and many other products for which there is a demand in a city; while it would not be profitable to raise the same products on a distant farm where there is no market to which products can be carried. Again, if there are towns or villages in the neighborhood, or even well-furnished lands and farmsteads of rich owners, from which you can purchase at a reasonable price what you need for the farm, and to which you can sell your surplus, such as props, or poles, or reeds, the farm will be more profitable than if they must be fetched from a distance; sometimes; in fact, more so than if you can supply them yourself by raising them on your own place. For this reason farmers in such circumstances prefer to have in their neighborhood men whose services they can call upon under a yearly contract—physicians, fullers, and other artisans—rather than to have such men of their own on the farm; for sometimes the death of one artisan wipes out the profit of a farm. This department of a great estate rich owners are wont to entrust to their own people; for if towns or villages are too far away from the estate, they supply themselves with smiths and other necessary artisans to keep on the place, so that their farm hands may not leave their work and lounge around holiday-making on working days, rather than make the farm more profitable by attending to their duties. . . .

I have now discussed the four divisions of the estate which are concerned with the soil, and the second four, which are exterior to the soil but concern its cultivation; now I turn to the means by which land is tilled. Some divide these into two parts: men, and those aids to men without which they cannot cultivate; others into three: the class of instruments which is articulate, the inarticulate, and the mute, the articulate comprising the slaves, the inarticulate comprising the cattle, and the mute comprising the vehicles. All agriculture is carried on by man —slaves, or freemen, or both; by freemen, when they till the ground themselves, as many poor people do with the help of their families; or hired hands, when the heavier farm operations, such as the vintage and the haying, are carried on by the hiring of freemen; and those whom our people called *obaerarii*,[8] and of whom there are still many in Asia, in Egypt, and in Illyricum. With regard to these in general this is my opinion: it is more profitable to work unwholesome lands with hired hands than with slaves; and even in wholesome places it is more profitable thus to carry out the heavier farm operations, such as storing the products of the vintage or harvest. . . .

Slaves should be neither cowed nor high-spirited. They ought to have men over them who know how to read and write and have some little education, who are dependable and older than the hands whom I have mentioned; for they will be more respectful to these than to men who are younger. Furthermore, it is especially important that the foremen be men who are experienced in farm operations; for the foreman must not only give orders but also take part in the work, so that his subordinates may follow his example but also understand that there is good reason for his being over them—the fact that he is superior to them in knowledge. They are not to be allowed to control their men with whips rather than with words, if only you can achieve the same result. Avoid having too many slaves of the same nation, for this is a fertile source of domestic quarrels. The foremen are to be made more zealous by rewards, and

8. Indentured laborers bound over until they worked off the debt.

care must be taken that they have a bit of property of their own, and mates from among their fellow slaves to bear them children; for by this means they are made more steady and more attached to the place. Thus, it is on account of such relationships that slave families of Epirus have the best reputation and bring the highest prices. The good will of the foremen should be won by treating them with some degree of consideration; and those of the hands who excel the others should also be consulted as to the work to be done. When this is done they are less inclined to think that they are looked down upon, and rather think that they are held in some esteem by the master. They are made to take more interest in their work by being treated more liberally in respect either of food, or of more clothing, or of exemption from work, or of permission to graze some cattle of their own on the farm, or other things of this kind; so that, if some unusually heavy task is imposed, or punishment inflicted on them in some way, their loyalty and kindly feeling to the master may be restored by the consolation derived from such measures. . . .

It was not without reason that those great men, our ancestors, put the Romans who lived in the country ahead of those who lived in the city. For as in the country those who live in the villa are lazier than those who are engaged in carrying out work on the land, so they thought that those who settled in town were more indolent than those who dwelt in the country. Hence they so divided the year that they attended their town affairs only on the ninth days[9] and dwelt in the country on the remaining seven. So long as they kept up this practice they attained both objects—keeping their lands most productive by cultivation, and themselves enjoying better health and not requiring the citified gymnasia of the Greeks. . . . As therefore in these days practically all the heads of families have sneaked within the walls, abandoning the sickle and the plow, and would rather busy their hands in the theater and in the circus than in the grain fields and the vineyards, we hire a man to bring us from Africa and Sardinia the grain with which to fill our stomachs, and the vintage we store comes in ships from the islands of Cos and Chios. And so, in a land where the shepherds who founded the city taught their offspring the cultivation of the earth, there, on the contrary, their descendants, from greed and in the face of the laws, have made pastures out of grain lands—not knowing that agriculture and grazing are not the same thing. . . .

9. That is, on market days *(nundinae)*, which were fixed at eight-day intervals.

I shall run over briefly and summarily the subject of cattle raising; and I shall the more readily do this because I have myself owned large stocks of cattle, sheep in Apulia and horses in the district of Reate. . . . For herds of larger cattle older men, for the smaller even boys; but in both cases those who range the trails should be sturdier than those on the farm who go back to the steading every day. Thus on the range you may see young men, usually armed, while on the farm not only boys but even girls tend the flocks. The herdsmen should be required to stay on the range the entire day and have the herds feed together; but, on the other hand, to spend the night each with his own herd. They should all be under one herdmaster; he should preferably be older than the rest and more experienced, as the other herdsmen will be more disposed to take orders from one who surpasses them in both age and knowledge. Still he should not be so much older that his age will prevent him from being as able to stand hard work; for neither old men nor boys can easily endure the hardships of the trail and the steepness and roughness of the mountains—all of which must be encountered by those who follow the herd, and especially herds of cattle and goats, which like cliffs and woods for pasturage. The men chosen for this work should be of a sturdy sort, swift, nimble, with supple limbs; men who can not only follow the herd but can also protect it from beasts and robbers, who can lift loads to the backs of pack animals, who can dash out, and who can hurl the javelin. . . .

As to the breeding of herdsmen: it is a simple matter in the case of those who stay all the time on the farm, as they have a female fellow slave in the steading, and the desires of herdsmen look no farther than this. But in the case of those who tend the herds in mountain valleys and wooded lands, and keep off the rains not by the roof of the steading but by makeshift huts, many have thought that it was advisable to send along women to follow the herds, prepare food for the herdsmen, and make them more diligent. Such women should, however, be strong and not ill-looking. In many places they are not inferior to men at work, as may be seen here and there in Illyricum, being able either to tend the herd, or carry firewood and cook the food, or to keep things in order in their huts. . . . All directions for caring for the health of human beings and cattle, and all sicknesses which can be treated without the aid of a physician, the head-herdsman should keep in writing. For one who does not know his letters is not fit for the place, because he cannot possibly keep his master's cattle accounts correctly. The number of herdsmen is determined differently, some having a smaller, some a larger number.

My own practice is to have a herdsman to every eighty wool-bearing sheep, while Atticus has one to every hundred. If flocks of sheep are very large (and some people have as many as 1,000) you can decrease the number of shepherds more easily than you can in smaller flocks, such as those of Atticus and mine. My own flocks contain 700, and yours, I think, had 800; but still you had one tenth of rams, as I do.

167. FINANCIAL DEALINGS OF AN EQUES

This case history is particularly revealing documentation on the intimate connection between foreign investments and foreign policy.

Cicero, *In Defense of Rabirius Postumus* ii, iii. 6, x. 28, xiv. 39–40; Adapted from *LCL*

In my boyhood my client's father, Gaius Curtius, was a powerful chief of the equestrian order and a very important tax farmer; and the magnanimity that marked his business relations would not have gained such approval from people, had he not also been filled with unparalleled philanthropy, which suggested that in increasing his wealth he sought not so much to gratify his avarice as to find the means to satisfy the kindness of his heart. My client was his son; and although he had never seen his father,[10] under the potent guidance of nature and the influence of constant talks in the household circle he was led to model himself after his father's life. His business interests and contracts were extensive; he held many shares in the farming of public revenues; whole peoples had him for creditor; his transactions covered many provinces; he put himself at the disposal even of kings. He had previously lent large sums to this very king of Alexandria;[11] but in the midst of all this he had never ceased enriching his friends, sending them upon commissions, bestowing shares upon them, advancing them by his wealth, and supporting them by his credit. In short, by his generosity as well as by his magnanimity he reproduced the life and practice of his father.

In the meantime Ptolemy had been expelled from his kingdom, and had come to Rome—"with guileful intent" as the Sibyl said [i.e., in a consultation of the Sibylline Books], and as Postumus learned to his

10. He was born after his father's death—hence his surname Postumus.
11. Ptolemy XI Auletes. He was expelled by the Alexandrian populace in 58 B.C., but was restored to the throne the following year by the army of the Roman proconsul of Syria, whose assistance he purchased for 10,000 talents.

cost. The king was in need and appealed to him; and my unhappy client lent him money—not for the first time, for he had already done so without seeing his debtor, when he was still on his throne. He thought the loan involved no risk, since no one doubted that the king was in process of being restored to his realm by the senate and people of Rome. But in his gifts and his loans he extended himself too far, lending not only his own money but also that of his friends.[12] A foolish thing to do, who denies? . . . Still, his debtor was a king, not a robber; and not a king who was hostile to the people of Rome, but one for whose restoration a mandate had, as he knew, been given to a consul by the senate; not a king who had no relations with this empire, but one with whom he had seen a treaty made in the Capitol. . . .

As soon as Postumus arrived at Alexandria [after Ptolemy's restoration], members of the jury, the king proposed to him, as the sole condition under which he might protect his wealth, that he should undertake the management and as it were the stewardship of the royal revenues. This he could do only by taking up the appointment of royal treasurer. The business was distasteful to Postumus, but it was absolutely out of the question for him to decline; the title itself, too, disgusted him, but it was the title attached in that country to that function, and not an invention of his own; he detested the dress as well, but without it he could retain neither the title nor the office. So to quote our poet [unknown],

> he bowed to Force,
> Which ever breaks and bends the mightiest power. . . .[13]

"He behaved like a despot at Alexandria," says the prosecutor. On the contrary he was victimized by the most arbitrary of despotisms. He himself had to endure imprisonment, he saw his friends thrown into chains, death was ever before his eyes, and finally, naked and needy, he fled the kingdom. "Yes," they say, "but in the end he realized profits in commerce; ships belonging to him put in at Puteoli; merchandise of his was reported and seen there. It is true that the goods invoiced were only cheap showy articles of paper, linen, and glass;[14] many ships were

12. Since the investment seemed such a "sure thing."

13. To run the Egyptian treasury must have presented itself to Rabirius as a limitless pork barrel, and the demand for the office may likely have come from himself, the creditor. Cicero's solemn portrayal of Rabirius as reluctant to become the servant of a foreign king verges on the ludicrous, as does his whole sympathetic account of the sufferings and anguish of Rabirius before he recouped his investment.

14. Papyrus, linen, and glass were the leading manufactured products exported by Egypt.

packed with these, but there was one small ship the cargo of which was not revealed." That voyage to Puteoli and the rumors at that time and the course taken by the crew and their big talk, together with the dislike shown to Postumus' name by spiteful people on account of vague impressions about his money, filled the public ear with such topics for one summer—not more.

168. Career of a Humble Roman Citizen-Soldier

Livy, *History of Rome* XLII. xxxiv

Spurius Ligustinus . . . requested the consul and the tribunes to permit him to say a few words to the people. With the permission of all he is reported to have spoken as follows: "Quirites, I, Spurius Ligustinus of the Crustuminian tribe, am of Sabine origin. My father left me a *iugerum* of land and a small cottage in which I was born and bred, and I am living there today. As soon as I came of age, my father gave me to wife his brother's daughter, who brought nothing with her but her free birth and her chastity, and together with these a fruitfulness which would be enough even for a wealthy house. We have six sons and two daughters, both of them already married. Four of our sons wear the *toga virilis,* two the *praetexta.*[15] I became a soldier in the consulship of Publius Sulpicius and Gaius Aurelius [200 B.C.]. For two years I served as a common soldier in the army which was taken over to Macedonia, fighting against Philip; in the third year Titus Quinctius Flamininus[16] made me, for my bravery, centurion of the tenth maniple of the *hastati.*[17] After Philip and the Macedonians were defeated and we were brought back to Italy and discharged, I at once volunteered to go to Spain with the consul Marcus Porcius [Cato the Elder, consul in 195 B.C.]. Those who during long service had experience of him and of other generals know that of all living commanders no one was a keener observer and judge of bravery. It was this commander who thought me worthy of being appointed centurion of the first century of the *hastati.* Again I served, for the third time, as a volunteer in the army which was sent against the Aetolians

15. The *toga virilis,* the national garment, was assumed by Roman boys at the age of 16 or 17; until that time they wore the *toga praetexta,* distinguished by a stripe. See Glossary.

16. For Flamininus, the "liberator of Greece," see § 68.

17. For the terms *hastati* and *principes* in this selection, see § 45.

and King Antiochus [see §§ 69–70]. I was made first centurion of the *principes* by Manius Acilius.[18] After Antiochus was driven out and the Aetolians subjugated, we were brought back to Italy, and after that I was in campaigns in which the legions served for a year. Then I served in Spain twice, once under the praetor Quintus Fulvius Flaccus, [181 B.C.], and again under the praetor Tiberius Sempronius Gracchus [180 B.C.]. I was brought home by Flaccus among those whom, as a reward for their bravery, he was bringing home for his triumph. I joined Tiberius Gracchus in the province at his request. Four times, within a few years, I held the rank of chief centurion; thirty-four times have I been rewarded for bravery by my commanders; I have received six civic crowns.[19] I have served for twenty-two years in the army and I am more than fifty years old. But even if I had not served my full time and my age did not yet give me exemption, still, Publius Licinius, as I was able to give you four soldiers to replace me, it would have been right that I should be discharged. But I want you to take what I have said simply as a statement of my case. For my part, as long as anyone who is enrolling troops judges me fit for service, I will never plead excuses. What rank the military tribunes think that I deserve is for them to decide; I will see to it that no man in the army surpasses me in bravery; and that I always have done so my commanders and those who have served with me are witnesses. And as for you, fellow soldiers, though you are within your rights in making this appeal, it is proper that, as in your youth you never did anything against the authority of the magistrates and the senate, so now, too, you should place yourselves at the disposal of the consuls and the senate, and consider any position in which you will be defending your country as an honorable one."

169. ROMAN AND ITALIAN BUSINESSMEN ABROAD

In the wake of the Roman armies went Roman and Italian businessmen. Beginning at the end of the second century B.C. and increasingly in the course of the next two centuries they established important business enterprises in the provinces and the "pacified" Hellenistic world; a considerable number even settled permanently in these foreign lands of opportunity. In the anti-Roman uprising in 88 B.C. (see § 81) 80,000 men, women, and children of Italian origin were massacred in the province of Asia alone.

18. For Manius Acilius Glabrio, see chapter 6, note 5.
19. The civic crown was awarded for saving the life of a fellow citizen.

"Narbonese Gaul," says Cicero (*In Defense of Fonteius* xi), "is packed with traders, crammed with Roman citizens. No Gaul ever does business independently of a citizen of Rome; not a penny changes hands in Gaul without the transaction being recorded in the books of Roman citizens." Found on the island of Delos, which in the second century became the chief center of the lucrative slave trade (cf. introduction to § 78), are numerous inscriptions stemming from the Italian colony that flourished there from 166 to 50 B.C., participating in the commercial, social, and religious activities of the island. Samples of these inscriptions are given here.

CIL, vol. I, 2d ed., no. 2239 (= *ROL,* 4:118–119); P. Roussel and M. Launey,
Inscriptions de Délos (Paris 1937), vol. 4, nos. 1526, 1527, 1645, 1688, 1725

i

[About 150 B.C. or earlier.] Lucius Oppius son of Lucius, Minatus Staius son of Ovius, Lucius Vicirius son of Tiberius, Aulus Plotius freedman of Marcus, Gaius Sehius freedman of Gaius, and Gaius Claudius freedman of Gaius, foremen, presented this [statue] to Mercury and Maia.

ii

[Shortly after 127 B.C.] The Roman shipowners and merchants who were protected during the occupation of Alexandria by King Ptolemy Euergetes [set up this statue] of Lochus son of Callimedes, "cousin"[20] of King Ptolemy and Queen Cleopatra, because of his goodness and kindnesses to them, [and dedicated it] to Apollo.

iii

[About 127 B.C.] [Statue of] Polemarchus, "cousin" of King Ptolemy Euergetes and Queen Cleopatra, *epistrategus,*[21] [dedicated] to Apollo, Artemis, [and Leto?] by Lucius and Gaius Pedius, sons of Gaius, Romans, on account of his goodness, his magnanimity, and his good will toward them.

20. Honorary title of the Hellenistic royal courts; cf. chapter 6, note 15.
21. Governor of a major administrative region of Egypt.

iv

[126/125 B.C.] [Statue of] Theophrastus son of Heraclitus, of the deme Acharnae, former superintendent of Delos, who laid out the market place and built piers around the harbor, [dedicated] by the Athenians residing in Delos and by the Romans and other foreign merchants and shipowners resident in Delos, because of his goodness, his magnanimity, and his kindnesses to them.

v

[About 100 B.C.] [Statue of] Gaius Ofellius Ferus son of Marcus, [dedicated] to Apollo by the Italians, because of his justice and his goodness to them. Work of Dionysius son of Timarchides and Timarchides son of Polycles, Athenians.[22]

vi

[Early first century B.C.] The merchants and those who do business in the square[?] market place [dedicated] to Apollo, Artemis, and Leto [this statue of] Maraeus Gerillanus son of Maraeus, Roman, banker at Delos, on account of his magnanimity to them. Work of Agasias son of Menophilus, Ephesian.

170. THE GROWTH OF WEALTH AND LUXURY

"The end of the Second Punic War and the defeat of Philip, king of Macedonia, gave our city the assurance of a more luxurious mode of life," says Valerius Maximus (*Memorable Deeds and Sayings* IX. i. 3). The gradual accumulation of wealth that flowed into Rome from the conquered areas and into the hands of the Roman ruling class transformed their lives from one of traditional agrarian simplicity to ostentatious display and unbounded luxury-spending. In the first century B.C. the growth of great fortunes and the parade of wealth in high society reached spectacular heights. This extravagance evoked a literary tradition of moralizing fulminations against luxury as the cause of Roman degeneracy (cf. chapter 5, note 13). Attempts to check such "conspicuous consumption" through sumptuary legislation proved futile (see § 171).

22. The final clause in this and the next inscription gives the names of the sculptors of the statues.

THE BEGINNINGS OF LUXURY

Livy, *History of Rome* XXXIX. vi. 3–9

At the end of the year [187 B.C.], after the new magistrates had been elected, Gnaeus Manlius Vulso celebrated his triumph over the Galatians on the fifth of March. The reason why he deferred his triumph to so late a date was his anxiety to avoid prosecution under the Petillian Law[23] while Quintus Terentius Culleo was praetor, and the possibility of being burned by the flames of the verdict by which Lucius Scipio was condemned. He thought the judges would be even more hostile to him than they had been to Scipio, owing to reports of his having completely destroyed military discipline, which his predecessor Scipio had maintained, by allowing his soldiers every kind of license. Nor were the stories being told of what had gone on in his province far away from men's eyes the only things that discredited him. Still worse things were being witnessed among his soldiers every day, for it was through the army serving in Asia that the beginnings of foreign luxury were introduced into the city. These men brought into Rome for the first time bronze couches, costly coverlets, bed curtains, and other fabrics, and— what was at that time considered gorgeous furniture—one-legged tables and sideboards. Banquets were made more attractive by the presence of girls who played on the lute and harp and by other forms of entertainment, and the banquets themselves began to be prepared with greater care and expense. The cook, whom the ancients regarded and treated as the lowest type of slave, was rising in value, and what had been a servile task began to be looked upon as a fine art.[24] Still what met the eye in those days was but the germ of the luxury that was coming.

Velleius Paterculus, *Compendium of Roman History* II. i. 1–2; From *LCL*

The first Scipio [Africanus] opened the way for the world power of the Romans; the second opened the way for luxury. For when Rome was freed of the fear of Carthage, and her rival in empire was out of the way, the path of virtue was abandoned for that of corruption, not gradually, but in headlong course. The older discipline was discarded to

---

23. This law (text in Livy, *History of Rome* XXXVIII. liv) concerned an investigation of the handling of booty obtained in the campaign of Asia Minor.

24. Cf. Pliny, *Natural History* XVIII. xi. 107: "There were no bakers at Rome until the war with King Perscus, more than 580 years after the founding of the city. The ancient Romans used to make their own bread, it being an especial occupation of the women, as even now among many peoples."

give place to the new. The state passed from vigilance to slumber, from the pursuit of arms to the pursuit of pleasure, from activity to idleness. It was at this time that there were built, on the Capitol, the porticoes of Scipio Nasica, the porticoes of Metellus . . . and, in the Circus, the portico of Gnaeus Octavius, the most splendid of them all; and private luxury soon followed public extravagance.

Pliny, Natural History XXXIII. xi. 147–150

Gaius Gracchus possessed some silver dolphins for which he paid 5,000 sesterces per pound. Indeed, Lucius Crassus, the orator, paid for two goblets engraved by the hand of the artist Mentor 100,000 sesterces, but he confessed that for shame he never dared use them. We know that he also had other articles of plate in his possession, for which he paid at the rate of 6,000 sesterces per pound. It was the conquest of Asia that first introduced luxury into Italy, for we find that Lucius Scipio exhibited in his triumphal procession [188 B.C.] 1,400 pounds' weight of engraved silver, together with golden vessels the weight of which amounted to 1,500 pounds. But that which inflicted a still more severe blow upon Roman morals was the legacy of Asia, which King Attalus left at his death, a legacy which was even more disadvantageous than the victory of Scipio. For upon this occasion all scruple was entirely removed in buying these things at the auction of the king's effects. This took place in the 622d year of the city [132 B.C.], the people having learned, during the fifty-seven years that had intervened, not only to admire but also to covet the opulence of foreign peoples. An immense impetus to the fashioning of morality was the conquest of Achaea, which during this interval, in the 608th year of the city [146 B.C.], had introduced both statues and pictures. That nothing might be wanting, the same year that saw the birth of luxury witnessed the downfall of Carthage, so that, by a fatal coincidence, at one and the same time the leisure for acquiring vices and the license for gratifying them came into being.

SOME ROMAN MILLIONAIRES

Pliny, Natural History XXXIII. x. 134–135

Marcus Crassus . . . used to say that no man was rich who could not maintain a legion upon his annual income. He possessed in land 200,000,000 sesterces, being the richest Roman next to Sulla. . . . We have known of many manumitted slaves since his time who were much more wealthy than he ever was; three, for example, all at the same time, in the reign of the Emperor Claudius [A.D. 41–54] . . . Callistus, Pallas, and Narcissus. . . .

Let us turn to Gaius Caecilius Isidorus, the freedman of Gaius, who, on the 27th day of January in the consulship of Gaius Asinius Gallus and Gaius Marcius Censorinus [8 B.C.], declared in his will that, though he had suffered great losses during the civil war, he was still able to leave behind him 4,116 slaves, 3,600 pairs of oxen, and 257,000 heads of other kinds of cattle, besides 60,000,000 sesterces in cash; he ordered 1,000,000 sesterces spent on his funeral.

Plutarch, Life of Crassus ii. 1–6

Now the Romans say that the many virtues of Crassus were obscured by his sole vice of avarice, and it seems that the one vice which became stronger than all the others in him dimmed the rest. The chief proofs of his avarice were the way in which he acquired his property and the size of it. For at first he was not worth more than 300 talents; then, during his consulship, he dedicated the tenth part of his property to Hercules, feasted the people, and gave to every citizen enough to live on for three months; still, when he made an inventory of his property before his Parthian expedition, he found it to have a value of 7,100 talents.

Most of this, if one must tell the scandalous truth, he gathered by fire and war, making the public calamities his greatest source of revenue. For when Sulla seized Rome and sold the property of those put to death by him, regarding and calling it booty, and wishing to make as many influential men as he could partners in the crime, Crassus refused neither to accept nor to buy such property. Moreover, observing how natural and familiar at Rome were the burning and collapse of buildings, because of their massiveness and their closeness to one another, he bought slaves who were builders and architects. Then, when he had more than 500 of these, he would buy houses that were on fire and those adjoining the ones on fire. The owners would let them go for small sums, because of their fear and uncertainty, so that the greatest part of Rome came into his hands. But though he had so many artisans, he never built any house but the one he lived in, and used to say that those that were addicted to building would undo themselves without the help of other enemies. And though he had many silver mines, and very valuable land with laborers on it, yet one might consider all this as nothing compared with the value of his slaves, such a great number and variety did he possess—

readers, amanuenses, silversmiths, stewards and table-servants. He himself directed their training, and took part in teaching them himself, accounting it, in a word, the chief duty of a master to care for his slaves as the living tools of household management.

"LUCULLUS DINES WITH LUCULLUS"

Plutarch, *Life of Lucullus* xxxix. 1-xli. 2 (abridged)

And, indeed, Lucullus' life, like the Old Comedy, presents us at the beginning with political acts and military commands, and at the end with drinking bouts and banquets, and what were practically orgies, and torch races, and all manner of frivolity. For I count as frivolity his sumptuous buildings, porticoes, and baths, still more his paintings and statues, and all his enthusiasm for these arts, which he collected at vast expense, lavishly pouring out on them the vast and splendid wealth which he acquired in his campaigns. Even now, with all the advance of luxury, the Lucullan gardens are counted the most costly of the imperial gardens. When Tubero the Stoic saw Lucullus' works on the seashore and near Naples, where he suspended hills over vast tunnels, encircling his residences with moats of sea water and with streams for breeding fish, and built villas into the sea, he called him Xerxes in a toga. . . .

Lucullus' daily dinners were ostentatiously extravagant—not only their purple coverlets, beakers adorned with precious stones, choruses, and dramatic recitations, but also their display of all sorts of meats and daintily prepared dishes—making him an object of envy to the vulgar. . . . Once when he dined alone, he became angry because only one modest course had been prepared, and called the slave in charge. When the latter said that he did not think that there would be need of anything expensive since there were no guests, Lucullus said, "What, do you not know that today Lucullus dines with Lucullus?"

171. SUMPTUARY LEGISLATION

The first manifestations of the growing luxury spending (see § 170) by the upper classes of Rome aroused the puritanic opposition of the old conservative families, led by Cato. That they were to fight a losing battle was revealed as early as 195 B.C., when they failed to prevent the repeal of the Oppian Law on the luxury of women—the first of a series of sumptuary laws, passed in 215 B.C., during the days of national catastrophe after

Cannae. The futility of attempting to check luxury by statute while the concentration of wealth steadily mounted is further revealed by the very frequency of such sumptuary laws.

THE REPEAL OF THE OPPIAN LAW

Livy, *History of Rome* xxxiv. i–viii (abridged)

Two tribunes of the plebs, Marcus Fundanius and Lucius Valerius, had brought in a proposal to the plebs to repeal the Oppian Law. This law had been passed on the motion of Gaius Oppius, a tribune of the plebs, during the consulship of Quintus Fabius and Tiberius Sempronius, in the midst of the heat of the Punic War. It forbade any woman to possess more than half an ounce of gold, to wear a dress of various colors, or to ride in a two-horsed vehicle in the city or any town or within a mile thereof, except in the case of public religious functions. The two Brutuses, Marcus Junius and Publius Junius, tribunes of the plebs, defended the Oppian Law and declared that they would not allow it to be repealed; many of the nobility came forward to speak in favor of the repeal or against it; the Capitol was filled with a crowd of supporters and opponents of the law; the matrons could not be kept indoors by either the authority of the magistrates or the orders of their husbands or their own sense of propriety. They blocked all the streets of the city and the approaches to the Forum, and implored the men as they descended to the Forum to allow the women to resume their former adornments, now that the commonwealth was flourishing and the private fortunes of all increasing every day. Their numbers were daily augmented, for women were assembling also from the towns and villages. They even ventured to approach the consuls and praetors and other magistrates with their demands. However, one of the consuls at all events was inexorably opposed—Marcus Porcius Cato.

[The lengthy rhetorical address put into Cato's mouth by Livy is here omitted, as well as the speech of the tribune Lucius Valerius advocating repeal of the law.]

After these speeches against and in favor of the law, the women poured out into the streets the next day in much greater number and in a body besieged the doors of the two Brutuses, who were vetoing the proposals of their colleagues, nor would they desist till the tribunes had withdrawn their veto. There was no doubt that the tribes would be unanimous in rescinding the law. It was repealed twenty years after it had been passed.

A CATALOGUE OF SUMPTUARY LAWS

Aulus Gellius, *Attic Nights* ii. xxiv; Adapted from *LCL*

Frugality among the early Romans and simplicity in food and banquets were secured not only by watchfulness and training at home but also by public penalties and the provisions of numerous laws. . . . An old decree of the senate, passed in the consulship of Gaius Fannius and Marcus Valerius Messala [161 B.C.] . . . provides that the leading citizens . . . should take oath before the consuls in set terms that they would not spend on each dinner more than 120 *asses,* exclusive of vegetables, bread, and wine; that they would not serve foreign but only native wine, nor use at table more than 100 pounds' weight of silverware. But subsequent to that decree of the senate the Fannian Law was passed, which allowed the expenditure of 100 *asses* a day at the Roman and plebeian games, at the Saturnalia, and on certain other days; of 30 *asses* on ten additional days each month; but on all other days of only ten. . . .[25]

Next the Licinian Law [between 113 and 97 B.C.] was passed, which, while allowing the expenditure of 100 *asses* on designated days, as did the Fannian Law, permitted 200 *asses* for weddings, and set a limit of 30 *asses* for other days; however, after decreeing fixed weights of dried meat and pickled fish for each day, it granted the indiscriminate and unlimited use of the products of the earth, vine, and orchard. . . .

Afterwards, when these laws were blotted out through neglect and when many men were dissipating huge fortunes in luxury and recklessly pouring their households and money into an abyss of dinners and banquets, the dictator Lucius Sulla proposed a law to the people [81 B.C.], which provided that on the Kalends, Ides, and Nones, on days of games, and on certain regular festivals it should be proper and lawful to spend 300 sesterces on a dinner, but on all other days no more than 30.[26]

Besides these laws we find also an Aemilian Law [78 B.C.], which set

---

25. Other provisions of the Fannian Law limited the number of guests at dinner to three, except on market days, when five were allowed (Athenaeus, *Savants at Dinner* vi. 274c), and forbade the use of certain foods (Pliny, *Natural History* x. l. 139).

26. This law also fixed maximum prices for delicacies (Macrobius, *Saturnalia* ii. xiii).

a limit not on the expense of dinners but on the kind and quantity of food.

Then the Antian Law [71 B.C.], besides curtailing outlay, contained the additional provision that no magistrate or magistrate-elect should dine out anywhere, except at the house of stipulated persons.

Lastly, the Julian Law came before the people, during the principate of Caesar Augustus, by which on working days 200 sesterces is the limit, on the Kalends, Ides, and Nones, and some other holidays 300, but at weddings and the banquets following them 1,000.

Ateius Capito says that there is still another edict—but whether of the deified Augustus or of Tiberius I do not exactly remember—by which the outlay for dinners on various festal days was increased from 300 to 2,000 sesterces, to the end that the rising tide of luxury might be restrained at least within these limits.

172. Lavish Public Expenditures: Games and Largess

A PLEA FOR MODERATION

Cicero, *On Duties* II. xvi. 55, 57, xvii. 58; From *LCL*

There are, in general, two classes of those who give largely: the one class is the lavish, the other the generous. The lavish are those who squander their money on public banquets, doles of meat among the people, gladiatorial shows, magnificent spectacles, and wild-beast fights —vanities of which but a brief recollection will remain, or none at all. . . .

I realize that in our country, even in the good old times, it had become a settled custom to expect magnificent entertainments from the very best of men in the year of aedileship. . . . Still we should avoid any suspicion of penuriousness. Mamercus was a very wealthy man, and his refusal of the aedileship was the cause of his defeat for the consulship. If, therefore, such entertainment is demanded by the people, men of right judgment must at least consent to furnish it, even if they do not like the idea. But in so doing they should keep within their means, as I myself did.

A ROMAN SPECTACLE

The magnificent games given by Pompey during his second consulship (55 B.C.), on the occasion of the dedication of his theater and the temple of Venus Victrix, are commented on by Cicero in this letter written in September or October of that year.

Cicero, *Letters to Friends* book VII, no. 1 (abridged); From *LCL*

If you ask me, the games were of course most magnificent; but they would not have been to your taste; that I infer from my own feelings. . . . For any feeling of cheerfulness was extinguished by the spectacle of such magnificence—a magnificence which, I am sure, it will not disturb you in the least to have missed seeing. For what pleasure can there be in the sight of 600 mules in the *Clytaemnestra,* or of 3,000 bowls in the *Trojan Horse,* or of the varied accoutrements of foot and horse in some big battle? . . .

There remain the wild-beast hunts, two a day for five days—magnificent; there is no denying it. But what pleasure can it possibly be to a man of culture, when either a puny human being is mangled by a most powerful beast, or a splendid beast is transfixed with a hunting spear? And even if all this is something to be seen, you have seen it more than once; and I, who was a spectator, saw nothing new in it. The last day was that of the elephants, and on that day the mob and crowd was greatly impressed, but manifested no pleasure. Indeed the result was a certain compassion and a kind of feeling that that huge beast has a fellowship with the human race.

EXTRAVAGANT LARGESS

Cassius Dio, *Roman History* XLIX. xliii. 1–4; From *LCL*

The next year [33 B.C.] Agrippa agreed to be made aedile and without taking anything from the public treasury repaired all the public buildings and all the streets, cleaned out the sewers, and sailed through them underground into the Tiber. . . . Furthermore, he distributed olive oil and salt to all, and furnished baths free of charge throughout the year for the use of both men and women; and in connection with the many festivals of all kinds which he gave . . . he hired barbers, so that no one should be at any expense for their services. Finally he rained upon the heads of the people in the theater tickets that were good for money in one case, for clothes in another, and again for something else, and he also set out immense quantities of various wares for all comers and allowed the people to scramble for these things.

173. THE BENEFITS OF ARISTOCRATIC GOVERNMENT

Belief in the advantages of aristocratic government is apparent throughout Cicero's *Republic,* and in this Cicero undoubtedly reflects the views of the senatorial class as a whole. In the opening statement on the three forms of government we read: "Either a just and wise king, or a select number of leading citizens, or even the people itself (though this is the least commendable type) can . . . it seems, form a stable government" (I. xxvi. 42). The selection given here applies a familiar Aristotelian doctrine that virtue is a mean, and exalts aristocratic government as the mean between monarchy and popular rule.

Cicero, *Republic* I. xxxiv. 52–53; From *LCL*

What can be nobler than the government of the state by virtue? For then the man who rules others is not himself a slave to any passion, but has already acquired for himself those qualities to which he is training and summoning his fellows. Such a man imposes no laws upon the people that he does not obey himself, but puts his own life before his fellow citizens as their law. If a single individual of this character could order all things properly in a state, there would be no need of more than one ruler; or if the citizens as a body could see what was best and agree upon it, no one would desire a selected group of rulers. It has been the difficulty of formulating policies that has transferred the power from a king to a larger number; and the perversity and rashness of popular assemblies that have transferred it from the many to the few. Thus, between the weakness of a single ruler and the rashness of the many, aristocracies have occupied that intermediate position which represents the utmost moderation; and in a state ruled by its best men, the citizens must necessarily enjoy the greatest happiness, being freed from all cares and worries, when once they have entrusted the preservation of their tranquillity to others, whose duty it is to guard it vigilantly and never to allow the people to think that their interests are being neglected by their rulers. For that equality of legal rights of which free peoples are so fond cannot be maintained (for the people themselves, though free and unrestrained, give very many special powers to many individuals, and create great distinctions among men and the honors granted to them), and what is called equality is really most inequitable. For when equal honor is given to the highest and the lowest—for men of both types must exist in every nation—then this very "fairness" is most unfair; but this cannot happen in states ruled by their best citizens.

174. THE PRACTICE AND PURPOSE OF WAR

In this statement there stands out not so much a theoretical analysis as the concrete implication that the expansion and wars of the Roman Republic were undertaken "in self-defense." Cf. Cicero, *Republic* III. xxiii. 35: "Our people, by defending its allies, has become master of the whole world."

Cicero, *On Duties* I. xi. 35–36; From *LCL*

Then, too, in the case of a state in its external relations, the rights of war must be strictly observed. For since there are two ways of settling a dispute—first, by discussion; second, by physical force—and since the former is characteristic of man, the latter of the brute, we must resort to force only in case we may not avail ourselves of discussion. The only excuse, therefore, for going to war is that we may live in peace unharmed;[27] and when victory is won, we should spare those who have not been bloodthirsty and barbarous in their warfare. For instance, our forefathers actually admitted to full rights of citizenship the Tusculans, Aequians, Volscians, Sabines, and Hernicans, but they razed Carthage and Numantia to the ground. I wish they had not destroyed Corinth; but I believe they had some special reason for what they did—its convenient situation, probably—and feared that its very location might some day furnish a temptation to renew the war.[28] In my opinion, at least, we should always strive to secure a peace that shall not admit of guile. And if my advice had been heeded on this point, we should still have at least some sort of constitutional government, if not the best in the world, whereas, as it is, we have none at all [written in 44 B.C.]

27. Similarly, a little later (I. xxiii. 80) Cicero remarks: "Diplomacy in the friendly settlement of controversies is more desirable than courage in settling them on the battlefield; but we must be careful not to take that course merely for the sake of avoiding war rather than for the sake of public expediency. War, however, should be undertaken in such a way as to make it evident that it has no other object than to secure peace." (Quoted from the Loeb Classical Library.)

28. For the Roman foreign policy leading to the destruction of Corinth, see §§ 76, 80.

Not only must we show consideration for those whom we have conquered by force of arms but we must also ensure protection to those who lay down their arms and throw themselves upon the mercy of our generals, even though the battering-ram has hammered at their walls. And among our countrymen justice has been observed so conscientiously in this direction that those who have given promise of protection to states or nations subdued in war become, after the custom of our forefathers, the patrons of those states.

As for war, humane laws touching it are drawn up in the fetial code of the Roman people under all the guarantees of religion [for the fetials, see § 51], and from this code it may be gathered that no war is just unless it is entered upon after an official demand for satisfaction has been submitted or warning has been given and a formal declaration made.[29]

175. RELIGIOUS CODE

In imitation of Plato, Cicero sets down in his *Laws* the outlines of a code of religious practices. These approximate, and at times idealize, the formal religious institutions of his own time.

Cicero, *Laws* II. viii. 19–ix. 22: From *LCL*

They shall approach the gods in purity, bringing piety and leaving riches behind. Whoever shall do otherwise, heaven itself will deal out punishment to him.

No one shall have gods to himself, either new gods or alien gods, unless recognized by the state. Privately they shall worship those gods whose worship they have duly received from their ancestors.

In cities they shall have shrines; they shall have groves in the country and homes for the *Lares*.[30]

They shall preserve the rites of their families and their ancestors.

They shall worship as gods both those who have always been regarded as dwellers in heaven, and also those whose merits have admitted them to heaven: Hercules, Liber, Aesculapius, Castor, Pollux, Quirinus; also those qualities through which an ascent to heaven is granted to

---

29. Cf. Cicero, *Republic* III. xxiii. 35: "Those wars are unjust which are undertaken without provocation. For only a war waged for revenge or defense can actually be just. . . . No war is considered just unless it has been proclaimed and declared, or unless reparation has first been demanded." (Quoted from the Loeb Classical Library.)

30. Tutelary deities of the real property of the household.

mankind: Intellect, Virtue, Piety, Good Faith. To their praise there shall be shrines, but none for the vices.

They shall perform the established rites.

On holidays they shall refrain from lawsuits; these they shall celebrate together with their slaves after their tasks are done. Let holidays be so arranged as to fall at regularly recurring breaks in the year. The priest shall offer on behalf of the state the prescribed grains and the prescribed fruits; this shall be done according to prescribed rites and on prescribed days; likewise for other days they shall reserve the plenteous offerings of the milk and the offspring.[31] And so that no violation of these customs shall take place, the priests shall determine the mode and the annual circuit of such offerings; and they shall prescribe the victims which are proper and pleasing to each of the gods.

The several gods shall have their several priests, the gods altogether their pontiffs, and the individual gods their flamens. The Vestal Virgins shall guard the eternal fire on the public hearth of the city.

Those who are ignorant as to the methods and rites suitable to these public and private sacrifices shall seek instructions from the public priests. Of them there shall be three kinds: one to have charge of ceremonies and sacred rites; another to interpret those obscure sayings of soothsayers and prophets which shall be recognized by the senate and the people; and the interpreters of Jupiter and Best and Greatest, namely the public augurs, shall foretell the future from portents and auspices, and maintain their art. And the priests shall observe the omens in regard to vineyards and orchards and the safety of the people; those who carry on war or affairs of state shall be informed by them beforehand of the auspices and shall obey them; the priests shall foresee the wrath of the gods and yield to it; they shall observe flashes of lightning in fixed regions of the sky, and shall keep free and unobstructed the city and fields and their places of observation. Whatever an augur shall declare to be unjust, unholy, pernicious, or ill-omened shall be null and void; and whosoever yields not obedience shall be put to death.

The fetial priests shall be judges and messengers for treaties, peace and war, truces, and embassies; they shall make the decisions in regard to war.

Prodigies and portents shall be referred to the Etruscan soothsayers, if the senate so decree; Etruria shall instruct her leading men in this art.

---

31. Milk, wine, and honey were offered to various divinities; some gods received as offerings full-grown victims, some sucklings.

They shall make expiatory offerings to whatever gods they decide upon, and shall perform expiations for flashes of lightning and for whatever shall be struck by lightning.

No sacrifices shall be performed by women at night except those offered for the people in proper form;[32] nor shall anyone be initiated except into the Greek rites of Ceres, according to the custom.[33]

Sacrilege which cannot be expiated shall be held to be impiously committed; that which can be expiated shall be atoned for by the public priests.

At the public games which are held without chariot races or the contest of body with body, the public pleasure shall be provided for with moderation by song to the music of harp and flute, and this shall be combined with honor to the gods.

Of the ancestral rites the best shall be preserved.

No one shall ask for contributions except the servants of the Idean Mother,[34] and they only on appointed days.

Whoever steals or carries off what is sacred or anything entrusted to what is sacred shall be considered as equal in guilt to a parricide.

For the perjurer the punishment from the gods is destruction; the human punishment shall be disgrace.

The pontiffs shall inflict capital punishment on those guilty of incest.

No wicked man shall dare to appease the wrath of the gods with gifts.

Vows shall be scrupulously performed; there shall be a penalty for the violation of the law.

No one shall consecrate a field; the consecration of gold, silver, and ivory shall be confined to reasonable limits.

The sacred rites of families shall remain forever.

The rights of the gods of the lower world shall be sacred. Kinsfolk who are dead shall be considered gods; the expenditure and mourning for them shall be limited.

---

32. The worship of Bona Dea, a strictly female rite, is meant.
33. This is a reference to the mystery cult at Eleusis, in Greece.
34. For Cybele, or the Great Mother, see § 177, third selection.

176. Suppression of Bacchanalia in Italy, 186 B.C.

Early in the second century B.C. the secret orgiastic rites of the Greek cult of Bacchus spread rapidly northward from southern Italy (Magna Graecia). Finding converts among the lowest strata of the population, including slaves, the Bacchic rites and secret associations reached Rome in 186 B.C. Roman conservatism in religious matters and aversion to orgiastic religious practices played a part in the Senate's decision to suppress the Bacchic societies. But fundamentally the senate was motivated by the fear that the growth of secret organizations (which were prohibited by Roman law), especially among the lower classes, might harbor or foster revolutionary movements. It accordingly dealt with the matter as a conspiracy against the state, using police powers to stamp out the societies. The decree passed by the senate, embracing all Italy, constituted direct interference in the internal affairs of the allies, even though the local governments may have welcomed it because of the outbreak of slave revolts in various parts of the peninsula about this time (cf. introduction to § 95).

Livy, *History of Rome* xxxix. viii–xix (abridged)

During the following year the consuls Spurius Postumius Albinus and Quintus Marcius Philippus were diverted from the army and the administration of wars and provinces to the suppression of an internal conspiracy. . . . A lowborn Greek came first into Etruria, a man possessed of none of the numerous arts which that most learned of all nations has introduced among us for the cultivation of mind and body, but a mere sacrificer and fortuneteller—not even one of those who imbue men's minds with error by publicizing their creed and professing openly their business and their teaching, but a hierophant of secret nocturnal rites. At first these were divulged to only a few; then they began to spread widely among men and women. To the religious content were added the pleasures of wine and feasting, to attract a greater number. When they were heated with wine, and all sense of modesty had been extinguished by the darkness of night and the commingling of males with females, tender youths with elders, then debaucheries of every kind commenced: each had pleasures at hand to satisfy the lust to which he was most inclined. Nor was the vice confined to the promiscuous intercourse of free men and women, but false witnesses and evidence, forged seals and wills, all issued from this same workshop; also poisonings and murders of kin, so that sometimes the bodies could not even be found for burial. Much was ventured by guile, more by violence, which was kept secret, because the cries of those calling for help amid the debauchery and murder could not be heard through the howling and the crash of drums and cymbals.[35]

This pestilential evil spread from Etruria to Rome like a contagious disease. At first the size of the city, with room and tolerance for such evils, concealed it, but information at length reached the consul Postumius. . . . Postumius laid the matter before the senate, setting forth everything in detail—first the information he had received, and then the results of his own investigations. The senators were seized by a panic of fear, both for the public safety, lest these secret conspiracies and nocturnal gatherings contain some hidden harm or danger, and for themselves individually, lest some relatives be involved in this vice. They decreed a vote of thanks to the consul for having investigated the matter so diligently and without creating any public disturbance. Then they commissioned the consuls to conduct a special inquiry into the Bacchanalia and nocturnal rites; they directed them to see to it that Aebutius and Faecenia suffered no harm for the evidence they had given, and to offer rewards to induce other informers to come forward; the priests of these rites, whether men or women, were to be sought out not only in Rome, but in every *forum* and *conciliabulum* [cf. chapter 7, note 38], so that they might be at the disposal of the consuls; edicts were to be published in the city of Rome and throughout Italy, ordering that none who had been initiated into the Bacchic rites should be minded to gather or come together for the celebration of these rites, or to perform any such ritual; and, above all, an inquiry was to be conducted regarding those persons who had gathered together or conspired to promote debauchery or crime.

These were the measures decreed by the senate. The consuls ordered the curule aediles to search out all the priests of this cult, apprehend them, and keep them under house arrest for the inquiry; the plebeian aediles were to see that no rites were performed in secret. The three commissioners[36] were instructed to post watches throughout the city, to see to it that no nocturnal gatherings took place, and to take precau-

---

35. The rumors here recorded by Livy about criminal and immoral practices connected with the Bacchanalia are doubtless wild exaggerations, to be compared with the similar charges directed against the early Christians.

36. The *triumviri capitales,* on whom see chapter 7, note 1.

tions against fires; and to assist them five men were assigned on either side of the Tiber, each to take charge of the buildings in his own district. . . .

The consuls then ordered the decrees of the senate to be read [in the assembly], and they announced the reward to be paid anyone who brought anyone before them or, in the absence of the person, reported his name. If anyone took to flight after being named, they would fix a day for him to answer the charge, and on that day, if he failed to answer when called, he would be condemned *in absentia*. If anyone were named who was beyond the confines of Italy at the time, they would set a more flexible date, should he wish to come and plead his cause. Next they ordered by edict that no one be minded to sell or buy anything for the purpose of flight, that no one harbor, conceal, or in any way assist fugitives. . . . Guards were posted at the gates, and during the night following the disclosure of the affair in the assembly, many who tried to escape were arrested by the three commissioners and brought back. Many names were reported, and some of these, women as well as men, committed suicide. It was said that more than 7,000 men and women were implicated in the conspiracy. . . .

So great, however, was the number of those who fled from the city that legal action was in numerous cases impossible because of default, and the praetors, Titus Maenius and Marcus Licinius, were compelled through the intervention of the senate to adjourn their courts for thirty days, until the consuls should complete their investigations. And since those whose names had been reported did not respond to summons and were not to be found in Rome, this same exodus compelled the consuls to make the rounds of the country villages and pursue their inquiry and conduct trials there. Those who had merely been initiated and repeated after the priest, following the ritual formula, the prayers in which was contained the execrable conspiracy to every crime and lust, but had not committed against themselves or others any of the acts to which they had bound themselves by their oath—these were left in prison. Those who had defiled themselves by debauchery or murder, who had polluted themselves by false witness, forged seals, substitution of wills, or other fraudulent practices, were sentenced to death. More were put to death than were thrown into prison. There was a large number of men and women in both groups. The women who had been found guilty were handed over to their relatives or guardians to be punished in private;[37] if

37. Cf. pp. 65–66, §§ 146 (first selection) and 191.

there was no one competent to exact it, the penalty was inflicted by the state.

Next the consuls were given the task of destroying all places of Bacchic worship, first at Rome, and then throughout the length and breadth of Italy, except where there was an ancient altar or a sacred image. For the future the senate decreed that there should be no Bacchic rites in Rome or in Italy. If anyone considered such worship a necessary observance that he could not neglect without fear of committing sacrilege, he was to make declaration before the urban praetor and the praetor would consult the senate. If permission were granted by the senate, with at least one hundred senators present, he might perform that rite provided no more than five persons took part in the service, and that they had no common fund and no master[38] or priest.

CIL vol. I, 2d ed., no. 581 (= ROL, 4:254–259)

[Letter of the Consuls Transmitting the Decree of the Senate
Concerning Bacchic Associations]

The consuls Quintus Marcius son of Lucius, and Spurius Postumius son of Lucius consulted the senate on the 7th day of October in the temple of Bellona. Present at the writing [of the decree] were Marcus Claudius son of Marcus, Lucius Valerius son of Publius, and Quintus Minucius son of Gaius.

In the matter of Bacchic orgies they passed a decree that the following proclamation should be issued to those who are allied with the Romans by treaty:

"Let none of them be minded to maintain a place of Bacchic worship. Should there be some who say they must needs maintain a place of Bacchic worship, they must come to the urban praetor at Rome, and our senate, when it has heard what they have to say, shall make decision on these matters, provided that at least one hundred senators be present when the matter is deliberated. Let no man, whether Roman citizen or of the Latin name[39] or one of the allies, be minded to attend a meeting of Bacchant women without approaching the urban praetor and obtaining his authorization with the approval of the senate, provided that not

38. The function of this Bacchic votary is uncertain: he may have been a presiding officer or conductor of ceremonies, or, as the juxtaposition of the mention of a common fund here and below suggests, a sort of business manager.

39. That is, from the Latin towns or Latin colonies.

fewer than one hundred senators be present when the matter is deliberated. Adopted.

"Let no man be a priest.[40] Let not any man or woman be a master; nor let any of them be minded to keep a common fund; nor let any person be minded to make either man or woman a master or vicemaster, or be minded henceforth to exchange oaths, vows, pledges, or promises with others, or be minded to plight faith with others. Let no one be minded to perform ceremonies in secret; nor let anyone be minded to perform ceremonies, whether in public or in private or outside the city, without approaching the urban praetor and obtaining his authorization with the approval of the senate, provided that not fewer than one hundred senators be present when the matter is deliberated. Adopted.

"Let no one be minded to hold services in a group larger than five men and women together, and let not more than two men and three women be minded to attend there among, except on authorization of the urban praetor and the senate as recorded above."

You shall proclaim these orders at a public meeting for a period covering not less than three market days, and that you may be cognizant of the decree of the senate, the decree was as follows: They decreed that should there be any persons who act contrary to the provisions recorded above, proceedings for capital offense must be taken against them; and the senate deemed it right and proper that you engrave this on a bronze tablet and that you order it to be fastened up where it can most easily be read; and that within ten days after the delivery of this letter to you, you see to it that those places of Bacchic worship which may exist are dismantled, as recorded above, except if there be anything holy therein. Ager Teuranus.[41]

177. RELIGIOUS DEVELOPMENTS

The hold of the traditional formal state religion upon the Roman populace began to be undermined by growing rationalism and skepticism during the third century B.C., especially among the upper classes. But the disas-

40. The votaries and priests of the cult of Bacchus were originally women; membership had only comparatively recently been opened to men.
41. This letter was received and inscribed on bronze by the people of Ager Teuranus in southern Italy, where it was found.

ters of the Second Punic War led to an upsurge of religious fervor.
Grasping after new ways of appeasing the gods, the Romans turned their
attention, with growing frequency, to prodigies and their expiation. For
this purpose they began increasingly to call upon the services of the
haruspices. These Etruscan diviners not only were concerned with the
interpretation and diverting of prodigies, but also greatly elaborated the
art of divination by lightning and introduced into Roman religion
the practice of extispice, that is, the interpretation of the entrails of sacrificial victims. In the desperate days of Hannibal's invasion recourse was
even taken to the primitive Italic practice of human sacrifice. Finally,
renewed impulse was given to the introduction of foreign rites, culminating in 205/204 B.C. in the first importation, under official auspices, of an
Oriental deity, the *Magna Mater* (Great Mother).

PRODIGIES AND THEIR EXPIATION IN THE SECOND PUNIC WAR

Livy, *History of Rome* xxi. lxii; From *LCL*

In Rome and near it many prodigies occurred that winter [218 B.C.], or
—as often happens when men's thoughts are once turned upon religion
—many were reported and too easily credited. Some of these portents
were that a free-born infant of six months had cried "Triumph!" in the
provision market; that in the cattle market an ox had climbed, of its own
accord, to the third story of a house and then, alarmed by the outcry of
the occupants, had thrown itself down; that phantom ships had been
seen gleaming in the sky; that the temple of Hope in the provision
market had been struck by lightning; that in Lanuvium a slain victim
had stirred, and a raven had flown down into Juno's temple and alighted
on her very couch; that in the district of Amiternum, in many places,
apparitions of men in shining raiment had appeared in the distance, but
had not drawn near to anyone; that in the Picentian country there had
been a shower of pebbles; that at Caere the lots had shrunk;[42] that in
Gaul a wolf had snatched a sentry's sword from its scabbard and run off
with it. For the other prodigies the decemvirs were commanded to
consult the [Sibyllinc] Books [§ 52], but for the shower of pebbles in the
Picentian country a nine days' sacrifice was proclaimed. They then set
about the expiation of the other portents, and in this virtually all the
citizens bore a part. First of all, the city was purified, and major victims
were offered up to designated gods; a gift of gold weighing forty pounds

42. These lots for divination were inscribed on small wooden or bronze tablets.

was carried to Lanuvium for Juno, and a bronze statue was dedicated to Juno by the matrons on the Aventine; a *lectisternium* [see § 53] was ordered at Caere, where the lots had shrunk; and a supplication was ordered to be made to Fortune on Mount Algidus; in Rome, too, a *lectisternium* was specially appointed for Juventas, and a supplication at the temple of Hercules, and later the whole people was commanded to observe this rite at all the *pulvinaria* [see § 53], also five major victims were slain in honor of the *genius* of the Roman people; and Gaius Atilius Serranus the praetor was ordered to make a vow, "if the commonwealth should abide for ten years in the present state." The making of these expiations and vows, as prescribed by the Sibylline Books, went far to alleviate men's anxiety concerning their relations with the gods.[43]

A HUMAN SACRIFICE

Livy, *History of Rome* XXII. lvii. 2–6; From *LCL*

They were terrified not only by the great disaster they had suffered [at Cannae in 216 B.C.] but also by a number of prodigies, and in particular because two Vestals, Opimia and Floronia, had in that year been convicted of unchastity. Of these one had been buried alive, as the custom is, near the Colline Gate, and the other had killed herself. Lucius Cantilius, a secretary to the pontiffs—one of those who are now called the lesser pontiffs—had been guilty with Floronia, and the *pontifex maximus* had him scourged in the Comitium so severely that he died under the blows. Since in the midst of so many misfortunes this pollution was, as happens at such times, converted into a portent, the decemvirs were commanded to consult the Sibylline Books, and Quintus Fabius Pictor was dispatched to Delphi, to inquire of the oracle with what prayers and supplications they might propitiate the gods, and what would be the end of all their calamities. In the meantime, by direction of the books of fate, some unusual sacrifices were offered; among others a Gallic man and

43. On the inconveniences caused by the reporting of prodigies, cf. especially Livy XXXIV. lv: "At the beginning of the year when Lucius Cornelius and Quintus Minucius were consuls [193 B.C.] there were such frequent reports of earthquake that men grew tired not only of the subject itself, but also of the holidays ordered on account of them. No meeting of the Senate could be held nor any public administration conducted, as the consuls were entirely occupied with sacrifices and expiations. At last the decemvirs received instructions to consult the Sacred Books, and in accordance with their answer three days of public prayer were proclaimed. Prayers were offered at all the shrines, the suppliants wearing wreaths, and it was decreed that all the members of a family should offer up their prayers together. Likewise, the Senate authorized the consuls to publish an edict forbidding anyone to report an earthquake on any day on which a holiday had been ordered on account of one already reported."

woman and a Greek man and woman were buried alive in the cattle market, in a place walled in with stone, which never before this time had been defiled with human victims, a sacrifice wholly alien to the Roman spirit.[44]

THE MAGNA MATER IS BROUGHT TO ROME

Livy, *History of Rome* XXIX. x–xiv (abridged)

At this time [205 B.C.] the state was much exercised by a religious matter which suddenly came up. Owing to the rather frequent showers of stones from the sky during the year, an inspection had been made of the Sibylline Books, and some oracular verses had been discovered which announced that whenever a foreign foe should carry war onto the soil of Italy he could be driven out of Italy and conquered if the Idean Mother were brough from Pessinus to Rome. The discovery of this prophecy by the decemvirs produced all the greater impression on the senators because the envoys who had taken the gift to Delphi reported on their return that when they sacrificed to the Pythian Apollo the indications presented by the victims were favorable, and, further, that the response of the oracle was to the effect that a far grander victory was awaiting the Roman people than the one from whose spoils they had brought the gift to Delphi. They regarded the hopes thus raised as confirmed by the action of Scipio in demanding Africa as his province as though he had a presentiment of the end of the war. In order, therefore, to secure all the sooner the victory which the fates, the omens, and the oracles alike were foreshadowing, they began to plan and to take measures for the best way of transporting the goddess to Rome.

Up to that time the Roman people had no allies among the communities of Asia. They had not forgotten, however, that they had sent to fetch Aesculapius from Greece [see § 53] for the health of the people though they had no treaty yet with that country, and now that they had formed an alliance with King Attalus against their common enemy

---

44. Human sacrifice was an Italic rite, but had been abandoned by the Romans very early. Cf. Pliny, *Natural History* XXX. i.12: "It is clear that there are still traces existing of the use of magic even among the Italic peoples. . . . At last, in the 657th year of the city, in the consulship of Gnaeus Cornelius Lentulus and Publius Licinius Crassus [97 B.C.], a decree forbidding human sacrifice was passed by the Senate; this proves that up to that time such monstrous rites were performed." But Pliny himself states (XXVIII. ii. 12) that human sacrifice was still practiced in Italy in his day (first century A.D.).

Philip, they hoped that he would do what he could in the interest of the Roman people. Accordingly, they decided to send a mission to him. Those selected for the purpose were Marcus Valerius Laevinus, who had been twice consul and had also been in charge of operations in Greece, Marcus Caecilius Metellus, an ex-praetor, Servius Sulpicius Galba, an ex-aedile, and two ex-quaestors, Gnaeus Tremellius Flaccus and Marcus Valerius Falto. It was arranged that they should sail with five quinque-remes in order that they might present an appearance worthy of the Roman people when they visited those states which were to be impressed with the greatness of the Roman name. . . .

The king gave the envoys a friendly welcome and conducted them to Pessinus in Phrygia.[45] He then handed over to them the sacred stone which the natives declared to be "the Mother of the Gods," and bade them carry it to Rome. Marcus Valerius Falto was sent ahead by the envoys to announce that the goddess was on her way, and that the best and noblest man in Rome must be sought out to receive her with all due honor. . . .

Publius Cornelius Scipio was ordered to go to Ostia, accompanied by all the matrons, to meet the goddess. He was to receive her as she left the vessel, and he was to place her when brought to land in the hands of the matrons to carry. As soon as the ship approached the mouth of the Tiber river, he put out to sea in accordance with his instructions, received the goddess from the hands of the priests, and brought her to land. Here she was received by the foremost matrons of the city. . . . The matrons, each taking their turn in bearing the sacred image, carried the goddess into the temple of Victory on the Palatine. All the citizens poured out to meet them, incense burners were placed before the doors wherever she was being carried, and, burning incense, they prayed that she would enter the city of Rome willingly and propitiously. The day on which this event took place was the 4th of April, and it was observed as a festival. The people came in crowds to the Palatine to bring gifts to the deity; a *lectisternium* was held and games were established which were called the Megalesian.[46]

---

45. The holy black meteorite, the symbol of the Phrygian goddess, was brought to Rome from Pergamum, not Pessinus. Attalus had already removed the stone to his capital, where a temple, called the Megalesion, had been established (Varro, *The Latin Language* vi. xv).

46. From the Greek word for "great"; cf. note 45.

178. DECLINE OF THE ROMAN STATE RELIGION

The hold of the state religion on the Roman citizenry was shattered by the economic and social developments of the second and first centuries B.C. — the rapid growth of latifundia and absentee landlordism, the consequent multiplication of a landless citizen mass in Rome (cf. introduction to § 166), and the rapid individualization of Roman society under the impact of Hellenism and of the extremes of wealth and poverty. The agricultural gods of the traditional religion were largely meaningless in urban life, especially for landless persons. Skepticism and superstitious fears mounted in the hundred years of internal and external crisis from the Gracchi to Augustus. Hence, Romans tended to satisfy their individual yearnings by other means, the educated through Greek philosophy, the lower classes in Hellenic and Oriental eschatological mystery cults. The ruling classes, however, though sympathetic themselves to Greek philosophy or extreme skepticism, frankly nurtured and manipulated the state religion as a political tool for the maintenance of their own power. Under these circumstances the state religion, fundamentally formalistic to begin with, became a lifeless body of mechanically observed ritual.

Polybius, *Histories* VI. lvi. 6–12; From *LCL*

But the quality in which the Roman commonwealth is most distinctly superior is in my opinion the nature of their religious views. I believe that it is the very thing which among other peoples is an object of reproach, I mean superstition, which maintains the cohesion of the Roman state. These matters have been so exaggerated and introduced to such an extent into their public and private life that nothing could exceed it—a fact which will surprise many. My own opinion at least is that they have adopted this for the sake of the common people. It is a course which perhaps would not have been necessary had it been possible to form a state composed of wise men, but as every multitude is fickle, full of lawless desires, unreasoned passions, and violent anger, the multitude must be held in by invisible terrors and suchlike pageantry. For this reason I think not that the ancients acted rashly and haphazardly in introducing among the people notions concerning the gods and beliefs in the terrors of hell, but rather that the moderns are most rash and foolish in banishing such beliefs.

Cicero, *On Divination* II. xxxii. 70

Experience, education, and the lapse of time have wrought changes in the art of augury; but with an eye to the opinion of the masses the practices, rites, discipline, and laws of augury and the authority of the college of augurs have been maintained for their great political usefulness. . . .

Dionysius of Halicarnassus, *Roman Antiquities* II. vi; From *LCL*

And this custom relating to the auspices long continued to be observed by the Romans, not only while the city was ruled by kings, but also, after the overthrow of the monarchy, in the election of their consuls, praetors, and other legal magistrates; but it has fallen into disuse in our days except as a certain semblance of it remains merely for form's sake. For those who are about to assume the magistracies pass the night out of doors, and rising at break of day offer certain prayers under the open sky; whereupon some of the augurs present, who are paid by the state, declare that a flash of lightning coming from the left has given them a sign, although there really has not been any. And the others, taking their omen from this report, depart in order to take over their magistracies, some of them assuming this alone to be sufficient, that no omens have appeared opposing or forbidding their intended action, others acting even in opposition to the will of the gods; indeed there are times when they resort to violence and rather seize than receive the magistracies.

179. CURSE BY ENCHANTMENT

This is an excellent early example of a *tabella defixionis,* or "enchantment tablet." It was found at Rome, and was written *c.* 75–40 B.C. This magic practice, sporadically known among the Greeks, was widely diffused among the Romans. It was the common practice to have this "binding" curse, prepared by a professional sorcerer, inscribed on a thin lead plate and wrapped around a nail.

CIL, vol. I, 2d ed., no. 2520 (=*ROL*, 4:280–285): From *LCL*

O wife of Pluto, good and beautiful Proserpina (unless I ought to call you Salvia), pray tear away from Plotius health, body, complexion, strength, faculties. Consign him to Pluto your husband. May he be unable to avoid this by devices of his. Consign that man to the fourth-day, the third-day, the every-day fever [malaria]. May they wrestle and wrestle it out with him, overcome and overwhelm him unceasingly until they tear away his life. So I consign him as victim to thee Proserpina, unless, O Proserpina, unless I ought to call thee Goddess of the Lower World. Send, I pray, someone to call up the three-headed dog[47] with request that he may tear out Plotius' heart. Promise Cerberus that thou wilt give him three offerings—dates, dried figs, and a black pig—if he has fulfilled his task before the month of March. All these, Proserpina Salvia, will I give thee when thou hast made me master of my wish. I give thee the head of Plotius, slave of Avonia. O Proserpina Salvia, I give thee Plotius' forehead, Proserpina Salvia, I give thee Plotius' eyebrows, Proserpina Salvia, I give thee Plotius' eyelids. Proserpina Salvia, I give thee Plotius' eye-pupils. Proserpina Salvia, I give thee Plotius' nostrils, lips, ears, nose, and his tongue and teeth so that Plotius may not be able to utter what it is that gives him pain; his neck, shoulders, arms, fingers, so that he may not be able to help himself at all; his chest, liver, heart, lungs, so that he may not be able to feel what gives him pain; his abdomen, belly, navel, sides, so that he may not be able to sleep; his shoulder-blades, so that he may not be able to sleep well; his sacred part, so that he may not be able to make water; his buttocks, vent, thighs, knees, legs, shins, feet, ankles, soles, toes, nails, that he may not be able to stand by his own aid. Should there so exist any written curse, great or small—in what manner Plotius has, according to the laws of magic, composed any curse and entrusted it to writing, in such manner I consign, hand over to thee, so that thou mayest consign and hand over that fellow, in the month of February. Blast him! damn him! blast him utterly! Hand him over, consign him, that he may not be able to behold, see, and contemplate any month further!

---

47. Cerberus, the mythical three-headed watchdog of Hades.

180. SOME ROMAN FESTIVALS[48]

LUPERCALIA — FEBRUARY 15

Plutarch, *Life of Romulus* xxi. 3–5

The Lupercalia, judging from the time of its celebration, would seem to be a feast of purification, for it is observed on the *dies nefasti* [see § 9] of the month of February, which one may interpret to signify *purification,* and the very day of the feast was in ancient days called *Februata;* but the name of the holiday was the meaning of the Greek Lycaea [feast of wolves], and it seems thus to be of great antiquity. . . . And we see the Luperci [priests of Faunus] begin their course from the place where they say Romulus was exposed. But the actual ceremonies make the reason for the name hard to surmise; for there are goats killed; then two youths of noble birth are brought to the priests, some of whom touch their foreheads with a bloody knife, while others at once wipe it off with wool dipped in milk. The youths must laugh after their foreheads are wiped. Next, having cut the goats' skins into strips, the priests run about naked, except for something about their middle, lashing all they meet with the thongs; and the young wives do not avoid their blows, fancying that they will thus promote conception and easy childbirth.

TERMINALIA—FEBRUARY 23

Ovid, *Fasti* II. 639–662; From *LCL*

When the night has passed, see to it that the god who marks the boundaries of the tilled lands receives his wonted honor. O Terminus, whether thou art a stone or a stump buried in the field, thou too hast been deified from days of yore. Thou art crowned by two owners on opposite sides; they bring thee two garlands and two cakes. An altar is built. Hither the husbandman's rustic wife brings with her own hands on a potsherd the fire which she has taken from the warm hearth. The old man chops wood, and deftly piles up the billets, and strives to fix the branches in the solid earth; then he nurses the kindling flames with dry bark; the boy stands by and holds the broad basket in his hands. When from the basket he has thrice thrown corn into the midst of the fire, the little daughter presents the cut honeycombs. Others hold vessels

48. For the names of these festivals, see p. 71.

of wine. A portion of each is cast into the flames. The company dressed in white look on and hold their peace. Terminus himself, at the meeting of the bounds, is sprinkled with the blood of a slaughtered lamb, and grumbles not when a sucking pig is given him. The simple neighbors meet and hold a feast, and sing thy praises, holy Terminus: thou dost set bounds to peoples and cities and vast kingdoms; without thee every field would be a cause of wrangling. Thou courtest no favor, thou are bribed by no gold: the lands entrusted to thee thou dost guard in loyal good faith.

ROBIGALIA—APRIL 25

Ovid, *Fasti* IV. 905–936; From *LCL*

On that day, as I was returning from Nomentum to Rome, a white-robed crowd blocked the middle of the road. A flamen was on his way to the grove of ancient Mildew *(Robigo)*, to throw the entrails of a dog and the entrails of a sheep into the flames. Straightway I went up to him to inform myself of the rite. Thy flamen, O Quirinus, pronounced these words' "Thou scaly Mildew, spare the sprouting corn, and let the smooth top quiver on the surface of the ground. O let the crops, nursed by the heaven's propitious stars, grow till they are ripe for the sickle! No feeble power is thine: the corn on which thou hast set thy mark, the sad husbandman gives up for lost. Nor winds, nor showers, nor glisten-ing frost, that nips the sallow corn, harm it so much as when the sun warms the wet stalks; then, dread goddess, is the hour to wreak thy wrath. O spare, I pray, and take thy scabby hands from off the harvest! Harm not the tilth; 'tis enough that thou hast the power to harm. Grip not the tender crops, but rather grip the hard iron. Forestall the de-stroyer. . . . But do not thou profane the corn, and ever may the husbandman be able to pay his vows to thee in thine absence." So he spake. On his right hand hung a napkin with a loose nap, and he had a bowl of wine and a casket of incense. The incense, and wine, and sheep's guts, and the foul entrails of a filthy dog, he put upon the hearth—we saw him do it.

LEMURIA—MAY 9

Ovid, *Fasti* v. 419–444: From *LCL*

When from that day the Evening Star shall thrice have shown his beauteous face, and thrice the vanquished stars shall have retreated before Phoebus, there shall be celebrated an olden rite, the nocturnal Lemuria: it will bring offerings to the silent ghosts. The year was formerly shorter, and the pious rites of purification *(februa)* were unknown, and thou, two-headed Janus, wast not the leader of the months. Yet even then people brought gifts to the ashes of the dead, as their due, and the grandson paid his respects to the tomb of his buried grandsire. It was the month of May, so named after our forefathers *(maiores),*[49] and it still retains part of the ancient custom. When midnight has come and lends silence to sleep, and dogs and all ye varied fowls are hushed, the worshipper who bears the olden rite in mind and fears the gods arises; no knots constrict his feet; and he makes a sign with his thumb in the middle of his closed fingers,[50] lest in his silence an unsubstantial shade should meet him. And after washing his hands clean in spring water, he turns, and first he receives black beans and throws them away with face averted; but while he throws them away, he says: "These I cast; with these beans I redeem me and mine." This he says nine times, without looking back; the shade is thought to gather the beans, and to follow unseen behind. Again he touches water, and clashes Temesan bronze [from southern Italy], and asks the shade to go out of his house. When he has said nine times, "Ghosts of my fathers, go forth!" he looks back, and thinks that he has duly performed the sacred rites.

181. ANCESTRAL IMAGES

Pliny, *Natural History* xxxv. ii

But on the contrary, in the days of our ancestors it was these that were to be seen in their reception halls, not statues made by foreign artists, or works in bronze or marble: portraits modeled in wax were arranged, each in its own niche, as images to accompany the funeral processions

49. A commonly accepted, though incorrect, derivation of the name of the month May. It was named after Maia, an old Italic divinity, later associated with the Greek Maia, mother of Mercury.

50. A charm to avert the evil eye, still practiced in Italy today.

of the family; and always, whenever some one died, every member of the family that had ever existed was present. The pedigree, too, of the individual was traced by lines to each of the painted portraits. Their record rooms were filled with archives and records of what each had done when holding the magistracy. Outside their houses and around the thresholds were placed other statues of those mighty spirits, together with the spoils taken from the enemy affixed there, memorials which a purchaser was not allowed to displace; so that the houses continued to triumph eternally even after they had changed masters. This was a powerful stimulus, when the walls each day reproached an unwarlike owner for having thus intruded upon the triumphs of another. There is still extant an indignant address by the orator Messala, in which he forbids the images of the Laevinii, who were strangers, to be included among those of his own family.

182. A ROMAN FUNERAL

Polybius, *Histories* VI. liii. i–liv. 2; Adapted from: *LCL*

Whenever any illustrious man dies, he is carried in the course of his funeral with all the paraphernalia into the Forum to the so-called Rostra,[51] sometimes conspicuous in an upright posture and more rarely reclined. Here with all the people standing round, a grown-up son, if he has left one and he happens to be present—otherwise some other relative—mounts the Rostra and delivers an oration on his virtues and successful achievements during his lifetime. As a consequence, the multitude, and not only those who had a part in these achievements but those also who had none, when the deeds are recalled to their minds and brought before their eyes, are moved to such sympathy that the loss seems to be not a private affair of the mourners, but a public one affecting the whole people. Next, after the interment and the performance of the usual ceremonies, they place the image of the departed in the most conspicuous place in the house, enclosed in a wooden shrine. This image is a mask reproducing with remarkable fidelity both the features and complexion of the deceased. On the occasion of public sacrifices they display these images and decorate them with much care, and when any distinguished member of the family dies they take them

---

51. The speaker's platform in the Forum, so called from the beaks *(rostra)* of captured ships which were attached to it.

to the funeral, putting them on men who seem to them to bear the closest resemblance to the original in stature and other traits. These representatives assume togas with a purple border if the deceased was a consul or a praetor, whole purple if he was a censor, and embroidered with gold if he had celebrated a triumph or achieved anything similar. These ride in chariots preceded by *fasces,* axes, and other insignia by which the different magistrates are wont to be accompanied according to the dignity of the rank in the state held by each during his life; and when they arrive at the Rostra they all seat themselves in order on ivory chairs. There could not easily be a more inspiring spectacle for a young man who aspires to fame and virtue. For who would not be inspired by the sight of the images of men renowned for their excellence, all together as if alive and breathing? What spectacle could be more glorious than this? Besides, he who makes the oration over the man about to be buried, when he has finished speaking of him, recounts the successes and exploits of the rest whose images are present, beginning from the most ancient. By this means, by this constant renewal of the good report of brave men, the fame of those who performed noble deeds is rendered immortal, while at the same time the fame of those who did good service to their country becomes known to the people and a heritage for future generations.

183. Funeral Eulogy of Turia

Though this funeral encomium in honor of Turia was delivered by her husband Quintus Lucretius Vespillo (some scholars doubt that it concerns this couple) in 8–2 B.C., most of the events referred to are of the last decades of the Republic. Vespillo was proscribed in 43 B.C., but after his pardon became consul, in 19 B.C. The legal matters concerned with the attempt of Turia's relatives to upset her father's will are omitted here.

CIL vol. VI, nos. 1527, 31670 (=Dessau, no. 8393)[52]

Before the day fixed for our marriage you were suddenly left an orphan, by the murder of both your parents in the solitude [of the country?].

Through your efforts chiefly the death of your parents did not remain unavenged. For I had departed to Macedonia, and Gaius Cluvius, your sister's husband, into the province of Africa.

52. Plus a fragment published in *American Journal of Archaeology* (1950), 54:223–226.

So zealous were you in the performance of this pious duty, in requesting and investigating and insistently demanding the punishment of
the guilty that, had we ourselves been present, we could not have
done more. You share the credit for this with that pious woman, your
sister.

While you were busy with these matters, to shield your honor, after
the punishment of the assassins, you at once retired from your father's
house to the home of my mother, where you awaited my return. . . .

Marriages of such long duration, not dissolved by divorce, but terminated by death alone, are indeed rare. For our union was prolonged
in unclouded happiness for forty-one years. Would that our long marriage had come to its final end by *my* death, and that *I* as the older—
which was more just—had yielded to fate.

Why recall your natural qualities, your modesty, deference, affability,
your amiable disposition, your faithful attendance to household duties,
your enlightened religion, your unassuming elegance, the modest simplicity of your attire? Need I speak of your attachment to your kindred,
your affection for your family—when you cherished my mother as you
did your own parents—you who share countless other virtues with
Roman matrons who cherish their fair name? These qualities which I
claim for you are your own; few have possessed the like and been able
to hold on to and maintain them; the experience of men teaches us how
rare they are.

With joint zeal we have preserved all the patrimony which you
received from your parents. Entrusting it all to me, you were not
troubled with the care of increasing it; thus did we share the task of
administering it, that I undertook to protect your fortune, and you to
guard mine. On this point I pass by many things in silence, for fear of
attributing to myself a portion of your deserts. Suffice it for me to have
indicated my sentiments.

You gave proof of your generosity not only towards very many of
your kin, but especially in your filial devotion. . . . You brought up in
our home . . . some worthy young girls of your kinship. And that these
might attain to a station in life worthy of your family, you provided
them with dowries. Gaius Cluvius and myself, by common accord,
executed your intention, and approving of your generosity, in order that
your patrimony might suffer no diminution, offered our own family
possessions instead and gave up our own estates to provide the dowries
settled upon by you. This I have related, not to sing my own praises,

but to show that we held ourselves in honor bound to execute from our property those obligations incurred by you out of the fulness of your heart. . . .

You helped my escape by selling your jewels and turning over to me all your gold and the pearls removed from your person; and thereupon the household furnished money; and deceiving the guards of our opponents, you made my absence comfortable. You ceased making trial of the violence of the soldiery, as your courage kept urging you to try; the clemency of those against whom you were planning this provided a safer path for you. In the midst of such a great disaster your spirit was so steadfast that no unbecoming word escaped your lips. . . .

[Rightly did Caesar say that you deserved the credit?] for my survival and for his restoration of me from exile to my native land. For unless you had prepared the way which he kept safe, looking out for my safety, his promises of assistance had been of no avail. So I owe no less a debt to your loyal devotion than to Caesar.

Why should I now conjure up the memory of the hidden counsels, concealed plans, and secret talks? How, aroused by the sudden arrival of messages from you to a realization of the present and imminent perils, I was saved by your counsel. How you did not allow me recklessly through excessively bold plans to face danger, and how, bent on more discreet plans, you provided for me a safe retreat, choosing as sharers in your plans for my safety—fraught with danger as they were for you all —your sister and her husband, Gaius Cluvius. Were I to attempt to touch on all these matters, it would be an endless task. Suffice it for me and for you that the retreat provided by you ensured my safety.

I should confess, however, that on this occasion I suffered one of the bitterest experiences of my life, in the fate that befell you. When the favor and decision of Caesar Augustus, then absent [from Rome], had restored me to my country, still a useful citizen perhaps, Marcus Lepidus,[53] his colleague, then present in the city, interposed objections to my pardon. Then, when you prostrated yourself at his feet, he not only did not raise you up—but, dragged along and abused, as though a common slave, your body all covered with bruises, yet with unflinching steadfastness of purpose you recalled to him Caesar's edict and the letter of felicitation on my pardon. Braving his taunts and suffering the most brutal insults and wounds, you denounced these cruelties publicly so

53. One of the members of the Second Triumvirate (see § 115).

that he became known as the author of all my perils. And his punishment for this was not long delayed.[54]

Could such courage remain without effect? Your unexampled patience furnished the occasion for Caesar's clemency, and, by guarding my life, branded the savage cruelty [of Lepidus]. . . .

When all the world was again at peace and the Republic reestablished, peaceful and happy days followed for us. We longed for children, which an envious fate denied us for some time. Had Fortune permitted herself to smile on us in the ordinary fashion, what had been lacking to complete our happiness? But advancing age put an end to our hopes. . . . Despairing of your fertility and disconsolate to see me without children . . . you spoke of divorce because of my unhappiness on this account, offering to yield our home to another spouse more fertile, with no other intention than that of yourself searching for and providing for me a spouse worthy of our well-known mutual affection, whose children you assured me you would have treated as though your own. . . . Nothing would have been changed, only that you would have rendered to me henceforth the services and devotion of a sister or mother-in-law.

I must admit that I was so angry that I was deprived of my mind, and that I was so horrified at your proposal that I scarcely regained control of myself. That you should have spoken of divorce between us before the decree of fate had been given; that you should have conceived of any reason why you, while you were still alive, should cease to be my wife, you who when I was almost an exile from life remained most faithful. . . .

Would that our time of life had permitted our union to endure until I, the older, had passed away — which was more just — and that you might perform for me the last rites, and that I might have departed, leaving you behind, with a daughter to replace me in your widowhood.

By fate's decree your course was run before mine. You left me the grief, the longing for you, the sad fate to live alone. . . .

The conclusion of this oration will be that you have deserved all, and that I remain with the chagrin of not being able to repay you all. Your wishes have always been my supreme law; and whatever it will be granted to me to do in addition, in this I shall not fail.

I pray that your *Manes* [protecting spirits of the dead] may assure and protect your repose.

---

54. Lepidus was deposed from power by Octavian in 36 B.C., and kept under house arrest in the resort town of Circeii in Latium until his death in 13 B.C.

184. EPITAPHS AND BURIAL PLACES

FROM THE TOMB OF THE SCIPIOS

The following are among the inscriptions found in the tomb of the distinguished patrician clan of the Scipios, just outside Rome.

CIL, vol. I, 2d ed., nos. 6–9, 12, 13, 15, 16 (= *ROL,* 4:2–9); *From LCL*

i

Lucius Cornelius Scipio son of Gnaeus.[55]

Lucius Cornelius Scipio Barbatus, Gnaeus' begotten son, a valiant gentleman and wise, whose fine form matched his bravery surpassing well, was aedile, consul, and censor among you; he took Taurasia and Cisauna from Samnium; he overcame all the Lucanian land and brought hostages therefrom.

ii

Lucius Cornelius Scipio son of Lucius, aedile, consul, censor.[56]

This man Lucius Scipio, as most agree, was the very best of all good men at Rome. A son of Barbatus, he was aedile, consul, and censor among you; he it was who captured Corsica, Aleria too, a city. To the goddess of Weather he gave deservedly a temple.

iii

Lucius Cornelius Scipio son of Lucius,[57] grandson of Publius, quaestor, tribune of the soldiers. Died at thirty-three years. His father vanquished King Antiochus.

iv

Gnaeus Cornelius Scipio Hispanus[58] son of Gnaeus, praetor, curule aedile, quaestor, tribune of soldiers (twice); member of the board of ten for judging law suits; member of the board of ten for making sacrifices.

55. Consul in 298 B.C., censor in 290.
56. Consul in 259 B.C., censor in 258.
57. Son of Lucius Scipio who defeated Antiochus at Magnesia in 190 B.C.
58. Probably a son of Scipio Hispallus, who was consul in 176 B.C.

By my good conduct I heaped virtues on the virtues of my clan; I begat a family and sought to equal the exploits of my father. I upheld the praise of my ancestors, so that they are glad that I was created of their line. My honors have ennobled my stock.

MISCELLANEOUS FUNERARY INSCRIPTIONS

CIL, vol. I, 2d ed., nos. 834, 1211, 1221, 1212, 1821, 2123 (= *ROL*, 4:8–9, 12–13, 22–25, 28–29, 42–43, 50–51); *From LCL*

i

[Rome; early second century B.C.] To Gaius Publicius Bibulus,[59] aedile of the plebs, son of Lucius, was granted, at the cost of the state by decree of the senate and by order of the people, to honor him because of his worthiness, a site for a memorial into which he himself and his posterity might be conveyed.

ii

[Rome; c. 135–120 B.C.] Stranger, my message is short. Stand by and read it through. Here is the unlovely tomb of a lovely woman. Her parents called her Claudia by name. She loved her husband with all her heart. She bore two sons; of these she leaves one on earth; under the earth has she placed the other. She was charming in converse, yet gentle in bearing. She kept house, she made wool. That's my last word. Go your way.

iii

[Rome; c. 80 B.C. or later.] Lucius Aurelius Hermia freedman of Lucius, a butcher of the Viminal Hill.

She who went before me in death, my one and only wife, chaste in body, a loving woman of my heart possessed, lived faithful to her faithful man; in fondness equal to her other virtues, never during bitter times did she shrink from loving duties.

Aurelia, freedwoman of Lucius.

Aurelia Philematium freedwoman of Lucius.

In life I was named Aurelia Philematium, a woman chaste and mod-

---

59. Probably tribune in 209 B.C.

est, knowing not the crowd, faithful to her husband. My husband was a fellow freedman; he was also in very truth over and above a father to me; and alas, I have lost him. Seven years old was I when he, even he, took me in his bosom; forty years old—and I am in the power of violent death. He through my constant loving duties flourished at all seasons.

iv

[On the Appian Way.] Stranger, stop and turn "your gaze towards this hillock on your left," which holds the bones of a poor man "of righteousness and mercy and love." Wayfarer, I ask you to do no harm to his memorial.

Gaius Atilius Euhodus freedman of Serranus, a pearl merchant of Holy Way, is buried in this memorial. Wayfarer, good bye.

By last will and testament: it is not permitted to convey into or bury in this memorial any one other than those freedmen to whom I have given and bestowed this right by last will and testament.

v

[Cádiz, Spain; first century B.C.] Hail! Herennia Crocine, dear to her own, is shut up in this tomb, Crocine dear to her own. My life is over; other girls too have lived their lives and died before me. Enough now. May the reader say as he departs, "Crocine, may the earth rest lightly on you." Farewell to all you above ground.

vi

[Sassina, Italy.] Horatius Balbus son of . . . is the giver to the citizens of this township and other residents therein, at his own expense, of sites for burial, except such as had hired themselves out as gladiators and such as had hanged themselves with their own hand or had followed a filthy profession for profit: to each person a site, 10 ft. in frontage and 10 ft. in depth, between the bridge over the Sapis and the upper monument which is on the boundary of the Fangonian estate. On sites where no one is buried, anyone who shall so desire shall make a tomb before he dies. On sites where persons have been buried it shall be permitted to build a memorial to him only who shall be buried there and to his descendants.

185. THE INFLUX OF HELLENISM
AND THE ANTI-HELLENIC MOVEMENT
OF THE SECOND CENTURY B.C.

When the conquest of Magna Graecia and Sicily in the third century B.C. and the expansion of Roman power into the eastern Mediterranean in the second century B.C. exposed the Romans to the cultural influences of the brilliant Hellenistic world, the ultraconservatives among the Roman nobility recognized that Hellenism, with its emphasis on intellectualism and individual happiness, represented a threat to their traditional doctrine of subordination of self to family, class, state, and gods, and hence a threat to the stability of their rule. Accordingly, they launched a vigorous but futile campaign to eradicate these "dangerous new ideas" from Roman life. "For indeed it was not a little rivulet that flowed from Greece into our city, but a mighty river of culture and learning," wrote Cicero *(Republic* II. xix. 34). The anti-Hellenic movement, of which Marcus Cato was for a time the leader (cf. pp. 10, 493), manifested itself in various ways, some of which are illustrated below; but by the end of the second century the ancestral Roman way of life had been transformed into a Greco-Roman culture that survived until the decline of the Roman Empire.

GREEK PHYSICIANS IN ROME

Pliny, *Natural History* XXIX. i. 12–14

Cassius Hemina, one of our most ancient writers, is authority for the statement that the first physician that came to Rome was Archagathus, the son of Lysanias, who came over from the Peloponnesus in the 535th year of the city, in the consulship of Lucius Aemilius and Marcus Livius [219 B.C.]. He states also that the Roman citizenship was granted him, and that he had a shop provided for his practice at the public expense at the Acilian Crossway; that he was a remarkable healer of wounds; that at the beginning his arrival was extraordinarily welcome, but that soon afterwards, from his cruelty in cutting and cauterizing, he acquired the name of *Carnifex* (executioner), and brought his art and physicians into disrepute.

This may be most clearly understood from the words of Marcus Cato, whose authority does not need to be bolstered by his triumph and censorship—so high does it rank of itself. I shall, therefore, cite his own words:

"Concerning those Greeks, son Marcus, I will speak to you in the proper place. I will show you the results of my own experience at Athens: that is a good idea to dip into their literature but not to learn it thoroughly. I shall convince you that they are a most iniquitous and intractable people, and you may take my word as the word of a prophet: whenever that nation shall bestow its literature upon us, it will corrupt everything, and all the sooner if it sends its physicians here. They have conspired among themselves to murder all foreigners with their medicine, a profession which they exercise for money in order that they may win our confidence and dispatch us all the more easily. They also commonly call us barbarians, and stigmatize us more foully than other peoples, by giving us the appellation of Opici.[60] I forbid you to have anything to do with physicians."[61]

DECREES AGAINST RHETORICIANS

Suetonius, *On Famous Rhetoricians* i; From *LCL*

The study of rhetoric was introduced into our country in about the same way as that of grammar, but with somewhat greater difficulty, since, as is well known, its practice was at times actually prohibited. To remove any doubt on this point, I shall append an ancient decree of the senate, as well as an edict of the censors:

"In the consulship of Gaius Fannius Strabo and Marcus Valerius Messala[62] the praetor Marcus Pomponius laid a proposition before the senate. Whereas speeches were made about philosophers and rhetoricians, the senate decreed on this matter as follows: that Marcus Pomponius, the praetor, should take heed and provide, as he deemed best in accordance with the interests of the state and with his own good faith, that they not be allowed to live in Rome."

Some time afterward the censors Gnaeus Domitius Ahenobarbus and Lucius Licinius Crassus [92 B.C.] issued the following edict about the same class of men: "It has been reported to us that there be men who have introduced a new kind of training, and that our young men frequent their schools; that these men have assumed the title of Latin rhetoricians and that young men spend whole days with them in idle-

---

60. A boorish Oscan tribe, familiar to the Greeks in Campania.

61. Cf. the primitive magic formulas preferred by Cato to the highly advanced Greek medical science of the time (see § 166, first selection).

62. 161 B.C. See § 171 for the Fannian Sumptuary Law passed in this year.

ness. Our forefathers determined what they wished their children to learn and what schools they desired them to attend. These innovations in the customs and principles of our forefathers do not please us nor seem proper. Therefore it appears necessary to make our opinion known both to those who have such schools and to those who are in the habit of attending them, that they are displeasing to us."[63]

LATIN THE OFFICIAL LANGUAGE

Valerius Maximus, *Memorable Deeds and Sayings* II. ii. 2

Indeed the manner in which the magistrates of olden times conducted themselves in order to maintain their dignity and the sovereign power of the Roman people can be understood by the fact that, among other evidences of how they acquired dignity, there was this practice, which they observed with great steadfastness, never to answer the Greeks except in Latin [for an instance see § 74]. Further, wresting from them the fluency of speech in which they excel, they forced them to speak through an interpreter, not only in our city, but also in Greece and Asia, in order, doubtless, to diffuse the Latin language among all peoples and to make it more respectable. Not that they lacked an interest in learning, but they thought that in every matter the Greek cloak should be subjected to the toga, thinking it an indignity that the weight and the majesty of the empire should be bestowed upon the allurements and delight of literature.

CATO'S HOSTILITY TO GREEK LEARNING

Plutarch, *Life of Cato the Elder* xxii. 1–xxiii. 3

When Cato was already an old man, Carneades the Academic and Diogenes the Stoic came as envoys from Athens to Rome. . . .[64] The most studious of the youth at once went to wait upon these men, and frequently heard them speak with admiration. But the charm of Car-

---

63. Similarly in 115 B.C. the censors Lucius Metellus and Gnaeus Domitius banned all dramatic performances from the city, excepting only a Latin flutist with singer, and also the dice game (Cassiodorus, *Chronicon*, Year 639).

64. These Greek philosophers, who came to Rome in 155 B.C., were accompanied by a third, Critolaus the Peripatetic. Cf. also Athenaeus, *Savants at Dinner* XII. 547a: "The Romans, therefore, the most virtuous of men in all things, did a good job when they banished the Epicureans Alcaeus and Philiscus from the city in the consulship of Lucius Postumius [173 B.C.] because of the pleasures which they introduced."

neades, which had boundless power and a reputation equal to it, won large and sympathetic audiences, and filled the city with its sound, like a wind. The report spread far and wide that a Greek of amazing talent, who charmed and disarmed everybody, had infused a powerful passion into the young men, so that forsaking their other pleasures and pursuits, they were in ecstasies about philosophy. This pleased the other Romans, and they were glad to see the youth participating in Greek culture and consorting with such remarkable men. But Cato, when this passion for discussion came flowing into the city, from the beginning was distressed, fearing lest the youth, by diverting their ambitions in this direction, should prefer a reputation for speaking well before that of deeds and military campaigns. And when the fame of the philosophers increased in the city, and a distinguished man, Gaius Acilius, at his own request became their interpreter to the senate at their first audience, Cato determined, under a specious pretext, to have all philosophers cleared out of the city. And coming into the senate he blamed the magistrates for letting these envoys stay so long a time without settling the matter, though they were such persuasive persons that they could easily secure anything they wished; that therefore a decision should be made and a vote taken on the embassy as soon as possible, so that they might go home again to their own schools and lecture to the sons of the Greeks, while the Roman youth listened, as hitherto, to their own laws and magistrates.

He did this not out of hostility, as some think, to Carneades, but because he wholly despised philosophy, and out of a patriotic zeal mocked all Greek culture and learning. . . . And to prejudice his son against anything that was Greek, in a rasher voice than became one of his age, he declared, as it were with the voice of a prophet or seer, that the Romans would lose their empire when they began to be infected with Greek literature. But indeed time has shown the vanity of this prophecy of doom, for while the city was at the zenith of her empire she made all Greek learning and culture her own.

186. ROMAN EDUCATION

Roman education was characteristically utilitarian. In the early period, before Rome became a world power, the home was the center of education. Here, under the personal tutorship of the *paterfamilias* and the *matrona,* the sons of the ruling-class families were prepared for their future political and military functions through physical training and the inculcation of the traditional Roman virtues. Especially important was the study of the examples of the national heroes of the past, and the memorization of the Twelve Tables (see introduction to § 32) as the foundation of the knowledge of civil law. The method was essentially that of imitation, and it included an informal apprenticeship to the father or to another distinguished statesman-soldier. In the third and second centuries B.C., under the impact of Hellenism, Roman education was gradually institutionalized and merged with Greek intellectualism. Despite conservative opposition (see § 185) schools were introduced; these were largely in the hands of Greek slaves and freedmen. Literature, both Greek and Latin, philosophy, rhetoric, and other aspects of the liberal arts became part of the formal curriculum. But the principal aim of the new Greco-Roman education was training in oratory—the key skill in the conduct of affairs. For increasing numbers, formal education culminated in a trip to the "university centers" of the Greek East. The early training of Cicero is a most instructive example of the Roman educational system of the last century of the Republic.

AN OLD-FASHIONED EDUCATION

Plutarch, *Life of Cato the Elder* xx. 3–6

As soon as Cato had a son, no business was so urgent, unless it was some public matter, but that he was present when his wife bathed the infant and dressed it in its swaddling clothes. For the mother herself nursed it and often, too, the infants of her slaves, in order to produce, by this common nurture, an affection in them toward her son. As soon as he showed signs of understanding, Cato himself took him in his charge and taught him to read, although he had an accomplished slave, Chilo by name, who was a teacher and taught many boys. But he thought it not proper, as he himself said, to have his son reprimanded by a slave, or to have his ears tweaked when he was slow in learning; nor would he have him under obligation to a slave for so priceless a thing as education. He himself, therefore, was his reading teacher, his law teacher, and his athletic trainer, and he taught his son not only how to hurl the javelin, to fight in armor, and to ride a horse, but also to box, to endure both heat and cold, and to swim through the eddies and billows of the river. He says, likewise, that he wrote his *History* in large characters with his own hand, that his son might thus have at home the means to acquaint himself with his country's ancient traditions; and that in his son's presence he refrained from obscene language no less than if he were in the presence of the Vestal Virgins. Nor would he ever bathe with him. This seems, indeed, to have been the common custom of the Romans, for even fathers-in-law used to avoid bathing with their sons-in-law, being ashamed to uncover their nakedness. But having afterwards learned of the Greeks to go naked, they have in turn infected the Greeks with this practice even in the presence of women.

Thus, like a beautiful work, Cato molded and fashioned his son to virtue.

THE TRAINING OF AN ORATOR

Tacitus, *Dialogue on Oratory* xxxiv

It was accordingly usual with our ancestors, when a lad was being prepared for public speaking, as soon as he was partially trained by home discipline, and his mind was stored with culture, to have him taken by his father or his relatives to an orator who held a leading position in the state. The boy used to accompany and attend him, and be present at all his public utterances, alike in the law court and the assembly, and thus he picked up the art of debate and became habituated to polemics, and indeed, I may almost say, learned how to fight in battle. Thereby young men acquired from the start great experience and much self-confidence and a very large stock of judgment, for they were studying in broad daylight, in the very thick of the conflict, where no one can safely say anything foolish or inconsistent without its being rejected by the judge or ridiculed by his opponent, or, last of all, repudiated by his legal aids. Thus from the beginning they were imbued with true and genuine eloquence, and, although they attached themselves to one man, nevertheless they became acquainted with all advocates of the same period in a multitude of civil and criminal cases. They had, too, abundant experience of popular audiences of the most diverse kinds, and from this they could easily perceive what was liked or disapproved in each speaker. Thus they did not lack a teacher of the very best and choicest kind. . . . And indeed it was under such teachers that the youth of whom I am speaking, the disciple of orators, the listener in the Forum, the attendant at the law courts, was trained and habituated by vicarious experience. The laws he learned by daily hearing; the faces of the judges were familiar to him; the ways of popular assemblies were continually before his eyes; he had frequent experience of the likes and dislikes of the people; and whether he undertook a prosecution or a defense, he was singly and alone at once equal to any case. We still read today with admiration the speeches in which Lucius Crassus in his nineteenth, Caesar and Asinius Pollio in their twenty-first year,[65] Calvus, when very little older, denounced, respectively, Gaius Carbo, Dolabella, Gaius Cato, and Vatinius.

CICERO'S STUDIES

Cicero, *Brutus* lxxxix–xci (abridged); From *LCL*

Though I wrote and read and declaimed daily with unflagging interest, yet I was not satisfied to confine myself only to rhetorical exercises. . . . For the study of civil law I attached myself to Quintus Scaevola, the son of Quintus; he took no pupils, but the legal opinions given to his clients taught those who wished to hear him. The year following this was the consulship of Sulla and Pompey.[66] Publius Sulpicius was tribune at that time and addressed the people daily, so that I came to know his style thoroughly. At this time Philo, then head of the Academy, along with a group of loyal Athenians, had fled from Athens because of the Mithridatic War and had come to Rome. Filled with great enthusiasm for the study of philosophy, I gave myself up wholly to his instruction. In so doing I tarried with him the more faithfully, for though the variety and sublimity of his subject delighted and held me, yet it appeared as if the whole institution of courts of justice had vanished for ever. . . . At this time too I devoted myself to study at Rome with Molo of Rhodes, famous as a pleader and teacher. . . .

For a space of about three years the city was free from the threat of arms. . . . During all this time I spent my days and nights in study of every kind. I worked with Diodotus the Stoic, who made his residence in my house, and after a life of long intimacy died there only a short time ago. From him, apart from other subjects, I received thorough training in dialectic, which may be looked upon as a contracted or compressed eloquence. Without it you too, Brutus, have held that eloquence properly so called (which your philosophers tell us is an expanded dialectic) is impossible. But though I devoted myself to his teaching and to the wide range of subjects at his command, yet I allowed no day to pass without some rhetorical exercises. I prepared and deliv-

65. The text is slightly in error. Crassus was twenty-one years of age at the time, Caesar twenty-three.

66. 89 B.C.; Cicero was then sixteen years old.

ered declamations (the term now in vogue), most often with Marcus Piso and Quintus Pompeius, or indeed with anyone, daily. This exercise I practiced much in Latin, but more often in Greek, partly because Greek, offering more opportunity for stylistic embellishment, accustomed me to a similar habit in using Latin, but partly too because the foremost teachers, knowing only Greek, could not, unless I used Greek, correct my faults nor convey their instruction.

Meantime, in the process of restoring orderly government, violence broke out again. . . . Measures were enacted for the reconstitution of the courts and stable government was at length restored. . . .[67] It was not until this time that I first began to undertake cases both civil and criminal, for it was my ambition, not (as most do) to learn my trade in the Forum, but so far as possible to enter the Forum already trained. At this time too I devoted myself to study with Molo; for it chanced that he came to Rome in the dictatorship of Sulla as a member of a commission to the senate with regard to the reimbursement of Rhodes. Thus my first criminal case, spoken in behalf of Sextus Roscius, won such favorable comment that I was esteemed not incompetent to handle any litigation whatsoever. There followed then in quick succession many other cases which I brought into court, carefully worked out, and, as the saying is, smelling somewhat of the midnight oil. . . .

However, having come to the conclusion that with relaxation and better control of my voice, as well as with modification of my general style of speaking, I should at once avoid risk to my health and acquire a more tempered style—to effect this change in habit of speaking was the reason for my departure for Asia Minor. Thus I had been active in practice for two years and my name was already well known in the Forum at the time when I left Rome.

Arriving at Athens I spent six months with Antiochus, the wise and famous philosopher of the Old Academy, and with him as my guide and teacher I took up again the study of philosophy, which from my early youth I had pursued, and had made some progress in, and had never wholly let drop. But at the same time at Athens I continued zealously with rhetorical exercises under the direction of Demetrius the Syrian, an experienced teacher of eloquence not without some reputation. Afterwards I traveled through all of Asia Minor and was with the most distinguished orators of the region, who were generous in giving

---

67. The reference is to the dictatorship of Sulla, who made the senatorial class once again eligible for jury service (cf. § 104 and introduction to § 158).

me opportunity to practice declamatory exercises with them. The chief of these was Menippus of Stratonicea, in my judgment the most eloquent man of all Asia in that time; and certainly, if to speak without affectation and without offense to good taste is Attic, he was an orator who could justly be placed in that category. But the one most constantly with me was Dionysius of Magnesia. There were also Aeschylus of Cnidus and Xenocles of Adramyttium. These men were at that time accounted the principal teachers of oratory in Asia. However, not content with them, I went to Rhodes and attached myself to Molo, whom I had already heard at Rome. . . . Thus I came back after two years' absence not only better trained, but almost transformed.

187. Why Oratory Flourished in the Late Republic

The dramatic date of this dialogue, in which Tacitus analyzes the decline of oratory in the imperial period, is A.D. 74/75. He looks back nostalgically to the heyday of Roman oratory in the dying days of the Republic.

Tacitus, *Dialogue on Oratory* xxxvi–xl (abridged); Adapted from *LCL*

Great oratory is like a flame: it needs fuel to feed it, movement to fan it, and it brightens as it burns.

At Rome too the eloquence of our forefathers owed its development to the same conditions. For although the orators of today have also succeeded in obtaining all the influence that it would be proper to allow them under settled, peaceable, and prosperous political conditions, yet their predecessors in those days of unrest and unrestraint seemed to accomplish more when, in the general ferment and without the strong hand of a single ruler, a speaker's political wisdom was measured by his power of carrying conviction to the unstable populace. This was the source of the constant succession of measures put forward by champions of the people's rights, of the harangues of state officials who almost spent the night on the speakers' platform, of the prosecutions of powerful defendants and hereditary feuds between families, of factions among the aristocracy and never-ending struggles between the senate and the commons. All this tore the commonwealth in pieces, but it provided a sphere for the oratory of those days and heaped on it what one saw were vast rewards. The more influence a man could wield by his powers of speech, the more readily did he attain to high office, the farther did he, when in office, outstrip his colleagues, the more did he gain favor with the great, authority with the senate, and name and fame with the common people. These were the men who had nations of foreigners under their protection, several at a time; the men to whom officials paid their respects on the eve of their departure for the provinces, and to whom they paid their respects on their return; the men who, without any effort on their own part, seemed to have praetorships and consulships at their beck and call; the men who even when out of office were in power, seeing that they could bend both the senate and the people to their will by their advice and authority. With them, moreover, it was a conviction that without eloquence it was impossible for anyone either to attain to a position of distinction and prominence in the community or to maintain it—and no wonder, when they were called on to appear in public even when they would rather not; when it was not enough to move a brief resolution in the senate unless one supported one's opinion in an able speech; when persons who had in some way or other incurred envy or else were charged with some specific offense had to put in an appearance in person; when, moreover, evidence in criminal trials had to be given not indirectly or by affidavit, but personally and by word of mouth. . . .

There was a further advantage in the high rank of the defendants and the importance of the interests involved, factors which are also in a great degree conducive to eloquence. For it makes a good deal of difference whether you are briefed to speak about a case of theft, or a rule of procedure, or an interlocutory order of a magistrate, or about electioneering practices, or extortion from the allies and the murder of fellow citizens. It is better, of course, that such horrors should not occur at all, and we must regard that as the most enviable political condition in which we do not suffer from such ills. Yet when these things did happen, they furnished the orators of the day with ample material. Hand in hand with the importance of the time goes the growing ability to cope with it, and it is a sheer impossibility for anyone to produce a great and glorious oration unless he has found a theme to correspond. . . .

Moreover, your public speaker can't get along without "hear, hear" and applause. He must have what I may call his stage. This the orators of former times could command day by day, when the Forum was packed by an audience at the same time numerous and distinguished, when persons who had to face the hazard of a public trial could depend on being supported by clients and members of the lower classes, and by deputations also from the municipalities and a section of Italy. These

were the days when the people of Rome felt that in quite a number of
cases they had a personal stake in the verdict. We know on good
authority that both the prosecution and the defense of Gaius Cornelius,
Marcus Scaurus, Titus Milo, Lucius Bestia, Publius Vatinius,[68] for example, brought the whole community together *en masse;* so that it
would have been impossible for even the most frigid of speakers not to
be enkindled and set on fire by the mere clash of partisan enthusiasm.
That is why, indeed, the quality of the published orations that have
come down to us is so high that it is by these more than by any others
that those who took part in the action are judged.

Think again of the incessant public meetings, of the privilege so freely
accorded of inveighing against persons of position and influence—yes,
and of the glory you gained by being at daggers drawn with them, in
the days when so many clever speakers could not let even a Publius
Scipio alone, or a Lucius Sulla or a Gnaeus Pompey, and when, taking a
leaf from the book of actors, they made public meetings also the opportunity of launching characteristically spiteful tirades against the leading
men of the state—how all this must have inflamed the able debater and
added fuel to the fire of his eloquence![69]

The art of our discourse is not a quiet and peaceable art, or one that
finds satisfaction in moral worth and unassuming conduct; no, really
great and famous oratory is a foster child of license, which foolish men
call liberty, an associate of sedition, a goad for the unbridled populace.
It owes no allegiance to any. Devoid of reverence, it is insulting, rash,
and overbearing. It is a plant that does not grow under a well-regulated
constitution. Does history contain a single instance of any orator at
Sparta or at Crete, states whose system and laws were exceedingly
stringent? It is equally true to say that in Macedonia and in Persia
eloquence was unknown, as indeed it was in all states that were content
to live under a settled government. Rhodes has had some orators, Athens a great many: in both communities all power was in the hands of the

68. All these were cases in which Cicero was involved in the years 65–54 B.C. Only the speech in
defense of Milo has survived entire.

69. Such freedom of speech was not as universal as this rhetorical passage implies; it was rather a
privilege which the ruling nobility accorded to itself but denied (at least at times) to others. There is,
for example, the famous case of the poet Naevius, "who wrote two plays . . . in prison when he had
been arrested in Rome because he constantly abused and insulted the leading public figures [i.e., in his
comedies]. He was later set free by the tribunes of the plebs, when . . . he apologized for his offenses
and for the impudent language with which he had previously insulted many men" (Aulus Gellius, *Attic
Nights* III. iii. 15).

populace—that is to say untutored persons—in both everyone, so to speak, had supreme power. Likewise at Rome, as long as the constitution was unsettled, so long as the country kept wearing itself out with factions and dissensions and disagreements, so long as there was no peace in the Forum, no harmony in the senate, no restraint in the courts, no respect for authority, no sense of propriety on the part of the magistrates, the growth of eloquence was doubtless sturdier, just as untilled soil produces certain vegetation in greater luxuriance. But the benefit derived from the eloquence of the Gracchi did not make up for what the country suffered from their laws, and too dearly did Cicero pay by the death he died for his renown in oratory.

188. ART COLLECTING

In 212 B.C. Marcus Marcellus captured Syracuse, and transported to Rome a large number of the art treasures of that city. "From that time," says Livy (xxv. xl. 2), "came the beginning of enthusiasm for Greek works of art and consequently of the general license to despoil all kinds of buildings, sacred and profane." In the two ensuing centuries the collection of Greek art objects by the Roman upper classes for the decoration of private homes and public places became a veritable mania with them (cf. § 80, last selection). It was not merely conquering generals who brought home art spoils from captured towns; provincial officials frequently took advantage of their positions to acquire what they wanted by persuasion or coercion; dealers and their agents (cf. Cicero, *Letters to Atticus* book I, no. 9) scoured the Greek world buying up antiques, copies, fakes — anything that went by the name of "art" fetched high prices at Rome.[70] Literary treasures, too, were in great demand; perhaps the best known "haul" of this kind was that of Sulla, who, after capturing Athens, carried off the philosophical library that had belonged to Aristotle and Theophrastus.

This insatiable Roman rapacity could not fail to arouse bitter resentment and hostility among the Greeks, and the Romans were far from unaware of this. But even principled Romans took the legal position that these acquisitions were legitimate if made either by purchase or as spoils of war and that, in the latter case, the loot was public property, and the victorious general was obligated to turn it over to the treasury (cf. § 89), but it is obvious that many neglected with impunity to do so.

70. Numerous examples of the prices of art objects in Rome are given in T. Frank, ed., *An Economic Survey of Ancient Rome*, 1:352–354.

Cicero, *Second Speech Against Verres* I. xix. 49–xxi. 55 (abridged); From *LCL*

Once Verres had reached Asia,[71] what need to go through the list of his dinner and supper parties, the horses and other presents made to him? I am not going to attack a man like Verres for every-day offenses. But I do assert that he carried off statues of great beauty from Chios, and also from Erythrae and Halicarnassus. From Tenedos—I make no reference to the money he seized—Tenes himself, the god for whom the people of Tenedos feel special reverence, who is said to have founded the city, and after whom Tenedos is named—this very Tenes himself, I say, a beautiful work of art, which you have on one occasion seen in the Comitium—this he carried off amid the loud lamentations of the citizens. And then mark how he stormed and sacked the ancient and glorious temple of Juno of Samos: how it plunged the Samians in grief, and distressed all Asia! how the story spread through the world, so that not one of you has not heard it! . . . The pictures, the statues he robbed that island of! I recognized the statues myself the other day in his house, on going there to do my sealing.[72] Where are those statues now, Verres? I mean those we saw in your house the other day, standing by all the pillars, and in all the spaces between the pillars too, yes, and even set about your shrubbery in the open air. . . . Did it never occur to you that on this point I was likely to subpoena your special friends who had continually been at your house, and make them say whether they knew of the previous existence of statues not now there? . . .

You are aware, gentlemen, that Aspendus is an old and famous town in Pamphylia, full of fine statuary. I shall not allege that from this town this or that particular statue was removed. My charge is that Verres did not leave one single statue behind; that from temples and public places alike, with the whole of Aspendus looking on, they were all openly loaded on wagons and carted away. Yes, even the famous *Harper* of Aspendus, about whom you have often heard the saying that is proverbial among the Greeks, of whom it is said that he made "all his music inside"—him too Verres carried off and put right inside his own house, so as to get the reputation of having beaten the *Harper* himself at his own game.[73] At Perga there is, as we know, a very ancient and much

---

71. Verres was in the East in 80–79 B.C. as legate to the governor of Cilicia.

72. That is, sealing the evidence against removal or destruction before the trial. Despite this Verres had, as the immediate sequel shows, removed most of the statues in question from his house after they had been sealed.

73. The point of the proverb here is that the statue was so lifelike that the *Harper* appeared to be

revered sanctuary of Diana: I assert that this too has been stripped and plundered by him, and that all the gold from the figure of the goddess Diana herself has been pulled off and taken away.

You villain, you knave, and you fool, what is the meaning of this? You visited these allied and friendly cities with the rights and rank of assistant governor; but had you forcibly invaded them as a general at the head of an army, even so, any statuary or works of art that you might take away from them you were surely bound to transport not to your own town house or the suburban estate of your friends,[74] but to Rome for the benefit of the nation. Need I quote the example of Marcus Marcellus, who captured Syracuse, that treasury of art?[75] Of Lucius Scipio, who conducted the war in Asia and overthrew that mighty monarch Antiochus? Of Flamininus, who conquered King Philip and Macedonia? Of Lucius Paullus, whose energy and bravery overcame King Perseus? Of Lucius Mummius, who took the beautiful city of Corinth, full of art treasures of every kind, and brought so many cities of Achaea and Boeotia under the empire and sovereignty of Rome?[76] These were men of high rank and eminent character, but their houses were empty of statues and pictures; while we still see the whole city, and the temples of the gods, and every part of Italy, adorned with the gifts and memorials that they brought us.[77]

enjoying his own music, inaudible to all others. The point of the pun is that Verres knew still better how "to play for himself alone."

74. The implication is that that is where the statues from Verres' house were taken after Cicero had sealed them in evidence for the trial (see note 72).

75. Cf. *Second Speech Against Verres* IV. liv: "As a conqueror he thought it proper to remove to Rome many objects that might fitly adorn our city; as a humane man, not to strip the place completely bare, especially as he had resolved to prevent its destruction. . . . All that was brought to Rome is to be seen near the temple of Honor and Virtue, or elsewhere. He set up nothing in his mansion, in his garden, in his country house near Rome; he felt that if he refrained from putting the city's adornments into his own home, his home would thereby become one of the city's adornments." (Quoted from the Loeb Classical Library.) Polybius says (*Histories* IX. x) of the art treasures taken from Syracuse [in 212 B.C.] that the Romans "used such as came from private homes to embellish their own homes, and those that were state property for their public buildings."

76. Cf. Aurelius Victor, *Famous Men* lx: "Mummius filled Italy with statues and paintings which he had taken as spoils from Corinth, but carried off none into his own house."

77. With this whole passage may be compared *Second Speech Against Verres* II. iv. 55–59, in which Cicero tells how Verres stripped Syracuse right down to the doors of its famous temple of Athena.

189. The Roman Theater

Vitruvius, *Architecture* v. vi. 1–9 (abridged); Adapted from *LCL*

The plan of the theater is to be thus arranged: that the center is to be taken of the dimension allotted to the orchestra at the ground level; the circumference is to be drawn; and in it four equilateral triangles are to be described touching the circumference at intervals. . . . Of these triangles the side of that which is nearest the stage will determine the front of the stage, in the part where it cuts the curve of the circle. Through the center of the circle a parallel line is drawn which is to divide the platform of the proscenium from the orchestra. Thus the stage will be made wider than that of the Greeks because all the actors play their parts on the stage, whereas the orchestra is allotted to the seats of the senators. The height of the stage is not to be more than 5 feet, so that those who are seated in the orchestra can see the gestures of all the actors. . . . As to the rows of the auditorium where the seats are placed, the seats are not to be lower than 16 inches nor more than 18. The width is not to be more than 2½ feet nor less than 2 feet. The roof of the colonnade, which is to be built on the top row of steps, is to be so planned as to be level with the top of the back wall of the stage, because thereby the voice will rise evenly until it reaches the top seats and the roof. . . . As to the orchestra, a sixth part is to be taken of its diameter between the lowest steps. On the wings at either side of the entrance, the inmost seats are to be cut back to a perpendicular height equal to that sixth. Whatever the amount of the cutting off is, fixes the spring of the arch over the passages. In this way their vaulting will have sufficient height. . . .

The scenery itself is so arranged that the middle doors are decorated like those of a royal palace, the doors on the right and left like those of guest chambers. Next on either side are the spaces provided for scenery. These the Greeks call *periaktoi* (revolving wings) from the triangular machines which revolve, each side having a different decoration. When there are to be scene changes in plays or when gods enter to the accompaniment of sudden claps of thunder, these are to turn and change the kind of scenery presented to the audience. Next to these are the projecting wings which afford entrances to the stage, one from the town square, the other from abroad. There are three kinds of scenery—one which is called tragic, a second, comic, a third, satyric. The scenes for these are different and unlike each other in plan. The tragic are designed with columns, pediments, and statues and other royal surroundings; the comic have the appearance of private buildings with balconies and views with windows, arranged in imitation of the plans of ordinary houses; the satyric are decorated with trees, caves, mountains, and other rustic surroundings, designed to imitate landscape.

190. PLANNING A TOWN HOUSE

Vitruvius, *Architecture* VI. iii. 1–4, 6–8, V. 1–2; In part from *LCL*

There are five different styles of inner courts, termed according to their construction as follows: Tuscan, Corinthian, tetrastyle, displuviate, and testudinate.

In the Tuscan, the girders that cross the breadth of the *atrium* (main hall) have cross beams on them, and valleys sloping in and running from the angles of the walls to the angles formed by the beams, and the rainwater falls down along the rafters to the roof opening in the middle.[78]

In the Corinthian, the girders and roof opening are constructed on the same principles, but the girders run in from the side walls and are supported all round on columns.

In the tetrastyle, the girders are supported at the angles by columns, an arrangement which relieves and strengthens the girders; for thus they have themselves no great span to support, and they are not loaded down by the cross beams.

In the displuviate, there are beams which slope outwards, supporting the roof and throwing the rainwater off. This style is suitable chiefly in winter residences, for its roof opening, being high up, is not an obstruction to the light of the dining rooms. It is, however, very troublesome to keep in repair, because the pipes, which are intended to hold the water that comes dripping down the walls all around, cannot take it quickly enough as it runs down from the channels, but get too full and run over, thus spoiling the woodwork and the walls of houses of this style.

The testudinate is employed where the span is not great, and where large rooms are provided in upper stories.

Atria are designed, in width and length, according to three classes. In

---

78. The roof opening *(compluvium)* was in the center of the *atrium;* in the *atrium* floor, directly under it, was a sunken basin or trough *(impluvium)* to catch the rainwater that came through the roof opening.

the first the ratio of the length to the width is 5:3, in the second the ratio is 3:2, and in the third the length equals the diagonal of a square whose sides equal the width. The height of *atria* up to the girders should be one fourth less than their width, the rest being the proportion assigned to the cciling and the roof above the girders.

The width of the *alae* (wings) to the right and left should be a fraction of the length of the *atrium,* as follows:

⅓, if length of *atrium* is 30–40 feet
²⁄₇, if length of *atrium* is 40–50 feet
¼, if length of *atrium* is 50–60 feet
²⁄₉, if length of *atrium* is 60–80 feet
⅕, if length of *atrium* is 80–100 feet

The lintel beams of the *alae* should be placed so as to make their height equal to their width. . . .

[Next proportions are set down for the width of the *tablinum* (record-alcove).]

The *fauces* (main entrance) in the case of smaller *atria* should be two thirds the width of the *tablinum;* for larger *atria,* one half. Let the busts of ancestors [see § 181] with their ornaments be set up at a height corresponding to the width of the *alae.* The proportionate width and height of doors may be settled, if they are Doric, in the Doric manner, and if Ionic, in the Ionic manner, according to the rules of symmetry which have been given about portals, in the Fourth Book. The roof opening should have a breadth of not less than one fourth nor more than one third the width of the *atrium,* and a length proportionate to that of the *atrium.*

Peristyles (open courtyards) lying crosswise would be one third longer than they are dcep, and their columns as high as the colonnades are wide. Intercolumniations should be not less than three nor more than four times the diameters of the columns. . . .

Triclinia (dining rooms) ought to be twice as long as they are wide. The height of all oblong rooms should be calculated by adding together their measured length and width, taking one half of this total, and using the result for the height. But in the case of *exedrae* (parlor rooms) or square *oeci* (large halls), let the height be brought up to 1½ times the width. Picture galleries, like *exedrae,* should be constructed of generous dimensions. Corinthian and tetrastyle *oeci,* as well as those termed Egyptian, should have the same symmetrical proportions in width and length as the *triclinia* described above, but, since they have columns in them, their dimensions should be ampler. . . .

After settling the positions of the rooms with regard to the quarters of the sky, we must next consider the principles on which should be constructed those apartments in private houses which are meant for the family itself, and those which are to be shared in common with outsiders. The private rooms are those into which nobody has the right to enter uninvited, such as bedrooms, dining rooms, bathrooms, and all others used for the like purposes. The common rooms are those which any of the people have a perfect right to enter, even without an invitation: that is, vestibules, inner courts, peristyles, and all intended for the like purpose. Hence men of everyday fortune do not need entrance courts, *tablina*, or *atria* built in grand style, because such men discharge their social obligations by going round to others rather than by having others come to them.

Those who are dependent on country produce must have stalls for cattle and shops in their entrance courts, with cellars, granaries, storerooms, and so forth in their houses, constructed more for the purpose of keeping the produce in good condition than for ornamental beauty.

For moneylenders and tax farmers, houses should be built rather comfortable and showy, and secure against robbery; for advocates and public speakers, handsomer and more roomy, to accommodate their audiences; for men of rank who, from holding offices and magistracies, have social obligations to their fellow citizens, lofty entrance courts in princely style, most spacious *atria* and peristyles, broad groves and walks, appropriate to their dignity, and in addition, libraries and porticoes, finished in a style similar to that of great public buildings, since private law suits, hearings before arbitrators, and even councils of state are quite frequently held in the houses of such men.

191. ROMAN WOMEN

TRADITIONAL STATUS

Most Roman women accepted their traditional passive role in Roman patriarchal society (see pp. 65–66, 520–22). Always subject to the guardianship of a male, they were noted for domesticity, chastity, and adherence to the ideal of *univira* ("one-man woman"), and the Roman *matrona* enjoyed an unusually respected status at the side of the *pater familias*. For

examples during the Republic, see §§ 183 and 184. Later Roman literature preserves instances of the earlier secluded, restricted, and subordinate role of Roman women. For the legal status and marriage of Roman
women, and for women in the imperial and early Christian periods see
in volume 2, chapter 5 and § 184.

Aulus Gellius, Attic Nights x. xxiii; From LCL

Those who have written about the life and civilization of the Roman
people say that the women of Rome and Latium lived an abstemious
life; that is, that they abstained altogether from wine, which in the early
language was called *temetum;* that it was an established custom for them
to kiss their kinsfolk for the purpose of detection, so that, if they had
been drinking, the odor might betray them. But they say that the
women were accustomed to drink the second brewing, raisin wine,
spiced wine, and other sweet-tasting drinks of that kind. And these
things are indeed made known in those books which I have mentioned,
but Marcus Cato declares that women were not only censured but also
punished by a judge no less severely if they had drunk wine than if they
had disgraced themselves by adultery.

I have copied Marcus Cato's words from the oration entitled *On the
Dowry,* in which it is also stated that husbands had the right to kill wives
taken in adultery: "When a husband divorces his wife," says he, "he
judges the woman as a censor would, and has full powers if she has been
guilty of any wrong or shameful act; she is severely punished if she has
drunk wine; if she has done wrong with another man she is condemned
to death." Further, as to the right to put her to death, it was thus
written: "If you should take your wife in adultery, you may with
impunity put her to death without a trial; but if you should commit
adultery or indecency, she must not presume to lay a finger on you, nor
does the law permit it."

Valerius Maximus, Memorable Deeds and Sayings VI. iii. 9–12

Egnatius Mecennius[79] . . . beat his wife with a cudgel and killed her
because she had drunk some wine, and not only did no one accuse him
in court because of this deed but he was not even censured, for every
man of good character believed that she had deserved the punishment

---

79. Supposedly of the time of Romulus; with this incident cf. pp. 65–66.

because of her example in violating temperance, and indeed any woman who has an immoderate desire for the drinking of wine closes the door to all virtues and opens it to transgressions.

There is also the blunt marital sternness of Gaius Sulpicius Gallus [consul in 166 B.C.]. He repudiated his wife, because he had detected her out of doors with her head uncovered, with an abrupt yet somewhat justified decision: "The law," he said, "prescribes my eyes only as the ones to which you may prove your beauty; it is for these that you should adorn yourself with embellishments of beauty, for these be good-looking, to the surer knowledge of these entrust yourself. If any one else looks upon you, because you have attracted him by a needless provocation, there needs must be suspicion and wrongful intent connected with it."

This was also the view of Quintus Antistius Vetus when he divorced his wife because he had seen her talking privately in public with some common freedwoman. For he was not so much disturbed by the fault itself as that he sought to punish, before any crime was committed, the swaddling clothes, as it were, and the nutriment of the fault, so that he might be able to avoid wrongdoing rather than punish it.

There should be added to these cases Publius Sempronius Sophus [consul in 268 B.C.], who inflicted upon his wife the ignominy of divorce for no other reason than that she had dared to be a spectator at the games without his knowledge. And so, when in the past such action was taken against women, their minds were far from transgressions.

THE "LIBERATED" WOMEN OF ROME

In the first century B.C., in consequence of the immense wealth of the senatorial and equestrian orders, upper-class Roman women achieved a degree of emancipation, socially and financially, rarely paralleled in antiquity. New forms of marriage law enabled such women to live as the equals of their men in marriage and divorce and without a legal guardian. Such women as Servilia, the mother of Marcus Brutus, and the notorious Clodia, mistress of the poet Catullus, who immortalized her in his impassioned lyrics, not only led independent lives but exerted behind the scenes a powerful influence on the politics of the times. Many threw themselves into unconventional living, luxury, and pleasure seeking. Many received through tutors the best liberal education of the times. But this Roman smart set had only limited freedom, for the professions and access to political power were closed to them. It is remarkable that the most famous woman in Roman history was not a Roman but Cleopatra, Queen of Egypt.

Sallust, Catiline xxxiv–xxxv

Catiline is said to have rallied to this cause . . . a number of women who in the beginning had lived very extravagantly. Later, when advancing age had moderated only their income but not their debauchery, they had accumulated huge debts. Through them Catiline believed he could stir up the slaves in the city, put the city to the torch, and add their husbands to his cause or kill them.

Among these was Sempronia, who had often committed many outrages with a male boldness. This woman was very fortunate in her lineage and beauty, and in addition in her husband and children. She was trained in Greek and Latin literature, playing the lyre, and dancing, more skilfully than is necessary for an upright woman, and in many other things that are the handmaidens of luxury. But dearer to her was everything but dignity and modesty. As for money or reputation, one would not easily discern which she cared for less. Her sexual appetite was so high that she more often solicited men than she was herself solicited. She had often previously betrayed her trust, disclaimed a debt, and had been an accomplice in murder. She had taken headlong plunges between luxury and poverty. But her native ability was not coarse. She could write poetry, make a jest, use language that was either modest or tender or provocative. She surely had much wit and much charm.

THE BONA DEA SCANDAL, 62 B.C.

Plutarch, Life of Julius Caesar ix. 1–x. 6

Publius Clodius . . . second to none in arrogance and insolence among those notorious for loathsome behavior, was in love with Pompeia, Caesar's wife, and she was not unwilling. . . .

The Romans have a goddess whom they call Bona Dea. . . . It is not lawful for a man to participate nor be in the house where the rituals are celebrated. The women by themselves are said to perform many rites in the service which are similar to the Orphic rites. And so when the time comes for the festival, either the consul or the praetor leaves his house, together with all the males, and his wife takes possession of the house and makes the arrangements. The most important of the rites are conducted at night, and mirth is mingled with the night revels, and there is much music.

At that time, when Pompeia was celebrating the festival . . . in the dress and with the instruments of a female entertainer, Clodius entered, looking like a young woman. . . . An attendant of Aurelia [Caesar's mother] came upon him and invited him to play with her woman to woman. When he refused, she dragged him into the midst and asked him who he was and where he came from. . . . When Clodius answered that he was waiting for Pompeia's maid named Abra, his voice betrayed him. The attendant at once sprang away with a scream toward the lights and the throng, shouting that she had caught a man. As the women were panic stricken, Aurelia halted the rites of the goddess and covered up the paraphernalia. Ordering the doors to be closed, she went about the house with torches searching for Clodius. He was found where he had fled, in the room of the slave girl who had let him in. When he was recognized by the women they drove him out of doors.

The women at once went away during the night and told their husbands what had happened. With the coming of day the talk spread throughout the city that Clodius had committed sacrilege. . . . And so one of the tribunes indicted Clodius for sacrilege . . . But the people defended Clodius. Caesar at once divorced Pompeia, but when he was summoned to Clodius's trial, he said he knew nothing of the things said against Clodius. Since his statement appeared strange, the prosecutor asked, "Why then did you divorce your wife?" "Because," he said, "I thought my wife should not even be under suspicion."

ORGANIZED PROTEST BY WOMEN, 43 B.C.

Appian, *Civil Wars* IV. xxxii–xxxiv

The triumvirs issued an edict affecting 1400 of the richest women. They were ordered to evaluate their property and pay for the needs of the war as much as the triumvirs should determine in each case. And it was provided that those who concealed any of their property or made a false evaluation would be fined, and rewards were to be given to those who informed, to both free persons and slaves. But the women decided to appeal to the women belonging to the triumvirs. They were successful with the sister of Octavian and the mother of Antony. But in the case of Fulvia, the wife of Antony, they were driven from the doors, and could hardly endure her arrogance. Then they forced their way into the Forum to the tribunal of the triumvirs, the people and the bodyguards making way for them. They spoke through Hortensia, who had been chosen beforehand for this.

"As is proper for women such as ourselves, in petitioning to you we had recourse to your women. Having been treated uncivilly by Fulvia, we have been driven to the Forum by her. You have already taken from us our fathers, our sons, and our husbands and our brothers, on the grounds that you have been wronged by them. If you also take away our property, you reduce us to a condition unworthy of our birth, our lifestyle, and our female nature. If indeed you have been wronged by us, as you say you were by our men, then proscribe us also as you did them. But if we women have not voted any of you a public enemy, nor torn down your house, nor destroyed your army, nor led another one against you, nor prevented you from obtaining your office and honors, why then do we share in the penalties if we did not participate in the guilt?

"Why should we pay taxes if we do not share in the magistracies, honors, military commands, in politics at all, for which you contend among yourselves with such great woe. It is a time of war, you say. But when have there not been wars? And when have women been taxed, we who are exempted among all men because of our nature? Our mothers once did rise above their nature when you were endangered with regard to the whole empire and the city itself at the time of the Carthaginian conflict. Then they contributed voluntarily, but not from their landed property, or dowries or houses, without which life is not livable for free women, but freely from the ornaments at home, without value being put on these, and not because of informers and accusers, not by compulsion or violence, but whenever they themselves wished. What fear is there even now among you for the empire and the country? Let there be war with the Gauls or the Parthians and we will not be inferior to our mothers for the common safety. But may we never contribute for civil wars, nor collaborate with you against each other. We did not contribute to Pompey, nor to Marius nor Cinna, nor Sulla, who had tyrannical power over the country. . . ."

As Hortensia was speaking thus, the triumvirs were angry that women when their men were silent should be so arrogant and bold at a public meeting and question the acts of magistrates, and should, while the men were serving in the army, not furnish money. They ordered the lictors to drive them away from the tribunal. But when there was an outcry from the multitude, the lictors desisted, and the triumvirs said they would postone the matter to the next day. The following day they reduced the number of women required to evalute their property, from 1400 to 400.

CLEOPATRA

Queen Cleopatra VII, Roman client ruler of Egypt, was a remarkably gifted woman, politically astute and ambitious. She was not especially beautiful, nor the "wanton Cleopatra" among Dante's gallery of the world's most lustful women. There were only two men in her life, Julius Caesar, by whom she had a son, and Mark Antony, who married her and had three children with her. To convert the impending civil war with Antony into a foreign war, Octavian unleashed a savage propaganda campaign against her, emphasizing lust, whoring, use of magic and drugs, drunkenness, animal worship and debauchery. This image of her has persisted in history, literature, and popular conception. Her suicide in 30 B.C. at the age of thirty-eight frustrated Octavian's ambition to exhibit her in his triumphal procession in Rome.

Plutarch, *Life of Antony* xxvii. 2–4

Her beauty, as is recorded, was not in and of itself incomparable, not such as to strike those who saw her. But conversation with her attracted attention, and her appearance combined with the persuasiveness of her talk, and her demeanor which somehow was diffused to others produced something stimulating. There was a freedom and ease in the tone of her speech, and she could turn her tongue easily, like an instrument of many strings, to whatever language she wished. At her meetings with barbarians she very rarely used interpreters at all, but she herself gave replies to most of them, for example, Ethiopians, Troglodytes, Hebrews, Arabians, Syrians, Medes or Parthians. And it is said that she knew the language of many others.

Cassius Dio, *Roman History* LI. xv. 4

Cleopatra was insatiable for sexual passion and money. She was swayed by great and laudable ambition, but also by overweening boldness. She gained royal power over the Egyptians by love, and hoped in the same manner to obtain royal power over the Romans. But she failed in the latter, and also lost the former. She captivated two of the greatest Romans of her day, and because of a third [Octavian] she destroyed herself.

Horace, *Odes* I. xxxvii

Now is the time to drink, now is the time to dance wildly stomping the ground, now is the time, my companions, to honor the couches of the gods with banquets *extraordinaires*. Before this day it was wrong to bring out Caecuban wine from ancestral cellars, while the queen was still preparing insane destruction for the Capitoline and destruction for the empire. She, with her polluted crew, men diseased and fouled, was mad enough to hope for anything, drunk as she was on sweet wine. But her madness soon abated with the escape of scarcely a single ship saved from the fires [of Actium]. And Caesar drove her mind, unbalanced by Egyptian wine, into fears of reality, and pursued her with his ships as she fled from Italy, just as the hawk chases the gentle doves or the quick hunter the hare on the snowy fields of Thessaly, to put the fateful monster in chains. But she sought to die in a more noble fashion; she did not shudder at the sword in womanly fashion, not did she hie away to secret shores with her swift fleet. Instead she had the courage to return, with calm expression on her face, to her palace lying in ruins, and bravely to handle the poisonous snakes, so as to drink in the dark venom in her body. Becoming more gallant when she resolved to die, she begrudged it to our tough Liburnian ships to be led, as a private citizen, in proud triumph—no ordinary woman she!

192. A Trip from Rome to Brundisium

This selection describes the journey through Italy in the fall of 38 B.C. or the spring of 37 B.C. that the poet Horace took in the entourage of Maecenas, who acted as mediator between Antony and Octavian in the negotiations that preceded the treaty of Tarentum.

Horace, *Satires* I. v

I left great Rome behind me, came to Aricia, and lodged in a modest inn. Heliodorus the rhetorician, by far the most learned among the Greeks, was my companion. From there we went to Forum Appii,[80] a place crammed with boatmen and rascally innkeepers. We took two days on a leisurely trip that better travelers make in one—the Appian

---

80. Forum Appii was about 40 miles from Rome. From here the party proceeded by canal-boat through the Pomptine Marshes to Feronia.

Way is less wearying, if taken slowly. Because of the water which was here most vile, I proclaimed war against my belly, waiting impatiently while my companions dined. Presently night was beginning to spread her shadows over the earth and to scatter the stars across the heavens. A babel of voices rose, slaves abusing boatmen and boatmen abusing slaves. "Bring to here!" "That's plenty. You've got three hundred on board now." We wasted a whole hour paying fares and harnessing the mule. The cursed gnats and frogs in the marsh made sleep impossible, while the boatman and the towpath attendant, soused with sour wine, rivaled one another in singing to their absent mistresses. Finally the towpath attendant became exhausted and dropped off to sleep while the lazy boatman tied the halter to a rock, turned out the mule to graze and lay on his back and snored. It was already dawn before we noticed that the craft was not moving. Then one hotheaded fellow jumped from the boat, and with a willow cudgel clubbed the mule and boatman over the head and back. At last we landed at ten o'clock and washed our hands and faces in your stream, Feronia.[81]

After breakfast we crawled along for three miles to arrive at Anxur which lies on her far-gleaming rocks. Maecenas and Cocceius were to meet us here, excellent fellows, both ambassadors on matters of great importance, accustomed to bring together estranged friends. Here I had to anoint my sore eyes with black salve. Meanwhile, Maecenas and Cocceius arrived, bringing with them Fonteius Capito, a polished gentleman and the closest friend of Antony.

We were delighted to leave Fundi, where Aufidius Luscus was magistrate, laughing at the insignia of this weak-headed clerk—his bordered robe, broad stripe, and pan of charcoal. Next, wearied with our journey, we stopped in the city of Mamurra's family where we had shelter with Murena and meals with Capito. Next day's sunrise was most welcome, for Plotius and Varius and Vergil met us at Sinuessa. No lovelier souls than these has the world ever produced, and no one can be more deeply attached to them than I. What hearty greetings and rejoicings! So long as I am in my right mind there is nothing that I prefer to a delightful friend.

We found shelter in the little house[82] alongside the Campanian bridge. Here the stewards gave us, as required, fuel and salt. Our next stop was Capua, where the mules were relieved of the packsaddles in good sea-

---

81. The southern terminus of the Pomptine canal.
82. Probably a public house used to entertain persons traveling on official business.

son. Maecenas went off to play. Vergil and I slept, for a game of ball is bad for sore eyes and dyspepsia. Next, we were welcomed by the well-stocked villa of Cocceius, which lies above the inns of Caudium. . . .

From that place we journeyed straight on to Beneventum, where our bustling host almost burned down his house while turning some scrawny thrushes on the spit. For the fire, when the logs fell apart, spread through the old kitchen and rushed on to lick the roof. Then you might have seen famished guests and scared slaves snatching up the supper, and everyone trying to extinguish the flames.

From this point Apulia begins to open up to me her familiar hills scorched by the sirocco. We could never have crawled through, if a villa near Trivicum had not taken us in for the night. Its smoke brought tears to our eyes, for the stove burned green boughs, leaves and all. . . .

From there we were whirled in carriages for twenty-four miles, to stop the night in a little town which I cannot name in verse but can describe easily by the following characteristics: water, the cheapest thing in the world, is sold here, but the bread is easily the best to be had, and the experienced traveler usually carries a load for the trip ahead, because Canusium, founded long ago by valiant Diomedes, has not a jugful more water and its bread is full of sand. Here Varius parted sorrowfully from his weeping friends. From this town we came, worn out, to Rubi, for the journey was long and made more difficult by rain.

Next day the weather was better but the road was worse, right up to the walls of Barium, a fishing town. Gnatia, built under the wrath of the water nymphs, gave us occasion for laughter and joking, for they wished us to believe that at these sacred thresholds incense melts without fire! Apella the Jew may believe this. I don't, for I have been taught that the gods live a carefree life, and that if nature produces a miracle, surely gods do not send it down from the high dome of heaven.

Brundisium is the end of a long trip—and my paper.

193. THE JULIAN CALENDAR

The most lasting of Caesar's reforms was his reorganization of the calendar with the assistance of his secretary Marcus Fulvius and the Alexandrian mathematician Sosigenes. The old Roman lunar calendar of 355 days (see § 9) had been traditionally harmonized, under the authority of the pontiffs, with the solar year by the addition of intercalary months of 22 and 23 days every second and fourth year. In 153 B.C. the beginning of the civil year was changed from March to January 1 (Praenestine Fasti, *CIL,* vol. I, 2d ed, p. 231: "The new year begins, because on that day the magistrates enter office; this began 601 years after the foundation of the city"). But the discretionary power of the College of Pontiffs in regulating the calendar led, in the middle of the first century B.C., to the manipulation of the calendar for political purposes. Since 58 B.C. there had been only one intercalation, with the result that the calendar year got to be 90 days ahead of the solar year. In 46 B.C., "the last year of confusion," Julius Caesar, by virtue of his authority as *pontifex maximus* and dictator, increased the year to 445 days, adding 23 days after February 2 and 67 days after September 27. Thus, by January 1, 45 B.C., the calendar was in alignment with the solar year. Thereafter, the intercalary month was abolished, a calendar of 365 days was established by lengthening 7 of the months by a day or two, and provision was made for an extra "leap-year" day to be added every fourth year between the 23d and 24th of February. This "Julian Calendar" is essentially our calendar of today.

Censorinus,[83] The Natal Day xx

Afterwards Numa, according to Fulvius, or Tarquin, according to Junius, instituted the year of 12 months and 355 days. . . . All the months . . . were composed of an uneven number of days, with the exception of February, which . . . was on that account regarded as more unlucky than the others. Finally, when it was decided to add an intercalary month of 22 or 23 days every two years, so that the civil year should correspond to the natural [solar] year, this intercalation was in preference made in February, between Terminalia and Regifugium [i.e., between February 23 and 24]; and this practice prevailed for some time before it was perceived that the civil years were a little longer than the solar.[84]

The care of correcting this inexactitude was given to the pontiffs and full power was vested in them for making the intercalation. But most of them were influenced by motives of enmity or else of partisanship, acting so that a magistrate might be forced out of office sooner or hold it a longer time. A tax farmer, for example, was made to gain or lose according to the duration of the year. In short, by capriciously making longer or shorter intercalations, they placed in disorder the very thing which was entrusted to them to regulate.

83. A grammarian of the third century A.D. His short antiquarian treatise, which was published in A.D. 238, is based on excellent sources, and is of great value for such topics as time reckoning, astrology, and music.

84. The lunar year contains 354 days, 8 hours, 48 minutes. The rough approximation of 355 days and the addition of 45 intercalary days in every four-year cycle resulted in an average of 366.25 days.

The calendar was so out of joint that Gaius Caesar, as *pontifex maximus,* in his third consulate and that of Marcus Aemilius Lepidus [46 B.C.], in order to correct the previous defect, placed between the months of November and December[85] two intercalary months of 67 days, having already intercalated 23 days in the month of February, which gave 445 days to that year. And at the same time he provided against the return of similar errors in the future by suppressing the intercalary months, and aligned the civil year with the course of the sun. Hence to the 355 days he added 10 days, which he divided among the seven months of 29 days as follows: two days were added to January, August, and December and one to the other months; and he placed these supplementary days at the ends of the months, so as not to disturb the religious festivals of each month. It is for this reason that today, although we have seven months of 31 days, yet there are only four which have retained the following peculiarity of the ancient system, namely, that the Nones fall on the seventh day, while in the other three it falls on the fifth. Moreover, to take account of the quarter of a day which, it seems, completes the solar year, Caesar ordered that after each period of four years there should be added, after Terminalia, instead of a month, as was the previous custom, an intercalary day, which is now called leap-year day. From this year, thus regulated by Julius Caesar, all those down to our time are called Julian, and they commence in his fourth consulate [45 B.C.].

85. The more probable position of Caesar's intercalary months of 46 B.C. is given in the introduction to this section.

9

THE AUGUSTAN AGE

194. "The Republic Restored": Establishment of the Principate

In January of 27 B.C. a major reorganization of the Roman government took place. Octavian laid down his *de facto* military dictatorship, and constitutional government was reestablished. In a historic, carefully staged meeting of the senate—"having first briefed his most intimate friends among the senators," as Cassius Dio puts it (LIII. ii. 7)—he proclaimed the "restoration of the Republic" and offered to retire to private life. His renunciation was, of course, not accepted; instead, a series of powers was voted him that firmly established him as ruler of the Roman Empire. He consented to accept the proconsular power (a special extended military command) for ten years, and the consulship annually together with modified tribunician power (which gave him effective control of the civil government). He was also awarded the honorary title of *Augustus,* which, together with the designation *Imperator,* subsequently became a fixed part of the official nomenclature of the emperors. Avoiding all official appellations suggestive of monarchy (though in the East he was called *autokrator*), Augustus preferred the informal title of *princeps* for himself in his new position. With its strong republican overtones—the leading senator under the Republic had been known as *princeps senatus*—this title had the effect of designating Augustus as "first citizen," *primus inter pares,* rather than a ruler over subjects. The senate, moreover, in theory retained its traditional functions and was to be the "partner in government" of the *princeps;* and the popular assemblies were to continue to meet as in the past. Thus, officially, the Principate, as the new regime is called, was the Republic restored. In reality, however, the trappings of republican government formed a politically expedient constitutional façade for a new imperial administration under the sovereignty of a monarch in all but name.

Four years later a new constitutional settlement made the position of the *princeps* permanent: Augustus resigned the consulship and derived his principal authority thereafter from full tribunician power, granted for life, and proconsular power, periodically renewed. Thus Augustus united under one authority both the powers wielded by the redoubtable republican tribunes such as the Gracchi (see §§ 97–100) and those exercised by the powerful generals of the civil war period. These were henceforth the dual bases of the emperors' authority.

TRANSITION FROM REPUBLIC TO PRINCIPATE

Tacitus *Annals* i. ii, iii. 7–iv. 2

After the death of Brutus and Cassius, there was no longer any army loyal to the Republic; Pompey[1] had been crushed at Sicily; and, with Lepidus deposed and Antony dead, not even the Julian faction had any leader left except Caesar. Then, laying aside the title of triumvir and parading as a consul, and professing himself satisfied with the tribunician power for the protection of the plebs, Augustus enticed the soldiers with gifts, the people with grain, and all men with the allurement of peace, and gradually grew in power, concentrating in his own hands the functions of the senate, the magistrates, and the laws. No one opposed him, for the most courageous had fallen in battle or in the proscription. As for the remaining nobles, the readier they were for slavery, the higher were they raised in wealth and offices, so that, aggrandized by the revolution, they preferred the safety of the present to the perils of the past. Nor did the provinces view with disfavor this state of affairs, for they distrusted the government of the senate and the people on account of the struggles of the powerful and the rapacity of the officials, while the protection afforded them by the laws was inoperative, as the laws were repeatedly thrown into confusion by violence, intrigue, and finally bribery. . . .

At home all was peaceful, the officials bore the same titles as before. The younger generation was born after the victory of Actium, and even many of the older generation had been born during the civil wars. How few were left who had seen the Republic!

Thus the constitution had been transformed, and there was nothing at all left of the good old way of life. Stripped of equality, all looked to

---

1. Sextus Pompey, son and political heir of Pompey the Great, is meant. See further notes 20, 24, 25, and 47.

the directives of a *princeps* with no apprehension for the present, while Augustus in the vigorous years of his life maintained his power, that of his family, and peace.

POWERS AND TITLES OF THE EMPEROR

Cassius Dio, *Roman History* LIII. xvii. 1–xviii. 3, xxi. 3–7; Adapted from *LCL*

In this way the power of both people and senate passed entirely into the hands of Augustus, and from this time[2] there was, strictly speaking, a monarchy; for monarchy would be the truest name for it, even if two or three men later held the power jointly.[3] Now, the Romans so detested the title "monarch" that they called their emperors neither dictators nor kings nor anything of this sort. Yet, since the final authority for the government devolves upon them, they needs must be kings. The offices established by the laws, it is true, are maintained even now, except that of censor; but the entire direction and administration is absolutely in accordance with the wishes of the one in power at the time. And yet, in order to preserve the appearance of having this authority not through their power but by virtue of the laws, the emperors have taken to themselves all the offices (including the titles) which under the Republic possessed great power with the consent of the people—with the exception of the dictatorship. Thus, they very often become consuls, and they are always styled proconsuls[4] whenever they are outside the *pomerium*.[5] The title *imperator* is held by them for life, not only by those who have won victories in battle but also by all the rest, to indicate their absolute power,[6] instead of the title "king" or "dictator." These latter titles they have never assumed since they fell out of use in the constitution, but the actuality of those offices is secured to them by the appellation *imperator*.[7]

2. January, 27 B.C. Dio's account of the prerogatives of Augustus as emperor, written early in the third century A.D., contains a number of anachronisms retrojected from his own day when emperors exercised more autocratic powers. For instances see the following footnotes to this selection.

3. Dio refers to the joint rule of Marcus Aurelius and Lucius Verus, and that of Severus, Caracalla, and Geta.

4. It was not until Trajan's principate that the title proconsul became part of the official nomenclature of the emperors.

5. For the *pomerium* of the city of Rome see § 6.

6. Actually the title *imperator*, while peculiar to Augustus' nomenclature, was disdained by Tiberius, Caligula, and Claudius. Though in common use unofficially, it did not become the standard title of the emperor until Vespasian's time.

7. In addition to the title of *imperator*, the official nomenclature of the emperors contains the number of times they were acclaimed *imperator* for military victories won under their auspices. Cf. Cassius Dio, *Roman History* XLIII. xliv. 4: "Those who are *imperatores* in the special sense employ this

By virtue of the titles named, they secure the right to make levies, collect funds, declare war, make peace, and rule foreigners and citizens alike everywhere and always—even to the extent of being able to put to death both *equites* and senators inside the *pomerium*[8]—and all the other powers once granted to the consuls and other officials possessing independent authority; and by virtue of holding the censorship [cf. note 74] they investigate our lives and morals as well as take the census, enrolling some in the equestrian and senatorial orders and removing others from these orders according to their will. By virtue of being consecrated in all the priesthoods and, in addition, from their right to bestow most of them upon others, as well as from the fact that, even if two or three persons rule jointly, one of them is *pontifex maximus,* they hold in their own hands supreme authority over all matters both profane and sacred. The tribunician power, as it is called, which once the most influential men used to hold, gives them the right to nullify the effects of the measures taken by any other official, in case they do not approve, and makes their persons inviolable; and if they appear to be wronged in even the slightest degree, not merely by deed but even by word, they may destroy the guilty party as one accursed, without a trial.[9] The emperors, it should be explained, do not think it lawful to be tribunes, inasmuch as they all belong to the patrician class, but they assume the power of the tribunes in its entirety, as it was at its height; and the number of the years of their rule is counted from the assumption of this power, the theory being that they receive it annually along with those who actually hold the office of tribune. These, then, are the institutions they have taken over from the Republic, each essentially in its traditional form and with the same title, so as to give the impression of possessing no power that has not been granted them. . . .[10]

Thus by virtue of these Republican titles they have clothed themselves with all the powers of the government, so that they actually possess all the prerogatives of kings without the usual title. For the appellation "Caesar" or "Augustus" confers upon them no actual power but merely shows in the one case that they are the successors of their

---

title once, as they do their other titles, and place it first. But those of them who also achieve in war some deed worthy of it acquire also the title handed down by ancient custom, and accordingly an individual is termed *imperator* a second or a third time, or as many more times as the occasion may arise."

8. Such arbitrary power was not acquired by the emperors until two centuries after Augustus.

9. Another of Dio's anachronisms (cf. note 2).

10. For the statute granting imperial powers to Vespasian, see vol. 2, § 4.

family line, and in the other the splendor of their rank. The name "Father"[11] perhaps gives them a certain authority over us all — the authority which fathers once had over their children; yet it did not signify this at first, but betokened honor and served as an admonition both to them to love their subjects as they would their children, and to their subjects to revere them as they would their fathers. . . .

Augustus did not enact all laws on his sole responsibility, but some of them he brought before the popular assembly in advance, in order that, if any features caused displeasure, he might learn it in time and correct them; for he encouraged everybody whatsoever to give him advice, in case anyone could think of any improvement in them, and he accorded them great freedom of speech; and he actually changed some provisions. Most important of all, he took as advisers for periods of six months the consuls (or the other consul, when he himself also held the office), one of each of the other kinds of officials, and fifteen men chosen by lot from the remainder of the senatorial body,[12] so that it was his custom to communicate proposed legislation after a fashion through these to all the other senators. For although he brought some matters before the whole senate, he generally followed this course, considering it better to take under preliminary advisement in a leisurely fashion most matters, and especially the most important ones, in consultation with a few; and sometimes he even sat with these men in trials. The senate as a body, it is true, continued to sit in judgment as before, and in certain cases transacted business with embassies and envoys from both peoples and kings; and the people and the plebs, moreover, continued to come together for the elections; but nothing was actually done that did not please Caesar. At any rate, in the case of those who were to hold office, he himself selected and nominated some;[13] and though he left the election of others in the hands of the people and the plebs, in accordance with the ancient practice, yet he took care that no persons should hold office who were unfit or elected as the result of factious combinations or bribery.

11. For the appellation "father of his country," see the selection from Suetonius below and § 195, paragraph 35.

12. This standing committee of the Senate, established by Augustus in 27 B.C. and reorganized on a new basis in A.D. 13, served as a privy council and ultimately developed into the equivalent of an imperial cabinet. For the Republican antecedents of such advisory councils see, for example, pp. 286, 374–75.

13. For the power of the emperors to nominate and commend candidates for office — recommendations that were tantamount to election — see also volume 2, §§ 4, 13. For Julius Caesar's practice in this regard see pp. 307–8.

Cassius Dio, *Roman History* LIII. xvi; Adapted from *LCL*

Such were the arrangements made, generally speaking, at that time; for in reality Caesar himself was destined to have absolute power in all matters for life, because he was not only in control of money matters (nominally, to be sure, he had separated the public funds from his own, but as a matter of fact he spent the former also as he saw fit) but also in control of the army. At all events, when his ten-year period[14] came to an end, there was voted him another five years, then five more, after that ten, and again another ten, and then ten for the fifth time, so that by the succession of ten-year periods he continued to be sole ruler for life. And it is for this reason that the subsequent monarchs, though no longer appointed for a specified period but for their whole life once for all,[15] nevertheless always held a celebration every ten years, as if then renewing their sovereignty once more; and this is done even at the present day.

Now, Caesar had received many privileges previously, when the question of declining the sovereignty and that of apportioning the provinces were under discussion. For the right to fasten laurels to the front of the imperial residence and to hang the civic crown above the doors was then voted him to symbolize the fact that he was always victorious over enemies and savior of the citizens. The imperial palace is called Palatium, not because it was ever decreed that this should be its name but because Caesar dwelt on the Palatine and had his military headquarters there. . . . Hence, even if the emperor resides somewhere else, his dwelling retains the name of Palatium.

And when he had actually completed the reorganization, the name Augustus was at length bestowed upon him by the senate and by the people. . . . He took the title of Augustus, signifying that he was more than human; for all most precious and sacred objects are termed *augusta*. For which reason they called him also in Greek *sebastos* . . . meaning an august person.

14. That is, of his proconsular power. From 23 B.C. on Augustus possessed *imperium maius* ("superior power"), that is, proconsular power over all the provinces of the Empire, including the authority to supersede the acts of governors of senatorial provinces.

15. The permanent grant of proconsular power began with the Emperor Tiberius.

Suetonius, *Life of Augustus* lviii; From *LCL*

The whole body of citizens with a sudden unanimous impulse proffered him the title of "father of his country"—first the plebs, by a deputation sent to Antium, and then, because he declined it, again at Rome as he entered the theater, which they attended in throngs, all wearing laurel wreaths; the senate afterwards in the senate house, not by a decree or by acclamation, but through Valerius Messala. He, speaking for the whole body, said: "Good fortune and divine favor attend thee and thy house, Caesar Augustus; for thus we feel that we are praying for lasting prosperity for our country and happiness for our city. The senate in accord with the Roman people hails thee 'Father of thy Country.'" Then Augustus with tears in his eyes replied as follows (and I have given his exact words, as I did those of Messala): "Having attained my highest hopes, members of the senate, what more have I to ask of the immortal gods than that I may retain this same unanimous approval of yours to the very end of my life?"[16]

195. THE ACCOMPLISHMENTS OF AUGUSTUS (RES GESTAE DIVI AUGUSTI)

The following document, from the hand of Augustus himself, is perhaps the most famous ancient inscription—"the queen of Latin inscriptions" Mommsen called it. A vast literature has grown up around it—numerous editions, commentaries, and discussions of its nature and purpose.[17] Shortly before he died, he left instructions for releasing to the public this "account of his accomplishments, which he desired to be inscribed on two bronze pillars to be set up before his mausoleum" (Suetonius, *Life of Augustus* iv). The *Res Gestae* is preserved in an almost complete copy, together with a Greek translation, inscribed on the walls of the temple of Rome and Augustus at Ancyra (modern Ankara in Turkey), in the province of Galatia (hence it is commonly called the *Monumentum Ancyranum*). Portions of the Greek and Latin texts have also been found in Apollonia and Antioch in Pisidia. Intended primarily for the people of the city of Rome, Augustus' account of his stewardship summarizes his career under three

16. The title of "father of his country" was bestowed on Augustus in 2 B.C. Cf. also note 11.

17. Discussions of the nature and purposes of this political autobiography, together with detailed commentaries on the text, may be found in P. A. Brunt and J. M. Moore, *Res Gestae Divi Augusti. The Achievements of the Divine Augustus* (Oxford, 1967); E. S. Ramage, *The Nature and Purpose of Augustus' "Res Gestae"* (Wiesbaden, 1987).

headings: the offices and honors conferred upon him (paragraphs 1–14); his expenditures out of his own funds for public purposes (paragraphs 15–24); his deeds in war and peace (paragraphs 25–35). Though largely factual, it is not a historical chronicle but a subjective political document. It is in the tradition of the inscriptions commemorating the achievements of distinguished Romans of the Republic and is similar in content to the well-known inscriptions set up by Oriental kings. Despite Augustus' profession of "restoring the Republic," a monarchical tone pervades the *Res Gestae*.

CIL, vol. III, pp. 769–799 (=EJ, pp. 1–31=*ADA,* pp. 20–63)

Below is a copy of the accomplishments of the deified Augustus by which he brought the whole world under the empire of the Roman people, and of the moneys expended by him on the state and the Roman people, as inscribed on two bronze pillars set up in Rome.[18]

1.[19] At the age of nineteen, on my own initiative and at my own expense, I raised an army by means of which I liberated the Republic, which was oppressed by the tyranny of a faction.[20] For which reason the senate, with honorific decrees, made me a member of its order in the consulship of Gaius Pansa and Aulus Hirtius [43 B.C.], giving me at the same time consular rank in voting, and granted me the *imperium.* It ordered me as propraetor, together with the consuls, to see to it that the state suffered no harm.[21] Moreover, in the same year, when both consuls had fallen in the war, the people elected me consul and a triumvir for the settlement of the commonwealth [cf. § 115].

2. Those who assassinated my father[22] I drove into exile, avenging their crime by due process of law; and afterwards when they waged war against the state, I conquered them twice on the battlefield [the two battles of Phillippi (42 B.C.)].

3. I waged many wars throughout the whole world by land and by

18. No trace of the original bronze inscription, set up before the mausoleum of Augustus in Rome, has been found.

19. The inscription is divided into paragraphs which, for convenience in citing, are numbered in the translation.

20. Antony and his adherents are meant. The period referred to is late 44 to early 43 B.C., when Octavian (as Augustus was then known) was in coalition with the Senate against Antony (cf. § 114) Noteworthy is the studied avoidance by Augustus in this document of the names of his opponents—such as Antony, Lepidus, Sextus Pompey, Brutus, Cassius—and the fact that the only Romans whom he names, other than consuls cited to date events, are members of the imperial family.

21. The formula for the "ultimate decree of the Senate"; see § 157. Augustus refers here to the war against Antony, which culminated in the two battles at Mutina in April of 43 B.C.

22. Julius Caesar, his adoptive father. Yet in general Augustus sought to distance himself from the image and policies of Julius Caesar.

sea, both civil and foreign, and when victorious I spared all citizens who sought pardon. Foreign peoples who could safely be pardoned I preferred to spare rather than to extirpate. About 500,000 Roman citizens were under military oath to me. Of these, when their terms of service were ended, I settled in colonies or sent back to their own municipalities a little more than 300,000,[23] and to all of these I allotted lands or granted money as rewards for military service. I captured 600 ships, exclusive of those which were of smaller class than triremes.[24]

4. Twice I celebrated ovations, three times curule triumphs,[25] and I was acclaimed *imperator* twenty-one times.[26] When the senate decreed additional triumphs to me, I declined them on four occasions. I deposited in the Capitol laurel wreaths adorning my *fasces,* after fulfilling the vows which I had made in each war.[27] For successes achieved on land and on sea by me or through my legates under my auspices the senate decreed fifty-five times that thanksgiving be offered to the immortal gods. Moreover, the number of days on which, by decree of the senate, such thanksgiving was offered, was 890. In my triumphs there were led before my chariot nine kings or children of kings. At the time I wrote this, I had been consul thirteen times, and I was in the thirty-seventh year of my tribunician power [A.D. 14].

5. The dictatorship offered to me in the consulship of Marcus Marcellus and Lucius Arruntius [22 B.C.] by the people and by the senate, both in my absence and in my presence, I refused to accept. In the midst of a critical scarcity of grain I did not decline the supervision of the grain supply, which I so administered that within a few days I freed the whole people from imminent panic and danger by my expenditures and efforts.[28] The consulship, too, which was offered to me at that time as an annual office for life, I refused to accept.

23. Tiberius inherited from Augustus an army of twenty-five legions (Tacitus, *Annals* IV. v), or about 125,000 men; cf. § 199.

24. The naval victories over Sextus Pompey (at Mylae and Naulochus), and over Antony and Cleopatra (at Actium) are meant.

25. The two ovations occurred in 40 and 36 B.C., the first after the Peace of Brundisium concluded with Antony, the second after the defeat of Sextus Pompey. Augustus celebrated a triple triumph in 29 B.C. for victories in Dalmatia, at Actium, and in Egypt.

26. In many cases the acclamation *imperator* was accorded to Augustus for victories gained by his legates; cf. note 7.

27. This is the well-known Republican custom, followed by victorious generals who were acclaimed *imperator,* of depositing laureled *fasces* (symbolizing victory) in the Capitol in accordance with vows taken there before they set out for their provinces.

28. This marks the beginning of the assumption by the Roman emperors of the *cura annonae* ("administration of the grain supply") of Rome as a permanent function of the imperial administration.

6. In the consulship of Marcus Vinicius and Quintus Lucretius, and again in that of Publius Lentulus and Gnaeus Lentulus, and a third time in that of Paullus Fabius Maximus and Quintus Tubero [in 19, 18, and 11 B.C.], though the Roman senate and people unitedly agreed that I should be elected sole guardian of the laws and morals with supreme authority, I refused to accept any office offered me which was contrary to the traditions of our ancestors.[29] The measures which the senate desired at that time to be taken by me I carried out by virtue of the tribunician power.[30] In this power I five times voluntarily requested and was given a colleague by the senate.[31]

7. I was a member of the triumvirate for the settlement of the commonwealth for ten consecutive years.[32] I have been ranking senator for forty years, up to the day on which I wrote this document. I have been *pontifex maximus,* augur, member of the college of fifteen for performing sacrifices, member of the college of seven for conducting religious banquets, member of the Arval Brotherhood, one of the *Titii sodales,* and a fetial.[33]

8. In my fifth consulship I increased the number of patricians, by order of the people, the senate. Three times I revised the roll of senators. And in my sixth consulship,[34] with Marcus Agrippa as my colleague, I conducted a census of the people. I performed the *lustrum*[35] after an interval of forty-two years. At this *lustrum* 4,063,000 Roman citizens were recorded. Then a second time, acting alone, by virtue of the consular power, I completed the taking of the census in the consulship of Gaius Censorinus and Gaius Asinius [8 B.C.]. At this *lustrum* 4,233,000 Roman citizens were recorded. And a third time I completed the taking of the census in the consulship of Sextus Pompeius and Sextus Appuleius [A.D. 14], by virtue of the consular power and with my son Tiberius Caesar as my colleague. At this *lustrum* 4,937,000 Roman citizens were recorded. By new legislation which I sponsored I restored many tradi-

29. In effect Augustus was thus offered permanent dictatorship in a new guise.

30. Augustus here refers to his moral and social legislation, the first installments of which were issued in 18 B.C.; see §§ 204–205.

31. Marcus Agrippa, twice; Tiberius, three times.

32. The triumvirate lasted officially from November 27, 43 B.C. to December 31, 33 B.C. The controversial question of the powers of Antony and Octavian in 32 B.C. has evoked heated scholarly discussion.

33. On these traditional priestly offices under the Republic, see §§ 11, 47, 48, 51, 52. All Roman emperors after Augustus held the first four of these priesthoods, the most important sacerdotal offices in the national religion.

34. 28 B.C. The last census had been taken in 70/69 B.C.

35. For this religious closing of the census, see § 56.

tions of our ancestors which were falling into desuetude in our generation; and I myself handed down precedents in many spheres for posterity
to imitate.

9. The senate decreed that vows for my health should be offered up
every fifth year by the consuls and priests. In fulfillment of these vows,
games were often celebrated during my lifetime, sometimes by the four
most distinguished colleges of priests, sometimes by the consuls. Moreover, the whole citizen body, with one accord, both individually and as
members of municipalities, prayed continuously for my health at all the
shrines.

10. My name was inserted, by decree of the senate, in the hymn of
the Salian priests. And it was enacted by law that I should be sacrosanct
in perpetuity and that I should possess the tribunician power as long as I
live.[36] I declined to become *pontifex maximus* in place of a colleague[37]
while he was still alive, when the people offered me that priesthood,
which my father had held. A few years later, in the consulship of Publius
Sulpicius and Gaius Valgius, I accepted this priesthood, when death
removed the man who taken possession of it at a time of civil disturbance; and from all Italy a multitude flocked to my election such as had
never previously been recorded at Rome.

11. To commemorate my return from Syria, the senate consecrated
an altar to Fortune the Home-bringer before the temple of Honor and
Virtue at the Porta Capena, on which altar it decreed that the pontiffs
and Vestal Virgins should make a yearly sacrifice on the anniversary of
the day in the consulship of Quintus Lucretius and Marcus Vinicius [19
B.C.] on which I returned to the city from Syria, and it designated that
day *Augustalia* from my name.

12. On this occasion, by decree of the senate, a portion of the praetors and tribunes of the plebs, together with the consul Quintus Lucretius and the leading men, was sent to Campania to meet me, an honor
which up to this time has been decreed to no one but myself. When I
returned to Rome from Spain and Gaul in the consulship of Tiberius
Nero and Publius Quintilius [13 B.C.], after successfully settling the
affairs of those provinces, the senate, to commemorate my return, or-

36. Augustus was accorded the *sacrosanctitas*, inviolability, of a tribune in 36 B.C. Modified tribunician power was conferred upon him in 30 B.C., but it was only after the constitutional settlement of 23
B.C. that he began to date his regnal years by the number of years he had held this power in its complete
form. Cf. paragraph 4 and § 194, second selection.

37. Lepidus was deposed from the Second Triumvirate in 36 B.C. but was permitted to retain the
office of *pontifex maximus*. Upon his death in 13 B.C. Augustus was elected chief pontiff the following
year. All subsequent emperors held this office.

dered an altar of the Augustan Peace[38] to be consecrated in the Campus Martius, on which it decreed that the magistrates, priests, and Vestal Virgins should make an annual sacrifice.

13. The temple of Janus Quirinus,[39] which our ancestors desired to be closed whenever peace with victory was secured by sea and by land throughout the entire empire of the Roman people, and which before I was born is recorded to have been closed only twice since the founding of the city, was during my principate three times ordered by the senate to be closed.

14. My sons Gaius and Lucius Caesar,[40] whom fortune took from me in their youth, were, in my honor, made consuls designate by the Roman senate and people when they were fifteen years old, with permission to enter that magistracy after a period of five years. The senate further decreed that from the day on which they were introduced into the Forum[41] they should attend its debates. Moreover, the whole body of Roman *equites* presented each of them with silver shields and spears and saluted each as *princeps iuventutis*.[42]

15. To the Roman plebs I paid 300 sesterces apiece in accordance with the will of my father [i.e., Julius Caesar]; and in my fifth consulship [29 B.C.] I gave each 400 sesterces in my own name out of the spoils of war; and a second time in my tenth consulship [24 B.C.] I paid out of my own patrimony a largess of 400 sesterces to every individual; in my eleventh consulship [23 B.C.] I made twelve distributions of food out of grain purchased at my own expense; and in the twelfth year of my tribunician power [12 B.C.] for the third time I gave 400 sesterces to every individual. These largesses of mine reached never less than 250,000 persons. In the eighteenth year of my tribunician power and my twelfth consulship [5 B.C.] I gave sixty *denarii* to each of 320,000 persons of the urban plebs. And in my fifth consulship [29 B.C.] I gave out of the spoils of war 1,000 sesterces apiece to my soldiers settled in colonies. This

38. Extensive parts of the famous Altar of Peace, dedicated in 9 B.C., are extant. The whole monument has been reconstructed *in situ*.

39. A small bronze shrine, with double doors on both ends, on the north side of the Forum. Cf. § 196, second selection.

40. Grandsons of Augustus, the sons of Agrippa and Julia, adopted by him in 17 B.C. and marked out as his successors. But Gaius died in A.D. 4, Lucius in A.D. 2. For honorary decrees to Gaius and Lucius, see § 209.

41. That is, introduced to public life. This traditional Roman ceremony, which occurred at puberty, involved among other things the assumption of the *toga virilis* ("toga of manhood"); cf. § 209, second selection.

42. That is, "leader of the youth." This title designated them as honorary heads of the young men of equestrian families who were organized in a kind of aristocratic Boy Scout movement.

largess on the occasion of my triumph was received by about 120,000 persons in the colonies. In my thirteenth consulship [2 B.C.] I gave sixty *denarii* apiece to those of the plebs who at that time were receiving public grain; the number involved was a little more than 200,000 persons.

16. I reimbursed municipalities for the lands which I assigned to my soldiers in my fourth consulship, and afterwards in the consulship of Marcus Crassus and Gnaeus Lentulus the augur [30 and 14 B.C.]. The sums involved were about 600,000,000 sesterces which I paid for Italian estates, and about 260,000,000 sesterces which I paid for provincial lands. I was the first and only one to take such action of all those who up to my time established colonies of soldiers in Italy or in the provinces. And afterwards, in the consulship of Tiberius Nero and Gnaeus Piso, and likewise of Gaius Antistius and Decimus Laelius, and of Gaius Calvisius and Lucius Passienus, and of Lucius Lentulus and Marcus Messalla, and of Lucius Caninius and Quintus Fabricius [in 7, 6, 4, 3, and 2 B.C.], I granted bonuses in cash to the soldiers whom after the completion of their terms of service I sent back to their municipalities; and for this purpose I expended about 400,000,000 sesterces.

17. Four times I came to the assistance of the treasury with my own money, transferring to those in charge of the treasury 150,000,000 sesterces. And in the consulship of Marcus Lepidus and Lucius Arruntius [A.D. 6; cf. § 199] I transferred out of my own patrimony 170,000,000 sesterces to the soldiers' bonus fund, which was established on my advice for the purpose of providing bonuses for soldiers who had completed twenty or more years of service.

18. From the year in which Gnaeus Lentulus and Publius Lentulus [18 B.C.] were consuls, whenever the provincial taxes fell short, in the case sometimes of 100,000 persons and sometimes of many more, I made up their tribute in grain and in money from my own grain stores and my own patrimony.

19. I built the following structures:[43] the senate house and the Chalcidicum adjoining it; the temple of Apollo on the Palatine with its porticoes; the temple of the deified Julius; the Lupercal; the portico at the Circus Flaminius, which I allowed to be called Octavia after the name of the man who had built an earlier portico on the same site; the state box at the Circus Maximus; the temples of Jupiter the Smiter and

---

43. To identify for the reader each of the public works listed in this and the two following paragraphs would require a series of footnotes longer than the text. A convenient source of information on the various structures is E. Nash, *Pictorial Dictionary of Ancient Rome*, 2 vols. (New York, 1961–1962).

Jupiter the Thunderer on the Capitoline; the temple of Quirinus; the temples of Minerva and Queen Juno and of Jupiter Freedom on the Aventine; the temple of the Lares at the head of the Sacred Way; the temple of the Penates on the Velia; the temple of Youth and the temple of the Great Mother on the Palatine.

20. I repaired the Capitol and the theater of Pompey with enormous expenditures on both works, without having my name inscribed on them. I repaired the conduits of the aqueducts which were falling into ruin in many places because of age, and I doubled the capacity of the aqueduct called Marcia by admitting a new spring into its conduit. I completed the Julian Forum and the basilica which was between the temple of Castor and the temple of Saturn, works begun and far advanced by my father, and when the same basilica was destroyed by fire, I enlarged its site and began rebuilding the structure, which is to be inscribed with the names of my sons; and in case it should not be completed while I am still alive, I left instructions that the work be completed by my heirs. In my sixth consulship [28 B.C.] I repaired eighty-two temples of the gods in the city, in accordance with a resolution of the senate, neglecting none which at that time required repair. In my seventh consulship [27 B.C.] I reconstructed the Flaminian Way from the city as far as Ariminum, and also all the bridges except the Mulvian and the Minucian.

21. On my own private land I built the temple of Mars Ultor and the Augustan Forum from spoils of war. On ground bought for the most part from private owners I built the theater adjoining the temple of Apollo which was to be inscribed with the name of my son-in-law Marcus Marcellus. In the Capitol, in the temple of the deified Julius, in the temple of Apollo, in the temple of Vesta, and in the temple of Mars Ultor I consecrated gifts from spoils of war which cost me about 100,000,000 sesterces. In my fifth consulship [29 B.C.] I remitted to the municipalities and colonies of Italy 35,000 pounds of crown gold[44] which they were collecting in honor of my triumphs; and afterwards, whenever I was acclaimed *imperator*, I did not accept the crown gold, though the municipalities and colonies decreed it with the same enthusiasm as before.

22. I gave a gladiatorial show three times in my own name, and five times in the names of my sons or grandsons; at these shows about 10,000

---

44. For the significance of "crown gold," see vol. 2, § 113, second selection.

fought. Twice I presented to the people in my own name an exhibition of athletes invited from all parts of the world, and a third time in the name of my grandson. I presented games in my own name four times, and in addition twenty-three times in the place of other magistrates.[45] On behalf of the college of fifteen, as master of that college, with Marcus Agrippa as my colleague, I celebrated the Secular Games[46] in the consulship of Gaius Furnius and Gaius Silanus. In my thirteenth consulship [2 B.C.] I was the first to celebrate the Games of Mars, which subsequently the consuls, in accordance with a decree of the senate and a law, have regularly celebrated in the succeeding years. Twenty-six times I provided for the people, in my own name or in the names of my sons or grandsons, hunting spectacles of African wild beasts in the circus or in the Forum or in the amphitheaters; in these exhibitions about 3,500 animals were killed.

23. I presented to the people an exhibition of a naval battle across the Tiber where the grove of the Caesars now is, having had the site excavated 1,800 feet in length and 1,200 feet in width. In this exhibition thirty beaked ships, triremes or biremes, and in addition a great number of smaller vessels engaged in combat. On board these fleets, exclusive of rowers, there were about 3,000 combatants.

24. When I was victorious I replaced in the temples of all the communities of the province of Asia the ornaments which my opponent [Mark Antony] in the war had seized for his private use after despoiling the temples. About eighty silver statues of myself, represented on foot, on horseback, or in a chariot, stood in the city; these I myself removed, and out of the money therefrom I set up golden offerings in the temple of Apollo in my own name and in the names of those who had honored me with the statues.

25. I brought peace to the sea by suppressing the pirates.[47] In that war I turned over to their masters for punishment nearly 30,000 slaves who had run away from their owners and taken up arms against the state. The whole of Italy voluntarily took an oath of allegiance to me and demanded me as its leader in the war in which I was victorious at Actium.[48] The same oath was taken by the provinces of the Gauls, the

---

45. These were games in the theatrical and circus shows.
46. For the Secular Games celebrated in 17 B.C., see § 206.
47. The naval war with Sextus Pompey (cf. note 1), which ended in 36 B.C.
48. The war against Antony and Cleopatra, who were defeated at Actium in 31 B.C.

Spains, Africa, Sicily, and Sardinia.[49] More than 700 senators served at that time under my standards; of that number eighty-three attained the consulship and about 170 obtained priesthoods, either before that date or subsequently, up to the day on which this document was written.

26. I extended the frontiers of all the provinces of the Roman people on whose boundaries were peoples not subject to our empire.[50] I restored peace to the Gallic and Spanish provinces and likewise to Germany, that is to the entire region bounded by the Ocean from Gades to the mouth of the Elbe river. I caused peace to be restored in the Alps, from the region nearest to the Adriatic Sea as far as the Tuscan Sea, without undeservedly making war against any people.[51] My fleet sailed the Ocean from the mouth of the Rhine eastward as far as the territory of the Cimbrians, to which no Roman previously had penetrated either by land or by sea. The Cimbrians, the Charydes, the Semnones, and other German peoples of the same region through their envoys sought my friendship and that of the Roman people.[52] At my command and under my auspices two armies were led almost at the same time into Ethiopia and into Arabia which is called Felix; and very large forces of the enemy belonging to both peoples were killed in battle, and many towns were captured. In Ethiopia a penetration was made as far as the town of Napata, which is next to Meroe; in Arabia the army advanced into the territory of the Sabaeans to the town of Mariba.[53]

27. I added Egypt to the empire of the Roman people.[54] Although I might have made Greater Armenia into a province when its king Artaxes was assassinated, I preferred, following the precedent of our ancestors, to hand over this kingdom, acting through Tiberius Nero, who was then my stepson, to Tigranes, son of King Artavasdes and grandson of King Tigranes. And afterwards, when this same people revolted and rebelled, after I subdued it through my son Gaius, I handed it over to the rule of King Ariobarzanes, son of Artabazus, king of the Medes, and

---

49. On the form of the oath of allegiance to Augustus, see § 201, second selection.

50. The emphasis is on the frontier policy in the West. The eastern provinces were hardly as well stabilized under Augustus. On the general frontier policy of Augustus, see § 203.

51. On these campaigns see further § 203.

52. The reference is to the campaign of A.D. 5, when Tiberius penetrated Germany as far as the Elbe River.

53. This is the disastrous expedition of Aelius Gallus in 25/24 B.C. against Arabia Felix (Yemen); the punitive Ethiopian expedition under Gaius Petronius in 24–22 B.C. achieved greater success; see further § 203.

54. On the death of Cleopatra in 30 B.C. On the special status of Egypt, see note 75.

after his death to his son Artavasdes. When the latter was killed, I dispatched to that kingdom Tigranes, a scion of the royal family of Armenia.[55] I recovered all the provinces extending beyond the Adriatic Sea eastward, and also Cyrenae, which were for the most part already in the possession of kings, as I had previously recovered Sicily and Sardinia, which had been seized in the slave war.[56]

28. I established colonies of soldiers in Africa, Sicily, Macedonia, in both Spanish provinces, in Achaea, Asia, Syria, Narbonese Gaul, and Pisidia. Italy, moreover, has twenty-eight colonies established by me, which in my lifetime have grown to be famous and populous.

29. A number of military standards lost by other generals I recovered, after conquering the enemy, from Spain, Gaul, and the Dalmatians. The Parthians I compelled to restore to me the spoils and standards of three Roman armies and to seek the friendship of the Roman people as suppliants.[57] The standards, moreover, I deposited in the inner shrine of the temple of Mars Ultor.

30. Through Tiberius Nero, who was then my stepson and legate, I conquered and subjected to the empire of the Roman people the Pannonian tribes, to which before my principate no army of the Roman people had ever penetrated; and I extended the frontier of Illyricum to the bank of the Danube River. An army of the Dacians which had crossed to our side of the river was conquered and destroyed under my auspices, and later on, my army crossed the Danube and compelled the Dacian tribes to submit to the orders of the Roman people.

31. Royal embassies from India, never previously seen before any Roman general, were often sent to me. Our friendship was sought through ambassadors by the Bastarnians and Scythians and by the kings of the Sarmatians, who live on both sides of the Don River, and by the kings of the Albanians and of the Iberians and of the Medes.[58]

32. The following kings fled to me as suppliants: Tiridates and afterwards Phraates son of King Phraates, kings of the Parthians; Artavasdes, king of the Medes; Artaxares, king of the Adiabenians; Dumnobellaunus and Tincommius, kings of the Britons; Maelo, king of the Sugumbrians,

55. On the Roman client states under Augustus, see further § 203.

56. Provinces held by Antony and Sextus Pompey. Cf. paragraph 25, above.

57. These were the standards lost by Crassus at the battle of Carrhae in 53 B.C. and in Mark Antony's disastrous operations against the Parthians in 36 B.C. They were restored as the result of diplomatic negotiations; Augustus' version is calculated to salve Roman pride.

58. The peoples named in this sentence inhabited the fringes of the Roman Empire from the Carpathians to the Caucasus.

and Segimerus[?], king of the Marcomannian Suebians.[59] Phraates son of Orodes, king of the Parthians, sent to me in Italy all his sons and grandsons, not because he was conquered in war, but seeking our friendship through pledge of his children. Under my principate numerous other peoples, with whom previously there had existed no exchange of embassies and friendship, experienced the good faith of the Roman people.

33. The peoples of the Parthians and of the Medes, through ambassadors who were the leading men of these peoples, received from me the kings for whom they asked: the Parthians, Vonones son of King Phraates, grandson of King Orodes; the Medes, Ariobarzanes son of King Artavasdes, grandson of King Ariobarzanes.

34. In my sixth and seventh consulships,[60] after I had put an end to the civil wars, having attained supreme power by universal consent, I transferred the state from my own power to the control of the Roman senate and the people. For this service of mine I received the title of Augustus by decree of the senate, and the doorposts of my house were publicly decked with laurels, the civic crown was affixed over my doorway, and a golden shield was set up in the Julian senate house, which, as the inscription on this shield testifies, the Roman senate and people gave me in recognition of my valor, clemency, justice, and devotion. After that time I excelled all in authority, but I possessed no more power than the others who were my colleagues in each magistracy.

35. When I held my thirteenth consulship,[61] the senate, the equestrian order, and the entire Roman people gave me the title of "father of the country" and decreed that this title should be inscribed in the vestibule of my house, in the Julian senate house, and in the Augustan Forum on the pedestal of the chariot which was set up in my honor by decree of the senate. At the time I wrote this document I was in my seventy-sixth year.[62]

---

59. Adiabenia was a district of Assyria; the Sugumbrians and Marcomannian Suebians were Germanic tribes.

60. 28 and 27 B.C. The reorganization of 28–27 B.C. (see § 194) put an end to the unlimited powers exercised by Augustus without legal title from the expiration of the triumvirate in 33 B.C. to that date. Augustus justifies his extralegal position by affirming that he held it "by universal consent."

61. 2 B.C. Cf. § 194, fourth selection.

62. Four appendices (not part of the original document of Augustus), which summarize the expenditures and public works of Augustus, are here omitted.

196. THE PRINCE OF PEACE AND THE NEW ORDER

The task of disseminating the official program of the new age among the educated portion of the population was undertaken by Maecenas, who, next to Agrippa (cf. §§ 208, 209), was the principal helper of Augustus in the first half of his reign. The literary coterie which Maecenas gathered about him rang the changes on the professed ideals of the new regime— peace and empire, rededication to the ancestral virtues, the traditions and religion of the idealized past, and the benevolent administration of the *princeps*.

Anonymous, *Panegyric on Piso*[63] 230–243; From *LCL*

The very bard [Vergil] who makes his poem on Aeneas resound among the Italian people, the bard who in his mighty renown treads Olympus and in Roman accents challenges venerable Homer, perchance his poem might have lurked obscure in the shadow of the grove, and he might have but sung on a fruitless reed unknown to the peoples if he had lacked a Maecenas. Yet it was not to one bard only that he opened his doors, nor did he entrust his destinies to Vergil alone. Maecenas raised to fame Varius,[64] who shook the stage with tragic mien; Maecenas drew out the grand style of the thundering poet and revealed famous names to the people of Greece. Likewise he made known to fame songs resonant on Roman strings and the Italian lyre of graceful Horace. Hail! ornament of the age, worshipful deservedly for all time, protection of the Pierian choir, beneath whose guardianship never did poet fear for an old age of beggary.

Horace, *Odes* IV. xv

When I wished to tell in lyric song of battles and the conquest of cities, Apollo rebuked me and forbade my spreading tiny sails upon the Tyrrhenian Sea. Thine age, O Caesar, has brought back fertile crops to the fields and has restored to our own Jupiter the military standards stripped from the proud columns of the Parthians;[65] has closed Janus' temple [cf.

---

63. Composed in the early part of the first century A.D.

64. Lucius Varius Rufus, eminent epic poet and dramatist of the Augustun Age, friend and literary executor of Vergil.

65. Cf. § 195, paragraph 29. This ode of Horace was written *c.* 13 B.C.

§ 195, paragraph 13] freed of wars; has put reins on license overstepping righteous bounds; has wiped away our sins and revived the ancient virtues through which the Latin name and the might of Italy waxed great, and the fame and majesty of our empire were spread from the sun's bed in the west to the east. As long as Caesar is the guardian of the state, neither civil dissension nor violence shall banish peace, nor wrath that forges swords and brings discord and misery to cities. Not those who drink the deep Danube shall violate the orders of Caesar, nor the Getae, nor the Seres,[66] nor the perfidious Parthians, nor those born by the Don River. And we, both on profane and sacred days, amidst the gifts of merry Bacchus, together with our wives and children, will first duly pray to the gods; then, after the tradition of our ancestors, in songs to the accompaniment of Lydian flutes we will hymn leaders whose duty is done, and Troy and Anchises and benign Venus' offspring.[67]

> Not as uncritical in his praise as were some of his contemporaries, Vergil in his poems reflects a cautious optimism, mingling enthusiastic hopes with brooding doubts. Augustus while yet a triumvir initiated his policy of restoring Italian agriculture after the ravages of the civil wars, and Vergil was invited to lend his support with a work glorifying the agricultural life. He responded by producing the *Georgics,* a masterpiece of poetic art imbued with a nostalgic idealization of the simple agrarian life, in which, he hoped, the ancestral virtues might flourish again.

Vergil, *Georgics* II. 458–474, 490–540

O happy beyond measure the tillers of the soil, if they but knew their blessings, on whom, far from the clash of arms, the earth most justly showers an easy livelihood from her soil! Even if no high mansion with proud portals pours forth from every room a mighty wave of men coming to pay their respects in the morning; even if men do not gape at pillars inlaid with lovely tortoise-shell, or at tapestries embroidered with gold, or at Corinthian bronzes; even if white wool is not dyed with oriental purple; even if the pure olive oil they use is not spoiled with perfume, yet they enjoy sleep without worry, and a life that cannot bring disillusionment but rather one that is rich in varied treasures, and peace in their broad farms, and grottoes, natural lakes, cool valleys, the

---

66. The Getae occupied the northern bank of the lower Danube; Seres is a generic name for peoples of central and east Asia, Chinese and Tibetans.

67. Horace refers to the Trojan prince Aeneas (see § 4), legendary ancestor of the Romans, from whom Julius Caesar and Augustus claimed direct descent.

lowing of cattle, and gentle slumber beneath a tree. Pastures are there and the haunts of wild game, and youth is hardy in toil and accustomed to simple fare; there the rites of the gods are observed and reverence for age survives; Justice took her last steps among these as she left the earth. . . .

Blessed was he who could discover the causes of things,[68] and trample upon all fears and inexorable death and the roar of greedy Hades' waters. Yet happy he too who had come to know the rustic gods, Pan, aged Sylvanus, and the sister nymphs. He is moved neither by the *fasces* which the people grant, nor by royal purple, nor by the conspiring Dacians swooping down from the Danube, nor by the affairs of Rome and the death throes of kingdoms. He has not had to grieve in pity for the poor nor to envy those who have. He plucks the fruits of the trees and reaps what the willing fields of their own accord produce and knows nothing of the rigor of the law, the frenzied Forum, and the public archives. Some ply unknown seas in their ships, rush to arms, make their way into the royal palaces of kings; another attacks and destroys cities and their hapless homes, to drink from jewelled cups and sleep on Tyrian purple; another hoards his wealth and broods over buried gold; another gapes with astonishment at the *Rostra;* another stands open-mouthed and is carried away by the applause that rings again and again through the theater from both plebs and senators; some rejoice when drenched in the blood of brothers, and go into exile, abandoning their dear hearths and homes and seeking another country underneath another sun.

But the farmer upturns the earth with his curved plow; this is his year-long toil, and thus he feeds his country and little grandchildren, his herds of cattle and bullocks that have served him well. Nor is there any halt throughout the year to the abundance of fruits or offspring of flocks or sheaves of grain, and his furrows are ever piled high with harvest and his granaries are filled to overflowing. When winter comes, the Sicyan olives are pressed by the mills, the pigs return well fed on acorns, the woods produce wild strawberries, and autumn drops her varied fruits, and high up on sunny rocks mellow grapes are ripened. Meanwhile, sweet children hang about his lips, his chaste household preserves its purity, the cows' udders hang full of milk, and the fat kids in the luxuriant meadow butt against each other locking horn with horn. The

68. Vergil here exalts peace of mind attainable through the natural philosophy of Epicurus and Lucretius.

master himself celebrates the festal days; stretched on the grass, while about a fire in their midst his comrades wreath the bowl, he pours libation and invokes thee, O Bacchus, and for the shepherds of his flock he holds a contest of throwing the swift javelin at a mark on an elm tree, and they bare their hardened bodies for the rustic wrestling match.

This is the life the ancient Sabines once cherished; so, too, Remus and his brother [Romulus, mythical ancestor of the Romans]; thus, surely, brave Etruria waxed strong, and Rome became the fairest thing on earth, and encircled together her seven hills with a wall. Yea, before the power of the Cretan kings and before impious mankind fed on slaughtered oxen, this was the life that was led on earth in the Golden Age of Saturn. Yea, not yet had they heard the blast of trumpet, not yet the ring of swords placed on hard anvils.

Vergil, *Aeneid* vi. 756–853 (abridged)

Now then, I[69] shall describe the future glory that is to attend the Trojan people, the descendants from the Italian people that await you, illustrious souls destined to succeed to our name, and I shall unfold to you your fate. . . . Romulus, son of Mars . . . do you see how a double plume stands on his helmet, and how his father marks him out even now by his distinctive badge as one of the gods? Yes, my son, it is under his auspices that glorious Rome will extend her empire to the ends of the earth and her heroism to the sky, and will encircle together her seven hills with a wall, fortunate in her brood of heroes. . . . Now turn your eyes here, behold this stock, your Romans. Here is Caesar and the whole progeny of Iulus,[70] destined to come under the great vault of the sky. This, this is he, the man you have heard promised to you so often, Augustus Caesar, son of a god, who will once again establish the Golden Age in Latium, in the region once ruled by Saturn, and will extend the empire beyond the Garamantes[71] and the Indians. . . .

Those souls, now, which you see equally agleam in armor, harmonious now and as long as they are confined in darkness, alas! how great a war will they wage against each other if they reach the light of day, what battles, what carnage will ensue, the father-in-law descending from the ramparts of the Alps . . . the son-in-law arrayed against him

69. The spirit of Anchises here foretells to his son Aeneas, who has come to visit him in Hades, the future glories of the Roman people.

70. Son of Aeneas, also named Ascanius and Ilus (from Ilium), to whom the Julian family sought to trace its origin

71. A remote North African tribe dwelling in the region now known as Fezzan.

with the forces of the east![72] Do not, do not, my children, cherish such wars in your hearts, do not turn your country's mighty power against the vitals of your country; and do you first, you who derive your descent from the gods, do you forbear, cast the weapons from your hand, my descendant. . . .

Others, doubtless, will mould lifelike bronze with greater delicacy, will win from marble the look of life, will plead cases better, chart the motions of the sky with the rod and foretell the risings of the stars.[73] You, O Roman, remember to rule the nations with might. This will be your genius—to impose the way of peace, to spare the conquered and crush the proud.

197. REORGANIZATION OF THE SENATE

The senatorial order, which had ruled the Roman Republic for hundreds of years, was absorbed into the Principate as a semihereditary aristocracy from which the emperors drew the highest imperial administrative and military officers. Together with the equestrian order, from which came the functionaries of the imperial civil service, the senatorial nobility formed the principal social base of the Principate. In three purgings of the rolls of the senate (29/28, 18, 13 B.C.), Augustus reorganized its personnel, weeding out unacceptable and politically unreliable members, reducing the membership to about 600, and establishing a property qualification of 1,000,000 sesterces. The reorganized senate, in addition to carrying out important administrative duties, became the principal legislative body of the state and a high court of justice (cf. volume 2, §§ 12–13).

Cassius Dio, *Roman History* LII. xlii. 1–7; Adapted from *LCL*

After this he held the office of censor,[74] with Agrippa as his colleague, and in addition to other reforms which he instituted he purged the senate. For as a result of the civil wars a large number of *equites* and even of men of lower rank were in the senate unjustifiably, so that the membership of that body had swollen to a thousand. Now, though it

72. The allusion is to the civil war between Julius Caesar and Pompey the Great, who had married Caesar's daughter.

73. Vergil here concedes to the Greek people superior achievement in the arts and sciences.

74. Dio is in error. Neither in 29 B.C., to which year Dio refers, nor at any other time did Augustus hold the office of censor. This high Republican magistracy had become virtually defunct during the last decades of the Republic. Augustus assumed the functions of the censors by virtue of his consular power. See further note 77.

was his wish to remove these men, he did not erase any of their names himself but urged them rather to become their own judges on the basis of their knowledge of their families and their lives; he thus first persuaded some fifty to withdraw from the senate voluntarily, and then compelled 140 others to imitate their example. He disfranchised none of them, but posted the names of the second group, sparing the members of the first group the reproach of the publication of their names, because they had not delayed but had straightway obeyed him. So these men returned to private life . . . and he made some other men senators. . . . And at the same time, ostensibly at the senate's bidding, he increased the number of patrician families, because the greater part of the patricians had perished (indeed no class is so wasted in civil wars as the nobility) and because the patricians are regarded as indispensable for the performance of our traditional institutions. In addition to these measures, he forbade all members of the senate to go outside Italy unless he himself commanded or permitted them to do so. This restriction is still observed down to the present day: no senator is allowed to go abroad to any place except Sicily and Narbonese Gaul. Since these regions are close at hand and the inhabitants are unarmed and peaceful, those who have any possessions there have been given the right to go there as often as they like without asking permission. . . .[75]

Suetonius, *Life of Augustus* xxxv. 1–3, xxxvii. 1–2; From *LCL*

Since the number of senators was swelled by a low-born and ill-assorted rabble (in fact, the senate numbered more than a thousand, some of whom . . . were wholly unworthy and had been admitted after Caesar's death through favor or bribery), he restored it to its former limits and distinction by two purges, one according to the choice of the members themselves, each man naming one other, and a second made by Agrippa and himself. (On the latter occasion it is thought that he wore a coat of mail under his tunic as he presided, and a sword by his side, while ten of the most robust of his friends among the senators stood about his chair. Cremutius Cordus[76] writes that even then the senators were not

---

75. In fact, however, under the Republic permission for senators to travel outside Italy and Sicily required action by the Senate, and Augustus transferred the authorization to the *princeps*. It was the Emperor Claudius who extended the range to Narbonese Gaul. Senators were explicitly excluded from Egypt. According to Tacitus (*Annals* II. lix. 4), "Augustus . . . set Egypt apart and forbade senators and high-ranking Roman *equites* from entering it without permission, for fear that whoever occupied that province, whose keys by land and sea [Pelusium and Alexandria] could be held with a very light garrison against mighty armies, would be able to distress Italy with famine."

76. See volume 2, § 6, fourth selection.

allowed to approach except one by one, and after the folds of their robes had been carefully searched.) Some he shamed into resigning, but he allowed even these to retain their distinctive dress, as well as the privileges of viewing the games from the orchestra and partaking in the public banquets of the order. Furthermore, that those who were chosen and approved might perform their duties more conscientiously and with less inconvenience, he provided that before taking his seat each member should offer incense and wine at the altar of the god in whose temple the meeting was held; that regular meetings of the senate should be held not oftener than twice a month, on the Kalends and the Ides; and that in the months of September and October none should be obliged to attend except a quorum drawn by lot, sufficient to pass decrees. He also adopted the plan of having privy councils [see note 12] chosen by lot for terms of six months, with which to discuss in advance matters which were to come before the entire body. . . .

To enable more men to take part in the administration of the state, he devised new offices: the supervision of public buildings, of the roads, of the aqueducts, of the channel of the Tiber, of the distribution of the grain dole to the people, as well as the prefecture of the city, a board of three for choosing senators, and another for reviewing the companies of *equites* whenever it should be necessary. He appointed censors, an office which had long been discontinued.[77] He increased the number of praetors.

198. THE NEW PREFECTURES

The administration of the imperial capital was placed on an efficient basis by Augustus and was gradually drawn under imperial control. Special administrative officials and permanent commissioners (cf. § 197) were developed by the first *princeps* to head bureaus which increasingly encroached upon the powers of the traditional Republican magistrates. The most important of these new departments were four prefectures established to take charge of various aspects of the security of Rome: the prefecture of the city, whose head was the chief constable of Rome and commanded the three urban cohorts of security police; the prefecture of the night patrol; the prefecture of the grain supply; and the prefecture of

---

77. Actually there were censors only once during the principate of Augustus, in 22 B.C. This date marks the end of the censorship as an independent office. Thereafter, though it was revived as an imperial prerogative by Claudius and the Flavians, the functions of this magistracy were absorbed into the imperial powers.

the Praetorian Guard (the emperor's bodyguard, nine cohorts of elite troops). The first of these great prefectures was held by senators of consular rank, the others by high-ranking *equites*. The duties of the first two are described in the following passages, which, being excerpted from the writings of the third-century jurists, Ulpian and Paulus, include some powers acquired by these prefects after the time of Augustus.

Justinian, *Digest* I. xii. I (abridged), xv. 3

The prefect of the city has jurisdiction over all offenses whatsoever, not only those committed inside the city but also those outside the city in Italy, according to a rescript of the deified Emperor Severus addressed to Fabius Cilo, prefect of the city. He shall hear complaints against masters by slaves who have sought asylum at sacred images or have been purchased with their own money for the purpose of being manumitted. He shall also hear the complaints of needy patrons concerning their freedmen, especially if they declare that they are ill and wish to be supported by their freedmen. The authority to relegate and deport persons to an island designated by the emperor is vested in him.

The same rescript begins as follows: "Inasmuch as we have entrusted our city to your care"; therefore any offense committed within the city is held to be under the jurisdiction of the prefect of the city; and likewise any offense committed within a hundred miles is under the jurisdiction of the prefect of the city; an offense committed beyond the hundredth milestone is outside the purview of the prefect of the city. . . .

Maintenance of the public peace and of order at the spectacles is also held to be under the jurisdiction of the prefect of the city; and indeed he should also have soldiers stationed at various points for the purpose of maintaining the public peace and to report to him whatever occurs anywhere. The prefect of the city can debar anyone from the city, as well as from any one of the official districts [of Rome] and can debar him from a business or profession or from the practice of law or from the Forum, either temporarily or permanently. He can also debar him from the spectacles. . . .

The deified Severus declared in a rescript that those who are accused of having held unlawful assemblies [cf. volume 2, § 51] must be prosecuted before the prefect of the city. . . .

Augustus held that the protection of the public security belonged to no one more than to the emperor, and that no one else was equal to the task; accordingly, he stationed seven cohorts in suitable places, so that each cohort protected two districts of the city;[78] in command of the cohorts were tribunes, and at the head of all was an official . . . called the prefect of the night patrol.

The prefect of the night patrol tries incendiaries, housebreakers, thieves, robbers, and harborers of criminals, unless the individual is so vicious and notorious that he is turned over to the prefect of the city. And since fires are generally caused by the negligence of occupants, he either punishes with beating those who have been unduly careless in the use of fire, or he suspends the sentence of beating and issues a severe reprimand.

Housebreaking is generally committed in apartment houses and in warehouses where men deposit the most valuable part of their property, when either a storeroom or a closet or a money box is broken into; in which case the guards are generally punished. The deified Antoninus stated this in a rescript to Erucius Clarus, saying that if warehouses are broken into he can examine by torture the slaves guarding them, even if some of them may belong to the emperor himself.

It should be noted that the prefect of the night patrol must be on duty the entire night, and should make his rounds appropriately shod and equipped with water buckets and axes. He must notify all residents to exercise care that no fire occur through any negligence; moreover, he is directed to give notice that each resident should keep water on his upper floor. He has also been assigned jurisdiction over those who take care of clothing in baths for a fee; and if while taking care of clothing they commit any fraud, he must try the case himself.

199. MILITARY REORGANIZATION

By 13 B.C. the demobilization of the huge civil war armies was completed, and Augustus undertook a definitive reorganization of the armed forces. "The system which existed at his death was modified only in detail by his successors during the first two centuries of our era, and traces of it remained till the last days of the Western Empire" (*Cambridge Ancient History*, 10:220). To some 300,000 men—c. 150,000 legionaries organized in twenty-eight legions (cf. note 81) and about the same number of provincial recruits in the auxiliary units—was entrusted the task of de-

---

78. Established in A.D. 6, the corps of 7,000 *vigiles*, all freedman, was distributed equally among the fourteen districts into which Augustus had divided Rome (cf. § 208, second selection).

fending the 4,000-mile-long frontier (cf. § 203) and of policing the provinces. In and about Rome were stationed several thousand troops comprising the emperor's bodyguard (called the Praetorian Guard) and the city guard. The whole was a professional, long-service standing army, the control of which was lodged firmly in the hands of the *princeps* (cf. § 201).

The expense of maintaining the military establishment was the largest single item in the imperial budget. It was a constant and increasingly difficult problem for Augustus and his successors to meet this expense without overstraining the civilian economy. In addition, the veterans had to be provided for after discharge. Until A.D. 6 a grant of land in a military colony continued to be the veteran's principal reward for service. In that year Augustus established the Soldiers' Bonus Fund *(aerarium militare),* financed by an initial grant of 170,000,000 sesterces from his own funds and by the income from a 1-percent tax on sales and a 5-percent inheritance tax. Thereafter, military colonies were still established on occasion, but normally the veteran received his discharge bonus in cash.

On all these matters, see further volume 2, chapter 7.

Suetonius, Life of Augustus xix, 1–2

Of the military forces he distributed legions and auxiliaries among the various provinces, stationed a fleet at Misenum and another at Ravenna to guard the Upper and Lower Seas,[79] and selected the remaining number for the protection partly of the city and partly of his own person. . . . However, he never allowed more than three [Praetorian] cohorts to remain in the city, and even those were without a permanent camp; the rest he regularly sent to winter or summer quarters in the neighboring towns. Furthermore, he placed all the soldiery everywhere on a specified scale of pay and bonuses and fixed the duration of military service and the rewards upon discharge according to each man's classification, in order to keep them from being tempted to revolution by age or by poverty after discharge. To have funds ready at all times without difficulty for their support and benefit he established the Soldiers' Bonus Fund, financed by new taxes.

Cassius Dio, Roman History LV. xxiii. 1–xxiv. 8 (abridged); Adapted from LCL

The soldiers were sorely displeased at the paltry character of the rewards given them for the wars which had been waged at this time, and none of them was willing to bear arms for longer than the stated period of his

---

79. The Adriatic and Tyrrhenian Seas, respectively.

service. It was therefore voted that 20,000 sesterces should be given to members of the Praetorian Guard [upon discharge] after they had served sixteen years, and 12,000 to the other legionaries after they had served twenty years.[80] Twenty-three or, as others say, twenty-five legions of citizen soldiers were being supported at this time. . . .[81] In the days of Augustus . . . there were also allied forces of infantry, cavalry, and sailors, whatever their number may have been (for I cannot state the exact figures). Then there were the [emperor's] bodyguards . . . and the city guards . . . and also picked foreign horsemen called Batavians (because the men from the island of Batavia in the Rhine are excellent horsemen). I cannot, however, give their exact number any more than I can give that of the *evocati*.[82] These last-named Augustus began to make a practice of employing from the time when he called again into service against Antony the troops who had served with his father, and he maintained them afterwards; they constitute even now a special corps and carry switches, like the centurions.

200. THE JULIAN LAW ON TREASON

With the advent of the Principate, revision of the statutes dealing with injury to the majesty of the Roman people and its representatives became necessary because of the emperor's status as the chief authority of the state. Augustus' Julian Law on Treason, the basic statute on the subject throughout the Empire, adapted Republican legislation to the new constitutional situation. The comprehensiveness and vagueness of the Roman concept of lese majesty rapidly led to an enormous extension of its application through interpretation, especially as it affected the majesty of the emperor; thus profession of Christianity, for example, was later treated as treasonable (cf. vol. 2, §§ 167–172). In the reign of Augustus the special treason court of the Republic soon fell into disuse, since treason cases were heard either by the emperor himself or by the senate (of which the emperor was the leading member). The penalty remained under Augustus the same as it had been from the time of Sulla—permanent banishment from Italy. Graver penalties were introduced in the reign of Tiberius—confiscation of property, deportation, loss of civic rights, and even death (see volume 2, § 6).

80. The time is A.D. 5. The periods of service were raised from twelve and sixteen years, respectively; see further the introduction to volume 2, § 138.

81. The figure twenty-five is the number of legions in existence at Augustus' death, after the annihilation of three legions in Germany (cf. § 203).

82. Literally, "recalled"—that is, veterans who constituted a reserve.

Justinian, *Digest* XLVIII. iv

The charge of treason . . . is lodged against a person through whose agency, with malice aforethought, a plot is formed whereby, without the order of the emperor, hostages perish, or whereby men armed with weapons or stones are present in the city or assemble against the state or occupy public places or temples, or whereby meetings or assemblies take place or men are gathered together for seditious purposes; or a person through whose agency, with malice aforethought, a plot is formed whereby any magistrate of the Roman people or a person possessing *imperium* or authority is slain or whereby anyone bears arms against the state; or a person who sends a messenger or letter or gives a signal to enemies of the Roman people, or who, with malice aforethought, causes the enemies of the Roman people to be aided with advice against the state; or a person who arouses or incites soldiers so as to cause sedition or an uprising against the state; or a person who does not depart from a province when he has been replaced by a successor; or [a soldier] who deserts from the army; or a civilian who goes over to the enemy; or a person who knowingly makes or cites a false entry in the public records. . . .

Moreover, the Julian Law on Treason directs that a person who injures the majesty of the state is liable to prosecution, such as one who abandons his post in time of war or fails to [?] hold a stronghold or gives up a military camp. Under the same law a person is also liable who, without the order of the emperor, wages war or levies soldiers or mobilizes an army; or who, when he has been superseded in his province, does not turn over his troops to his successor; or who deserts his command or an army of the Roman people; or a person not holding public office who knowingly and with malice aforethought exercises any function belonging to an authority or magistrate; or who causes any of the aforementioned acts to be done; or by whom with malice aforethought anyone is bound by oath to act against the state; or by whom, with malice aforethought, an army of the Roman people is led into ambush or betrayed to the enemy; or by whom, with malice aforethought, information is given whereby an enemy is prevented from coming into the power of the Roman people; or through whose agency, with malice aforethought, enemies of the Roman people are assisted with provisions, arms, weapons, horses, money, or anything else, or friends are turned into enemies of the Roman people; or who with malice aforethought so acts as to weaken the allegiance of a king of a foreign country to the Roman people; or whose action with malice aforethought results in facilitating the giving of hostages, money, or pack animals to enemies of the Roman people against the interests of the state; likewise, one who releases a defendant who has been imprisoned as a result of his confession of guilt before a court. . . .

A charge is extinguished by the death [of the accused], except in the case of a person accused of treason; for unless he is cleared of this charge by his heirs, the estate is confiscated by the privy purse. Clearly, not everyone accused of treason under the Julian Law is in this position, but only a person who is accused of high treason, that is, one motivated by hostile intent against the state or the emperor; but if a person is accused of treason under any other section of the Julian Law, his death extinguishes the charge.

201. ASPECTS OF PROVINCIAL ADMINISTRATION

The historic division of the Empire in 27 B.C. into imperial and senatorial provinces was a political safeguard against the menace to Augustus and the new regime of the reemergence of the rival proconsuls and war lords whose ambitions had convulsed the Roman world in the last century of the Republic. In acquiring the proconsular power (cf. § 194) Augustus assumed the titular proconsulship over the Spanish and Gallic provinces, Egypt, and Syria (together with a small section of Asia Minor), and thus concentrated in the hands of the *princeps* the bulk of the military forces of the Empire, which were stationed in these strategic and generally less pacified provinces. Thus, with one stroke, Augustus placed under his control not only the standing armies but also the foreign policy of the Empire. It is true that some legions continued to be commanded by the proconsuls of the senatorial provinces of Africa, Macedonia, and Illyricum, but the *princeps* through his *maius imperium* exercised effective control in these areas also (cf. note 14 and § 202). Within the provinces Augustus continued the traditional Roman policy of supporting the propertied classes and of fostering local self-government in the variously constituted urban communities of the Empire. An important aspect of Augustus' provincial reorganization was his suppression of the flagrant abuses and the ruthless exploitation which had characterized the provincial administration of the Republic (cf. chapter 6).

Cassius Dio, *Roman History* LIII. xii–xv (abridged); Adapted from *LCL*

Augustus declared that he would not personally govern all the provinces, and that in the case of such provinces as he should govern he would not do so indefinitely. And he did, in fact, restore to the senate the weaker provinces, on the ground that they were peaceful and free from war, while he retained the more powerful ones, alleging that they were insecure and precarious and either had enemies on their borders or were able on their own account to begin a serious revolt. His professed motive in this was that the senate might enjoy without fears the finest portion of the empire, while he himself had the hardships and the dangers; but his real purpose was that by this arrangement the senators should be unarmed and peaceful, while he alone had arms and maintained soldiers. Accordingly, Africa, Numidia, Asia, Greece with Epirus, the Dalmatian and Macedonian districts, Sicily, Crete, and the Cyrenaic portion of Libya, Bithynia with the adjoining Pontus, Sardinia, and Baetica[83] were held to belong to the people and the senate; while to Caesar belonged the remainder of Spain—that is, the districts of Tarraco and Lusitania—and all the Gauls—that is Gallia Narbonensis, Gallia Lugdunensis, Aquitania, and Belgica. . . . These provinces, then, together with Coele-Syria, as it is called, Phoenicia, Cilicia, Cyprus and Egypt, fell at that time to Caesar's share;[84] for afterwards he gave Cyprus and Gallia Narbonensis back to the people, and for himself took Dalmatia instead. . . . All of those which came into the Roman Empire after this were added to the provinces of the one who was emperor at the time.

Such then, was the division of the provinces. And wishing even so to divert the Romans far away from the idea that he was at all monarchical in his purposes, Caesar undertook for only ten years the government of the provinces assigned him; for he promised to reduce them to order within this period, and boastfully added that, if they should be pacified sooner, he would the sooner restore them, too, to the senate. Thereupon he first appointed the senators themselves to govern both classes of provinces, except Egypt. This province alone he assigned to an *eques*. . . .[85]

83. There are anachronisms in Dio's list. In 27 B.C. there were only eight senatorial provinces. Greece was still attached to Macedonia; Numidia, then a client kingdom, was annexed to the province of Africa in 25 B.C.; Baetica did not become senatorial until later in Augustus' reign.

84. This list, too, contains anachronisms (cf. note 83) in the divisions and names of provinces.

85. Cf. § 203, third selection. Later in Augustus' principate several smaller imperial provinces, garrisoned only by auxiliary troops, were assigned equestrian procurators or prefects as their governors.

Next he ordained that the governors of senatorial provinces should be annual magistrates, chosen by lot, except when a senator enjoyed privileges because of the large number of his children or because of his marital status [cf. § 204]. These governors were to be sent out by action of the senate in public meeting; they were to carry no sword at their belt nor to wear military uniform; the name of proconsul was to belong not only to the two ex-consuls but also to the others who had merely served as praetors or who held the rank of ex-praetors. . . . The other governors, on the other hand, were to be chosen by the emperor himself and were to be called his legates with the rank of praetor, even if they were ex-consuls. Thus, of these two titles which had been in vogue so long under the Republic, he gave that of praetor to the men chosen by him, on the ground that from very early times it had been associated with warfare, calling them propraetors; and he gave the name of consul to the others, on the ground that their duties were more peaceful, styling them proconsuls. For he reserved the actual titles of consul and praetor for Italy, and designated all the governors outside of Italy as acting in their stead. So, then, he caused the appointed governors to be known as propraetors and to hold office for as long beyond one year as he wished;[86] he made them wear the military uniform and a sword, which gives them the power of inflicting punishment even on soldiers. . . .

It was thus and under these circumstances that the custom was established of sending out ex-praetors and ex-consuls as governors of the two classes of provinces. In the one case, the emperor would commission a governor to any province he wished and whenever he wished. . . . In the case of the senatorial provinces, he assigned Asia and Africa on his own responsibility to the ex-consuls, and all the other provinces to the ex-praetors, but by public decree, applicable to all the senatorial governors, he forbade the allotment of any senator to a governorship before the expiration of five years from the time he had held office in the city. . . .[87]

This is the system followed in the case of the provinces of the people. To the others, which are called the imperial provinces and have more than one citizen-legion, are sent officials who are to govern them as legates; these are appointed by the emperor himself, generally from the ex-praetors. . . .

86. An extreme case is known of a man who held a series of such governorships for twenty-four years under Augustus and Tiberius.

87. This was a reenactment of a measure passed by the Senate and Pompey in 53/52 B.C. Ex-consuls probably were required to wait ten years.

These, then, are the positions which belong to the senators. Passing now to the *equites,* the emperor himself selects *equites* to be sent out as military tribunes (both those who are prospective senators and others . . .), despatching some of them to take command of purely citizen troops, and others of the auxiliary troops as well. . . .[88] The procurators (for this is the name we give to the men who collect the public revenues and make disbursements according to the instructions given them) he sends out to all the provinces alike, to those of the people as well as to his own, and to this office *equites* are sometimes appointed and sometimes even freedmen, except where the proconsuls exact the tribute from the people they govern. The emperor gives instructions to the procurators, the proconsuls, and the propraetors, in order that they may go out to their provinces under definite orders. For both this practice and the giving of salaries to them and to the other officials was established at this time. In former times, of course, certain persons had contracted with the state to furnish the officials with all they needed for the conduct of their office; but under Caesar these officials for the first time began to receive a fixed salary. . . . The following regulations were laid down for them all alike: they were not to raise levies of soldiers or to exact money beyond the amount assessed, unless either the senate should so vote or the emperor so order; and when their successors arrived, they were to leave the province at once, and not to delay on the return journey, but to return within three months.

OATH OF ALLEGIANCE TO AUGUSTUS

When the client-king Deiotarus of Paphlagonia died in 6 B.C., his domain was annexed to the Empire and assigned to the province of Galatia. Three years later this oath of allegiance to Augustus was taken, first at Gangra, the administrative seat, by delegates from all the cities of the region, and subsequently by all the Paphlagonians in their local communities. Introduced by Augustus in the days of his death struggle with Antony, this personal oath of allegiance to the chieftain from the civilian population as well as the military became a standard ritual of the Principate (cf. volume 2, § 3).

---

88. Prospective senators were required to serve in the army at least one year as tribunes of legionary or auxiliary cohorts or as prefects of auxiliary cavalry.

Dittenberger, *OGIS,* no. 532 (=Dessau, no. 8,781)

In the third year from the twelfth consulship of the Emperor Caesar Augustus, son of a god, March 6, in the . . .[89] at Gangra, the following oath was taken by the inhabitants of Paphlagonia and the Roman businessmen dwelling among them:

"I swear by Jupiter, Earth, Sun, by all the gods and goddesses, and by Augustus himself, that I will be loyal to Caesar Augustus and to his children and descendants all my life in word, in deed, and in thought, regarding as friends whomever they so regard, and considering as enemies whomever they so adjudge; that in defense of their interests I will spare neither body, soul, life, nor children, but will in every way undergo every danger in defense of their interests; that whenever I perceive or hear anything being said or planned or done against them I will lodge information about this and will be an enemy to whoever says or plans or does any such thing; and that whomever they adjudge to be enemies I will by land and sea, with weapons and sword, pursue and punish. But if I do anything contrary to this oath or not in conformity with what I swore, I myself call down upon myself, my body, my soul, my life, my children, and all my family and property, utter ruin and utter destruction unto all my issue and all my descendants, and may neither earth nor sea receive the bodies of my family or my descendants, or yield fruits to them."

The same oath was sworn also by all the people in the land at the altars of Augustus in the temples of Augustus in the various districts. In this manner did the people of Phazimon, who inhabit the city now called Neapolis,[90] all together swear the oath in the temple of Augustus at the altar of Augustus.

In 6/5 B.C. the people of the town of Conobaria in Baetica, Spain, took an oath for the safety of Augustus, as recorded in this somewhat fragmentary inscription, the first such oath found in the western part of the Empire. It would appear that at this time an empirewide demonstration (even including Judaea, where sacrifices were made to Jehovah for the safety of Augustus) of allegiance to Augustus and his designated heirs was orchestrated.

89. "Camp" and "civic center" have been proposed for the word lost in the lacuna.
90. Modern Mersivan in Turkey, where this inscription was found.

Zeitschrift für Papyrologie und Epigraphik (1988), 72:113–127

In the proconsulship of Publius Petronius Turpilianus sons of Publius, and the . . . of Marcus Alfius Laches son of Gaius, and Titus Quinctius Silo son of Titus, . . . the magistrates, senate and people of Conobaria swore in the following words:

Of my own volition I express my regard for the safety, honor and victory of the Emperor Caesar Augustus son of the Deified [Julius Caesar], *pontifex maximus*, and of Gaius Caesar son of Augustus, leader of the youth, consul designate, pontiff, and of Lucius Caesar son of Augustus, and of Marcus Agrippa grandson of Augustus. I will take up arms, and I will hold as friends and allies the same ones I understand are theirs. And I will consider those to be my enemies, those whom I observe to be theirs. And if anyone does or plans anything against them, I will pursue them to the death by land and by sea.

202. The Cyrene Edicts

This long Greek inscription from Cyrene, first published in 1927 and widely discussed since, constitutes the most important epigraphical find for the reign of Augustus since the famous *Res Gestae*. It contains four imperial edicts of 7/6 B.C. and a fifth, appending a decree of the Senate, of 4 B.C. The first edict revises the judiciary system of the province, patterned after the criminal courts of Rome, by providing for mixed juries of Greeks and Romans in capital cases. The second concerns a case which apparently established the precedent for the prosecution (attested under subsequent emperors) of affronts to imperial statues under the law of *maiestas* (lese majesty: cf. § 200 and volume 2, § 6). The third edict, which limits the privileges of newly created Roman citizens, is an important document on the subjects of multiple citizenship and compulsory public services in the provinces. The fourth edict, dealing with the jury system in Cyrene, supplements the first. The decree of the Senate appended to the fifth edict established a new, accelerated procedure by judicial commissions of Roman senators in extortion cases limited to a claim for recovery and involving no concomitant capital charges against the accused public official. Altogether these edicts shed invaluable light on the fusion of Hellenistic and Roman law in the eastern provinces; since Crete–Cyrene was a senatorial province, they also constitute important evidences of the emperor's *maius imperium* (cf. note 14).

SEG, vol. IX, no. 8 (=*FIRA*, vol. I, no. 68)

i

The Emperor Caesar Augustus, *pontifex maximus,* holding the tribunician power for the seventeenth year, acclaimed *imperator* fourteen times, declares:

Since I find that there are all told in the provincial territory of Cyrene 215 Romans of all ages with a census rating of 2,500 *denarii* or more, from whom the jurors are chosen;[91] and since embassies from the cities of the province have complained bitterly that among these same Romans there exist certain conspiracies to oppress the Greeks in trials on capital charges, the same individuals acting in turn as accusers and as witnesses for one another; and since I myself have ascertained that some innocent people have in this way been oppressed and carried off to the supreme penalty, it is my view that, until the senate makes a decision on this matter or I myself find some better solution,[92] it will be the right and proper procedure for those governing the province of Crete and Cyrene to impanel in the provincial territory of Cyrene the same number of Greek jurors from the highest census rating as of Romans—no Greek or Roman to be less than twenty-five years of age, and none to have a census rating and property of less than 7,500 *denarii,* if there is a sufficient number of such persons, or, if the full number of jurors who need to be impaneled cannot be made up on this basis, they shall impanel men possessing half this census rating, but not less, as jurors in trials of Greeks on capital charges.

A Greek under indictment shall be given the right to decide, the day before the prosecution opens its case, whether he wants his jurors to be all Romans or half Greeks; and if he chooses half Greeks, then the balls shall be checked for equal weight[93] and the names shall be written on them, and from one urn the names of the Romans and from the other those of the Greeks shall be drawn until a total of twenty-five is obtained in each group. Of these the prosecutor may, if he wishes, dismiss one from each group, and the accused three out of the total, provided he does not dismiss either all Romans or all Greeks. Then all the others

91. This low census rating for jury service is indicative of the low level of wealth prevailing among Roman citizens in the province of Crete-Cyrene. At Rome the minimum property rating for jury duty was 100,000 denarii.

92. This clause reflects the principle of collaboration between Senate and *princeps* inherent in the constitution of the Principate (cf. p. 555).

93. The lots ("balls") were checked for equal weight to equalize the chance of selection.

[after hearing the case] shall separate for the balloting, the Romans casting their votes separately in one box, the Greeks separately in a second; then a separate count shall be made of the votes on either side, and the governor shall pronounce in open court the verdict of the majority of all the jurors.

Furthermore, since the kinsmen of murdered persons generally do not leave unjustifiable deaths unavenged and it can be expected that those responsible will not lack Greek prosecutors to demand justice on behalf of their slain relatives or fellow citizens, it is my view that all who in the future govern Crete and Cyrene will act rightly and fittingly if in the provincial territory of Cyrene they do not permit a Roman to act as a prosecutor of a Greek for the murder of a Greek man or woman, except where someone who has been honored with Roman citizenship takes action concerning the death of one of his relatives or fellow citizens.

ii

The Emperor Caesar Augustus, *pontifex maximus,* holding the tribunician power for the seventeenth year, declares:

Publius Sextius Scaeva does not merit reproach or censure for ordering Aulus Stlaccius Maximus son of Lucius, Lucius Stlaccius Macedo son of Lucius, and Publius Lacutanius Phileros, freedman of Publius, to be sent on to me from the province of Cyrene under guard because they had said that they had knowledge concerning my security and the commonwealth and wished to declare it.[94] In so doing Sextius performed his duty conscientiously. However, since they have no information that concerns me or the commonwealth but have declared and convinced me that they had misrepresented and lied about this in the province, I have set them free and am releasing them from custody.[95] But as for Aulus Stlaccius Maximus, whom the envoys of the Cyrenaeans accuse of having removed statues from public places, among them even the one on the base of which the city inscribed my name, I forbid him to depart without my order until I have investigated this matter.

94. Cf. in § 201 the oath of allegiance in which the inhabitants of the Roman provinces promised to report any such information that might come to their attention.

95. It seems strange, at first sight, that Augustus should release these Romans without punishment when they have confessed that they have lied, presumably to implicate Greeks in Cyrene in charges of lese majesty. Augustus' action is to be explained as one of his conciliatory measures intended to calm the seething animosity between Greeks and Romans in the province. His concessions to the Greeks in the other edicts were directed toward the same end.

iii

The Emperor Caesar Augustus, *pontifex maximus,* holding the tribunician power for the seventeenth year, declares:

Persons from the province of Cyrene who have been honored with [Roman] citizenship I order nonetheless to perform in their turn the personal compulsory public services of the Greeks. Excepted are those to whom, by decree of my father or myself in accordance with a law or a decree of the senate, exemption was granted together with citizenship. And even for those to whom such exemption was granted, it is my pleasure that they shall be exempt only as to the property they possessed at the time, but for all subsequent acquisitions they shall be subject to the usual charges.[96]

iv

The Emperor Caesar Augustus, *pontifex maximus,* holding the tribunician power for the seventeenth year, declares:

Regarding disputes which occur henceforth between Greeks within the province of Cyrene, excluding indictments for capital crimes, where the governor of the province must himself conduct the inquiry and render a decision or else set up a panel of jurors [as detailed in the first edict]—for all other cases it is my pleasure that Greek jurors shall be assigned unless some defendant or accused desires to have Roman citizens as jurors; and for those to whom in accordance with this decree of mine Greek jurors are assigned, it is my pleasure that no juror shall be assigned from the city from which either the plaintiff or the accuser or the defendant or the accused comes.

96. Compulsory public services in the Roman Empire were of two kinds: those based on personal status *(munera personalia* or *corporalia)* and those based on property holdings *(munera patrimonialia):* cf. volume 2, §§ 66, 77, 115, 128. In this edict Augustus enunciates the important principle, maintained by his successors, that a provincial's acquisition of Roman citizenship was compatible with retention of his original citizenship (cf. p. 421) and did not exempt him from the performance of *munera* in his local community unless the grant of citizenship was specifically accompanied by such exemption. Roman citizens of Italian origin residing abroad did at first enjoy exemption from such community obligations, but with the deterioration of municipal finances in the first and second centuries (see volume 2, § 69) this privilege was progressively reduced by the emperors, until finally the universal citizenship edict of Caracalla in A.D. 212 (Volume 2, § 106) placed all Roman citizens on the same plane.

v

The Emperor Caesar Augustus, *pontifex maximus,* holding the tribunician power for the nineteenth year, declares:

A decree of the senate was passed in the consulship of Gaius Calvisius and Lucius Passienus, with me as one of those present at the writing.[97] Since it affects the welfare of the allies of the Roman people, I have decided to send it into the provinces, appended to this my prefatory edict, so that it may be known to all who are under our care. From this it will be evident to all the inhabitants of the provinces how much both I and the senate are concerned that none of our subjects should suffer any improper treatment or any extortion.

Decree of the Senate

Whereas the consuls Gaius Calvisius Sabinus and Lucius Passienus Rufus spoke "Concerning matters affecting the security of the allies of the Roman people which the Emperor Caesar Augustus, our *princeps,* following the recommendation of the council which he had drawn by lot from among the senate,[98] desired to be brought before the senate by us," the senate passed the following decree:

Whereas our ancestors established legal process for extortion [see §§ 100, 146, 158] so that the allies might more easily be able to take action for any wrongs done them and recover moneys extorted from them, and whereas this type of process is sometimes very expensive and troublesome for those in whose interest the law was enacted, because poor people or persons weak with illness or age are dragged from far-distant provinces as witnesses, the senate decrees as follows:

If after the passage of this decree of the senate any of the allies, desiring to recover extorted moneys, public or private, appear and so depose before one of the magistrates who is authorized to convene the senate, the magistrate—except where the extorter faces a capital charge —shall bring them before the senate as soon as possible and shall assign them any advocate they themselves request to speak in their behalf before the senate; but no one who has in accordance with the laws been excused from this duty shall be required to serve as advocate against his will.

---

97. Augustus' being recorded in the preamble as one of "those present at the writing" of the decree means that he was one of the sponsors of the decree in the Senate; cf. the first paragraph of the decree, below. This is the only extant example of an emperor's participation in this formality.

98. On the emperor's *consilium* see note 12.

In order that the cases of those bringing such charges in the senate may be heard, the magistrate who grants them access to the senate shall the same day in the presence of the senate, with not less than two hundred [members] on hand,[99] choose by lot four from all those of consular rank who are in Rome itself or within twenty miles of the city; likewise three from all those of praetorian rank who are in Rome itself or within twenty miles of the city; likewise two from all the other senators and those possessing the right to voice opinion in the senate who are then either in Rome or less than twenty miles from the city.[100] But he shall not choose anyone who is seventy years of age or over, or is the incumbent of a magistracy or an authority, or presiding officer of a law court, or commissioner of grain distribution;[101] or anyone prevented by illness from performing this duty, who excuses himself on oath before the senate and presents three members of the senate to attest this on oath; or anyone who is so closely related by family or marriage to the accused that he may not, in accordance with the Julian Judiciary Law,[102] be compelled to give evidence in a public action against his will; or anyone who the accused swears before the senate is hostile to him (but he shall not by such oath eliminate more than three). From the nine selected in this manner, the magistrate who does the drawing shall see to it that within two days those claiming the money and the one from whom they claim it make rejections in turn until five are left. If any of these judges dies before the case is decided, or some other cause prevents him from rendering his decision and his excuse is approved by the sworn statement of five members of the senate, then the magistrate, in the presence of the judges and of those claiming the money and the man from whom they claim it, shall again choose by lot from those members who are of the same rank or have held the same magistracies as the man who is being replaced, provided he does not thus choose a member who may not by this decree of the senate be chosen to try the accused.

The judges chosen shall hear and inquire into only those cases in which a man is accused of having appropriated money from a community or from private parties; and, rendering their decision within thirty days, they shall order him to restore such sum of money, public or

---

99. That is, about one third of the membership; cf. introduction to § 197.

100. *Recuperatores* was the Latin term for judges of such *ad hoc* tribunals. The three-category system by which their names were drawn was that used in appointing senatorial commissions. The twenty-mile radius from Rome was meant to correspond to a day's journey.

101. Such high officials were generally exempted from legal process during tenure of office.

102. This law of 17 B.C. regulated the procedures of the criminal courts.

private, as the accusers prove was taken from them. Those whose duty it is to inquire into and pronounce judgment in these cases shall, until they complete the inquiry and pronounce their judgment, be exempted from all public duties except public worship.

The senate decrees also that the magistrate who does the drawing of the judges—or, if he cannot, the ranking consul—shall preside over the proceedings and shall grant permission to summon those witnesses who are in Italy, with the proviso that he shall allow a man making a private claim to summon not more than five, and those pressing public claims not more than ten.[103]

The senate likewise decrees that the judges who are selected in accordance with this decree of the senate shall pronounce in open court each his several finding, and what the majority pronounces shall be the verdict.

203. FRONTIER AND FOREIGN POLICY

Augustus, the "prince of peace," annexed more territory to the Roman Empire than did any of the famous conquering generals of the Republic. But his conquests were based on the essentially defensive strategic plan—to which his successors held with few exceptions (cf. vol. 2, §§ 7–10)—of protecting the Empire by means of strong, easily defensible natural barriers. In the west the Roman conquest of Spain, begun nearly two centuries earlier, was completed when the last vestiges of resistance surviving in remote mountain fastnesses were suppressed. In the east diplomatic negotiations with the Parthians led to the fixing of the Euphrates River as the frontier between the two empires and to recognition of the Roman protectorate over Armenia. To the south, an expedition aimed at acquiring the fabled riches and lucrative trade of Arabia Felix (modern Yemen) was a dismal failure; in Ethiopia, however, after a number of years of frontier warfare, Roman garrisons were established in a buffer zone south

---

103. This and the two preceding paragraphs reduce drastically the delays and expenses in which the procedures of the extortion courts of the Republic involved the provincials. The Republican practice allowed sixty days for constituting the jury; here the senatorial tribunal is constituted in final form within two days from the presentation of the complaint in the Senate. The Republican practice gave the parties the right to subpoena large numbers of witnesses from any part of the Empire (up to 120 witnesses under the Julian Law of 59 B.C.) and allowed them generous amounts of time. Cicero in his prosecution of Verres, for example, was given 110 days to collect witnesses. Here the number of witnesses is reduced to a maximum of five or ten; only persons within the borders of Italy can be subpoenaed as witnesses (*voluntary* witnesses from the provinces are of course not excluded); and the whole hearing is to be over and the verdict rendered within thirty days from the constitution of the tribunal.

of the Egyptian border. In the north the frontier was advanced to the Danube, and in A.D. 5 Roman armies stood on the Elbe. But the great rebellion in Pannonia (A.D. 6–9) and the annihilation of three Roman legions in the Teutoburg Forest of Germany in A.D. 9 caused Augustus to pull in his horns. The conquest of Germany was abandoned, and the northern frontier of the Empire thereafter remained based on the Rhine and Danube rivers.

Suetonius, *Life of Augustus* XXI, xxiii; Adapted from *LCL*

He subdued Cantabria, Aquitania, Pannonia, Dalmatia, and all Illyricum, as well as Raetia and the Vindelici and Salassi (Alpine tribes), some under his personal leadership, some by generals acting in his name. He also put a stop to the inroads of the Dacians, slaying great numbers of them together with three of their leaders, and forced the Germans back beyond the river Elbe, with the exception of the Suebi and the Sigambri, who submitted to him and were taken into Gaul and settled on lands near the Rhine. Other peoples, too, that were not entirely peaceful he reduced to submission. But he never made war on any people without just and due cause, and he was so far from the desire of increasing his dominion or his military glory at any cost that he forced the chiefs of some of the barbarians to swear in the temple of Mars the Avenger that they would faithfully keep the peace for which they asked. In some cases, indeed, he tried exacting a new kind of hostages, namely women, because he realized that they disregarded pledges secured by males; but he always allowed them to take back their hostages as many times as they wished. On those who rebelled often or with unusual treachery he never vindictively visited any severer punishment than that of selling the prisoners on the conditions that they should not live while slaves in a country near their own nor be set free within thirty years. The reputation for prowess and moderation which he thus gained led even the Indians and the Scythians, nations known to us only by report, to send envoys voluntarily to sue for his friendship and that of the Roman people. The Parthians, too, readily yielded to his claim to Armenia, and at his demand surrendered the military standards which they had taken from Marcus Crassus and Mark Antony [cf. note 57]; they offered him hostages besides, and once when there were several claimants of their throne they accepted only the one chosen by him.

. . . . .

He suffered but two severe and ignominious defeats, both in Germany — those of Lollius and of Varus. The former was more humiliating than serious,[104] but the latter was almost fatal, since three legions were slaughtered with their general, his lieutenants, and all the auxiliaries.[105] When the news of this arrived, Augustus posted night watches throughout the city to prevent any disturbance, and he prolonged the terms of the governors of the provinces so that the allies might be held to their allegiance by experienced men with whom they were acquainted. Also, as had been done in the Cimbric and Marsic wars,[106] he vowed great games to Jupiter Best and Greatest if the condition of the commonwealth should improve. In fact, they say he was so overcome that for months on end he refused to cut his beard or hair and would from time to time dash his head against the door, crying: "Quintilius Varus, give me back my legions!" And he observed the day of the disaster each year as one of sorrow and mourning.

THE DISASTER IN GERMANY

Cassius Dio, *Roman History* LVI. xviii–xix; Adapted from *LCL*

The following are the events that took place in Germany during this period. The Romans were holding portions of it . . . and soldiers of theirs were wintering there and cities were being founded. The barbarians were adapting themselves to Roman ways, were becoming accustomed to hold markets, and were meeting in peaceful assemblages. They had not, however, forgotten their ancestral habits, their native manners, their old life of independence, or the power derived from arms. Hence, so long as they were unlearning these old ways gradually and progressively under the eyes of the Roman garrisons, they were not disturbed by the change in their manner of life and were becoming different without noticing it. But when Quintilius Varus became governor of the province of Germany and was administering the affairs of these peoples as part of his duties, he strove to change them more rapidly. He issued orders to them as if they were enslaved, and exacted money as he would from subjects. To this they were in no mood to submit. The leaders

104. In 17 B.C. three German tribes launched a raid across the Rhine and defeated Marcus Lollius, governor of Gaul.

105. According to Velleius Paterculus (*Compendium of Roman History* II. cxvii) the auxiliaries numbered six cohorts of infantry and three companies of cavalry.

106. The Cimbrians, a Germanic people, in the course of their migrations toward the end of the second century B.C. inflicted several defeats on Roman armies in the Alpine regions and threatened to invade Italy until crushed by Marius near Vercellae (101 B.C.; cf. p. 219). The Marsic War was another, probably the earliest, name by which the Romans designated the Italic War (§ 103).

longed for their former ascendancy, and the masses preferred their accustomed conditions to foreign domination. But they did not openly revolt, since they saw that there were many Roman troops near the Rhine and many within their own borders; instead, they received Varus as if prepared to do everything demanded of them, and thus they drew him far away from the Rhine into the land of the Cherusci, toward the Weser, and there by behaving in a most peaceful and friendly manner led him to believe that they would live submissively even without soldiers present.

Consequently he did not keep his legions together, as was proper in hostile country, but distributed many of the soldiers to helpless communities, which asked for them for the alleged purpose of guarding various points, arresting robbers, or escorting provision trains. . . . Then there came an uprising, first, by design, on the part of those who lived far off from him, so that Varus should march against them and so be more easily overpowered by them while proceeding through what was supposed to be friendly country, instead of putting himself on his guard as he would do if all became hostile to him at once. And so it came to pass. They escorted him as he set out, and then begged to be excused on the pretense that they would mobilize their allied contingents and quickly come to his aid. Then they took charge of their forces, which were held in readiness somewhere, and, after the men in each community had put to death the [Roman] soldiers in their midst for whom they had previously asked, they came upon Varus who was by now in almost inextricable forests. And there, at the very moment of revealing themselves as enemies instead of subjects, they wrought great and dire havoc.

THE SOUTHERN FRONTIER

The following is a vainglorious inscription in Latin and Greek, erected in 29 B.C. on the island of Philae, near the first cataract of the Nile, by Cornelius Gallus, the first Roman prefect of Egypt (he was also a poet, and a friend of Vergil). In it he celebrates his suppression of the Thebaid's revolt against the introduction of the Roman taxation system and his establishment of a Roman protectorate over a buffer zone south of the cataract (see further note 110). In addition to the present inscription, Gallus "set up statues of himself practically everywhere in Egypt, and inscribed the list of his achievements on the pyramids" (Cassius Dio LIII. xxiii. 5). For reasons which (despite scholarly debate) remain unclear he was recalled in disgrace, and he committed suicide (26 B.C.).

CIL, vol. III, no. 14,147 (5) (=Dessau, no. 8,995)

Gaius Cornelius Gallus son of Gnaeus, Roman *eques,* first prefect of Alexandria and Egypt after the overthrow of the kings by Caesar, son of a god—having been victorious in two pitched battles in the fifteen days within which he suppressed the revolt of the Thebaid, capturing five cities—Boresis, Coptus, Ceramice, Diospolis Magna, and Ophiëum[107]—and seizing the leaders of these revolts; having led his army beyond the Nile cataract, a region into which arms had not previously been carried either by the Roman people or by the kings of Egypt;[108] having subjugated the Thebaid, the common terror of all the kings;[109] and having given audience at Philae to envoys of the king of the Ethiopians, received that king under [Roman] protection, and installed a prince over the Triacontaschoenus,[110] a district of Ethiopia—dedicated this thank offering to his ancestral gods and to the Nile his helpmate.

CLIENT STATES

As the preceding inscription indicates, Augustus continued the policy, begun under the Republic, of buttressing some frontiers with buffer zones under Roman protectorate (see § 195, paragraphs 27, 32–33). The Romans preferred to control these remote and economically backward frontier regions indirectly through native princes because it would have been much more expensive to install and maintain the administrative machinery of Roman rule. But their very weakness made them in the long run unreliable bases of Roman power, and in the course of the first century most of these vassal states—by this time considerably Romanized in their ways—were annexed to the Empire.

---

107. Diospolis Magna was the Latin name of the city of Thebes; Ceramice and Ophiëum were two of its districts.

108. Here Gallus' boastfulness degenerates into sheer untruth. Both Pharaohs and Ptolemies had extended their rule south of the cataract at times.

109. The powerful priesthood of Amon, centered in Thebes, had been a constant thorn in the side of the Egyptian kings from very early times.

110. "Thirty-schoenium Land," the region from the first to the second cataract (c. 165 miles), which thus became a Roman protectorate under an Ethiopian client-king. This arrangement was impermanent, however. Nine years later, after an Ethiopian raid on the Egyptian frontier and the consequent Roman invasion of Ethiopia in force, this buffer zone was reduced by Augustus to twelve *schoenia* (c. 66 miles). In this the Romans maintained a string of military posts that successfully prevented any further violation of the southern frontier until the middle of the third century.

Suetonius, *Life of Augustus* xlviii; From *LCL*

Except in a few instances he either restored the kingdoms of which he gained possession by right of conquest to those from whom he had taken them, or joined them to other foreign nations. He also united with mutual ties the kings with whom he was in alliance and was very ready to propose and favor marriages or friendships among them. He never failed to treat them with all consideration as integral parts of the empire, regularly appointing guardians for such as were too young to rule or feeble-minded until they grew up or recovered, and he brought up the children of many, educating them together with his own.

Strabo, *Geography* xiv. v. 6; Adapted from *LCL*

The region [of Cilicia Trachea] was naturally well adapted to the business of piracy both by land and by sea [cf. § 131]—by land because of the height of the mountains and the populous tribes living beyond them on plains and farm lands that are large and easily overrun; and by sea because of the wealth of ship-building timber, harbors, fortresses, and secret recesses. With all this in view, the Romans deemed it better for the region to be ruled by kings than to be under Roman prefects sent to administer justice, who were not likely always to be present or to have armed forces with them.

CIL, vol. V, no. 7,231 (= Dessau, no. 94); 9/8 B.C.

This inscription is found on an arch at Segusio (Susa) in the Cottian Alps.

[Dedicated] to the Emperor Caesar Augustus, son of a god, *pontifex maximus,* holding the tribunician power for the fifteenth year, acclaimed *imperator* thirteen times, by Marcus Julius Cottius, son of King Donnus, prefect[111] of the following tribes—the Segovii, Segusini, Belacori, Caturiges, Medulli, Tebavii, Adanates, Savincates, Ecdinii, Veaminii, Venisami, Iemerii, Vesubianii, and Quadiates—and by the tribes which are under his command.

111. Apparently Cottius had been placed in charge of these tribes with the rank of a Roman perfect. In A.D. 44 he was allowed to assume the title of king, which his father had borne.

204. Social Legislation: Fostering the Family

In 18 B.C. Augustus launched his program of social and moral regenera-
tion. Its goals were to restore public morality and to encourage marriage
and family life, especially in the upper classes, and to assure the domination of the Italian stock in the Empire by increasing the birth rate. To
these ends he enacted three laws. In the Julian Law on Curbing Adultery
he took the unprecedented step of making adultery a criminal offense
punishable by exile and loss of property and even sanctioned the killing of
an adulterer caught in the act. The Julian Law on Classes Permitted to
Marry, supplemented in A.D. 9 by the Papian–Poppaean Law, with which
its provisions are frequently fused in the sources, eliminated some (but not
all) class barriers to marriage, penalized celibacy, granted privileges to
married people, and rewarded childbearing (see volume 2, § 46). Though
these laws remained on the books down to the time of Justinian and were
included in his codification, their efficacy was at best limited—Juvenal
(*Satires* ii. 37) called them "dormant"; Tertullian (*Apology* iv) called them
"most futile." The essence of their futility lay in the fact that the moral
symptoms which they attempted to abate by legislative fiat were produced
by underlying socioeconomic conditions that remained unaltered. (The
situation is neatly epitomized by the fact that the consuls from whom the
Papian–Poppaean Law took its name were both bachelors.) The result
was widespread evasion and opposition, to which the emperors responded
with occasional palliatives and numerous individual dispensations.

THE SLACKENING OF THE MARRIAGE BOND

In this ode, published in 23 B.C., Horace comments on the prevalence of
marital infidelity as part of the general decline of religion and morality in
Roman society.

Horace, *Odes* iii. vi (abridged); Adapted from *LCL*

Thy father's sins, O Roman, thou though guiltless shalt expiate, till
thou dost restore the crumbling temples and shrines of the gods and
their statues soiled with grimy smoke. 'Tis by holding thyself the servant of the gods that thou dost rule; with them all things begin; to them
ascribe the outcome! Outraged by neglect, they have visited unnum-
bered woes on sorrowful Italy. . . . Teeming with sin, our times have
sullied first the marriage bed, our offspring, and our homes; sprung

from this source, disaster's stream has overflowed the people and the fatherland. . . . The young maiden even now trains herself in coquetry and, impassioned to her finger tips, plans unholy amours. Anon she seeks young paramours at her husband's board, nor stops to choose on whom she will swiftly bestow illicit joys when lights are banished, but openly when bidden, and not without her husband's knowledge, she rises, be it some peddler summons her, or the captain of some Spanish ship, lavish purchaser of shame. . . . What do the ravages of time not injure! Our parents' age, worse than our grandsires', bore us still less worthy and destined soon to produce an offspring still more wicked.

THE JULIAN LAW ON CURBING ADULTERY

Various legal sources, collected in ADA, pp. 112–128 (abridged)

"No one shall hereafter commit debauchery or adultery knowingly and with malice aforethought." These words of the law apply to him who abets as well as to him who commits debauchery or adultery.

The Julian Law on Curbing Adultery punishes not only defilers of the marriages of others . . . but also the crime of debauchery when anyone without the use of force violates either a virgin or a widow of respectable character.

By the second section [of the law] a father, if he catches an adulterer of his daughter . . . in his own home or that of his son-in-law, or if the latter summons him in such an affair, is permitted to kill that adulterer with impunity, just as he may forthwith kill his daughter.

A husband also is permitted to kill an adulterer of his wife, but not anyone at all as is the father's right. For this law provides that a husband is permitted to kill [a procurer, actor, gladiator, convicted criminal, freedman, or slave] caught in the act of adultery with his wife in his own home (but not in that of his father-in-law). And it directs a husband who has killed any one of these to divorce his wife without delay. Moreover, he must make a report to the official who has jurisdiction in the place where the killing has occurred and he must divorce his wife; if he does not do this, he does not slay with impunity.

The law punishes as a procurer a husband who retains his wife after she has been caught in adultery and lets the adulterer go (for he ought to be enraged at his wife, who violated his marriage). In such a case the husband should be punished since he cannot claim the excuse of ignorance or feign patience on the pretext of not believing it.

He by whose aid or advice with malice aforethought it is made possible for a man or woman caught in adultery to evade punishment through bribe or any other collusion is condemned to the same penalty as is fixed for those who are convicted of the crime of procuring.

He who makes a profit from the adultery of his wife is scourged. . . . If a wife receives any profit from the adultery of her husband she is liable under the Julian Law as if she were an adultress. . . . Anyone who marries a woman convicted of adultery is liable under this law.

The law prescribes that when notice of divorce has been sent on suspicion of the crime of adultery, the emancipation of slaves who belong to the wife or husband or their parents is to be delayed for a space of two months, reckoned from the date of the divorce, to allow for employing examination under torture if the need arises.

It was enacted that women convicted of adultery be punished by confiscation of half of their dowry and a third of their property and by relegation to an island, and that the male adulterers be punished by like relegation to an island and by confiscation of half of their property, with the proviso that they be relegated to different islands.

THE JULIAN LAW ON CLASSES PERMITTED TO MARRY AND THE PAPIAN-POPPAEAN LAW

Suetonius, *Life of Augustus* xxxiv

Among the laws which he revised or enacted were a sumptuary law and laws on adultery and chastity, on bribery, and on classes permitted to marry. The last of these he amended somewhat more severely than the others, but in the face of the clamor of opposition he was unable to push it through until he had withdrawn or mitigated some of the penalties and increased the rewards. . . . And when he saw that the intent of the law was being evaded by betrothal with immature girls and by frequent changes of wives, he shortened the duration of betrothals[112] and set a limit on divorces.

---

112. He ordered that girls might not be betrothed before the age of ten, and he limited the duration of engagements to a maximum of two years. Tacitus adds (*Annals* III. xxviii) that the rewards offered for successful prosecution of evaders of these laws stimulated the rise of professional spies and informers (cf. volume 2, § 6).

Cassius Dio, *Roman History* LIV. xvi. 1–2; From *LCL*

He laid heavier assessments upon the unmarried men and women and on the other hand offered prizes for marriage and the begetting of children. And since among the nobility there were far more males than females, he allowed all [free men] who wished, except senators, to marry freedwomen, and ordered that their offspring should be held legitimate.

Tacitus, *Annals* III. xxv

Augustus in his old age supplemented the Julian Laws with the Papian– Poppaean Law in order to increase the penalties on celibacy and enrich the treasury. But people were not driven thereby to marriage and the rearing of children in any great numbers, so powerful were the attractions of the childless state. Instead the number of persons courting danger grew steadily greater, for every household was undermined by the denunciations of informers; and now the country suffered from its laws, as it had previously suffered from its vices.

Various legal sources, collected in *ADA*, pp. 166–198 (abridged)

The Julian Law provides as follows: No one who is or shall be a senator, or a son, grandson born of a son, or great-grandson born of a son's son of any one of these, shall knowingly and with malice aforethought have as betrothed or wife a freedwoman or any woman who herself or whose father or mother is or has been an actor. And no daughter of a senator or granddaughter born of a son or great-granddaughter born of a grandson (a son's son) shall knowingly and with malice aforethought be betrothed or married to a freedman or to a man who himself or whose father or mother is or has been an actor, and no such man shall knowingly and with malice aforethought have her as betrothed or wife.

Freeborn men are forbidden to marry a prostitute, a procuress, a woman manumitted by a procurer or procuress, one caught in adultery, one convicted in a public action, or one who has been an actress.

Conditions added contrary to laws and imperial decrees or to morality—such as, "if you do not marry," or "if you have no children"— carry no weight.

In the seventh section of the Julian Law priority in assuming the *fasces* is given not to the consul who is older but to the one who has more children than his colleague either in his power [i.e., minors or unmarried females] or lost in the war. . . . But if both are married and the fathers of the same number of children, then the time-honored practice is restored and the one who is older assumes the *fasces* first.

Persons are exempted from serving as guardians or trustees for various reasons, but generally because of their children, whether they are in the father's power or free from his power. For anyone who has three living children in Rome, or four in Italy, or five in the provinces, can, after the example of the other compulsory public services, be exempted from serving as guardian or trustee.

No freedman who has two or more sons or daughters of his own in his power (excepting one who has been an actor or who has hired out his services to fight with animals) shall be obliged to give, do, or perform for his patron or patroness or their children services as gift or duty, or anything else which he may have sworn, promised, or bound himself to in return for his freedom.

A freedwoman who is married to her patron shall not have the right of divorce . . . as long as the patron wants her to be his wife.

A man or wife can, by virtue of marriage, inherit a tenth of the other's estate. But if they have living children from a previous marriage, in addition to the tenth which they take by virtue of marriage they receive as many tenths as the number of children. Likewise a common son or daughter lost after the day of naming adds one tenth, and two lost after the ninth day add two tenths. Besides the tenth they can receive also the usufruct of a third part of the estate, and whenever they have children the ownership of the same part.

Sometimes a man or wife can inherit the other's entire estate, for example, if both or either are not yet of the age at which the law requires children—that is, if the husband is under twenty-five and the wife under twenty; or if both have while married passed the age prescribed by the Papian Law—that is, the man sixty, the woman fifty. . . . They enjoy testamentary freedom in each other's favor if they have obtained the "right of children" from the emperor, [cf. volume 2, §§ 46, 91], if they have a common son or daughter, or if they have lost a fourteen-year-old son or twelve-year-old daughter or two three-year-olds or three after the day of naming . . . [cf. volume 2, § 64, second selection]. Likewise if the wife has a child by her husband within ten months after his death she takes the whole of his estate.

Sometimes they inherit nothing from each other, that is, if they contract a marriage contrary to the Julian and Papian–Poppaean Law (for example if anyone marries a woman of ill repute or a senator marries a freedwoman).

Bachelors also are forbidden by the Julian Law to receive inheritances or legacies. . . . Likewise by the Papian Law childless persons, precisely because they have no children, lose one half of inheritances and legacies.

The Julian Law exempted women from marriage for one year after the death of a husband and six months after a divorce; the Papian Law [raised these to] two years after the death of a husband and a year and six months after a divorce.

In keeping with the thirty-fifth section of the Julian Law, those who without just cause prevent any children in their power from marrying or refuse to give a dowry . . . are compelled to give them in marriage and bestow dowry.

Since the [passage of the] Papian Law the portion of one who is ineligible lapses and belongs to those named in the will who have children.

If there is no one entitled to the possession of an estate, or if there is someone but he has failed to exercise his right, the estate passes to the public treasury.

205. SOCIAL LEGISLATION: RESTRICTIONS ON MANUMISSION AND CITIZENSHIP

In keeping with his policy of preserving and invigorating the Italian stock as a core of imperial administrators and soldiers (cf. §§ 199, 204), Augustus placed brakes on the traditional practice of granting Roman citizenship to manumitted slaves, establishing at the same time a hierarchy of status in the freedman class. For a variety of reasons there had been an extraordinarily high rate of manumissions, especially of Greeks and Orientals, in the last decades of the Republic and in the early years of the Principate. A large class of freedmen, enjoying actual but not statutory freedom, had come into being through the widespread practice of informal manumission (see volume 2, § 49). By the Junian Law (probably of 17 B.C.) the status of these freedmen was regularized, but they were assigned to a new social category, that of the Junian Latins, who possessed limited civic rights with the opportunity for advancement to full citizenship. Augustus' most important measures for limiting the admission of ex-slaves into the Roman body politic were the Fufian–Caninian Law of 2 B.C., which restricted testamentary manumissions (the commonest of the formal methods of emancipating slaves), and the Aelian–Sentian Law of A.D. 4, which placed checks on the freeing of slaves during the lifetime of their masters and on the acquisition of full citizenship by freedmen. The latter statute also created a new category for freedmen of questionable character, assimilated to the *dediticii peregrini* (surrendered foreigners), who were permanently debarred from Roman citizenship and forbidden to live within one hundred miles of Rome.

THE FREEDMAN PROBLEM: A CONTEMPORARY VIEW

Dionysius of Halicarnassus, *Roman Antiquities* IV. xxiv. 4–8; Adapted from *LCL*

Things have come to such a state of confusion and the noble traditions of the Roman commonwealth have become so debased and sullied that some who have made a fortune by robbery, housebreaking, prostitution, and every other base means, purchase their freedom with the money so acquired and straightway are Romans. Others, who have been confidants and accomplices of their masters in poisonings, murders, and crimes against the gods or the state, receive from them this reward. Some are freed so that they can receive the monthly allowance of grain given at the public expense, or any other largess distributed by the leading men to the poor among the citizens, and bring it to those who have granted them their freedom. And others owe their freedom to the levity of their masters and to their vain thirst for popularity. I, at any rate, know of some men who have allowed all their slaves to be freed after their death, so that when dead they might be called good men and their funerals might be attended by a throng of mourners wearing liberty caps[113] on their heads. . . .

Such great reproaches and disgraces hard to wipe out should not be allowed into the body politic. I should like to see the censors, preferably —or, if not they, then the consuls, for it requires some important magistracy—take this matter in hand, inquiring into those freed each year, who they are and why and how they were freed, just as they inquire into the lives of the *equites* and the senators; after which they should enroll in the tribes such of them as they find worthy of citizenship and allow them to remain in the city, but should expel from the city the foul and corrupt herd.

---

113. The *pilleus*, a cap worn by emancipated slaves as a symbol of their freedom.

THE FUFIAN–CANINIAN LAW

Various legal sources, collected in *ADA*, pp. 202–205

By the Fufian–Caninian Law a limitation on manumitting slaves by will was established. A person who has more than two but not more than ten slaves is permitted to manumit up to one half of this number. And a person who has more than ten but not more than thirty slaves is permitted to manumit up to one third of this number. And a person who has more than thirty but not more than one hundred is given the power of manumitting up to one fourth. Finally, a person who has more than one hundred but not more than five hundred is permitted to manumit not more than one fifth. The law takes no account of a person who has more than five hundred nor does it establish a ratio therefor, but it prescribes that no one is permitted to manumit more than one hundred. On the other hand, if anyone has only one or two slaves, he is not affected by this law, and therefore has unrestricted power of manumission.

If anyone desires to manumit by will more than the above-indicated number entails, the order [in which they are listed] shall be followed, freedom being effective only for those who were named first, up to the number entailed in the explanation outlined above. Similarly, if the names of slaves granted freedom by a will have been written in a circle, none shall be free, since no order of manumission is to be found; for the Fufian–Caninian Law nullifies what has been done to evade the law.

THE AELIAN–SENTIAN LAW

Various legal sources, collected in *ADA*, pp. 205–219 (abridged)

Under the [Aelian–Sentian] Law a master under twenty years of age is not permitted to manumit a slave in any other manner except by the rod[114] after proof of adequate cause for manumission before a council.[115]

When the emperor manumits a slave he does not apply the rod, but at his pleasure a person becomes free who is manumitted in accordance with the law of Augustus.

Moreover, the age requirement for [the manumission] of a slave was

114. A formal method of manumission before a praetor or other competent official; cf. further the introduction to volume 2, § 49.

115. The manumission councils created by this law consisted of five senators and five *equites* in Rome and of twenty Roman citizens in the provinces, chosen by the magistrate who presided at the hearings.

introduced by the Aelian–Sentian Law. For this law did not allow slaves under thirty to become manumitted Roman citizens in any other way except through emancipation by the rod, after proof of adequate cause for manumission before a council.

The same law provides that a slave under thirty years who has been manumitted by the rod shall not become a Roman citizen unless cause has been proved before a council . . . but it stipulates that a person manumitted by will is in the same status as if he were free with the consent of the master, and therefore he becomes a Latin.

In accordance with the Aelian–Sentian Law, anyone under thirty who has been manumitted and has become a Latin, if he marries either a Roman citizen or a Latin colonist or a woman of the same status as himself, and so attests with not less than seven adult Roman citizens as witnesses, and begets a child, when this child reaches the age of one the right is granted him by this law to come before a praetor, or in the provinces before the provincial governor, and prove that, in accordance with the Aelian–Sentian Law, he has married and has a one-year-old child from this marriage; and if the one before whom the case is proved finds that this is so, then the Latin himself and his wife, if she also is of the same status, and the child, if it also is of the same status, are ordained to be Roman citizens.[116]

206. Reinvigoration of Religion

The essence of Augustus' religious policy was an "alliance of the throne and the altar." Chracteristically, he restored the façade of the decaying state religion (cf. § 178), imposing new content upon the old forms, deftly fusing the ancestral state cult and its Hellenic incrustations with the rapidly growing ruler cult (see § 207). Oriental cults were banished from Rome; obsolete priesthoods, religious traditions, and rituals were revived; many temples were restored and new ones built (cf. § 208). Of particular significance was Augustus' elevation of the temple of Apollo on the Palatine Hill (where the imperial palace stood) to a position of importance rivaling that of Jupiter on the Capitoline. The most spectacular manifestation of Augustus' religious policy—and perhaps the most spectacular event in the entire religious history of Rome—was the epochal celebration of the *Ludi Saeculares* (Secular Games) in 17 B.C.[117] This solemn pageant, traditionally

116. The Aelian–Sentian Law also required birth declarations; for examples see volume 2, § 149, third and fourth selections.
117. The Secular Games, last celebrated in 146 B.C., were not held in 46 because of the civil war.

a centennial expiatory rite commemorating the end of an era, was transformed by Augustus into a thanksgiving ceremonial ushering in a new golden age, to coincide with the completion of his basic reforms. And throughout the Empire not only was the traditional toleration of the numerous civic, ethnic, and tribal cults reaffirmed, but respect for and protection of religious practices were fostered.

Suetonius, *Life of Augustus* xxxi. 1–4; Adapted from *LCL*

After he had finally assumed the office of *pontifex maximus* . . . he collected whatever prophetic writings of Greek or Latin origin were in circulation anonymously or under the names of irresponsible authors and burned more than 2,000 of them, retaining only the Sibylline Books and making a selection even among these; and he deposited them in two gilded cases under the pedestal of the Palatine Apollo. . . .[118] He increased the number and prestige of the priests and also their privileges, in particular those of the Vestal Virgins. Moreover, when there was occasion to choose another Vestal in place of one who had died, and when many used all their influence to avoid submitting their daughters to the hazard of the lot, he solemnly swore that if anyone of his granddaughters were of eligible age he would have proposed her name. He also revived some of the ancient rites which had gradually fallen into disuse, such as the augury of safety,[119] the office of the *flamen Dialis,*[120] the ceremonies of the Lupercalia, the Secular Games, and the festival of the crossroads.[121] At the Lupercalia he forbade beardless youths to join in the running, and at the Secular games he would not allow young people of either sex to attend any entertainment by night except in the company of some adult relative. He ordained that the protecting deities of the crossroads should be decorated with flowers twice a year, in spring and summer.[122]

By the convenient discovery of an oracle certifying that the last games had occurred in 126, coupled with the learned advice of Ateius Capito, an eminent jurist and expert on religious law, that the ancient Etruscan *saeculum* (century) was 110 years, the year 17 B.C. was more or less harmonized with the tradition of a centennial celebration.

118. Augustus thus transferred the sacred oracular books from the temple of Jupiter on the Capitol, where they had been stored during the Republic (cf. § 52), to the shrine of the "imperial" god.

119. An ancient augural ceremony conducted annually in times of peace to determine whether it was proper to pray for the safety of the Roman people.

120. Because of the numerous taboos imposed upon this priest of Jupiter (see § 49) no one could be found to fill this office between 87 and 11 B.C.

121. The Compitalia, a festival of the lower classes held at street corner shrines (cf. chapter 8, note 6; volume 2, chapter 3, note 1), had been abolished by Caesar. On the Lupercalia see § 180.

122. This revived cult (cf. note 121) was associated henceforth with the imperial cult.

THE SECULAR GAMES

This huge marble inscription contains the official records of the board of fifteen for performing sacrifices, headed by Augustus and Agrippa, which conducted the Secular Games of 17 B.C. The beginning of the inscription is lost. Of the extant portion, lines 1–49, too fragmentary to warrant translation, contain a letter of Augustus to the board of fifteen informing it of the dates and the arrangements to be made for the celebration, and a series of edicts by the board to the populace announcing the celebration and informing it of arrangements for the distribution of purificatory materials, the offering of first-fruits, and the games, festivals, and sacred banquets to be presented. Next are recorded the two following decrees of the Senate.

CIL, vol. VI, no. 32,323, lines 50–63, 90–168 (= *FIRA*, vol. I, no. 40; = Dessau, no. 5,050)

May 23, in the Julian Voting Hall.[123] . . . Present at the writing were . . . Aemilius Lepidus, Lucius Cestius, and Lucius Petronius Rufus. . . .

Whereas the consul Gaius Silanus reported that after a lapse of many years the Secular Games would be celebrated in the present year under the direction of the Emperor Caesar Augustus and Marcus Agrippa [cf. § 195, paragraph 22], holders of the tribunician power, and that, because as many as possible ought to view these games out of religious duty and also because no one will attend such a spectacle again [i.e., during the lifetime of that generation], it seemed proper to permit . . . those who were not yet married to be present with impunity on the days of these games; and whereas he asked the senate what it was pleased to do in the matter, concerning this matter the senate decreed as follows: Since these games have been ordained for religious purposes and since it is not granted to any mortal to view them more than once . . . those who are liable under the Law on Classes Permitted to Marry[124] shall be permitted to view with impunity the games which the masters of the board of fifteen for performing sacrifices will present.

And on the same day in the same place, the same were present at the writing, and the following decree of the senate was passed.

---

123. Planned by Julius Caesar, this enormous structure was completed by Augustus and Agrippa in 26 B.C. With the obsolescence of the popular assemblies in the early Empire, it was converted to other uses, such as meetings and shows.

124. See § 204. Unmarried men and women were forbidden by this law to attend public spectacles.

Whereas the consul Gaius Silanus declared that it was appropriate for the preservation of the memory of this great benevolence of the gods that a record of the Secular Games be inscribed on a bronze and on a marble column, both to be erected for the future remembrance of the event in the place where the games would be held, and asked the senate what it was pleased to do in the matter, concerning this matter the senate decreed as follows: The consuls, one or both, for the future remembrance of the event shall erect in that place a column of bronze and a second of marble on which a record of these games has been inscribed, and they shall likewise contract for this work and shall order the praetors who are in charge of the treasury[125] to pay to the contractors the sum for which they have contracted.

[Lines 64–75 record another edict of the board, dated May 25, clarifying details of the participation of the populace in the celebration; lines 76–89 describe the distribution of purificatory materials and the offering of firstfruits on May 26–31.]

On the following night[126] in the Campus Martius near the Tiber the Emperor Caesar Augustus sacrificed to the Fates according to the Greek rite[127] nine ewes as whole burnt offerings, and by the same rite nine female goats, and he uttered the following prayer:

"O Fates! As it has been prescribed for ye in those [Sibylline] books —and by virtue of this may every good fortune come to the Roman people, the Quirites—let sacrifice be made to ye with nine ewes and nine female goats. I beseech and pray ye, just as ye have increased the empire and majesty of the Roman people, the Quirites, in war and in peace, so may the Latins ever be obedient; grant everlasting safety, victory, and health to the Roman people, the Quirites; protect the Roman people, the Quirites, and the legions of the Roman people, the Quirites, and keep safe and sound the state of the Roman people, the Quirites; be favorable and propitious to the Roman people, the Quirites, to the board of fifteen, to me, to my house and my household; and deign to accept this sacrifice of nine ewes and nine female goats, perfect for sacrificing. To these ends be ye honored by the sacrifice of this

125. In 23 B.C. Augustus transferred the management of the public treasury from the quaestors, who were usually relatively young men near the beginning of their public careers, to two of the annual praetors, who would be men of greater experience in public office.

126. May 31. Our translation of the remainder of this inscription incorporates restorations based on the similar text in volume 2, § 161.

127. So conducted since the ceremony was ordained by a Sibylline oracle (cf. §§ 52–53), which has been preserved (see Zosimus II. vi). In the inscription the Fates are called by their Greek name.

ewe,[128] become ye favorable and propitious to the Roman people, the Quirites, to the board of fifteen, to me, to my house and my household."[129]

After the sacrifice was completed, the presentation of plays was begun at night on a stage without the addition of a theater and without setting up seats;[130] and 110 matrons,[131] who had been designated by the board of fifteen, held *sellisternia*,[132] setting up two seats for Juno and Diana.

One June 1 in the Capitol the Emperor Caesar Augustus sacrificed a perfect bull to Jupiter Best and Greatest, and in the same place Marcus Agrippa sacrificed another, and they uttered the following prayer:

"O Jupiter Best and Greatest! As it has been prescribed for thee in those books—and by virtue of this may every good fortune come to the Roman people, the Quirites—let sacrifice be made to thee with this splendid bull. I beseech and pray thee," the rest as above.

At the sacral vessel were Caesar, Agrippa, Scaevola, Sentius, Lollius, Asinius Gallus, Rebilus.[133]

Then the presentation of Latin plays was begun in a wooden theater, which had been erected in the Campus Martius along the Tiber; and the mothers of families held *sellisternia* in the same manner; and the theatrical performances which had been begun at night were not interrupted.

[Lines 110–114] contain an edict of the board ordering a suspension of mourning during the celebration.]

Further, at night near the Tiber the Emperor Caesar Augustus made a sacrifice to the *Ilithyiae* [Greek goddesses of childbirth] of nine sacrificial cakes, nine *popana,* and nine *phthoes*[134] and uttered the following prayer:

"O *Ilithyia!* As it has been prescribed for thee in those books—and by virtue of this may every good fortune come to the Roman people,

128. Roman formalism would require the repetition of the prayer for each animal sacrificed.

129. For earlier examples of this archaic formula, see § 54 and p. 157.

130. This was the ancient Roman custom before the erection of formal theaters under Greek influence.

131. One for each year of the Etruscan *saeculum* (cf. note 117).

132. Sacred banquets for female divinities at which their images were seated on chairs. For the similar *lectisternium,* at which images of the gods were placed on couches, see p. 149.

133. Members of the "Board of Fifteen," which, enlarged in keeping with Augustus' policy of increasing the number of priesthoods, had at least twenty-one members at this time.

134. Both of these were special sacrificial cakes of Greek origin.

the Quirites—let sacrifice be made to thee with nine *popana,* nine sacrificial cakes, and nine *phthoes.* I beseech and pray thee," the rest as above.

On June 2 in the Capitol the Emperor Caesar Augustus sacrificed a cow to Queen Juno, and in the same place Marcus Agrippa sacrificed another, and he uttered the following prayer:

"O Queen Juno! As it has been prescribed for thee in those books—and by virtue of this may every good fortune come to the Roman people, the Quirites—let sacrifice be made to thee with a splendid cow. I beseech and pray thee," the rest as above.

Then Marcus Agrippa[?] led the 110 married mothers of families who had been designated by the board of fifteen [?] in the following prayer:

"O Queen Juno! If there be any better fortune that may come to the Roman people, the Quirites . . . we married mothers of families on bended knees beseech and pray [?] thee . . . just as thou hast increased the empire and majesty of the Roman people, the Quirites, in war and in peace, so may the Latins ever be obedient; grant everlasting safety, victory, and health to the Roman people, the Quirites; protect the Roman people, the Quirites, and the legions of the Roman people, the Quirites, and keep safe and sound the state of Roman people, the Quirites; be favorable and propitious to the Roman people, the Quirites, to the board of fifteen for performing sacrifices, to us. . . . This we 110 married mothers of families of the Roman people, the Quirites, on bended knees beseech and pray of thee. . . ."

Further, at night near the Tiber the Emperor Caesar Augustus sacrificed a pregnant sow . . . to Mother Earth and uttered the following prayer:

"O Mother Earth! As it has been prescribed for thee in those books —and by virtue of this may every good fortune come to the Roman people, the Quirites—let sacrifice be made to thee . . . with a perfect pregnant sow. I beseech and pray thee," the rest as above.

The matrons held *sellisternia* on this day in the same manner as on the previous day.

On June 3 on the Palatine the Emperor Caesar Augustus and Marcus Agrippa offered sacrifice to Apollo and Diana with nine sacrificial cakes, nine *popana,* and nine *phthoes,* and they uttered the following prayer:

"O Apollo! As it has been prescribed for thee in those books—and by virtue of this may every good fortune come to the Roman people, the Quirites—let sacrifice be made to thee with nine *popana,* nine sacrificial cakes, and nine *phthoes.* I beseech and pray thee," the rest as above.

"O Apollo! Just as I have offered thee *popana* and have uttered the proper prayer, to this same end be thou honored by the offering of these sacrificial cakes and become favorable and propitious." Likewise with the *phthoes*. [Prayer] to Diana with the same words.

And when the sacrifice was completed, twenty-seven previously designated boys and the same number of girls, with both parents living, sang a hymn [on the Palatine Hill], and in the same manner in the Capitol. The hymn was composed by Quintus Horatius Flaccus.[135]

When the theatrical performances had ended at the . . . hour near the place where the sacrifice had been offered on the previous nights and where the theater and stage had been erected, turn posts were set up and chariot races were presented, and Potitus Messalla presented trick riders.

And an edict was issued as follows:

"The board of fifteen for performing sacrifices declares: We have supplemented the customary games with seven days of additional games, commencing on June 5: Latin plays in the wooden theater which is near the Tiber, at the second hour; Greek informal shows in the theater of Pompey, at the third hour; Greek stage plays in the theater which is in the Circus Flaminius,[136] at the fourth hour. . . ."

On June 11 an edict was issued as follows: "The board of fifteen for performing sacrifices declares: On June 12 we shall present an animal hunt in . . . and circus games . . ." [i.e., chariot races].

All these celebrations were conducted by the board of fifteen for performing sacrifices: the Emperor Caesar Augustus, Marcus Agrippa . . . Gnaeus Pompey, Gaius Stolo, Gaius S . . ., Marcus Marcellus. . . . [The rest is lost.]

PROTECTION OF TEMPLES

This inscription in Greek and Latin contains in the second paragraph a letter from the governor of the province of Asia to the city of Cumae regarding the purchase of a temple by a private individual, and, as a preamble to the letter, a general order issued by Augustus and Agrippa in regard to such matters.

---

135. The famous Secular Hymn by Horace is extant.

136. That is, the theater of Marcellus, which was, however, not fully completed until some years later.

AE, 1979, no. 596 (= *SEG,* vol. XVIII, no. 555); 27 B.C.

The Emperor Caesar Augustus son of the deified [Julius Caesar] and Marcus Agrippa son of Lucius, the consuls, have ordered: In the cities of each province, if there are any public or sacred places belonging to a cult association or a city, and if there are or shall be any votive offerings in these places, no one is to seize, purchase or receive them as security or gift. As for anything removed therefrom or purchased or given if gift, the governor of the province is to see to its restoration to the public or sacred property of the city, and is not to recognize as legal any such thing given in pledge.

The proconsul Lucius(?) Vinicius greets the magistrates of Cumae. Apoleonides Noraceius son of Lucius, one of your citizens, has come and informed me that a shrine of Father Bacchus is, by virtue of a sale, in the possession of Lysias Tucalleus son of Diogenes, one of your citizens, and the cult-association members want to restore the sanctuary to the god, in keeping with the order of Augustus, by paying the price which was inscribed on [the wall of] the shrine of the god Bacchus by Lysias. I order you to see to it that, if it is so, Lysias receive the price which is recorded in the shrine and restore the shrine to the god, and that it is inscribed "The Emperor Caesar Augustus son of the deified restored [this]." But if Lysias opposes what Apollonides demands, I deem it just that Lysias post bond for his undertaking to appear where I shall be.[137]

PROTECTION OF BURIAL PLACES

This Greek inscription, first published in 1930, was reported to have come from Nazareth, though its provenance is uncertain. It has been assigned by most scholars to the time of Augustus, but it may have been issued as much as a century later. In Hellenistic law and in Roman law, at least until the second century B.C. (cf. § 164), violation of sepulture was a civil offense punishable by a monetary fine. Augustus (if indeed the "Caesar" is he), though in so many other matters he continued traditional legal institutions in the eastern provinces of the Empire, in this case sharply increased the rigor of the law. In the Roman imperial period thereafter profanation of cemeteries was treated as a serious crime, with penalties including condemnation to the mines, deportation, and even death. Efforts to connect this edict with Jesus are without substance.

137. That is, at the governor's assizes *(conventus),* on which see volume 2, § 75.

SEG, vol. VIII, no. 13 (=*FIRA*, vol. 1, no. 69)

Ordinance of Caesar. It is my pleasure that graves and tombs prepared
for the cult of ancestors or children or kinsmen shall remain undisturbed
in perpetuity. And if anyone brings information that someone has caused
destruction, or has in any other manner cast out the buried dead, or has
with malice aforethought removed them to other places to the detriment
of the interred, or has removed tombstones or other stones, I order that
such a person be brought to trial for [violating] the cult of [dead]
persons, just as is done in the case of gods. The buried dead must in the
future be accorded much more respect. Absolutely no one shall be
allowed to disturb them. If anyone does, I desire him to be sentenced to
capital punishment for violation of sepulture.

EGYPTIAN CULTS

Though Augustus succeeded Cleopatra as monarch of Egypt in 30 B.C.,
the traditional Egyptian cults continued undisturbed. In addition to the
cults of Sarapis and Isis, this papyrus emphasizes the cult of the goddess
Thoëris, the hippopotamus deity of the town Oxyrhynchus. This is the
earliest extant papyrus of the Roman period; the date is 30/29 B.C.

Oxyrhynchus Papyrus, vol. XII, no. 1453

Copy of oath. Thonis (also called Patoïphis) son of Thonis, and Heraclides
son of Totoës, both lamplighters of the temple of Sarapis, the most great
god, and of the shrine of Isis in the same place, and Paäpis son of Thonis,
and Poëosirir son of the aforementioned Patoïphis, both lamplighters of
the temple of Thoëris at Oxyrhynchus, the most great goddess, all four
swear by Caesar, god, son of a god, swear to Heliodorus son of Heliodorus, and to Heliodorus son of Ptolemaeus, caretakers of the temples
of the Oxyrhynchite and Cynopolite nomes, that we will carefully look
after the lamplighting of the aforementioned temples as prescribed, and
will provide the proper oil for the lamps burning in the indicated temples [for the year] from Thoth 1 to Mesore [intercalary] 5 of the present
first year of Caesar. . . . If I observe the oath may it be well with me, if
I swear falsely, the opposite. First year of Caesar. . . .

PROTECTION OF FREEDOM OF WORSHIP OF JEWS

The Jewish people were under the overlordship and protection of the Romans for about 200 years from the Maccabaeans to the reign of the Roman client king Herod the Great, enjoying the privileges of their monotheistic religion and ancestral customs. They had enjoyed Caesar's favor. Under Augustus, from whose time all the Jews around the Mediterranean were under Roman sovereignty, they continued to receive equality of civic status with the Greeks in the Asiatic provinces. But the privileges of the Jews in the Diaspora were frequently challenged in the provinces by Greek cities, and Roman officials were frequently called upon to reaffirm their status. Sacrifices to Jehovah for the safety and health of Augustus were standard practice. In 15 B.C. Marcus Agrippa visited Jerusalem at the invitation of Herod; there he was hailed with enthusiastic acclaim by the populace and he offered a sacrifice of 100 oxen to the god of the Jews. In 14 B.C. he reaffirmed the privileges of the Jews in the provinces.

Josephus, *Jewish Antiquities* XVI. 162–170

Caesar Augustus, *pontifex maximus* holding the tribunician power . . . , decrees: Whereas the Jewish people have been found well-disposed to the Roman people, not only at the present time but also in the past, and especially in the instance of Hyrcanus, their high priest in the time of my father Imperator Caesar, it was decided by me and my council, in accord with the treaty rights passed by the Roman people, that the Jews are to enjoy their own customs in accordance with their ancestral law, just as they enjoyed them under Hyrcanus the high priest of the Most High God, and that their sacred monies are to be inviolate and transmitted to Jerusalem, and be delivered to the officials of Jerusalem, and that they not have to post bond for appearance in court on the Sabbath or on the day of preparation for it from the ninth hour. And if anyone is caught stealing their sacred books or their sacred monies from a synagogue or from an ark of the Law, he shall be deemed a sacrilegious person, and his property shall be confiscated to the public treasury of the Roman people.

And with regard to the decree granted by them to me on account of the piety I have toward all men . . . , I order it and this edict to be posted in a most conspicuous place, that prepared for me by the pro-

vincial council of Asia in Ancyra. And if anyone violates any of the
aforesaid, he shall suffer a severe penalty. . . .

Agrippa to the magistrates, council and people of the Ephesians,
greeting. It is my will that the Jews in [the province of] Asia, in
accordance with their ancestral custom, should provide for the care and
protection of the sacred monies transmitted to the temple in Jerusalem.
And as for those who steal sacred monies of the Jews and flee to places
of asylum, it is my will that they be removed and handed over to the
Jews, in accordance with the law by which sacrilegious persons are
removed. I have also written to the proconsul Silanus that no one shall
compel a Jew to give sureties for appearance in court on the Sabbath.

Marcus Agrippa to the magistrates, council and people of the
Cyrenaeans, greeting. The Jews of Cyrene . . . appealed to me that they
are being harassed by some informers and are being prevented from
sending their sacred monies on the pretext of taxes due that are not
actually owed. I order that restitution be made to them, and that they
not be molested in any way. And if sacred monies have been removed
from any cities, I order those persons responsible for these matters to
correct them for the Jews there.

207. EMPEROR WORSHIP

The Principate brought with it an important new element in Roman
religion—emperor worship. This institution endured in the form in which
Augustus organized it as long as the Principate itself (cf. volume 2, § 162).
In the eastern provinces Augustus was naturally regarded as the successor
of the divine monarchs of the Oriental and Hellenistic dynasties. Alive to
the centralizing and unifying force of this bond of devotion to the reigning
house, Augustus sanctioned the continuance of the ruler cult in the east by
a series of *ad hoc* directives and fostered its spread in the west in a modified
form that would not clash with Roman religious tradition. When the
passage of time had brought familiarity and acceptance, he was able in 12
B.C., as *pontifex maximus,* to organize the imperial cult as part of the state
worship. In Italy and the west the imperial cult was fitted into Roman
tradition by being devoted not to the living emperor, but to his *genius,* or
tutelary spirit; the emperor himself, after the precedent of Julius Caesar,
was deified after death (cf. § 211). In the Greek-speaking provinces, on the
other hand, Augustus himself was worshipped officially as a god— com-

monly in association with the goddess Roma—from the very beginning of his sole rule. "The different forms the worship of Augustus took in Rome, Italy and the provinces illustrate the different aspects of his rule— he is Princeps to the Senate, Imperator to army and people, King and God to the subject peoples of the Empire" (R. Syme, *The Roman Revolution*, p. 475). There was, however, no formal empirewide cult of the ruler in the Roman Empire. Freedom of worship in a highly polytheistic world was the norm. Provinces, cities, groups, individuals expressed their homage to Augustus at their own will. Often the ruler cult was merely an expression of loyalty and gratitude to the *princeps* and his family, or an act of political and diplomatic expediency, not genuine religious veneration. In Rome and Italy deification came to Augustus posthumously.

Cassius Dio, *Roman History* LI. xx. 6–8; Adapted from *LCL*

Octavian meanwhile, besides attending to the general business, gave permission for sacred precincts to Rome and to his father Caesar, whom he named the hero Julius,[138] to be dedicated in Ephesus and Nicaea. (These cities had at that time attained chief place in Asia and Bithynia, respectively.) And he ordered the Romans resident in these cities to pay honor to these divinities. But the aliens, whom he styled Hellenes, he allowed to consecrate certain precincts to himself—the Asians in Pergamum, the Bithynians in Nicomedia. This practice, beginning under him, has continued under other emperors not only among the Hellenic peoples but also among all the others subject to the Romans. For in the capital itself and in the rest of Italy no emperor, however worthy of renown, has dared to do this; still, even there various divine honors are bestowed after their death upon such emperors as have ruled uprightly, and in fact shrines are even built to them.

NARBO HONORS AUGUSTUS' BIRTHDAY

Altars were erected to the divine spirit *(numen, genius)* of Augustus in various places in Italy and the western provinces. The altar at Narbonne, in southern France, contains two inscriptions, the first celebrating the erection of the altar in A.D. 11, the second its formal dedication in 12/13. The altar is stated to have been erected in gratitude for Augustus' reconciliation of some local class dispute about which no details are given.

138. In Latin *Divus Julius* ("the deified Julius"). The time is 29 B.C.

CIL, vol. XII, no. 4,333 (=Dessau, no. 112)

i

In the consulship of Titus Statilius Taurus and Lucius Cassius Longinus, September 22. Vow taken to the divine spirit of Augustus by the populace of the Narbonensians in perpetuity: "May it be good, favorable, and auspicious to the Emperor Caesar Augustus, son of a god, father of his country, *pontifex maximus,* holding the tribunician power for the thirty-fourth year; to his wife, children, and house; to the Roman senate and people; and to the colonists and residents of the Colonia Julia Paterna of Narbo Martius, who have bound themselves to worship his divine spirit in perpetuity!"

The populace of the Narbonensians has erected in the forum at Narbo an altar at which every year on September 23—the day on which the good fortune of the age bore him to be ruler of the world—three Roman *equites* from the populace [i.e., not members of the local senate][139] and three freedmen shall sacrifice one animal each and shall at their own expense on that day provide the colonists and residents with incense and wine for supplication to his divine spirit. And on September 24[140] they shall likewise provide incense and wine for the colonists and residents. Also on January 1 they shall provide incense and wine for the colonists and residents. Also on January 7, the day on which he first entered upon the command of the world [cf. "Calendar of Holidays," pp. 625–26], they shall make supplication with incense and wine, and shall sacrifice one animal each, and shall provide incense and wine for the colonists and residents on that day. And on May 31, because on that day in the consulship of Titus Statilius Taurus and Manius Aemilius Lepidus[141] he reconciled the populace to the decurions, they shall sacrifice one animal each and shall provide the colonists and residents with incense and wine for supplication to his divine spirit. And of these three Roman *equites* and three freedmen one. . . . [The rest of this inscription is lost.]

139. The animals sacrificed to the *genius* of the emperor were bulls (the characteristic sacrifice to Jupiter, most solemn and most expensive of the sacrifices).

140. The birthday of Augustus was regularly celebrated for two days: cf. the "Calendar of Holidays," § 207. The *genius* was associated with a Roman from birth and was especially honored on his birthday.

141. A.D. 11. Lepidus, consul during the first part of the year, was replaced by Longinus, who is cited at the beginning of the inscription. Since the consulship was largely an honorary office under the Empire, the emperors frequently resorted to this practice of appointing several consuls, each to hold office for a part of the year, as a means of (1) rewarding more men with this honor and (2) providing the requisite number of men of consular rank to fill the high administrative posts.

ii

The populace of Narbo has dedicated the altar of the divine spirit of Augustus . . . under the regulations recorded below.

"O divine spirit of Caesar Augustus, father of his country! When this day I give and dedicate this altar to you, I shall give and dedicate it under such regulations and such rules as I shall here this day publicly declare to be the groundwork both of this altar and of its inscriptions: If anyone wishes to clean, decorate, or repair it as a voluntary service, it shall be lawful and permissible.[142] If anyone sacrifices an animal without making the customary additional offering, it shall nevertheless be accounted properly done. If anyone wishes to donate a gift to this altar or honor it, he shall be permitted, and the same regulation as applies to the altar shall apply to such gift. The other regulations for this altar and its inscriptions shall be the same as those for the altar of Diana on the Aventine Hill. Under these regulations and these rules, just as I have stated, on behalf of the Emperor Caesar Augustus, father of his country, *pontifex maximus,* holding the tribunician power for the thirty-fifth year; of his wife, children, and house; of the Roman senate and people; and of the colonists and residents of the Colonia Julia Paterna of Narbo Martius, who have bound themselves to worship his divine spirit in perpetuity, I give and dedicate this altar to you that you may be favorably and kindly disposed."

ASIA HONORS AUGUSTUS' BIRTHDAY

Beginning in 29 B.C. in the eastern provinces and in 12 B.C. in the west, Augustus authorized the establishment of provincial assemblies. These bodies, organized on a representative basis, possessed no legislative, judicial, or administrative powers. Annual meetings were held at which the principal business was the maintenance of the imperial cult, review of the administration of the governor and procurators, and appeals to the emperor on behalf of the entire province. The following decree was passed (probably in 9 B.C.) by the league of the Greek cities in the province of Asia in response to a letter from the governor suggesting that it would be a suitable token of their gratitude for Augustus' many benefactions if they

---

142. The Latin phrase *ius fas* means that something is in accordance with the laws of man and the dictates of religion, respectively.

adopted his birthday as their New Year's Day. To accomplish this the cities had to realign their Macedonian lunar months in conformity with the Julian solar calendar.

OGIS, no. 458, lines 30–62 (= EJ, no. 98 = *RGDE*, no 65)

It was decreed by the Greeks in the province of Asia, on motion of the high priest Apollonius son of Menophilus, of Azanium: Whereas the providence which divinely ordered our lives created with zeal and munificence the most perfect good for our lives by producing Augustus and filling him with virtue for the benefaction of mankind, blessing us and those after us with a savior who put an end to war and established peace; and whereas Caesar when he appeared exceeded the hopes of all who had anticipated good tidings, not only surpassing the benefactors born before him but not even leaving those to come any hope of surpassing him; and whereas the birthday of the god marked for the world the beginning of the good tidings through his coming, and [the cities of] Asia decreed in Smyrna, when Lucius Volcacius Tullus was high priest and Papias was secretary, that a crown be awarded to the one suggesting the greatest honors for the god; and whereas Paullus Fabius Maximus, proconsul of the province sent for its preservation by that god's right hand and purpose,[143] benefited the province with his own suggestions—the extent of which benefactions no one could succeed in telling adequately—and suggested for the honor of Augustus a thing hitherto unknown by the Greeks, namely, beginning their calendar with the god's nativity;

Therefore—may Good Fortune and Safety attend!—it has been decreed by the Greeks in the province of Asia that the New Year shall begin in all the cities on September 23, which is the birthday of Augustus; that, to be sure that the day corresponds in every city, they use also the Greek date along with the Roman date; that the first month—named Caesar, as previously decreed—be reckoned beginning with September 23, the birthday of Caesar; that the crown decreed for the one suggesting the greatest honors in behalf of Caesar be given to the proconsul Maximus, and that he also be proclaimed in these words at every celebration

---

143. In his equally fulsome letter that evoked this decree, the governor speaks of Augustus coming as, *inter al.*, "the end of men's regretting that they had been born." Similarly, the city of Myra in Lycia hailed him as "the god Augustus Caesar, son of a god, ruler of land and sea, benefactor and savior of the whole world" (*IGRR*, vol. 3, no. 719). Augustus' reorganization of provincial administration (§ 201) had eliminated, if not all, at least the grossest of the abuses of Republican times.

of the athletic games held at Pergamum in honor of Rome and Augustus: "Asia crowns Paullus Fabius Maximus for having most piously invented the honors for Caesar;" that he be proclaimed in like manner also at the games held in the city in honor of Caesar; that the communication of the proconsul and the decree of Asia be inscribed on a stele of white marble, which is to be set up in the sacred precinct of Rome and Augustus [in Pergamum]; and that the public advocates for the year shall see to it that in the leading cities of the assize districts the communication of Maximus and the decree of Asia are inscribed on steles of white marble, and that these steles are set up in the temples of Caesar.

THE MONTH AUGUST

This decree of the Senate, changing the name of the month Sextilis to Augustus, was passed in 27 B.C., but the honor was not officially accepted by the emperor until 8 B.C., when he made some necessary adjustments in the calendar.

Marcrobius, *Saturnalia* I. xii. 35 (=*FIRA*, vol. I, no. 42)

"Whereas in the month Sextilis the Emperor Caesar Augustus entered upon his first consulship and conducted three triumphs into the city, and the legions were brought down from the Janiculum and served under his aegis and oath, and also in this month Egypt was brought into the power of the Roman people, and in this month an end was put to the civil wars; and whereas for these reasons this month is and has been most fortunate for this Empire, the senate decreed that this month be named August." Likewise a plebiscite was passed on the same subject on motion of Sextus Pacuvius, tribune of the plebs.

CALENDAR OF HOLIDAYS

Fragments are extant from some twenty different calendars of Augustan festivals. The following calendar comes from Cumae in Italy and dates probably from some time after A.D. 4. Its list of holidays is representative, not comprehensive; many others are recorded in other *fasti*. Cities often honored Augustus by making the day of his visit their New Year, and this may be the reason why this calendar begins in August.

CIL, vol. X, no. 8,375 (= Dessau, no. 108)

August 19. On this day [in 43 B.C.] Caesar entered upon his first consulship. Thanksgiving.

September . . .[144] On this day [in 36 B.C.] the army of Lepidus surrendered to Caesar. Thanksgiving.

September 23 and 24. Birthday of Caesar [63 B.C.] Sacrifice of an animal to Caesar. Thanksgiving.

October 7. Birthday of Drusus Caesar [15–11 B.C.]. Thanksgiving to Vesta.

October 18 [or 19th]. On this day [in 48 B.C.?] Caesar assumed the toga of manhood. Thanksgiving to Hope and Youth.

November 16. Birthday of Tiberius Caesar [42 B.C.]. Thanksgiving to Vesta.

December 15. On this day [in 19 B.C.] the altar of Fortune the Homebringer, who brought Caesar back from the overseas provinces, was dedicated. Thanksgiving to Fortune the Home-bringer.

January 7. On this day [in 43 B.C.] Caesar first assumed the *fasces*. Thanksgiving to Jupiter the Eternal.

January 16. On this day [in 27 B.C.] Caesar was named Augustus. Thanksgiving to Augustus.

January 30. On this day [in 9 B.C.] the Altar of the Augustan Peace was dedicated. Thanksgiving to the sovereignty of Caesar Augustus, guardian of the Roman citizens and of the world.

March 6. On this day [in 12 B.C.] Caesar was elected *pontifex maximus*. Thanksgiving to Vesta and to the public household gods of the Roman people, the Quirites.

April 14. On this day [in 43 B.C.] Caesar won his first military victory. Thanksgiving to Augustan Victory.

April 16. On this day [in 43 B.C.] Caesar was first acclaimed *imperator*. Thanksgiving to the Good Fortune of his rule.

May 12. On this day [in 19 B.C.] the temple of Mars was dedicated. Thanksgiving to the Labors of Mars.

May 24. Birthday of Germanicus Caesar [15 B.C.]. Thanksgiving to Vesta.

July 12. Birthday of the deified Julius [Caesar. 100 B.C.]. Thanksgiving to Jupiter, to Mars the Avenger, and to Venus the Procreator.

[The rest of the inscription is too framentary for restoration.]

---

144. Some day between the 4th and the 22d.

ASIA MOURNS THE GOD AUGUSTUS

This inscription, found at Halicarnassus in the province of Asia, is a copy
of a decree of the provincial council passed probably in A.D. 15, shortly
after the death of Augustus.

EJ, no. 98a

It was decreed by the Greeks in Asia on motion of Gaius Julius M . . . ,
loyal to the emperor, high priest of the goddess Roma and Imperator
Caesar Augustus, son of a god, *pontifex maximus,* father of his country
and of the whole world:

Whereas the immortal and eternal nature of the universe, in addition
to other immense benefactions, has bestowed the greatest good upon
mankind by producing Caesar Augustus for a happy life for us, the
father of his own country, namely the Goddess Roma, Zeus Patroos and
the savior of the whole human race; and whereas his providence has not
only fulfilled the vows of all, but exceeded them . . . for peace has been
brought to land and sea, cities flourish, well governed, harmonious and
prosperous, and there is prosperity and the peak of all that is good; and
whereas there are high hopes for the future, good cheer in the present,
with men showing their loyalty in full measure with games, poems,
sacrifices and hymns. . . . [The rest is lost.]

208. PUBLIC WORKS

On Augustus' public works see § 195, paragraphs 19–21. The construction of public works at their own expense was a traditional practice of
prominent citizens under the Republic. Augustus, actively assisted by his
associates (notably Agrippa), carried on this tradition with unprecedented
splendor and munificence. He thereby established a precedent for future
emperors, who bestowed innumerable adornments and improvements—
aqueducts, harbors, temples, colonnades, streets, markets, arches, etc.
(many of them still standing)—upon the city of Rome, Italy, and the
provinces (cf. also volume 2, § 22).

VITRUVIUS' DEDICATION TO AUGUSTUS

Vitruvius, *Architecture* I. Preface 2–3; From *LCL*

I observed that you cared not only about the common life of men and the constitution of the state but also about the provision of suitable buildings; so that the state was not only made greater through you by its new provinces, but the majesty of the empire also was expressed through the eminent dignity of its public buildings. Hence I conceived that the opportunity should be taken at once of bringing before you my proposals about such things. . . .

Since, then, I was indebted to you for such benefits that to the end of my life I had no fear of poverty, I set about the composition of this work for you. For I perceived that you have built, and are now building, on a large scale. Furthermore, with respect to the future, you have such regard to public and private buildings that they will correspond to the grandeur of our history, and will be a memorial to future ages.

"A CITY OF MARBLE"

Suetonius, *Life of Augustus* xxviii. 3–xxx. 2; *Adapted from LCL*

Since the city was not adorned as befitted the majesty of the empire and was exposed to flood and fire, he so beautified it that he could justly boast that he had found it a city of brick and left it a city of marble,[145] and he certainly made it safe for the future, so far as human foresight could provide.

He erected many public works, foremost among them the following: his Forum, with the Temple of Mars the Avenger; the Sanctuary of Apollo on the Palatine; and the Temple of Jupiter the Thunderer on the Capitol. His reason for building the Forum was the increase in the number of people and the lawsuits, which seemed to call for still a third Forum, since two[146] were no longer adequate. . . . He vowed the Temple of Mars when he undertook the war of Philippi to avenge his father; accordingly, he decreed that in it the senate should deliberate on wars and requests for triumphs, from it men on their way to the provinces and military commands should be escorted, and to it victors on their return should bring the tokens of their triumphs. He erected the Sanc-

---

145. This is, of course, a rhetorical exaggeration.
146. That is, the original Roman Forum and the adjacent Forum of Julius Caesar.

tuary of Apollo in that part of his abode on the Palatine for which the soothsayers declared that the god had shown his desire by striking it with lightning; and he joined to it colonnades with Latin and Greek libraries, and when he was getting to be an old man it was there that he often held meetings of the senate or certified the panels of jurors. He dedicated the temple to Jupiter the Thunderer because of a narrow escape; for on his Cantabrian expedition during a march by night a flash of lighting grazed his litter and struck dead the slave who was lighting the way. He constructed some works too in the name of others—his grandsons, his wife, and his sister—such as the colonnade and basilica of Gaius and Lucius, the colonnades of Livia and Octavia, and the theater of Marcellus. More than that, he often urged other prominent men to adorn the city with new monuments or to restore and embellish old ones, each according to his means. And many works were erected at that time by many men: for example, the Temple of Hercules and the Muses by Marcius Philippus, the Temple of Diana by Lucius Cornificius, the Hall of Liberty of Asinius Pollio, the Temple of Saturn by Munatius Plancus, a theater by Cornelius Balbus, an amphitheater by Statilius Taurus, and by Marcus Agrippa in particular many magnificent structures.

He divided the area of the city into districts and neighborhoods and arranged that the former should be under the charge of annual magistrates selected by lot and the latter under captains elected by the people of the respective neighborhoods. To guard against fires he devised a system of stations of night watchmen [see § 198], and to control the floods he widened and cleared out the bed of the Tiber, which had for some time been filled with rubbish and narrowed by jutting buildings. Further, to make the approach to the city easier from every direction, he personally undertook to rebuild the Flaminian Road as far as Ariminum and assigned the rest of the highways to men who had been honored with triumphs to pave out of their spoils money.

He restored sacred edifices which had gone to ruin through lapse of time or had been destroyed by fire and adorned both these and the other temples with most lavish gifts; for example, in a single donation he deposited in the shrine of Jupiter Capitolinus 16,000 pounds of gold and precious stones and pearls worth 50,000,000 sesterces.

THE ADMINISTRATION OF THE AQUEDUCTS

Frontinus, *The Water Supply of Rome* II. xcviii–cxxix (abridged)

First Marcus Agrippa, after his aedileship (which he held after his consulship), served as a sort of permanent commissioner of works and services which he himself had created.[147] Inasmuch as the available supply now warranted it, he determined how much water should be allotted to the public structures, how much to the collection basins, and how much to private consumers. He also kept his own private gang of slaves for the maintenance of the aqueducts, reservoirs, and collection basins. This gang was given to the state as its property by Augustus, who had inherited it from Agrippa.

After him, in the consulship of Quintus Aelius Tubero and Paullus Fabius Maximus [11 B.C.], decrees of the senate were passed and a law was promulgated on this subject. . . . Augustus also subsumed in an edict the rights to be enjoyed by those drawing water according to Agrippa's records, thus making the whole matter subject to his own grants. . . .

I shall now indicate what the water commissioner must attend to, and the law and decrees of the senate which serve to establish his procedures. With regard to the right of drawing water in private establishments he must see that no one draws water without a written authorization from Caesar—that is, that no one draws public water which he has not been authorized to and that no one draws more than he has been authorized to. . . . He must exercise great vigilance against manifold forms of fraud. The channels outside the city must be frequently inspected with great care to check on the granted quantities. The same must be done in the case of the reservoirs and the public fountains, so that the water may flow day and night without interruption. . . .

The right to granted water does not pass [automatically] to an heir, a buyer, or any new owner of the property. But public baths long ago received the privilege that water once granted them should remain theirs in perpetuity. . . .

No one doubts, I am sure, that the aqueducts nearest the city—that

147. In 33 B.C. Agrippa undertook the aedileship in order to help win over the Roman populace to the side of Octavian against Antony. Among his vast expenditures of that year (cf. § 172), he repaired and enlarged the water supply of Rome. Thereafter, Agrippa maintained unofficial supervision of the Roman aqueducts until his death in 12 B.C. The office of commissioner of water supply was created the following year (cf. the next paragraph); some of the pertinent legislation of that year is cited herein.

is, the last seven miles, which are built of squared-stone masonry—must be especially protected, both because they are structures of the greatest magnitude and because each one carries several water courses. If it is ever necessary to interrupt these, they will deprive the city of the greater part of its water supply. But there are remedies even for this difficulty: a temporary structure is built up to the level of the inoperative aqueduct and a channel made of lead troughs is connected to by-pass the interrupted section. . . .

Very often, moreover, damages arise from illegal acts of property owners who injure the channels in numerous ways. In the first place, they obstruct the space around the aqueducts, which by decree of the senate is to be kept clear, with buildings or trees (the trees do the greater damage, because their roots break apart the vaultings and the sides). Again, they run local and country roads right over the aqueducts themselves. Finally, they shut off access for maintenance and repairs. All such acts have been provided against in decrees of the senate.[148]

209. THE HELPERS OF AUGUSTUS

MAECENAS

A trusted friend and counselor, who preferred to remain in the equestrian order, Maecenas was Augustus' representative in matters involving personal and political disputes. Maecenas was also the leading patron of letters during the Augustan Age. Vergil, Horace, Propertius, and several other major and minor figures of the period were members of his literary circle.

Cassius Dio, *History of Rome* LV. vii. 1–5

Augustus lamented the passing of Maecenas [8 B.C.], for he had received many benefits from him, and for this reason he had entrusted to him (although he was a member of the equestrian order) the city's administration for an extended period. Maecenas was particularly serviceable to him in view of his uncontrollable temper. For he was always able to dispel his anger and turn him to a gentler mood. . . . In fact, he was not at all annoyed at such actions, but was actually happy, for whenever he

---

148. One decree (quoted by Frontinus II. cxxv) mentions that Augustus, following Agrippa's example, undertook to defray the cost of aqueduct repairs from his own privy purse (cf. § 195, paragraph 20).

became unduly angered because of his nature or the press of affairs these were corrected by the freedom of speech of his friends. This was the supreme proof of Maecenas's excellence, that he ingratiated himself with Augustus although he countered his impulsive actions and pleased all the others. Maecenas was particularly influential with him, so that he was able to obtain for many men offices and political power; though pretentious, he remained to the end of his life in the equestrian order. For these reasons Augustus missed him very much, and also because Maecenas, although he was annoyed at his wife's affair with Augustus, left his entire estate to him.

MARCUS AGRIPPA

For three decades, until his sudden death at the age of fifty-one, Agrippa was the closest friend and associate of Augustus. A "new man", like many others in Augustus's entourage, he distinguished himself as a famed general and Rome's greatest admiral, provincial administrator, imperial geographer, and city-planner and builder. In 21 B.C. he married Julia, Augustus's only child, becoming not only the son-in-law of the *princeps* but also presumptive successor, occupying the position of "vice emperor." His great fortune was expended largely in building up and adorning the capital city (see §§ 172, 208) and on benefactions to many other cities in Italy and the Empire. At his death in 12 B.C. the buoyancy and dynamism of the new order began to fade away. It was said of Agrippa later that he "was the only one of all whom the civil wars had made famous and powerful who was felicitous for the public good" (Seneca, *Moral Epistles* lxxxxiv. 46).

Cassius Dio, *History of Rome* LIV. xxviii. 1–xxix. 2

Meanwhile Augustus enhanced the status of Agrippa, who had come back from Syria, by giving him the tribunician power again for another five years, and sent him out to Pannonia, which was on the verge of war, granting him *imperium* greater than that of officials everywhere outside of Italy. . . . Agrippa returned [from Pannonia], and when he was in Campania he fell ill. Learning of this, Augustus . . . set out, and finding him already dead, he had his body carried to the city, and caused it to lie in state in the Forum. He spoke the eulogy over him, with a curtain hanging in front of the corpse. And he conducted his funeral in the same manner in which his own was later conducted, and he buried him in his own mausoleum, even though Agrippa had provided his own in the Campus Martius.

Such was the end of Agrippa, who had become clearly in every way the noblest man of his time, and used the friendship of Augustus for the greatest advantage to Augustus himself and to the country. For the more he surpassed others in virtue, the more he voluntarily kept himself below Augustus, and, devoting all his wisdom and valor to the highest advantage of Augustus, he expended all the power and honor he received from him upon benefactions to others.

FUNERAL ORATION OF AUGUSTUS OVER AGRIPPA

A papyrus fragment found in Egypt contains part of a Greek translation of the oration that Augustus pronounced at the funeral of his son-in-law and associate-*princeps*.

Cologne Papyrus 10 + *Zeitschrift für Papyrologie und Epigraphik* (1983), 52: 60–62

. . . The tribunician power was given to you for five years by decree of the senate in the consulship of the two Lentuli [18 B.C.]. And again the same power was granted to you for a second five-year term in the consulship of Tiberius Nero and Quinctilius Varus [12 B.C.], your sons-in-law.[149] And it was confirmed by a law that into whatever province the affairs of the Roman people might take you, no one in those provinces should have greater power than you. But you rose to the summit by my favor, by your own virtues, and by the consensus of all men.

[The rest is too fragmentary to yield continuous sense.]

210. PROVISION FOR THE SUCCESSION

Augustus' carefully laid plans to hand on the Principate in a direct line of descent were frustrated by a series of premature deaths which in the end left his wife's son, Tiberius Claudius Nero, as the nearest reliable person to whom he could turn for a successor. A further irony is the fact that, whereas Augustus' successor was not a descendant of his, less than thirty years after his death a grandson of Mark Antony ascended the throne as the Emperor Claudius.

149. Tiberius was married to Vipsania Agrippina, a child of Agrippa's first marriage. Publius Quinctilius Varus was married either to her sister or to a daughter of Agrippa's (second) marriage to Claudia Marcella.

AUGUSTUS' DYNASTIC POLICY

Tacitus, Annals I. iii. 1–5

To consolidate his control Augustus raised his sister's son Claudius Marcellus, who was still a mere stripling,[150] to the pontificate and curule aedileship, and Marcus Agrippa, not a noble by birth but a good soldier and his partner in victory, to two consecutive consulships. On Marcellus' death soon afterward,[151] he took Agrippa as his son-in-law. His stepsons, Tiberius Nero and Claudius Drusus, he honored with imperial titles, even though his own family was still intact—for he had admitted Agrippa's children, Gaius and Lucius, into the house of the Caesars, and even before they had laid aside the purple-bordered toga of boyhood he had had a consuming desire, beneath a pretense of reluctance, to have them named leaders of the youth and consuls designate.[152] After Agrippa departed his life and premature death (or their stepmother Livia's treachery)[153] cut off Lucius and Gaius Caesar—the former while on his way to our armies in Spain, the latter while returning, weakened by a wound, from Armenia—since Drusus had long since perished, Nero alone remained of the stepsons, and everything centered on him.[154] He was adopted as a son, as colleague in *imperium,* as associate in the tribunician power, and was paraded before all the armies. . . . But in addition, mind you, in order to provide himself with additional safeguards, Augustus

150. Marcellus' marriage to Augustus' only child, Julia, did not produce any children.

151. In 23 B.C. Two years after Marcellus' death Julia was married to Agrippa, who, to further Augustus' dynastic purpose divorced his second wife—Augustus' niece Marcella—whom he had married some eight years before and who had already borne him children. At the time of their marriage Julia was about eighteen years old, Agrippa was slightly older than her father. This marriage produced five children.

152. Gaius and Lucius Caesar, the two oldest sons of Julia and Agrippa, were born in 20 and 17 B.C., respectively, and were formally adopted by Augustus in the latter year. The honors mentioned here were accorded them when they came of age in 5 and 2 B.C., respectively. A letter is extant (in Aulus Gellius, *Attic Nights* XV. vii. 3) in which Augustus, writing to Gaius in A.D. 1, remarks, "I pray the gods that I may be permitted to pass whatever time is left me with us all in good health and the state flourishing, while you learn to play the part of upright men and prepare to succeed to my position."

153. An allegation, for which there is no evidence, of the type that proliferated in the atmosphere of dynastic aspiration and intrigue characteristic of the Empire.

154. Agrippa died in 12 B.C., Drusus in 9 B.C., Lucius Caesar in A.D. 2, and Gaius Caesar in A.D. 4. Tiberius was adopted by Augustus in A.D. 4, four months after the last of those deaths. The clause of his will (recorded in Suetonius *Life of Tiberius* xxiii) in which he named Tiberius as his heir reveals the bitter frustration of Augustus' dynastic hopes: "Since a cruel fortune has snatched from me my sons Gaius and Lucius, Tiberius Caesar is to be my heir to two thirds of my estate."

placed Drusus' son Germanicus in command of the eight legions on the Rhine and ordered Tiberius to adopt him, even though there was a grown son in Tiberius' house.

RESOLUTION ON THE COMING OF AGE
OF GAIUS CAESAR

When Gaius and Lucius Caesar, the grandsons whom Augustus adopted as his sons and heirs apparent, reached the age of fifteen and assumed the toga of manhood, the cities of the Roman Empire resounded with ringing resolutions of public joy. The following inscription was erected at Sardis in 5 B.C.

IGRR, vol. IV, no. 1,756, lines 6–27 (= EJ, no. 99)

On motion of the *strategi* Metrodorus son of Conon, Clinius, Musaeus, and Dionysius—

Whereas Gaius Julius Caesar, the eldest of the sons of Augustus has —as has been fervently prayed for—assumed in all its splendor the pure-white toga [of manhood] in place of the purple-bordered toga [of youth], and all men rejoice to see the prayers for his sons rising together to Augustus;

And whereas our city in view of so happy an event has decided to keep the day which raised him from a boy to a man as a holy day, on which annually all shall wear wreaths and festal garb, and the annual *strategi* shall offer sacrifices to the gods and render prayers through the sacred heralds for his preservation; to unite in consecrating an image of him set up in his father's temple; also on the day on which the city received the good news and the decree was ratified, to wear wreaths and perform most sumptuous sacrifices to the gods; and to send an embassy concerning these matters to go to Rome to congratulate him and Augustus;

Therefore it was resolved by the council and the people to dispatch envoys chosen from the most distinguished men for the purpose of bringing greetings from the city, of delivering to him the copy of this decree sealed with the public seal, and of discussing with Augustus the common interests of the province of Asia and of the city. . . .

The Emperor Caesar Augustus, son of a god, *pontifex maximus,* holding the tribunician power for the nineteenth year, to the chief magistrates and council of Sardis, greeting. Your envoys, Iollas son of Metrodorus and Menogenes son of Isidorus, grandson of Menogenes, had an audience with me in Rome and presented me with the decree sent by you in which you make known your resolutions concerning yourselves and express your joy on the coming to manhood of the elder of my sons. I commend you, therefore, for your earnest endeavor to demonstrate your gratitude to me and all my house for the benefits you receive from me. Farewell.

RESOLUTION ON THE DEATH OF GAIUS CAESAR

The untimely deaths of Augustus' adopted sons evoked extravagant manifestations of patriotic grief throughout the Empire. The following is the resolution passed by the town council of Pisa on the death of Gaius Caesar in A.D. 4 (the parallel resolution adopted two years earlier for Lucius Caesar is also extant: *CIL,* vol. XI, no. 1,420 = Dessau, no. 139). We omit the introduction of the resolution, which follows the form used by the senate at Rome for its decrees.

CIL, vol. XI, no. 1,421 (= Dessau, no. 140)

Whereas observations were made that the actions recorded below were taken when there were no magistrates in our colony on account of the election campaign—

Since on April 2 the news reached us that Gaius Caesar, son of Augustus (father of his country, *pontifex maximus,* guardian of the Roman Empire and protector of the whole world), grandson of a god— after the consulship which he had auspiciously completed by waging war beyond the farthest dominions of the Roman people and after he had administered the state well and had conquered or received under our protection most warlike and mighty peoples—had been wounded defending the state and had as a result of this mischance been snatched by cruel fates from the Roman people when he had already been designated *princeps* most just and most like his father in virtues, and sole protector of our colony; and since this event, coming when the mourning had not yet subsided which the entire colony had undertaken as a result of the death of his brother Lucius Caesar, consul designate, augur, our patron, leader of the youth, has renewed and increased the grief of all, individually and collectively;

For these reasons, all the decurions and colonists (since at the time of this misfortune there were in the colony no duovirs or prefects or anyone in charge of the administration of justice) agreed, in consideration of the magnitude of so great and unexpected a calamity, that from the day on which his death was announced to the day on which his bones are brought back and buried and the due rites are performed to his departed spirit all should wear mourning, keep the temples of the immortal gods, the public baths, and all shops closed, and abstain from festivity, and the matrons in our colony should make public lamentation; that the day on which Gaius Caesar died, viz., February 21, should go down in history and be observed at the present time by order and wish of all as a day of mourning like that of the Allia [cf. p. 79], and that it should be expressly forbidden to hold, plan, or announce for or on that day, viz., February 21, any public sacrifice, thanksgivings, weddings, or public banquets or to hold or view on that day any theatrical performances or circus games; that every year on that day solemn public sacrifice shall be offered to his departed spirit by the magistrates or by those who are in charge of the administration of justice at Pisa in the same place and in the same manner as the solemn sacrifice established in honor of Lucius Caesar; that an arch adorned with the spoils of the peoples conquered or received under our protection by him shall be erected in a much-frequented place in our colony, and that upon it shall be placed a statue of him standing in his triumphal attire and, flanking this, two gilded equestrian statues of Gaius and Lucius Caesar; that, as soon as we can lawfully elect and have duovirs for the colony, the first duovirs elected shall submit this decision of the decurions and all the colonists to the [body of] decurions so that it may be legally enacted by the exercise of their public authority and entered by their authorization in the public records; and that meanwhile Titus Statulenus Juncus, flamen of Augustus, *pontifex minor* of the public worship of the Roman people, shall be requested to go with envoys, explain the present unavoidable circumstances of the colony, and report this proper public action and disposition of all by delivering a notification to the Emperor Caesar Augustus, father of his country, *pontifex maximus,* holding the tribunician power for the twenty-sixth year (and this Titus Statulenus Juncus, leader of our colony, flamen of Augustus, *pontifex minor* of the public worship of the Roman people, has done, delivering the notification, as stated above, to the Emperor Caesar Augustus, *pontifex maximus,* holding the tribunician power for the twenty-sixth year, father of his country).

It is hereby decreed by the decurions that all that was done, enacted, and decided by the unanimous agreement of all classes on April 2 in the consulship of Sextus Aelius Catus and Gaius Sentius Saturninus, shall be so done, carried out, conducted, and observed by Lucius Titius son of Aulus and by Titus Allius Rufus son of Titus, the duovirs, and by whoever hereafter shall be duovirs, prefect, or any other magistrates in our colony, and that all these things shall be done, carried out, conducted, and observed in perpetuity; and that Lucius Titius son of Aulus and Titus Allius Rufus son of Titus, the duovirs, shall see to it that everything recorded above shall in accordance with our decree be in the presence of the proquaestors entered by the town clerk in the public records at the earliest opportunity. Adopted.

THE WILL AND LAST DOCUMENTS OF AUGUSTUS

Cassius Dio, *Roman History* LVI. xxx. 5–xxxiii. 5 (abridged)

On the 19th of August, the day on which he had first become consul, he passed away. He lived 75 years, 10 months, and 26 days (he had been born on the 23d of September) and was sole ruler, from the time of his victory at Actium, 44 years less 13 days. . . . The body of Augustus was borne from Nola by the leading men of each city in succession, and when it reached the outskirts of Rome the *equites* received it and conveyed it by night into the city.

The next day there was a meeting of the senate. . . . Drusus took his will from the Vestal Virgins, with whom it had been deposited, and brought it into the senate. Those who had witnessed the document examined their seals, and then it was read in the hearing of the senate. . . . Polybius, an imperial freedman, read the will, as it was not proper for a senator to perform any such function. In it, according to some, two thirds of the inheritance was left to Tiberius and the remainder to Livia; for, in order that she too might have some enjoyment of his estate, he had asked the senate for permission to leave her so much, which was more than the amount allowed by law.[155] These two, then, were named as heirs. He also directed that many articles and sums of money should be given to many persons related and unrelated to him, not only to senators and *equites* but also to kings; to the people he left

---

155. The Voconian Law of 169 B.C. allowed a woman to inherit a maximum of 100,000 sesterces. In addition, Livia was by the will admitted into the Julian family with the name of Augusta (Suetonius, *Life of Augustus* ci).

40,000,000 sesterces,[156] and to the soldiers 1,000 sesterces apiece to the Praetorians, half that amount to the city guard, and 300 each to the rest of the citizen soldiery.[157] Moreover, he ordered that to the children whose patrimony he had inherited while they were still small the whole amount should be paid back with accumulated interest when they reached manhood. (This, in fact, had been his practice even in his lifetime; for whenever he succeeded to the estate of anyone who had offspring he would restore it all to the man's children, immediately if they were already grown up, otherwise later.) Nevertheless, though such was his attitude toward the children of others, he did not restore his own daughter from exile,[158] although he did hold her worthy of bequests, and he instructed that she should not be buried in his own mausoleum. So much was made clear by the will.

Four more documents were then brought in, and Drusus read them. In the first were written detailed instructions for his funeral. In the second, which moreover he ordered to be inscribed on bronze tablets to be set up in front of his mausoleum, were recorded all the acts which he had performed.[159] The third contained an account of military matters, of the public revenues and expenditures, the amount of money in the treasuries,[160] and all other such matters relating to the Empire. The fourth contained commands and injunctions for Tiberius and for the public, such as not to free many slaves, lest they fill the city with a promiscuous rabble, and not to naturalize large numbers of citizens, so that there should be a marked difference between themselves and their subjects [cf. § 205]. He exhorted them to entrust the public business to all men of intellectual and practical ability and not to let it depend on any one person; in this way no one would set his mind on absolutism, nor would the state, on the other hand, go to ruin if one man fell. He advised them to be satisfied with the *status quo* and to suppress completely any desire to increase the Empire to greater size; for then, he said, it would be difficult to guard, and as a result they would run the risk of losing what they already had [cf. § 204].

---

156. Suetonius (*Life of Augustus* ci) mentions in addition a bequest to the tribes of 3,500,000 sesterces. The individual legacies, he reports, ran as high as 20,000 sesterces.

157. That is, the legionaries, see the introduction to vol. 2, § 150.

158. In 2 B.C., in keeping with his social legislation (cf. § 204), Augustus banished his notorious daughter Julia for adultery. Political as well as moral considerations may have been involved.

159. This document, the only one of the four that has been preserved, is the famous "Accomplishments of Augustus" (§ 195).

160. That is, the state treasury (*aerarium*) and the emperor's privy purse (*fiscus*).

211. THE DEIFICATION OF AUGUSTUS

Cassius Dio, *Roman History* LVI. xlvi; Adapted from *LCL*

[The senate[161]] declared Augustus immortal, assigned to him a college
of priests and sacred rites, and made Livia, who was already called Julia
and Augusta [cf. note 155], his priestess; they also permitted her to
employ a lictor when she exercised her sacred office. On her part, she
bestowed a million sesterces upon a certain Numerius Atticus, a senator
and ex-praetor, because he swore that he had seen Augustus ascending
to heaven in the manner of the traditions concerning Proculus and
Romulus.[162] A shrine voted by the senate and built by Livia and Tiberius
was erected to him in Rome, and others in many different places, some
of the communities building them voluntarily and others unwillingly.
Also the house at Nola where he passed away was made a precinct
sacred to him. While his shrine in Rome was being erected, they placed
a golden image of him on a couch in the temple of Mars and to this they
paid all the honors that they were afterwards to give to his statue. Other
honors voted him were that his image should not be borne in anybody's
funeral procession, that the consuls should celebrate his birthday with
games like those in honor of Mars, and that the tribunes of the plebs,
since they were sacrosanct, should manage these Augustan Games. These
officials conducted everything in the customary manner. . . . Besides
this Livia had a private festival in his honor for three days in the palace,
and this ceremony is still continued down to the present day by whoever
is emperor.

161. Meeting on September 17, five of six days after the funeral.
162. The legend was that Julius Proculus, a Roman senator, declared that Romulus had appeared
to him shortly after his death as the god Quirinus.

10

COINS

In the fifth century B.C. (or possibly earlier) bronze began to be used in central Italy as a medium of exchange valued by weight. The first Roman coins, didrachmas, modeled on the Italo-Greek coinages of southern Italy, were issued c. 300 B.C. In the second century an annually elected board of "three men for the casting and striking of bronze, silver, and gold" was created to control the issuance of the currency. For particular needs the right to coin money was sometimes delegated to—or, in the tumultuous years of the dying Republic, arrogated by—other magistrates, such as quaestors and praetors. Additionally, special issues were decreed by the senate for special purposes.

Under Augustus the mints and the entire monetary system were reorganized. From then on the emperor issued the gold and silver coinage, leaving the bronze to be authorized by the senate on his recommendations.

Under these circumstances there was a constant, virtually annual change in coin types and in their pictorial images and legends. The moneyers of the Republic, members of the senatorial nobility, took to using coins as vehicles for spreading family and personal renown or for recording religious themes or political messages. In the first century B.C. the Roman dynasts began to use the coins for blatant self-advertising, and beginning with Julius Caesar personal portraiture appears on Roman coinage. But it was Octavian/Augustus who proved himself to be the world's first great master of the art of political propaganda, which he spread through coins, as well as through the written word and sculpture and architecture. Under his reign coinage became a systematic instrument of policy to mold public opinion with a myriad of messages of imperial achievements, policies, and promises.

Legends are given in capital letters, as they appear on the coins. OBV. = obverse, REV. = reverse, r. = facing right, l. = facing left.

c. 300 B.C. Silver
   OBV. Helmeted head of bearded Mars l.
   REV. Horse's head r. OF THE ROMANS

c. 300 B.C. Bronze
   OBV. Head of Apollo or helmeted head of Minerva r.
   REV. Man-headed bull r. OF THE ROMANS [in Greek or Latin]

c. 274 B.C. Cast bronze bar weighing c. 6.5 lb.
   OBV. Elephant r.
   REV. Sow l.

This issue commemorates the Romans' first encounter with elephants in the war with Pyrrhus. According to one tradition the elephants were frightened by the grunting of the Romans' swine.

211–200 B.C. Silver
   OBV. Helmeted head of goddess Roma r.
   REV. Castor and Pollux on horseback charging with spears r.

This issue celebrates the protection of the Dioscuri in the defeat of Hannibal.

c. 197 B.C. Gold
   OBV. Bearded head of Flamininus r.
   REV. Winged goddess of Victory standing l. holding wreath and palm.
   OF T(itus) QUINCTIUS (Flamininus).

This series of coins, struck in Greece after Flamininus' defeat of Philip V of Macedon at Cynoscephalae, is the first to depict a living Roman. The next such portrait is that of Julius Caesar in January of 44 B.C.

c. 150 B.C. Silver
   OBV. Helmeted head of goddess Roma r.
   REV. She-wolf standing r. suckling the twins Romulus and Remus;
   the shepherd Faustulus standing at left. SEX(tus) POM(peius)
   FOSTLUS

This is an early instance of self-glorification on Roman coins: the moneyer, Fostlus, celebrates his claimed descent from Faustulus, the shepherd who, in the legend, found the twins being suckled by the wolf.

150–125 B.C. Silver
    OBV. Helmeted head of goddess Roma r.
    REV. Venus, crowned by Cupid, in a chariot drawn by two horses r.
      (above) ROME (below) SEX(tus) Juli(us) CAISAR [*sic*]

Here is an early reference to the Julian family's claim to be descended, through Aeneas, from Venus.

C. 105 B.C. Silver
    OBV. Helmeted head of goddess Rome r. P(orcius) LAECA, ROME.
    REV. A cuirassed soldier standing l. with his hand on the head of a
      man in a toga r.; to their r. a lictor holding fasces l. I APPEAL

The moneyer here celebrates the Porcius Laeca, who, ninety years earlier, introduced the law guaranteeing Roman citizens their right of appeal even against magistrates exercising military authority outside Rome.

46 B.C. Gold
    OBV. Veiled head of goddess Piety r. CAESAR THRICE CONS(ul)
    REV. Sacrificial implements A(ulus) HIRTIUS PR(efect of the city)

This was issued to celebrate Caesar's quadruple triumph for his victories in Gaul, Egypt, Pontus, and Africa.

January 44 B.C. Silver
    OBV. Laureate head of Caesar r. CAESAR FOURTH TIME
      DICT(ator)
    REV. Juno Sospita r. on a two-horse chariot with shield and spear
      M(arcus) METTIUS [the moneyer]

February–March 44 B.C. Silver
    OBV. Head of Caesar r. laureate and veiled as pontifex maximus
      CAESAR DICT(ator) FOR LIFE
    REV. Venus with scepter and shield standing l., holding statue of
      Victory in r. hand P(ublius) SEPULLIUS MACER [the moneyer]

42 B.C. Silver
    OBV. Head of Brutus r. BRUT(us) COM(mander); L(ucius)
      PLAET(orius) CEST(ianus) [the moneyer]

REV. Cap of freedom between two naked daggers ON THE ID(es)
OF MAR(ch)

42 B.C. Gold
OBV. Head of Octavian r. G(aius) CAESAR TRIUMVIR FOR THE
S(ettlement of) THE C(ommon)W(ealth)
REV. Aeneas advancing r. carrying his father Anchises on his shoulder
L(ucius) REGULUS OF THE BOARD OF FOUR FOR STRIK-
ING PUBLIC GOLD

42 B.C. Silver
OBV. Head of Antony r. M(arcus) ANTONI(us) COM(mander)
REV. Temple enclosing bust of sun god TRIUMVIR FOR THE
S(ettlement of) THE C(ommon)W(ealth)

32–31 B.C. Silver
OBV. Head of Antony. ANTONY. ARMENIA CONQUERED
REV. Bust of Cleopatra. CLEOPATRA QUEEN OF KINGS AND
HER SONS, KINGS

29 B.C. Silver
OBV. Victory standing r. holding wreath and palm
REV. Octavian standing r. in a four-horse chariot EMP(eror) CAESAR

28 B.C. Silver
OBV. Head of Augustus EMP(eror) CAESAR S(on) OF THE DEI-
FIED, CONS(ul) 6TH TIME, CHAMPION OF THE LIBERTY
OF THE R(oman) P(eople)
REV. PEACE. Mystic box for holding sacred utensils

27 B.C. Gold
OBV. Head of Augustus r. with capricorn [his zodiac sign] CAESAR
S(on) OF THE DEIFIED, CONS(ul) 7TH TIME
REV. Crocodile between the words EGYPT CAPTURED

18–17 B.C. Silver
OBV. Head of Augustus CAESAR AUGUSTUS
REV. Symbol of comet DEIFIED JULIUS

18 B.C. Silver

    OBV. Head of the god Liber. TURPILIANUS MONEYER

    REV. Kneeling Parthian extending Roman standard CAESAR AUGUSTUS, STAN(dards) REC(overed)

17 B.C. Gold

    OBV. Herald. AUGUST(us) S(on) OF THE DEIFIED. THE SE(cular) GAMES

    REV. Head of Iulus(?) M(arcus) SANGUINIUS MONEYER

2 B.C. Gold

    OBV. Head of Augustus. CAESAR AUGUSTUS S(on) OF THE DEIFIED, FATHER OF HIS COUNTRY

    REV. Gaius and Lucius Caesar standing. G(aius) CAESAR, L(ucius) CAESAR S(ons) OF AUGUSTUS CONS(uls) DESIGN(ate), LEADERS OF THE YOUTH

A.D. 13–14 Gold

    OBV. Head of Augustus CAESAR AUGUSTUS S(on) OF THE DEIFIED, FATHER OF HIS COUNTRY

    REV. Head of Tiberius TI(berius) CAESAR S(on) of AUG(ustus) TR(ibunician) POW(er) 15TH [Year]

GLOSSARY

NOTE: More common terms (e.g., *consul, senate, latifundia*) will be found in the index.

AERARIUM, the treasury of the Roman state, kept in part of the temple of Saturn at the foot of the Capitoline Hill.

AMPHORA, a Greek and Roman liquid measure, 8 *congii*, or *c.* 6 gallons, 7 pints.

AS, plur. ASSES, a Roman monetary unit; originally 1 lb. weight of copper, it dropped through successive devaluations from the middle of the third century B.C. to ½ ounce in 89 B.C., and was suspended a few years later until its revival in the imperial period; in the meantime it had been replaced (about the Second Punic War) by the *sestertius* as the Roman unit of reckoning.

ASIA, the Romans' designation of Asia Minor; or of that part of Asia Minor constituting the Roman province of Asia.

AUSPICES, divination, particularly by observation of the flight of birds.

CAMPUS MARTIUS ("Field of Mars"), so called from the very early altar of Mars located there, this plain between the Tiber and the Capitol was the meeting place of the *comitia centuriata*. In the course of time it was adorned with numerous public buildings and temples.

CAPITOL, the temple of Jupiter Optimus Maximus (Jupiter Best and Greatest) situated on the southwest summit of the Capitoline Hill in Rome, and sacred to the "Capitoline Triad": Jupiter, Juno, and Minerva. Many Roman colonies and municipalities had a Capitol modeled on that in Rome as their center of worship.

CENTURION, the principal professional Roman military officer, in charge of a century (100 men at maximum strength). Each Roman legion had 60 centurions.

COMITIA, public assembly of the Roman people summoned in groups.

COMITIUM, the open-air meeting place in the Forum.

CONGIUS, a Roman liquid measure, 6 *sextarii*, or c. 3½ quarts.

CONSCRIPT FATHERS *(Conscripti)*, Roman senators; variant name of members of governing council of Roman municipalities.

CROWN MONEY, a supposedly voluntary contribution in gold expected of provincials and conquered peoples to pay for victory crowns for triumphant Roman generals.

CURIA, (1) one of thirty local units of the Roman people, a division dating from the era of the kings; also, the meeting place of such a unit or, later, other body. Hence, (2) the senate house of Rome, situated in the Forum, on the north side of the Comitium. It was an elegant structure, *c.* 25 by 18 meters in extent.

CURULE CHAIR, ivory folding seat, one of the badges of office of Roman magistrates possessing the *imperium*.

DECURIO, member of local senate of Roman municipalities, composed usually of 100 decurions.

DENARIUS, "tenpiece," a Roman silver coin, originally worth 10, later 16 *asses;* equivalent of the Greek drachma.

DRACHMA, a Greek silver coin, approximately equal to the Roman *denarius.*

DUOVIR, member of two-man board; most commonly, *duoviri iure dicundo,* "two-man board with judicial power," the two chief magistrates of Roman municipalities.

EQUES, plur. EQUITES, originally "cavalrymen," or "knights," a census classification in the "Servian" constitution (see § 27); by the second century B.C. the term had come to designate a member of a definite social and economic class —the equestrian order, intermediate between the senatorial order and the plebs—which was engaged in banking and large-scale business operations, especially in tax collection and other public contracts let by the state (see publican). The minimum census for qualification as an *eques* in the last century of the Republic was probably 400,000 sesterces.

FASCES, a bundle of rods with an ax protruding from the upper part, carried by lictors in front of magistrates possessing *imperium* as symbols of the power of these magistrates to scourge (rods) or behead (ax) Roman citizens.

FORUM, the Roman Forum, civic center in Rome (also in Roman municipalities), situated between the Capitoline and Palatine Hills; in early times it served as market, in the late Republic as the place for the transaction of public business.

GENIUS, a tutelary spirit which, according to Roman belief, each man was assigned at birth as his personal protecting deity and which he worshiped accordingly, especially on his birthday.

IDES, division of Roman month; 15th of the month in March, May, July and October, 13th in other months.

IMPERATOR, commander-in-chief, a title bestowed on a victorious general by his soldiers.

IMPERIUM, the right or power to command (in military, civil, religious, and judicial matters), supreme administrative power held first by the Roman kings, and in the Republic by dictators, masters of the horse, consuls, proconsuls, praetors, and propraetors.

INTERREX, a provisional head of the state, appointed by the senate during a vacancy in the kingship or both consulships.

IUGERUM, a Roman land measure, 28,800 square Roman feet, or c. ⅝ acre.

KALENDS, first day of Roman month.

LEGATUS, (1) lieutenant to a general or provincial governor; (2) envoy or member of an embassy.

LICTOR, an attendant who carried the *fasces* before a Roman magistrate invested with *imperium* and who served as his apparitor; praetors were accompanied by six lictors, consuls by twelve, dictators by twenty-four.

MEDIMNUS, a Greek dry measure, 6 *modii*, or c. 1½ bushels.

MILE, *Roman*, in Latin *mille passus* (1,000 paces), i.e., 5,000 Roman feet or c. 4,850 English feet, or *c.* 0.92 English mile.

MINA, a Greek weight (c. 1¼ lb.) and monetary unit worth 100 drachmas.

MODIUS, a Roman dry measure, 16 *sextarii*, or c. 1 peck.

NEW MAN *(novus homo)*, the first member of an equestrian family to be elected to the consulship, thereby making his whole family one of the ruling nobility. See *Nobles*.

NOBLES *(nobiles,* "the well known"), an unofficial term in general use to describe the tightly knit oligarchy of patrician and plebeian families whose members had held the consulship. These families usually controlled the elections, held the major magistracies, and effectively ruled Rome in the last two centuries of the Republic.

NOME, an administrative division of Egypt, in charge of a *strategus*.

NONES, a division of the Roman month; 7th of the month in March, May, July and October, 5th in the other months.

OBOL, a Greek coin, ⅙ of a drachma.

OVATION, a triumph for a less than definitive victory. Instead of riding in a chariot, the victorious general walked in the procession or, after the privilege was granted Julius Caesar, rode on horseback.

PRAETORIAN GUARD, the emperor's bodyguard, consisting of several military cohorts stationed in and near Rome. The Guard was headed by (usually) two prefects, men of equestrian rank, who early in the Principate and increasingly in times of crisis, intervened to act as emperor makers.

PREFECT, (1) the title of an army officer commanding any of several military units; (2) the holder of one of three top-echelon equestrian administrative posts created by Augustus: prefect of Egypt, of the grain supply, and of Rome's night watch. See also *Praetorian Guard*.

PROCURATOR, a government agent, especially in the financial services.

PROMAGISTRATE, the title of a consul, praetor, or quaestor after his year of office. In the late Republic authority was regularly extended for a year or more beyond the year of elected office. Proconsuls and propraetors continued to exercise *imperium* in command of armies and provinces.

PUBLICAN, strictly, any public contractor, but used especially of a collector of the public revenues.

QUADRIREME, a galley having groups of four rowers; similarly, the *trireme* used groups of three oarsmen, the *quinquereme* groups of five, the *septireme* groups of seven.

QUATTUORVIR, member of four-man board; especially the board of magistrates of Roman municipalities from 89 B.C., consisting of *duoviri iure dicundo* and two aediles.

QUINQUEREME, the standard warship of the Roman fleet; see also *quadrireme*.

QUIRITES, Roman citizens.

RECUPERATOR, a member of a tribunal (usually of three or five) to try civil cases.

SEPTIREME: see *quadrireme*.

SESTERTIUS, a Roman silver coin, originally 2½ *asses,* later 4 *asses,* which from the time of the Second Punic War replaced the copper *as* as the unit of monetary reckoning. It was usually abbreviated HS (i.e., IIS = 2½). The English plural is sesterces.

SEXTARIUS, a Roman liquid measure, ⅙ *congius,* or *c.* 1 pint; also a dry measure, ¹⁄₁₆ *modius*.

STADE or STADIUM, a Greek linear measure, 625 Roman feet, or ⅛ Roman mile.

STRATEGUS, a Greek title of a military and civil official; especially the head of the Achaean League.

TALENT, a Greek weight (80 Roman lb., or *c.* 57 lb. avoirdupois) and monetary unit worth 60 minas or 6,000 drachmas. Euboeic and Attic talents are variant designations of this unit.

TOGA PRAETEXTA, a toga with a purple border, worn by boys before coming of age and by magistrates and senators.

TOGA VIRILIS, the plain white toga assumed by Roman boys on reaching manhood.

TRIBUTUM, a direct property tax to meet war costs levied on Roman citizens until 167 B.C.; thereafter it was a tax paid to Rome by conquered peoples.

TRIREME, the standard Greek war galley until Hellenistic times; see also *quadrireme*.

TRIUMPH, the procession—from the Campus Martius to the Capitol—of a Roman general celebrating a major victory, if so ordered by the senate. The victor rode in a chariot and was accompanied in the parade by his army, the magistrates and senators, and displays of the spoils (including fettered captives), all proceeding on foot.

VECTIGAL, revenue accruing to the Roman state from rentals of state property, customs duties, and other indirect taxes.

SELECT BIBLIOGRAPHY

GENERAL BIBLIOGRAPHY

Included in this list are books pertinent to more than one chapter of this volume. Books noted here are as a rule not repeated in the individual chapter bibliographies.

Adcock, F. E. *The Roman Art of War Under the Republic*. Cambridge, 1940, reprint 1960.

Bailey, C., ed. *The Legacy of Rome*. 7th ed. Oxford, 1947.

Boardman, J. et al., eds. *Oxford History of the Classical World*. Oxford, 1986.

Bowder, D., ed., *Who Was Who in the Roman World, 753 B.C.–A.D. 476*. Oxford and Ithaca, 1980.

Broughton, T. R. S. *The Magistrates of the Roman Republic*. 2 vols. and Supplement. New York, 1951, reprint 1986; 1952, reprint 1984; 1986.

Cambridge Ancient History. Vols. 7–10 and vols. 3–4 of Plates. Cambridge, 1928–1934.

Cary, M. *The Geographic Background of Greek and Roman History*. Oxford, 1949.

Croon, E., ed. *The Encyclopedia of the Ancient World*. New York, 1965.

Frank, T., ed. *An Economic Survey of Ancient Rome*. Vol. 1: *Rome and Italy of the Republic*. Baltimore, 1933; reprint, Paterson, N.J., 1959.

Hammond, M. *City-State and World State in Greek and Roman Political Theory until Augustus*. Cambridge, Mass., 1951; reprint New York, 1966.

Heitland, W. E. *Agricola: A Study of Agriculture and Rustic Life in the Greco-Roman World from the Point of View of Labour*. Cambridge, 1921; reprint Westport, Conn., 1970.

Larsen, J. A. O. *Representative Government in Greek and Roman History*. 2d ed. Berkeley, 1976.

Lemprière's Classical Dictionary of Proper Names Mentioned in Ancient Authors. 3d ed., rev. by F. A. Wright. Boston, 1984.

MacKendrick, P. L. *The Mute Stones Speak: The Story of Archaeology in Italy*. 2d ed. New York, 1983.

Oxford Classical Dictionary. 2d ed. Oxford, 1970.

Petrie, A. *An Introduction to Roman History, Literature and Antiquities.* 3d ed. New York, 1961.

Platner, S. B., and T. Ashby. *A Topographical Dictionary of Ancient Rome.* London, 1929.

Reinhold, M. *History of Purple as a Status Symbol in Antiquity.* Brussels, 1970.

Rostovtzeff, M. and E. Bickerman. *A History of the Ancient World: Rome.* New York, 1961.

Sherwin-White, A. N. *The Roman Citizenship.* 2d ed. Oxford, 1973.

Starr, C. G., Jr. *The Emergence of Rome as Ruler of the Western World.* 2d ed. Ithaca, 1953.

Starr, C. G., Jr. *The Roman Empire 27 B.C.–A.D. 476: A Study in Survival.* Oxford and New York, 1982.

Wylie, J. K. *Roman Constitutional History from Earliest Times to the Death of Justinian.* Pasadena, 1948.

INTRODUCTION

Historiography

Barnes, H. E. *A History of Historical Writing.* 2d ed. New York, 1962.

Cambridge Ancient History. Vols. 7–12. Cambridge, 1928–1939.

Cary, M. and A. H. McDonald. "Historiography, Roman," in *Oxford Classical Dictionary.* 2d ed. Oxford, 1970.

Fornara, C. W. *The Nature of History in Ancient Greece and Rome.* Berkeley, 1983.

Laistner, M. L. W. *The Greater Roman Historians.* Berkeley, 1947.

Histories of Roman and Later Greek Literature

See bibliography for chapter 8.

Christian Writers

Goodspeed, E. J. *A History of Early Christian Literature.* Chicago, 1942.

Pfleiderer, O. *Primitive Christianity, Its Writings and Teachings in their Historical Connections.* 4 vols. New York, 1906–1911; reprint Oxford, 1965.

Tyson, J. B. *The New Testament and Early Christianity.* New York and London, 1984.

Wolfson, H. A. *The Philosophy of the Church Fathers.* Cambridge, Mass., 1956.

Legal Sources and Commentaries

See bibliography for volume 2 chapter 8.

Inscriptions

Gordon, A. E. *Illustrated Introduction to Latin Epigraphy*. Berkeley, 1983.
Rushforth, G. M. *Latin Historical Inscriptions Illustrating the History of the Early Empire*. 2d ed. Oxford, 1930.
Sandys, J. E. *Latin Epigraphy*. 2d ed., rev. by S. G. Campbell. Cambridge, 1927.

Papyri and Similar Documents

David, M., and B. A. van Groningen. *Papyrological Primer*. 4th ed. Leiden, 1965.
Hunt, A. S., and C. C. Edgar. *Select Papyri*. 2 vols. London, 1932–1934. Loeb Classical Library.
Kenyon, F. G. *Books and Readers in Ancient Greece and Rome*. 2d ed. Oxford and New York, 1951.
Lewis, N. *Papyrus in Classical Antiquity*. Oxford, 1979.

Coins

See bibliography for chapter 10.

1. FROM THE BEGINNINGS TO 509 B.C.

Alföldi, A. *Early Rome and the Latins*. Ann Arbor, 1965.
Boardman, J. *The Greeks Overseas*. Harmondsworth and Baltimore, 1964.
Dumézil, G. *Archaic Roman Religion, with an Appendix on the Religion of the Etruscans*. Chicago, 1970.
Fowler, W. W. *The Religious Experience of the Roman People*. London, 1911.
Gjersted, E. *Legends and Facts of Early Roman History*. Lund, 1962.
Hooker, E. M. "The Significance of Numa's Religious Reforms." *Numen* (1963), 10:87–132.
Momigliano, A. "An Interim Report on the Origins of Rome." *Journal of Roman Studies* (1963), 53:95–121.
Ogilvie, R. M. *Early Rome and the Etruscans*. London, 1976.
Richardson, E. *The Etruscans, Their Art and Civilization*. Chicago, 1964; reprint 1976.
Rose, H. J. *Ancient Roman Religion*. London, 1948.
Westrup, C. W. *Introduction to Early Roman Law*. 4 vols. Copenhagen and London, 1934–1950.
Woodhead, A. G. *The Greeks in the West*. London and New York, 1962.

2. THE CONQUEST AND ORGANIZATION OF ITALY TO 264 B.C.

Alföldi, A. *Early Rome and the Latins*. Ann Arbor, 1965.

Boardman, J. *The Greeks Overseas*. Harmondsworth and Baltimore, 1964.

David, M. "The Treaties Between Rome and Carthage and Their Significance for Our Knowledge of Roman International Law," in *Symbolae . . . Van Oven Dedicatae*. Leiden, 1946, pp. 231–250.

Heurgon, J. *The Rise of Rome, to 264 B.C.* London, 1973.

McDonald, A. H. *The Rise of Roman Imperialism*. Sydney, 1940.

3. DOMESTIC AFFAIRS TO 264 B.C.

For works on Roman religion see also bibliography for chapter 1.

Cohen, D. "The Origin of Roman Dictatorship." *Mnemosyne* (1957), 10:300–318.

Develin, R. *The Practice of Politics at Rome 366–167 B.C.* Brussels, 1985.

Jashemski, W. F. *The Origins and History of the Proconsular and the Propraetorian Imperium to 27 B.C.* Chicago, 1950.

Raaflaub, K. A., ed. *Social Struggles in Archaic Rome: New Perspectives on the Conflict of the Orders*. Berkeley, 1986.

Wagenvoort, H. *Roman Dynamism: Studies in Ancient Roman Thought, Language and Custom*. Oxford, 1947.

Westrup, C. W. *Introduction to Early Roman Law*. 4 vols. Copenhagen and London, 1934–1950.

4. OVERSEAS CONQUESTS, 264–27 B.C

Badian, E. "Rome and Antiochus the Great: A Study in Cold War." *Classical Philology* (1959), 54:81–99.

Caven, B. *The Punic Wars*. London and New York, 1980.

David, M. "The Treaties Between Rome and Carthage and Their Significance for Our Knowledge of Roman International Law," in *Symbolae . . . Van Oven Dedicatae*. Leiden, 1946, pp. 231–250.

Dorcy, T. A., and D. R. Dudley. *Rome Against Carthage*. London, 1971.

Dubs, H. H. "An Ancient Military Contact Between Romans and Chinese," *American Journal of Philology* (1941), 62:322–330.

Dyson, S. L. *The Creation of the Roman Frontier*. Princeton, 1985.

Ellis, P. B. *Caesar's Invasion of Britain*. New York, 1980.

Errington, R. M. *The Dawn of Empire: Rome's Rise to World Power*. London, 1971.

Gruen, E. S. *The Hellenistic World and the Coming of Rome.* 2 vols. Berkeley, 1984.

Harris, W. V. *War and Imperialism in Republican Rome 327–70 B.C.* Oxford, 1979.

Heichelheim, F. M. "New Evidence on the Ebro Treaty." *Historia* (1954), 3:211–219.

McDonald, A. H. *The Rise of Roman Imperialism.* Sydney, 1940.

Radin, M. "The International Law of the Gallic Campaign." *Classical Journal* (1916/7), 12:8–33.

Rodgers, W. L. *Greek and Roman Naval Warfare.* Annapolis, 1937; reprint 1964.

Rostovtzeff, M. *The Social and Economic History of the Hellenistic World.* 3 vols. Oxford, 1941; reprint 1967.

Tarn, W. W., and G. T. Griffith. *Hellenistic Civilization.* 3d ed. London, 1952.

Thiel, J. H. *Studies on the History of Roman Sea Power in Republican Times.* Amsterdam, 1946.

Walbank, F. W. *Philip V of Macedon.* Cambridge, 1940; reprint Hamden, Conn., 1967.

Warmington, B. H. *Carthage.* Baltimore, 1965.

5. THE DECLINE AND FALL OF THE ROMAN REPUBLIC

Balsdon, J. P. V. D. *Julius Caesar: A Political Biography.* New York, 1967.

Brunt, P. A. "The Army and the Land in the Roman Revolution." *Journal of Roman Studies* (1962), 52:69–86.

Earl, D. C. *Tiberius Gracchus: A Study in Politics.* Brussels, 1963.

Evans, J. K. "Wheat Production and Its Social Consequences in the Roman World." *Classical Quarterly* (1981), 31:428–442.

Gelzer, M. Caesar, *Politician and Statesman.* Cambridge, 1968.

Holmes, T. R. *The Architect of the Roman Empire.* Vol. 1. Oxford, 1928; reprint New York, 1977.

Holmes, T. R. *The Roman Republic and the Founder of the Empire.* 3 vols. Oxford, 1923.

Huzar, E. G. *Mark Antony: A Biography.* Minneapolis, 1978; reprint London, 1986.

Lacey, W. K. *Caesar and the End of the Roman Republic.* London and New York, 1978.

Lewis, N. *The Ides of March.* Toronto, 1985.

Lintott, A. *Violence in Republican Rome.* Oxford, 1968.

Rawson, E. *Cicero: A Portrait.* Rev. ed. Ithaca, 1983.

Scott, K. "The Political Propaganda of 44–30 B.C." *Memoirs of the American Academy in Rome* (1933), 11:1–49.

Scullard, H. H. *Roman Politics 220–150 B.C.* Oxford, 1951; reprint Westport, Conn., 1987.

Suolahti, J. *The Junior Officers of the Roman Army in the Republican Period: A Study on Social Structure*. Helsinki, 1955.

Stockton, D. *The Gracchi*. Oxford, 1979.

Syme, R. *The Roman Revolution*. Oxford, 1939.

Taylor, L. R. *Party Politics in the Age of Caesar*. Berkeley, 1949.

Toynbee, A. "Economic and Social Consequences of the Hannibalic War." *Bulletin of the John Rylands Library* (1954), 37:271–287.

Toynbee, A. *Hannibal's Legacy: The Hannibalic War's Effects on Roman Life*. 2 vols. Oxford, 1965.

Westermann, W. L. *The Slave Systems of Greek and Roman Antiquity*. Philadelphia, 1955.

Wirszubski, C. *Libertas as a Political Idea at Rome During the Late Republic and Early Principate*. Cambridge, 1950.

Yavetz, Z. "The Failure of Catiline's Conspiracy." *Historia* (1963), 12:485–499.

6. THE ADMINISTRATION OF THE IMPERIAL REPUBLIC: FOREIGN DOMINATION AND PROVINCES

Badian, E. *Foreign Clientelae (264–70 B.C.)*. Oxford, 1958; reprint 1984.

Badian, E. *Roman Imperialism in the Late Republic,* 2d ed. Oxford and Ithaca, 1968.

Braund, D. C. *Rome and the Friendly Kings: The Character of Client Kingship*. London and New York, 1984.

Gabba, E. *Republican Rome, the Army, and the Allies*. Oxford and Berkeley, 1976.

Hammond, M. "Ancient Imperialism: Contemporary Justifications," *Harvard Studies in Classical Philology* (1948), 58–59:105–161.

Jones, A. H. M. *The Cities of the Eastern Roman Provinces*. 2d ed., rev. by M. Avi-Yonah et al. Oxford, 1971.

Jones, A. H. M. *The Greek City from Alexander to Justinian*. Oxford, 1940.

Magie, D. *Roman Rule in Asia Minor*. 2 vols. Princeton, 1950; reprint Salem, N.H., 1975.

Rostovtzeff, M. *The Social and Economic History of the Hellenistic World*. 3 vols. Oxford, 1941; reprint 1967.

Sherwin-White, A. N. *Roman Foreign Policy in the East 168 B.C. to A.D. 1*. London and Norman, Okla., 1984.

Stevenson, G. H. *Roman Provincial Administration*. 2d ed. Oxford, 1949.

Tarn, W. W., and G. T. Griffith. *Hellenistic Civilization*. 3d ed. London, 1952.

7. THE ADMINISTRATION OF THE IMPERIAL REPUBLIC: THE GOVERNMENT AT ROME

Badian, E. *Publicans and Sinners: Private Enterprise in the Service of the Roman Republic.* Rev. ed. Ithaca, 1983.

Bauman, R. A. *The Crimen Maiestatis in the Roman Republic and Augustan Principate.* Johannesburg, 1967.

Brunt, P. A. *Italian Manpower 225 B.C.–A.D. 14.* Oxford, 1971; reprint 1987.

Collins, J. H. "Caesar and the Corruption of Power." *Historia* (1955), 4:445–465.

Cramer, F. H. *Astrology in Roman Law and Politics.* Philadelphia, 1954.

Ehrenberg, V. "Imperium Maius in the Roman Republic." *American Journal of Philology* (1953), 74:113–136.

Gelzer, M. *The Roman Nobility.* Oxford, 1969.

Jonkers, E. J. *Social and Economic Commentary on Cicero's De Imperio Gn. Pompei.* Leiden, 1959.

Smith, R. E. *Service in the Post-Marian Army.* Manchester, 1958.

Suolahti, J. *The Roman Censors: A Study on Social Structure.* Helsinki, 1963.

Szemler, G. J. *The Priests of the Roman Republic: A Study of the Interactions Between Priesthoods and Magistracies.* Brussels, 1972.

8. SOCIETY AND CULTURE, 264–27 B.C.

For works on Roman religion, see also bibliographies for chapters 1 and 3.

Brown, F. E. *Roman Architecture.* New York, 1961.

Brunt, P. A. *Social Conflicts in the Roman Republic.* London, 1971.

Brunt, P. A. *The Fall of the Roman Republic.* Oxford, 1988.

Casson, L. *Travel in the Ancient World.* London, 1974.

Clark, D. L. *Rhetoric in Graeco-Roman Education.* New York, 1957.

D'Arms, J. H. *Commerce and Social Standing in Ancient Rome.* Cambridge, Mass., 1981.

D'Arms, J. H. *Romans on the Bay of Naples.* Cambridge, Mass., 1970.

Duff, J. W. *A Literary History of Rome from the Origins to the Close of the Golden Age.* 3d ed. London, 1960.

Earl, D. C. *The Political Thought of Sallust.* Cambridge, 1961; reprint Amsterdam, 1966.

Farrington, B. *Science and Politics in the Ancient World.* 2d ed. London, 1965.

Finley, M. I., ed. *Slavery in Classical Antiquity.* Cambridge, 1960; reprint 1968.

Gabriel, M. M. *Masters of Campanian Painting.* New York, 1952.

Grant, F. C. *Ancient Roman Religion.* New York, 1957.

Gruen, E. S. *The Last Generation of the Roman Republic.* Berkeley, 1974.

Gwynn, A. O. *Roman Education from Cicero to Quintilian*. Oxford, 1926; reprint New York, 1960.

Kenyon, F. G. *Books and Readers in Ancient Greece and Rome*. 2d ed. Oxford and New York, 1951.

Lilja, S. *Homosexuality in Republican and Augustan Rome*. Helsinki, 1983.

MacMullen, R. *Roman Social Relations, 50 B.C. to A.D. 284*. Corrected reprint. New Haven and London, 1981.

Nicolet, C. *The World of the Citizen in Republican Rome*. Berkeley, 1980.

North, J. A. "Religious Toleration in Republican Rome." *Proceedings of the Cambridge Philological Society* (1979), 25:85–103.

Paoli, U. E. *Rome: Its People, Life and Customs*. New York, 1964.

Rawson, E., ed. *The Family in Ancient Rome*. London, 1986.

Rawson, E., ed. *Intellectual Life in the Late Roman Republic*. London, 1985.

Richter, G. M. A. *Ancient Italy: A Study of the Interrelations of Its Peoples as Shown in Their Arts*. Ann Arbor, 1955.

Robinson, L. *Freedom of Speech in the Roman Republic*. Baltimore, 1940.

Rose, H. J. *A Handbook of Latin Literature*. 5th ed. London, 1962.

Rostovtzeff, M. *The Social and Economic History of the Hellenistic World*. 3 vols. Oxford, 1941; reprint 1967.

Rostovtzeff, M. *The Social and Economic History of the Roman Empire*. 2d ed., rev. by P. M. Fraser, 2 vols. Oxford, 1957.

Scullard, H. H. *Festivals and Ceremonies of the Roman Republic*. London and Ithaca, 1981.

Smith. W. A. *Roman Education*. New York, 1955.

Syme, R. *Sallust*. Berkeley, 1964.

Treggiari, S. *Roman Freedmen During the Late Republic*. Oxford, 1969.

Wardman, A. *Rome's Debt to Greece*. London, 1976.

Wheeler, R. E. M. *Roman Art and Architecture*. New York, 1964.

Winspear, A. D. *Lucretius and Scientific Thought*. Montreal, 1963.

Yavetz, Z. "The Living Conditions of the Urban Plebs in Republican Rome." *Latomus* (1958), 17:500–517.

Yavetz, Z. *Slaves and Slavery in Ancient Rome*. New Brunswick, N.J., 1987.

9. THE AUGUSTAN AGE

Bauman, R. A. *The Crimen Maiestatis in the Roman Republic and Augustan Principate*. Johannesburg, 1967.

Bowersock, G. W. *Augustus and the Greek World*. Oxford, 1965; reprint Westport, Conn., 1981.

Burn, A. R. *The Government of the Roman Empire from Augustus to the Antonines*. London, 1952.

Campbell, J. B. *The Emperor and the Roman Army, 31 B.C.–A.D. 235*. Oxford, 1984.

Carter, J. M. *The Battle of Actium: The Rise and Triumph of Augustus Caesar*. New York, 1970.

Charlesworth, M. P. "The Refusal of Divine Honours, an Augustan Formula." *Papers of the British School at Rome* (1939), 15:1–10.

Chilver, G. E. F. "Augustus and the Roman Constitution, 1939–50." *Historia* (1950), 1:408–435.

Crook, J. A. "Some Remarks on the Augustan Constitution," *Greece and Rome* (1953), 22:10–12.

Duff, J. W. *A Literary History of Rome from the Origins to the Close of the Golden Age*. 3d ed. New York and London, 1960.

Earl, D. C. *The Age of Augustus*. New York, 1968; reprint 1980.

Hammond, M. *The Augustan Principate in Theory and Practice During the Julio-Claudian Period*. Reprint with Appendix. New York, 1968.

Hannestadt, N. *Roman Art and Imperial Policy*. Aarhus, 1986.

Holmes, T. R. *The Architect of the Roman Empire*. 2 vols. Oxford, 1928–1931; reprint New York, 1977.

Jones, A. H. M. "The Imperium of Augustus." *Journal of Roman Studies* (1951), 41:112–119.

Jones, A. H. M. *Augustus*. London and New York, 1970.

Millar, F., and E. Segal, eds. *Caesar Augustus: Seven Aspects*. Oxford, 1984.

Ramage, E. S. "Augustus' Treatment of Julius Caesar." *Historia* (1985), 34:223–245.

Reinhold, M. *The Golden Age of Augustus*. Toronto, 1978.

Reinhold, M. *Marcus Agrippa: A Biography*. Geneva, N.Y., 1933; reprint Rome, 1965.

Stevenson, G. H. *Roman Provincial Administration till the Age of the Antonines*. 2d ed. Oxford, 1949.

Syme, R. *The Roman Revolution*. Oxford, 1939.

Syme, R. *The Augustan Aristocracy*. Oxford, 1985.

Taylor, L. R. *The Divinity of the Roman Emperor*. Middletown, Conn., 1931; reprint New York, 1975.

Wilkinson, L. P. *Horace and His Lyric Poetry*. 2d ed. Cambridge, 1968.

Woodman, T., and D. West. *Poetry and Politics in the Age of Augustus*. Cambridge, 1984.

Yavetz, Z. *Plebs and Princeps*. Oxford, 1969. Rev. ed. New Brunswick, 1988.

Zanker, P. *The Power of Images in the Age of Augustus*. Ann Arbor, 1988.

10. COINS

Carson, R. A. G. *Principal Coins of the Romans*. 3 vols. London, 1978–1981.

Grant, M. *Roman History from Coins*. Cambridge, 1958.

Grueber, H. A. *Coins of the Roman Republic in the British Museum*. 3 vols. London, 1910; reprint 1970.

Mattingly, H., ed. *Coins of the Roman Empire in the British Museum.* 6 vols.
   London, 1923–1963.
Mattingly, H., ed. *Roman Coins from the Earliest Times to the Fall of the Western
   Empire.* 2d ed. London, 1960.
Mattingly, H., E. A. Sydenham, C. H. V. Sutherland et al. *The Roman Imperial
   Coinage.* 9 vols. London, 1923–
Robertson, A. S. *Roman Imperial Coins in the . . . University of Glasgow.* 5 vols.
   Oxford, 1962–1982.
Sutherland, C. H. V. *Roman History and Coinage 44 B.C.–A.D. 69.* Oxford, 1987.
Sydenham, E. A. *The Coinage of the Roman Republic.* Rev. ed. London, 1952;
   reprint Salem, N.H., 1975.

INDEX